Essentials of Marketing Research

Essentials of
Marketing Research

Tony Proctor PhD

Visiting Professor in Marketing,
Chester Business School

Third Edition

FT Prentice Hall
FINANCIAL TIMES

An imprint of **Pearson Education**
Harlow, England • London • New York • Boston • San Francisco • Toronto • Sydney • Singapore • Hong Kong
Tokyo • Seoul • Taipei • New Delhi • Cape Town • Madrid • Mexico City • Amsterdam • Munich • Paris • Milan

Pearson Education Limited
Edinburgh Gate
Harlow
Essex CM20 2JE
United Kingdom

and Associated Companies throughout the world

Visit us on the World Wide Web at:
www.pearsoneduc.com

First published 1997
Second edition 2000
Third edition 2003

ISBN 0 273 67400 5

British Library Cataloguing-in-Publication Data
A catalogue record for this book is available from the British Library

10 9 8 7 6 5 4 3 2 1
11 10 09 08 07 06 05 04 03

Typeset in 10/12 $^1/_2$ pt Palatino by 68
Printed by Ashford Colour Press Ltd., Gosport

Contents

Case studies

FURTHER CASE STUDIES

Preface

Marketing research has often been called market research, and there has been much confusion about what is market research and what is marketing research. Some writers have been so worried about the terminology that they have even called their books 'research for marketing decisions' to overcome the problems. I refer to the subject matter as marketing research and I am quite sure in my own mind to what I am referring.

There have been vast changes in marketing research, largely as a result of the development of information technology. Marketing research can be to some extent a quantitative subject and, while many of the techniques used have been around for many years, the ease of using them has been frustrated by a lack of powerful and easily available computational aids. Looking back, it is a sobering thought to remember that in the mid-1960s the slide rule was the tool of the day and electronic calculating aids had only just appeared. At that time mainframe computers were in their infancy and the mechanical Burroughs' comptometers had only just given way to more sophisticated electronic ones. Now the problem is not so much lack of computing power as the need to acquire the skills to make use of all the sophisticated analytical methods that are available, as and when appropriate.

This book looks at the traditional approach to marketing research and the traditional tools of analysis. It also discusses new developments – particularly in the areas of qualitative data analysis and marketing decisions' support systems. I have tried to make the book into a teaching/study book designed primarily for undergraduates but of interest to MBA and other postgraduate or post-experience students wanting to get some idea of the subject matter. In writing such a book, getting the balance right between different topics and the depth into which to go is constrained by what we can physically include in a book of this length. Because it is designed as a teaching book, I have paid attention to the provision of case studies, illustrations and questions, all of which take up space.

The various chapters address different topics in marketing research:

- Chapter 1 looks at the nature of marketing research and the need for marketing research. An overview is given of the process of marketing research and the chapter concludes by looking at the role of agencies and ethical issues in marketing research.

- Chapter 2 pays attention to planning the research project and in particular to the use of PERT analysis to guide the management of the project.
- Chapter 3 examines the uses and limitations of secondary data, indicating when secondary data may be useful in research and giving details of useful internal and external sources of data.
- Chapter 4 examines the process of sampling. Attention is given to all aspects of sampling, including the sampling frame, sampling unit selection, sampling method, the sample size and the sampling plan.
- Methods and applications of surveys are dealt with in Chapter 5. Sources of error, methods of data collection, dealing with non-response, panel/syndicated marketing research, and omnibus surveys are among the topics discussed.
- Chapter 6 covers measurement, scales and attitude measurement. The process of measurement is discussed along with levels and variations in measurement. Validity, reliability and sensitivity are also considered. The chapter also looks at the nature of attitudes and their measurement.
- Chapter 7 looks at questionnaire construction and development. Particular attention is given to question content, question phrasing, kinds of response format, question sequence, question layout, pretesting and revising.
- Qualitative research methods are outlined in Chapter 8. Focus-group discussions, individual depth interviews and projective techniques are considered.
- Chapter 9 looks first at observation as a research method and then at experimentation. Details of many different experimental designs are given. The chapter also looks at test marketing both in the market place and under simulated conditions.
- Chapter 10 examines data interpretation and the various tools of quantitative data analysis. A wide range of statistical methods is examined. It is presupposed that the reader is familiar with statistics at an introductory level.
- Chapter 11 presents an aspect of marketing research that is not usually discussed in a textbook of this kind. Qualitative data analysis is an important dimension to marketing research. The chapter looks at a variety of tools and methods which can assist in the analysis of qualitative data.
- Chapter 12 discusses evaluation reports and their presentation. Emphasis is placed on the use of information technology to help prepare and present good reports.
- Chapter 13 looks at a variety of examples of applied marketing research, including product research, segmentation research, competition research and promotion research.
- Business-to-business marketing research, services research and research for internal marketing are the subject matter of Chapter 14.
- Global marketing research is the subject matter of Chapter 15.
- Chapter 16 discusses marketing decision-support systems. Among the most interesting developments here are applications of neural network software as expert systems.
- Further case studies are included to promote thought on how marketing research as an entity can be applied in practice.
- A glossary and a full bibliography are included.

My thanks are due to Jim Blythe for the case studies that he has contributed, and also to Lucy, Carol and Zoë for their contributions.

A downloadable *Instructor's Manual* and accompanying *PowerPoint slides* are also available free of charge to lecturers and tutors adopting the main book. They can be accessed at www.booksites.net/proctor_emr.

Tony Proctor

Acknowledgements

We are grateful to the following for permission to reproduce copyright material:

Figure 11.3 from QRS NUD*IST, Version N6, *Work Interactions Project*, QSR Pty Limited; Figure 15.2 from SNAP, Mercator Research Group Ltd.

The future lies abroad from *The Financial Times Limited*, 30 June, 1997, © Sir Martin Sorrell; The 'Market Research Services Classification' of Social Class from *National Readership Survey* (JICNARS, 1981); Selected ACORN types and group from *Market Analysis*, CACI Limited (2002), all rights reserved, ACORN and CACI are registered trademarks of CACI Limited (CACI, 1989); SNAP from SNAP, Mercator Research Ltd; Lake Lucerne Navigation Company (SGV) case study from Lake Lucerne Navigation Company (SGV).

The American Marketing Association for a definition on 'Marketing Research'; Business Opportunity World for an extract adapted from 'Safety letterbox' published in *Business Opportunity World* May 1996; Zoe Cooper for an extract adapted from her MBA dissertation, Keele University; Lucy Double for an extract adapted from her MBA dissertation, Keele University 1991; Editions Rebondir for extracts adapted from 'Small business ideas and studying the local market' published in *Rebondir* no12 p.35, 1996 and 'Un restaurant de gambas, Ouvrir un commerce' published in *Rebondir* no12 p.42, 1996; Carol Fry for extracts adapted from her MBA dissertation, Keele University; Guardian Newspapers Limited for an extract adapted from 'Second rescue for spluttering Reliant' by Chris Barrie published in *The Guardian* 6 April 1996 © Chris Barrie 1996; The Insider Group for an extract adapted from 'Best of the bunch' by R. Hutton published in *The Scottish Business Insider* March 1994; International Wrist Watch for an extract adapted from 'The French Connection' published in *International Wrist Watch* 1995, Issue 31; Management Decision for an extract adapted from 'Forecasting: the key to managerial decision-making' by D. Waddell and A. S. Sohal published in *Management Decision*, 32(1) 1994; The Market Research Society for extracts adapted from *Research Plus* 'Homelink' September 1993, 'Get a helping of the sugar-free chips game' by Sue White September 1993, 'Don't ask consumers to supply your answers' by Simon Sylvester November 1993, 'The cascade theory that shows practical gains' by Peter Gorle October 1995, 'Now business research is every agency's research' by D. Jamieson October 1995, 'Research that becomes part of a company's strategy' by N. Perrott October 1995, 'The markets are emerging – and research is hard on their heels' by Mia Bartonova January 1996, 'Quality will mark the route to deeper client relationships' by Bryan Bates March 1996, 'In Europe's complex market, check the price is right' by A. J. Bowditch April 1996, 'Why we won't keep taking pills' by A. Branthwaite and J. Bruggemann April 1996, 'Now that India's got GATT, a massive market beckons' by Sue Bunn April 1996, 'How a spoonful of research helps the medicine go down' by Tracey Sanderson April 1996, 'The launch went fine – then the devil's in the dealing' by Andrew Scott April 1996, 'The world shrinks, maybe, but there's still the need to travel' by M. Goodyear May 1996, and 'With growing demands for data, will purity prove only theoretical?' by Peter Mouncey May 1996; Marketing for extracts adapted from 'Research propels innovation', and 'Avon ads praise the real woman' by Ruth Nicholas published in *Marketing* 27 January 1994; Marketing News for an extract adapted from 'Delphi technique can work for new product development' by Gianni Bolongaro published in *Marketing News* 3 January 1994; Marketing Week for extracts adapted from *Marketing Week* 'PepsiCo needs new strategy for iced tea' by Jon Rees 16 April 1996, 'Poster watch' 26 April 1996, 'Working on site' 26 April 1996, 'Commercial TV audiences rise' by Paul McCann 26 April 1996, and 'The data game' by David Reed 3 May 1996; South Africa Tourism Board for an extract adapted from *South Africa: a World in One Country*, 1996; Rene Spindler for an extract adapted from her M.Sc. dissertation, Odense University 1991; and Rushuang Xiong for an extract adapted from their MBA dissertation, Keele University 1994.

We are grateful to the Financial Times Limited for permission to reprint the following material:

Management: Marketing wake-up, © *Financial Times*, 3 June, 1997; Management: The English Bear Company, © *Financial Times*, 28 April, 1997; Why researchers are so jittery, © *Financial Times*, 3 March, 1997; Golden nuggets on a long and winding road, © *Financial Times*, 2 December, 1997; Data loss, © *Financial Times*, 23 January, 1997; Opinion polling faces new scrutiny, © *Financial Times*, 21 March 1997; Baby boomers get the message, © *Financial Times*, 26 May, 1997; Shoppers under the microscope, © *Financial Times*, 5 December, 1997; Caught in the neighbours' tangled web, © *Financial Times*, 15 August, 1997; Public puts faith in brand names, © *Financial Times*, 13 October, 1997; Soft drinks switch to PET leaves industry struggling, © *Financial Times*, 22 October, 1997; Newspapers are a source of information about competitors, © *Financial Times*, 20 December, 1997; Electronic revolution in the retailing world, © *Financial Times*, 3 September, 1997; British divided into four types, © *Financial Times*, 5 September, 1997; Deceptive appearance, © *Financial Times*, 3 February, 1997; Orchestras aim to pass the baton, © *Financial Times*, 20 May, 1997; The decline and fall of frills, © *Financial Times*, 28 April, 1997; Breakthroughs in business intelligence, © *Financial Times*, 7 May, 1997; Watching paint fly, © *Financial Times*, 25 September, 1997; China's future dragons, © *Financial Times*, 14 August, 1997; When time means money, © *Financial Times*, 24 May, 1997; The growing business, © *Financial Times*, 23 December, 1997; Canal Satellite, © *Financial Times*, 12 September, 1997; Saffron revivalists turn to genetic engineering, © *Financial Times*, 15 January, 1997; World tyre industry may face shake-out, © *Financial Times*, 14 March, 1997.

In some instances we have been unable to trace the owners of copyright material, and we would appreciate any information that would enable us to do so.

1 The nature of marketing research

OBJECTIVES

After reading this chapter you should be able to:

- define marketing research, understand the philosophy of science and understand how marketing research relates to marketing decision-making and planning;

- appreciate the major divisions of marketing research and how it is part of marketing strategy;

- understand the role played by marketing research agencies and the kind of services they provide;

- be aware of the ethical issues involved in marketing research;

- be aware of how the Internet can be used in marketing research;

- appreciate the need for creativity in marketing research;

- appreciate the problems created by non-response in marketing research.

KEY WORDS

risk reduction	secondary research
market research	quantitative research
customer research	agencies
preliminary research	in-house research
conclusive research	research proposal
performance research	ethics
primary research	creativity

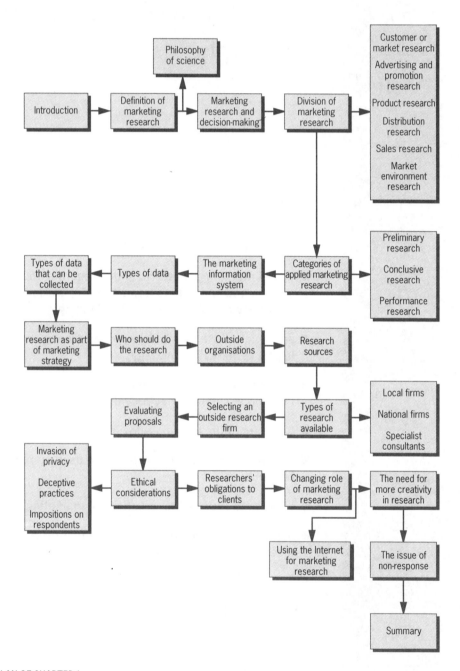

PLAN OF CHAPTER 1

INTRODUCTION

Marketing research aims to take some of the risk out of marketing decisions by providing information that can form part or all of the basis of decision-making. It is applicable to all aspects of marketing-mix decisions and should be an integral part of the process of formulating marketing strategy. Marketing research can help in a variety of studies and makes use of both primary and secondary data sources. It can be conducted either in-house by a firm's own staff or by outside marketing research companies that specialise in marketing research activities. Outside research companies, or agencies, offer a wide range of services, ranging from off-the-peg studies to tailor-made studies to meet the needs of individual clients. As is the case with many other services involving obtaining information from firms and members of the public, ethical considerations are an important issue. In a rapidly changing environment the need to come up with new ideas is also extremely important, and priority needs to be given to introducing creativity into marketing research.

MARKETING RESEARCH: A DEFINITION

Peter Chisnall[1] points out that although the term 'market research' is now largely used as a synonym for 'marketing research' there was originally a distinct difference between the scope of the activities they covered. Some confusion has been caused by the term 'market research' being rather freely used to describe the full range of activities properly covered by marketing research. Chisnall notes, however, that market or marketing research is essentially about the disciplined collection and evaluation of specific data in order to help suppliers understand their customer needs better. Moreover, since decision-making necessarily involves some element of risk, the collection and evaluation of such data should be used to reduce and control, to some degree, the parameters of risk surrounding particular marketing proposals.

Marketing research as defined by the American Marketing Association

Marketing research is the function that links the consumer, customer and public to the marketer through information – information used to identify and define marketing opportunities and problems; generate, refine, and evaluate marketing actions; monitor marketing performance; and improve understanding of marketing as a process. Marketing research specifies the information required to address these issues; designs the method for collecting information; manages and implements the data-collection process; analyzes the results; and communicates the findings and their implications.
Source: AMA.[2]

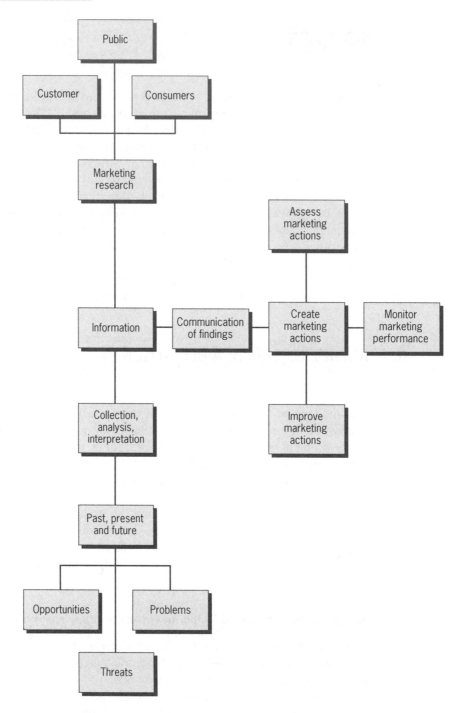

Figure 1.1 Role of marketing research

Any definition of marketing research has to take account of the changing role of research in modern marketing. Marketing research connects the consumer, the customer and the public to the marketer through the medium of information. This information is used to distinguish and define marketing opportunities and threats or problems. It is also used to create, improve and assess marketing actions and to monitor marketing performance. It also helps to improve understanding of marketing as a process. Marketing research identifies the information required to address these issues. It comprises methods for collecting data, analysis of the data collected and its interpretation, and communication of the findings and their implications. It takes account of past experience, the present situation and the likely future so that marketing executives can make sound decisions.

This definition of marketing research underlines the role of research in all phases of marketing, assisting and guiding the marketing efforts of the organisation (Figure 1.1). Marketing research involves more than studies of specific problems or specific situations, for it prevents problems arising in the first place. There is a need for marketing research to be at the centre of decision-making.[3,4] It is a fact-finding and forecasting function that is used by all phases of marketing and even by other functional aspects of an organisation.

PHILOSOPHY OF SCIENCE

All academic research is said to be grounded in a philosophical perspective. Easterby-Smith et al.[5] provide a useful summary as to why a philosophical perspective to any research study is important. For example, it can help to clarify research design in terms of its overall configuration, what kind of evidence is gathered and from where, and how this can be interpreted to provide answers to the question(s) asked. It can help recognise which designs are likely to work and which will not, and also highlight limitations of particular approaches, it can help the researcher identify research designs which may be outside his or her past experiences.

There continues, however, to be a great deal of debate among academic researchers around the most appropriate philosophical position from which methods of research should be derived. In this instance the competing *schools of thought* are often described as *positivist* and *phenomenological*. These schools of thought are perhaps best viewed as extremes on a continuum. Each school has its own set of assumptions and a range of methodological implications associated with its position. However, there is a danger of oversimplification if this distinction is taken too literally. It is important to recognise that rarely does any piece of research work fit neatly into a particular school of thought. Rather a piece of research tends to subscribe to a particular school of thought.

The researcher's methodological, epistemological and ontological premises can be termed a paradigm or interpretive framework that basically encompasses a set of beliefs that guide the research action. This comprises:

- *Methodology* – focuses on how we gain knowledge about the world.

- *Epistemology* – asks: how do we know the world? What is the relationship between the inquirer and the known? (It is concerned with how things can be made known to the researcher.)

- *Ontology* – raises basic questions about the nature of reality. (It is concerned with assumptions about the kind of things there are in the world.)

Research methodologies will differ according to both their ontological and epistemological assumptions, though generally there are two types of research methodology:

- positivist
- phenomenological

Positivism

Positivism is a more dominant approach in natural science and is concerned with causal explanation such as patterns and regularities in events. As such, this is an important methodology in the social sciences and particularly in business research. Within a positivist methodology the ontological assumptions view the social world as an external environment, where definite structures affect people in similar ways, and where people understand and react to these structures in similar ways. The epistemological assumptions in this approach are that the researcher is independent of what is being researched and their role is to observe and measure social structures. A positivist approach is therefore deductive in nature – for example, taking a theory from literature and researching it to confirm or refute the proposition.

Phenomenology

Phenomenology is the main alternative to the positivist approach in social research and is an interpretavist methodology. The ontological assumption here is that people are not passive in simply responding to structures but instead reality is itself socially constructed. The epistemological assumption is that the researcher interacts with the subjects of the research, and that his or her role is to understand people's interpretation of events rather than the events themselves. The focus with this approach is to discover meaning rather than measurement. A phenomenological approach is therefore inductive in nature, as the investigation will guide the construction of a theory.

To fully understand the traditions of each school of thought, and its theoretical basis, is a significant field of study in its own right and is beyond the scope of this piece of work. To gain a fuller appreciation of the theoretical foundations of each school of thought see Allison *et al.*,[6] Bekesi[7] and Embree.[8]

It is an important consideration that the research study and its findings are fully accepted by its target audience, if it is to have any actionable value. A positivist approach will help to overcome some of these reservations given that this approach is widely adopted in this environment as a means of research. Allison *et al.* argued that positivism and phenomenology are in fact complementary rather than incompatible, and that there are many similarities between the two schools of thought. Hannabuss,[9] citing the work of Gummesson,[10] provides a useful summary of the differences between a positivistic and a hermeneutic approach. The positivistic approach stresses rules by which we can explore and explain phenomena objectively, defining valid knowledge and inquiry in scientific terms. It focuses on description and explanation. There exist clear distinctions between facts and values, rationality and logic, statistical techniques and detachment, and explicit theories and hypotheses.

Academics agree that there is no research method which is the most appropriate for all research problems. Each research study has its own distinctiveness, assumptions, bias and degrees of usefulness. It is generally argued that the choice of research design imposes intellectual and practical constraints on a researcher in terms of reliability, validity and generalisability.[11]

MARKETING RESEARCH AND DECISION-MAKING

There are elements of uncertainty and risk attached to all business decisions and the main difficulty is how to reduce the risk involved in the choices that are made. Common sense suggests that the availability of good information reduces the risk. After all, having perfect information all the time would make the job of exercising choice much easier since there would be no risk in making marketing decisions. Correct answers to such questions as how much to spend on advertising and what message should be contained in the advertising would always be known.

The first step in the decision-making process is the identification of needed information. Incorrect specification of requirements will provide only useless information, so it is necessary to ensure that the specification is correct. Poor or misleading information not only costs time and money but also generates confusion, chaos and badly informed decisions. One must determine what information is needed to make a particular decision. Next, consideration has to be given to whether the information can be obtained within a reasonable time and at a reasonable cost, and whether one can afford to spend both the time and the money to obtain it.

Information used in the right way can be a powerful aid to marketing. A competitive advantage can be achieved with the help of accurate, relevant information since it helps marketers make better decisions. Inaccurate, irrelevant information is both misleading and dangerous in the extreme.

The potential benefits of market research

Plastics chemist Graham West thought marketing was an expensive exercise in woolly thinking.

He is the managing director of Belgrade Insulations, a plastics and vacuum-forming company based in Wellingborough. In 1991 a Department of Trade and Industry official called to talk about the department's Marketing Initiative to help smaller businesses write a marketing plan. As a result of changes partly inspired by the programme, West says: 'I realised I had been lacking direction for years. We had been simply unable to look for markets where we could apply the company's skills.' A recent study by the Marketing Council and Warwick Business School looked at companies, including Belgrade Insulations, that had taken part in the DTI scheme. It found that some simple marketing tasks had fostered significant sales growth.

John Stubbs, chief executive of the Marketing Council, thinks the findings should encourage personal business advisers at Business Links, the government-led support service, to think hard about how to help sharpen marketing skills.

West had been running his own company for 20 years without a thought of marketing. In 1991 the building industry, to which he supplied a variety of products including lids for cold water tanks, 'stopped dead'. Worse, Belgrade Insulations was dependent for at least 60 per cent of its sales – and 'far more' of its profits – on a single customer. The company had a healthy balance sheet, with no borrowing, but turnover seemed to have plateaued at about £3m – producing pre-tax profits of about £230,000.

West hired a sales development manager. But he already had a sales executive. 'All I had done was put another man in the field with a scatter-gun approach. We had to look outside the building industry, but we did not know where.'

So West was receptive when he heard about the DTI scheme. A marketing consultant was allocated to him and spent part of two or three weeks producing a report. The government paid half the consultant's fee. 'He was very sharp. He could see our problems and didn't talk down to us. But he probably went too far. There was such an enormous list of things to do.' More pertinently, the report assumed marketing knowledge. 'It didn't quite get us off the ground.'

Shortly after, attracted by cheap training, he took part in the Investors in People scheme, one of whose consultants had a marketing background. Building on the DTI report, West says: 'We sat down and identified the company's strengths and weaknesses and what we could bring to the table that our competitors could not – which was actually very little.'

The car components industry looked relatively promising – and, unlike the building trade, was still ticking over, in spite of the recession. A telephone survey was conducted, and West followed up every inquiry, however small – 'odds and ends, orders no one else wanted'.

At the same time, West decided that he needed to bolster research and development capabilities, and hired a pattern maker who could concentrate on developing prototypes from the new customers' requests. Some sizeable orders materialised. 'I have to say we lost money on the majority, but we had gone up a very steep learning curve. The ideas were tumbling out.' Now the company could produce a prototype in a week or less – rather than the month or two it had previously taken.

Eighteen months ago West brought in a full-time marketing man with a brief to hunt out growth industries where the company's skills – including its sharper research and development capabilities, could be used. In addition to car components, Belgrade Insulations is now selling to the leisure industry, to heating and ventilation companies and to the general engineering sector. It has recently focused on waste disposal as another growth area where it is working with customers to fashion new products. 'We can charge whatever is the going rate, we are not beholden to one customer.' The company to which West was once selling 60 per cent of his goods now accounts for less than 25 per cent of sales, and he hopes that will reduce further as expansion continues elsewhere.

In the year to August 1996 pre-tax profits rose to about £500,000 on sales of £4.8m, and he is aiming for sales of £7m by 1999. Belgrade Insulation's financial strength, its R&D skills and, as West puts it, the 'team effort', have played a crucial role in its development. But it was some simple marketing, he reckons, that really awoke the business.

Source: Katharine Campbell.[12] Reprinted with permission.

DIVISIONS OF MARKETING RESEARCH

Marketing research has developed a number of broad divisions covering the range of problems and decisions with which executives have to deal. These are indicated in Figure 1.2.

Customer or market research

Customer or market research can produce quantitative facts about particular markets and market segments – for example, the size of the market both in terms of unit sales and value. When this data is collected over time it allows one to identify trends and helps to predict future sales. It can also provide information on where customers are located, their spending patterns, earnings and their credit worthiness. It can also explain why customers prefer one brand to another and what price they are willing to pay. Market research can also provide information about market share of all the firms operating in a market or market segment.

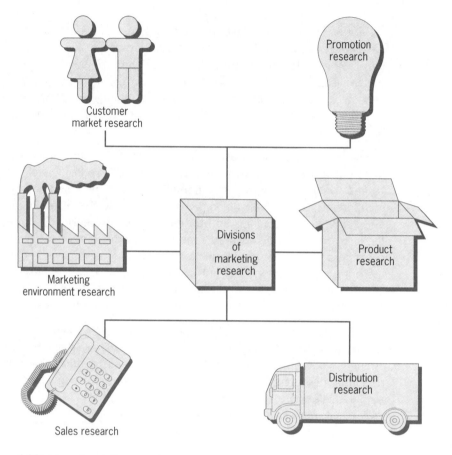

Figure 1.2 Divisions of marketing research

Customer market research provides information on:

- market and market segment sizes
- trends in the market which can be used for forecasting
- brand shares
- customer characteristics and motivations
- competitors' brands shares

Advertising and promotion research

Advertising research measures the success of advertising campaigns in relationship to their objectives. It also helps users of advertising in selecting the most appropriate promotional media and methods that are likely to produce the most effective results. Advertising research can provide information on which medium is most likely to reach the target audience for specific campaigns. It also provides information about what messages are most likely to appeal to the target audience. Research also helps in the process of evaluating in advance the likely impact of a campaign by testing out advertisements on a limited scale. Through tracking studies the effectiveness of a campaign can be monitored at all stages of its implementation.

Promotional research provides information on:

- the most suitable method of promotion
- the most suitable copy and campaign material
- the most suitable media to use
- the effectiveness of the communications in achieving objectives

Product research

Product research helps to find additional uses for existing and potential products or services. It also helps, in the case of new product ideas, to test out the product concept with potential users and purchasers before the expensive process of product development. If a product concept is found to be sound and is then developed, product research can test the product out on potential users before the launch. This latter information can be used to remove any apparent design faults in a product. Product research helps to provide an effective assessment of the strengths and weaknesses of a product or service in comparison with competitors' products or services. Research also provides information on the appropriate packaging of a product, helping to design it in such a way as to promote the image of the product (or service).

Product research provides information on:

- opportunities for new product development
- product design requirements
- comparative performance *vis-à-vis* competitors' offerings
- packaging

Distribution research

Research helps to find the best channels of distribution for a product and helps in the selection of distribution channel members. With regard to physical distribution, research indicates the best sites for warehouse and retail locations.

Distribution research provides information on:

- suitable distribution methods
- the appropriateness of channel members
- the best location for warehouses and retail outlets

Sales research

Sales research helps to assess and measure the effectiveness of different methods or techniques of selling. It helps to ensure that sales patches are roughly equivalent in size so that sales staff are not unfairly discriminated against when it comes to setting sales targets. Sales research provides information on the suitability of remuneration methods and levels for motivating the sales force. Research is also concerned with sales training and can provide extensive feedback on the quality of sales presentations made by sales staff.

Sales research provides information on:

- the effectiveness of sales methods and techniques
- establishing sales territories
- the adequacy of remuneration methods
- sales training requirements

Marketing environment

This division of marketing research examines the political, economic, social and technological influences which may have an impact on a firm's marketing operations.

In the case of the political aspect of the environment, changes in government can affect trading conditions and these need to be anticipated on a worldwide basis. Clearly, the economic climate within which a business operates exerts an effect. These effects may be temporary or more permanent. Attention has to be given to such influences when planning, and research helps to assess the impact of political and economic factors.

Social influences can also have a substantial impact on some businesses. Population explosions or declines directly influence the demand for certain goods. Research provides information on which factors are relevant and how they impinge on the organisation's activities.

Technological influences can have a sudden and dramatic impact on the fortunes of a business. A sudden technological breakthrough can make currently successful products and processes obsolete in a very short space of time. Research can monitor technological progress and provide advance notice of new developments.

Market environment research provides information on:

- political influences
- economic influences
- social influences
- technological influences

CATEGORIES OF APPLIED MARKETING RESEARCH

Preliminary research

Preliminary research is often necessary before a final statement and definition of a problem can be agreed upon. For example, someone may come up with the idea for a new service. Preliminary research may concern such matters as whether the market for such a service is regional or national, who would use the service, and what substitute services people use. Answers to these kinds of questions can help to define the nature and scope of more complete research.

A review of earlier research may be helpful. It is possible, for example, that the suggestion put forward as an idea for a new service has been previously researched. There may even be already published sources of information that can provide pertinent information. Government publications might mention the service, for example, or some trade publication may have mentioned it and even considered its use.

Conclusive research

Conjectures or hypotheses are developed in the preliminary research and in the course of defining the marketing problem. Conclusive research is carried out to produce evidence to support these hypotheses. In conducting conclusive research, a thorough search of already published data is made. Fieldwork may also be conducted.

Performance research

Performance research is concerned with assessing how well recommended marketing actions are being carried out and what benefits in terms of objectives set are being realised. Performance research monitors the effectiveness of marketing management. It questions the definition of the problem that has directed the work to date. It makes one review whether a new study is desirable because certain questions remain unsatisfactorily resolved.

Marketing research provides information for marketing decision-making and problem-solving and may thus be regarded as part of the marketing information system. In the last chapter in the book we look in detail at the marketing information system. However, because of its relationship to marketing research we introduce the subject in this chapter.

Small business ideas and studying the local market

When you have got some idea of the national market for your idea and some insights into the most suitable openings that relate to the activities in which you are interested, the next step is to study possibilities in the local market.

You need to immerse yourself in the environment. Start by making a tour of the streets in the town and the town's commercial centres. Note the neighbouring kinds of businesses, particularly those that offer similar or complementary kinds of products or services to those you want to offer. Take note of the kind of clientèle they attract.

This study will give you a better understanding of the neighbourhood. You can then find out from your local Chamber of Commerce how long certain kinds of businesses on particular streets have been there – a good indicator of your own particular chances of long-term survival. You may also find out what kind of businesses have been unsuccessful either in general or in particular areas and, more to the point, why this has been the case.

Source: Rebondir.[13]

THE MARKETING INFORMATION SYSTEM

Marketing information systems have been around for a long time – conceptually, there is nothing particularly new about them. The original ones were paper-based systems in which summarised information was stored in large banks of filing cabinets. In comparison with current notions of information systems, the early paper-based systems were relatively inefficient. With the advent of computers, particularly desktop computers, the opportunity developed for marketing information systems to become more sophisticated and efficient.

A marketing information system is a way of systematically gathering and giving helpful marketing information to the right people on a continuous basis and at the right time. Since information needs, sources and costs alter with time, a review of any information system is desirable from time to time. Such a review should specify individual people's information requirements, at what times information is required and where it can be found.

Marketing managers use many different types of information and there are many ways of putting together a marketing information system. The required information can be classified in a number of different ways. One way of classifying the information is:

- internal information
- external information

- position information
- decision information
- forecast information

Internal information is made up of sales reports, sales analyses and cost analyses related to sales. Most of the raw data already exists within the organisation and needs to be processed or analysed so that it becomes helpful information. An information system facilitates this process.

External information refers to the size, structure, trends, opportunities and threats in the environment. It also includes information on competitors and customers, both existing and potential. Employees, customers and distributors contribute this form of marketing information.

Position information is created by combining internal and external information. For example, one might combine the enterprise's sales and the overall sales of the enterprise and its competitors in the market to calculate market share. In a similar fashion, internal strengths and weaknesses can be compared to those of competitors to find competitive advantage, unique selling points, and whether any competitive advantage is sustainable.

Decision information results from various analyses, which can involve mathematical and statistical treatment of data.

Forecast information can be based on either subjective opinions, ascertained by survey, or on statistical analysis of trends.

Some of this information can be obtained cheaply, while other forms take time to gather and analyse. There is a trade-off between the value of information and its cost – in terms of time and money. Executives must know which information affects which decisions and which information is essential.

TYPES OF DATA

Research can be categorised into primary and secondary; and qualitative and quantitative. Primary research is usually carried out for the specific use of a client company or even by the company itself. Secondary research makes use of research already carried out by someone else for some other purpose.

Quantitative research produces numbers and figures – such as numbers and percentages of consumers who are aware of particular products or services. Qualitative research, on the other hand, provides data on why people buy – what motivates them to buy – or their impressions of products, services or advertisements. Both forms of research produce information on markets, competitors, distributors and customers. For example, reports provide information on markets, their size, structure, key producers and distributors, their market share, trends and prices. They also provide information on behaviour, attitudes and intentions.

In the case of consumer goods, retail audits measure market sales, week by week or day by day, competitor's sales, market shares, prices, special offers and stock levels. Customer surveys use structured questionnaires to assess, among other

DECIDING WHO SHOULD DO THE RESEARCH

Research may be undertaken by a firm's own research staff alone, given to an outside agency to perform, or some combination of both of these options. Where both an outside agency and internal personnel undertake research on the same problem, consultation between the outside agency and internal personnel is essential. Handing over a complex study completely to an outside firm can be fraught with problems. On the other hand, allowing internal personnel to have too much of an input may prevent new and useful insights emerging. The research proposal should identify who should do what.

Where company personnel are used in the research, even though a competent agency has been hired, there are several advantages to be gained. Using people from departments that will be affected by the study will help 'sell' the results. Using company personnel can also direct and redirect the progress of the study into the most useful and profitable areas. Using people from departments other than marketing will educate them about the ways and benefits of marketing research.

NEED FOR ASSISTANCE FROM OUTSIDE RESEARCH ORGANISATIONS

In recent years there has been a trend towards using outside suppliers. This has probably occurred because of the more complex and sophisticated research techniques that have recently been developed and the fact that people in organisations do not usually have the necessary skills for these techniques. Computerisation has produced ways of finding and analysing information that could not have been dreamed of only a few years ago. While computers have been adopted almost universally, their use for marketing research has developed as a specialised field of knowledge and few firms have developed this expertise for themselves. Companies are also reducing their middle and top management staff. For financial reasons, many companies believe that an outside research firm can perform market research better and more cheaply than the companies' own personnel. Because of the wealth of information now available to clients on a continuing basis from agencies that specialise in gathering, analysing and reporting information, it is too costly and time-consuming for any single company to attempt to collect such information itself. The use of outside firms is desirable when confidentiality is of paramount importance. This is very important where knowing the company and its products has an effect on the responses given by subjects participating in the research.

RESEARCH SOURCES

Outside research firms specialise in one or more forms of research assistance, and relatively few firms can offer all methods with equal expertise. The specialised research assistance that can be given is as follows:

- mail surveys
- personal interview studies
- telephone studies
- panels
- omnibus studies
- sampling
- focus groups

Specialisation in overall marketing measurements might include the following:

- test marketing
- scanner test marketing
- controlled test marketing
- simulated test marketing

There are also research firms that specialise in the problems of market segmentation, customer/prospect databases, advertising media studies and audience studies.

TYPES OF RESEARCH AVAILABLE

A number of types of marketing research are offered by specialist agencies:

- *Custom-designed studies.* These studies are designed to meet the specific needs of the buyer.

- *Syndicated studies.* These are ongoing surveys conducted continuously or periodically, using the same basic data, that are reported separately to multiple clients. The reports can be adjusted to meet the needs of the client.

- *Standardised studies.* These are studies based on a method of doing things (usually a unique method) such as copy testing, simulated test marketing, or setting up a consumer panel or an omnibus study. Special equipment or facilities may be a built-in part of the service.

Outside agencies offering research may be categorised according to their type and location.

Local firms offering special types of assistance

These firms may specialise in interviewing, mall intercepts, telephone research, etc. They may take on special local assignments for large, nationwide research companies. Such firms often offer facilities for focus and other types of research groups and may handle research other than their specialities.

National research firms

Agencies of this kind may be able to do almost all forms of marketing research. The companies often offer consulting in marketing and even general management. They also may offer computer-based information for use in databases, marketing strategy decisions and the like.

Consultants in various specialities

These firms may consult and advise about packaging, advertising and personnel problems. They also may offer to do some research relating to their specialities. These firms may have a major field of interest, such as engineering or electronics. The research offered by consultants can include necessary outside studies, both marketing and technical.

SELECTING AN OUTSIDE RESEARCH FIRM

In the case of selecting an ongoing research service, the buyer must think not only of the dependability of the research method offered, but also whether the research firm is likely to stay in business. For services with standardised procedures, the crucial element is whether the concept of the procedure selected can produce the information deemed necessary. Quality of work is important but the probability is that a research firm would not still be in business if the quality of its work were poor.

In selecting an outside agency account should be taken of the degree to which an in-depth knowledge of the employing company and its field is required and the agency's skill in the type of study to be undertaken. An outside agency often needs some weeks of training or instruction about the company and its marketing problems before it can understand what the client requires.

Steps in choosing a research firm

1   Check sources for finding names of research companies.
2   Compile a list of firms and decide on two or three that appear to be the most promising.
3   Contact the research firm in writing, giving as full a description as possible of the problem.
4   Arrange an interview with the research firm, preferably in its office.
5   Find out more about the research supplier and about its previous clients.
6   Explore how the research firm prefers to work with clients.
7   Ask for a written proposal.
8   Come to a clear understanding that further discussions may change the proposal in some ways.
9   Agree about who will be the prime contacts between client and researcher.
10   Make it clear to a firm submitting a proposal that proposals from other firms are also being considered when this is the case.

EVALUATING THE PROPOSALS

In evaluating proposals one should consider the factors shown in the box.

Factors to consider when evaluating proposals

1   Whether the proposal shows an understanding of the problem and its marketing implications.
2   The nature of the organisation undertaking the research and the skills the researchers possess.
3   Whether the total price is reasonable and acceptable. Whether there are large price differences among different proposals and, if so, whether they signal different assumptions by different firms.
4   Whether the proposal contains a procedure for changes if they are required and whether this procedure is acceptable to the client.

ETHICAL CONSIDERATIONS IN MARKETING RESEARCH

Coinciding with the rise of consumerism and equal rights legislation, people have become more assertive of their rights, especially in the market place. An increased concern for privacy, a reluctance to be used as guinea-pigs for new products and an increased reluctance to accept research claims for new products in advertisements characterise the new outlook of many consumers.

In applying the term 'ethics' to marketing research, it is assumed that ethics involves the assessment of an action in terms of that action being morally right or wrong. Each society possesses standards to which it expects its members to adhere. Sometimes, these standards are quite precise and there is little dispute about their meaning. At other times, however, these standards are quite general and can be interpreted in different ways. The area of greatest concern is marketing researchers' treatment of participants. The abuses that arise in this area tend to fall into three broad categories: invasion of privacy, deceptive practices and impositions (Figure 1.3).

Invasion of privacy

Invasion of privacy is not an issue that is unique to marketing research. It also occurs in many other aspects of business and has heightened people's sensitivity to the privacy issue. However, actually defining when a person's privacy is invaded may be difficult. For example, is observing the actions of a shopper in a supermarket an invasion of their privacy? Is questioning a person about their income, product use or future purchase plans an invasion of privacy?

Up to the present, it has been felt that observing a person's public actions (e.g. shopping in a supermarket) does not infringe on their privacy. It is also maintained that information willingly provided by respondents in a survey does not constitute an invasion of privacy, since the person's participation implies their consent. However, questions are currently being raised about whether many respondents in

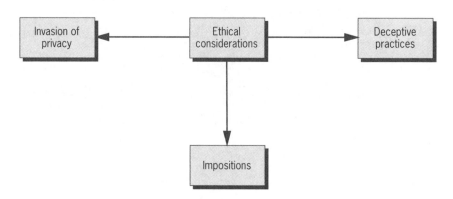

Figure 1.3 Ethical considerations in marketing research

surveys appreciate when they are in situations where they must provide information (as is the case in government census studies) and when they are in situations where they have a real choice of whether to provide information. Since there is no widely acceptable definition of privacy, the invasion of privacy issue is of considerable concern for marketing researchers.

Deceptive practices

It is a deceptive practice when a researcher misrepresents the purpose of the research, its sponsorship, its promises of anonymity, the amount of time required to participate in the research, or inducement for participating in it. Perhaps the most notorious deception is obtaining a sales pitch under the guise of marketing research.

An operational definition of deception in marketing research may be difficult to make with absolute precision. A code of ethics should, however, clarify what actions might be considered acceptable practice.

A code of ethics – is there a breach of ethics involved?

■ A potential telephone respondent is told that the questioning will only take a few minutes, when it takes twenty minutes.

■ Return envelopes in an 'anonymous' mail survey are coded so that respondents and non-respondents can readily be identified in order to save money when sending out second requests.

Impositions on respondents

Here we are looking at actions by researchers that show a lack of concern for the participants. Under this heading are such actions as contacting respondents at inconvenient times, wasting participants' time because of inappropriate research, and poorly prepared interviews.

Ethical considerations in taste-testing with drugs

The Market Research Society makes no reference to the testing of medicines in its Code of Conduct. Butterworth's *Law of Food and Drugs* details the requirements for clinical trials of the efficacy of products, but does not provide any definition of requirements for the testing of other aspects of pharmaceutical products such as flavour acceptability. Indeed, there are no real guidelines for taste-testing pharmaceuticals. The responsibility for designing safe consumer research resides with the agency doing the work. Moreover, providing an agency takes sufficient steps to ensure the safety of the research protocol, responsibility for the safety of the actual product and product ingredients lies with the manufacturer.

Increasingly, over-the-counter medicines are becoming more important to pharmaceutical firms. Manufacturers can increase sales and market share by improving the appeal of their products to consumers. There is an increase in research activities into the reformulation of products to achieve better taste characteristics and subsequent testing with consumers to investigate preference or prove claims made about taste. Nevertheless, this type of research produces ethical concerns since many of the products tested contain active drugs. However, the issues involved in showing that one product is preferred to another in terms of taste are completely different from clinical trial issues.

Reading Scientific Services Ltd (RSSL) is a multidisciplinary scientific consultancy providing research and analytical services to the food, drink, consumer goods, chemical and healthcare industries. It has expertise in both routine and investigative pharmaceutical analysis including sensory evaluation and consumer research. When conducting consumer research on pharmaceutical products the dose each respondent receives has to be limited. In practice this means controlling the amount and number of products tasted. Prescreening of product prototypes is essential in order to ensure the selection of the best samples to research with consumers. Sensory evaluation, making use of trained panels, is an efficient way of prescreening. Panellists are selected for their taste sensitivity and are trained to describe and measure flavour and mouthfeel characteristics. Results of the sensory evaluation are used to make sure that only prototypes that seem to have the required range of flavour and mouthfeel characteristics are taken forward to the stage of consumer research. Moreover, because sensory evaluation gives an objective and precise description of the flavour and mouthfeel characteristics of each product, the task of consumer research is simplified to preference judgements and opinions about key product characteristics. At the same time the dose administered can be kept to a minimum.

Nonetheless, consumers must give their 'informed consent' to take part in such research and interviewers must explicitly inform respondents of any restrictions or exclusions. Respondents must also read and sign a consent form which states the restrictions and tells consumers of the nature of the research. If appropriate, a GP supervises the tasting sessions.

Source: Tracey Sanderson.[15]

Ethics is also involved in the type of marketing research carried out and/or whether it is carried out in an ethically correct manner. When the research involves the testing of products which might have potentially dangerous side effects on consumers, considerable care has to be taken to ensure that procedures adopted are ethically acceptable and that they are not open to criticism.

RESEARCHERS' OBLIGATIONS TO CLIENTS

As well as ethical obligations to respondents, researchers also have obligations to their clients. Among the obligations are:

- *Methods used and results obtained must be accurately represented.* Researchers must use effective research procedures in obtaining and analysing the data. There is also an obligation to tell clients when they make ill-advised research requests. The researcher must also inform the client of any critical weakness or limitation in the collected data, especially those that could lead to major errors if the information is acted upon without reservation.

- *The client's identity as well as the information obtained must be held in confidence.* Any actual or prospective client approaching or using a research firm has the right to expect that what is revealed to that firm as part of this relationship is confidential.

- *Research should not be undertaken for competition if such research will jeopardise the confidential nature of the client–researcher relationship.*

ICC/ESOMAR Code

This is a professional code of practice for market researchers, published by the European Society for Opinion and Marketing Research (ESOMAR). It is based on the following eight principles:

1 Personal data has to be processed fairly and lawfully.
2 Personal data has to be obtained only for lawful purposes and should not be processed in any manner that is incompatible with such purposes.
3 Personal data has to be adequate, relevant and not excessive in relationship to the purpose for which it is being used.
4 Personal data has to be accurate and up to date where this is appropriate.
5 Personal data should not be kept on file any longer than is necessary for the purpose for which it was acquired.
6 Personal data has to be processed in accordance with the requirements of the Data Protection Act (see below).
7 Appropriate technical and organisational measures have to be in place to prevent unauthorised or unlawful processing of personal data, and to protect it against accidental loss, destruction or damage.
8 Personal data should not be transferred anywhere outside the European Economic Area unless there are preventive measures in place to ensure the rights and freedoms of data subjects in relation to the processing of personal data.

Data Protection Act

In 1999 the Data Protection Act 1998 was extended. The definition of data now includes all manual and electronic records – including video recordings and group discussions. Under the new provisions there is now specific reference to sensitive personal data – information carried regarding racial or ethnic origin, political opinions, religious or other similar beliefs, physical or mental health, sex life, and criminal convictions or proceedings. Conditions are laid down under which sensitive personal data may be lawfully processed. The 1984 Act set out a system of registration for all users of personal data covered by the Act – data user's name and address, description of personal data held, purpose for which the data is held, description of sources from which the data are derived, description of people to whom the data may be disclosed, names of places outside the UK to where the data may be sent, and an address for the receipt of requests from data subjects who wish to have access to the data. The 1998 Act introduced a new system of notification. It should be noted that it is against the law to hold or use any data in a way that is inconsistent with the registered entry. Registered entries are valid for specific periods and changes have to be recorded officially.

The Act is concerned with individuals, not corporate bodies, and does not refer to the processing of data by manual means. Useful guides to the Data Protection Act are available from the Data Protection Registrar, Springfield House, Water Lane, Wilmslow, Cheshire SK9 5AX.

Trends in marketing research

- A movement away from probability sampling towards quota sampling, along with a fall in sample sizes.
- Because of cost and time pressures less use of the integrated survey model of qualitative, pilot and full survey in projects.
- More qualitative research as a 'stand-alone' method in a wider number of applications.
- Growing use of databases for sampling.

  Source: Peter Mouncey.[16]

THE CHANGING ROLE OF MARKETING RESEARCH

Organisations are dynamic entities existing within a continuous, changing state of flux and trying to adapt to the requirements of rapidly changing environments. This very much applies to marketing research organisations, whether they are in-house departments or agencies. The last twenty-five years has witnessed vast changes in the way in which information is handled in organisations of all types and sizes. Alongside this revolution in information management, the role of marketing research has undergone substantial change. The change is not complete and it is impossible to say that the role of marketing research is now a fixed, static entity: its role is certain to change further in the future.

Adapting to the changing conditions of the business environment means dealing with new problems and decisions that may not previously have arisen. This accentuates the need for creativity in marketing research to enable new ways of researching new problem situations.

Changing role of market research

In the years ahead, successful research suppliers will need to develop close cooperation with their research clients. It is likely that much of the day-to-day work formerly carried out by in-house market research departments will be out-sourced to specialist research agencies. This will entail agencies having to have a much better understanding of their clients' problems and the manner in which research survey data can contribute towards the solution of such problems. Researchers are not primarily data gatherers though data gathering is essential and the work must be properly organised and controlled. The specialist skill of researchers, however, is being able to spot how research can help resolve a problem and help a firm make better decisions. It is the skill and creativity that is part of knowing how to get worthwhile information, how to help clients understand what data are telling them and what decisions they should consider making as a result.

Substantial changes have occurred in the market research business over the past decade. In particular there has been considerable change in the way research is bought and sold and the manner in which research is conducted. During the 1980s there was a slimming down in the size of market research departments and research suppliers often found themselves dealing with brand and marketing management, rather than in-house market research managers. For a long time, research suppliers had bemoaned the fact that they seldom dealt directly with executives who used research data they supplied. The change in circumstances meant that researchers had to deal directly with brand and marketing managers and help them make the best use of research.

Unfortunately, things have not worked out as well as might have been anticipated. There have been practical difficulties, such as research needs not being anticipated early enough within research users' companies. Research suppliers have also had to acknowledge that brand and marketing managers make use of information of which market research data is only a part. Executives are not research specialists and do not have the same depth of interest in the research process. In practice, market research data is now bought more as a component input to a company's overall activity rather than to meet specific client needs for a particular project.

Data collection methods are likely to change in the future, with an increasing use of computer assisted techniques, e-mail and the Internet as a means of communicating with customers, retailers and consumers. The trend of the last ten years, in which many market research departments have been abolished or combined with marketing departments, is also likely to be reversed. The unique skills of the specialist market researcher will come to be better understood and appreciated. It is unlikely that large in-house market research departments will develop again, but the establishment of small, high-level specialist teams of researchers within medium-sized and major companies is likely. Such teams will have a specialist role to play in the development of research briefs which will enable information to be made available as and when it is required. They will also contribute significantly to the way information is used within a marketing organisation.

Source: Bryan Bates.[17]

USING THE INTERNET FOR MARKETING RESEARCH

The Internet has remarkable potential as a tool for marketing research. It enables primary marketing research to become much less expensive to conduct than by using traditional media. Such research can, however, only really be exploratory. In using the Internet for collecting data and information, the scope of the sampling frame is restricted to those members of the Internet community who agree to respond. It has to be borne in mind that the demographics of users of the Internet are different from the general population. Results from Internet marketing research should not usually be generalised to the entire population. However, as more and more households gain access to the Internet this is a problem which may resolve itself in due course.

Web page self-completion forms facilitate the assessing of attitudes, wants and values of an organisation's customers. For example, a firm might use a self-completion form to learn about its customers' demographics and product preferences. Using such data the firm might employ it as a basis for segmenting its market.

The Internet might be used during product/service development. A company can quickly assess customers' thoughts about product changes or new products before any research and development investments are made. This can be done globally. In the same way a firm can gain much information through monitoring discussion groups made up of members of the firm's customer base. Executives can use this information to learn not only of the perceived strengths and weaknesses of their own products or services, but those of their competitors as well.

THE NEED FOR MORE CREATIVITY IN RESEARCH

We live in a world that is undergoing continuous and rapid change. Situations are regularly encountered that have not previously arisen. Technology, competition, changes in social values, new expectations of customers, economic upheaval and all the other kinds of changes that can occur in the business environment produce new problems for management. Solutions to such problems often require insight that traditional, well-used problem-solving techniques are unable to provide. Under such circumstances the need for creative problem-solving assumes a greater importance than ever before. Developments in world markets, shorter production cycles, the need to find new ways to resource the exploitation of opportunities, and the scarcity and cost of basic resources are just a few of the new challenges for the modern day executive. In order to respond to such challenges there is a need to think creatively.

Research findings have provided support for the argument that there is a direct link between creative thinking and organisational efficiency and effectiveness.[18] In particular, creativity helps to improve the value of solutions to persistent organisational problems. It has also been found that creativity helps to encourage profitable innovations, rekindles employee motivation and improves personal skills and team performance. All these can contribute towards a continuous flow of ideas for new products and services and, by improving work processes, provide the platform on which an organisation can develop its competitive advantage.

There are few aspects of organisational activity where the need for creativity does not make itself felt. While the need for new ideas often predominates problem tasks, old ideas, too, need to be re-examined. After all, creativity is the process of revealing, selecting, swapping around and combining our store of facts, ideas and skills. Rickards[19] has described creativity as an 'escape from mental stuckness', an operational definition that is very much in keeping with its role in decision-making and problem-solving.

Creative research

One of the key reasons for the lack of genuine innovation in the 1990s is that researchers keep asking the same questions and using the same processes, with the result that predictable responses are obtained from consumers. Since there are nowadays so many 'expert' consumers, a new creative focus is required to encourage new kinds of consumer responses to be made. It is necessary to inject creativity into research, making use of both environmental stimuli and people, for it is these elements that make creative research more effective. It is essential, however, that researchers should be familiar with and confident in the use of creativity techniques.

A step in the right direction is to introduce a high level of interaction into consumer workshops in order to interpret the sensory experiences of the consumer. It is often the case that what consumers say and actually do conflict with one another. Knowing this and observing it may help us to intuitively read between the lines and make research more efficient and meaningful.

Source: Claire Nuttall.[20]

The need for creativity in research is no less than in any other area of marketing or management. If research is to provide really useful information for helping organisations to gain a competitive advantage, it needs to be imaginative and capable of bringing forth equally new ideas, insights and viewpoints from respondents.

NON-RESPONSE AS AN ISSUE IN THE EFFECTIVENESS OF MARKETING RESEARCH

In a society where people are becoming more and more cynical towards marketing research, non-response is becoming an issue that is relevant to the effectiveness of such research. Answers to questions posed in surveys, for example, may differ considerably between those who respond and those who do not. In busy shopping malls, those who spend time helping the researcher fill in questionnaires may have totally different ideas and concerns to those who rush rapidly by and decline to cooperate. Moreover, in the case of business to business research, the non-respondent may be an organisation of major significance, whose lack of participation renders the research comparatively meaningless. While training of interviewers, extra incentives and even patience can sometimes overcome potential non-response, pressure of time, apathy, scepticism and greater feelings of rights to privacy all contribute to the potential problems posed by non-response.

SUMMARY

This chapter has explored how marketing research can take some of the risk out of marketing decision-making by providing information that can contribute to sound marketing decision-making. This may be achieved in all elements of the marketing-mix and, through involvement in problem formulation and solution-finding, marketing research becomes an integral part of the process of formulating marketing strategy. Marketing research can perform a variety of studies and makes use of both primary and secondary data sources. It can be applied either in-house or by marketing research companies that specialise in this form of consultancy. The latter offer a wide range of services, from off-the-peg studies to tailor-made studies to meet the needs of individual clients. Like many other services involving the generation of confidential information and reports, ethical considerations are an important issue and need to be fully explored. New ways of asking questions pose challenges for marketing researchers and the introduction of creativity into marketing research is paramount.

Questions

1   What is marketing research?
2   What do you understand by the philosophy of science?
3   How does marketing research help reduce the risk in decision-making?
4   Indicate the ways in which marketing research can help marketing management.
5   What are the main divisions of marketing research?
6   What kind of information is provided through customer or market research?
7   What kind of information does promotion and advertising research provide?
8   Indicate the nature of product research.
9   What kind of information is made available through distribution research?
10 Discuss the nature of sales research.
11 What kinds of information does environment research try to elicit?
12 What is meant by the following terms?
    a   Preliminary research.
    b   Conclusive research.
    c   Performance research.
13 What is the difference between marketing research and marketing information systems?
14 Indicate the typical elements of a marketing information system.
15 Differentiate between primary and secondary data.
16 Describe the different types of consumer data that can be collected.
17 Discuss how marketing research is part of marketing strategy.
18 When might it be desirable to use outside marketing research services as opposed to doing research in-house?
19 What factors should be taken into account when selecting an outside agency?
20 Indicate the kind of specialist services that marketing research agencies might be able to supply.
21 How should a marketing research proposal be evaluated?
22 What are the ethical considerations that should be taken into account in marketing research?
23 How might the Internet be used in marketing research?
24 Why is there a need for more creativity in marketing research?
25 What kind of problems and issues are created by the fact that many people often refuse to take part in a research study? How might these problems be addressed?

Case study 1.1   Lampelichter AG, Essen

All manufacturers of lamps are frantically trying to maintain and protect their share in a shrinking market. Each manufacturer has a large number of production facilities across Europe and the profitability of the companies is determined by production loading. In this industry economies of scale play a major role and the over-capacity of the manufacturers ensuing from the shrinking market has brought about aggressive price competition. This has been reflected in lower unit selling prices and reduced margins, and has put further emphasis on achieving economies of scale. Currently, lamp manufacturing is not a profitable industry. Companies are fighting for market share and high exit barriers prevent withdrawal. However, whenever the upturn occurs, those firms that survive the recession will be in a good position to take advantage of future growth and new markets.

Recently, Philips has entered the Polish market both to access the emerging ex-Comecon markets and to obtain a lower cost base to aid its price competitiveness in established European markets. Similarly, GE has invested heavily in Hungary and Osram has expanded its distribution into the former East Germany and purchased the North American operations of GTE, which has retrenched its business activities to its core of telecommunications. The acquisition of GTE's share of the North American market was critical to Osram to prevent its being marginalised as a European producer. The North America move countered GE's expansion into Europe. GE has also acquired controlling interests in manufacturing sites in Italy, Japan and China. Philips and Osram are also investing in joint ventures in China and the Far East.

As manufacturers have moved into areas of lower cost production, the unit selling price of the manufacturers since 1993 has fallen in real terms – a trend that is expected to continue. However, while the unit production cost of the product has fallen, the distribution and sales costs associated with it have risen.

Lampelichter employs around 100 personnel and was established in 1970. As one of the leading independent suppliers of replacement lamps to independent electrical retailers in Germany, the firm undertakes marketing and distribution but has no manufacturing capacity. It has a single warehousing and office facility in Essen and uses carriers to deliver its consignments to customers. In 1993, 65 per cent of its annual sales were under its own-label brand. In 1995 the firm was looking towards a sales revenue target of DM30m. In 1994 the firm's sales revenues were made up as follows:

- light bulbs 74 per cent
- plugs, sockets and other accessories 10 per cent
- security, task lighting, etc. 12 per cent
- torches, batteries, etc. 4 per cent

In Europe generally, the independent electrical retailers have chosen to reduce stockholding, thereby holding stock back at their suppliers. This has produced an increase in the number of orders placed but a reduction in the average order value. Unless suppliers can break the trend of falling selling prices coupled with rising sales and distribution costs, the long-term net margin position of the suppliers in the independent market will continue to worsen. The lamp supply industry is very seasonal – November's turnover is approximately twice that of June. The period September to March is critical to the success of the organisation, but the resources available to allow it to take advantage of the season are carried throughout the year. This makes it a high-fixed-cost organisation that actually budgets to lose money in the spring and summer periods.

Lampelichter differs from the majority of its competitors. It markets its products on a national basis rather than the more usual local or regional basis adopted by the competition. Competition comprises manufacturers (competing directly for major accounts), national electrical wholesalers, local electrical wholesalers, special lamp distributors, and appliance and accessory distributors. Within the company's organisational structure there are board representatives for sales, marketing, finance and operations. Approximately 60 per cent of the company workforce is directly related to the sales/sales support roles. The remaining 40 per cent is taken up in staffing the following departments: data processing, accounts and finance, quality assurance, warehousing and transport.

The sales budget in 1995 split the total revenue targets as follows:

Distribution channel	1995 Target	1994
Independent electrical retailer	60%	65%
Commercial user	32%	25%
Onward distributor	8%	10%

Lampelichter considers that it has committed and talented management and employees, a good reputation in the trade, excellent goodwill and significant customer loyalty. It also has a substantial field sales force, its own branded product range, consistent attractive barcoded own-brand packaging and excellent supplier relationships with all major lamp suppliers. The firm is a financially strong private company with limited borrowings. It has high stock inventory coupled with an extensive product range. Furthermore, it has expertise in fragile products. The firm has a market-led culture (with the object of being customer led).

Lampelichter's historic customer base is in decline and the firm is reluctant to accept added-value products. Within the company there is a lack of internal performance standards. Profitability is declining and there is an under-utilisation of assets. Compared with competition the firm is a relatively high-fixed-cost operation. Moreover, delivery performance is poorer than that of competitors. Under-manning of the sales force is causing ineffective sales management. The sales force is also an ageing one in terms of selling skills and professionalism, and exhibits an absence of any customer segmentation and associated objectives and strategies. The company has a weak planning structure and skills base and a poor training culture.

There are a range of possible opportunities in the market place. These include range extension into complementary non-lamp products, supply-chain integration and new markets. However, the firm faces increased competition from lower cost distributors, increased competition from manufacturers on direct contracts with large users, increased seasonality of the core business, falling real costs of lamps, centralisation of supplier power with fewer own-brand suppliers, and fewer independent retailers.

Following discussion between the top management of the company and a European management consultancy organisation, the consultancy firm recommended that Lampelichter should commission marketing research to explore the various avenues open to it.

Question

What kind of marketing research information do you think Lampelichter should try to obtain?

Case study 1.2 | Reliant

Reliant Motors, one of Britain's last car companies, came back from the verge of extinction for the second time in two years yesterday, when three businessmen bought the Staffordshire firm from administrators for an undisclosed sum that is thought to be less than £500,000. In January, last year, Reliant was bought by the Gloucestershire engineering group, Avonex, from receivers appointed after the parent company, Beans Industries, was hit by bad debt. Yesterday's sale, by administrators Finn Associates, follows fresh difficulties.

Jonathan Heynes, a former Jaguar engineer, and two anonymous businessmen intend to increase production of the three-wheeler Robin to thirty cars a week and plan to introduce a three-wheeler pick-up truck and city delivery vehicle. The factory in Tamworth, currently employing ten workers, has fifty cars to complete before production restarts. Before lay-offs began the firm employed 110 people and Mr Heynes hopes to rehire up to ninety.

It was Mr Heynes' intention that the three-wheeler, immortalised in the comedy programme 'Only Fools and Horses', would remain the core of the business although Reliant did plan to expand into sports car production, albeit using four wheels per car. The new sports car would be priced around £18,000, some three times the price of the Robin.

The Robin

- Top speed: in excess of 70 miles an hour
- Acceleration: 0–60 mph in 14 seconds
- Production: more than 44,000 current runners
- Fuel consumption: 72.5 mpg at 56 mph

- Standard equipment on top range models: radio-cassette, instrumentation including clock
- Price: from £6,000

Mr Heynes said that the Robin appealed to motorists who wanted a simple vehicle that would not rust. Reliant owners are typically over forty years of age, often prefer the DIY approach and are often former motor-cyclists who have concluded that some protection on the road was better than none. Some 70 per cent of sales are top-of-the-range models that have more instruments than the basic model and a heated rear window.

A consortium of Far East businessmen has already secured the rights to produce the cars outside Britain.

Source: Chris Barrie.[21]

Question

Discuss the value of marketing research for a firm in Reliant's circumstances.

Case study 1.3   Shell fish restaurant

Jean-Patrick Mazzaoli got his idea in the USA where he had been at university studying marketing. On the other side of the Atlantic he had discovered a chain of restaurants that only served lobsters, shrimps and other shell fish. He was convinced that this might well catch on in France. On returning to France he decided that he wanted to adopt the formula and set up a restaurant in his home town, Marseilles. He was very friendly with Yves Tarallo, a trained chef, and together they decided to study the market to establish the viability of such a project.

Source: Rebondir.[22]

Question

Indicate the kind of marketing research Jean-Patrick and Yves might reasonably carry out.

Case study 1.4   Reading Scientific Services Ltd (RSSL)

RSSL is a multidisciplinary scientific consultancy providing research and analytical services to the food, drink, consumer goods, chemical and healthcare industries. It has expertise in both routine and investigative pharmaceutical analysis including sensory evaluation and consumer research. One of its clients has developed a new variant of a pharmaceutical over-the-counter product and wishes to assess whether it has a more acceptable flavour than the market leaders. The product is aimed at children from three to eight years of age. It is to be evaluated against four competitors, all of which are over-the-counter medicines with the same level and type of active drug.

Source: Tracey Sanderson.[23]

Questions

1 Discuss the ethical considerations involved.

2 What steps might be taken to ensure proper testing in this case?

Case study 1.5 | The English Bear Company

The English Bear Company was founded in 1991 by Alise Crossick, 29, and her husband Jonty, 28. They now have 10 shops in cities including Bath, Cambridge and London and have recently opened in Tokyo. Their annual turnover is £4m.

Jonty: 'Alise and I met at Cambridge in 1988 when we were both impecunious students. We knew we wanted to be in business on our own and that whatever we did, we would have to start with nothing. Designing and selling T-shirts was the obvious choice because it didn't need any capital, only an understanding supplier. The bear idea grew out of that. Our most popular T-shirt featured a bear which Alise had drawn, yet she'd never actually made one when we decided to launch the bear company.

'Being a typical Antipodean, she just got on with it: advertised for bear-makers, then sat down with a bear manual. Most of the applicants patiently watched her demonstrate, then showed her how it could be done 100 per cent better.

'We always wanted to create a company that would communicate something from the heart, something magical. I think the bears do that because they express fun and cuddles. We make them out of distressed mohair which makes them look old and loved. Our customers don't want something pristine, they're looking for character.

'We initially made mistakes in identifying our customers. Our first outlet was a kiosk in Whiteley's which we thought was perfect as it gave us a start in London. The rent was so cheap that we didn't bother to carry out market research. It wasn't until we opened in Cambridge that we realised the tourist trade was much more lucrative.

'Our sites are now picked with greater care. It's about 50 per cent strategic choice, 30 per cent gut feeling and 20 per cent scientific data.'

Alise: 'It was never just about selling bears, our vision was the whole concept of people wearing bear clothes, eating bear marmalade and drinking bear tea.

'When people love bears, they personify them and become absorbed in the lifestyle. We get young businessmen coming into our shops who look like they want to quickly buy a bear and run out again. The next minute they're captivated and umming and ahhing over which face they like the best.

'Occasionally we get people bringing old bears for repairs, like the chap who rushed in with something his dog had half-eaten.

'There's not enough people in retail trying to help their customers, it's all take, take, take. We put our hearts into the business and believe passionately in the products. If you put enough energy and care into something it should work.

'We're not in business to suffer so we only work with people we like. Bears bring out the best in people because they cross gender and race and represent unconditional love. If we weren't working together I wouldn't find it so worthwhile. We generate so much love between us that it makes it wonderful for everyone around.'

Source: Fiona Lafferty.[24] Reprinted with permission.

Questions

1 Discuss how marketing research may have been used beneficially by the English Bear Company.

2 How might marketing research still prove a useful tool to the company?

Case study 1.6 | Twenty-first-century market research

Market research is coming out of the closet. Direct marketing firms have emerged to service the new phenomenon of relationship marketing – lifestyle databases underpinning the mailings of the firms to provide a direct interface between research and practice.

Direct marketing company databases hold a mass of fine detail on customers' purchasing habits. Advances in computer technology have given firms the ability to combine databases to give a fuller picture of customer purchasing habits without ever having to approach a respondent with a questionnaire – the information is directly available. Researchers no longer need to reassure respondents about anonymity, either; instead they offer rewards to consumers in exchange for giving personal information to the researchers.

Data mining is the new catchword for market researchers. Using what used to be considered as secondary sources of information, the researchers analyse direct marketing company records to build up an in-depth picture of the lifestyles of millions of consumers. New ways of segmenting markets based on lifestyles and attitudes are being discovered, and ways of translating market research into market action are working more quickly and effectively. Because of the speed of analysing such research, market researchers are able to offer high-quality tailored research packages to small firms who previously could not have afforded professional market research.

Another area in which market research is being revolutionised is through the Internet. On one Web-based project 160 out of 400 respondents replied to an e-mail survey within three hours – formerly, this many responses would have taken days to obtain, or even weeks using normal postal services. An additional advantage is that such surveys cost around one-third the price of telephone surveys. Currently most of this research is being conducted in the United States, where more people are connected to the Net than is the case in Europe, but eventually Web-based research is expected to outperform all other methods of conducting surveys.

The relatively new activity of category management has also thrown up new challenges for market researchers. The Institute of Grocery Distribution defines CM as 'The strategic management of product groups through trade partnerships which aim to maximise sales and profits by satisfying consumer needs.' In practice, what this means is that manufacturers and retailers need to co-operate in managing certain product categories, rather than concentrating solely on brands. For example, Van den Bergh Foods (manufacturers of margarine and other fats) saw a need to establish retailer-specific market research programmes to develop an understanding of consumers' motivations to buy margarine. The research programme involved 1200 interviews conducted as customers left the stores, 1300 interviews at the margarine display fixtures in the stores, 200 depth interviews, 76 accompanied shopping trips, and 36 hours of video observation. The research was carried out in seven major retail chains. Marked differences between the different retailers were found, so Van den Bergh were able to conclude that marketing, merchandising and even pricing might need to be varied between retailers to take account of differences in consumer motivation between store chains.

Ultimately, it seems that such research would be more efficiently carried out if the retailers themselves participated in the costs and shared the benefits – this would, of course, require agreements between the retailers to share information. Such agreements do not present a problem if the work is carried out by an independent market research company, of course, but the result for the market researchers is that they may find themselves forced into a tight brief which allows little room for creativity.

Increasingly, the business community is becoming more information-orientated. In a constantly changing world, the need for up-to-date and accurate information is more important than ever before, and market researchers are using (and seeking) new tools for collecting and analysing that information.

(Case contributed by Jim Blythe)

Questions

1 What might be the limitations on using Web-based research in the UK?

2 What are the advantages and disadvantages of research for category management purposes?

3 How might the disadvantages of CM research be reduced?

4 What ethical problems might arise from the combination of direct-mail databases to generate detailed information about consumers?

5 How might creative approaches to Web research increase response rates?

Further reading

Achrol, R S and Stern, L W (1988) Environmental determinants of decision making uncertainty in marketing channels, *Journal of Marketing Research*, 25, pp 36–50.

Anderson, P F (1983) Marketing, scientific progress, and scientific method, *Journal of Marketing*, 47(4), 18–31.

Aschenbaum, A A (1993) The future challenge to market research, *Marketing Research: A Magazine of Management and Application*, 5(2), pp 12–18.

Bogda, P and Meyers, G C (1991) Grab a partner for more effective research, *Marketing News*, 7 January, p 2ff.

Brown, S (1996) Art or science? Fifty years of marketing debate, *Journal of Marketing Management*, 12(4), 243–67.

Hill, A, Roberts, H, Ewings, P and Gunnell, D (1997) Nonresponse bias in a lifestyle survey, *Journal of Public Health Medicine*, 19(2), 203–7.

Hirschman, E C (1986) Humanistic inquiry in marketing research: philosophy, method and criteria, *Journal of Marketing Research*, 23, pp 237–49.

Jackson, P (1994a) *Buying Market Research*, London: Kogan Page.

Jick, T D (1979) Mixing qualitative and quantitative methods: triangulation in action, *Administrative Science Quarterly*, December, 24, 602–11.

Macht, J (1999) The new market research, *Inc*, 20(10), pp 86–94.

Marek, D (1998) We all need to address declining respondent co-operation, http://www.mra-net.org.

McDaniel, C and Gates, R (2002) *Marketing Research: The impact of the Internet* (5th edn), Cincinnati, OH: South-Western.

Perry, C, Reige, A and Brown, L (1999) Realism's role among scientific paradigms in marketing research, *Irish Marketing Review*, 12(2), 16–23.

Peter, P J and Olson, C (1989) The relativist/constructionist perspective on scientific knowledge and consumer research, in E Hirschman (ed) *Interpretive Consumer Research*, Provo, UT: ACR, pp 24–8.

Piercy, N and Evans, M (1993) *Managing Marketing Information*, London: Croom Helm.

Robson, S (1991) Ethics: informed consent or misinformed compliance?, *Journal of the Market Research Society*, 33, 19–28.

Shea, C Z and LeBourveau, C (2000) Jumping the hurdles of marketing research, *Marketing Research*, 12(3), pp 22–30.

Singer, E, Von Thurn, D R and Miller, E R (1995) Confidentiality assurances and response. A quantitative review of the experimental literature, *Public Opinion Quarterly*, 59(1), pp 67–77.

Weible, R and Wallace, J (1998) Cyber research: the impact of the Internet on data collection, *Market Research*, 10(3), pp 19–27.

Weinman, C (1991) It's not an 'art', but marketing research can be creative, *Marketing News*, 25(8), pp 9, 24.

West, C (1995) Marketing research, in M J Baker (ed) *Companion Encyclopaedia of Marketing*, London: Routledge.

References and notes

[1] Chisnall, P (1992) *Marketing Research* (4th edn), Maidenhead: McGraw-Hill, pp 5–6.

[2] AMA (1987) New marketing research definition approved, *Marketing News*, 21, 2 January.

[3] Cowan, D (1994) Good information, *Journal of the Market Research Society*, 36(2), pp 105–14.

[4] Freeling, A (1994) Marketing is in a crisis – can marketing research help?, *Journal of the Market Research Society*, 36, pp 97–104.

[5] Easterby-Smith, M, Thorpe, R and Lowe, A (1991) *Management Research: An introduction*, London: Sage, p 21.

[6] Allison, B, O'Sullivan, T, Owen, A, Rice, J, Rothwell, A and Saunders, C (1996) *Research Skills for Students: Transferable and learning skills*, London: Kogan Page.

[7] Bekesi, J (1997) Gruppe Phänomenologie. Society for the Advancement of the Critical Development of Phenomenology and its Impulses, http://gph.freezope.org.

[8] Embree, L (1997) What is phenomenology?, Center for Advanced Research in Phenomenology, http://www.phenomenologycenter.org/phenom.htm.

[9] Hannabuss, S (1995) Approaches to research, *Aslib Proceedings*, 47(1), p 3.

[10] Gummesson, E (1990) *Qualitative Methods in Management Research*, London: Sage.

[11] Cresswell, J W (1994) *Research Design: Qualitative and quantitative approaches*, London: Sage.

[12] Campbell, S (1997) Management: marketing wake-up, *Financial Times*, 3 June.

[13] *Rebondir* (1996) no 12, p 35.

[14] Samways, A and Whittcome, K (1994) UK brand strategies, a *Financial Times* management report, p 60.

[15] Sanderson, T (1996) How a spoonful of research helps the medicine go down, *Research Plus*, April, pp 6–8.

[16] Mouncey, P (1996) With growing demands for data, will purity prove only theoretical?, *Research Plus*, May, p 9.

[17] Bates, B (1996) Quality will mark the route to deeper client relationships, *Research Plus*, March, pp 9, 14.

[18] Raudsepp, T (1987) Establishing a creative climate, *Training and Development Journal*, April, pp 50–3.

[19] Rickards, T (1988) *Creativity and Innovation: A transatlantic perspective*, Manchester Business School: Creativity and Innovation Yearbook.

[20] Nuttall, C (1996) Research needs more creativity, *Marketing Week*, 29 April, p 32.

[21] Barrie, C (1996) Second rescue for spluttering Reliant, *Guardian*, 6 April, p 2.

[22] *Rebondir* (1996) Un restaurant de gambas, ouvrir un commerce, *Rebondir*, no 12.

[23] Sanderson, T (1996) How a spoonful of research helps the medicine go down, *Research Plus*, April, pp 6–8.

[24] Lafferty, F (1997) Management: The English Bear Company: Partners, *Financial Times*, 28 April.

2 Planning the research project

OBJECTIVES

After reading this chapter you should be able to:

- understand how marketing research helps in allaying uncertainty;

- appreciate the cost and value of marketing research;

- appreciate the need to plan, schedule and control a marketing research project, probably with the aid of computer-based PERT in this process.

KEY WORDS

problem definition	research limitations
uncertainty	research schedule
value of research	PERT
research plan	research control
research proposal	

might have expected. The fault may lie with the price or the packaging, but the firm does not really have any precise ideas. It is even wondering whether it should drop out of the jellies market entirely. If this last action is seriously contemplated it needs to know how this would affect the firm's other product lines and, in particular, what effect it would have on distributors' readiness to stock the firm's other products.

A systematic approach to problem definition can help to direct marketing research staff in their efforts to obtain relevant information. It is also informative to all those people in the organisation who will be affected by the findings and recommendations.

Many parties may be involved in helping to define a marketing problem and it has to be approached in a systematic manner

A firm manufactures high-quality crystal glassware and wants to expand and become more profitable. It is considering manufacturing and distributing a line of lower-quality, lower-price products. It is unsure, however, whether it has the manufacturing and marketing experience to make such a venture successful.

In defining such a problem we have to adopt a systematic approach. The first step is to find out what the firm needs to know. Certainly, the firm needs a complete knowledge of the market. What competitive lines are being sold? Are competitors' lines profitable? Is there room for another line? How strong are brand names? How strong would the firm's brand name be in this lower-price line? Should the firm even use its brand name for this product? Can current distribution channels handle the new line? How strong are lines coming in from other countries?

The definition of the marketing problem must cover these questions together with additional questions posed by other involved parties.

Problem definition must take into account the situation of the company and its ability to take sound action. Poorly thought-out marketing decisions can cause major problems, sometimes with disastrous consequences. Many things can go wrong and many opportunities can be missed. The marketers in the firm need to anticipate and prevent as many of these as possible, and in each case the first action should be a precise definition of the problem.

Swiss watch industry – missing an opportunity through incorrect perception of the problem

The Swiss watch industry chose to ignore the application of a new technology even though it had itself created the technology in the first place. Although the

Swiss watch industry invented the quartz movement it did not initially make use of the invention because it felt that this invention would have strong negative effects on its existing product markets.[1] The Swiss argued that anyone else could make the quartz movement, whereas only the Swiss themselves had the skills to make the clockwork components required for automatic and mechanical movements.

With the benefit of hindsight we can appreciate that the Swiss were right in their thinking but wrong in their strategy. Watchmakers in Japan and Hong Kong immediately adopted the quartz movement, and in one year the sales of Swiss watches dropped by some 25 per cent.

Swiss watch manufacturers became entrapped because the executives in the firms did not really understand the nature of the market. They did not appreciate or understand customer wants and needs. The Swiss Swatch company rescued the Swiss watch industry by providing a bulk outlet for quartz movements so that prices could be brought down. The firm also recognised that telling the time was no longer the most important thing in a watch. Swatch was not selling 'an indicator of the time' as much as fun and costume jewellery.

From the very beginning of awareness and consideration of a marketing problem, research should be an integral part of the problem-solving approach.

Example of a marketing decision – a new product for a manufacturer

Marketing research can find information that helps to answer the following questions:

- Does an obvious need for the product exist?
- Has the company sufficient financial resources to design, manufacture and push the product through the early sales growth years?
- What will be the best design to adopt?
- What will be the best price level(s) for the market or market segments?
- How should the firm choose between volume, price and profit?
- What will be the probable market life for the product?
- What level of quality will be required?
- Who are the competitors, who is about to enter the market and how strong are actual and potential competitors?
- What will be required in the way of promotion? What will it cost?
- How will this new product affect current lines?

Table 2.1 Problem definition: goal orientation

• Write down description of problem Then ask:	• Problem: sales/profits of main product are stagnating
• What do we need to accomplish (needs)?	• Need: increased sales and profits
• What are the obstacles?	• Obstacles: competition intense so increase in market share unlikely; market saturated; home market in recession
• What constraints must we accept to solve the problem?	• Constraints: lack of funds for internal new product development
• Redefine the problem, bearing the . above in mind	• Problem redefinition: possible avenues to explore: new markets, market segments, diversification, licensing, joint ventures, integrative strategies

PROBLEM DEFINITION: GOAL-ORIENTED APPROACH

Rickards[2] suggests that a useful way in which to approach problem definition is the technique–goal orientation. Essentially the method employs identifying needs, obstacles and constraints in the search for an adequate definition of the problem. The procedure, along with an illustration, is given in Table 2.1.

See also Proctor[3] for an extensive coverage of problem-definition techniques.

STEPS IN SOLVING PROBLEMS

It is usually possible to solve problems in more than one way. For example, a new range of furniture may be produced for sale in the domestic market, the domestic market and Europe, or for worldwide distribution. A decision has to be taken as to which of these options is the best strategy to adopt. The decision here reflects the nature of the problem and, in such a problem statement, there are three possible options.

The problem statement illustrates the important point that the various options need to be identified and set out. Information then has to be obtained that is pertinent to each of the identified courses of action so that an objective evaluation can then be made about the course of action to follow. There may be some disagreement about the nature of the options and it is therefore of paramount importance that these disagreements are resolved as soon as possible. Before the final definition of the marketing problem, those involved in the decision must also agree on the nature and quality of the information needed to make a sound decision.

DECIDING WHETHER TO UNDERTAKE A RESEARCH STUDY

Whether marketing research makes organisations more profitable is open to question for there are other factors to consider. Profits are associated not just with increased revenues but also result from controlling or even cutting costs – just to name two sources! Many of these factors may have nothing to do with marketing research. However, in theory decision-making based on good information should be better than decision-making made on the basis of no information or poor information. Of course, in practice, this may not hold true. Even information which is thought to be good may not necessarily be useful. People's attitudes and opinions do not always match with their actions so that information collected can sometimes be misleading. For example, people may say that they will buy a new car in the next year and that they will buy a specific model. Many factors can then intervene in the meanwhile which will mean that the appropriate actions are not followed through.

The above, however, is a negative picture and it is argued that in many instances – hopefully the majority – marketing research will lead to better information, which will in turn lead to better decisions. The better decisions may in turn lead to increased revenues or lower costs and hence to more profits. For example, group discussions may indicate the need for additional features that can be built in to a product. The additional features will enhance the product's competitive advantage in the market place, which in turn will enhance its sales. The additional cost of including the features may involve a price increase to the customer but the overall effect is an increase in profits associated with the product.

It is arguably better to make decisions based on objective data than purely subjective feelings – and better still to use both in decision-making. Better research and better management judgement, for example, might have prevented the disaster when the Sinclair C5 car was introduced in the UK some years ago.[4] Similar comments also apply in the case of the Swiss watch industry and its failure to exploit the opportunities presented by the quartz movement.

UNCERTAINTY IN DECISIONS

Marketing decisions are made under conditions of uncertainty. We can never be sure whether a new product will be successful or whether an advertising campaign will be effective in terms of meeting its objectives. In fact, in marketing there is very little of which we can be certain.

Marketing research helps to dispel uncertainty

A producer of gourmet foods encounters uncertainty when contemplating a new product containing large percentages of saturated fat and cholesterol. How strong is consumer awareness of these dangers to health? Are people likely to become rapidly more health conscious? Marketing research would be very advisable for this new product.

PROBABLE PAY-OFF OF EACH OPTION

Attention to the probable pay-off of each new product, service or other option should be considered. The greatest potential pay-off, other things being equal, is the determining factor in exercising choice. We should attempt to estimate the probable pay-off of each option before we specify the necessity of researching material that is relevant to that option. Past product successes or failures can give clues about what might happen.

The cost of getting information should be weighed against the possible sales and profits that may result from implementing a proposed course of action. Hence, the nature and amount of marketing research to be undertaken must be strictly controlled by cost and profit considerations. In many cases the cost of research is small compared with the possible benefits to be derived from adopting a course of action. The profits associated with the introduction of new products can run into many millions of pounds whereas the cost of marketing research may be measured in thousands of pounds. However, there may be instances where marketing research is relatively costly in relationship to expected benefits. In such cases, decision trees like the one in Figure 2.1, including the options of 'with' or 'without' research, can be set up to estimate the benefits of undertaking research.

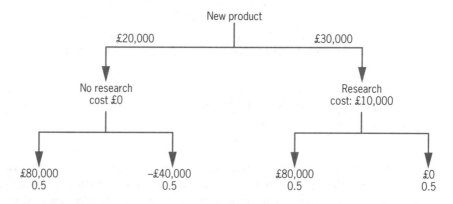

Figure 2.1 Value of marketing research

- Determine previous recommendations
- Determine research questions

Method/analysis for research

- Select data collection method
- Select analysis method
- Select supplier/field service
- Choose facility location(s)
- Prepare focus group materials
- Supervise recruiting
- Supervise/conduct sessions
- Review sessions

Data analysis and interpretation

- Choose appropriate analysis
- Run analysis
- Interpret results
- Choose report format
- Highlight findings

Report: write up research method and management

- Present overview
- Review literature
- Design and execute
- Describe population, sampling frame, sampling method/size
- Detail collection method
- Report completion rate
- Explain data processing

Report: write up analysis and interpretation

- Present data
- Present data manipulations
- Present interpretations
- Summary/conclusion
- Review significant findings
- State major discovery
- Report study limitations
- Prepare tables
- Prepare illustrative graphs

- List references
- Write abstract
- Edit report
- Revise report
- Print report

Research project: presentation to management

- Highlight findings
- Prepare slides/overheads
- Rehearse presentation
- Present report

THE PROPOSAL

The producers of the proposal and plan should take into account how the findings and recommendations should be presented and to whom. These details impinge on how collected information is subsequently organised and best presented as charts, tables, slides or in other ways. A study that will be presented solely to top management may require important differences in method of presentation and details. Some thought has to be given to the types of personalities that will examine the proposal. This means assessing the extent to which the proposal will have to 'prove itself' to certain management members and what will be needed to convince them to accept it.

Research proposal

1   Clear statement of the marketing problem or problems to be investigated
2   Contributory factors and constraints related to the problem
3   Definition of the product/service to be investigated
4   Definition of the survey population to be sampled
5   Major areas of measurement – consumption, beliefs about products, expectations, attitudes, motivations, classifications of buyers, etc.
6   Methodology to be adopted (types of data, method of sampling, research instruments, etc.)
7   Expected degree of accuracy of research findings
8   Cost and time involved in conducting the research
9   Conditions applying to research
10 Previous experience of researchers

USE OF PERT IN PLANNING RESEARCH

A marketing research plan is a form of project and as such may be thought of as a combination of interrelated activities that have to be carried out in a certain order so that the entire task is completed. There is a logical sequence to the interrelated activities in the sense that some of them cannot start until others are completed. Projects and planning activities have become extremely complex and require systematic and effective management techniques to help optimise the efficiency of executing such activities. Efficiency amounts to bringing about the greatest reduction in the time to complete the scheduled activities while taking into account the economic feasibility of using available resources.

Planning, scheduling and control can be assisted by a network-analysis tool such as the project evaluation and review technique (PERT). This tool provides help to monitor and organise resources in order to enable a project or activity to be completed on time and within budget limits. Projects and planning activities are complex entities that often have extensive duration times, involve many different and interrelated costs, and comprise work of a distinctive, unique, non-repetitive nature. It is customary to model projects and planning activities as networks to capture the nature of the interrelationships and the sequencing of their various component parts.

PERT is basically a three-part technique:

1 *Planning*: this incorporates an in-depth analysis of the project or planning task and the construction of the network to describe it.

2 *Scheduling*: this involves the analysis of the project or exercise to determine completion time, critical activities, and the start and finish times for each activity.

3 *Controlling*: this includes using the network and the schedule to keep track of progress and making any revisions necessary to keep the project or exercise on schedule and within budget.

The planning stage involves three parts:

1 identifying and sequencing all activities;
2 drawing the network to represent the exercise;
3 estimating activity times and costs.

Once the network has been constructed and the expected times decided, it becomes possible both to determine the minimum completion time for the exercise and to schedule each activity. This stage is handled well by a computer program.

At some stage in the project it may be thought desirable to shorten the completion time. This can usually be achieved by allocating additional resources to critical activities. A minimum duration for the project or exercise will exist and further expenditure will not be able to reduce completion time below this minimum. It also has to be realised that the efficient allocation of resources requires further analysis of the project or exercise, examining time/cost trade-offs in order to obtain the greatest time reduction per amount of money expended.

A significant impact on the process of project management and planning has been made by computers, and specialised software packages – more specifically, packages that run on desktop computers – have been developed. In applying the PERT technique, the networks produced are often large and require many revisions for replanning and updating. Making such revisions by hand can be time-consuming, confusing and costly. The process is much accelerated by the use of appropriate computer software, making changes and comparisons much easier. There are many relevant software packages available, some specifically designed for use with the desktop computer. A useful guide to have when selecting a package is that provided by Smith and Gupta.[6]

An example of a sophisticated project management computer software package is Time Line for Windows.[7] It possesses convenient graphing tools that make it easy to build and revise schedules and to assign and coordinate resources, dependencies and due dates across multiple projects and planning exercises. Multiple views also allow us to see many aspects of a complex model simultaneously. There are six types of view permissible:

- the Overview
- the Gantt view
- the PERT view
- the Time-Scaled PERT view
- the Resource view
- the Cross-tabulation view.

The package also includes Guide Line software that enables the user to generate project and planning schedules just by answering a series of questions. The Guide Maker add-on enables the user to create custom guides for any business situation. Guide Line is based on the idea that most projects and planning exercises have been done before. Once the user has specified project or planning exercise requirements, it produces task lists, resource allocations and time estimates for the project or exercise.

Information about projects is stored in a database. Taking various views of the database, coupled with appropriate graphical representations, enables detailed and informative analysis to take place (see Figures 2.3–2.6).

Figure 2.3 shows the standard cross-tabulation view of a marketing research plan. Two views or windows on the data are being displayed simultaneously. Moreover, the two views are synchronised to examine the same set of records. The two windows can be expanded or contracted to show more or fewer fields and further records can be viewed by scrolling down through the records to ones that are not currently displayed on the screen. The cross-tabulation view allows the user to examine the tasks that have to be completed in their logical sequence and to see how the costs will arise over time and affect cash-flow requirements.

Figure 2.4 shows the standard resource view of the data along with availability and cost of each person involved in the exercise.

Figure 2.5 shows the standard Gantt view of the data. Here again two windows on the database are simultaneously displayed. The right-hand window shows

Figure 2.3 Standard cross-tabulation

Figure 2.4 Standard resource

11   Indicate what might be contained in a research proposal. What is the significance of a research proposal?

12   What role might PERT play in planning a marketing research study? What would be its value to the study?

| Case study 2.1 | New shoe company |

The New shoe company, based in the English Midlands, is experiencing a fall in profits. The company measures profits in terms of the annual pretax return on capital employed earned by the company.

The sales director says that falling profitability is a reflection of the current slump in the market. Total demand in the market place is much less than it was twelve months ago and the company has struggled to maintain its market share at the previous level as competition has intensified. Competition from European manufacturers has been sharpened by changes in EU trading regulations and Spanish manufacturers, in particular, have taken advantage of their lower cost structure to make inroads into the British market. At the same time the New shoe firm has failed to take full advantage of opportunities in Europe. It has not fully developed its market niching strategy where it can gain a competitive advantage. The sales director blames the firm's lack of competitiveness on the poor performance of the R&D team and the inability of the manufacturing departments to control costs.

The technical director claims that the firm's products are competitive with any that are produced worldwide. Indeed, in her view, the firm's products are by far the best available at the price offered. She points to the lack of marketing effort expended by the firm in the past year, pointing to the necessity to keep the firm's name before the public at all times, especially when competition is increasing in strength. At the same time she recognises that marketing effort requires financing and that this was not adequately provided during the period in question.

The production director points out that the company has been able to lower its manufacturing costs substantially through the introduction of new technology into the manufacturing process. However, he points out that the accounting practices adopted by the firm distort the true picture. Profitability, in his view, has improved though this is not truly reflected in the company's management accounts.

The finance director feels that the drop in profitability is attributable to recent acquisitions the firm has made. Ventures into retailing have not been as profitable as had first been supposed. This might to some extent have been reflective of bad timing on behalf of the company, given the current recession, in making such acquisitions.

The managing director points out that clearly there is a problem and that perhaps one should pay particular attention to what competitors are doing and how the firm is responding from a marketing viewpoint.

Questions

1 Given the limited information in this case, what do you think could be the real problem or problems in this example?

2 Depending on the real nature of the problem identified, how might marketing research help in this case?

Case study 2.2	The interface between researching and facilitating

Novo Nordisk is a relatively small pharmaceutical company with three main product groups: insulin, HRT and growth hormone. The firm was experiencing a decline in customer loyalty and a business consultancy firm was asked to investigate and deal with the problem. The managing director of Novo recognised that customer care was a strategic differentiator for the firm in the very specialised market that it served and wanted end-to-end problem resolution, not research.

Novo competes with Eli Lilly, Ciba-Geigy, Wyeth, CP (Fisons), Kabivitrum and Sereno for business and although product efficacy and cost are of paramount importance, in this market context customer care is equally important. Novo Nordisk's managing director asked the business consultants to sort out the firm's customer-care programme. This involved investigating the problem, identifying the need and helping to implement changes.

The business consultants conducted face-to-face interviews with more than 100 professionals in the field of diabetes, HRT and growth hormone in thirteen UK hospitals. Respondents were medical consultants, registrars, nurses and pharmacists. A postal survey of more than 600 GPs and practice nurses was also carried out by the business consultants. Among the findings were the following:

- Medical professionals were uncomfortable with the term customer care.
- Typical comments were 'good but not as good as they used to be' and 'good, but becoming complacent'.
- Medical professionals did not like the reps who seemed more concerned about sales than patient welfare.
- Registrars felt treated as second-class customers by the reps who paid more attention to consultants.
- Customers wanted a fact-based information line for fast response to medical queries.
- Professionals want non-promotional information.

The business consultants also carried out a comprehensive examination of Novo's internal operation. This comprised face-to-face interviews, two top-team workshops and a quantitative survey of staff. All the company's senior management were interviewed. At the top-team workshop, the group was asked to rank the importance of the different customer groups and to generate a list of customer-care activities, which was subsequently used in the quantitative research. The business consultants then carried out a quantitative survey with non-board-level staff at Novo with a sample structured to be representative of the whole workforce.

It was discovered that:

- Customer-care activities were not formally measured and most staff had received no customer-care training.
- There was a lack of coordination between divisions and individuals in their contact with the most significant customer groups and some rivalry between divisions.
- There was an awareness of Novo's desire for professional customer service and support.

Findings from both the customer and staff research studies were fed directly into the second top-team workshops, where each director gave a short presentation covering the five issues arising from the survey which they considered to be the most important to Novo. The directors also suggested the appropriate steps to be taken. Indeed, where the generating ideas for solutions is concerned, the approach has to be so involving that the distinction between researching and facilitating becomes blurred.

The business consultant's findings from the employee survey and the top-team workshops led to the development of detailed action plans in seven areas: customer care, teamwork, delegation, communication, organisational clarity, human resource policies and flexibility.

Source: N Perrott.[8]

Questions

1 Describe the kind of planning that you think must have been conducted before this project began.
2 To what extent are the subsequent stages of the research dependent on earlier stages? How might this be anticipated during the planning stages of the research?
3 In what ways is a marketing researcher a facilitator as well as a researcher?

Case study 2.3   Why researchers are so jittery

With a general election looming, Britain's market research wizards are on tenterhooks. The latest issue of the UK's Market Research Society magazine is titled: '1997: Year of decision for MR', and the lead article starts by asking whether 1997 will be a year of 'further embarrassment'. The second article is titled: 'Laying the ghost of the nightmare of '92', a reference to the way UK opinion polls were all at sea with their predictions of the 1992 UK election result.

Having celebrated their society's 50th birthday last year with much braggadochio, researchers now have a hangover. This being election year, the opinion polls are on trial again, and if researchers get things wrong – which hardly seems possible, but then it did not seem possible last time – their credibility will be in smithereens.

Inevitably, the entire market research business will be seen as guilty by association, and market research is now pretty big business. With £7bn in turnover and steady, compound growth of 8–10 per cent a year, the UK research business has done extremely well of late. Moreover, the Association of Market Survey Organisations (Amso) forecasts growth of 15–20 per cent this year.

Research is a nice little export earner, too. As with other marketing activities, Britain is a world leader. According to Amso, about 20 per cent of UK market research turnover comes from international surveys, and international work is growing faster than domestic.

Today there are few manufacturing companies, media houses, government departments, public bodies, academic institutions or even retailers in Britain which do not integrate research into their decision-making processes. For many years, retailers were market research Cinderellas. They believed they could learn from their store traffic everything they wanted to know. As a result, they felt they did not need to ask any questions. But retailers now account for some 5 per cent of total research expenditure, and their share is growing steadily.

However, not everything is rosy. Though other market researchers strive to distance themselves from the political pollsters, they know they share their problems, and many of those problems are fundamental. On one hand, some members of the public manifestly enjoy taking part in research surveys and focus groups. The paid interviewers know who they are, and return to them again and again. This leads to bogus results.

On the other hand, more people are becoming refuseniks. In Britain the industry now conducts well over 15m interviews per year, and 100m questionnaires are mailed out by database companies. Although there are no published figures, most experienced researchers will confirm that refusal rates are rising steadily.

Even in flagship studies like the National Readership Survey, response rates are now just over 60 per cent after eight or more calls on respondents. (When the survey started in 1954 they reached 85 per cent after six calls.) So 40 per cent of the NRS universe is nowadays uncanvassed. Political polls suffer similarly high non-response rates, which was one of the reasons for the 1992 debacle.

More worryingly, a welter of evidence shows that a growing proportion of the public is now playing games with market researchers. They understand the processes (which are hardly rocket science) and consciously manipulate their responses. Like voters in by-elections, they deliberately send messages to companies and political parties, using the researchers as conduits. It takes only a small percentage of such respondents to invalidate results. None too soon, the research industry has started to investigate these problems. Several of the key papers at last month's Amso annual conference addressed the increasingly uncertain relationship between market researchers and their raw material – the public.

It is by no means clear what, if anything, can be done, and that is why so much hangs on the election pollsters' accuracy this time round. Polls capture the headlines. Polls have also captured politicians. Nobody pays more attention to surveys than politicians. Contrary to conventional wisdom, market research is a far more potent influence in modern politics than advertising. Politicians read, mark, learn and inwardly digest the voters' views on everything from abortion to traffic crossings. And the pollsters revel in their influence.

Behind the Oval Office, the new sell-and-tell pot-boiler by President Bill Clinton's former chief electoral strategist, Dick Morris, shows Clinton messily awash with market research findings in the run-up to last year's election. Indeed, Clinton often felt himself drowning in them.

The pollsters tried to control his every waking moment. They told him to become a father figure with a powerful red tie and dictated how he should spend his holidays. 'Can I golf?' the president asked the pollsters, his tone dripping sarcasm. 'Maybe if I wear a baseball cap?' He was told: 'No, sir, go rafting.'

In compensation, market research has given political leaders, both in western and ex-communist democracies, new power over their parties. In Britain, former prime minister Margaret Thatcher was able to march on with confidence during the Falklands war because she tracked public opinion throughout. Neil Kinnock, the former Labour leader, was able to defeat Militant extremists because he knew that the vast majority of the electorate, and the vast majority of Labour voters, supported him. The ability of the present Labour leader, Tony Blair, to ride roughshod over Labour's historic articles of faith has, again, been built on firmly researched foundations. When zealous and partisan supporters claim 'the party'll never buy that,' the leader, research data in hip-pocket, can nowadays ignore them with insouciance.

All of this emphasises the present symbiosis between market research and politics. It will last as long as the politicians continue to have faith in the researchers' wizardry. The politicians influence a great deal of business, both directly, via government departments, and indirectly, via publicity and the media.

So the researchers wait – and worry – for 1992 was not their only cock-up. They also bombed in 1970. And in the 13 elections between 1945 and 1987, some 40 per cent of pollsters' forecasts were inaccurate by more than plus or minus 2 per cent – a small margin, but usually sufficient to swing the result, which is all that matters.

Most of the time the researchers' findings cannot be verified. They cannot be proved right or wrong. Except at elections. That is why market researchers are now so jumpy. Their outlook is far from bleak, but it is distinctly unsettled.

Source: Winston Fletcher.[9] Reprinted with permission.

Question

If most of the time the researchers' findings cannot be verified, how does this affect the true value of market research?

Case study 2.4   Tracking the railways

Since the British railway system was privatised in 1996, the new rail companies have been plagued with problems. Poor rolling stock, delayed trains, disaffected passengers, and poor coordination between the different companies regarding timetabling and through ticketing have all contributed to the feeling of malaise that plagues the industry.

Some of the directors of the train operating companies (TOCs) have been less than sympathetic towards their customers – one director went so far as to suggest that the 40,000 complaints a year his company was getting were being written during people's working time, and that he was considering writing to their bosses about it. Another director said that the non-functioning toilets on his trains were 'a detail' which would have to wait. The same director raised fares by five per cent, justifying this on the grounds that he was acting within the terms of his operating contract – apparently ignoring the moral obligation he has to his customers. The reason for these attitudes could be that the TOCs have only been given a seven-year franchise – a period of time hardly conducive to making major long-term investments in capital goods such as rolling stock and locomotives. The temptation to take a short-term view is clearly a strong one.

Equally problematically, each company seems to be trying to establish its own brand, and even competing with other companies, at a time when the industry needs to present a united front in order to stave off competition from road transport.

One of the problems facing the TOCs is that branding may not be very effective when approaching customers who prefer to be called passengers and only want to get from A to B in the most efficient way possible. Design company Wolff Olins found that the most popular layout for the Heathrow Express was the most practical one rather than the most luxurious, and Virgin Trains report that the poor image of their rail services has damaged the previously invulnerable Virgin brand.

Some commentators believe that the TOCs need to segment their market more clearly and respond better to customer needs. 'People must be very careful to distinguish superficial marketing from true marketing,' says Fiona McAnena of the Added Value Company. Both Great North Eastern Railway and Great Western Trains have modelled themselves on British Airways; market research showed that people wanted a more personal approach, and GNER have taken these findings on board to the extent of asking staff to seek out opportunities to add a personal touch.

Market research has not always worked for the railways, though. When the Gatwick Express was being redesigned, customers were asked how the service could be improved. They were unable to come up with anything beyond the obvious, whereas the researchers were hoping that they would be able to suggest radical changes to the service. The researchers responded by setting up a panel (a think-tank) of advertisers, researchers and psychologists in the hope that they would be able to second-guess the consumers. So far the results of this panel have not been divulged.

In the longer term, the TOCs will need to work out the problem of short-termism. This will probably require a change of heart on the part of Government, allowing longer franchises to be granted – the catch-22 is that the Government is unlikely to do so until standards improve. In the meantime, the TOCs and the passengers (or customers) will need to make the best of a difficult situation.

Questions

1 Why might the Gatwick Express research have failed?

2 How would you plan a research programme to identify the needs of the different market segments for rail transport?

3 What are the problems inherent in running a research programme for the railways?

4 Given the negative attitudes of some rail bosses towards their customers, what might be the problems of presenting the findings of the research?

5 How might market research help in effecting a reconciliation between the TOCs and their passengers?

Further reading

Andreasen, A (1983) Cost-conscious marketing research, *Harvard Business Review*, 61, p 4.

Butler, P (1994) Marketing problems: from analysis to decision, *Marketing Intelligence and Planning*, 12(2), pp 4–13.

Chapman, R G (1989) Problem definition in marketing research studies, *Journal of Services Marketing*, 3(3), pp 51–9.

McCulough, D (1999) Why marketing research is a waste of money (and what you can do about it) *Marcom Today*, November.

Markland, R E (1983) *Topics in Management Science*, New York: Wiley.

Taha, H A (1992) *Operations Research: An introduction*, New York: Macmillan, Ch 13.

Zemke, R (1978) How market research techniques can pay off for trainers, *Training*, 15(12).

References and notes

[1] De Bono, E (1992) in Peters, T, *Liberation Management*, London: Macmillan, p 635.

[2] Rickards, T (1974) *Problem Solving through Creative Analysis*, Aldershot: Gower.

[3] Proctor, T (1999) *Creative Problem-Solving for Managers*, London: Routledge.

[4] Marks, A P (1990) The Sinclair 5 – why did it fail?, *Management Decision*, 28(4), pp 9–14.

[5] Kerlinger, F (1973) *Foundations of Behavioral Research*, New York: Holt, Rinehart & Winston, Ch 2.

[6] Smith, L A and Gupta, S (1985) Project management software in P & IM, *P & IM Review and APICS News*, June, pp 66–8.

[7] Time Line 6 for Windows, Symantec Corporation, 10201 Torre Avenue, Cupertino, CA 95014, USA.

[8] Perrott, N (1995) Research that becomes part of a company's strategy, *Research Plus*, October, pp 6ff.

[9] Fletcher, W (1997) Why researchers are so jittery, *Financial Times*, 3 March.

3

Secondary data

OBJECTIVES

After reading this chapter you should be able to:

■ appreciate the various sources of secondary data;

■ understand how to start systematically to collect this data.

KEY WORDS

secondary data	libraries
internal data	bibliographies
external data	on-line
government statistics	databases
abstracts	CD-ROM
indexes	

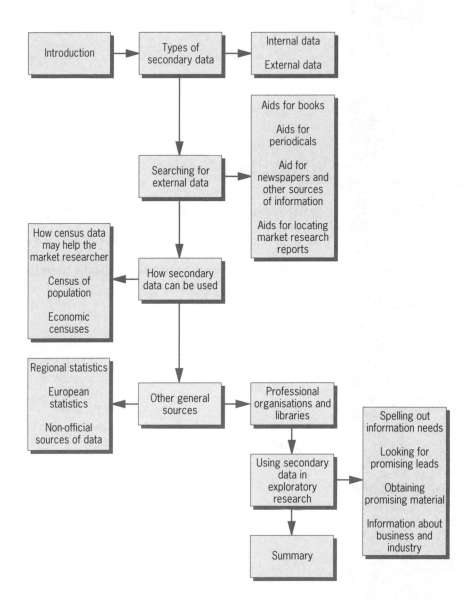

PLAN OF CHAPTER 3

INTRODUCTION

In this chapter we review the various sources of secondary data. Information helps an organisation to solve its marketing problems and to make marketing decisions. A distinction between information and data has to be made. Data comprises unorganised news, facts, and figures about any kind of topic you could possibly name. Information, by comparison, is quite different from data. It is a body of facts that is organised around a specific topic or subject. It comprises facts organised and presented to help solve a problem or develop a plan.

When we read about something that has happened, for example, new products that have been launched, we are looking at secondary data. Actually being involved in launching a new product and noting our experience in this connection amounts to generating and collecting primary data. When doing research we never collect primary data if the material has already been collected by someone else, since it is a waste of time and effort. We should always start, therefore, by examining secondary sources of information.

TYPES OF SECONDARY DATA

There is a large amount of secondary data available to the marketing researcher. While only a very small proportion of existing secondary data may be useful in any one project, marketing researchers should know where to obtain relevant data and should be familiar with procedures to reduce the amount of time required to search for data. A starting point is to separate secondary data into either *internal* or *external* sources.

Internal data

Internal secondary data is produced by an organisation in its day-to-day operations. Data on sales, advertising expenditures, inventory records, salespeople's reports, distribution costs and prices are just some examples of the type of internal data that is produced.

In many instances internal data is gathered in a relatively unorganised manner and people in the organisation may have little knowledge of what data is actually available. The growth of marketing information systems alongside the trend towards the computerisation of all records in a business has done and can do much to simplify the organisation and accessibility of internal data.

External data

External data refers to data that comes from a wide variety of sources outside an organisation. So numerous are the various forms of external data that in order to

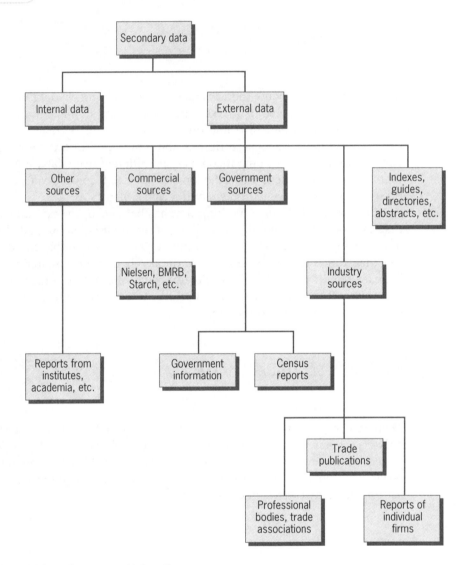

Figure 3.1 Secondary sources of information

use them effectively a researcher needs to be skilled in the use of indexes, abstracts and directories to locate relevant material. Without the use of these aids much time and effort is invariably wasted and much relevant information may be overlooked.

SEARCHING FOR EXTERNAL DATA

The complexity of the search operation will very much depend on the type of data that is sought. Where specific data is sought, the search may be quite narrow and of short duration. The researcher may often be unaware of specific information sources so it is important to undertake the search in an organised and systematic manner.

In the course of searching for information, the use of indexes, abstracts, directories and other available guides is helpful. You need to appreciate the difference between an abstract and an index. Whereas an abstract presents the basic contents of a publication in a few lines, an index presents only the minimum of data about the publication: author, publisher, date of publication, and so on. Today collections of abstracts may be searched for electronically on CD-ROM disks or the Internet and saved to a floppy disk or hard disk file. Since the stored information is in ASCII format, these files may subsequently be read into word processors or databases for further analysis or exploration.

The starting point in reviewing secondary data is to make sure that you have correctly identified the topic on which you need information. This first involves listing all the possible categories or headings under which the topic might be discussed by other researchers or authors. It is a good idea to make the topics fairly wide-ranging in the first instance so that important aspects are not overlooked. Once these headings have been established, attention can then be turned to aids that will point you in the right direction.

First you should ascertain whether or not a bibliography on the subject already exists. A publication called *Bibliographies Index: A Cumulative Bibliography of Bibliographies*, published by the HH Wilson Company, New York, is a useful starting point. This publication lists various books, periodicals and other publications that are relevant to topics that have been identified. *The British National Bibliography* has been published since 1950 and is generally available for consultation in public libraries. There are cumulative volumes and it is also advisable to use the index, which will list terms or topics you may not have considered. Most academic libraries have a wide range of bibliographies and indexes that cover major fields of study. If the subject is somewhat unique it is possible that a bibliography may not exist. In this case you will need to construct a bibliography for yourself.

Abstract available on CD-ROM – permitting electronic searches of thousands of abstracts

Access No: 01075313 ProQuest ABI/INFORM (R) Research

Title: Breaking away

Authors: Selwyn, Padi

Journal: *Successful Meetings* [SMM] ISSN: 0148–4052 Vol: 44 Iss: 9 Date: Aug 1995 pp: 79–83

Reprint: Contact UMI for article reprint (order no. 9753.02) Restrictions may apply

Subjects: Business community; Meetings; Planning; Creativity; Success

Geo Places: US

Codes: 9190 (United States); 2310 (Planning); 2200 (Managerial skills)

Abstract: A 1993 Porter/Novelli survey of 100 Fortune 500 executives revealed that creativity is the most important element for business success. Six tips to help meetings planners to enhance their own and others' creativity are offered: 1. Open your mind. 2. Diversify. 3. Clear your mind for each day. 4. Stop looking for the right answer. 5. Discover your creative rhythm. 6. Health makes wealth.

Specific sources of information include books, periodicals, newspapers, government information, directories, and statistics and information stored for use with a computer. There are many different aids that can help you find information that is most appropriate to your needs. But remember that the availability and comprehensiveness of these aids vary from country to country. For example, while there are a vast number of aids available in the USA for such purposes their relevance to the needs of researchers in, say, Europe is not always guaranteed.

Aids for books

Every library keeps a *card catalogue* file on what it contains and this should usually be the starting point for most library research. Most catalogue systems present information on books in at least two ways: an author–title section for those looking for works of a particular author, and a subject section for those looking for information on a specific subject. Where books are not held by a library, interlibrary loan facilities usually exist. Many UK libraries possess facilities to enable researchers to examine a database on a CD-ROM. *Boston Spa* details the 500,000 books in the British Library's national interlibrary loan collection. Another database, *Bookbank*, also provides details of books published in Britain. *Books in Print* (UK and USA) enables researchers to identify all books that have been published and that are currently in print. Equivalent systems operate in most other countries. The interlibrary loan facility may operate on a reciprocal basis between a number of regional and/or local libraries. Alternatively, the British Library at Boston Spa in Yorkshire operates a service for books and periodical articles. Researchers may find it useful to visit the British Library Centre at Boston Spa but it should be noted that advance notice of a visit is appreciated.

Aids for periodicals

The large number of periodicals and their variety of articles mean that the researcher has to rely on indexes in searching for appropriate data. Most of these indexes are to be found in the reference areas of libraries.

Ulrich's *International Periodicals Directory* (New York: Bowker) is a good place to start because it lists subject specialisms and publication details of journals that are currently available. In the case of specifically British journals, *Current British Journals: A subject guide to periodicals* is helpful. Other indexing services list all the material published in specified periodicals and are produced on a regular basis with annual accumulations. They are arranged by subject matter and author but do not give detailed information on the contents of the article.

Abstracting services provide the same information as indexes and also a summary or abstract of the article that provides enough detail for the researcher to know if it is relevant. A rapidly increasing number of indexes and abstracts are now available as databases on CD-ROM disks. These include:

- ABI-Inform: Business and management
- Bookbank: British books in print
- PSYCLIT: Psychological abstracts
- UK Official Publications: Parliamentary, non-parliamentary and non-TSO publications
- Indexes and abstracts are also becoming available on the Internet

Aid for newspapers and other sources of information

For some researchers the material sought will be contained in newspapers, national census reports or other statistical databases. Most universities, for example, have access to a retrieval system for the national census.

The National Online Management Information System (NOMIS) is a computerised employment information system developed at Durham University on behalf of the Department of Employment. It has been in national use since 1982 and permits access to official statistics on employment, vacancies and population, together with facilities to compare and analyse data on a wide range of areas from local to national levels. The information is available at a wide range of geographical levels, and some data analysis facilities, such as graphs and percentages, are available within the system itself. Among the data that NOMIS can provide are:

- Census of population data to ward level
- Census of employment total since 1971 – specifically employment by industrial classification for local travel to work areas
- Annual population projections
- National Health Service migration datasets.

Such data are available for many scales of study, including the following:

- wards
- travel-to-work areas
- local authority districts
- parliamentary constituencies
- regions.

When searching for UK government statistics, researchers should start with the free *Government Statistics, a Brief Guide to Sources* or the *Guide to Official Statistics*, which can be bought from The Stationery Office (formerly HMSO).

The UK market for fitted bathrooms: the use of secondary data and its limitations

At first the idea was to concentrate on the market for fitted bathrooms, but as this market in the UK is still in its infancy the market structure is very fragmented, so it is difficult to obtain information about this segment. Because of this problem the research concentrated on the British market for baths and sanitary-ware. The objectives of the research were to provide the reader with a general understanding of:

■ the market structure
■ the distribution system
■ the buyer behaviour of private customers

Using the Aslib directory a list of eight libraries that could be of help was drawn up. Four of these were in London: London Business School, Overseas Trade Library, London Commercial Library and British Library – the science and business department. Two libraries were in Manchester: Manchester Business School and the Central Library commercial section. One library was in Birmingham – Birmingham Central Library – and the other library was the British Library in Boston Spa.

Being based in the north of England I started in the local area and visited the two libraries in Manchester and the one in Birmingham. The result was quite good in terms of identifying the available material as there were several good publications about available market reports, newspaper articles and magazines. The search words used during this part of the desk research were:

■ bath(s)
■ showers
■ sanitary-ware
■ ensuite bathroom
■ bathroom
■ ceramics
■ toilet
■ WC

The initial desk research was followed by a three days stay in London. The material obtained in London comprised market analyses made by professional companies and articles from magazines. On average the reports were one to two years old. All the reports more or less followed the same structure:

1   Introduction
2   Market size
3   Demand composition: the customers
4   Distribution: concentrating on the merchants
5   Manufacturers
6   Prospects and recent developments.

The information in reports was to a large extent a replication of the same facts and figures. This at least suggested that the data was reliable. However, the major problem was that none of the reports looked into the distribution system in depth nor did they describe the consumer buying behaviour in a systematic way.
Source: Rene Spindler.[1]

Aids for locating market research reports and other marketing information

There are many thousands of reports available and they can be located through several sources, for example, Market Search,[2] Reports Index[3] and Findex.[4] Information on organisations providing marketing information and on-line data can be found in *The UK Marketing Source Book*[5] and *The Source Book*.[6] Database source books include: *On-Line Business Source Book*,[7] *On-Line Business and Company Databases*[8] and *Directory of On-Line Databases*.[9]

Golden nuggets on a long and winding road

Getting lost on the information superhighway? Online business information services can provide the shortcuts to show business users where they need to go.

The Internet is a goldmine of information, but searching for that elusive nugget often yields nothing but frustration.

Online business information services provide better and quicker ways of finding information on the Internet – albeit at a price. And through the Internet, these companies can reach a global market of information seekers and offer new products.

Business information has been available online for many years. Initially, access was only via proprietary terminals and private networks, on Reuters and Lexis-Nexis, for example. But the growth of the personal computer has led most services to move to PC-based access with a Windows-based interface design to make searching for information easier.

Many information services use agency distributors, including big online networks such as CompuServe, to extend their reach around the globe. But in the Internet age, these traditional delivery channels are costly and old-fashioned. So providers of business information are adapting their proprietary services to allow access from the web.

'The Internet allows us to serve our existing market with new products,' says Gerard Buckley, marketing director with Dun & Bradstreet, a leading US business information provider. The company opened its global information database to the Internet in July.

Web surfers can search free of charge the D&B GlobalSeek database, which has details on more than 45m companies in 200 countries. They also can buy a synopsis of the business operations of a particular company. The report is purchased by credit card directly from the web for $5 (£2.95). D&B's existing contract subscribers can also buy reports on the web using the password they use to access the traditional proprietary service.

FT Information, the business information division of Pearson, publisher of the *Financial Times*, recently announced a new Internet-based product: FT Discovery for the Web. It provides users with news alerts and international business information including news, company information and market intelligence. The product is designed to appeal to smaller businesses and is thus offered at a fixed price – £99 a month for each user – and can be accessed using a standard web browser and Internet connection. Dialog, which claims to be the world's oldest and largest online information service, celebrated its 25th anniversary this year by launching an Internet-based service. Called Dialog Web, the service is accessed via a standard web browser using the same command language adopted for the proprietary Dialog service.

Dialog comprises more than 470 databases from a broad range of disciplines, including business news, patents and trademarks, science and technology, as well as consumer news. It is the flagship product of Dialog Corporation, formed last month from the merger of MAID, a fast-growing UK information provider, and Knight-Ridder Information, the online division of US newspaper publisher Knight-Ridder and previous owner of Dialog.

KRI's information empire comprises more than 900 databases, 9 terabytes of data and 160,000 customers. The smaller MAID has 4,700 corporate subscribers – a single subscription may, however, cover hundreds of users. Its core product is Profound, which offers around 100m pages of information from more than 5,000 content publishers, including market research reports, business news, company statistics, brokerage research and stock market prices. Profound uses MAID's proprietary InfoSort data indexing technology that allows fast, accurate searching across all the databases. The service was launched in 1995, initially just as a dial-up service. But in mid-1996, MAID added access via the Internet.

At the end of 1996 an intranet version of Profound was launched that can be custom designed for an organisation at a fixed price and offers the security advantage of an intranet. The intranet (a private network) system also uses the InfoSort technology to allow each company to define its information needs and index information in predetermined categories. This facility aims to overcome the information overload problem common to online information services, and ensure that only information relevant to the company is provided on its intranet. British Telecom plans to use the intranet version of Profound to offer large business customers a complete managed intranet service, including customised information.

Financial analysts were surprised when loss-making MAID, whose 1996 sales were just £21m, announced in August its plan to buy the much larger KRI, with revenues last year of almost $290m. KRI's parent Knight-Ridder justified the sale by saying it wanted to focus resources on expanding its newspaper empire.

Online information services have proved a thorn in the side of many media groups because of their heavy up-front development costs. The Internet creates further uncertainty in the online market, and the big consumer-oriented services, such as CompuServe, have lost subscribers because of the Internet's growth.

Analysts say business-oriented online services are not as vulnerable because of their sophisticated search engines and high-value data. However, much of the bread-and-butter information they offer, such as company results, and magazine and newspaper articles, can often be found for free on the web. This is, however, assuming users have the patience to search for it. The rapid rise of the web browser as a standard, easy-to-use interface has left online service providers wondering whether they should continue to sink money into developing and supporting proprietary software.

CompuServe, for example, announced in October it would make many of its databases and technical forums available to web surfers on a pay-as-you-go basis, as well as continuing with its traditional proprietary service. Gerard Buckley, of Dun & Bradstreet, believes proprietary services still have the edge because of the effort that has gone into optimising the software used to acess the service. But their longer term future looks less certain.

'There will always be people who will need value-added (proprietary) software, but increasingly we are moving to the Internet,' he says.
Source: Geoffrey Nairn.[10] Reprinted with permission.

HOW SECONDARY DATA CAN BE USED

Secondary data can be useful in one or more of three ways in marketing research: in exploratory work, as a news source or in marketing decisions. When secondary data is used as part of an exploratory study it is often associated with long-range consider- ations of a firm, such as whether to think seriously about developing a completely new product or service. A manufacturer of leather goods, for example, might want to consider the feasibility of establishing a chain of leather-ware shops. The first step in the research process would involve a great deal of secondary research.

There is one secondary source – the census – that is both so extensive and intensive that it cuts across all three categories. There are also some other general sources that can apply to one or more of the three categories.

The census

The census is the largest single source of secondary data. The range and amount of information available from the census is too great to describe in depth here. The material covers both population and business. First we consider how census data may help the marketing researcher, and then we list the major types of information available in the census.

How census data may help the marketing researcher

- Studying the growth trends of production data over a period of years can help a manufacturer to identify new product lines or additions to a product line.
- Census data may help in determining business location. Studying demographic data for an area before deciding to open a retailer outlet in that particular area is a case in point. Furthermore, a firm may establish sales territories for its sales staff on the basis of census of population data.

All countries will have censuses of one type or another. Here we choose illustrations from the UK.

Census of population

Conducted every ten years, the census of population provides details on the nature of the population. It covers demographics such as sex, age, ethnicity, family size, marital status, occupation, income and education.

Economic censuses

Economic censuses include the census of production and the census of distribution.

The census of production, taken every five years, provides data on shipments (in both units and money terms) of thousands of manufactured products. Shown by SIC numbers and descriptions, these data can pinpoint exactly where particular items are produced.

The census of distribution provides basic information on the structure of retail areas of distribution. Since 1976 it has been superseded by annual sample enquiries.

OTHER GENERAL SOURCES

Other general sources include local government sources and chambers of commerce (Table 3.1). For business and professional markets, another possibility is trade, business or professional associations.

In the UK, a very useful government publication, published by The Stationery Office, is the *Guide to Official Statistics*: this covers all official and significant non-official sources of statistics, both regular and occasional, published during the past ten years. It attempts to give the user a broad indication of whether the statistics required have been compiled and, if so, whether they have been published. It does not contain statistics but it does indicate where to find them.

Table 3.1 Useful UK government sources of information

Annual Abstract of Statistics	Data on housing, manufactured goods, population, etc.
Monthly Digest of Statistics	As above but published monthly
Abstract of Regional Statistics	Economic and social regional statistics for UK
Economic Trends	Monthly review of the economic situation
Social Trends	Annual collection of social statistics – population, households, education, health, housing, environment, leisure, etc. Useful for indicating changes in expenditure
Digest of Health Statistics for England and Wales (annually)	
Agricultural Statistics: England and Wales (annually)	
Financial Statistics (monthly)	UK monetary and financial statistics
Digest of Energy Statistics (annually)	
Highway Statistics (annually)	
Passenger Transport in Great Britain (annually)	
Housing and Construction Statistics (quarterly)	
Monthly Bulletin of Construction Statistics	
Key Data	Overview of statistics produced by government at a modest cost
Overseas Trade Statistics of the UK (monthly)	
Food Survey	Trends in expenditure on food
The General Household Survey	A continuous sample survey providing a picture of changing social conditions in many aspects of everyday life
Family Expenditure Survey Reports (annually)	Trends in expenditure on consumer products – indicates changes in patterns of expenditure
National Income and Expenditure Blue Book (annually)	
Annual Estimates of the Population of England and Wales and of Local Authority Areas (annually)	
Department of Employment Gazette (monthly)	

Bill of Entry Service	Customs and Excise data
Business Monitor	Information on different UK industries – provides performance indicators and trends against which one can compare one's own performance. Helps to answer the question: How large is the market?

Data loss

Next week, *Social Trends*, the annual snapshot of life in the UK, will be published, significant parts of its data drawn from the General Household Survey. The edition due in two years' time will not be as good, for the Office of National Statistics has just announced that this year's GHS, a survey of more than 10,000 households a year, is to be suspended. It is a suspension, furthermore, that sounds worryingly like a death-knell. The survey will be resumed the following year, its users have been told, 'if this is appropriate'.

This is a short-sighted and damaging decision. The GHS is a prime source of continuous survey data since 1971. Its value lies in an unbroken series embracing income, housing, family composition, health, employment status, education, disability, use of social services, informal care and much else. It provides a window into the growing world of self-employment, the effects of widening inequality and the growth and impact of lone parenthood, while providing measures of social integration and exclusion. It is used in government, in academia and in market research.

Over the past five years it has been the most used of the wealth of data sets held in the Economic and Social Research Council's archive. While other surveys duplicate some of the GHS's coverage, none provides its ability to combine such disparate elements of British life over time in measures which can inform public policy.

Its suspension, to save £500,000, follows a cut in ONS's £100m budget. It goes on hold while a rapid and wide-ranging review is held of future social survey needs. Such a review, to avoid unneeded duplication and ensure value for money, is sensible.

It is not sensible for the ONS to have to act first and consider afterwards. At a time when reform of welfare policies is centre stage, it cannot be right to suspend the survey that can inform those policies and measure their outcomes. The ONS should be given the chance to think again, even if that means a temporary budget reprieve.
Source: Financial Times.[11] Reprinted with permission.

Regional statistics

The Office for National Statistics also publishes a useful booklet entitled *Government Statistics: A brief guide to sources*. This publication lists the government ministries and departments responsible for gathering specific economic and social data, such as annual statistics in retail trades, and a classified list of manufacturing businesses.

European statistics

The *Eurostat Catalogue*[12] appears annually and comprises monographs, collections, CD-ROMs and computer output products published by Eurostat. The catalogue provides a summary of each available publication or statistical document. Where statistics in printed form are also available as computer output products on magnetic tape, disks or on-line this is also indicated. The organisations disseminating the information are also given. The useful sources of information listed are shown in Table 3.2.

Table 3.2 European statistical sources

European Official Statistics: A guide to databases	Almost 100 publicly accessible databases within the field of official statistics are listed. The information contained in these databases covers virtually all economic and social sectors
European Official Statistics: Sources of information	Lists the addresses of about 250 bodies: statistical offices of international and supranational organisations; national statistics institutes; regional statistics institutes; and national ministries and central banks that publish information
Eurostat – Your Partner for European Statistics: A guide to the Statistical Office of the European Communities	The guide shows where to obtain statistical information about the EU – the sort of facts that are needed to be really well informed about the EU
Portrait of the Regions	Some 200 regions, comprising the entire territory of the EU, feature in this publication in the form of maps and illustrations in colour, general and harmonised statistical tables, commentaries and analyses on territory, strengths and weaknesses of a region, changes in population, employment and unemployment and structure of the economy
Portrait of the Islands	This provides information on all inhabited islands of the EU
Europe in Figures	This presents figures on the most important aspects of the EU. It uses diagrams, tables, maps, illustrations and text to summarise the process of European integration, its achievements and the important facts about the Union today. It is essential for understanding current and future developments in Europe
Facts through Figures	Illustrates the life of people in Europe under five headings: the environment, men and women, education and employment, the economy, and day-to-day life

Atlas GIS for Windows and DOS, Eurostat edition	Displays socioeconomic data on city, region, country or Europe on maps. Displaying data on maps pinpoints patterns and relationships between data elements. *Regio* statistics include population, births, deaths, employment, gross value added and GDP as well as NUTS boundaries covering three levels of the EU regions
Eurostat Yearbook	The contents are organised into five chapters: the people, the land and environment, the national economy, trade and industry, and the Union
Basic Statistics of the Community	Gives all the main statistics on the EU and provides comparisons of a number of European countries. Covers general statistics, economy and finance, population and social conditions, forestry and fisheries, external trade, services and transport and the environment
Regions: Statistical Yearbook	Gives the latest statistics relating to economic and social factors in the regions of the EU
Eurostat-CD	Contains economic and social statistics, regional data, external trade data at product level and the nomenclatures used to classify the different data
Reports on ACP Countries	Various: e.g. Bulgaria, Hungary, Poland

Eurostat data are stored in different databases, for example *New Cronos, COMEXT, Regio, Gisco, Eurofarm, IOT and Eurocron*. Data are offered on magnetic tapes, on diskettes, on paper and, in some cases, on-line.

- *New Cronos* contains around 55 million statistical data covering every sector of the economy. The data may be monthly, quarterly, half yearly or yearly depending on the statistical field covered.
- *COMEXT* exists on CD-ROM and contains statistics on trade between the Member States of the Union and their trade with some 300 non-member countries.
- *Regio* contains socioeconomic information on the various regions of the European Union. These are classified in line with a specific system called Nomenclature of Territorial Units for Statistics (NUTS). The subjects covered by *Regio* are demography, economic accounts, unemployment, labour force sample survey, industry, agriculture and transport. The entire database of approximately 100 tables is available on magnetic tape, diskette or printout.
- *Gisco* is the Geographic Information System of the Commission of the European Communities. Geographical data files provide a digital backcloth to many types of cartographic applications and spatial analyses. Eurostat holds several completely integrated subsets of data.
- *Eurofarm* is a database containing the results, in tabular form, of the Union surveys on the structure of agricultural holdings.

- *IOT* contains the input–output tables of Eurostat that appear every five years.
- *Eurocron* contains the latest data for the main macroeconomic indicators in the major statistical sectors.

Further information on the databases is available from the European Commission, rue de la Loi 200, B-1049, Brussels, Belgium, or at 2 rue Mercier, L-2985 Luxembourg.

Non-official sources of data

There are also many non-government sources of data published by a variety of bodies: trade associations, banks, academic institutions, the trade and professional press, newspapers, and surveys produced by commercial research organisations. Some of these are shown in Table 3.3.

An interesting new partnership has formed between the Office for National Statistics (ONS) and Taylor Nelson Sofres. These two bodies are the largest gatherers and analysers of data in the UK in their respective sectors – public and private. The ONS's mission is to improve decision-making in business by providing quality statistics. Taylor Nelson Sofres, as the UK's largest market research firm, has set the standard for market data analysis for more than twenty years. These two organisations have joined forces to produce *UK Markets*, published by Taylor Nelson Sofres from data provided by the ONS. The data relates to 4800 products taken from 28 500 statistical returns made by the ONS under the Products of the European Community (PRODCOM) inquiry. The returns provide 90 per cent coverage of UK manufacturers' sales (the remaining 10 per cent is estimated). The aggregated UK product sales totals are passed to Taylor Nelson Sofres, which processes the data further, adding derived tables, analysis, commentary and charts.

Table 3.3 Useful sources of information provided by commercial organisations

Mintel Market Intelligence Reports (monthly)	Reports on consumer products
Retail Intelligence (Mintel) (quarterly)	Special studies of various market sectors
ADMAP (monthly)	Covers all advertising media with regular analyses of advertising expenditures by product categories and media
Media Expenditure Analysis (MEAL)	Advertising expenditure across media types
Retail Business (monthly)	Specific aspects of markets
Marketing in Europe (monthly)	Specific aspects of markets
Euromonitor: Market research Great Britain (monthly)	Studies of specific markets
Euromonitor: Market research Europe (bi-monthly)	Studies of specific markets

BLA Group: Market Assessment (bi-monthly)	Home, office and leisure sectors in the UK
Financial Times: Business Information Service	Business intelligence service: national and international commerce and industry data. Brand shares, advertising expenditure, production, import and exports
Keynotes Reports	Consumer and industrial market sizes and trends
BRAD (British Rate and Data)	Detailed information on newspapers, magazines, television and other advertising media
Market Research Society Yearbook	Mainly useful for providing comprehensive lists of organisations providing market research services in Britain
Kompass Directory	Provides information on firms in different industries and also geographically. Available for the UK, Europe and elsewhere. Useful for identifying competitors
Kompass On-line	Provides company names and addresses for thousands of firms throughout Europe, along with other pertinent information about the companies

---

UK Markets: A joint venture between the Office for National Statistics and Taylor Nelson Sofres

UK Markets is a series of 91 annual and 34 quarterly reports on UK manufacturers' sales, export/import and net supply. Data is provided for every manufacturing sector of the UK on:

■ total manufacturers' sales for each of 4800 products;

■ export/import totals in terms of both value and volume, inside and outside the EU;

■ the value of net supply to the UK market;

■ import and export ratios, inside and outside the EU;

■ average values of the product for each category;

■ trend data for up to the last five periods, both as actual figures and indices;

■ analysis and interpretation, with user-friendly commentaries, charts and graphs.

The data and analyses in each report enable a firm to:

■ compare its own performance with that of the total market;

■ assess market share in every category;

■ compare unit sales with the industry and market norms;

■ monitor trends and more accurately forecast the future;

- measure share of exports;
- measure share of the UK market held by imports.

UK Markets is available in three formats: hard copy, CD-ROM, and Intelligent fax.

PROFESSIONAL ORGANISATIONS AND LIBRARIES

Various professional organisations and libraries are also useful sources of data. Professional organisations that are particularly useful in the UK include:

- Association of Market Survey Organisations
- Institute of Management
- Market Research Society
- Confederation of British Industry
- Chartered Institute of Marketing
- Institute of Practitioners in Advertising
- Advertising Association

Main libraries in major UK cities, such as Manchester, have substantial commercial libraries attached and these provide large quantities of relevant data. The following specialist libraries are also of interest:

- City Business Library, Brewers Hall Gardens, London EC2
- Science Reference Library, Chancery Lane, London WC2
- Statistics and Market Intelligence Library, 1 Victoria Street, London SW1
- Libraries attached to London, Manchester and Warwick Business Schools

Academic researchers also publish research findings on various aspects of the marketing process, often within specific industry sectors, at an even lower cost. Government departments collect, analyse and publish a vast array of facts, figures, surveys and reports. Newspapers, trade journals and trade associations regularly publish surveys and market reports for as little as the cover price. The burden of scanning the press, wandering through libraries and searching among mountains of journals can be reduced with database search facilities. Both CD-ROM databases and on-line databases can search newspapers, magazines and journals for key words. Some databases cover books, research reports and dissertations. Other on-line services, such as the Internet, are a great source of marketing intelligence. However, much of the information required by marketing researchers is only available from commercial providers who charge for access, for example, Infoplus[13] and Dialog.[14]

Secondary sources are cheaper and faster, whether it is a complete market report or just a key fact, figure or name. However, the accuracy and reliability of the secondary source must also be considered.

USING SECONDARY DATA IN EXPLORATORY RESEARCH

Exploratory research provides a broad understanding of an industry, a service or an area in which a firm wants to expand its limited knowledge. Three steps are involved:

1 spelling out information needs;
2 looking for promising leads by title or apparent content;
3 getting hold of promising published material.

One often has to choose between print format and computer format when choosing how to capture the data. Although readily available print sources are usually inexpensive, checking out print sources takes considerable time. Use of on-line sources, by comparison, is much quicker and can often provide more pertinent information. However, it costs money to obtain data in this way, and the novice or even the person with computer experience is likely to need some expert assistance.

Spelling out information needs

Marketing research begins with a statement of the problem. A statement of the marketing problem indicates the nature of the marketing decisions to be made. In turn, this leads to a statement of the kind of information that is required to reach these decisions. The nature of the information requirement always has to be specified. Failure to do this will make the search for secondary information unfocused and indefinite.

Looking for promising leads

Libraries are the best source for printed material. Libraries include the public library, the college or university library and the specialist library. The public library is often a good starting point. Even in a small town, the public library may have commercial directories and other sources of data. Even better is the college, university or business school library, if there is one readily available – in the larger ones, on-line searches may be possible. In major cities there is probably an excellent commercial library. The commercial library in a large city usually has not only good materials, but good general facilities as well.

An investigator will also want to see if there is a specialist library nearby. Typically found in industrial and commercial areas, these are usually privately maintained (by a business or an association) and carry considerable depth of material within some specialised topic, such as advertising or direct-mail selling. A good public library may give information on specialist libraries that may be prepared to make their services available.

When visiting a library you should arrive armed with a complete knowledge of the business problem. When talking with the library staff about the problem, it will soon become clear whether they know how to help. If the person at the desk cannot help, they will generally refer you to someone else. Your enquiry may also indicate that there are specialists in other library systems who can be of help.

Obtaining promising material

The economy

In order to have an understanding of the economic climate, since all marketing effort operates within this framework, the marketer or marketing researcher must have a continuing and current understanding of the state of the economy. Several newspapers and periodicals can be used for this purpose – for example, the *Financial Times* and the *Economist*. Libraries retain numbers of the major publications and these can be easily accessed.

Particular fields of business

Keeping up to date with knowledge about a particular field of business makes it a necessity to read trade papers covering the field on a regular basis. These also can be helpful in getting a general feel of a particular business or industry field that the firm is considering entering.

Consumer geographics, demographics and psychographics

The term *geographics*, in terms of consumers, means where people live. The word *demographics* concerns the statistics of an area's population, such as number of households along with their composition, income, sex, age, education and occupation. Combining geographics and demographics has coined the word geodemographics, which is simply a demographic description of those within specific geographic areas. The data are sometimes presented as descriptions of localities; in other cases the marketer predefines the characteristics of what are considered their best customers or prospects and obtains a list of where such people live.

The term *psychographics* is used by psychologists to mean the personality characteristics of an individual. Now that its usage has been adapted to marketing research, its meaning has been expanded. It is used to describe people not only in terms of their personality characteristics, but also in terms of their interests and lifestyles as a reflection of these characteristics.

Lifestyle databases and geodemographic information

Data on sales and purchases underpin many databases and this is usually overlaid with a considerable amount of profile data. This is known as *biographics* – the fusion of profile and data on sales and purchases. As a result of associating people's names, addresses, purchasing behaviour and lifestyles and placing it all together on a single record we can obtain an idea of someone's lifestyle. We can also create data fusion by linking such data with a Geographic Information System database. Linking purchasing behaviour data with lifestyle, geodemographics and panel data helps to produce patterns of purchasing buying in various regions.

Information sources for statistics

The census and private sources provide statistics about consumers. Since the census provides details about where and who consumers are – specific geography by characteristics such as age, sex, ethnicity, size and nature of the living unit, type of dwelling, and rental or value of dwelling unit – it has many immediate marketing applications. A firm can use local data to tailor neighbourhood promotions. A bank can make use of local data to obtain a demographic picture of the neighbourhoods surrounding its various locations. With this information it can single out neighbourhoods most closely matching its profiles of typical purchasers of personal loans, mutual funds, and other banking services. It can effectively target its advertising and direct-mail efforts.

Information about business and industry

General categorisation of business and industry

Grouping by kind of business is just as important for business and industry as demographics is for consumers. One of the best and most commonly used methods of classifying business and industry by type is the Standard Industrial Classification (SIC), which lists all types of business and assigns classification numbers to each.

Using the SIC classification

- Group 27 is Printing, Publishing and Allied Industries.
- The first broad category below 27 is 271, referring to Newspapers: Publishing, or Publishing and Printing.
- The digits 2711 represent the next subdivision; in this case they cover the same category. However, Books are 273, followed by 2731, meaning Books: Publishing, or Publishing and Printing; and then 2732, covering book printing.
- The broad category of 27 continues down to 279, Service Industries for the Printing Trade.

The categorisation of the SIC is formulated so that no industry is missed. Only with knowledge of the SIC number is it possible to search most sources for material relevant to the particular marketing problem.

Directories

The *Yellow Pages* of the telephone directory is a good source of company names by type of business. In the UK even local public libraries usually have most of the *Yellow Pages* for the entire country. A limitation of the use of the *Yellow Pages* should, however, be borne in mind. There is no quality control of the companies listed: a listed firm might be a sole-trader operation handled on a part-time basis. Many other business directories may also be found on library shelves in the reference section. For example, the *Kompass Directories* provide useful information on businesses and their products.

SUMMARY

This chapter has considered the various sources of secondary data and suggested systematic ways of searching for appropriate data or information relevant to a marketing problem. Attention has been drawn to both government and commercial sources of data and to libraries, bibliographies, indexes and abstracts as important aids in the search for information process. Detailed information has been presented about many secondary information sources.

Questions

1   Define secondary and primary data.

2   When might you use secondary as opposed to primary data?

3   Indicate the main sources of secondary data that may be used in marketing research.

4   When searching for secondary data, what steps should be followed to ensure that data sources are not overlooked?

5   What are the following resources?

   a   bibliographies

   b   abstracts

   c   indexes

6   When might you use a card catalogue in the course of library research?

7   What is NOMIS?

8   What is a census?

9   What do the main UK censuses cover?

10   How might census information be useful to marketers?

11   Outline some of the main UK government published statistics and reports and how they might be useful to marketers.

12   What are the main UK sources of information produced by commercial organisations that are useful to marketers? How might they be used by marketers? Give examples.

13   How might generalist or specialist libraries be useful to marketers? Indicate some of the establishments and the relevant information they might contain.

14   Indicate how you would start a search for European statistics.

15   Academic institutions undertake research and publications in a variety of fields. To what extent might the information that is produced be useful to marketing management?

16   Outline the role of secondary data in exploratory research.

17   What kind of information would you find in directories? How might this information be applied in marketing research?

Case study 3.1   Montres d'Occasion

The Jewellery Quarter in Birmingham is one of the last surviving British examples of the transition from an essentially domestic to an industrialised economy. Three centuries of industrial innovation, growth and decay can be traced in its streets and buildings. It typifies the essential character of entrepreneurial activity in Victorian Birmingham and it throws out a challenge to any ability to plan for the future. Working in precious metal in Birmingham dates from at least the fourteenth century, but the industry did not attain national importance until the second half of the eighteenth century.

Charles is contemplating taking up the lease on workshop/retail premises in the Jewellery Quarter of Birmingham at Hockley. He wants to refurbish and repair second-hand wrist-watches under the French name for second-hand watches, 'Montres d'Occasion'. Birmingham is the UK's second largest city with over one million inhabitants and its Jewellery Quarter has a national and some say even international reputation for the breadth and variety of jewellery goods and services it can offer.

In the Jewellery Quarter many businesses are engaged in buying, selling and repairing jewellery items, including watches. Charles' interest in the idea stems from his own experience as an amateur horologist and the skills he developed at college in working with gold and silver. He has been an avid collector of wrist-watches for the past twenty years and has a comprehensive collection of more than 500 wrist-watches of different kinds. These range from modern-day quartz Swatches to First World War officers' wrist-watches. He plans to offer many of these watches for sale as part of his opening stock. Naturally, there are three or four favourite ones that he plans to keep for himself.

Charles visited Hockley to get some idea of the kind of place he would be working in if he did decide to go ahead with the venture. Now he wants to obtain more detailed information that will help him make a sensible decision.

Question

What difficulties might Charles encounter in doing this?

The Web

You first need an understanding of what the Internet is and what it is not. You have to be conversant with the concept of networking – building relationships around common interests. The World Wide Web is the part of the Internet that is likely to be of particular interest to marketers, because it brings together sound, vision, text and direct communication with individuals: in other words, multimedia. At least 100,000 companies around the world launched Web sites during 1995–6.

Firms can design and run a Web site themselves. The big investors include companies with international brands, such as drinks manufacturers, who recognise that the Web is a cost-effective global communication tool. Another Web site is the Yell International directory site for *Yellow Pages*. Other companies include Rank Xerox, whose site has already generated sales worth nearly £200,000. Rank Xerox markets colour laser printers and multifunctional faxes – which means it needs to target early adopters. Research showed the firm that these are exactly the sort of people who are likely to be using the Internet. The Glaxo Wellcome site invites you to choose from the following options:

- *Science:* browse a selection of information relevant to those involved in pharma-cology, or find out about scientific research at Glaxo Wellcome.
- *Healthcare:* take a look at this collection of informative reports relating to disease and disease management issues.
- *News:* keep yourself up to date with our latest developments.

Perhaps one of the faults with many sites is that they try to be all things to all people. Many Web site launches promote the fact that a company's information is being presented to twenty or thirty million people worldwide, as if it were some kind of global television broadcast. However, the Web is different to TV and press communication. It is 'narrowcasting' in the sense that the audience is self-selecting: the audience chooses to visit the site and, once in, the user chooses what information they want to look at.

Running a site is time-consuming if it is to be done properly and it is imperative to keep information up to date. Virgin Atlantic fell foul of a US court for failing to update its fare information.

Source: Marketing Week.[15]

Question

Discuss the possibility of using a Web site to provide secondary marketing information. What kind of difficulties are there in doing this?

Case study 3.3 | Salaries

In 1996 the James Market Research Organisation was trying to put together a list of published figures relating to people's earnings. They were looking for information for the occupations shown in Table 3.4.

Table 3.4

Army
Private
Colonel

Prison service
Prison Officer
Principal Officer

Police
Constable
Superintendent

Health
Nurse
General practitioner
Dentist
Consultant

Education
Teachers
(Primary/secondary)
Head teacher (secondary)
University lecturer
Professor

Council workers
Road sweeper
Office cleaner
Filing clerk
Senior officer
Chief executive

Retail
Sales assistant
Storekeeper

Transport
Tyre/exhaust fitter
Car mechanic

Airline stewardess
Airline captain

Media
Reporter (national)
National TV reporter

Advertising
Product manager
Marketing manager
Marketing director

Civil Service
Graduate civil servant
Permanent Secretary

Fire service
Firefighter
Senior divisional officer

Construction
Labourer
Carpenter/joiner
Civil engineer
Architect

Food and Restaurants
Barman
Chef

Football players
Top Premier League
Third Division

Computing
Programmer
Computing manager

Accountancy
Accountant
Chief Accountant

Lawyers
Solicitor
Criminal QC
High Court Judge

Politicians
Member of Parliament

Prime Minister

Miscellaneous
Hairdresser
Receptionist
Postman
Social worker
Librarian

Questions

1 Indicate likely data sources for each one of the figures.
2 What will the figures in each case actually represent?
3 In each case do you think that the figures will represent a true picture of actual earnings? Why or why not?

Case study 3.4 | **PowerUp Electricity plc**

The deregulation of the UK electricity supply industry in 1988 allowed new suppliers to enter the energy market and compete with the traditional (though now privatised) electricity supply companies. PowerUp Electricity plc is a subsidiary of a French utility company, and was formed specifically to take advantage of the new competitive environment.

For the French company, the UK was an unknown territory. Having seen some of the mistakes made by French utility companies during the privatisation of water supplies in Britain, the parent company's management were nervous about making the same errors, so they decided to carry out a major market research exercise in order to ascertain the likely acceptability of PowerUp plc. The company's target market was home owners with family incomes in excess of £25,000 p.a.; an analysis of the French utility company's own records showed that these households (or at least, their French equivalents) had the lowest rate of default on credit, were relatively large consumers of electricity, and were usually prompt payers. PowerUp needed to identify these customers, establish ways of reaching them, and (more importantly) find out what would attract them to switch electricity suppliers.

In the first instance, the firm's researchers set out to find out how many such households exist within the UK. This proved straightforward enough; Government statistics supplied the answer, at 2.2 million households. This was more than enough to make entering the market worthwhile; PowerUp could go to the next stage.

ACORN statistics were bought in to find out where the households were located, but then the work of surveying the households began. The researchers decided to opt for a quota sample, using the ACORN classifications to establish the quotas.

This meant considerable travel was involved, but since the survey was intended to establish parameters for a national company, this was only to be expected – PowerUp certainly did not want to skimp on research that might save the company millions in the long term.

Unfortunately, although the ACORN data was extremely reliable for judging the type of housing and the lifestyles of the inhabitants, it did not prove a successful predictor of income. For this the firm needed another source of data, which it was able to buy in from a specialist mailing list supplier. By combining details from the mailing list with those supplied by ACORN, PowerUp's researchers were able to generate a more refined mailing list of customers within the target market and use this to run a questionnaire-based survey to determine their needs.

Also, some doubt was expressed at board level as to whether the figures for France could be applied to the UK – the directors were not naive enough to believe that credit ratings in the UK could be calculated in exactly the same way as they were in France, or that UK consumers would have the same consumption profiles as their French equivalents, even if other details such as income and home ownership were similar. Apart from any other considerations, the rate of home ownership in the UK is much higher than that in France, which would alone be enough to distort the comparisons.

Overall, the directors felt that the research as conducted so far was inconclusive to say the least, and downright inaccurate to say the worst. Their feeling was that the UK should be considered as a completely separate market, with its own rules and parameters; very little could be carried over from experience of the French market, and indeed it might be dangerous to attempt to do so.

(Case contributed by Jim Blythe.)

Questions

1 How might PowerUp have used secondary sources to check the comparability of the French target market with the British target market?
2 What other sources of secondary data might PowerUp have used to find out about their target market?
3 What information needs did the secondary research reveal?
4 What sources are available for PowerUp to find out how to promote the product to the target market?
5 Why did PowerUp need to use primary research at all?

Further reading

Abdel-Ghany, M and Sharpe, D L (1997) Consumption patterns among the young–old and old–old, *Journal of Consumer Affairs*, 31(1), pp 90–112.

Abraham, M and Lodish, L (1990) Getting the most out of advertising and promotion, *Harvard Business Review*, 68(3), pp 50–63.

Baker, K (1989) Using geodemographics in market research, *The Journal of the Market Research Society*, 31, pp 37–44.

Blattberg, R and Deighton, J (1991) Interactive marketing: exploiting the age of addressability, *Sloan Management Review*, 33(1), pp 5–14.

Blattberg, R and Hoch, S (1990) Database models and managerial intuition: 50% Model + 50% Manager, *Management Science* 36(8), pp 887–99.

Crouch, S (1985) *Marketing Research for Managers*, London: Pan Books.

Government Statistics: A brief guide to sources, London: Office for National Statistics.

Jackson, P (1994b) *Desk Research*, London: Kogan Page.

Larson, E (1992) Watching Americans watch TV, *The Atlantic Monthly*, March.

Mayer, M (1990) Scanning the future, *Forbes*, 15 October.

Marketing Pocket Book, published annually by The Advertising Association in conjunction with NTC Publications, Farm Road, Henley-on-Thames, Oxfordshire RG9 1EJ. *See also* the *Lifestyle Pocket Book*, *The Media Pocket Book* and the *Regional Marketing Pocket Book*.

References and notes

[1] Spindler, R (1991) unpublished MSc dissertation, Odense University.

[2] *Market Search*, Arlington Publications, 25 New Bond Street, London W1Y 9HD.

[3] *Reports Index*, Business Surveys Ltd, Osmington Drive, Broadmayne, Dorset DT2 8ED.

[4] *Findex:* available through Euromonitor, 87 Turnmill Street, London EC1 5QU.

[5] *UK Marketing Source Book*, NTC Publications, Farm Road, Henley-on-Thames RG9 1EJ.

[6] *The Source Book*, Keynote Publications, 72 Oldfield Road, Hampton, Middlesex TW12 2HQ.

[7] *On-Line Business Source Book*, Headland Press, Henry Smith's Terrace, Headland, Cleveland TS24 0PD.

[8] *On-Line Business and Company Databases*, ASLIB, 20 Old Street, London EC1V 9AP.

[9] *Directory of On-Line Databases*, Gale Research International, PO Box 699, North Way, Andover, Hampshire SP10 5YE.

[10] Nairn, G (1997) Golden nuggets on a long and winding road, *Financial Times*, 3 December.

[11] *Financial Times*, 23 January 1997.

[12] *Eurostat Catalogue: Publications and Electronic Services*, Office for the Official Publications of the European Communities, L-2985 Luxembourg.

[13] *Infoplus*, PO Box 12, Sunbury on Thames, Middlesex TW16 7UD.

[14] Dialog, Plaza Suite, 114 Jermyn Street, London SW1Y 6HJ.

[15] Working on site, *Marketing Week*, 26 April 1996, pp 51ff.

4   Sampling

OBJECTIVES

After reading this chapter you should be able to:

■ appreciate the key elements involved in devising a sampling plan;

■ understand the important features of both probability and non-probability samples;

■ understand the major types and primary practical uses of both probability and non-probability sampling;

■ understand the primary approaches for determining sample size;

■ appreciate the nature of the sources of sampling and non-sampling error and how to minimise them.

KEY WORDS

census	cluster sample
sample	stratified sample
population	social classification
universe	ACORN
frame	convenience sample
random sample	judgement sample
quota sample	response error
probability sample	non-response error
non-probability sample	call-backs

PLAN OF CHAPTER 4

INTRODUCTION

Once the researcher has decided how primary data is to be collected, the next task is to obtain a sample of respondents that is representative of the target population of interest. This chapter discusses the major sampling techniques and how they are used in marketing research. The techniques can be divided into probability and non-probability methods. In probability sampling each element of the population has a known non-zero chance of being selected. In such cases it is possible to compute sampling variation and project the results to the entire population. In the case of non-probability sampling, the chance of selection of a particular population element is known and, strictly speaking, results cannot be projected to the entire population. Although sampling can be technically rigorous the need to be so does depend on the particular application.

This chapter discusses the key elements involved in devising a sampling plan and explores the importance of properly defining the target population of interest. It illustrates the important features of both probability and non-probability samples and describes the major types and primary practical uses of both probability and non-probability sampling. The chapter outlines the primary approaches to determining sample size, defines the concept of sampling and non-sampling error and explains the nature of the factors contributing response and non-response errors. Finally, it suggests how response rates can be improved and discusses ways of remedying non-response errors.

Census and samples

When we want to uncover information about the attitudes, ideas, beliefs and habits of a population, one way is to ask every member of it to participate in our study. Such an approach is called taking a census.

A census

A census is a count of people, houses, business firms or other items of interest taken at a particular time. Governments of different countries often take censuses of population and production every ten years. A census of the population, for example, tries to count everyone in the country at a specific time. A questionnaire is sent to every household asking how many persons are living there at the designated time and asking for information about gender, age and other details.

Census data are used for market research and changes in the data are indispensable in forecasting trends in demand for goods and services. Almost every country now conducts a census of some kind, usually at intervals of five or ten years. The information obtained ranges from basic data on the size, ages and locations of a country's population to information on migration, family composition, income and standard of living. Censuses can vary in their accuracy; questions have to be skilfully framed to obtain objective answers or at least to minimise the degree of inaccuracy.

> ### Sampling
>
> ■ Marketing research of a whole population is impractical.
> ■ Sampling allows us to obtain valid data on a representative section of a population from which we can draw valid conclusions about the whole population.
> ■ Random and quota sampling methods are usually applied in marketing research.

SAMPLING

Some so-called census information is in fact obtained by sampling. Computer-assisted statistical procedures make it possible to obtain useful information about many characteristics of the population by questioning only a selected sample of persons. Samples cost only a fraction of what it would cost to interrogate everyone.

To sample something is to examine a small portion of it, usually for the purpose of judging the nature or quality of the whole. In statistics, a collection of elements that have one or more specified characteristics is called a population. A sample, then, is some portion of a population. Because many populations of interest are too large to work with directly, techniques of statistical sampling have been devised to obtain samples taken from larger populations.

Unless a sample is chosen by a random mechanism, however, the results that are obtained from a study are likely to be biased in some direction. It is for this reason that methods of random sampling have been devised. A random sample can be chosen, for example, by throwing dice. Most commonly, however, when a list of names exists from which a sample can be chosen, the actual technique is to use random numbers generated by a computer. The list is numbered, and the computer provides a string of numbers from this list in such a way that various batches of entries in the list have an equal chance of being drawn.

Suppose that a market survey is being taken. A sample group is chosen from the population in the above manner, and the individuals who make up the sample are then interviewed. For example, an individual may be asked about washing powder brand choice. The arithmetic mean of the total answers provided by the individuals yields the proportion preferring one brand or the other. Any statistical population asked this question will also have an average response to it. The responses of the individuals in the population vary about this average response. The variability of the response is described by a quantity called the population variance. The arithmetic mean varies from one sample to the next, but it varies about the average response. In addition, the bigger the sample relative to the population size, the more accurate is the estimate determined by sampling.

Some situations permit the population to be split into a few very homogeneous groups or strata. The sample may then consist of a random sample taken within each stratum. Such a sample is called a stratified random sample.

Thus far we have assumed that a list, or sampling frame, is available. This is not true, however, in all cases. For example, no list exists of the pony population of Dartmoor. Thus the important topic of estimating the size of some populations must be handled differently. Areas are usually chosen at random.

The basic notion of a random sample

If the population is (1,2,3), there are three possible two-member samples: (1,2), (2,3) and (1,3).

Each of them has a one-out-of-three chance of being drawn. This is called random sampling.

Key elements involved in devising a sampling plan

Surveys attempt to find things out about a population. For marketing research purposes populations may consist of people or firms. A population for a survey comprises all the persons or companies to which you would like to direct questions. It would be highly advantageous to contact all members of a population and ask them to answer all the questions we want to put. If this could be done we could produce very accurate results. However, only seldom is it possible to contact or gain a response from all the members of a population. The exception is in the case of industrial market research, where it may be possible to contact all the firms that make up a particular population because the population may be very small.

Usually, large populations are encountered in marketing research and it is impractical or too expensive to contact all the members. In such cases we have to take a sample from the population – but we must ensure that the sample we choose represents the population as a whole.

There are three decisions to be taken in drawing up a sampling plan:

- Who is to be surveyed? This defines the target population. Once this has been done the next step is to develop a sampling frame: that is, a way of giving everyone in the target population a known chance of inclusion in the sample.
- How many people/companies should be surveyed? Large samples give better results than smaller ones. However, samples of less than 1 per cent of a population can often provide good, reliable information provided that the sampling procedure is credible.
- How should the respondents be chosen? Probability samples allow the calculation of confidence limits for sampling error. Thus in taking probability samples we can attach probabilities to any point estimates that are made. Cost and time often make it impractical to collect data through probability samples. Researchers often use non-probability samples – particularly quota samples. Strictly speaking, sampling errors cannot be measured in such cases.

Figure 4.1 Steps in developing a sample

Sampling plan

- Who is to be surveyed?
- How many people/companies should be surveyed?
- How should respondents be chosen?

Definition of the population

The population is the total group to be studied, the target population (sometimes referred to as the universe). It is the grand total of what is being measured: people, stores, homes or whatever. But since most samples in marketing research are of people, homes or stores, the term population, as we use it here, typically refers to one of these. If the purpose of the study has been well defined, the population is also well delineated. This is crucial if the study is to be significant and practical for the guidance of marketing management.

Importance of properly defining the target population of interest

A sample should reflect the characteristics of the population of interest to the study – that is, the target population. It is essential to define the target population precisely since failure to do so is likely to lead to the ineffective solving of a research problem.

A population needs to be defined in terms of elements, units and time. The population for a new quiz TV programme, for example, may be defined as:

- males or females;
- aged between eight and eighty;
- who have watched an existing quiz TV programme in the past thirty days in their own homes.

Population for a new quiz TV programme

Elements: males or females, aged between 8 and 80, who have watched an existing quiz programme in the past 30 days

Units: household

Time: January 1997

The elements that constitute the population are referred to as sampling units. In the new quiz TV programme example, households are designated as the sampling units. It is easier to select households, the place where the programmes are watched, than to interview everyone who qualifies as a member of the population. In some situations, population elements and the sampling unit will be the same, while in others they will be different.

It is up to the marketing researchers to provide explicit instructions to the field workers about the qualifications of the target population. This is achieved with the help of a list of screening questions that can be used to qualify respondents. Screening questions specifically define who should be included in the sample and who should be excluded. Most marketing research surveys exclude certain individuals for a variety of reasons. For example, in the case of a TV sports programme, if a member of a household works for a TV company then they are excluded. This is usually the first question asked and the interview is terminated at this point if this is the case. These individuals may be excluded for security reasons since they may work for competitors and the researchers would not want them to find out what the study is about.

THE SAMPLING FRAME

Obtaining a sample involves selecting some elements from the target population. In order to do this, it is assumed that it is possible to identify the target population of interest. A sampling frame is simply a list that identifies the target population. It can be a list of names and telephone numbers, as in telephone surveys, an area map of housing or a list of addresses purchased from a mailing-list supplier. It could also be a database. The frame defines the sampling unit, the unit used in the design of the sample. The frame, and therefore the sampling unit, may take the form of households, students, retail stores of a particular defined type (nature and size, for instance), businesses or transactions.

Although lists or other geographic breakdowns can be found, the list rarely matches the target population exactly. For instance, a list of residents of a given district naturally does not include new arrivals or households living in dwellings built since the list was compiled. Lists are rarely up to date and often contain duplication, such as households with more than one telephone number or individuals whose names appear on two or more lists.[1]

No sampling frame is perfect. For example, the listing in a telephone book omits unlisted numbers and is outdated on the day of publication because of moves in and out of the area it covers (for implications, see McKenzie[2]). Good research planning requires knowledge of the shortcomings of the sampling frame in order to make adjustments in the sampling design. The sampling frame or list that is used defines what may be termed the operational or working population. The difference between the operational population and the target population is usually referred to as the sampling gap. This gap appears in most marketing research studies, and efforts should be applied to try to minimise the gap since its presence increases the potential for misleading results. This can sometimes be done by combining two or more lists, taking care to remove one set of the names that appear on both lists.

Sampling frame optimisation

■   Target population – operational population = sample gap
■   Combine lists to minimise sample gap

Sometimes no sampling frame is available. As a rather extreme example, suppose that for some reason it is desirable to conduct a study of those who are overweight. No such list exists. But it is possible to use screening as a method of locating such people. A general frame of individuals can be used, and filter questions (with standards of overweight set up in advance) can be used, asking age, height and weight to determine those who qualify.

One frame that might be used is the telephone directory. The typical approach is to randomly select a number from the alphabetical list – say that this is 578 343 – and then to add a predetermined number, say +3, to this. The number actually used in the frame then becomes 578 346. The logic seems reasonable – but the list should include unlisted as well as listed numbers.

Another possibility for a frame is the mailing list. Depending on the needs for the particular study, it is possible to obtain, on the consumer side, lists as varied as camera-club members, computer owners, home owners (by value of home), prime investors (by nature of interest) and magazine subscribers (for many magazines).

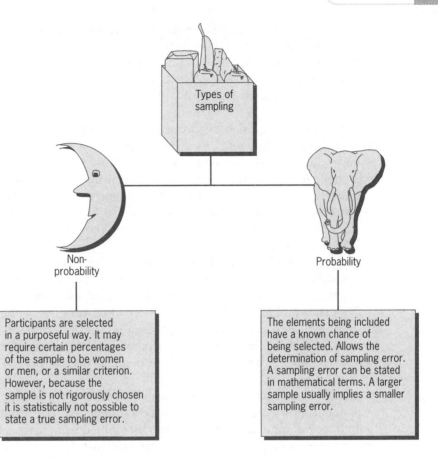

Figure 4.2 Types of sampling

On the business and professional side, we can find lists of small-town business persons, personnel executives, retailers and plumbers.

An obvious sampling frame is the self-accumulated list: a list already in the hands of the marketing firm. It may include the names and addresses of those who have made purchases, have had deliveries made, used credit cards or registered at trade shows.

SAMPLING METHODS

There are two major types of sampling methods: probability sampling and non-probability sampling.

Probability samples comprise samples in which the elements being included have a known chance of being selected. A probability sample enables sampling error to be estimated. This, in simple terms, is the difference between the sample value and the true value of the population being surveyed. A sampling error can be stated in mathematical terms: usually plus or minus a certain percentage. A larger sample usually implies a smaller sampling error.

Non-probability samples are ones in which participants are selected in a purposeful way. The selection may require certain percentages of the sample to be women or men, housewives under thirty or a similar criterion. This type of selection is an effort to reach a cross-section of the elements being sampled. However, because the sample is not rigorously chosen it is statistically impossible to state a true sampling error.

Today, most samples chosen for applied research are non-probability samples. If carefully done – with quotas, for example, of persons to be studied – the findings are usually valid. A true probability sample, because of the stringent requirements, is likely to be far too expensive and too time-consuming for most uses. The sampling method chosen for any particular study, therefore, must be explained carefully, with the reasons for its acceptability and likelihood of supplying accurate data.

The research plan may not require that the whole country be sampled. Cost and time factors may lead to the decision to cover only part of a country. Past experience for the products or services being studied may indicate that the selected areas are representative of the nation with respect to what is being studied. However, the more specific the description of those to be studied, the larger the sample must be.

The major problem with the quota method of sampling is that the interviewers are allowed discretion in choosing the individual respondents within the quota categories. This discretion introduces a possible source of bias, because the resulting sample can largely omit some types of people, such as those who are difficult to contact.

A much better approach is the probability method of sampling, in which specific respondents are chosen by random selection methods. The result of this method is that no type of individual is systematically omitted from the sample, and the likely amount of error in the resulting data can be calculated.

Statistical laws have established that no matter how large the population being studied (from a small city to a whole country), the size of the sample is the main factor that determines the expected range of error in a probability sample. Most current polls use samples ranging in size from 1000 to 2000 individuals. Many polling organisations have adopted probability methods in selecting their samples, but the less reputable polls still use quota methods or even non-scientific haphazard methods of sample selection – and the quality of their findings suffers accordingly.

The forms of probability sampling

There are five forms of probability sampling (Figure 4.3):

1 simple random
2 random walk
3 stratified random
4 cluster
5 systematic.

The following are illustrative of the kind of sampling approach that might be taken.

Simple random sample

In this case all members of the population have a known and equal chance of being included in the sample. For example, the names of every firm in a given population could be written on slips of paper and the slips deposited in a box. The box could then be shaken so that all the slips of paper become thoroughly mixed up. A blindfolded person drawing successive slips of paper from the box would be taking a random sample of the population.

Simple random sampling works well when we are dealing with relatively small populations. For large-scale consumer populations, however, the method is not appropriate since it is difficult to obtain a list of all the people in a given population.

Random walk sampling

This form of sampling is used extensively in market research as a cheap approximation to true random sampling. The sample involves conducting random walks in small areas. These areas are usually wards within constituencies. First, a random sample of constituencies is drawn from a list of constituencies and then within each of the randomly selected constituencies a random selection of wards is chosen. Next, selected random starting points within these areas (wards) are chosen and interviewers are given fixed routes to follow and instructions to obey. The instructions specify the interval of households to contact (for example, every seventh house) and the action to take at each street junction (turn alternatively left or right). Special instructions are given about blocks of flats and what to do when non-residential buildings are encountered. Although the resulting sample is not truly random it is usually treated as if it were.

Stratified random sample

This approach is more suitable for sampling large consumer populations. It entails dividing the population into mutually exclusive groups and drawing random samples from each group. For example, the population might be divided into six groups, A, B, C1, C2, D and E, reflecting the social background of the people involved. Random

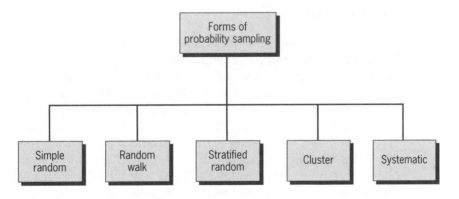

Figure 4.3 Types of probability sample

samples are then drawn from each group. Again, however, there still remains the problem of obtaining suitable lists of people who make up the population and the various groups within it. Stratified sampling may be used in industrial marketing research where it is possible to identify a population of firms. A stratified sample is usually adopted to make sure that minority groups are adequately represented.

The 'Market Research Services Classification' of Social Class

Grade	Percentage of population	Status	Head of household's occupation
A	3	Upper middle class	Higher managerial, administrative or professional
B	13	Middle class	Intermediate managerial, administrative or professional
C1	23	Lower middle class	Supervisory or clerical junior managerial, administrative or professional
C2	32	Skilled working class	Skilled manual workers
D	19	Working class	Semi- and unskilled manual workers
E	10	Those at lowest level of subsistence	State pensioners or widows; casual or lowest grade workers

Source: JICNARS.[3]

The ABCDE classification conceived by Market Research Services Ltd has been the system most frequently used to classify people into social classes for marketing purposes. Its failure to capture the complexity of class differences has led to new systems such as SAGACITY and ACORN.

Cluster sample

In this case the universe and the frame are defined and classified into homogeneous segments. Random samples are then chosen from each segment. The method offers a sharpening of sampling, virtually guaranteeing that the use of these cells of units – done in two dimensions or more – will provide a cross-section of each.

Cluster sampling is a suitable approach to sampling large consumer populations. Here the population is divided into mutually exclusive groups and the researcher draws a sample of the groups to interview. This time we are not interested in a person's social class but in where they live or some other characteristic. Assuming that residence is the key factor and that the objective is to interview household heads, then the first step is to divide up the locality under study into individual areas of housing. A random or stratified sample of the areas identified is then taken and interviews are held with every household head within each sampled area.

This is a 'single-stage' cluster sample since only a sample of the blocks or areas of housing is taken. A 'two-stage' cluster sample might involve undertaking the same number of interviews, making sure that a large number of blocks are covered but that only a sample of households in each block is interviewed. For example, if an area comprises three high-rise tower blocks of flats, we might randomly select one of the three blocks and interview all household heads within that block.

Systematic sampling

In the systematic sampling method, the sampling units are chosen from the sampling frame at a uniform interval at a specified rate. For example, we might use the residential telephone directory. Perhaps the book has 400 pages in it, with an average, after a check of perhaps ten widely dispersed pages, of 400 listings per page, for an estimated total of 160 000 listings (400×400). The particular study requires a list of 2000 for sampling purposes. (For simplicity at this point, we forget the number of completions required.) This means that every 80th listing (160 000/2000) should be drawn.

So that the method is a true probability method, where every sampling unit has an equal chance of coming into the sample, there also must be a random starting point. Thus, if we are using every 80th listing, we must select a random starting number of between 1 and 79.

Forms of non-probability sampling

There are three forms of non-probability sampling (Figure 4.4):

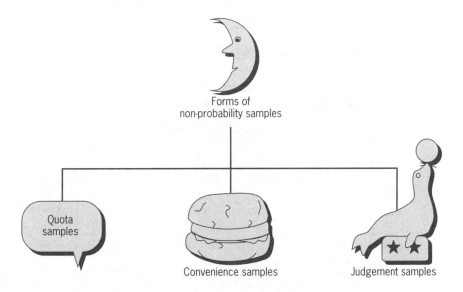

Figure 4.4 Non-probability sampling methods

1 quota sampling
2 convenience sampling
3 judgement sampling.

Quota sampling

In the case of quota sampling the researcher starts with the knowledge of how the universe is divided by strata. The investigators are instructed simply to fill the cells, so that the sample obtained is indeed representative in terms of the cells. The procedures used in quota sampling make the choice of respondents the responsibility of the interviewers. Unfortunately, this can lead to substantial bias which cannot be objectively measured. Wide use of quota sampling has been made in marketing research since it is relatively cost effective compared with other methods. However, with the development of random sampling techniques, researchers have become more critical of the drawbacks of this method. If properly applied, the method can be successful because it is possible to introduce representativeness by stratifying the quota sample by objective and known population characteristics such as age, sex, family status and socioeconomic group. Quota samples may be accurately constructed using classifications such as ACORN. This is because such classifications are based on objective distributions of statistical variations in demographic, housing and occupational factors.

The first step is to estimate the sizes of the various subclasses or strata in the population. This is usually done through reference to some outside source – for example, a census of population data. The relevant strata to the study has to be specified. For instance, a person's age may be something that a researcher may think is relevant to a particular study. As a consequence, age will have to be taken into account when drawing up the sample. For example, if it is found that in the population 25 per cent of people are aged between twenty-five and thirty, then the aim should be to make sure that 25 per cent of the people in the sample fit into this age band. There are similar requirements for other age bands reflecting the proportions with which they appear in the population under study. Other factors as well as age might also be considered.

Selected ACORN types and groups	
Group	
C	Older housing of intermediate status
Type	
C 8	Mixed owner occupied and council estates
C 9	Small town centres and flats above shops
C 10	Villages with non-farm employment
C 11	Older private housing, skilled workers

Group	
J	Affluent suburban housing
Type	
J 33	Interwar semis, white-collar workers
J 34	Spacious interwar semis, big gardens
J 35	Villages with wealthy older communities
J 36	Detached houses, exclusive suburbs
Source: CACI.[4]	

Convenience sampling

In convenience sampling, there is no sample design. It is similar to an interviewer questioning people as they meet them on the street or in shopping precincts. Choice of the respondent is left entirely to the interviewer. Some methods, such as this, allow potential respondents to decide for themselves whether or not to respond.

The researcher takes the most accessible population members from which to obtain information. This happens, for example, when a firm producing a prototype new domestic appliance gets some of its employees to test out the product in their own homes. Such a sample provides useful information to the researcher as long as the sample seems to be reasonably representative of the population being studied. However, asking a convenience sample of students about their reading habits might not be appropriate if you are interested in the reading habits of the population as a whole – i.e. all ages and occupations.

Judgement sampling

This type of sampling relies on sound judgement or expertise. It depends on selecting elements that are believed to be typical or representative of the population in such a way that errors of judgement in the selection will cancel each other out. Judgement samples tend to be used more often in industrial market research than in consumer market research. In industrial market research a firm may get 50 per cent of its business from ten large purchasers and the remaining 50 per cent from 300 smaller firms. A judgement sample might therefore comprise five of the large purchasers (50 per cent) and 150 of the remainder (50 per cent). Judgement would be exercised to ensure that the firms chosen in the sample represented the subgrouping.

Sampling and non-sampling error

The quality of the data in a particular survey is a function of what is termed the *total survey error*. Total survey error reflects the difference between the overall population's true mean value of the characteristic of interest and its mean observed value obtained from the particular sample of respondents. What is of interest is what causes the information obtained from a sample of respondents to differ from that of the entire population. Total survey error is composed of random sampling error and non-sampling error.

Random sampling error occurs because the selected sample is not a perfect representation of the overall population. It represents how accurately the chosen sample's true mean value reflects that of the population. Random sampling error can be controlled by employing an appropriate statistical design and by increasing the sample size.

Non-sampling error represents the extent to which the mean observed value (on the characteristic of interest) for the respondents of a particular sample disagrees with the mean true value for the particular sample of respondents. The size of the non-sampling error depends on two factors: non-response errors and response errors. Non-response errors occur because not all those included in the sample do in fact respond. Moreover, the mean true value of those respondents who do not respond may be different from the entire sample's true mean value. Response error, on the other hand, occurs when respondents give inaccurate answers.

Non-response errors

Very few studies ever achieve a 100 per cent response success rate. The problem of non-response error occurs because those who agree to participate in the study are in some respects different from those who decline to participate. Usually, the higher the response rate, the lower the probability of non-response error effects. Nevertheless, response rates are not always a good indicator of non-response error. First, response rates do not reflect whether the respondents are good representatives of the target sample. Second, an increase in response does not always lead to a reduction in the non-response error. Third, the notion of response rate is ambiguous since the number of eligible respondents used in the calculation of response rates frequently differs across studies. Unfortunately, the extent of the difference between respondents and non-respondents can seldom be directly determined (see Hahlo[5] for a discussion of non-response errors).

Non-response errors

■ Low response rates: those not responding differ in some way from those who do
■ Unrepresentative sample

Response errors

■ Wanting to give an answer that pleases the researcher
■ Faulty memory, fatigue or nature of the questions
■ Lack of knowledge/familiarity with subject matter
■ Wanting to give socially acceptable answers
■ Interviewer influence

Response errors

People may give an inaccurate response either intentionally or unintentionally simply because they are being interviewed. For example, respondents may deliberately not report their duly considered answer because they want to help or please the researcher. This is often encountered in new product tests. In another instance, even though the respondent intends to respond accurately, response error arises because of faulty memory, fatigue, question format or even question content. It also arises when people have little or no experience with the survey topic, for example, asking a low-income respondent about comparatively expensive goods.

Interviewers can influence respondents' answers, incorrectly record respondents' answers and even falsify respondents' answers. People may also be influenced by their attitude to the organisation conducting the study. Last, the wish to give socially acceptable answers to sensitive or potentially embarrassing questions can also lead to response errors.

A variety of factors can cause errors in survey results. The onus is on the researcher to:

- determine whether respondents have enough information about the topic on which to base their opinions;
- word and/or pose the questions carefully;
- avoid biases in wording that suggest a socially desirable answer, or lead respondents to agree with one side of an issue;
- pretest questions in pilot studies to ensure their clarity and impartiality;
- train interviewers to avoid influencing respondents' answers.

SAMPLING IN PRACTICE

So far we have examined some of the methods of applying sampling in a study. We now consider the choice of a sampling method.

Required precision is a factor in influencing the choice of sampling method. Getting a clear-cut answer about the most likely effect of a proposed price reduction on market share demands a sampling design where precision of results can be measured – some kind of probability sample. However, an exploratory study that is trying to obtain some rough idea about which price reduction method is most promising for further development and testing can use a non-probability sample. It would not be cost effective to spend additional money on a more precise sample. The availability of an appropriate sampling frame is another factor. Drawing a sample without a frame can be difficult and expensive.

Some factors specific to the study may dictate the form of data collection to be used, such as personal interviews in shopping precincts, postal questionnaire or telephone study. If the study requires the placement of a product with people for in-home trial, the telephone and postal methods (except in combination with other methods) are not feasible. These methods also cannot be used for testing television advertisements.

However, if the study intends to measure the number of people reached by a particular radio or television advertisement, the telephone procedure, with its easy access and low unit cost, may be the right method. On the other hand, if the study is aimed at measuring the readership of a publication, then a meeting between interviewer and respondent is essential to show and go through the publication. Finally, the cost of collecting the information has to match the value of the study to the sponsor.

Sampling small populations

The above sampling methods are standard procedures to adopt when sampling populations that occur reasonably often. Sometimes, however, the population sought after is not that easy to find. Special sampling methods may be required in these cases. A good illustration is to be found by a researcher who is interested in ascertaining attitudes and other information about prescription drug brands used by only a very small number of patients. There are likely to be few of them and, without special sampling methods, it will be too difficult and expensive to study them.

There are six techniques that can be applied in such a case:

1 direct screening
2 two-phase screening
3 stratification
4 multiframe sampling
5 selection of high-yield clusters
6 multiplicity sampling.

There is also a seventh approach which could involve using data from an existing database.

Direct screening

Here, people are approached, on the telephone or in a shopping precinct, to ascertain whether they meet the requirements for being part of the sample and, if so, they are subsequently questioned. The method has the drawback that if the incidence is too low it will mean a lot of non-productive interview time, progress will be slow and costs will be high.

Two-phase screening

In this case, one survey is followed by a second among those who qualify. The first contact defines the qualifiers. The second produces the responses sought from those who qualify.

Three approaches to two-way screening

1. Cluster sampling

Where users of barbecues are to be questioned, clusters of neighbourhoods where barbecues are likely to be common can be identified. Either by telephone interviewing (using clusters by postal code, perhaps) or by personal interviewing within clusters, those having barbecues can be located efficiently.

2. Omnibus study

A continuing study, it is done either personally or by telephone. It makes it possible to ask a screening question and have the research firm follow up with those who qualify. It is an inexpensive way to accumulate lists of those who qualify. However, there are limitations. If the study requires follow-ups, in-home placement of a product, exposure of a television commercial, or the like, the research firm may not be able to do this at reasonable cost, if at all.

3. Panels

The panel typically is a national list of families that have agreed to participate in mail and telephone studies, and the sponsoring research firm tries to make sure that the total panel represents national and regional demographics. The screening and follow-up can be over the telephone or by post.

Stratification

Stratification entails sorting out those with specific demographic characteristics from selected small geographic areas where there seem to be concentrations of specific groups of people with certain characteristics. Using census data it may be possible to do this for postal code areas.

Multiframe sampling

A list of the desired rare population is seldom complete or even available. So the answer, both in terms of costs and a good sample, is to work with two frames.

High-yield clusters

This is almost trial-and-error. It is useful in residential telephone surveys where the costs of an initial qualifying call are low. Let us say that a random-digit dialling system is intended to produce a sample of residences only. Such a system is almost certain to produce non-residence numbers as well. To minimise the proportion of non-residence numbers, clusters of perhaps 100 numbers are set up. Within each cluster, a 10-digit number is randomly chosen.

Multiplicity sampling (snowballing)

Members of the rare population are located by screening within each individually designated enumeration unit. A respondent who qualifies for the sample is asked to provide the names of others who also presumably qualify. A network of contacts is produced, which might include all households containing parents or their children. Each network of households then becomes the sampling unit, from which information about the other members of the network can be obtained.

A major drawback to this method is that there is no way of checking to be sure that the sample is representative of the population of interest.

Conducting sampling

Here, we consider the problems associated with obtaining the right respondent, gaining the respondent's cooperation, the completion rate, and handling the problems of people who are too busy to cooperate and no answers (in telephone surveys).

Obtaining the right respondent

We should firmly establish in the minds of researchers the qualifications for being a respondent in a study. If a telephone survey requires a specific person in a household, the questioning procedure should establish the position of the person answering the call, and not allow the interviewer to assume that any voice on the phone belongs to the desired person. If a heavy user of instant puddings is required, the questions and questioning procedures must be objective and thorough. The interpretation of the term 'heavy' is not something that should be left to either interviewer or respondent. There should be strict guidelines about classifying respondents into heavy, medium or light users, for example, so that this objective definition can be used in deciding who qualifies for questioning.

In a shopping-precinct study where interviewers stop shoppers to question them, investigators can be given instructions about the ratio of men and women to interview. However, there can be special problems in shopping-precinct interviews. The Monday shopper is likely to be different from the Saturday shopper and the morning shopper is different from the afternoon or evening shopper. The interviewing should be scheduled to represent all the varying categories.

When carrying out consumer telephone surveys, it is essential to make use of a recording form to ensure that the prescribed steps are properly carried out. This ensures that the consumer telephone sample is carried out as planned. The same kind of attention is required with a sample of business respondents. In a telephone survey where executives are the target sample, it is often difficult to get past the secretary or the assistant to the executive. A personal visit to the office often presents the same problem. Making a telephone call or sending a letter ahead of time, to see if a specific time can be set for that telephone call or personal visit, can help to resolve the problem. The nature of the questioning can be outlined. This not only gives the secretary a chance to clear it with the boss, but gives the executive time to obtain materials and documents ready for the interview. However, advance notice may also cause problems. It is often difficult for the potential respondent to arrange time ahead. Moreover, the advance call may provide the person with the means of postponing or refusing the interview outright.

Respondent cooperation

A large proportion of the public often refuses to participate in market surveys. Non-participation rises with interview length and varies with subject matter. This presents the possibility of a serious sampling problem.

The completion rate

The completion rate is the proportion of those in the potential sample who actually participate in the research. The sampling is ineffective if too few candidates end up being questioned or observed. We would expect at least 50–60 per cent of those designated as potential respondents to participate. The problem is that non-respondents are often different in some way from those who participate. The way in which this problem is tackled depends on how both the first contact with the person and the follow-up contacts are made.

In consumer telephone surveys, the timing of the call may be a critical factor. If the study involves working mothers, the hours of dinner preparation and serving should be avoided in order to gain cooperation. Evenings and weekends provide a better opportunity to secure interviews where the male household head is to be questioned. However, evening calls to retired people may be unproductive since some senior citizens retire early and will not be pleased if prevented from doing so or if awakened from their sleep.

Achieving a 50 per cent response rate on the first call is good going. Call-backs are a necessity, as are specific plans and record-keeping to ensure that the call-back plan is properly carried through. Where a postal survey is involved, records should be kept for each individual showing the original date of posting. After a set number of days without a response, a second letter or even a telephone call is made. In the case of telephone and personal interview studies, you need to have some idea about why there is a non-response. It may be that there is no one at home (or no answer to the telephone), or the qualified respondent is not available. In the former case, the call-back is made on a random basis, following a predetermined plan that may schedule the follow-up attempt at a time when someone is there. It may be a different day, a different hour. If the non-response is because the qualified person is not available, there should be a procedure in which the individual who is at home can suggest a good time to make the call.

Where a person is busy or there is no answer

One of the major reasons for no answers is the increasing proportion of couples who both work, and the proportion is greater among high-income groups and in towns. At evenings and weekends young couples may form a dining-out or a shopping team. Weather is also a consideration: in the good weather during the summer months, people spend less time in the house and more outdoors, while in the cold season, the reverse is true. Call-backs are the solution but they have to be planned systematically.

In the case of telephone studies, interviews should be conducted only between 9 a.m. and 9 p.m. Interviewers should be thoroughly trained, and an emphasis should be put on making the interviewing experience pleasant and appealing to the respondent so that further cooperation is encouraged. The respondent should be told the topic at the start of the questioning and the questionnaire should be kept to a reasonable length.

THE SIZE OF THE SAMPLE

Primary approaches for determining sample size

Marketing researchers use at least four different methods of determining sample size. Sample size determination can be based on:

1 intuition
2 statistical precision
3 cost limitations
4 industry standards.

Intuition

This is the most unsatisfactory method of determining sample size. It uses informed intuition as the basis for determining how many units to sample. The method of determining sample size is completely arbitrary and does not consider the likely precision of the survey results or the cost of obtaining them.

Statistical precision

The size of a sample affects the quality of the research data and it is not simply a question of applying some arbitrary percentage to a specific population. The sample size that needs to be taken should reflect the basic characteristics of the population, the type of information required and the costs entailed. The larger the sample size, the greater its precision or reliability, but practical constraints of time, staff and other costs intervene.

When computing the size of a sample, the size of the non-response factor should be borne in mind. If, for example, a final sample of 3500 is planned and the non-response is estimated at 30 per cent then it would be advisable to increase the original factor to 5000. Such a correction will help to obtain the number of responses required but it will not correct the bias that arises from non-response errors – the fact that those who do not respond may have significantly different opinions from those who do respond.

The error of a sample varies inversely with the square root of the sample size. A sample of 9000 is more accurate than a sample of 1000. After a certain sample size has been reached, additional large increases in size do not significantly improve the statistical precision of a given sample. Costs, on the other hand, increase with larger samples.

The precision of the survey is a function of the sample size (although see Chisnall[6]). Precision is related to the square of the number in the sample. That is, the accuracy of results increases proportionately to the square of the sample size. If the sample size is doubled, let us say from 500 to 1000, accuracy rises only to the square root of the doubled sample size (2), or a bit less than half (1.4). While technically the rationale applies only to probability sampling, it is usually used as a guide in planning the size of non-probability samples as well. By sampling precision we do not mean how accurate the results are, for accuracy depends on too many factors: how good the questions are, whether or not the interviewer (if there is one) affects the results, etc. What is referred to here is the degree to which data on a simultaneously replicated study parallel those of another study, or how similar the results of two simultaneous studies are.

Sampling error

Sampling error is the difference between a survey result and its parameter (a known statistic of the universe) – that is, the difference between the true value of a parameter of a population and that estimated from a sample. The error occurs because the value has been calculated from a sample rather than from the whole parent population.

The confidence interval

The confidence interval is an interval within which a parameter of a parent population is calculated (on the basis of sample data) to have a stated probability of lying. Generally, the researcher settles for a 95 per cent probability – meaning that there are 95 or more chances in 100 that the reported figure falls within the range of a stated numerical value from the parameter.

For simplicity and because it answers almost all needs, our discussion here is limited to a discussion of percentages. But another measure of the confidence interval might be in terms of means. The confidence interval can be calculated only when the study has used probability sampling to obtain the results.

Overall precision required

Once the overall precision (range of the confidence interval) has been defined for the particular study, it is possible to make some tentative decisions on sample size. We say tentative only because there are still other aspects to be considered. In principle this approach can be used only with probability sampling, since there is no way of knowing whether a non-probability sample produces a sample similar to one based on selection probabilities. Practically, however, it is often used as a guide in determining the sample size of non-probability samples. As the sample size is quadrupled the confidence interval is cut in two. The confidence interval decreases as the expected percentage of results moves away from 50 per cent (either plus or minus). This has some practical implications. First, increasing the required accuracy places a heavy premium on the price of the survey because of the effect it has on sample size requirements. Second, if the expected result cannot be predicted, 50 per cent is the correct percentage to use. That is where the greatest error margin is experienced. So if results cannot be predicted in advance, sample size planning should be on the conservative side: in this case, the larger, more expensive side.

Cost limitation

This method determines sample size on the basis of the budget allocated to the project. It involves first subtracting from the available budget all non-sampling-related costs (for example, the fixed cost of designing the survey, questionnaire preparation, data analysis and report generation), then dividing this amount by the estimated cost per sampling unit to arrive at the desired sample size. The approach is unsatisfactory because it emphasises cost to the exclusion of all other factors, especially precision.

Industry standards

These refer to those rules of thumb, developed from experience, that have become standard industry guidelines for determining how large a sample to draw. Conventional guidelines on sample size vary with the type of marketing research study as well as with the number of cells included in the study. The conventional approach to determining sample size is frequently used in non-probability designs, especially in quota samples. In quota samples, for example, the minimum number of respondents per cell is usually 50. A cell of 1000–1500 is usually considered as a reasonable sample for a national (probability) market study. Also, 200–300 per cell is the convention for a typical concept or product test.

Other factors

Deciding on sample size is not simply a statistical matter. The actual decision is a judgement call by marketing management or top management, depending on the importance of the particular problem. In any case, the decision will not be based on such points as sampling size: it will centre on costs versus value.

SUMMARY

This chapter has introduced the idea of sampling, contrasting it with a census. The key elements involved in devising a sampling plan have been discussed and the importance of properly defining the target population of interest has been emphasised. Illustrations of the important features of both probability and non-probability samples have been given and the major types and primary practical uses of both probability and non-probability sampling have been outlined. The primary approaches for determining sample size have been discussed and the concept of sampling and non-sampling error has been considered. The nature of the factors contributing to response and non-response errors have been described and suggestions made as to how response rates can be improved and non-response errors minimised. Particular attention has been given to sampling methods that are most appropriate for small populations. Attention has also been paid to the management of the sampling process and the determination of sample size.

Questions

1 Differentiate between a sample and a census.

2 What are the major arguments for undertaking research using sample data as opposed to census data?

3 Explain the notion of a random sample.

4 What are the key elements involved in developing a sample plan?

5 What is a sampling population?

6 How would you try to properly define a population?

7 How would you set about determining a sample frame?

8 Why is no sampling frame perfect? What can you do to compensate for this?

9 What are the limitations and advantages of using the telephone directory as a sampling frame?

10 Differentiate between probability and non-probability sampling.

11 Differentiate between the following:

   a straight random sample

   b random walk sample

   c stratified sample

   d cluster sample

   e systematic sample.

   What do they all have in common?

12 Differentiate between:

   a quota sampling

   b convenience sampling

   c judgement sampling

   What do they have in common?

13 What use might be made of ACORN types and groups and social class grade systems in sampling?

14 Indicate the main sources of sampling and non-sampling errors in survey research.

15 Indicate the sampling methods more appropriate for small populations. Why are such approaches more appropriate?

16 What are the essential components of ensuring that the sampling process is well managed?

17 What methods might be employed to determine the best size of sample to take?

Case study 4.1   Research Consultants

Research Consultants has been commissioned to determine the following: Why do people select one estate agent over another? Do customers know or care if an estate agent is a member of a particular institute or professional body? And what additional services would customers like to receive from estate agents?

Research Consultants underbid four other research firms to obtain the contract: in fact, its bid was some 50 per cent of the next lowest bid. The main reason that Research Consultants was able to do this was because of the sampling methodology it selected. In its proposal the company said that university students would be used to gather the survey data. The company said that it would randomly select twenty universities from across the UK and contact the head of the business or management department at each college. The head would be asked to submit a list of ten students who would be interested in earning some extra money and then a senior consultant in the company would contact the students individually. The company's aim was to identify five students at each institute, who would ultimately complete ten interviews each. When the students were contacted by the senior consultant they were told that they would be given £5 for each completed interview. The only requirement about who would be interviewed was that it must be someone who had had some experience of dealing with an estate agent in the previous twelve months. In fact, the consultant said that probably the easiest thing to do was for students to visit local pubs during the lunch hour and go from table to table asking for people who might be interested in being interviewed.

Questions

1 How would you describe this method of sampling?
2 What problems do you see arising from this approach?
3 Suggest a much better sampling method.

Case study 4.2   Jerome's department store

Jerome's customers are in the middle and upper middle income bracket and the store bases its reputation on having good, serviceable and not too fashionable clothing. The store also sells popular lines of cosmetics. Like all good department stores, the firm has a variety of departments ranging from china and jewellery to soft furnishings. At one time the firm also sold major electrical appliances but competition became too cut-throat and the firm decided to withdraw from that market.

In the last twelve months the store has experienced a slowing down of sales of clothes. Management felt that perhaps this was because it was not really very fashion conscious in what it had to offer. As a result a decision was taken to have a market research study conducted to ascertain whether the store should stock more designer clothing in the men's, women's and children's departments.

It was intended that the survey interviews were going to be conducted in the consumers' homes and would last more than an hour and a half. Jerome planned to show respondents a number of potential lines that could be added, including examples of clothing and information about the clothes' designers. The cost of the proposed survey was of some concern to management. As a result, management was particularly concerned about the number of interviews that should be taken since this would obviously influence the total cost of the exercise.

Question

How should Jerome proceed with respect to the market research survey? Specifically, what approach should it take to sampling?

Case study 4.3 | McBain's fast food restaurant

McBain's is considering opening a fast food restaurant in Liverpool and, as part of the viability study, it wants to assess people's attitudes to a new fast food restaurant. There are to be 200 completed interviews and as far as possible the sample should be as follows:

Gender	50 per cent should be male
	50 per cent should be female
Age	40 per cent between 16 and 24
	40 per cent between 25 and 50
	10 per cent to be under 16
	10 per cent to be over 50
Occupation	20 per cent to be students
	80 per cent to be non-students

The interviews are to be conducted at the St Johns shopping precinct.

Question

Indicate how such a quota sample might be achieved.

Case study 4.4 | Student research projects

A marketing lecturer set his students the task of thinking up an idea for a new product, then researching the market for it. The students were allowed to use any research methods that seemed appropriate, but all were expected to carry out secondary research before designing their primary research programmes. Most of the groups of students found that thinking up the product ideas was fun, but the research was more like hard work – on the other hand, they appreciated the opportunity to put some of their own ideas to work.

Altogether, there were 42 ideas for new products; some of these were not technically feasible, or would be unlikely to be profitable, but some of the ideas seemed viable. In any case, the assignment was about research, not about the technical design of products, so the feasibility or otherwise of the products was irrelevant.

The students carried out the necessary secondary research, then designed their own primary research programmes. Most used questionnaire-based surveys, a few used focus groups, and a tiny number used depth interviews, observation, experimentation or other techniques.

The students were left to their own devices somewhat; the idea was to allow them to learn from their mistakes and find out for themselves what the pitfalls of market research are. In most cases, students managed to produce fairly good results, but quite obviously some of them had serious difficulties.

The questionnaire surveys turned out to be the ones that caused the most difficulty. Apart from the problems of designing the questionnaire, many of the students had made basic sampling errors. Here are some examples, taken from the students' written-up assignments:

- 'We conducted a random sample of shoppers by stopping people in the High Street on Saturday morning.' (New type of shopping basket)
- 'In order to find out the views of young people, we asked for volunteers and interviewed 23 students from the university.' (Radio station)
- 'We surveyed 10 women and 10 men. The women were 20 per cent more likely to like the product than were the men, and people over 60 were 10 per cent more likely to like the product. Overall, 40 per cent of the respondents liked the product.' (Gardening tool)
- 'Telephone interviews with 100 respondents revealed that 32 per cent of those interviewed would buy the roof sealer. Unfortunately, a further eight people who were interviewed later turned out to be grown-up children of the household rather than the home owner.' (Emergency roof sealing tarpaulin)
- 'The main problem we had with the interviews was that most people were too busy to stop and talk to us. Eventually, we managed to complete 70 useable questionnaires, however.' (Banking services)
- 'Having obtained the permission of the crèche to conduct our research, we gave the questionnaire to the mothers when they arrived to collect their children. The following day we collected the questionnaires; unfortunately only about half were returned. However, these were enough to enable us to draw some conclusions.'

The focus groups were rather better, but even here some problems became apparent.

- 'Our group consisted of six boy and two girls, aged between eighteen and twenty. We showed them the model of the product and asked them to comment on it; at first they seemed to find it difficult to say much, but after some prompting they began to discuss it more freely.' (Car vacuum cleaner)
- 'When we showed them the product most of them seemed puzzled. We had six housewives in the group, all of them from a coffee-morning group of friends.' (Safety device for lawnmowers)
- 'Our group often strayed from the subject. We had a representative sample consisting of three teenagers (one male, two female), two middle-aged people, and three old-age pensioners.' (Carpet cleaning device)

Although the students were able (in most cases) to work out what had gone wrong, they did not always know what to do to put matters right. This meant that the lecturer needed to spend considerable time with them to correct misconceptions and to help them understand the issues raised by the research; despite that, all those concerned, both lecturer and students, felt that the exercise had been a useful introduction to market research.

(Case contributed by Jim Blythe.)

Questions

1 In each of the above cases, say what you think is wrong with the sampling.
2 For each of the above cases, say what you think the students should have done instead of what they actually did.
3 For each of the above cases, say what additional research you could do to correct the sampling errors or minimise their effect.
4 How can sampling errors such as these be avoided in future?
5 Is it possible to obtain a perfect sample?

Further reading

Adcock, C J (1997) Sample size determination – a review, *Statistician*, 46(2), pp 261–83.

Bailar, B A (1997) Does sampling work?, *Business Economics*, 32 (1), January, pp 47–53.

Bolton, R N (1994) Covering the market, *Marketing Research: A Magazine of Management and Applications*, 6(3), pp 30–5.

Butcher, B (1994) Sampling methods – an overview and review, *Survey Methods Centre Newsletter*, 15, pp 4–8.

Cowan, C D (1991) Using multiple sample frames to improve survey coverage, quality and costs, *Marketing Research: A Magazine of Management and Applications*, 3(4), pp 66–9.

Dent, T (1992) How to design for a more reliable customer sample, *Business Marketing*, 17(2), pp 73–6.

Dutka, S and Frankel, L R (1988) *Techniques for the Cost Efficient Sampling of Small or Rare Populations*, New York: Audits & Surveys.

Hague, P N (1985) *The Industrial Market Research Handbook* (2nd edn), London: Kogan Page.

Hoinville, G, Jowell, R and Associates (eds) (1978) *Survey Research Practice*, Oxford: Heinemann, ch 4.

Kress, G (1988) *Marketing Research* (3rd edn), Upper Saddle River, NJ: Prentice-Hall, chs 8–9.

Marsh, C and Scarborough, C (1990) Testing nine hypotheses about quota sampling, *Journal of the Market Research Society*, 32, October, pp 485–506.

Rowland, M L and Forthofer, R N (1993) Adjusting for non-response bias in a health examination survey, *Public Health Reports*, 108 (3), May–June, pp 380–6.

Semon, T T (1994a) Save a few bucks on sample size, risk millions in opportunity loss, *Marketing News*, 28(1), p 19.

Watson, M A (1992) Researching minorities, *Journal of the Market Research Society*, 34(4), pp 337–44.

References and notes

[1] Semon, T T (1994b) A good sample of accounts may not always be a good sample of your customers, *Marketing News*, 28(9), pp 8–11.

[2] McKenzie, J (1988) Study of characteristics of ex-directory telephone owners, *Market Research Newsletter*, December.

[3] JICNARS (1981) *National Readership Survey*, London: JICNARS.

[4] CACI (1989) *Market Analysis*, London: CACI.

[5] Hahlo, G (1992) Examining the validity of re-interviewing respondents for quantitative surveys, *Journal of the Market Research Society*, 34, pp 99–118.

[6] Chisnall, P M (1992) *Marketing Research* (4th edn), Maidenhead: McGraw-Hill, p 107.

5 Surveys

OBJECTIVES

After reading this chapter you should be able to:

■ appreciate the various approaches to collecting primary data through surveys: postal surveys, personal interviews, telephone surveys, completely self-administered surveys, panels and omnibus studies;

■ understand the criteria used for selecting the data collection method best suited to the specific marketing research problem on hand;

■ understand that, when using surveys to help answer a marketing problem, relevance, accuracy, timeliness and cost must be taken into account;

■ appreciate the merits of different survey methods.

KEY WORDS

facts
opinions
interpretations
bias
questionnaire
interviews

telephone surveys
panels
syndicated research
omnibus surveys
interactive research

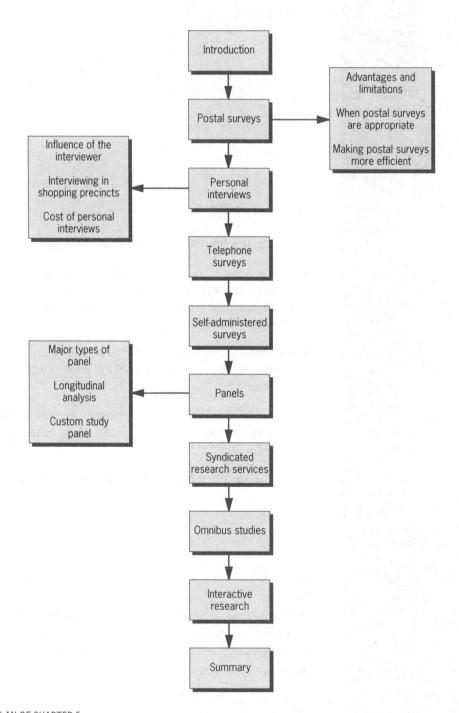

PLAN OF CHAPTER 5

INTRODUCTION

In this chapter we explore some of the various methods of collecting primary data through surveys: postal surveys, personal interviews, telephone surveys, completely self-administered surveys, panels and omnibus studies. The importance of and criteria for selecting the data collection method best suited to the specific marketing research problem are considered. When using surveys to help answer a marketing problem, relevance, accuracy, timeliness and cost must be taken into account. The chapter discusses the merits of different survey methods. Each method has its advantages and limitations.

Figure 5.1 Survey methods

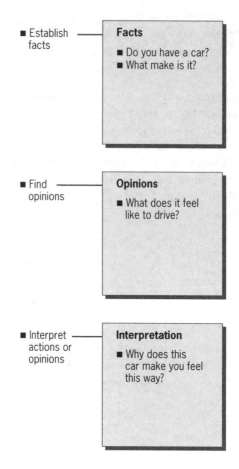

Figure 5.2 What surveys can do

POSTAL SURVEYS

In the case of postal surveys a questionnaire is sent to a potential respondent and the person writes in the replies and posts it back.

Advantages and limitations

Low cost per response

The costs of a postal survey are low. However, it is assumed that the user is an expert in postal surveys and understands how to get a high rate of return. On this assumption, the costs per return are low compared with most other survey methods. It is the going-in cost that is high; once the basic costs have been paid, the additional cost per unit is minimal. Once envelopes and paper costs are paid, though postage costs rise proportionately with numbers, printing costs rise only minimally.

No interviewer bias or cost

Since no interviewers are used in postal surveys, interviewer bias is absent in the responses. Moreover, the lack of interviewers means that one of the largest cost elements in the interviewer survey is eliminated.

Questionnaire scope

It is possible to request information about, and get answers to, a breadth of topics. The lack of a face-to-face situation removes any reticence to reveal personal habits and feelings. Both men and women freely respond to questions about their personal financial affairs and other relatively private personal matters.

Questionnaire length

Provided the subject matter interests the respondent, the person responding will spend considerable time filling in the questionnaire. This means that there is an opportunity to ask a reasonably long sequence of questions.

Respondent interaction

There is no interruption of what the respondent may be doing in order to respond to the series of questions, and the person can reply whenever it is convenient to do so. There is an opportunity for a considered response, since the respondent is under no pressure to make an immediate reply. The postal survey makes it easy to present exhibits, such as advertisements and product models.

Sampling problems

Unlike many other survey methods, the sampling frame is either a good list or a not-so-good list. As a result the adequacy of the postal survey is dependent on the quality of the postal list. In reality, few sampling frames for postal surveys – telephone books, city directories, industrial directories or purchased postal lists – are complete or current.

Response problems

The response rate is low, unless the researcher/marketer knows how to get good responses to a postal study. A problem with a low response rate is that those who respond are not necessarily similar to those who do not. The results, therefore, may be misleading. Experience often indicates that people who reply to a survey are those who are most interested, or those with extreme feelings or opinions about the survey's subject matter. It is essential to compare the reactions of those who respond immediately and those who respond only on follow-up. Moreover, it can be dangerous to depend on the findings of a postal survey.

Advantages and limitations of postal surveys

Advantages

- Low cost
- No interviewer bias
- Questionnaire length

Limitations

- Questionnaire scope
- Respondent interaction
- Sampling problems
- Response rate problems
- Lack of control over respondents
- Wrong respondents – wrong information

Another response problem concerns the market definition for the particular product or service. Partial illiteracy is a feature of many populations in the West. It is also greater among households with lower incomes. If the product or service is one whose market extends into the lower income levels, people simply cannot or will not respond, leading to a non-measurement of that segment of the market.

Lack of control over respondents

Since the recipient of a postal questionnaire can see and examine all the questions before answering any, there is no control over the sequence in which the questions are exposed. This lack of control limits the scope of questions in the postal questionnaire. For instance, we cannot ask for unaided recall of advertising slogans for household goods and then ask about the names of household goods recalled, showing a list. Such a list would help people connect household goods' names with advertising messages.

Wrong respondents, wrong information

Another limitation of the postal survey is that the questionnaire may be answered by someone other than the addressee. For the executive or professional, it might be the secretary. For a specific member of a household, it might be someone else in it. These self-substitutions can rarely be detected. The postal questionnaire recipient may also consult others before responding to the questionnaire.

When postal surveys are appropriate

The postal survey is also used to get information from people who are difficult to interview in person: those insulated from personal contact by a 'gatekeeper' (doorman, security guard, receptionist, secretary), including groups such as management, professionals (lawyers, physicians) and those living in exclusive quarters.

The postal survey may be able to handle difficult questionnaire content. If the topic concerns delicate or personal topics – such as birth control, sexual behaviour or personal finances – the postal questionnaire may be the best way of eliciting desired information.

In the case of an industrial survey, a question about sales or purchases of a particular item will almost certainly require the checking of records, if an accurate response is to be obtained. The postal questionnaire, once again, may serve such a purpose well, but the rate of response will probably fall if records must be consulted.

Making postal surveys more efficient

Notifying people in advance increases the rate of return in a survey and should be communicated to recipients a few days ahead of the postal questionnaire. The simplest approach is to make use of a personally addressed advance postcard, which alerts the recipient that a questionnaire will soon be on its way. There is a tendency to ignore post sent to 'the occupant' or job title in a place of business, so efforts should be made to personalise the approach. Where a long questionnaire is to be used, advance notice by telephone may be worthwhile.

The cover letter must motivate the recipient to complete and return the questionnaire. It must look interesting and important and seem short so that the recipient need spend little time in finding out what message it contains. The purpose of the study should be described briefly and the benefits to the recipient should be highlighted. Sometimes the recipient can be offered a small token for participation and this is generally included in the posted materials. It is important to retain the impression of quality, so a good quality return envelope should be used.

Follow-ups are intended to increase the proportion of respondents, thereby ensuring a more representative survey. However, the researcher should ensure that enthusiastic respondents do not reply twice. Most often this can be handled by keying, a method of identifying those who respond to the first posting, and approaching only the non-respondents in the follow-up procedure.

PERSONAL INTERVIEWS

In the personal interview, respondent and interviewer speak face-to-face. At one time it was a very popular way of conducting surveys, particularly in-home interviews for consumer products. Today, the in-home personal interview is no longer a popular research method. It is expensive and generates a low response rate unless a great deal of time is spent in making call-backs. Fewer people are at home when interviewers are most likely to want to call.

Personal interviews now are largely conducted in shopping precincts. Shopping precincts are now a way of life in metropolitan areas, as is personal interviewing in these locations. Personal interviews are also conducted at business and professional locations.

Influence of the interviewer

The interviewer is the chief factor in the value of the obtained data. The accuracy of the data obtained is influenced by the manner in which the questions are put to the respondents and the skill with which follow-up and probing questions are handled. The interviewer must act in a neutral way to avoid exerting a bias on the replies.

Advantages and limitations of personal interviews (in shopping malls)

Advantages

- Low cost
- Little of the investigator's time is wasted
- Procedures are standardised and specific
- Monitoring of the interviewers
- Possible to use illustrative materials during the course of the interview

Limitations

- Time pressure – those in a hurry can be difficult people to question
- Interviewer may be tempted to seek out those shoppers who do not appear to be in such a hurry
- Per-interview cost is the highest of any survey method
- Refusal rate is high, running anywhere from 5 per cent to 30 per cent

A good interviewer should be able to establish rapport with others. They also need to be trained, and training should cover the role and nature of marketing research, what surveys are and how they are conducted, and the role and importance of the interviewer. Training for a specific study is also necessary. An example of training for a specific study is given in the box.

Training for a specific study

Interviewing instructions are provided with regard to:

- Introduction to the particular study
- Interviewer timing requirements (dates and hours of work assignments)
- General purpose of the study

- The process of interviewing
- Selection of prospective respondents
- Specific procedures for the initial contact and for securing cooperation

Interviewing in shopping precincts

The process is easy and fast and it can be set up and carried out in a hurry. The approach makes it easy to spread the geographic distribution of respondents without having to take steps such as paying for interviewer travel. Compared with most other methods, the approach is generally low cost. Little of the investigator's time is wasted, procedures are standardised and specific, and there is monitoring of the interviewees. All these augur well for efficiency. Whatever the form of personal interview, one major advantage of interview surveys is that it is possible to use illustrative materials, such as advertisements or illustrations of the product, during the course of the interview.

Interviews in shopping precincts are not based on a probability sample. Usually it is a quota sample and the interviewer is given instructions about the proportions they are expected to get by demographics (such as gender and age). There are problems with sampling with personal interviews in shopping precincts. On weekdays there may be greater proportions of the elderly and teenagers and if, in the case of a shopping centre, it has a number of entrances, those shoppers coming in from the parking lot will typically be of a higher income level than those entering from the bus-stop entrance. The strategic placement of interviewers to cover key thoroughfares is therefore critically important.

Many shopping precinct interviews have to be conducted quickly. Shopping precinct shoppers are there to shop and to get back to their homes or offices. They can be difficult people to question. They don't have time and it is not the right point in their activities to interrupt them. So even when the interviewer gets their attention, they are under pressure to speed up the questioning – which does not make for high-quality interviewing. There is also the problem that the interviewer may be tempted to seek out those shoppers who do not appear to be in such a hurry – they may be the ones who are shopping at leisure and are not in a hurry to get anywhere.

Costs of personal interviews

The per-interview cost of personal interviewing is the highest of any survey method. A considerable amount of non-productive time has to be paid for. The refusal rate is high, running anywhere from 5 per cent to 30 per cent. Moreover, more non-productive time is paid for returning for recall interviews where in-home or business interviews are sought. Indeed, if the potential respondent is in a business or profession, the time spent on the interview is often excessive. If an appointment has not been arranged in advance, many hours may be spent in a waiting-room hoping for a session.

TELEPHONE SURVEYS

If the study is one requiring a broad geographic sample, national or regional, the telephone survey may be ideal. The telephone survey can also be used as an efficient follow-up method in connection with another basic method of data collection. Telephone surveys involve a team of interviewers working from a central location, with workstations provided along with outgoing telephone lines for each.

Today, almost all telephone interviewing is computer-controlled. The interviewer works with a computer. In a consumer survey, when the interviewer gets an answer to a call, they check to make sure that it is a household and then ask to speak to the desired respondent. Then use is made of the computer. Each question is shown on the monitor in sequence, and the interviewer reads the question exactly as it appears on screen. Since most questions designed for telephone surveys are short-answer questions, where the respondent's replies are limited to a choice of possibilities, these are also shown on the screen. All the responses go immediately into the computer for later analysis.

Telephone interviews have many advantages. There is a compulsion to answer the telephone, regardless of what a person happens to be doing at the time: the ringing sound compels action. Some 95 per cent of households have telephones and the business telephone coverage is practically 100 per cent. In the telephone method, efficient call-backs are the rule; they are made at times when the desired respondent is more likely to be at home. A very high response rate is not unusual in the case of telephone interviewing. As no travel time is needed for the interviewer to make contact with the respondent, it is neither wasteful of interview time nor costly travel expenses. As a result the amount of time needed for the study and interviewing costs are reduced.

Advantages and limitations of telephone interviews

Advantages

■ Compulsion to answer the telephone
■ Efficient call-backs
■ High response rate
■ No travel
■ Question modification possible

Limitations

■ List of telephone numbers outdated
■ Demanding nature of the telephone ring may announce an unwanted sales pitch
■ Limit to the length of the typical telephone interview
■ No way to provide visual aids

With a computerised interviewing program, it is generally possible to modify the questions during the survey process. Sometimes, the order in which a list of possible answers is given to respondents can affect their response. The first item on the list usually gets more responses than it should and the last position on the list may also bias replies. The first and last positions are the most likely to be affected. Computerised interviewing can be programmed to provide for equal average position, eliminating any such bias.

Telepost: an adjunct to personal interviews

The aim of the research was to gather information that would ultimately help to define an effective marketing strategy for the sponsoring firm's market offering supplied either as a product or service, or some combination of both. The research studied both the actions and reactions to the market offering as well as the degree of sophistication, in sales and marketing, of the companies interviewed.

The first stage of the research process was conducted using personal interviews, primarily because of their high degree of flexibility. The method used is termed as a guided or focused interview that, while allowing the respondent to talk freely around each topic, successfully covers the topics of crucial context in a more or less systematic way. The number of respondents was small and only partially representative of the population of interest. However, it was especially effective with busy business executives and was ideal for this research as the respondents were chosen as experienced and authoritative executives from the field of sales and marketing in industrial and business-to-business marketing. Thirty names and addresses were located. Of the companies chosen, some were named by the sponsoring firm as ones that they wanted to interview. Others were located in *Key British Enterprises – British Business Rankings* (Dun & Bradstreet International).

The telepost combination technique was the method used for the second stage of the research. This method is very effective in obtaining a high quality response in complex markets. A sample frame was developed which was supportive of the personal interviews and which widened the sample base. The information gathered from the personal interviews allowed the sponsoring firm to produce revised documentation on the market offering. This second document was used and sent out as the material for the Telepost survey. A questionnaire, to be administered by telephone, was prepared to cover what had been established in the personal interviews, as the key dimensions. Letters were then sent to named respondents within the sample frame, informing them that they would be contacted by telephone and providing details of the nature of the interview and requesting that they read the revised documentation before the interview.

The telephone interviews therefore provided a quantification, extension and verification of the findings of the personal interviews.
Source: Zoe Cooper.[1]

Despite all its strong points, telephone interviewing does have limitations. Unless special steps are taken, the list of telephone numbers used in a survey will be outdated on the day of publication, with omissions of new listings and inclusion of outdated ones. Although the demanding nature of the telephone ring is an advantage, it can all too often signal an unwanted sales pitch and the owner may not answer the call. There is also a limit to the length of the typical telephone interview and usually it cannot run for more than about fifteen minutes. Moreover, there is no way to provide visual aids, such as advertisements or other display materials.

SELF-ADMINISTERED SURVEYS

These kinds of studies are often conducted by service firms such as restaurants, motels or hotels, and occasionally by health and financial institutions or even retail stores. In these cases questionnaires are left in convenient places for the potential respondent to pick up, fill in and return either in a convenient depository or by a prepaid-postage return envelope.

PANELS

A panel is a continuing group that responds to questioning from time to time. It can be made up of persons, households or business firms. A panel may exist, for questioning purposes, for as little as a week or as long as a year or more. The panel may be set up by telephone, postal or personal interview. Some research firms offer the use of their ongoing panels to provide syndicated information available to all subscribers, while other research companies make their panels available for custom use. The user can specify the demographics or even require specific category or brand users.

Syndicated panel services measure such things as buying volume by brand and television viewing and use consumer diaries or electronic devices to obtain the desired data. The consumer diary is a form for the consumer to record their purchases or some other form of behaviour. An electronic device attached to the television set may monitor television tuning. In the case of retail-store panels, the data collection method may be through the use of either scanners or physical audits.

Cable TV has the most viewers

According to the first *Cable Audience Measurement Survey*, published this week, the main cable-exclusive channels reach over half of all people. Moreover, research shows that more TV is watched in cable homes than non-cable households. In total, cable and satellite channels achieve a combined average weekly reach of 93.6 per cent of all cable home individuals.

Target audiences are relatively well-satisfied with cable-exclusive channels according to research findings. The Box achieves a higher viewing share than MTV among 10–15-year-olds: 1.8 per cent compared with 1.5 per cent for MTV and 0.8 per cent for VH-1.

The survey also shows that cable householders make extensive use of technology: 34 per cent have a games console, and 29 per cent have a computer compared with the national average of 24 per cent, according to TGI.

The findings are based on diary research commissioned by the Cable Research Group. Research was conducted in January among 997 adults and 315 children by research company RSMB.

Source: Paul McCann.[2]

Major types of panel

The major ongoing panels are divided into panels used for syndicated offerings and those used for custom studies. The panel method has some great advantages, several of which are unique.

Longitudinal analysis

A custom panel or a syndicated panel enables us to monitor the reactions or behaviour of the same person, household or business respondent over a period of time. The panel approach makes it possible to get a continuing series of reports from the same people.

Where one-off studies are used, the researcher may encounter people who are not consistent users of the brand in question. Researchers might then question them about their inconsistent patterns of purchase. However, the panel method gives an opportunity to ask the question at the time the purchase behaviour has changed, and to obtain a current and immediate reply rather than one that is dependent on memory.

Purchase of a brand by exposure to early advertising

(Measured in first wave)

	End of first month	End of second month
Total panel members	(6000)	(6000)
Total exposed to early advertising	(600)	(600)
Purchases by total sample	9.6%	10.8%
Purchases by those exposed to early advertising	15%	18%
Purchases by those not exposed to early advertising	9%	10%

Suppose you wanted to ascertain the impact of advertising on purchases. The introduction of a new product in the market might use an advertising blitz concentrated in the first month. On two successive one-shot surveys, done at the end of the first month and again a month later, questions about advertising recall and brand purchase could be asked, with results showing that brand advertising recall for the test product dropped from 10 per cent to 5 per cent in the two sweeps, while brand purchases went from 9.6 per cent to 10.8 per cent.

People would be unlikely to recall whether they were exposed to the blitz advertising, even though they could recall brand purchase within the week. The panel results among 6000 customers are shown above. The table shows clearly that the blitz advertising had a continued impact.

Panels cost less than a comparable series of parallel but separate samples. There is only a one-time basic sampling cost, be it households or stores, and continuing cooperation may also be high. The sample is the most serious limitation of the panel. With consumer panels, annual loss of members can be substantial. Some panel members soon lose interest and others are sometimes so self-conscious about their participation that their behaviour is affected.

Nielsen homescan grocery consumer panel

Typical of the kind of data provided by this panel are the following. The reports produced refer to the research purchaser's specific products.

For the information purchaser's particular brand, up to date data is provided on such things as the total households buying the brand, the penetration, the brand volume, market share, the percentage of the volume on offer, the average price, the purchase occasions per buyer, and the market volume per buyer. A demographic analysis is provided for all buyers broken down by social class, household size, age of housewife and region. For example, the report might identify the percentage of a firm's plastic products sold to different sizes of households.

A trend report is also produced showing consumer expenditure on specific product items, such as the firm's plastic bags and plastic bags in total. It might also show sales trends through different types of outlets, for example, ASDA, Boots, Gateway, etc.

Custom study panel

The postal panel can be specific for two types of small segments of the population: one is demographic and the other is behavioural. The research firm may already have information in its files identifying such households of people. If this is not the case, most research firms offering custom panel use provide postal screening. Alternatively, most of these firms will make a fast telephone survey to locate those who qualify.

A postal panel does have some definite drawbacks. It is usually self-administered, so the questionnaire is filled in by the respondent without supervision and can clearly be seen in its entirety before any questions are answered. Where careful sequencing through the questioning steps is required to obtain reliable information, the postal panel, like the postal questionnaire, can produce misleading findings. Moreover, as is the case with all postal questionnaires, it is unlikely that a person's response to an open-ended question will be very deep. No opportunity exists for an interviewer to probe to get a full and meaningful reply. An inherent disadvantage of the custom panel is the time it takes for results. It is at least as slow as the outgoing and returning post. Another disadvantage is that the typical custom panel has no way of showing its members television commercials, and so has no way of getting reactions to these.

SYNDICATED RESEARCH SERVICES

Most syndicated research services are owned by the research companies that run them and, in the main, are continuous panels. The main problem for people wanting to make use of these services lies in identifying which services are available and who provides them. The *Market Research Society Yearbook* contains a list of providers of these services. In effect, syndicated research services are off-the-peg research studies.

Syndicated service firms collect and distribute information for many different users. The firms specialise in making available secondary information and other services at a lower price than it would cost a user of the information if the latter had to conduct the study itself. An example of a syndicated service firm is AC Nielsen. Syndicated research firms can provide excellent information. For example, a producer of consumer packaged goods – inexpensive items that are branded, packaged and sold via self-service in grocery stores, mass-merchandise outlets and other retail stores – may subscribe to Nielsen's retail research services in order to get a variety of information about its brands and their comparative competitive performance with other brands. The manufacturer receives much valuable information, including:

- industry volume
- sales trends
- sales by package size
- competitors' sales
- local or regional sales
- inventory figures
- market share information
- distribution and out-of-stock figures.

The costs of conducting the research are shared among the entire client base.

Lifestyle marketing

Many brands are sponsoring questions on surveys about the use of competing brands. Companies such as Procter & Gamble, Imperial Tobacco, Guinness and Premier Beverages have all taken the exclusive rights for a year on answers by consumers about their branded products. Information on specific buying behaviour remains the strongest element of lifestyle data.

There is currently very little interest in attitudinal questions. Clients are looking for specific information on potential buyers or buyers of competitors' products. There is less interest in attitudinal data than four or five years ago. This view is expressed at CMT, which runs the National Shoppers' Survey and markets a lifestyle database called Behaviour Bank. The managing director of the firm says that it does not tend to get too involved in attitudinal questions over and above what they already ask, such as reasons for purchase. Questions that are very important concern whether the consumer buys on price, or promotion or brand name or whether the consumer simply rotates products. The power of the grocery multiples and electrical goods chains has helped to stimulate the market for lifestyle data and manufacturers need to be able to understand what share of customers they have and what is stimulating purchase.

Geodemographic profile providers have been motivated to respond to the recent upsurge in interest in lifestyle data. CACI indicates that their base is in census data and that this is still very much needed, for example in retail planning. The advantage geodemographics still has over lifestyle is that it is based on data on every individual in the country whereas the closest that lifestyle can get is data for households from the MIC database, formed by pooling CMT and NDL's surveys. CACI, however, is among a number of suppliers that have developed and launched systems that draw on both sets of data. CensusLifestyle combines CACI's ACORN geodemographics with lifestyle data licensed from ICD. This enables bias to be taken out of lifestyle data. One new product to flow from this fusion of data is PayCheck, which enables marketers to predict the likely income for every postcode, something that has always been difficult to achieve in the UK.

In an effort to expand use of targeting and profiling beyond direct marketing and store planning, some suppliers are now combining market research products with lifestyle and census information. Taylor Nielsen AGB, for instance, is marketing 'SmartBase' that bridges the gap between market research and database marketing. By licensing data on 13 million households from MIC and linking it to the AGB SuperPanel, SmartBase combines both breadth and depth of information. MIC has information on 60 per cent of households, and has a match to 7,000 of the households on the SuperPanel. A similarly complex process has been used by Equifax Europe to build its Dimensions database, which incorporates census, lifestyle, and market research from MORI and other data sources.

Source: David Reed.[3]

OMNIBUS STUDIES

An omnibus study is an ongoing sudy through which a buyer can ask a limited number of questions at a very reasonable cost, because the general overhead costs of fielding the study are shared by a number of clients. Omnibus studies are often scheduled on a weekly, monthly or quarterly basis. Some are conducted through personal interviews but most omnibus services collect data by telephone interviews, so it is impossible to show display materials such as advertisements or products.

Omnibus studies assist in finding small segments of the population and the costs of locating a sufficient number of such respondents are low. If the incidence is too low to produce a sufficient number in one survey, the questions are retained in subsequent ones at a modest cost. Most omnibus services offer follow-up probes of those giving specific replies. These probes are usually conducted on a follow-up basis rather than at the time of original questioning (unless there are only a few questions) so as not to delay completion of fieldwork for the standard service.

Omnibus research is a hybrid between off-the-peg research, where data has already been collected and the researcher simply purchases whatever is available, and primary research, where the researcher collects data first hand. The term describes regular research surveys undertaken with a certain frequency and definite method and which use a set number of respondents and sampling points.

Omnibus research is particularly suitable for fairly robust data – for example, the usage and purchase of products – but it is less useful for attitudinal and opinion studies. A typical omnibus survey might last for forty minutes or more and during that time the respondent might be asked about six or more entirely different topics. The superficiality of some questions can prevent respondents from gaining the amount of concentration necessary to pursue any particular topic in depth. The *Market Research Society Newsletter* provides a list of organisations offering omnibus services.

INTERACTIVE RESEARCH

In interactive research the participant interacts, via a computer connection, to questions or other stimuli presented on a screen or by some other means. The process may provide a response by means of a keyboard, a computer mouse or a touch-sensitive screen.

There is no interviewer with most interactive research systems and this helps to remove potential problems associated with such matters as the cost of interviewers, the need for supervision and potential biasing influence. There is no risk of the influence of inflection or accent, nor is there any limitation on delicate subject matter, often present with an interviewer.

As responses are automatically entered into the system, there is no need for the expensive process of the individual coding of each answer and all interactive systems ask the questions in the same form and order. Most interactive research systems provide questionnaire skip patterns, so that subsidiary questions are always asked when they should be asked and skipped when they should not be asked. As all computer-based systems do, these interactive methods provide a rapid reporting of results. The responses are barely in the system before the summary tables are produced.

Interactive methods have their limitations: only a reasonably straightforward series of questions can be asked. A complicated questionnaire cannot be handled through this medium. Moreover, since the method is almost a self-administered exercise, no opportunity exists for asking open-ended questions.

SUMMARY

This chapter has explored some of the various methods of collecting primary data through surveys: postal surveys, personal interviews, telephone surveys, completely self-administered surveys, panels and omnibus studies. The importance of and criteria for selecting the data collection method best suited to the specific marketing research problem have been considered. When using surveys to help answer a marketing problem, relevance, accuracy, timeliness and cost have to be taken into account. The chapter has discussed the merits of different survey methods, since each method has its own advantages and limitations. Attention has also been given to the use of panels, syndicated research services, omnibus studies and interactive research.

Questions

1   What are the main ways of conducting surveys?
2   Indicate the advantages and limitations of postal surveys.
3   What do you consider to be the most appropriate applications for postal surveys?
4   Suggest ways in which postal surveys can be made more efficient.
5   How are personal interview surveys usually conducted these days? How is this different from what it was some years ago? What do you think brought about the change?
6   When training interviewers to undertake a specific personal interview survey, what kind of training is necessary?
7   What are the advantages and limitations of telephone surveys?
8   What do you consider to be the best kinds of applications for telephone surveys?

9   What is a consumer panel?

10   What kind of facts are consumer panels best at eliciting?

11   Indicate the main types of consumer panels and their purpose.

12   How do syndicated research services differ from other kinds of marketing research services? What kinds of information do they collect?

13   What are omnibus studies?

14   What are the advantages and limitations of making use of omnibus studies?

15   Indicate what is meant by interactive research. What are its advantages and limitations?

Case study 5.1 | Central Training College (A)

The Central Training College is the headquarters of a training group which is part of a consultation, recruitment and training company. One of the recruiting divisions of the company carries out the recruitment of permanent and temporary sales, construction, finance and management personnel, as well as office personnel. The Central Training College offers a wide range of general office courses as well as more specialised courses such as languages, business administration and desk-top publishing. The consultation, recruitment and training company has been developing its activities in training and recruitment through organic and acquisitional growth. It has been proposed to move into the London market in time to take advantage of any improvements in industry growth. The most cost-effective method is thought to be to develop the property in central London already owned by the firm – the Central Training College – rather than pay for new premises.

At the moment, graduates of the college are left to find their own employment contacts or they are referred to a suitable employment agency. No financial gain is received by the college from this arrangement. If there were a recruitment agency that was part of the same company operating in the college, all students would be referred to it rather than to rival firms' recruitment agencies. This would increase the potential turnover per student. (Turnover refers to the money received through tuition and placement fees.)

A consultant was called in to advise on the viability of opening a recruitment agency in central London. On the basis of initial discussions the consultant produced the following research proposal.

Research proposal

Summary of brief

1   To determine the viability of opening a recruitment agency in central London.
2   To determine if the Central Training College would be a good location.
3   To find out if the name Central Recruitment would be acceptable.

Proposed research objectives

1 Investigate current and future demand for recruitment agencies.
2 Investigate actual intentions to use the service.
3 Discover if the name of the recruitment agency is an important factor in the purchase decision.
4 Investigate student and business attitudes to the provision of such a service.
5 Obtain demographic details of both students and businesses interested in the service.

Proposed research design

Conduct two surveys, one of the students at the college and the other of the employers. Students to be interviewed face-to-face and the employers to be contacted through the post.

Source: Carol Fry.[4]

Question

Evaluate the research proposal.

Case study 5.2 | Consumer Products

Phil Rice, marketing manager of Consumer Products, wants to have as much information as he can about purchasers of aluminium wrapping foil and plastic wrapping bags. This covers both his own firm's products and those of competitors. Competitive products include retailers' own brands and this makes up a substantial proportion of sales in the market.

Phil would like to have information on such things as the total households buying his firm's brand, the penetration of the market, the brand volume, the market share, the average price, the purchase occasions per buyer and the market volume per buyer, all by different demographic characteristics of consumers – i.e. broken down by social class, household size, age of housewife and region. For example, he would like to know such things as the percentage of the firm's wrapping foil sold to different sizes of households. He also needs to have a good idea of trends including, for instance, consumer expenditure on specific product items such as the firm's aluminium foil sales by region. Information on sales through different types of retails outlets is also desirable.

In addition to such things as usage rates, purchase patterns and their relationship to consumer characteristics, he also wants to know what customers think about the various brands already on the market.

Question

What might be the best way for Phil Rice to obtain such data? Explain your answer.

Case study 5.3 | Liptonjuice (A)

In March 1994 Britvic felt that all its research indicated that it was on to another winning brand in the iced tea drink Liptonjuice, a joint venture between Unilever, the maker, PepsiCo, and its part-owned distributor Britvic. It was expected that the product would achieve a sales volume of £20m in its first year and the producers mistakenly saw the British tradition of tea-drinking as an advantage. Liptonjuice, it was believed, would play on the public's love of tea in combination with an increasing preference for more varied soft drinks. Despite initial optimism, the brand's future is now in serious jeopardy since PepsiCo and Britvic have said they will no longer distribute it. Unilever now has to go it alone or find a new partner. It was first launched in March 1994 and subsequently relaunched after radical changes to give a cleaner, more refreshing taste, better suited to British palates. But all this has been to no purpose.

PepsiCo might consider introducing its own iced tea as part of its Radical Fruit range. The range – minus an iced tea – is already available in Spain. The feeling as far as the UK market is concerned is that the British take a singular view of tea: it is something to be drunk hot, at any time of the day. Moreover, it was felt that even a multi-million pound advertising campaign that had been used to back Liptonjuice had failed to persuade the British to change their minds.

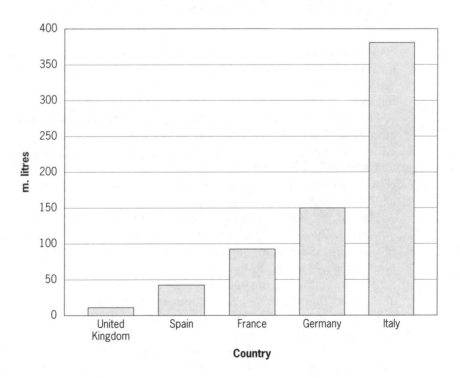

Figure 5.3 Iced tea consumption in Europe in 1995

However, other European countries take their tea without milk and, as in the case of the US, at specific times of the day. For Europeans and Americans the idea of drinking cold tea, without milk, as just another drink is far more acceptable, since the associations with hot, milky tea are not as strong. It has also been easier to position the product as a sports drink in Europe and to sell it through sports clubs.

In Italy, in 1995, iced tea was the fastest growing soft drink.

Coca-Cola has its own iced tea in the US and Europe, where it is called Nestea. Liptonjuice was launched in Spain in 1994, a year after Nestea's Spanish début but sales have been disappointing, as in the UK. PepsiCo's Radical Fruit range has, however, been a success in Spain.

Source: Jon Rees.[5]

Questions

1 Britvic's original enthusiasm based on research seems to have been misguided. Discuss the kinds of things that might have gone wrong.

2 Do you think that survey research might have a role to play in guiding any of the companies still interested in marketing iced tea to European countries, including the UK? Explain your answer.

Case study 5.4 | **Opinion polling faces new scrutiny**

'The general election will determine which techniques will be used for opinion polling in future, although the diversity of current practices may make it more difficult for the polling industry as a whole to win credibility,' Mr John Curtice, a reader in politics at Strathclyde University, said yesterday.

He said that because pollsters had changed their methodologies in different ways after getting the 1992 election wrong, this election would be a test of which of the various methods now in use was most accurate.

The polling industry was as diverse in its methodologies as it had ever been, in contrast to the last election, when there was a broad consensus about how polling should be conducted, Mr Curtice said.

He told the Market Research Society conference in Birmingham that the election would provide an opportunity to assess the relative merits of telephone and face-to-face polling, and of sampling on a random basis or by setting certain quotas for the types of people to be questioned.

A study following the debacle of 1992 said the surveys did not identify hidden Tories and that the controls in quota sampling were not enough to counter the possibility that people questioned in a quota poll were more likely to be Labour than the population in general.

The polls' failure in 1992 to reflect the Conservative victory has allowed the Tory party to cast doubt on the credibility of the overwhelming Labour lead which most have shown for many months.

Among changes brought in since 1992, NOP and Mori have altered how they weight the quotas they set, by making more use of government surveys, such as the Labour Force Survey.

ICM and Gallup have both switched to using a form of random sampling rather than quota sampling, and to telephone polling instead of face-to-face interviews. Pollsters have also adjusted how they weight figures depending on how people say they voted in the last election.

Source: Alison Smith.[6] Reprinted with permission.

Question

Discuss the problems associated with quota sampling in surveys. How might such problems be solved?

Case study 5.5 | Volvo Car UK

Volvo Car UK is the British marketing arm of the Volvo company, the Swedish manufacturer of high-quality, reliable cars. Volvo cars have a reputation for being solid, extremely safe, reliable, long-lasting and comfortable; they also hold their value well. For many drivers (and fleet operators) this makes Volvo the ideal prestige company car.

In terms of its long-term corporate strategy, Volvo aims to become 'the most desired and successful speciality car brand and the most customer-focused organisation in the world, achieving exemplary standards and support which will match or exceed customer expectations.' The problem for Volvo lies in deciding who is the customer – is it their extensive dealer network, who sell the cars, is it the corporations and fleet operators who specify Volvo as company cars, or is it the world's motorists, who ultimately buy the cars?

Volvo believes that a major market for it in the UK is the corporate customer; 70 per cent of sales of Volvos in the UK are to corporations. Ultimately, these sales are to corporate employees who would like to choose Volvo as their company car. To meet the needs of these customers, Volvo runs two programmes; firstly, the Corporate Account Relationship Experience (CARE) which is aimed at corporate customers and fleet operators, and secondly the One Customer One Relationship (Oncore) programme which is a dealer programme designed to satisfy the drivers of the cars. CARE is aimed at encouraging corporate customers and fleet operators to specify Volvo, but once the cars are sold and the drivers take possession of them, the Oncore programme takes over. Oncore is concerned with the relationship between the dealers (some of which are directly owned by Volvo, but most of which are independent businesses) and the drivers.

Volvo deals directly with the largest corporate customers, but dealers are involved both before and after sales with all the organisations that run fleets of Volvos. Some dealerships have in-house corporate specialists who have the expertise to understand the needs of fleet operators; typically, these dealerships are located in large cities where there are plenty of potential corporate customers.

Market research has shown that drivers of company Volvos are involved in six relationships which Volvo has input into. These relationships are as follows:

1 Volvo and its corporate customers.
2 Corporate customers and their employees.
3 Corporate customers and Volvo dealers.
4 Volvo and Volvo drivers.
5 Volvo and its dealers.
6 Volvo dealers and Volvo drivers.

The Oncore and CARE programmes help to ensure consistency across these relationships. Oncore is about the drivers, CARE is about the corporations, but in each case the approach must remain consistent because of the close relationship between the corporations and the drivers (who are employed by the corporations). Currently Volvo is still behind Mercedes and BMW in terms of numbers of cars sold to corporate clients, but the firm hopes to improve on this over the next few years.

From Volvo's viewpoint, the drivers are of crucial importance even though they do not always make the decision to specify Volvo. The reason for this is that the drivers will have some influence on the decisions (if they don't like the cars or are dissatisfied with Volvo's dealer service they might discourage their firms from specifying Volvo next time). Also, the drivers have families and friends who will see the cars and ride in them, and each satisfied driver becomes an ambassador for Volvo.

In the longer term, Volvo seeks to refine both its corporate programme and its driver-care programme to provide maximum repeat business. To do this successfully, the company must take account of its input into each of the six relationships identified above, and must maintain a clear message and service to its corporate customers and their employees.

(Case contributed by Jim Blythe.)

Questions

1 How might Volvo find out why some customers prefer Mercedes or BMW?
2 What types of market research might help Volvo to refine the Oncore programme?
3 What types of market research would help Volvo to refine the CARE programme?
4 How could Volvo find out how to improve each of the six relationships identified above?
5 How might Volvo find out how effective the drivers are at acting as ambassadors for the cars?

Further reading

Albaum, G (1987) Do source and anonymity affect mail survey results?, *Journal of the Academy of Marketing Science*, 15, pp 74–81.

Albaum, G and Strandskow, J (1989) Participation in a mail survey of international marketers: effects of pre-contact and detailed project explanation, *Journal of Global Marketing*, 2(4), pp 7–23.

Arnett, R (1990) Mail panel research in the 1990s, *Applied Marketing Research*, 30(2), pp 8–10.

Bachmann, D P (1987) Cover letter appeals and sponsorship effects on mail survey response rates, *Journal of Marketing Education*, 9, pp 45–51.

Churchill, V B (1988a) How good is mail panel research? Address before Advertising Research Foundation Conference.

Churchill, V B (1988b) Learning to live with continuing household panels, *Telenation Reports*, Summer, pp 1–2.

Collins, M (1997) Interviewer variability: a review of the problem, *Journal of the Market Research Society*, 39, 67–84.

Davis, G (1997) Are Internet surveys ready for prime time?, *Marketing News*, 7 April, p 5.

Deming, W E (1950) On errors in surveys, *American Sociological Review*, 9(4).

Dillman, D A, Singer, E, Clark, J R and Treat, J B (1996) Effects of benefits appeals and variations in statements of confidentiality on completion rates for census questionnaires, *Public Opinion Quarterly*, 60(3).

Flaherty, J (1990) Computer administration of questions: more desirable or more socially desirable, *Journal of Applied Psychology*, 75, pp 310–14.

Fletcher, K. (1995) Jump on the omnibus, *Marketing*, 15 June, pp 25–8.

Gold L N (1996) Do it yourself interviewing, *Marketing Research: A magazine of Management and Applications*, 8(2), pp 40–1.

Mehta, R and Sivadas, E (1995) Comparing response rates and response context in mail vs electronic mail surveys, *Journal of the Marketing Research Society*, 37(4), pp 429–39.

Oppermann, M (1995) E-mail survey – potentials and pitfalls, *Market Research*, 7(3), pp 29–33.

Parker, L (1992) Collecting data the e-mail way, *Training and Development*, July, pp 52–4.

Riche, M F (1990) A bigger role for telephone interviews, *American Demographics*, September, p 17.

Rothenberg, R (1989) The trouble with mail interviewing, *New York Times*, 16 August.

Sheehan, K B and McMillan, S J (1999) Response variation in e-mail surveys: an exploration, *Journal of Advertising Research*, 39(4), pp 45–54.

Synodinos, N E and Brennan J E (1988) Computer interactive interviewing in survey research, *Psychology and Marketing*, 5, 115–38.

Taylor, H (2000) Does Internet research work? Comparing online survey results with telephone survey, *International Journal of Market Research*, 42(1), pp 51–63.

Tse, C B, Tse, K C, Yin, C H, Ting, C B, Yi, K W, Yee, K P and Hong, W C (1995) Comparing two methods of sending out questionnaires: e-mail vs mail, *Journal of the Market Research Society*, 37(4).

Warner, S L (1965) Randomised response: a survey technique for eliminating evasive answer bias, *Journal of the American Statistical Association*, 60, pp 63–9.

References and notes

[1] Cooper, Z (1991) Unpublished MBA dissertation, Department of Management, Keele University, September.

[2] McCann, P (1996) Commercial TV audiences rise..., *Marketing Week*, 26 April, p 15.

[3] Reed, D (1996) The data game, *Marketing Week*, 3 May, pp 47–51.

[4] Fry, C (1991) Unpublished MBA dissertation, Department of Management, Keele University, September.

[5] Rees, J (1996) PepsiCo needs new strategy for iced tea, *Marketing Week*, 16 April, p 23.

[6] Smith, A (1997b) Opinion polling faces new scrutiny, *Financial Times*, 21 March.

6 Measurement and scaling

OBJECTIVES

After reading this chapter you should be able to:

- **appreciate the basic concepts of measurement and scaling;**

- **distinguish between the various types of measurement scales;**

- **describe and illustrate the comparative types of measurement scales;**

- **distinguish and illustrate the non-comparative types of measurement scales;**

- **appreciate the difference between single-item versus multiple-item scales.**

KEY WORDS

scaling	projective techniques
measurement	ratings
nominal scale	semantic differential
ordinal scale	Q-sort
ratio scale	staple scale
interval scale	Likert scale
comparative scale	Thurstone scale
non-comparative scale	graphic scale
attitude scale	

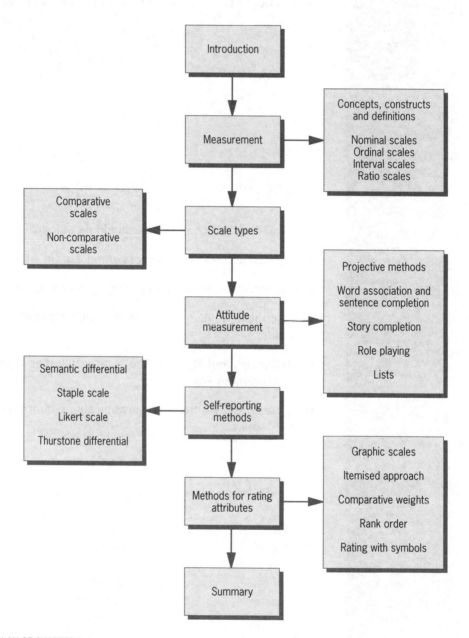

PLAN OF CHAPTER 6

INTRODUCTION

In this chapter the basic concepts of measurement and scaling are introduced and defined, distinguishing between the various types of measurement scales. The chapter goes on to describe and illustrate the comparative types of measurement scales, distinguishing and illustrating non-comparative types of measurement scales. Finally, single-item versus multiple-item scales are discussed.

Measurement is the process by which scores or numbers are assigned to the attributes of people or objects. How this is done is strongly influenced by the sort of information that is being sought. For example, if precise information on cigarette consumption is being sought, it is better to ask people to say how many cigarettes they smoke in a day. By contrast, when trying to collect information on the perceptions of cigarette smokers, it is better to ask people to classify themselves as heavy or light smokers. The two methods produce quite different kinds of measurement.

There are many different kinds of measurement-scaling techniques. These scaling techniques often have different properties. It is necessary to understand the correct way to employ a technique because how a characteristic or trait is measured has implications for the interpretation and analysis of the data collected from using the technique.

First we look at some basic concepts of measurement and scaling and then distinguish between comparative and non-comparative scales. We then illustrate how these different scales are used and finally we compare single-item and multiple-item scales.

MEASUREMENT

Numbers given as answers to questions help in the analysis and interpretation of information that is collected by research. When taking measurements there are rules for assigning numbers to objects to represent the quantities of attributes. The rules apply to the procedure used to assign numbers that reflect the amount of an attribute possessed by an object, a person, etc. Attention must to be paid to the objectives of the study, the precise definition of the characteristic to be measured and the correspondence between the measurement rule and the characteristic.

Concepts, constructs and definitions

A concept or construct refers to characteristics that we wish to measure and a definition of the precise meaning of the concept or construct. Many of the constructs measured in typical marketing research studies are directly observable and many are not. The concepts of sales and market share can be directly linked to observable events. In contrast, the concepts of attitude, product perception or other customer-satisfaction factors are measured indirectly.

Depending on the characteristics being measured, the numbers assigned have different properties that affect the kind of statements that can be made about the amount of a characteristic possessed by one individual relative to another. The scales used in these different types of measurement are termed nominal, ordinal, interval and ratio.

Nominal scales allow us to place an object in one and only one of a set of mutually exclusive classes with no implied ordering. For example, a car's registration plate is an example of nominally scaled data. The numbers assigned have no other specific properties other than to identify the car assigned that number. Nominal-scaled variables include examples such as gender, religious denomination and political affiliation. The numbers assigned do not actually reflect the amount of the attribute possessed by the object under scrutiny. Because nominal data does not possess order, distance or origin, only a limited number of statistics are allowable. It is not meaningful, in this case, to compute the mean because it has no significance. However, a nominal variable can be counted: it would, for example, be legitimate to say that 50 per cent of a sample is female. The correct measure of central tendency is the mode, the value that occurs most frequently.

Nominal data

Given three ratings 1, 2 and 3 we cannot say that the distance between 1 and 2 is the same as between 2 and 3, nor can we say that the magnitude of 2 is proportional to both 1 and 3. There is no implied ordered sequence. The numbers assigned have no other specific properties than to identify the object.

Ordinal-scaled data involves ranking. This means we can say that an object has more or less or the same amount of an attribute as some other object. There is an implied ordered sequence so that the option listed first is less or greater than the objects listed second and subsequently. No property of distance between the numbers is implied, nor do the numbers reflect the magnitude of a characteristic possessed by an object.

Ordinal data

Given three ratings 1, 2 and 3 we cannot say that the distance between 1 and 2 is the same as between 2 and 3, nor can we say that the magnitude of 2 is proportional to both 1 and 3. There is, however, an implied ordered sequence so the option listed first is less or greater than the objects listed second and subsequently.

Interval-scaled data reflects how much more one object has of an attribute than another object. It is possible to tell how far apart two or more objects are with respect to the attribute. Interval data has order and distance properties and the most frequent type of measure of central tendency is the arithmetic mean. The standard deviation is also used to measure dispersion about the mean. Almost the whole range of statistical analysis can be applied to interval measurement scales but interval data does not allow comparisons of the absolute magnitude of the measurements to be made across objects. We cannot say that an object assigned the number 6 has twice as much of the characteristic being measured as the object assigned the number 3. While interval data possesses the characteristic of order and distance there is no absolute origin (zero point). Interval scales are often used in commercial marketing research studies, especially when a researcher collects attitudinal and overall brand rating information.

Interval-scaled data

Given three ratings 1, 2 and 3 we *can* say that the distance between 1 and 2 is the same as between 2 and 3 but we *cannot* say that the magnitude of 2 is proportional to both 1 and 3. There is an implied ordered sequence so the option listed first is less or greater than the objects listed second and subsequently.

Ratio-scaled data possess the same kind of properties as interval-scaled data but also possess an absolute or natural origin. Thus we can say in this case that the number 6 has twice the characteristic being measured as the object assigned the number 3 on a ratio scale. Ratio data are commonly associated with directly observable physical events or entities. Measures of market share, sales, income, etc. possess characteristics that lend themselves to ratio scaling. Ratio scales have all the properties of the other measurement scales, since they possess the characteristics of order, distance and unique origin (zero point).

Ratio-scaled data

Given three ratings 1, 2 and 3 we *can* say that the distance between 1 and 2 is the same as between 2 and 3, and we *can* say that the magnitude of 2 is proportional to both 1 and 3. There is an implied ordered sequence so the option listed first is less or greater than the objects listed second and subsequently.

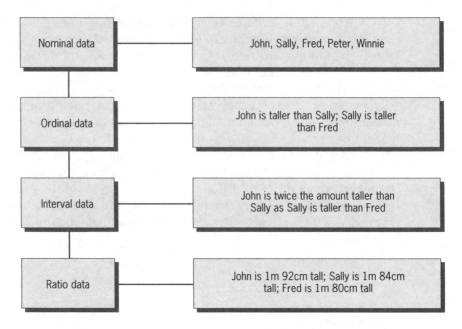

Figure 6.1 Four types of data

SCALE TYPES

There are two broad classes of measurement scale: comparative and non-comparative scales (Figure 6.2).

With *comparative scaling* the respondent is asked to compare one set of objects against another. For example, a respondent might be required to compare one brand of butter against the other brands that they consider when making a purchase in a supermarket. Results have to be interpreted in relative terms and have ordinal or rank-order properties. The scores obtained indicate that one brand is preferred to another, but not by how much. In the case of this type of scale relatively small differences among the objectives being compared can be detected.

In *non-comparative scaling* respondents are required to evaluate each object independently of other objects being investigated. Non-comparative scaling is often referred to as *monadic scaling*.

Comparative scales

This type of scaling ensures that all respondents approach the rating task from the same known reference point. There are several variations in the technique used.

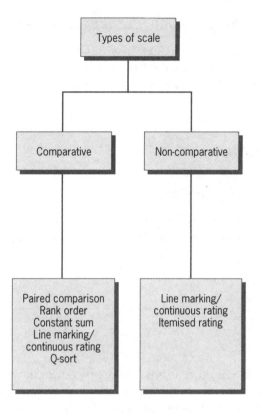

Figure 6.2 Types of scale

Paired comparisons

The respondent is presented with two objects at a time and is required to indicate a preference for one of the two according to some stated criterion. The method yields ordinal scaled data, for example, brand A is better than brand B, or, brand A is cleaner than brand B, and so on. It is often applied in cases where the objects are physical products. One important point about data obtained through paired comparisons is that the ordinal data can be readily converted into interval-scaled data.

Rank-order scales

In this case, respondents are presented with several objects simultaneously and required to order or rank them.

Constant sum scales

Respondents are asked to allocate a number of points – say, for instance, 100 points – among objects according to some criterion, for example, preference or importance. They are instructed to allocate the points such that if they like brand A twice as much as brand B, they should assign twice as many points to brand A.

Line marking/continuous rating comparative scale

This is often used to obtain similarity judgements. Usually, respondents are presented with object pairs and asked to judge their similarity by marking a five-inch line anchored by the phrases 'Exactly the same' and 'Completely different'.

Example

Rolex and Longines

Please indicate how similar you believe these two brands of watch are by placing an X on the line below at the point that approximates your judgement.

Exactly
the same

Completely
different

Q-sort scale

This scale employs a rank-order procedure in which objects are sorted into piles based on similarity with respect to some criterion. Respondents are presented with a set of objects (brands, concepts, words or phrases) and are told to sort them into piles, according to some criterion. For instance, a respondent might be given a set of brands and asked to sort them according to which are the most similar to the person's ideal brand.

Once the respondent has completed the Q-sort, each item is assigned a rank order. The data are ordinal in nature and can be analysed with statistical procedures that are suitable for this type of data.

Non-comparative scales

The respondent is not instructed to compare the object of interest either against another object or some specified criteria. In rating an object, the respondent assigns the rating based on whatever criteria are appropriate for that individual. In assigning a rating, each respondent must use some criteria of their own: it is not provided by the researcher.

Line marking/continuous rating scales

A line marking or continuous rating scale can be used in a non-comparative format. In this case the respondent is required to assign a rating by placing a mark at the appropriate position on a line, usually five inches long, that best describes the subject under study. No standard for comparison is given. The resulting scores are usually analysed as interval data.

Itemised rating scale

Here the respondent is provided with a scale that has numbers and/or a brief description associated with each category. They are asked to select one of the categories, ordered in terms of scale position, that best describes the object under study. The scale can take on various formats reflecting the number of categories used, the nature and degree of verbal description, the number of favourable and unfavourable categories, and the presence of the neutral position. This kind of scale can have any number of response categories. However, the controlling factor concerns the respondent's ability to discriminate among categories.

Various types of verbal descriptions and numeric formats can be employed and the former do help to ensure that respondents are operating from the same base. However, the presence of verbal descriptions will influence the responses obtained. Pictures and other types of graphics may also be used.

If an equal number of favourable and unfavourable classes is used, a scale is balanced; otherwise the scale is unbalanced. You might want to use an unbalanced scale when the distribution of responses is likely to be skewed. More categories might be used in the direction of the skewness. Unbalanced scales are often used when asking socially threatening questions or in cases where most of the respondents are likely to have positive, or conversely negative, opinions about a subject.

When a balanced rating scale is used, there is a choice between using an even or an odd number of scale items. In the case of an odd number of scale items, the middle scale position is usually designated as a neutral point.

Itemised rating scales are often used to measure purchase intentions. Purchase-intention scales represent an attempt to measure a respondent's interest in a brand or product.

Multiple-item scales

A multiple-item scale consists of a number of statements to which the respondent must react. For example, a respondent might be asked to indicate how favourable or unfavourable each statement is. An overall score is then determined by combining the reactions to each.

ATTITUDE MEASUREMENT

Attitudes are assumed to be a precursor of behaviour and are considered to express a person's beliefs and, in some sense, to influence the person's ultimate behaviour. Most commercial market research studies contain questions to measure the respondent's attitude.

People have different notions about what constitutes an attitude but it often involves feelings, emotions and likes or dislikes. Attitudes reflect a person's evaluation of an object based on their beliefs about that object. To some degree, attitudes influence how the person will respond when they encounter the object.

An attitude might therefore be looked on as a learned predisposition to respond in a consistently favourable or unfavourable manner to a given object.[1] Such a description assumes that attitudes are learned, that they are a forerunner to behaviour, and that they are stable.

There are several types of scaling techniques that can be used to measure attitudes. Here we discuss and illustrate some of them.

Projective methods

The basic premise of projective methods is that the best way to obtain the true feelings and attitudes of people is to enable them to indirectly present data about themselves by speaking through others.

Projective techniques such as sentence, story and picture completion are taken from the domain of abnormal psychology. They were devised in the belief that people have various psychological blockages that prevent them from verbalising their true feelings. The assumption is that normal people, too, experience blockages and that the method is also valuable in these circumstances.

In the case of picture completion or cartoon techniques the respondents are shown a picture of one or more people in a situation related to the subject under study. They are then told to describe what is occurring or to answer a question asked by one or other of the cartoon characters. The characters are usually drawn to be as neutral as possible (no smiles or frowns). Picture frustration (putting one of the cartoon figures in a frustrating position) and thematic apperception tests (depicting more general situations than the frustrating method) are the most generally used methods (Figure 6.3).

What do you think is going on?

Figure 6.3 Thematic apperception

Word association and sentence completion

In the case of word association a respondent is given a series of single words and then asked to match each with one of their own. The goal is to elicit quick, unrestrained answers. For example:

Carnation: *perfume*

Flower seller: *anniversary*

Sentence completion follows the same kind of pattern.

The kind of flower I prefer is ⎯⎯⎯⎯⎯⎯⎯⎯⎯⎯

Men who buy flowers are ⎯⎯⎯⎯⎯⎯⎯⎯⎯⎯

Story completion, role-playing and reactions to lists

Story completion is a longer version of sentence completion in which participants are presented with partial scenarios and asked to complete the story. For example:

It was a dark day and the headlamps of the cars moved like will of the wisps in the murky twilight. Candice stepped almost unconsciously into a limousine which stood, door ajar, at the curb...

Role-playing

Participants are asked to assume the role of another person and to behave in a manner in which they feel that person would act. For example, to identify people's attitudes towards a particular brand a small group of respondents is asked to provide the conversation they feel would occur in a similar same-sized group of consumers discussing their feelings about the brand.

Lists

Lists of various products or activities are shown to participants and they are asked to describe the type of person who would have used such a list. Their answers will shed light on their feelings about the items on the list and what type of people such items appeal to.

Lists

What kind of shoppers are A and B? Examine the two shopping lists below and suggest characteristics for each of the shoppers.

Shopper A	Shopper B
1 tin baked beans (Heinz)	2 kilos new potatoes
2 large cartons of semi-skimmed milk	1 packet of baby corn
6 apples – cox's	1 box of tea bags (large)
2 packets white sugar	2 cartons of milk (large)
1 jar of Nescafé	1 tub of margarine
2 tins of sardines	1 bottle of aerated water
4 cans of Lager (Skol)	1 packet of Special K cereal
1 tub of chocolate ice-cream (large)	1 tin of tuna chunks
1 packet of PG Tips tea bags (large)	4 yoghurts – organic (fruit)
2 loaves (white – from bakery dept)	6 eggs (medium)
2 packets of pork sausages	

A variation on this method is to have two identical shopping lists, except for one single item. The lists are shown to different samples of respondents – i.e. no one person sees both the lists. This helps to spot what people associate with the one item that is different on the two lists.

SELF-REPORTING METHODS

Semantic differential scale

The scaling technique was originated by Osgood, Suci and Tannenbaum.[2] The originators of the technique discovered that the perceived meaning of a variety of words and concepts could be decomposed in terms of three components: potency, activity and evaluation. In marketing research, the semantic differential is often used to measure attitudes towards the imagery surrounding products and services. In general, only the evaluative (e.g. good/bad) component is measured.

The scale consists of a number of bipolar adjectival phrases and statements that could be used to describe the objectives being evaluated. In the original work of Osgood *et al.*, only single-word bipolar adjectives, not phrases, were used. However, common practice in marketing research applications is to use adjectival phrases as well. An example is shown in Figure 6.4. Each bipolar adjective rating scale consists of seven categories, with neither numerical labels nor category descriptions other than for the anchor categories. To remove any position bias, favourable and unfavourable adjectival phrases are randomly distributed to the

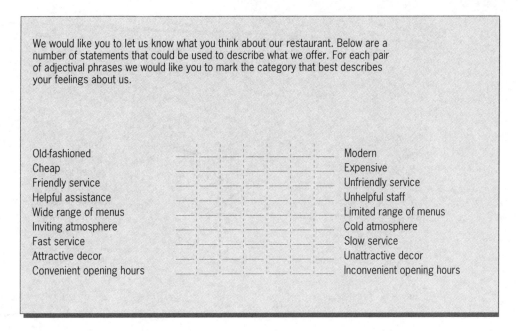

We would like you to let us know what you think about our restaurant. Below are a number of statements that could be used to describe what we offer. For each pair of adjectival phrases we would like you to mark the category that best describes your feelings about us.

Old-fashioned		Modern
Cheap		Expensive
Friendly service		Unfriendly service
Helpful assistance		Unhelpful staff
Wide range of menus		Limited range of menus
Inviting atmosphere		Cold atmosphere
Fast service		Slow service
Attractive decor		Unattractive decor
Convenient opening hours		Inconvenient opening hours

Figure 6.4 Semantic differential

left-hand and right-hand anchor positions. The respondent is asked to mark one of the seven categories that best describes their views about the object along the continuum implied by the bipolar object pair. An overall attitude score is computed by summing the responses on each adjective pair. Before computing the overall score, the response categories must be coded. Usually the categories are assigned values from 1 to 7, where 1 is assigned to the unfavourable adjectival phrase and 7 is assigned to the favourable adjectival phrase. Thus, before assigning codes and summing, the researcher must be careful to reverse the individual scale items where necessary so that each attitude continuum ranges from unfavourable to favourable or vice versa.

Ratings on each of the bipolar adjective pairs are often used to provide a profile or image of the objects being investigated. This is achieved by plotting the mean ratings on each of the bipolar adjective pairs for each of the objects. Figure 6.5 shows an example of such profiling. In order to facilitate interpretation of the profile, all the favourable adjectival phrases are positioned on the same side. From this kind of plot it is possible to obtain an overall impression of people's perceptions of the object.

In Figure 6.5, a comparison is made between two restaurants. Not only does the scale permit such comparisons to be taken in at a glance but it also allows us to see fairly readily where more in-depth research is required. The decor of 'our restaurant', for example, is perceived to be at or about the neutral point. Further research is needed to uncover how it might be improved to the taste of its clientele.

Figure 6.5 Semantic differential profile

Staple scale

This technique differs from the semantic differential because it uses just one term and asks the respondent to describe how well that term describes the subject. Circling +5 means that the respondent agrees very strongly that the term is an appropriate description, while circling −4 indicates the reverse. The scores for each respondent can be summed and compared with the total scores of other respondents.

Staple scale

Our restaurant

+5	+5
+4	+4
+3	+3
+2	+2
+1	+1
Awkward	Helpful
−1	−1
−2	−2
−3	−3

−4	−4
−5	−5

Select a plus number for words that you think describe the restaurant accurately. The more accurate you think the description is, the larger should be the plus number selected. Conversely, select a minus number for words which do not describe the restaurant. The less accurate you believe the description to be, the larger should be the minus number you select.

Likert attitude scales

These measure attitudes and comprise statements with which the respondent has to agree or disagree.

Likert scale

'Persil washes whiter than white'

Strongly disagree	Disagree	Don't Know	Agree	Strongly agree
−2☐	−1☐	0☐	+1☐	+2☐

In the Likert[3] method a series of statements is provided and interviewees are required to rate each statement on the basis of the strength of their personal feelings toward it. The numbers assigned to the responses are numerical values associated with each possible answer. When analysing the results, the signs of these numbers are reversed when a statement is unfavourable.

Thurstone differential

In this method interviewees are asked to select those statements with which they agree from a list of between 20 and 25 statements. The statements are derived from an original list of 100–200 statements that are evaluated by a panel of 15–20 judges. Each judge is asked to place those statements in 11 nearly equal piles. These piles represent the judgements of the panel members as to which statements are more favourable and which are least favourable about the subject. The sixth or middle pile is the neutral position.

Mean scores for each of the original 100–200 statements are determined on the basis of the piles in which they were placed by the judges. The 20–25 statements with the smallest dispersion are chosen to be included in the survey. From this latter list the interviewee is asked to check only those with which they agree, enabling a mean score for each interviewee to be obtained. This score quantifies the attitude of each interviewee toward the subject under study. Many people argue that the scale is an *ordinal* rather than interval scale.

The 20–25 statements used in the scale must all deal with the same subject. If attitudes towards a variety of subjects are sought – firm's products, personnel, etc. – a separate list of statements would be required for each subject.

Thurstone scale

Suppose attitudes towards a restaurant are being assessed using a Thurstone scale. An interviewee indicates three statements with which they agree:

Statement	Value assigned by judges
1 The restaurant has a friendly atmosphere	3.0
15 The restaurant offers a good choice of menus	1.5
21 Always rely on the quality of the food	2.7
Average	2.4

Some general comments relating to these techniques

When administering these techniques, respondents are provided with a number of alternative choices – words, statements, numbers – and required to select the one that most closely describes their attitude toward the subject. When applying these techniques, the researcher must decide how many choices to include as well as their wording.

There is disagreement on the ideal *number of choices* that should be offered to respondents. Four to eight choices appears to be preferred, with five the number used most often. There is also a lack of consensus on whether there should be an *even or odd number of choices*. An even number of choices compels the respondent to declare a position, whereas an odd number usually provides a middle position for those in situations where the respondent cannot identify their feelings. The drawback to offering a neutral position is that this choice attracts many respondents who do not have strong feelings on the issue and hence it does not allow the researcher to distinguish between answers.

There is a related issue which is relevant to the point about the 'odd versus even' number of questions: this concerns the provision of a category headed *'don't know'*. There are many situations in which respondents do not have an opinion or are not sufficiently informed on a topic to have an opinion about it. A neutral position and a 'don't know' choice *are not the same thing*. Where both can occur, provision has to be made to record both.

Attention should also be given to the *wording of choices*. There should usually be an equal number of favourable or unfavourable statements. Responses can easily be biased if the majority of choices are either favourable or unfavourable. An unbalanced set of categories might be preferred, however, when there is prior evidence that, in general, attitudes held are at extreme positions. For example, if all viewpoints are likely to be positive, then more precision may be obtained by offering the categories:

1 outstanding
2 well above average
3 above average
4 average
5 below average

METHODS FOR RATING ATTRIBUTES

Thus far we have examined techniques that allow respondents to express their feelings on the extent to which an item or topic possesses certain attributes. However, in trying to obtain an overall score for the subject matter under scrutiny, we have assumed equal weighting for all the attributes or statements. It is necessary, however, to measure how important each attribute or statement is for the overall attitude being measured.

Rating scales enable respondents to disclose the intensity of their feelings about certain attributes or about the subject itself.

Graphic scales

The respondent indicates the intensity of their feelings toward some attribute or object by placing a mark at some point along a continuum that includes all possible ratings.

Graphic scale

Please indicate how important each attribute is to you in your selection of a restaurant. Place an X on each line at the position that best reflects your feelings.

Attribute	Not important	Very important
Low prices	_____	
Courteous service	_____	
Varied menu	_____	
Convenient location	_____	

Itemised approach

Here, a list is prepared of the object's attributes and the respondents are asked to identify how important each item is to them in their final attitude toward the object.

Itemised approach

Attribute	Very important	Fairly important	Somewhat important	Not important
Price	___	___	_X_	___
Durability	_X_	___	___	___
Appearance	___	___	___	_X_

Comparative weights

Here the respondent is forced to rate the attributes on the basis of their perceived relative importance.

Comparative weights

Price	22
Weight	16
Durability	12
Material	21
Looks	29
Total	100

The respondent is asked to divide 100 points among five attributes to denote the relative importance of each attribute.

Rank order

In this case the respondent is asked to arrange a number of objects according to some criterion. This produces strictly ordinal scaling, since no data are presented about the relative difference between any of these objects. The procedure is easy for the respondent to perform if the comparison is limited to six or seven objects.

Multiple-item scales are often used in attitude measurement.

Rank order

Please rank the following restaurants according to the friendliness of their personnel. Place the number 1 beside the restaurant that you feel has the most friendly personnel, 2 by the restaurant with the next most friendly personnel, and so on until all restaurants have been rated.

——   Rembrandt

——   Silver Moon

——   Hole in the Wall

——   Barny's Place

——   Il Seraglio

Rating with symbols

In cases where there may be language or literacy difficulties, an alternative to using words in scales is to use symbols instead. The example in Figure 6.6 illustrates this.

SUMMARY

This chapter has defined and discussed the basic concepts of measurement and scaling, distinguishing among the various types of measurement scales. A description and illustration of comparative types of measurement scales have been given, as have descriptions and illustrations of non-comparative types of measurement scales. Single-item versus multiple-item scales have been compared and discussed. Various attitude measurement scales have also been examined.

Great   OK   Unsure   Poor   Ghastly

Figure 6.6 Example of symbols representing ratings

Questions

1 What do you understand by the term measurement in marketing research?
2 Differentiate between concepts, constructs and definitions.
3 Differentiate between nominal, ordinal, interval and ratio-scaled data, and indicate when each might appropriately be used in marketing research.
4 Describe the two main types of scaling.
5 Differentiate between paired comparisons, rank-order scales, constant sum scales, continuous rating, comparative scale or line marking, and Q-sort scales. What do all these scales have in common?
6 What are itemised rating scales?
7 What are multiple-item scales?
8 What are attitudes? Indicate the different ways in which they can be measured.

Case study 6.1 | Summit Motors (A)

Summit Motors' records indicate that less than 40 per cent of its new car buyers remain loyal service customers after the first free service. The dealer is keen to increase the percentage to at least 50 per cent. A number of different attributes have been identified as affecting the patronage of a service facility and the dealer wants to conduct a small survey among new car purchasers who have bought cars during the past two years to assess customer views.

The attributes affecting patronage are considered to be whether or not:

- the job is done first time;
- complaints are dealt with speedily;
- warranty work is attended to promptly;
- the dealer can do any job required;
- service is available when required;
- the service is friendly and courteous;
- a car is ready when promised;
- only necessary work on a car is performed;
- service prices are low;
- the car is cleaned up after service;
- the service facility is convenient for home;
- the service facility is convenient for work;
- courtesy cars are available;
- maintenance reminders are posted.

Question

Construct a scale that would be helpful to the dealer and that could be the focal point of the survey.

Case study 6.2   Barny's Café

Barny's Café is just off the promenade at Eastbourne. It is tucked away down a side street and although it does not enjoy the prominence of many of the cafés in the town, there are a good number of passers-by during the season and many stop for a drink or even a meal. Out of season, however, the café suffers from the usual, perhaps to be expected, seasonal drop in sales. However, Barny has noticed that, unlike many of his competitors, he does not have any regular customers who help to offset the seasonal drop in sales. In the summer, when the town is crowded, it is difficult to get a seat in a café and virtually all the cafés are full to overflowing around lunchtime and in the afternoon. Virtually anyone who can offer a seat and a rest for half-an-hour can get customers.

Barny sees his problem as one of establishing a customer base – in other words: how to get regular customers and keep them. As far as he can see there does not appear to be anything especially different about the 'more successful' cafés from what he has to offer. One thought that has crossed his mind is the idea of conducting a small survey to find out people's attitudes towards his café and, if possible, their attitudes to other cafés in the town.

Question

Draw up a suitable attitude measurement scale that might help Barny have a better idea of how he might tackle this problem.

Case study 6.3   Liptonjuice (B)

Before making any further decisions imagine that PepsiCo had decided to undertake an extensive survey of people's attitudes to iced tea in the United States, the United Kingdom, Spain, France, Germany and Italy.

Question

Suggest how PepsiCo might go about measuring people's attitudes to Liptonjuice.

Case study 6.4   Chinese imports

East-West Connections Ltd specialise in the import of novelties and small household products from the Far East, notably from Korea and mainland China. The company's Chinese agents have for some time been suggesting that the firm's range could be extended to include Chinese white goods – washing machines, refrigerators, freezers and so forth – since these were now being produced to high standards and in substantial quantities within the People's Republic. Following in the footsteps of Changhong, the largest TV manufacturer in China (now exporting to the USA), the agents believe that the Western world is ready for Chinese consumer durables.

The directors of East-West are somewhat less enthusiastic. Although they are well aware that firms such as Wuxi Little Swan (washing machine makers) and Qingdao Haier or Guangdon Kelon (refrigerator manufacturers) are seeking opportunities outside China, they feel that the British public still think of Chinese goods as being in the 'cheap and nasty' category. For the firm to make the considerable leap from dealing in cheap fans and ceramic ornaments to dealing in consumer durables would require some fairly solid evidence; the capital cost alone could bankrupt the firm if the idea went wrong. On the other hand, being first to introduce the products into Britain could have very substantial advantages in terms of long-term viability of the firm. After all, there is a limit to how many substandard vases can be sold, and in the long run the firm would need to seek new opportunities.

The obvious answer to the problem was to conduct some research among UK consumers to see what their perception of Chinese goods is. The consultants brought in to do the research decided to begin by using a Q-sort to assess perceptions of Chinese goods against perceptions of 23 other nationalities including European, American and Far Eastern countries. The perceptions of the countries' goods were assessed across the following criteria: reliability, design quality, durability, price, availability, and prestige value. The Q-sort revealed that Chinese goods ranked higher than some countries on price and availability, and even ranked higher on design than did a few countries', but in almost all cases China ranked low on durability and reliability.

The country which appeared to be closest to China in terms of public perception of the goods was Korea. Since Korean engineering has become more acceptable in the West over the past ten to fifteen years (with the advent of Korean cars such as Daewoo and Kia), the researchers decided to concentrate further efforts on investigating the relationship between perceptions of China and perceptions of Korea. For this, the researchers decided to use a multidimensional scaling approach so that they could see how great the differences were between China and Korea on the attributes identified above.

China was perceived as having a very large advantage on price, a small disadvantage on design, a small disadvantage on prestige, and big disadvantages on reliability, durability and availability. For Chinese goods to be successful in the UK, therefore, East-West Connections would need to change the perception of unreliability. In fact, quality testing showed that the Chinese goods were no more unreliable than Korean goods, but the Koreans had the advantage of being able to ride on the back of Japan's reputation for high-quality goods. The Chinese might not have a similar advantage – but without a doubt they were going to be in the market within the next ten years or so.

The directors of East-West Connections were unsure whether the firm would be able to make the substantial changes in public perceptions that appeared necessary; on the other hand, the prospect of being first to market in a potentially huge growth area was very tempting indeed.

(Case contributed by Jim Blythe.)

Questions

1 Why might the research team not have used multidimensional scaling across all the comparison countries instead of a Q-sort?
2 What does multidimensional scaling tell us that a Q-sort does not?
3 Draw up a semantic differential scale for assessing attitudes to Chinese goods.
4 What other techniques might have been appropriate to the study?
5 What are the limitations of Q-sort and multidimensional scaling?

Further reading

Churchill, G A (1979) A paradigm for developing better measures of marketing constructs, *Journal of Marketing Research*, 16, pp 64–73.

Gofton, K (1997) If it moves measure it, *Marketing*, 4 September, p 17.

Green, P A, Tull, D S and Albaum, G (1988) *Research for Marketing Decisions*, Upper Saddle River, NJ: Prentice Hall.

Ohanian, R (1990) Construction and validation of a scale to measure celebrity endorsers' perceived expertise, trustworthiness and attractiveness, *Journal of Advertising*, 19(3), pp 39–52.

Oppenheim, A N (1968, 1969, 1984) *Questionnaire Design and Attitude Measurement*, Oxford: Heinemann.

References and notes

[1] Fishbein, M and Azjen, I (1975) *Belief, Attitude, Intention and Behavior*, Reading, MA: Addison-Wesley, p 6.

[2] Osgood, C, Suci G and Tannenbaum, P (1987) *The Measurement of Meaning*, Urbana, IL: University of Illinois Press.

[3] Likert, R (1932) A technique for the measurement of attitudes, *Archives of Psychology*, 140.

7 Questionnaires

OBJECTIVES

After reading this chapter you should be able to:

- understand the principles involved in designing and constructing questionnaires;

- understand the principles involved in testing and debugging questionnaires.

KEY WORDS

questionnaire	closed-ended questions
survey	open-ended questions
pretesting	scales
phrasing	dichotomous questions
layout	multiple choice
sequence	semantic differential
response format	projective techniques

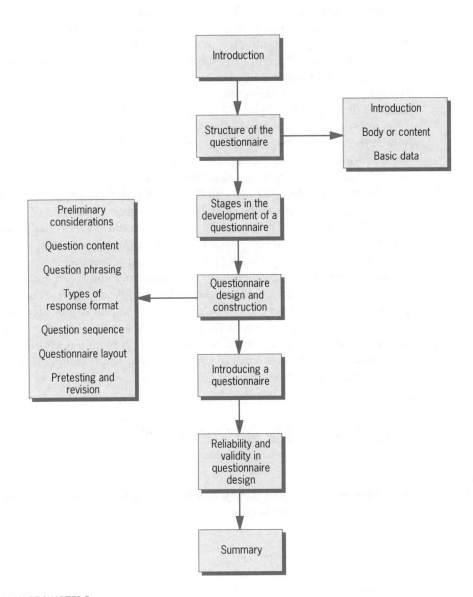

PLAN OF CHAPTER 7

INTRODUCTION

In this chapter we look at the design and construction of questionnaires. Questionnaires are used in a variety of contexts in marketing research. They can be employed during the conducting of surveys, which include mail surveys, telephone interviews, formal structured personal interviews, and self-administered studies. Irrespective of the context in which survey research is conducted, the ways in which the questionnaire is constructed are very broadly similar. However, questionnaires must be developed carefully, tested and debugged before they are administered.

A questionnaire is a data-collection instrument. It formally sets out the way in which the research questions of interest should be asked. Even simple questions need proper wording and organisation to produce accurate information. Consideration needs to be given to how questions should be worded, in the light of the objectives of the research, and the target group of respondents who are to be questioned. Attention also needs to be given to the organisation of the questionnaire and to its pretesting. The procedures recommended in this chapter apply to mail, telephone, personal and computer-assisted telephone interviews.

There are definite guidelines for preparing a questionnaire. First, there are limitations to what a questionnaire can measure. People can accurately report the make or brand of a fashion item they have bought for some time after the actual purchase. If it is a frozen-food item, their memory span will be considerably shorter. If it is a commodity-type product such as salt or sugar, where the brands are almost indistinguishable, it will probably have been completely forgotten. Depending on the subject, there may be recall of something that respondents think they have seen when actually they have not.

STRUCTURE OF THE QUESTIONNAIRE

The three major parts of the questionnaire are the introduction, the body of the questionnaire and its basic data.

The introduction

To be successful, the introduction to the questionnaire must achieve two things:

1 It must be persuasive.
2 Usually it must qualify the respondent as someone who belongs in the sample.

The starting point of the questionnaire is self-identification. In a one-to-one interview, the investigator has to explain who they are and the firm doing the study. The introduction states the topic of the study. If it is a one-to-one survey, the person may have to be qualified to ensure that they really belong in the sample. Possibly only users of a particular type of product or service are wanted.

The body or content

The body or content consists of questions that cover information needed to solve the marketing problem. The range of topics covers facts, knowledge, opinions and attitudes, motives and possible future behaviour. Factual questions include such things as ownership, shopping/buying behaviour, and media exposure as well as knowledge possessed by respondents. Questions also attempt to measure opinions and attitudes – feelings about products, firms and advertising. There is also the measurement of motives, still more difficult and uncertain in dependability of results. Finally, there is possible future behaviour. Questioning in this last area must bear in mind that results are an expression of attitude and not an accurate prediction of behaviour. People are often willing to describe their plans, but these are often not carried out.

Designing the questionnaire

First, the problem to be tackled by the survey has to be defined. This will enable you to decide which questions to ask. It is always tempting to cover too much in a questionnaire. However, too long a questionnaire can be demoralising for both interviewer and respondent. A questionnaire should only be as long as is absolutely essential for its purpose. Moreover, the aim of the questionnaire should always be borne firmly in mind when constructing it and each question should make contributions to the research objectives.

The information obtained as a result of administering the questionnaire will depend on the respondent's ability and willingness to respond. The aim should be only to ask opinions if the interviewer is reasonably sure that the respondent understands what is involved and is able to give meaningful answers. The interviewer should also aim to ask questions only from those who are able to answer them accurately. It should always be borne in mind that a willingness to respond is not a guarantee of the accuracy of the answers.

Basic data

The last section of the questionnaire is mainly information about the household and the individual. It almost always includes demographics about the household, aspects such as family size, nature and income. Typically, it also covers demographics about the respondent and it may include questions about lifestyle and psychographics.

This section of the questionnaire has three purposes. First, where there are known and dependable statistics about the population from which the sample has been selected, such data provide a rough check on the representativeness of the sampling. Second, through analysis of subgroups, it provides a method for identifying differences of key results in response by subgroups such as gender and age. Third, there is identification material such as the respondent's name, address and telephone number.

Impact of survey method on questionnaire design

Whether survey data is collected through personal interview, telephone, mail or self-administration, it will have an impact on questionnaire design. In a shopping centre interview, for example, there are time limitations which are not encountered in other situations. In the case of a self-administered questionnaire the questions have to be very explicit and short. In the case of a telephone interview a rich verbal description of a concept may be necessary to ensure that the respondent understands what is being discussed.

STAGES IN THE DEVELOPMENT OF A QUESTIONNAIRE

The stages involved in the design of a questionnaire and how they fit in with the general research process are outlined in the box. This provides an overview of what should have been done prior to the development of the questionnaire. It also examines what is involved in questionnaire development and testing.

Stages in the development of a questionnaire

1　Identification and specification of the research problem/research objectives
2　Selection of the population to be studied
3　Choice of data collection: face-to-face, telephone, mail, computer approach
4　Ordering of the topics to be addressed
5　Establishing the cross-tabulations that will be required
6　Deciding how the topics will be covered – direct/indirect questions, open-ended questions, closed-ended questions – and how they will be precoded
7　Questionnaire layout and the design of any supporting material, such as showcards
8　Pretesting of the questionnaire to obtain feedback on the ordering of questions, responses to questions, instructions to interviewers, efficiency of layout and to assess the time taken by the interviewers and the cost of interviews

QUESTIONNAIRE DESIGN AND CONSTRUCTION

On reaching this stage in the conducting of a research study it is expected that the research problem has already been expressed in terms of an appropriate set of research questions. These questions have now to be put in a suitable format for the respondents to answer and then arranged into a questionnaire in a valid, logical fashion that will produce meaningful answers. Considerable thought needs to go into the process of constructing a questionnaire: it is not as simple as might appear at first sight. Indeed, the process involves going through the following sequence of steps (Figure 7.1):

1 preliminary considerations;
2 question content;
3 question phrasing;
4 types of response format;
5 question sequence;
6 questionnaire layout;
7 pretest, revision and final version of the questionnaire.

Preliminary considerations

Attention must be paid to the kind of information that is required, the nature of the respondents who are to be surveyed and the method by which the survey is to be conducted. *These three considerations are interdependent.* For instance, in order to answer questions in a meaningful way, a respondent must have access to relevant information and it must be appropriate for the person concerned to make a response. By way of illustrating the last point, asking the male partner in a household about shopping habits is not appropriate if the female partner does all the shopping.

The questionnaire must address all the data requirements that are specified in the research objectives and attention must be given to ensuring that this is done. It is also important to take account of how the questionnaire is to be tabulated after collection of the data. Each topic should be taken in turn and it should be decided which groups in the survey population warrant individual attention when it comes to discussing this topic.

Question content

When looking at the content of questions you should ask the following questions:

1 *Is the question necessary?* If the answer provided by a question does not contribute to satisfying the research objectives, the question itself should be omitted.
2 *Does the respondent understand the question?* The language of the question should be at the level of the respondent being interviewed.

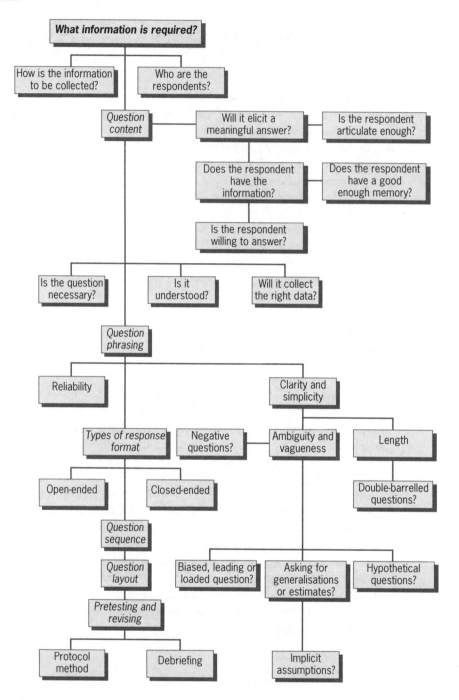

Figure 7.1 Questionnaire design and construction

3   *Will the question suffice to elicit the required data?* Questions may be badly phrased or too ambiguous to produce specific information; for example, 'When do you shop?' Asking the same question, but with the words in a different order, may also produce different answers. For example, asking whether it is right to 'drink

and drive' may elicit a different answer to asking whether it is right to 'drive and drink'. You should also avoid questions that pose more than one question; for example, 'When and where do you shop?'

4   *Does the respondent have the necessary information to answer the question?* The ability of a respondent to provide a meaningful answer will reflect:

(a)   *The extent to which the respondent is informed.* Some respondents may not wish to disclose ignorance and may try to bluff their way through certain questions. In constructing and asking questions it is therefore important to ensure that there is no suggestion that the respondent should know the answer.

(b)   *How good is the respondent's memory?* People forget and need something to jog their memories. It is better to ask people if they recognise something rather than to ask them to recall it.

(c)   *How articulate is the respondent?* People vary considerably in this respect. Where open-ended questions are being asked it is inevitable that some people will be better than others at getting over the point they wish to make. Closed-ended questions, where an individual has to indicate a predetermined answer, help to alleviate this particular problem.

5   *Is the respondent willing or able to answer the questions?* Non-response or distorted answers are sometimes made by respondents. Embarrassment or loss of face are strong motivators that influence how a person responds to questions. Ways of alleviating this problem include:

(a)   removing or redrafting questions that are likely to create these kinds of problems.

(b)   reassuring respondents of the importance of the questions and the confidentiality of the data provided. Anonymity of the responses can help.

Question phrasing

Clarity and simplicity

The style of language used should be appropriate for the target population. You should not appear to be condescending, nor should you assume that respondents are as well informed on the subject as the person who asks the questions.

> **Clarity and simplicity**
>
> Don't ask respondents what viscosity of oil they put in their cars. Ask them what grade they use.

Length of questions

Keep the sentences short and to the point.

Ambiguity and vagueness

Ambiguity and vagueness in question wording must be avoided at all costs. If the meaning of a question is unclear, you cannot expect the respondent to provide a clear, unambiguous answer. Avoid confusing words – words that are spelt the same but can have different meanings or words that sound the same but are spelt differently.

> **Ambiguity and vagueness**
>
> The word light can mean both light in weight and light in colour. Using the word on its own can be confusing.

Biased words and leading or loaded questions

Biased words have emotional connotations such that the respondent may respond to the word rather than to the question in which it is contained: 'bosses' and 'interference' are two such words. Such words should be avoided. Leading questions are those that either suggest the way in which the respondent should answer, or strongly suggest what the questioner's position on the subject is. These too should be avoided.

> **Leading questions**
>
> Avoid leading questions such as: 'Most people believe that advertising puts up the price of goods in the shop. Do you?'

Negative questions

Questions with a negative formulation, with which respondents are asked to agree or disagree, can be confusing. Confusion leads to the respondent guessing and thence to measurement error. Questions phrased in a negative fashion should be avoided.

> **Negative questions**
>
> Questions with the format: 'You don't think…do you?' are not only confusing but also leading.

Questions asking for estimates or generalisations

These should be avoided since they are a potential source of error.

Estimates and generalisations

Do not ask people how much they usually spend on their green groceries on average every week. This can be accurately ascertained by keeping consumer diaries.

Hypothetical questions

The words 'would' or 'could' should be avoided in questions since they encourage the respondent to guess and speculate.

Hypothetical questions

Do not ask people if they would purchase something if it were available.

Implicit assumptions

When phrasing questions, do not do so in a manner that assumes that all respondents are well informed and in possession of all the facts. Questions that make an implicit assumption of a respondent's background knowledge will not produce valid, accurate results. Different respondents will make different assumptions, so the questions will not generate useful responses. Indeed, it is advisable, wherever appropriate, to state the essential assumptions on which the question is dependent.

Implicit assumptions

'Would you prefer a holiday in Spain to a holiday in Greece?' is a difficult question to answer unless you know the various assumptions relating to the two holiday venues. For example, that the cost of the holidays is similar.

Response choices should not overlap

This applies to closed-ended questions where a number of answers are provided from which the respondent has to select the most appropriate (see below).

Overlapping responses

If the categories of response given are in ranges such as:

1 0–5   ☐

2 5–10   ☐

3 10 or more   ☐

then there is clearly overlap between category 1 and category 2, and between category 2 and category 3. Redrafting the categories of response as:

1 less than 5 ☐

2 5 to under 10 ☐

3 10 or more ☐

removes the problem.

Double-barrelled questions should be avoided

These are questions where two opinions are joined together in the one question.

Double-barrelled questions

'Do you think the service provided in the hotel is friendly and efficient?'

There are really two questions in one here. Is the service friendly? Is the service efficient? Two questions are warranted to avoid confusion in recording and analysing answers.

Reliability and validity of questions

Reliability reflects whether asking the same question of the same person on a subsequent occasion will elicit the same response. Validity reflects whether you are ascertaining through a question what you think you are ascertaining. Both are influenced by the respondent's ability to answer a question accurately. If a respondent is not informed on a topic or exhibits poor memory recall relating to the topic, the accuracy of responses will be impeded. Under such circumstances the reliability and validity of the question is in doubt.

Questionnaire wording

Care has to be taken with how questions are phrased since careful question design can substantially reduce the bias arising from confusion or lack of understanding. It will also help to minimise response bias which is a function of the respondent's perceptions and predispositions. Questions should be simple, intelligible and clear. The trade-off between the desire to secure a maximum amount of information from a respondent and the need to keep the interview clear has a major bearing on questionnaire design in respect of its length, complexity, layout and wording.

Types of response format

Questions can be open-ended, where the respondent may answer in their own way, or closed-ended, where all possible answers are prespecified. Open-ended questions can reveal more information and are often worthwhile during exploratory work when you want to discover what people think. On the other hand, closed-ended questions are easier to interpret and tabulate.

There is evidence that respondents react differently to the two types of question. When the same question is put to matched samples of respondents, responses vary with the approach used.[1]

Closed-ended

In a closed-ended question, the question is followed by a structured response. All possible answers are given with the question. Such questions are easy to use, reduce interviewer bias, reduce the bias exhibited by respondents in answering questions, and facilitate coding and tabulation.

Dichotomous question

This is a question suggesting two answers, usually yes and no. These types of questions are excellent where a fact is to be determined and where the views of the respondents are likely to be clear-cut.

Dichotomous question

Did you buy your hi-fi on credit terms?

Yes ☐   No ☐

Multiple choice question

Here the respondent is offered a list of answers from which to select one that is closest to their view. This format reduces any bias that can be introduced by the respondent's ability to articulate. It also simplifies the coding of responses. Three or more answers are offered and the respondent usually has to select one of them.

Multiple choice question

Which of the following cities do you think might be the most interesting for someone to visit for the first time:

| London ☐ | Paris ☐ | New York ☐ | Lisbon ☐ |
| Munich ☐ | Ankara ☐ | Beijing ☐ | Dublin ☐ |

In this same category are scales. There is a variety of scales (see Chapter 6):

- Likert scale: this measures attitudes
- Semantic differential: this also assesses people's attitudes
- Rating scale
- Staple scale.

Open-ended

Open-ended questions do not suggest an answer and allow people to write whatever they wish. The main purpose of this type of question is to obtain the respondent's own verbalisation of, comprehension of, and reaction to stimuli such as advertisements, packages, products and concepts.

Unstructured question

Unstructured questions allow the respondent to reply in whatever format they prefer.

Unstructured question

'What do you think about Fry's Turkish Delight?'

Projective techniques

Projective techniques include word association, sentence completion, story completion and picture completion, all of which are discussed in Chapters 6 and 8.

Question sequence

The sequencing of questions is important. The earlier questions should attempt to create interest in the respondent. The questions should also follow a logical order. Questions about age, salary, etc. should be left until last, except where use is being made of a quota sampling, in which case it is necessary to establish this information at the outset of the interview.

To enhance preparedness to participate in a study, questionnaires should appear logical and carefully thought out. The typical flow in market research surveys involves a progression from evaluative to diagnostic questioning, or vice versa, and then on to classification questions (see the box relating to a questionnaire for a new product concept).

Example of moving from evaluative through diagnostic to classification questions

Questionnaire concerns consumer opinions of a new product concept.

■ *Evaluative*

purchase interest or intent

■ *Diagnostic*

reasoning behind the level of purchase intent or interest

considered uniqueness of the concept

considered credibility of the concept

perceived importance of the main benefit

anticipated frequency/quantity of purchase/usage

ratings of the concept with respect to different product benefits

■ *Classification*

age of respondent

family size of respondent

educational attainment of respondent

occupation of respondent

income group of respondent

The initial questions should be used to engage interest, to reassure and to give a foretaste of what is to follow. Potentially embarrassing questions should be left until later in the questionnaire. Questions that suggest answers to subsequent questions should be avoided. Overall the questions should move from the general to the specific and there should be a logical flow from question to question and from topic to topic. All questions relating to a particular topic should be asked before moving on to another topic, thus making it easy for the respondent to follow and develop a line of thought.

Flowcharts can help to highlight groups of questions that are relevant to some respondents and not to others. They aid in the sequencing and routeing of questions as well as in providing instructions to the interviewer (Figures 7.2 and 7.3).

Funnelling and *inverted funnelling* are also important features of sequencing, although the approach is only really suitable for personal and telephone interviews. A funnel sequence is adopted when the respondent is assumed to possess some ideas about a topic. It refers to the procedure of asking the most general questions about the topic first, followed by successively more specific and restricted questions. Such an approach minimises the possibility that

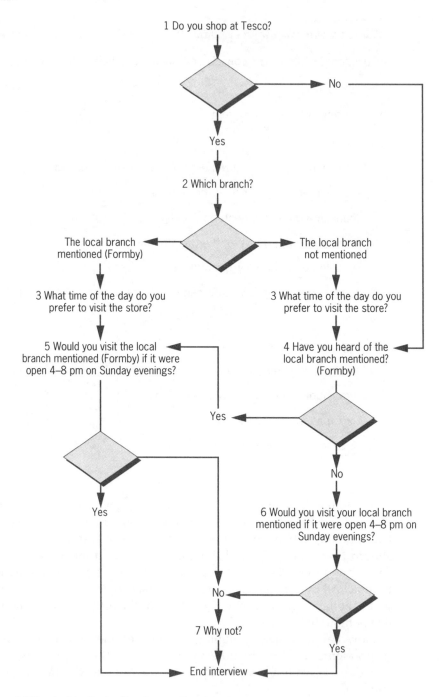

Figure 7.2 Flowchart for Sunday shopping questionnaire

early questions will bias responses to later questions. It is a useful approach when the interviewer needs to ascertain the nature of the respondent's frame of reference.

Sunday evening shopping

1 Do you shop at Tesco?

Yes ☐

No ☐

(If 'No' go to question 6)

2 Which branch(es) do you use?

(SHOW CARD)

Formby ☐

Other (please state) ☐

_____

_____

_____

3 What time of day do you prefer to visit the store?

Mornings ☐

Lunch time (12–2) ☐

Afternoons ☐

Evenings ☐

4 (Only ask this question if Formby is not indicated in the answer to question 2)

Have you heard of the local branch mentioned? (Formby)

No ☐

Yes ☐

(If 'No' go to question 6)

5 Would you visit the local branch mentioned (Formby) if it were open 4–8 pm on Sunday evenings?

Yes ☐

No ☐

(If 'No' go to question 7

If 'Yes' end interview)

6 Would you visit your local store if it were open 4–8 pm on Sunday evenings?

Yes

No

(If 'Yes' end interview)

7 Why not?

_____

_____

_____

_____

_____

_____

_____

_____

_____

_____

_____

_____

_____

END INTERVIEW

Figure 7.3 Flow of questionnaire resulting from the flowchart of the same questionnaire shown in Figure 7.2

Example of funnelling

Questionnaire relates to assessing customer impressions of a new airline service.

1   What is your overall reaction to the new service we are operating from Manchester to Istanbul?
2   Do you find anything about the new service to your distaste?
3   Do you find the kind of in-flight entertainment to your taste?

Inverted funnelling moves from the specific to the general. Since this approach makes respondents consider certain specific points in reaching their evaluations, it is useful in those instances where the interviewer wishes to ensure that all respondents base their evaluations on similar factors. This approach works best where respondents are questioned about topics about which they do have strong feelings.

Questionnaire layout

Questionnaires should be easy to use and encourage the user either to answer questions posed by an interviewer or to self-complete. A questionnaire that is badly presented or printed is likely to cause non-response or measurement error. Design considerations include the following:

- using good quality paper;
- keeping the body of the questionnaire as trim as possible;
- using spacing to break up text and improve its presentation;
- using different typefaces to assist reading;
- adding colour to promote interest;
- using routeing and/or branching instructions to guide a respondent;
- making it easy for respondents to answer the questions.

Pretesting and revising a questionnaire

When they are first drafted, questionnaires often contain questions that are ambivalent, cumbersome and vague. Instructions may also be confusing: the questionnaire may be too long and questions that should have been included may have been omitted. The pretest is a means of discovering the faults in a questionnaire before it is administered. To pretest a questionnaire a small subsample of the intended respondent group is selected: perhaps a dozen or so people. A good range of respondents is needed. The pretest can be run as a debriefing session or by using the protocol method.

The debriefing method

Here the questionnaire is presented to respondents in exactly the same manner as it would in a real study. After completing the questionnaire, respondents are asked about their thought processes while they were completing it and whether there were any problems with such items as routeing and branching instructions, understanding questions, and so on.

The protocol method

This involves respondents thinking aloud as the interview proceeds or as they fill in the questionnaire.

In examining the findings of a pretest, particular attention should be given to ensuring that:

- the meaning of the questions is clear;
- the questions are easy to answer;
- the questions flow logically from one to another;
- the routeing/branching instructions are clear;
- the questionnaire is not too long;
- the questionnaire engages and retains the respondent's interest.

There are at least five considerations to be taken into account when conducting a pretest of the questionnaire:

1 All aspects of the questionnaire should be included, most specifically:

    (a) layout
    (b) question sequence
    (c) word meaning
    (d) question difficulty
    (e) branching instructions.

2 The pretest should be administered and conducted in an environment and context that is identical to the one to be used in the final survey.
3 The majority of the pretest interviews should be undertaken by regular staff interviewers. This should include experienced and relatively new interviewers.
4 Respondents in the pretest should resemble and be representative of the target population. This means that they should be familiar with the topic and possess similar characteristics, attitudes and opinions to those in the target population.
5 The size of the sample used for pretesting will depend on the variation of the target population. The more heterogeneous the target population, the larger the pretest sample required. And the more complex the questionnaire is, the larger the pretest sample should be.

Computer-assisted questionnaires

Computer-assisted programs can handle long and complicated questionnaires of practically any length and can also accommodate very large samples. They can also be personalised or seem to act in an intelligent manner. In the latter respect, answers from previous questions can be inserted automatically into the text of later questions. For instance, a questionnaire about computers may ask whether the respondent has used any particular makes recently and ask him or her to name the makes. A later portion of the questionnaire may probe into each such computer experience and the program can be structured so that the name of each computer tried is inserted automatically into the questionnaire at the right point. Another useful feature is that the replies to an open-ended question are available to an interviewer for later access, if required. Any interview temporarily terminated at the respondent's request, for instance a telephone interview, can be rescheduled for completion at a later time.

INTRODUCING A QUESTIONNAIRE

Any questionnaire must be properly introduced to the respondent, whatever method of data collection is employed. Interviewers must introduce themselves to the respondent, indicating the purpose of the study, and must establish their credentials. This is also true of postal questionnaires, where either the introductory part of the questionnaire must do this or else an accompanying letter must explain its purpose and benefits.

Exercise

Critique the questionnaire in Figure 7.4 relating to cycling in Mudchester and suggest how it might be improved. You should pay attention to the various points about questionnaire design and construction that have already been mentioned.

RELIABILITY AND VALIDITY IN QUESTIONNAIRE DESIGN

Reliability refers to the consistency in reaching the same results when the measurement is made over and over again. Validity refers to the degree to which the question measures what it is supposed to be measuring. While a valid measure is always reliable, a reliable measure is not necessarily a valid one. While pretesting,

Mudchester Cycle Questionnaire

To help us to carry out our policy of improving conditions for cyclists in
Mudchester we should be grateful if you could complete this questionnaire.
A prepaid envelope is attached.
Thank you for your cooperation.

Q1 About you

Q1a What sex are you?   ☐ Male   ☐ Female

Q1b Age   ☐ 0–16   ☐ 17–24   ☐ 25–34

                                             ☐ 35–44   ☐ 45–59   ☐ 60 plus

Q1c How long have you been cycling regularly in Mudchester? ⌐⊤⌐ years
Q1d How long have you been cycling altogether?   ⌐⊤⌐ years

Q2 About your journey

Q2a How far have you cycled?   ☐ km
Q2b How long did it take you?   ☐ mins
Q2c What is the purpose of your journey?

    1☐ Work   2☐ Education   3☐ Shopping

    4☐ Leisure   5☐ Other   6☐ Not stated

Q2d Other (please specify)   _____

    _____

Q2e How many days a week do you cycle? ☐ days

Q3 Your opinion

Q3a Where do you/would you like to park your bicycle?

_____

_____

_____

Q3b What improvements do you think the Mudchester Council should make?

_____

_____

_____

_____

Figure 7.4 Mudchester Cycle Questionnaire

revising and further testing a questionnaire may increase its reliability, it will not
necessarily increase its validity. One way to ensure that an instrument really does
measure what it is supposed to measure is to compare the results with a 'yardstick' –
an external measurement.

Key points on questionnaire design, construction and pretesting

Preliminary considerations

- information required
- nature of the target respondents
- type of data-collection method required to survey the respondents

The questions

- reason for asking each and every question
- clarity and conciseness in expression
- exclusivity of response choices
- use of natural, familiar language
- exclusion of bias in phraseology
- avoidance of double-barrelled questions
- alternatives to be stated explicitly
- reliability and validity of questions

Questionnaire construction

- when to use open-ended as opposed to closed-ended questions
- determination of the appropriate number of response categories and their description in the case of closed-ended questions
- ensuring a movement through the questionnaire from evaluative to diagnostic to classification type questions

Pretesting questionnaire

- ensuring the testing of all aspects of the questionnaire
- pretesting in an environment and context that is identical to the one that will be used in the final survey
- establishing a debriefing procedure

An assessment of the validity of factual answers usually requires the researcher to consult other sources of information, secondary data or census reports. Nevertheless, while a measure may have excellent validity, in the descriptive sense at the time it was taken, it may possess poor validity in terms of its ability to accurately predict an outcome. In the time between the measurement and the actual event, many factors may have had an impact.

SUMMARY

Questionnaire design is a craft. Many factors have to be taken into account when assembling a questionnaire. These include such things as the overall research objectives, the kinds of data analysis that are to be employed, the amount of money that can be spent on the research project and the time in which the research has to be completed. There are no hard and fast rules about designing a questionnaire but there is a set of guidelines that can be followed to help overcome the risk of poor questionnaire design.

In this chapter we have examined issues in questionnaire design and construction. The major activities involved in questionnaire design are: (1) preliminary considerations, (2) question content, (3) question phrasing, (4) types of response format, (5) question sequence, (6) questionnaire layout, and (7) pretest, revision and final version of the questionnaire. The discussion emphasised general guidelines and suggested basic principles involved in asking questions. For questionnaire construction, attention was focused on response formats, logical flow and layout considerations. In discussing the pretesting of questionnaires emphasis was placed on what items should be pretested, the manner in which the pretest should be conducted, who should be the respondents in the pretest, and how large a sample is required for the pretest. Finally, attention was paid to establishing the reliability and validity of questionnaires.

Questions

1   In what contexts are questionnaires used in marketing research?

2   Explain the initial considerations that have to be taken into account before embarking on the construction of a questionnaire.

3   What are the factors that should be taken into account when deciding on the content of questions?

4   What factors should be taken into account when looking at the phrasing of questions?

5   Give examples of:

   (a)   a loaded question

   (b)   a double-barrelled question

   (c)   an ambiguous question.

6   Distinguish between closed-ended questions and open-ended questions.

7   Select from the following list of open-ended questions those that would be better posed as closed-ended questions. Rewrite the ones you choose to make them closed-ended.

- Exactly how much is the journey going to cost?
- What are your favourite kinds of holidays?
- Where have you been in previous years for your holiday?
- How satisfied are you with your travel agent?
- Which day of the week do you prefer to travel?

8   Give examples of:

   (a)   dichotomous questions

   (b)   multiple choice questions.

9   What factors should be taken into account when considering question sequence?

10   How ought questionnaire layout be specified in order to encourage respondents to answer the questions?

11   Describe the two approaches to pretesting and revising a questionnaire. What are the five considerations that should be taken into account when undertaking a pretest?

12   Distinguish between reliability and validity in questionnaire design.

13   How should a questionnaire be introduced?

14   Here is a poorly worded set of questions attempting to establish how customers rate and perceive the products and services of a supermarket. The questions have to be answered by someone who has only a few minutes to spare while waiting at the till. Determine what the questions should be trying to elicit, cut down the number of questions asked and see if you can design a short questionnaire that will elicit the kind of information you need.

   Hand the completed questions to the cashier as you leave.

   Q1   What is your name?

   Q2   How old are you?

   Q3   Do you come here often?

   Q4   What don't you like?

   Q5   How much do you have to spend?

   Q6   Would you come on Friday nights after 6 o'clock if you thought we were open?

   Q7   Have you a car?

   Q8   What do you think about the quality of our service?

   Q9   Where do you go for your holidays?

   Q10   Can you park your car all right?

   Q11   Are the trolleys the right size?

   Q12   Do you bring your children with you?

   Q13   Have you any complaints?

   Q14   Do you like our green products?

Q15   Do you not think that we should not close on every other Sunday?

Q16   What is your sex?

Q17   How often do you come here?

Q18   Do you think we are a clean shop?

Q19   Do you think we should diversify?

Q20   What promotional offers would you like?

Case study 7.1 | Central Training College (B)

In Case Study 5.1, a consultant was called in to advise on the viability of opening a recruitment agency in central London. On the basis of initial discussions the consultant produced the following research proposal.

Research proposal

Summary of brief

1 To determine the viability of opening a recruitment agency in central London.
2 To determine if the Central Training College would be a good location.
3 To find out if the name Central Recruitment would be acceptable.

Proposed research objectives

1 Investigate current and future demand for recruitment agencies.
2 Investigate actual intentions to use the service.
3 Discover if the name of the recruitment agency is an important factor in the purchase decision.
4 Investigate student and business attitudes to the provision of such a service.
5 Obtain demographic details of both students and businesses interested in the service.

Proposed research design

Conduct two surveys, one of the students at the college and the other of the employers. Students to be interviewed face-to-face and the employers will be contacted by post.

Source: Carol Fry.[2]

Question

Produce a flowchart and questionnaires that could be used in this research.

Case study 7.2   The Roland watch company

Roland believes there is a growing and substantial market for mechanical and automatic wrist-watches for both ladies and gentlemen. For the past five years he has produced and marketed watches with quartz movements under the label 'Roland' using the Greek letter ρ as his trademark.

There is a large and growing market for second-hand mechanical and automatic watches and there are a growing number of 'houses' producing and marketing new models. Most of the major manufacturers now have a token item in their product line – at least as far as the men's wrist-watch market is concerned. The new market for mechanical and automatic watches is made up as follows:

Segment 1

Watches usually priced at more than £2,500 which do not contain expensive jewellery adornments such as diamonds. This tends to be a specialist market for the connoisseur. Long-established, well-known companies offering watches to this market include Jaeger, Blancpain, Breguet, Patek Philippe, Audemars Piguet, Girard Perregaux and Vacheron Constantin. A number of small, less well-known houses also produce for this market segment. They include Alan Silberstein, Daniel Roth and Frank Muller.

Segment 2

Watches priced between £1,000 and £2,500. This represents a fairly substantial market and is dominated by Rolex. Other competitors in this price segment include Bretling, which differentiates itself from Rolex by offering sports mechanical and automatic sports watches. Omega has a range of mechanical and automatic watches in this segment. A relative newcomer to the market, Chronoswiss, offers a range of connoisseur watches to this segment.

Segment 3

Watches priced between £500 and £1,000. This represents a popular price range and there are many firms making offerings to this segment including Eterna, Maurice Lacroix, Oris and Baume & Mercer. Many of the well-known 'mass production' houses also have at least one offering to this segment. Included in the latter category are Longines and Ebel.

Segment 4

In this segment are found mechanical and automatic watches priced at between £150 and £500. Manufacturers such as Oris, Maurice Lacroix and Michel Herbelin have a presence here.

Segment 5

This segment comprises watches priced between £75 and £150. It has the interest of several small houses, including Claude Helier and Le Cheminant.

Segment 6

This is the cheapest section of the market where watches are priced at less than £75. At the top end of the segment are mechanical and automatic fashion models produced by Swatch along with utility models produced by Seiko. At the ultra cheap end of the market are models by Limit and Sekonda.

Only a few houses manufacture their own mechanical and automatic movements. The majority buy the movements from the Swiss Eta manufacturing company.

Roland would like to start producing and selling mechanical and automatic watches and has decided to survey his dealers and concessionaires for their opinions.

Question

Produce a flowchart and questionnaire that Roland could send to dealers and other intermediaries to help him decide what to do.

Case study 7.3 | ## Researching the sports market

Westbourne Research Consultants is a small market research consultancy based in the west of England. Recently, they were approached by the local authority's Leisure and Amenities Department to solve a market research problem.

Leisure and Amenities had decided to conduct a survey of their own to find out which sports local people participated in most frequently. They had conducted the research outside local sports centres, and had come up with some surprising results; for one thing, it appeared that far more local people claimed to participate in sports than could be accounted for by the usage figures obtained from the sports centres themselves. Secondly, the researchers had the impression that respondents had had real difficulty answering some of the questions. These are the questions that proved problematical:

Q4: Why do you play your favourite sport?
Q8: How can sporting facilities be improved in the area?
Q12: What is your opinion of the Leisure and Amenities Department, and why?
Q23: Who do you think should have the most say in deciding which new facilities can be developed?

In fact, the study seemed to be so flawed (and was proving so difficult to analyse) that the Leisure and Amenities Department wanted Westbourne to run a new research project altogether.

Westbourne's research manager asked Leisure and Amenities' management the following questions:

1 What are you hoping to gain from this research?
2 What management decisions will be based on the research?
3 Who are the people whose opinions you wish to canvass?

The managers of the Leisure and Amenities Department explained that the research aim was to improve their knowledge of the needs of the local population in terms of sports provision; they would be basing investment decisions on the results, particularly in the area of sports centre design and playing-field provision; and they expected that a representative sample of the local population, including children and the elderly, should be included. In particular, Leisure and Amenities were interested in those people who rarely (or never) took part in sport, since there was a possibility that their needs were not being met at all by the present provisions.

Westbourne Research immediately identified a sampling problem; the original Leisure and Amenities survey had been conducted close to the sports centres, and therefore the sample had contained a very high proportion of people who were either entering or leaving the centres. This sampling bias accounted for the very high proportion of people who participated in sport regularly, since clearly people who were entering or leaving the sports centre would be likely to participate in sport.

Leisure and Amenities had not pretested their questionnaire, which possibly accounted for some of the problems, but Westbourne immediately saw a need to redesign the questionnaire somewhat and re-run it. Unfortunately, Leisure and Amenities indicated that they had only very limited funds remaining; having spent considerable staff time on their own questionnaire, the management found it financially embarrassing (and embarrassing from a career viewpoint) to admit that the original study had gone wrong, and asked Westbourne if they could make any use at all of the data already collected.

Overall, Westbourne agreed that the original questionnaire was not entirely useless; apart from the questions already identified, the remainder of the questionnaire seemed to have been reasonably well designed and they had no reason to doubt its worth. They agreed to seek ways to use the information in some way, in order to save costs.

(Case contributed by Jim Blythe.)

Questions

1 What should Westbourne do to minimise the sampling bias?
2 How might Westbourne be able to comply with Leisure and Amenities' request to use some of the existing data?
3 What was wrong with the questions that could not be analysed?
4 What are the problems associated with designing a questionnaire to be completed by such a broad range of respondents?
5 What preparatory work should Westbourne do before redesigning the questionnaire?

| Case study 7.4 | Attitudes of cat owners to catfood |

The following cover letter and questionnaire was made available for self-completion at numerous pet shops throughout the UK. The purpose of the survey was:

1 To identify cat owners' knowledge about the ingredients of cat foods and their cats' dietary requirements.
2 To discover what factors are most important in their choice of cat foods.

Rapid Research
Chester

Dear Cat Owner

This questionnaire is part of a research project on cat foods being conducted to (a) find out more about the feeding procedures followed by cat owners and (b) determine the attitude of cat owners toward existing cat food products. Your cooperation and participation in this study will enable cat food manufacturers to better meet your cat's food requirements. Your name is not required in this study since we are only interested in aggregate replies. Please complete the questionnaire at leisure and place it in the box provided at the checkout next time you visit the shop. Your immediate cooperation in this study will be greatly appreciated.
Sincerely,

Mark Twain
Enclosure

1 Precisely how many cats are there in your household?
2 Indicate each cat's breed and estimated value; then indicate the description that most closely describes the cat.

Description of cat

Breed	Estimated value	Show cat	Just a pet	Other
[1]				
[2]				
[3]				
[4]				

3 Indicate the percentage of each type of cat food and frequency with which you feed each type of food to your cat.

	Never 0%	Seldom 1–30%	Frequently 30–70%	Usually 70–90%	Always 90–100%
Table scraps					
Canned					
Dry					

4   Indicate the brands of cat food you presently use [e.g. Tucker's treats, Paws].

5   What is the major health benefit to your cat from each of the following ingredients? [Indicate "don't know" if applicable.]

Vitamins   [i] Benefit   [ii]   [ ] Value unknown
Minerals   [i] Benefit   [ii]   [ ] Value unknown
Fats   [i] Benefit   [ii]   [ ] Value unknown
Proteins   [i] Benefit   [ii]   [ ] Value unknown
Carbohydrates   [i] Benefit   [ii]   [ ] Value unknown

6   Which ingredients do you feel are the most important requirements in your cat's diet.

[ ] Carbohydrates [ ] Vitamins [ ] Minerals [ ] Proteins [ ] Fats [ ] Don't know

7   If you buy canned cat food, indicate how important each of the following factors is in your purchase.

	No influence	Some influence	Important	Very important
Price				
Content [% of meat, etc.]	—	—	—	—
Brand name [Paws]	—	—	—	—
Who makes it [e.g. Smith]	—	—	—	—
Nutritional value of the cat food	—	—	—	—

8   What type of meat do you think is generally used in most canned cat food?

———————   The same as we eat
———————   Meat that has not been passed for human consumption
———————   Inedible by-products [e.g. intestines, bones, etc.]
———————   Don't know
———————   Other

9   Do you think canned cat foods satisfy the dietary requirements of your cat?
[ ] yes [ ] no [ ] don't know

10   Do you think some breeds of cat require special cat food?
[ ] yes [ ] no [ ] don't know

11   Do you supplement your cat's diet with vitamin drops or pills?
[ ] yes [ ] no [ ] don't know

12   Who usually purchases your cat food?
——————— Husband
——————— Wife
——————— Children

13   How do you think canned cat food can be improved?

Question

What are the strengths and weaknesses of this questionnaire and cover letter?

Further reading

Bolton, R (1991) An exploratory investigation of questionnaire pretesting with verbal protocol analysis, *Advances in Consumer Research*, 18, pp 558–65.

Booth-Kewley, S, Edwards, J E and Rosenfeld, P (1992) Impression management, social desirability and computer administration of attitude questionnaires: does the computer make a difference?, *Journal of Applied Psychology*, 77(4), pp 562–6.

Churchill, G (1995) *Marketing Research: Methodological Foundations* (6th edn), Fort Worth, TX: Dryden Press.

Hague, P (1987) Good and bad in questionnaire design, *Industrial Marketing Digest*, 12(3), pp 161–70.

Hague, P (1993) *Questionnaire Design*, London: Kogan Page.

Holtgraves, T, Eck, J and Lasky, B (1997) Face management, question wording and social desirability, *Journal of Applied Social Psychology*, 27(18), pp 1650–71.

Kalton, G and Schuman, H (1982) The effect of the question on survey responses: a review, *Journal of the Royal Statistical Society*, 145 (part 1), pp 42–73.

Locander, W, Sudman, S and Bradburn, N M (1976), An investigation of interview method, threat and response distortion, *Journal of the American Statistical Association*, 71, 269–75.

Morton-Williams, J (1978) Questionnaire design, in R Worcester and J Downham (eds) *Consumer Market Research Handbook*, Wokingham: Van Nostrand Reinhold.

Oppenheim, A N (1968, 1984) *Questionnaire Design and Attitude Measurement*, London: Heinemann.

Payne, S L (1951) *The Art of Asking Questions*, Princeton, NJ: Princeton University Press.

Tull, D S and Hawkins, D I (1990) *Marketing Research: Measurement and Method*, New York: Macmillan.

Vinten, G (1997) The threat in the question, *Credit Control* 18(1), pp 25–31.

Wilkinson, S, (1998) Focus group methodology: a review, *International Journal of Social Research Methodology*, 1(3), pp 181–203.

References and notes

[1] Morton-Williams, J and Sykes, W (1984) The use of interaction coding, *Journal of the Market Research Society*, 26(2), April.

[2] Fry, C (1991) Unpublished MBA dissertation, Department of Management, Keele University, September.

8 Qualitative research

OBJECTIVES

After reading this chapter you should be able to:

- understand the nature and uses of focus groups;

- understand the possible misuse of focus groups;

- appreciate the techniques used in moderating group discussions;

- understand the difference between focus groups used for consumer-product research and those used for industrial research.

KEY WORDS

focus groups
moderator
exploratory
clinical
experiencing
teleconferencing
video-conferencing

guide
industrial focus groups
depth interview
projective techniques
word association
cartoon test

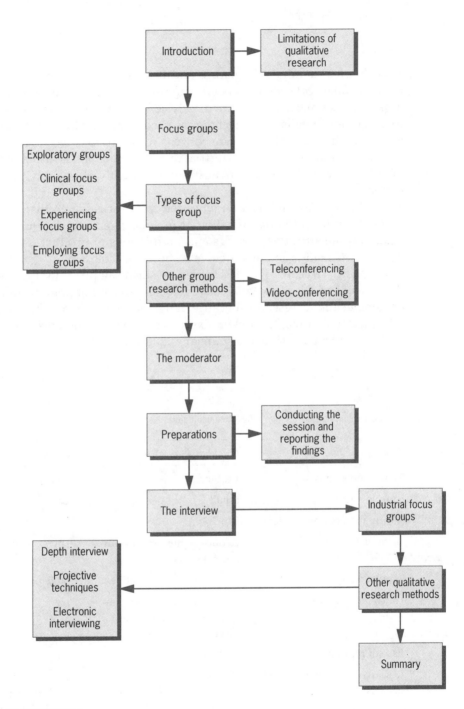

PLAN OF CHAPTER 8

INTRODUCTION

This chapter examines the nature and uses of focus groups, showing how this method of data collection can obtain information that is largely unavailable through other types of marketing research. Advice is offered about the possible misuse of focus groups, details of the techniques used in moderating group discussions are given and the distinction is made between focus groups used for consumer-product research and those used for industrial research. Attention is also drawn to a variety of other qualitative research techniques, notably those relying on projective methods.

Qualitative research is a widely used term for research that does not subject research findings to quantification or quantitative analysis. Qualitative research examines the attitudes, feelings and motivations of product users. The contrast between qualitative and quantitative is shown in Table 8.1.

Qualitative research is characterised by small samples and this has always been the focus of criticism. Executives are reluctant to base important strategy decisions on small-sample research because it relies so much on the subjectivity and interpretation of the researcher. Executives show a preference for a large sample with computer analysis and a summary table of results.

Table 8.1 A contrast between qualitative and quantitative research

Comparison dimension	Qualitative research	Quantitative research
Type of questions	Probing	Non-probing
Sample size	Small	Large
Information per respondent	Much	Varies
Administration	Requires interviewer with special skills	Fewer special skills required
Type of analysis	Subjective, interpretative	Statistical
Hardware required	Tape recorders, projection devices, video, pictures, discussion guides	
Ease of replication	Difficult	Easy
Researcher training necessary	Psychology, sociology, social psychology, consumer behaviour, marketing, marketing research	Statistics, decision models, decision-support systems, computer programming, marketing, marketing research
Type of research	Exploratory	Descriptive or causal

Despite the apparent preferences of executives, qualitative research has grown in popularity, for three reasons. First, it is usually much cheaper than quantitative research. Second, it produces a good mechanism for coming to an understanding of customer attitudes and motivations. Third, it can improve the efficiency of quantitative research.

Qualitative and quantitative research are often combined into a single study or series of studies. The patterns displayed in quantitative research can be enriched with the addition of qualitative information. Qualitative research combines with quantitative measures by providing a thorough understanding of the customer. The techniques of qualitative research involve open-ended questioning and the data is rich and often very revealing.

Limitations of qualitative research

Qualitative research does not pick out small differences quite as well as large-scale quantitative research. Nevertheless, qualitative research can detect minor problems that are not apparent in a quantitative study. Another limitation is that qualitative studies do not provide samples that are representative of the target population of the research. In terms of the sort of data produced, small sample size and free-flowing discussion can lead qualitative research projects along many different avenues of thought. Influential or dominant characters within a discussion group can also lead the group off on tangential discussions or bias the 'group view'. There is also the problem of the discussion leader's competence. The usefulness of qualitative research depends very much on the skills of the researcher.

Baby boomers get the message

Thirty years ago they were listening to the Beatles and enjoying the Sixties after growing up in postwar austerity. Now, 45- to 55-year-olds in the 'baby boomer' generation are looking at their circumstances and worrying about growing old in an increasingly insecure society.

That general conclusion comes from a study based on qualitative research into the attitudes of this group across 16 markets, including the US, Japan, Australia, the UK, and several countries in continental Europe. It carries strong marketing messages for those seeking to address this group, whose spending power outstrips its numbers. In the UK, for example, it makes up 14 per cent of the population but accounts for almost one-quarter of household expenditure. In France, the 'boomers' account for 20 per cent of spending on goods and services, while in the US the figure is 17 per cent.

Jane Gwilliam, the author of the report, says there is a striking similarity not only in the cares and concerns expressed by the boomers across all the countries where they were questioned but also about the most effective ways to communicate with them.

The prime media for reaching the boomers are television and newspapers. They spend a substantial amount of leisure time at home, and though they regard radio as more reliable than TV, the lack of 'grown up commercial' stations makes it less relevant for advertising.

Most still take at least one newspaper a day, and are more inclined to pay attention to press advertisements than to inserts and fliers.

While fliers and 'junk mail' are likely to go straight in the bin, the group seems to have a more positive attitude towards catalogues.

The study concludes that neither cinema nor sponsorship is particularly effective in marketing to boomers. That is partly because they spend so much time at home, but also because they fear their concerns will be ridiculed by the young.

Boomers' attitudes towards brands, as expressed in the study, are in sharp contrast to younger people's views. Gwilliam says that while young people value the brand name itself, and may buy the product without thinking about other brands, for boomers brand names are only as valuable as the goods and services they represent and are likely to have been chosen after other brands have been considered.

The research found that boomers do not like being patronised by advertising. According to Gwilliam, the boomers grew up with television and saw advertising evolve to become more sophisticated. They are therefore more discriminating and more alert to subtly patronising overtones than young people.

'I sometimes wonder whether a 30-year-old account manager really has an understanding of what boomers have gone through.'

Source: Alison Smith.[1] Reprinted with permission.

FOCUS GROUPS

A focus group comprises seven to twelve persons who are led by a moderator in an in-depth discussion on a particular topic or concept. The aim of focus-group research is to learn and understand what people have to say about a topic and understand their arguments. The moderator has to get people to talk about a topic at length and in detail. The purpose is to discover how they feel about a product, concept, idea or organisation and how it forms part of their lives. The moderator wants to discover the amount of emotional involvement people possess with the topic under discussion.

Most marketing research companies use the focus-group technique in consumer marketing research. It is often fairly easy to bring together a knowledgeable group of people who can discuss the topic of interest. However, the method is used much less among industrial goods companies: understandably, since the task of getting together executives covering such diverse areas as engineering, sales management or financial management is both costly and time-consuming.

The participants in the group have some common characteristics that relate to the topic discussed in the group. A focus group permits free discussion about a problem or topic and, guided by the moderator, participants' minds can range freely. Interaction with each other can produce ideas and suggestions that exhibit synergy.

A moderator has to keep a discussion alive and guide it towards a conclusion on which all participants can agree. Effective guiding, not leading, is what a good moderator must do. Discussion must be kept to a topic of interest to the sponsor. The sponsoring firm is paying for the exercise and expects relevant results. The moderator must move the group away from irrelevant discussion that is not helpful to the sponsor – and still leave the group free to air valuable new ideas.

TYPES OF FOCUS GROUP

Exploratory groups

Focus groups are often used at the exploratory phase of marketing research to help to define the problem precisely. For example, focus groups may be employed to identify the questions to be included in a survey. They may also be used to help generate hypotheses for testing. The various types of focus groups and their applications are summarised in Table 8.2.

Clinical focus groups

Clinical focus groups are used because a person's true motivations and feelings are subconscious. We cannot take at face value what many customers have to say and

Table 8.2 Types of focus groups and their characteristics

Characteristics	Exploratory	Clinical	Experiencing
Experience a real consumer	No	No	Yes
Obtaining a high level of interaction among the group members is essential	No	Yes	Yes
When a homogeneous group of people is required	No	No	Yes
The moderator's interviewing technique is critical	No	Yes	No
A moderator must have scientific credentials	Yes	Yes	No
Observation by management is appropriate	No	No	Yes
Verbatim quotes should be emphasised in the reports	No	No	Yes

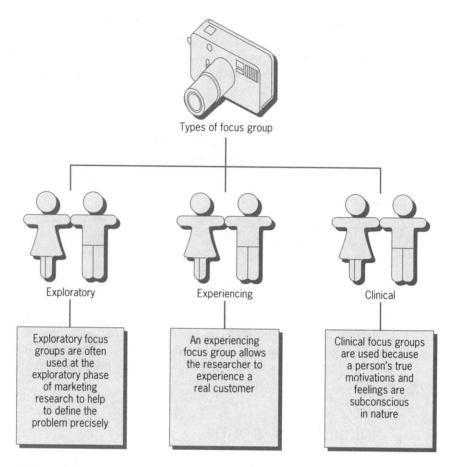

Figure 8.1 Types of focus group

the research needs to probe beneath the level of consciousness. It is assumed that a person's real motives can be uncovered using clinical judgement. The focus group provides data for clinical judgement and the moderator has to be highly skilled to persuade participants to reveal their inner thoughts and feelings.

Some applications for focus groups

New product ideas

Focus groups can give the client firm ideas for new products. A gap in the market may be identified and further research can then seek to identify the true size or potential gap in the market. If several focus groups should come up with the same idea it may well be worth serious consideration, even though it may have been considered before and rejected. It may be possible to adjust costs, perhaps, so that profitability is more positive.

Focus groups can indicate the likelihood of success with a new product. It would be possible, for example, to test the concept of a new product for the current market. You would seek answers to questions such as:

- What would be its advantages?
- Would people accept the drawbacks of the product?
- How does the idea compare with other products?
- What is the reaction of the group to various product features?
- What does the group think about the product's performance capabilities?

Problems with decreasing sales

When sales have declined rapidly on certain products, focus groups can help uncover the reasons. The products, for example, might seem to be doing the job they were intended to do, but other problems might become apparent. Minor inadequacies in product design or packaging can cause customers to switch to competitors' products. A focus group can be given several competitors' products to examine (without identification) and their positive and negative comments about the products can then be noted.

Price

In a time of inflation or recession, a producer may be looking for ways to cut costs and lower prices. Unnecessary product features may need to be eliminated. Focus groups can be used to identify these unnecessary features.

Customer attitudes

Focus groups can uncover consumer attitudes toward the sponsoring firm sufficiently to warrant further research that can lead to beneficial and remedial action.

Experiencing focus groups

An experiencing focus group allows the researcher to experience a real customer. It gives the researcher an opportunity to experience the emotional framework in which the product is being used. Effectively the researcher can experience all the satisfactions, disatisfactions, rewards and frustrations undergone by the actual customer when the product is used.

Employing focus groups

Focus groups provide data about problems through the mechanism of group dynamics. By talking among themselves and with a moderator, a relatively small group of interested people can produce more valuable thoughts and ideas than if each participant were interviewed separately. Nothing is quite the same as what can happen when a group interested in a topic or a product sit around a table for one to two hours discussing how they feel about it. In terms of bringing out suggestions, an experienced moderator can produce a degree of interaction and cooperation that produces unanticipated ideas.

Focus groups are unique: they can explore customary ways of doing things or customary beliefs, and possible reactions to something new. They can try to determine why such conditions and reactions exist and what can be done to change them. Focus groups can highlight attitudes, prejudices, changing ways of using products and changing ways of viewing pricing and distribution.

OTHER GROUP RESEARCH METHODS

While the typical focus group still involves seven to twelve or thirteen participants, a moderator, an agenda for discussion, a room equipped with a one-way mirror in which sponsors listen and watch, suitable electronic equipment, and chalkboards, there have recently been new ideas and new techniques. For example, Option Technologies Inc offers a system incorporating the following steps.

A group of people, often a focus group, generates a list of items relevant to the topic under discussion. The list is entered into a computer and the system generates a systematic set of questions about the list that is projected on to a large-screen monitor. This provides a visual stimulus for group members to register their opinions. Participants vote on individual, hand-held keypads linked to the computer, which organises the votes into graphics that are fed back to the group by a projection system. Participants orally interpret the meaning of their opinions as projected on the monitor. Group discussion clarifies the issues under research and leads to a systematic and organised basis for further research.

Teleconferencing

Respondents are invited to participate in a group telephone discussion at a specific day and time. At that time they are contacted at their office or home anywhere in the country over a telephone conference system. The moderator guides the discussion using techniques designed to create maximum interaction between the participants. The sponsor can give inputs to the moderator's assistant without being heard by the participants. The session lasts for about an hour-and-a-half and provides about as much information as a two-hour face-to-face session.

Video-conferencing

In different locations, usually different parts of the country, groups gathered around tables are asked to sample new or improved products. Video cameras and microphones are installed at the locations. Executives at remote locations are able to watch the groups and hear them and can speak to the moderator, sharpening up the direction the group discussion is taking.

All these systems have their strengths and weaknesses. Using the telephone obviously allows hard-to-reach experts to be involved in the research, since they do not have to leave their homes or offices. Each participant can hear all the others and each has a chance to contribute without being identified. The sponsor can listen in on the actual session or later via a tape-recording. However, face-to-face groups offer the opportunity for more personal contact – and perhaps the group dynamic works better when all the participants are seated around the table and can see each other. Facial reactions and visible muscular reactions often tell us what the participant is thinking more clearly than words, and other participants can and do react to these signs.

Marketing research and innovation

There is a danger in relying too heavily on research during the creative process. Hugh Seymour-Davies, a director of Innovation and Development, a new product development company that commissions much marketing research, argues that novel ideas do not come from market research. In his view the consumer can only give a retrospective response about what they use and how it influences their buying decisions. The point is echoed in a slightly different way by John Boult, a director of industrial design company Product First. He argues that research cannot design a new product, but it can act as a catalyst and indicate the direction the innovation should take.

Innovation and Development uses two different research techniques to deal with new product innovations. Market researchers are commissioned through Innovation and Development's clients to run consumer discussion groups. During these sessions participants may be 'fooled' into thinking a product idea already exists by being presented with fake newspaper clippings describing it. In this way the researchers discover what consumers like and dislike about the idea.

Discussion groups are also used to prompt representative consumers to fantasise about new products. A skilled discussion leader is required in these situations as eliciting such responses from research consumer groups is an art. It is very easy for such discussion groups to fizzle with embarrassment and awkwardness rather than sizzle with ideas. With an experienced group leader and a productive session, the respondents give the product-development specialists clues about possible new product developments.

However, one of the biggest problems in using discussion group feedback is interpreting exactly what consumers mean. When Innovation and Development was working on new product development for Cadbury's chocolate cream liqueur, it included a hint of hazelnut flavouring to give the drink a unique flavour. When the researchers verbally suggested that the liqueur should have this slight flavouring, consumers reacted negatively as they were not used to the idea of mixing the two flavours. However, when taste tests were conducted, without revealing what the extra flavours were, consumers loved the chocolate liqueur laced with hazelnut.
Source: Marketing.[2]

Practicalities of focus group sessions

Seven to twelve participants is ideal. With fewer than seven, there is not enough interplay to provide worthwhile information. It is difficult to work with larger groups, for under such circumstances one or two people tend to dominate the conversation and the discussion is difficult to control.

The group of participants should have enough knowledge of and experience with the type of problem to produce meaningful ideas and reactions.

The participants must feel they are taking part in something that is both worthwhile and interesting, that they are contributing to the solution of the sponsor's problem. Payments to the respondents are perfectly in order and necessary to get a good representative group together.

THE MODERATOR

The role of the moderator in a focus session is to get the best and most innovative ideas about the focal problem from the group. The moderator must bring the session to a close with suggestions that will be of value to the sponsor in guiding further research or further thinking.

The moderator should have the following characteristics

- be acceptable to the group as a person with whom they can work easily
- have a quick mind capable of noting new ideas that come from the group and pressing for further discussion, even though it means leaving the fixed agenda
- have a good memory for names. Group dynamics will flourish if each participant can feel the importance of what they are saying and thinking. This is reinforced when participants are known by their names
- have the prestige and ability to control a group if it wanders, bringing it back to the topic under discussion without appearing to dominate unduly. The moderator must also be able to recognise the importance of new ideas that were not expected but appear significant
- be as neutral as possible

The moderator should be selected with the particular problem in mind. Selecting a moderator who has no interest in or knowledge of the subject would be pointless: they might easily miss some good ideas that arise unexpectedly from the group.

PREPARATION

Groups should be carefully screened to get the best people for the problem under discussion. The moderator and the sponsor should manage the choice of participants in the group. The most valuable thoughts and ideas arise when a group is fairly homogeneous. Usually, more than three groups discussing the same problem will add very little, though if there are known or suspected regional differences, for example, more than three may be necessary. It may often be advisable to form the different groups by age and sex.

Discussion guide for acceptability of a new product concept

1 Warm up

- explain focus groups
- no correct opinions – only opinions
- need to hear from everyone
- associates are watching from behind the mirror. They are very interested in the group's opinions
- audiotapes – so notes are not necessary
- one person to talk at a time. No side discussions or some important comments will be missed
- no questions to the moderator. What they know is unimportant
- participants not to worry if they don't know much about the topic. If there are different views in the group that is also important to know
- no one will contact participants after the session
- any questions

2 What comes to mind when this product concept is mentioned?

- likes and dislikes?
- problems?
- changes you would like to see?
- how do you feel about current brands available?
- what are your likes and dislikes about them?
- how would you change them?
- do you use more than one brand? What alternatives do you use? Why did you choose those particular brands?
- what factors are important in determining the brands you use?

3 Present a description of the new product concept. Ask how the group feels about it.

- how many of you would consider using this product?
- why do you say that? What do you like or dislike about it?
- do you see any distinct advantages in this product over the brands you are currently using?
- how would you expect this product to be priced?
- use of product, frequency of purchase, etc. need to be explored next: expand on this example.

4 Give them the opportunity for final questions and comments.

5 Thank them for their cooperation.

Preparation of the moderator's guide should be a joint effort of the sponsor, the agency (if one is involved) and the moderator. It should contain open, non-leading questions designed to stimulate thinking and discussion. Such questions might not be used verbally at all; rather, they may serve as a reminder to the moderator of matters the sponsor wants to be covered.

The moderator's guide should consider the types of participants in the group – their knowledge and experience. It should not show bias or reflect already formed opinions and should be developed with the counsel of those people who will have to implement the findings of the research study. All interested parties are responsible for making sure that everything pertinent is included in the guide, which should also contain suggestions on the timing of the session.

The client firm should ensure that the moderator understands the problem and the importance of the findings of each session. The moderator should be guided in preparation for the various directions in which the discussion may go. This does not mean that the moderator should prejudge how the discussion should or should not go. The moderator must know enough about the industry and the problem to recognise the unexpected and valuable points that may be aired.

Most professional research firms that offer focus group sessions will have a room dedicated for the purpose. The room will include one-way mirrors so that the client may watch and listen without being seen. It will contain chalkboards, a decent sized table, appropriate television and projection equipment, and pads and pencils for taking notes.

A useful aid to the moderator is the provision of name cards. Initially, there should be a brief discussion of the ground rules for the session. The moderator tells the group about its purpose, stating that the sponsoring firm looks forward to the group's discussion on this topic as an aid in deciding a crucial matter. The use of a one-way mirror should be explained to the participants. There may be a brief account of who the sponsoring firm is, what it does and why problems such as these make so much difference. Some mention should also be made of how the results of the session will be used. The participants then usually introduce themselves with a few brief remarks.

Conducting the session and reporting the findings

The moderator's guide should be used to steer participants into discussion of the areas the sponsor wants covered. It should not be necessary for the moderator to spend time merely asking questions and receiving answers. Participants should be encouraged to voice their thoughts without prodding. A well-chosen moderator will be experienced enough to draw out the quiet ones and to quiet the talkative. At the end of the discussion, the moderator should summarise the group's suggestions, ideas and attitudes.

THE INTERVIEW

It can be difficult to record informal interviews. Should the interviewer record everything that the respondents say, only those remarks that they consider relevant, or should the respondents' answers be paraphrased? The last two procedures introduce the danger of interviewer bias, so in most cases the verbatim report is probably the best solution.

Tape-recording is particularly useful in informal interviews as long as none of the respondents object. The use of tape-recorders permits the recording of everything that respondents say, thus enabling the interviewer to concentrate on the interview. On average it may take two to three times as long to transcribe tapes as it does to record the conversation. Thus an hour-long interview may take two to three hours to transcribe. In transcribing the tapes, everything that the interviewer and the respondents say has to be written down. However, when writing up transcriptions, views, attitudes and factual answers may be put into a logical order for the ease of the reader.

The debriefing and wrap-up should be carried out immediately after the session. Strong points can be emphasised and errors noted while they are fresh in everyone's minds. Debriefing and wrap-up can also come after the conclusion of a number of sessions on the same research problem. Here the emphasis will be on those ideas and attitudes that were common to all groups. There may be a written or video-screen report which should emphasise all the important attitudes and issues expressed by one or more of the groups. The report should also recommend further necessary research.

Formal written reports can take on one of several formats according to the client's needs, the researcher's style and what was formally agreed on in the research proposal. At one extreme, the investigator can prepare a brief impressionistic summary of the main findings, relying mainly on memory. This type of report is often used with experiencing groups, where the main objective is for the clients to experience real customers. The client can retain the tape-recordings of the sessions and listen to the groups several times to become immersed in what the customers are saying. At the other extreme, the researcher listens to the tapes, copying down salient quotations and fitting the participants' thoughts into a more general scheme derived from the research objectives and the researcher's training.

A method between the two extremes, and the most common, is often called the cut-and-paste technique. It lacks the in-depth psychological analysis of the clinical report, but still requires considerable skill and insight on the part of the researcher. The first step is to have the group sessions transcribed. Next, the researcher reviews the transcripts, looking for common threads or trends in response patterns. Similar patterns are then cut apart and matched between the groups. The researcher then produces folders containing relevant material by subject matter.

The last step is to write the actual report: the introduction describing the purpose of the research, the major questions the researcher sought to answer, the nature and characteristics of the group members and how they were recruited. This is followed by a two- or three-page summary of findings and recommendations. The report concludes with the main body of findings.

INDUSTRIAL FOCUS GROUPS

Focus groups that deal with industrial research problems are much like those covering consumer products, but with several important differences. First, the moderator must be knowledgeable in the field being discussed. Most moderators know about fast-moving consumer goods or shopping in supermarkets, but not all of them know enough about machine tools to conduct a discussion with a group of technicians and engineers. The screening of possible moderators in industrial areas must be even more thorough than for those in consumer-product areas.

Preparing the moderator and the moderator's guide about the industrial problem must also be very thorough. It may be advisable to have an in-house moderator lead the discussion, or at least to have one in the room to help the moderator with difficult technical points. The participants in industrial focus groups must also be carefully chosen to make sure that each can speak about the problem. Time considerations are important: a group of people will become impatient if a session runs overlength or becomes too wordy and repetitive.

OTHER QUALITATIVE RESEARCH METHODS

Depth interview

Historically, the term 'depth interview' has meant a relatively unstructured one-to-one interview. The interviewer is thoroughly trained in the skill of probing and eliciting detailed answers to each question. Sometimes psychologists are used in depth interviews. They use clinical non-directional techniques to uncover hidden motivations.

Some advantages of depth interviews relative to focus groups

1   Group pressure is eliminated so that each respondent reveals more honest feelings.

2   The personal one-to-one situation gives the respondent the feeling of being the focus of attention, whose personal thoughts and feelings are important and genuinely wanted.

3   The respondent attains a heightened state of awareness in a personal interview because they are in constant rapport with the interviewer and there are no group members to hide behind.

4   The extra time devoted to individual respondents encourages the revelation of new information.

5   Respondents can be probed at length to reveal the feelings and motivations that underlie their statements.

6   Without the restrictions of cultivating a group process, new directions of questioning can be improvised more easily. Individual interviews allow greater flexibility in exploring casual remarks and tangential issues, which may provide critical insights into the main issue.

7   The closeness of the one-to-one relationship allows the interviewer to become more sensitive to non-verbal feedback.

The direction of the depth interview is guided by the interviewee's response. As the interview progresses, the interviewer thoroughly probes each answer and uses the replies as a basis for further questioning.

The success of any depth interview depends entirely on the interviewer. A second factor that determines the success of depth research is correct interpretation. The unstructured nature of the interview and the clinical nature of the analysis increase its complexity.

Projective techniques

Projective techniques are sometimes incorporated in depth interviews. The origins of projective techniques lie in the field of clinical psychology. In essence, the objective of any projective test is to delve below the surface responses in order to obtain true feelings, meanings or motivations. The rationale behind projective tests comes from knowledge that people are often reluctant to or cannot reveal their deepest feelings. In other instances they are unaware of those feelings because of psychological defence mechanisms.

Projective tests are techniques for penetrating a person's defence mechanisms and allowing their true feelings and attitudes to emerge. A subject is usually presented with an unstructured, nebulous situation and asked to respond. Because the situation is ill-defined and has no true meaning, the respondent must use their own frame of reference to answer the question. In theory, the respondent projects their feelings into the unstructured stimulus. Because the subjects are not talking directly about themselves, defence mechanisms are purportedly bypassed. The interviewee is talking about something else or someone else, yet revealing their own inner feelings in the process.

The most commonly applied projective tests used in marketing research are word-association tests, sentence and story completion, cartoon tests, third-person techniques and analogies.

Word-association tests

Word-association tests are used to select brand names, advertising campaign themes and slogans (see Chapter 6 for an explanation of the test).

Sentence and story completion

These can be used in conjunction with word-association tests. The respondent is furnished with an incomplete story or group of sentences and asked to complete them (see Chapter 6 for more information).

Cartoon tests

Cartoon tests create a highly projective mechanism by means of cartoon figures or strips, similar to those in comic books. They can be used to measure the strength of an attitude toward a particular product or brand (see Chapter 6 – thematic apperception test – for more information).

Third-person techniques

Perhaps the easiest projective techniques to apply, other than word association, are third-person techniques. Rather than asking someone directly what they think, it is couched as 'your neighbour' or 'some people' or some other third party. Rather than asking a housewife why she does not typically provide a nutritionally balanced breakfast, a researcher would ask, 'Why don't many housewives provide their families with nutritionally balanced breakfasts?' The third-person technique is often used to avoid issues that might be embarrassing or evoke hostility if answered directly by a respondent.

Analogies

The use of analogies helps us to reveal people's inner feelings. For example, a person may buy a car to suit their personality. Through the purchase, the person is able to express their personality and thereby benefit. The use of the 'personal analogy' technique can sometimes enable researchers to uncover the relationship between people's personalities and potential purchase objects, such as a car.

We all have emotions and feelings. The personal analogy mechanism harnesses the use of our emotions and feelings in order to obtain insights into how people perceive decisions or problems. The idea is to identify ourselves with a non-human object which is the subject of the problem. We have to transfer our own feelings into the entity, imagine how it might feel and act in the problem situation.

For example, we might be asked to imagine what it would feel like to be a new BMW car. Answers might be:

- 'I feel powerful'
- 'I feel extremely fit and raring to go'
- 'I feel ready for my new executive owner'

Based on such an analysis it might then be possible to develop advertising themes to aim at specific customer groups. Through such a technique, we can release ourselves from looking at a problem in terms of its previously analysed elements.[3]

Electronic Interviewing

Electronic interviewing can involve both one-to-one interviews and focus groups, and offers practical advantages. In the first place it is not constrained by geographical locations or time zones, and electronic interviewing requires no additional transcription. Not only does this save money but it can also eliminate errors introduced through transcription. Secondly, electronic interviewing diminishes the problem of interviewer effect. It can also reduce problems caused by dominant or shy participants, particularly in electronic focus groups.

The skills required to conduct on-line discussions are different skills for both the interviewer and the subject since lack of verbal communication can be a problem. Often tacit information that would be conveyed in a conventional interview situation will be lost in electronic conversations. Non-verbal communication and active listening are essential elements of effective interviewing. No doubt, as technology progresses and videocam equipment becomes commonplace, even some non-verbal communication will be transportable.

SUMMARY

This chapter has examined the nature and uses of focus groups, showing how this method of data collection can obtain information that is largely unavailable through other types of marketing research. Advice has been offered about the possible misuse of focus groups, and details of the techniques used in moderating group discussions have been described. The distinction between focus groups used for consumer-product research and those used for industrial research has been made. Attention has also been drawn to a variety of other qualitative research techniques, notably those relying on projective methods. Finally consideration has been given to a new way of collecting qualitative data through the medium of electronic interviews.

Questions

1 Define qualitative research.

2 What are the main differences between qualitative and quantitative research?

3 Indicate the limitations of qualitative research.

4 What are focus groups? What is their purpose?

5 Outline the different types of focus groups.

6 Discuss the kind of problems where focus groups may be able to provide useful insights.

7 What is teleconferencing? How does it operate?

8 Discuss the role of the moderator in focus groups.

9 What preparations are necessary before a focus group session?

10 What is the moderator's guide? What does it contain and how is it used?

11 Indicate the important points that should be made when briefing a moderator.

12 What are the important points to bear in mind about industrial focus groups?

13 What are depth interviews and what are their purpose? What advantages and limitations do they have when compared with focus groups?

14 Explain the nature of projective techniques.

15 What are the advantages and disadvantages of electronic interviewing?

Case study 8.1   Avon cosmetics

Some important questions about consumers that need to be answered in the cosmetics industry include:

- Do women buy cosmetics to cover up or to enhance what nature has provided?
- Do women have different wants and needs as far as cosmetics are concerned?
- What kind of advertising gimmicks are likely to be most effective?
- Is there an element of fantasy in buying and using cosmetics?

Glamour appeal in the advertising of cosmetics products to women usually features the faces of attractive celebrities or good-looking young women. Nevertheless, the advertising agency handling Avon's account maintains this is not what women want to see. Avon's group marketing communications manager believes that 'real beauty' comes from the inside and the company is intent on reflecting this in their advertising strategy.

In an attempt to modernise its image, Avon is developing two important themes in its advertising. First, it wants to show that the products it has to offer are for 'real women' and, second, it wants to show that it appreciates the nature of female friendship. After all, many of Avon's 160,000 representatives make most of their sales to friends.

Avon's target audience is essentially women over 25 and under 50, positioned in the mid-market. Its main competitors are Boots and Body Shop. Avon's approach is novel: it challenges the traditionally accepted notions of women's attractiveness. The managing partner of the agency handling the account was quoted as saying that the advertisements spurned the way in which imagery was associated with cosmetic products and, in particular, 'the preying on women's feelings of inadequacy'. He argued that cosmetics were not about hiding inadequacies but rather about making the best of what women have.

In an attempt to bring female friendship and 'real women' into the advertising, one advertisement presents two friends talking about a new romance, along with the 'great for kissing' lipstick with moisturiser. In another advertisement an upset young mother, seeing her child off to school for the first time, is featured. In the latter advertisement a friend offers her a tear-proof mascara. Friendship and 'realness' are also emphasised in press advertisements, where genuine friends are featured talking about each other. The actresses used in sequences have the appearance of 'real women'.

Source: Ruth Nicholas.[4]

Question

What kind of qualitative research do you think might have been used in this instance?

Case study 8.2	IBM

'Butterfly was great technology, but very expensive to implement,' according to a Dell spokesman.

IBM's extensively praised Butterfly expandable notebook keyboard design seems ready to die shortly after emerging from its chrysalis and IBM have no plans to replace it. The product was considered an important advance in portable PC design when it appeared in IBM's Think Pad 701C in March 1995 since it offered a reasonable sized keyboard in a sub-A4 system. However, its high price is thought to have reduced anticipated sales and the appearance of larger screens than the 701C's 10.4 inch display have allowed notebook manufacturers to produce very slim A4 or slightly larger designs which allow more room for keyboard space.

Source: PC Direct.[5]

Question

Is marketing research really of any value to a firm such as IBM when it comes to designing new PCs?

Case study 8.3 | Muller

Muller, a successful German yoghurt brand, established a UK operation in 1987,[6] launching its two brands Muller Fruit Corner and Muller Crunch Corner into the UK market the following year. By 1990 the brand had captured more than 10 per cent of the UK yoghurt market, becoming market leader ahead of the previously dominant Ski brand from Eden Vale. In 1993 the brand was the clear market leader with a share of 23 per cent. Sales increased from around £75m in the UK in 1992, to over £100m in 1993.

An important tenet of Muller's success was its adoption of a marketing approach contrary to the style used by existing yoghurt brands in the UK. While many other yoghurt brands emphasised health issues such as low fat, live bacteria and real fruit, Muller brought new momentum to the market with a product that was high in calories and sold as an indulgence product. In 1993 Joanna Lumley was used in the £5m 'pure and sinful' campaign that was seen by industry commentators as a welcome break from the 'squeaky clean' yoghurt marketing campaigns of the past. Muller also sponsors Aston Villa football club.

The rest of the market soon followed Muller's lead: there have been recent launches of 'twin-pot' yoghurt by own-label suppliers and other brands, as well as an increase in yoghurts marketed as indulgence treats rather than as a means of abstaining from calories.

Source: A Samways and K Whittcome.[7]

Question

What kind of marketing research might have led Muller to adopt a strategy that was contrary to the style used by existing yoghurt brands in the UK?

Case study 8.4 | Brand valuation

The brand acts as a focus for all marketing activities; consumers identify with brands, and have a mental image of what the brand means not only in terms of its utilitarian values, but also in terms of intangible values such as prestige, value for money, or self-image. For example, research shows that in blind taste tests most people prefer Pepsi Cola to Coca-Cola, but when they are able to see the can or bottle (and hence identify the brand) most people prefer the Coke.

For many years, managers have recognised that such brands have a value which is independent of the physical product, and most firms have tried (for internal accounting purposes) to place a value on the 'goodwill' generated by the brand itself. Unfortunately, the accounting methods used have varied from one firm to another, which has led to problems when a firm wishes to sell a brand, or when the company is being valued for tax purposes or for shareholders' reports.

During 1999, a new accounting standard was introduced in the UK for the valuation of brands. For many years, standards have existed for the valuation of such intangibles as goodwill and patents, but until now no agreed method has been in place for measuring the value of a brand.

For many companies, this is a major breakthrough in asset valuation; it has been estimated that brands and intellectual property make up 96 per cent of the total value of the Coca-Cola Corporation, 95 per cent of the value of Microsoft, and even for heavy industrial corporations such as BP the figure may be as high as 74 per cent.

Shell Oil realise the importance of the brands. Simon Saville, global brand manager for Shell International, says 'For some years Shell has tracked the health of its brand through market research surveys in key countries. We are extending this to include a tracking of brand value on an annual basis. In order to estimate the Shell brand value, we must first understand how that value is derived: why customers buy our products and services, what they prefer about Shell, and how important this is to them in their purchase decisions.'

Brand value is an important part of franchising and licensing negotiations, and most firms recognise that they are managing an asset which has value. Investment in promoting the brand will increase its value, and having an accounting standard for valuing brands means that marketing managers are better able to argue their case for more investment in the brand, even with the most traditional of finance managers.

For finance managers, the main purpose of brand valuation is to establish a more accurate balance sheet; brands as assets can be included, and the finance managers know that other firms are using the same valuation methods. From a marketing management viewpoint, the main purpose of brand valuation is to see the trend over time, rather than to establish an absolute valuation figure. This allows the manager to control what is happening to the brand, perhaps by increasing investment in it or (if the brand's value is low) reducing investment. In the absence of agreed methods for valuing, firms have been operating with a degree of uncertainty, according to many managers.

On the other hand, Alex Batchelor (brand valuation director of consultants Interbrand Newell & Sorrell) says, 'Brand valuation is very much like business valuation with a couple of tweaks. Sure, there are judgements in it but there are judgements in everything. The accounting profession has done a wool-pulling act where people think it's a perfect science when it is not.'

The new accounting standard draws a distinction between intangible assets which have a limited life (for example most patents) and those which have an indefinite life (which would be true of many brands). The standard defines limited life as being less than twenty years. In practice, market research has a major role to play in the valuation of brands, because the consumer's view of the brand will determine not only whether the brand will be purchased during the next few years, but whether the brand is robust enough to survive in the very long term.

Whichever methods marketers use to determine the brand value, it seems that the new accounting standard will not only add more rigour to the estimates, but will also help to focus the minds of managers more keenly on brand management issues.

(Case contributed by Jim Blythe.)

Questions

1 How might qualitative research be used to value brands?
2 What methods could be used to determine the most effective routes for investing in brands?
3 What differences in research approach would be needed to meet the differing needs of brand managers and finance managers?
4 How might the robustness of a brand be measured?
5 How might the objectiveness and accuracy of qualitative research into brand valuation be ensured?

Case study 8.5 | # Hi-fi systems

Marketers often seem to be inordinately fond of the word 'new'. Newness appears to be a desirable feature of products, yet the word is difficult to define – is it about freshness, or about novelty? Does it refer to something that the particular manufacturer has not made before, does it refer to something that has been brought in from another industry, or does it refer to something that the consumer has never seen before? These questions are of crucial importance to high-tech industries such as consumer electronics and photography.

Hi-fi purchase involves a substantial investment on the part of the customer. Apart from the obvious monetary cost of buying a top-of-the-range system (which is counted in thousands of pounds rather than hundreds) hi-fi buffs (or audiophiles) are often highly involved in the product purchase. This means that their choice of hi-fi system reflects on them as individuals; they naturally want to be seen with the latest, most technically advanced system as well as own a system that sounds good and lasts.

It appears that the audiophiles' perception of 'newness' of the equipment is a factor, and research was conducted by a UK university to find out how consumers judge newness in hi-fi equipment. Several focus groups were invited to examine three hi-fi systems and comment on which was the most innovative, and why. The groups were allowed to examine the equipment, play CDs on it, and (of course) discuss what they thought about the equipment. The focus groups were recorded on video tape, and full transcripts of everything that was said were made; a separate analysis was carried out on the movement and body language of the focus group members, and the ways they used the equipment.

The following is a brief extract from the transcripts of one of the focus groups; this group was composed entirely of males aged 20 to 25.

Which is the most innovative?

Hard to tell unless, you know, unless you study the brochures.

You'd go for the looks.

But it isn't only looks is it?

But it's innovative design, but like you said earlier, that's been around. You've seen that for absolutely years.

Saying that, that's a new colour, whether it'll take off...

The thing is we're not going to find out which is the most innovative unless we read the manuals.

But then I don't understand the jargon they use anyway.

But this one's got this tape thing. I like the tape-to-tape thing.

This one's innovative with the size; they're making them even smaller than that nowadays.

Compared to this one, yeah.

But then you could add to it.

Well, I think I can solve the problem.

This one's more innovative because of the size and because it's more compact and that.

They're making them even smaller than that nowadays.

I'm not too sure about these small buttons.

I don't like the small buttons.

The thing is you can't have a small system with really big buttons.

But this has gone too far the other way; with these they're almost pin size.

But with a remote control you just sort of sit there and press that.

But half the time I don't understand the remote control either.

I reckon this one's more innovative, then.

Yeah, but are you going on looks alone?

Yeah, it is swaying me a bit but no. Like the fact that it's more compact and everything, you're going into smaller things now, all your microchips and everything.

That's all we can say really because we don't know about the sound and that.

But if I went into a shop and they, um...

That one's more fuddy-duddy, this one's more modern and probably people see that as being more innovative.

There's a record player option on it.

If you go into a shop and they have stacks of stuff there you'd just like listen, I wouldn't know, I wouldn't have a clue which would be the best sound for me really. And the ones that sounded best to me might not be the ones that have the bass and everything on.

I don't like it not being adjustable.

I'd go for this one, I'd go for the adjustable one.

This one looks like the one I've got, five, six or seven years old.

That's quite an old one, isn't it.

Whereas this, this one uses computer interfacing which is quite different.

That's right, yes.

So this one must be more innovative, if it's using digital impulses.

Yeah, very right.

Why, what's the point?

Is it just to cut down...

Yeah, that is more innovative.

There are design functions that I like. I like the drawer, I think that's brill, but some of the gimmicks to me are useless, like this search and find a tape thing. I wouldn't use that at all.

It's got a lot of plusses. A lot of it's gimmicks, you've got your sliding out drawer thing which is nice, you've got your buttons which I tend to like, the big ones and your laser display.

Which is the most innovative?

The Denon definitely.

It's the looks.

Which do you think is the most innovative?

Why is it the most innovative?

It's the colour, its image, these sort of little touch controls...

This is new.

I agree with what you're saying.

These little touch controls.

Is it really functional, your tape coming out like that, it's quicker just to push a button.

This drawer sliding out and that...

It must be a real bummer if your tape gets chewed, I mean how do you manage with head cleaning and that? You sort of take it along to the bloke and say stick your head-cleaning tape in?

I would have thought that came out easily.

This is practical and in a way it hides all its innovations, whereas that one shouts at you this is new, this is Gary Glitter music!

This one doesn't appear to have anything, your stop, your play, your forward. It's programmable, it repeats your scan, it's all standard, maybe it's all inside, whereas that one shouts out what it's got but it doesn't particularly explain why.

There's a thing on – what's that programme called where they test all the cars? Top Gear – saying a sports car could be like a cappuccino, looks great but doesn't taste so good, but that sort of tastes good but doesn't look so good.

At the end of the day I'd still stick with that.

But this one's more innovative, just on presentation.

(Case contributed by Jim Blythe.)

Questions

1 Using the data above, extract the key issues in judging innovativeness.
2 Build a causal model for the judgement of innovativeness.
3 What other information would be helpful in analysing this data?
4 What other analysis could be undertaken?
5 How might the data be re-ordered to make analysis easier?
6 What computer software would be available for analysing this type of data?

Further reading

Albrecht, T L, Johnson, G M and Walther, J B (1993) Understanding communication processes in focus groups, in Morgan, D L (ed), *Successful Focus Groups: Advancing the State of the Art*, Newbury Park, C A: Sage, pp 51–63.

Bhaduri, M, de Souza, M and Sweeney, T (1993) International qualitative research: a critical review of different approaches, *Marketing and Research Today*, 21(3), pp 171–8.

Blum, A G and Law, K (1984) Making focus groups even more effective, *Agri Marketing*, March, p 24 ff.

Byers, P Y and Wilcox, J R (1991) Focus groups: a qualitative opportunity for researchers, *Journal of Business Communication*, 28(1), pp 63–78.

Cahill, D (1998) When to use qualitative marketing research: how about at the midpoint?, *Marketing News*, 32(1), 5 January, pp 15, 17.

Clark, L G (1986) Focus groups are a phone call away, *Marketing News*, 3 January.

Collins, L F (1991) Everything is true, but in a different sense: a new perspective on qualitative research, *Journal of the Market Research Society*, 33, pp 31–8.

Colwell, J (1990) Qualitative market research: a conceptual analysis and review of practitioner criteria, *Journal of the Market Research Society*, 32.

Day E (1998) Know consumers through qualitative research, *Marketing News*, 32(1), 5 January, p 14.

Gabriel, C (1990) The validity of qualitative market research, *Journal of the Market Research Society*, 32, pp 507–20.

Greenbaum, T L (1984) Keys to improving the effectiveness of focus group research, *Marketing Review*, June–July, 23.

Greenbaum, T L (1988) *The Practical Handbook and Guide to Focus Group Research*, Lexington, MA: Heath.

Hammond, M (1986) Creative focus groups: uses and misuses, *Marketing and Media Decisions*, July, pp 154–6.

Kaushik, M and Sen, A (1990) Semiotics and qualitative research, *Journal of the Market Research Society*, 32, pp 227–43.

Mathews, A (1997) Academic xenophobia and the analysis of focus group data, *Journal of Targeting, Measurement and Analysis for Marketing*, 6(2), pp 160–71.

Mazzella, G F (1997) Show and tell focus groups reveal core boomer values, *Marketing News*, 3(12), 9 June, H8.

McDonald,W (1993) Focus groups research dynamics, *Journal of the Academy of Marketing Science*, 21(2), pp 161–8.

Murray, P J (1997) Using virtual focus groups in qualitative research, *Qualitative Health Research*, 7(4), pp 542–9.

Schindler, R M (1992) The real lesson of new Coke: the value of focus groups for predicting the effects of social influence, *Marketing Research: A Magazine of Management and Applications*, December, pp 22–7.

Strauss, A and Corbin, J (1990) *Basics of Qualitative Research*, London: Sage.

Sykes, W (1990) Validity and reliability in qualitative marketing research: a review of the literature, *Journal of the Market Research Society*, 33, pp 3–12.

The Teleconference Network (1990) Orangeburg, NY: The Market Navigator.

Tillet, L S (2000) A 24-hour focus group – sites dig into search queries to learn consumer preferences, *Internet Week*, 808, 10 April, p 170.

References and notes

[1] Smith, A (1997a) Baby boomers get the message, *Financial Times*, 26 May.

[2] Research propels innovation, *Marketing, 27* January 1994, pp 33–5.

[3] Proctor, T (1992) *Essential Marketing*, London: Collins Educational.

[4] Nicholas, R (1994) Avon ads praise the real woman, *Marketing*, 27 January, p 6.

[5] IBM's Butterfly gets crushed on the wheel *PC Direct*, May 1996, p 57.

[6] Wheatley, K and Flexmer, W A (1987) Option Technologies, Inc, *Marketing News*, 27 February, p 23.

[7] Samways, A and Whittcome, K (1994) UK brand strategies, *A Financial Times Management Report*.

9 Observations and experiments

OBJECTIVES

After reading this chapter you should be able to:

- understand the role played by observational techniques in marketing research;

- appreciate how experimentation can be applied in marketing;

- understand the function and limitation of different experimental designs;

- understand the different kinds of approaches that can be taken to test-marketing.

KEY WORDS

pupilometer	basic designs
psychogalvanator	statistical designs
scanning	Latin square
experimental designs	randomised design
validity	factorial design
reliability	test-marketing
maturation	controlled test-marketing
mortality	simulated test-marketing
regression effects	consumer-tracking studies

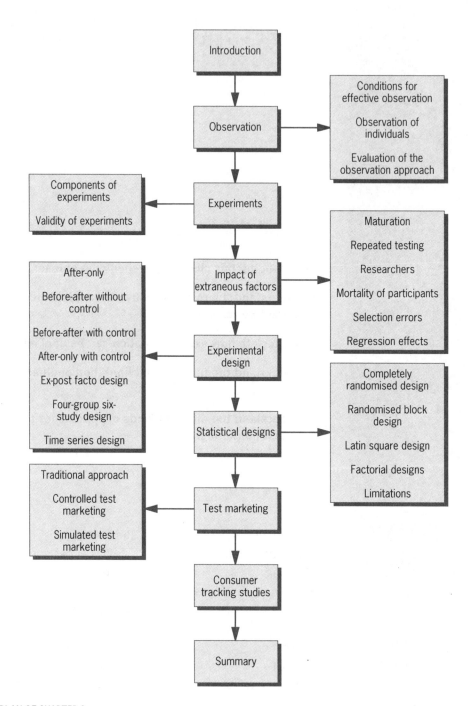

PLAN OF CHAPTER 9

INTRODUCTION

This chapter examines a variety of observational methods including those using mechanical means and scanning. It then looks at experimentation as a research method. Different types of experimental design are examined, together with a variety of approaches to test-marketing.

OBSERVATION

One drawback of the survey method is that much of the information obtained is based on interviewees statements describing what they have done or expect to do in the future. With respect to past actions, the interviewees can make mistakes in trying to recall what has happened, particularly when some time has elapsed since the event. The same kind of problem also applies to their intended actions, since these may also differ markedly from what actually happens. This is a common occurrence when people are asked about their purchase intentions for such items as cars, homes or major appliances. Many intended purchases never actually take place for a variety of reasons. The observation method does not suffer from these shortcomings since it records events as they actually happen.

Observation involves the personal or mechanical monitoring of selected activities. It records actions as they occur and thus there is no lack of accuracy caused by a respondent's faulty recollection of their past actions or inadequate estimate of future ones.

Shoppers under the microscope

The scene is a US convenience store: 'cappuccino devotees' stride confidently towards the coffee dispenser, while 'clandestine consumers' consider a range of snacks after choosing their main purchase, and 'explicit treaters' wander in search of something to satisfy a vague desire before selecting the familiar comfort of a chocolate bar.

Clearly, researchers wanting to understand more about consumer habits would learn little about these shoppers merely by analysing how often people visited the store. But by using a technique called observational research – watching how different types of people use goods and services – a fuller picture can be obtained.

By watching what happened in the convenience store, E-Lab, a Chicago-based research consultancy, was able to advise PepsiCo, the international food and soft drinks group, on where and how to position its products in order to get higher sales.

Observing how people behave in different surroundings or how they handle pieces of equipment is valuable in helping a company meet a specified aim, such as entering a new market, and in developing products to meet future needs that consumers have not yet recognised.

Observational research ranges from the distant to the intimate. For some projects, studying footage of people browsing in a shopping mall or negotiating their way through an airport can be appropriate. For others, researchers spend time with subjects as they use the product at home or work.

'It's a matter of trying to get under the skin of real people,' says Tim Brown, European director of Ideo, a product development company. For example, watching a travel agent set up a conference call by arranging a speaker phone for each person and putting the handsets together demonstrated how she equated one phone with one person – an insight Ideo used in its advice on phone software to AT&T, the US telecoms operator. Finding the right people to watch is critical for techniques that involve observation of a few individuals or households. In contrast to conventional market research, where consumers are chosen because they fit squarely in the middle of particular categories, consumers picked for shadowing are intended, as Mr Brown says, to 'hit the edges'.

This might involve selecting people who are 'early adapters' to new technology, and those most resistant to it; or people using the product in an unusual environment.

In the UK the process can still be informal, while in the US selection is itself a business. 'We use an outside agency – which mainly handles focus groups – to screen and recruit participants,' says Liz Sanders, head of research at Fitch, the design consultancy, in Ohio. One factor driving the growth of observational research is technology. Advances in photography and video recording make it easier to obtain and analyse the observations, increasing the research's value. Secondly, technology is itself an area where consumers may not be well-placed to articulate needs that could be met by a new generation of computers, telephones or other machines.

Fitch used observational research when it was advising Compaq, the computer company, on the design of the Presario personal computer. 'By working with consumers in their homes, we came to the realisation that a computer should be more friendly for home use,' says John Fillingham, director of policy research at Fitch in the UK. 'For example, the Presario's features include a compact disc rack and a great pair of speakers – it looks more like a consumer product.'

He adds, however, that while observation shows researchers what people do, it does not tell them why. 'A combination of observation and what consumers say about what they do gives you an ability to cross-check.'

Dorothy Leonard, writing in the current issue of the *Harvard Business Review*, identifies five types of information available from observation. Apart from needs that consumers have not yet articulated, they are: the triggers that prompt people to use a product or service; how the product relates to the consumer's environment; how consumers customise the product (and so how manufacturers can make those modifications for them); and the intangible qualities consumers value in the product.

Some consultants believe observational techniques can contribute even in the area of brand identity, provided the observations are evaluated properly. This goes well beyond whether packaging is convenient to open or whether a software program is easy to use.

'Every kind of behaviour has a particular framework and theory,' says Rick Robinson of E-Lab. 'It's a matter of finding the meaningful pattern.' Steelcase, the US office furniture company, wanted to shift from being rooted in manufacturing excellence to being based on understanding work processes. Observational research helped it develop the new identity, and design its showrooms to encourage customers to buy on the basis of that understanding.

Observing how people behave is valuable in helping a company meet a specified aim.

Source: Alison Smith.[1] Reprinted with permission.

Conditions required for effective observation

Three conditions usually exist if the observation method is to be effectively carried out:

1 The event must be observable: attitudes, motives and other mental activities are difficult to record with the observation method.
2 The event must occur frequently or be predictable.
3 The event must be completed over a short period of time.

One way in which we can ensure that all three of these conditions are met is to set up an experiment in which all the conditions can be controlled and manipulated. The laboratory environment is often the best setting for observational studies.

Observation is used in shopping studies, especially in stores, when the customer is looking at the shelves and deciding what to buy. It is used to find out how things are done in practice.[2]

Types of observation procedure

- normal versus controlled conditions
- structured versus unstructured observation
- use of mechanical devices to aid observation
- measuring response latency – indicator of certainty of preference

Types of observation procedures

Activities really need to be observed under normal conditions. However, as some activities are not easily observed under normal conditions it is often necessary for the observation to take place in a controlled environment – for example, inviting people into a specially equipped room in order to observe the manner in which they use a product.

When people are aware they are being observed it is argued that they behave in different ways to how they would under normal circumstances where they are not being observed. In some cases this awareness will have little effect on their actions. However, there are many situations in which people change their activities if they know they are being watched. Salespeople in a clothing store may be especially polite to customers if they know their performance is being monitored.

There is also the choice between a structured and an unstructured observation. In a structured situation, the observers are told how and what to observe. Usually a checklist is given to them to record what happens. Structured methods are used where a hypothesis is tested. In an unstructured observation, which is most useful in research of an exploratory nature, the observer is given much latitude with respect to what to note.

A variety of mechanical devices are used to observe people's actions or responses. For example, a psychogalvanator measures a person's emotional reactions to various stimuli by measuring changes in a person's perspiration rate. It is used to assess people's reactions to different advertisements. The pupilometer measures changes in the size of a person's pupils as they are looking at an advertisement, package or product design. A change in pupil size reflects the person's interest in the object. Eye cameras can monitor a person's eye movements while reading, identifying the parts the reader perceived first, the parts dwelt on and the amount of copy actually read.

One fairly simple observation method is called response latency. It measures the amount of time a respondent takes to answer a question. Quick answers indicate certainty of preference. This observation technique is especially useful in telephone interviews, since latency can be measured with voice-stimulated stopwatches.

Electronic scanning

Electronic scanning is an observation method that is rapidly developing in popularity. Scanners were intended to improve productivity in retail shops, but they have also become valuable tools for researchers. Many retail stores will even sell research firms the data obtained from their own scanning records. There are, however, some limitations in scanner data. For example, not all sales data provided by the scanners are accurate. Three conditions must exist for real accuracy: each item must be precoded correctly by the manufacturer, the code must be correctly entered into the retailer's system, and every item must be scanned at the checkout counter.

Scanners are universal in large supermarkets and provide the store and its central office with an immediate record of sales by product (units and value). Data from scanners at checkout counters can be used to assess the impact that a price cut, coupon blitz or store display has on sales and profits. A scanner analysis system allows managers to determine almost instantly how well a promotion is working and what effect price changes, amount of inventory and arrangement on shelves will have on sales. Scanner data can be linked with demographics of areas to guide consumers on what to buy. Foods on supermarket shelves can be tied more closely to the demographics of the particular area. Thus inventory can be matched to local needs, and turnover rate can be increased.

Auditing is a method of measuring the amount of movement of merchandise, by category and brand, through a retail outlet. It requires someone to check the amount of goods on hand (both on-shelf and in store) at the start of a sales period, the addition to stock during the period (from checking receipts for goods delivered to the store), and the amount of goods on hand again at the end of the sales period.

Observation of the in-store environment

Observations include:

- distribution (and out-of-stock)
- shelf price
- shelf facings (reported in number and share)
- shelf location
- display activity
- presence of point-of-purchase material.

Results, depending on user needs, can be shown by category, brand and types/sizes. These are reported by total, by individual markets, and by major chains. Breaks by sales regions and other special analyses can be provided on order.

Mystery shoppers

Retailers send out employees to shop at competitors' stores. The purpose is to observe fixture layouts, merchandise displays, store traffic and special promotions. Some organisations even send out specially trained staff to pose as customers. In the latter case the interest is in the quality of the customer service. A mystery shopper not only observes a shopping environment but also how employees react and behave based upon the shopper's actions. It could involve visiting a bank and reporting that one had left at home (many miles away) one's wallet and cheque book and requesting emergency cash. Some large retail organisations employ many part-time mystery shoppers.

Observation of individuals

There are many applications of personal observation techniques. Hand counters were employed for many years in making counts of pedestrians in and around shopping centres. Personal observation is used in most surveys: the interviewer, for example, records observations about gender, age and apparent socioeconomic status. Another personal observation method which has become fashionable is called the 'anthropological' approach.[3] It is almost totally subjective and amounts to an almost live-in approach within a few households or shopping places. It is used to arrive at generalisations about living styles relevant to the specific product.

Personal observation at work

A well-known car producer 'discreetly' observed car shoppers as they inspected cars in showrooms. Observations included how shoppers were dressed, whether they appeared confident or timid, whether they kicked the tyres and what questions they asked.

Evaluation of the observation approach

Observation within both households and stores typically requires the setting up of a panel, making it subject to sampling difficulties and problems with maintaining participation. Another problem is the quality of the data obtained. There may be serious questions about the quality and completeness of store scanner data. Large items may not readily scan and may be incompletely or inaccurately entered by hand; some brands with multiple forms are similarly labelled; and so on.

EXPERIMENTS

In experiments the researcher manipulates selected independent variables and measures the effect of these manipulations on the dependent variables. In the survey and observation methods, the information is usually obtained under normal or near normal conditions and the researcher intervenes only to gather data, not to alter the environment. Causality means that a relationship exists between two or more events. The first event can be seen as a cause of the second if the occurrence of the first increases the likelihood of the occurrence of the second. The objective is to provide evidence that suggests a high probability of one event leading to another. It does not have to be demonstrated conclusively.

Three types of evidence are used to demonstrate the existence of a causal relationship:

1 Concomitant variation, which reflects the extent to which a cause (x) and effect (y) occur together or vary together in some predictable way.
2 Time order of occurrence of the causal factor (x), which must either precede or take place simultaneously with the effect (y). This is a logical requirement for a causal relationship, but there are situations where things become confusing because the two factors seem to affect one another.
3 Absence of other causal factors, which is the most difficult type of evidence to demonstrate. It states that no other factors could have caused a similar change in the dependent variable (y). This demands extensive testing to eliminate all

Figure 9.1 Experiments should have three components

other possible explanations for the change in x. It accounts for the importance of selecting an appropriate experimental design.

As well as the three types of evidence indicated above, if a causal relationship is to be useful to management the relationship should be operative in a variety of environments. It should also be a relationship that is stable enough so that it makes future actions by executives worthwhile.

Components of experiments

Experiments should have three components (Figure 9.1):

1 The variable being acted upon – variously called the test unit, the dependent variable or the subject.
2 The change being imposed – the treatment or the independent variable.
3 The results related to the change – the effect, outcome or observation.

Validity of experiments

Experiments should have both internal and external validity. Internal validity refers to whether the experiment treatment is solely accountable for the changes occurring or whether some extraneous factors were also at work. If there were outside factors as well, then internal validity is affected by the ability to measure their impact. External validity is to do with whether the findings can be applied to the real-world situation. Experiments can be conducted either in the field or under controlled laboratory conditions. In the former case the establishment of internal validity can be quite difficult. Laboratory experiments, by contrast, may lack external validity because of their controlled environment.

Validity of experiments

It is customary for tests or experiments involving new products to be carried out under laboratory conditions. Unfortunately, because in actual usage the operating conditions for the products may be very different to those in the laboratory, the external validity of such tests and experiments is difficult to assess.

IMPACT OF EXTRANEOUS FACTORS

Two considerations affect an experiment's internal validity:

1 The influence the treatment had on the actual outcome.
2 The influence of extraneous factors.

Extraneous factors can take a number of forms (Figure 9.2).

History and maturation

The changes associated with the passage of time are described as history and maturation. The influence of history is typified by changes in current events external to the experiment but that still may have affected its outcomes. The impact of history becomes greater as the length of the experiments increases. Maturation is primarily concerned with changes occurring within the individual subjects.

Repeated testing

This applies in experiments where the same people are tested a number of times. As they become familiar with the testing procedure, their performances may change solely because of this familiarity.

Figure 9.2 Extraneous factors influencing validity

Impact of the researchers themselves

The researchers themselves may cause some of the change. Their very presence may influence the actions of the subjects being observed.

The mortality of participants

A problem with experiments carried out over a long period is that some of the original participants may drop out. The problem is often encountered with consumer panels. There is no way of knowing whether the test units lost would have responded similarly to the treatment as those units that remained.

Selection errors

The test units may be chosen in a manner that biases the results. They may not be representative of the desired population or the treatments are assigned to them in such a way that they influence the outcome.

Regression effects

This occurs when test units are chosen on the basis of their extreme score or performance on some earlier test. The outliers, especially those with very low performance, tend to move to a more average position over time.

All these factors represent causes for error in the experiments. Many of them can be controlled if the appropriate experimental design is used. Experiments should be designed primarily to control those extraneous factors most likely to seriously influence the outcome and not try to eliminate all sources of error.

EXPERIMENTAL DESIGNS

These are blueprints for the experiments. They define both the pattern for applying the treatment to the test units and how to measure the treatment's impact. Experimental designs fall into two broad categories:

1 Basic (informal) designs
2 Statistical (formal) designs.

The main difference between these two categories is that basic designs concentrate on measuring only the impact of the treatment, whereas statistical designs also measure the impact of other factors in addition to the treatment.

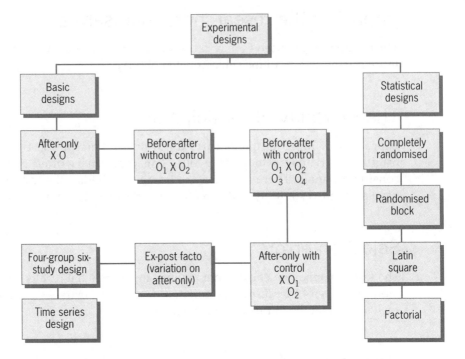

Figure 9.3 Types of experimental design

There are a number of basic experimental designs that attempt to measure the effect of the treatment (Figure 9.3). The methods differ in terms of the approaches they employ to isolate the treatment's impact. Some of the more popular designs are now described (see Cochran and Cox[4] for more designs).

The following symbols are used to help in presenting these designs:

X = the period in which the treatment is applied
O = the observation periods before and/or after the treatment. Subscripts are used to identify the time of each observation
EG = the experimental group: the subjects receiving the treatment
OG = control group: the subjects matched up with the experimental group, but not receiving the treatment

After-only design

This is used by researchers who are not overly concerned about the strength of their findings or internal/external validity. Symbolically the design appears as:

$$X \qquad O$$

A single group of subjects is exposed to a treatment, and the subjects' responses are recorded once. The subjects are usually selected in a subjective (non-random) manner.

After-only design

Special pence-off coupons for a shampoo are hand-distributed to women in a shopping mall. The number of these coupons turned in is recorded and a judgement is made of the success of the coupon promotion.

With this form of design, no data exists that can be used to assess the influence of extraneous factors during the period. There is also no evidence about the subject's behaviour before the treatment. The design is simple to use, but its results are not very enlightening. There is no indication, for example, of how the treatment may have changed customer behaviour.

Before-after without control

This involves measuring the test unit before and after treatment.

$$O_1 \: X \: O_2$$

An example here would be the collecting of sales data for a period of time before the application of, say, a special sales promotion. Let us say that average sales were £450 per day. During the next two weeks a special sales promotion was offered and average daily sales rose to £510 per day.

$$O_1 = £450$$

$$O_2 = £510$$

$$O_2 - O_1 = \text{effect of the treatment}$$

$$£510 - £450 = £60 \text{ per day}$$

It appears that the inclusion of the special sales promotion had a positive effect: daily sales increased by £60. This assumes that any changes in the units sold were caused solely by the introduction of the special promotional offer. Realistically, at least part of the difference could have been caused by such extraneous factors as the unavailability of the main competitor's product during the two weeks in question.

Before-after with control

A control group is selected and observed over the entire testing period. This control group is comparable in make-up to the group who will receive the treatment. The major assumption in the design is that both groups are affected in a similar manner by extraneous factors. For this assumption to be correct, the subjects must be randomly selected and the treatments randomly assigned.
The statement of the design is:

$$\text{EG:} \quad O_1 \quad X \quad O_2$$

$$\text{OG:} \quad O_3 \qquad\quad O_4$$

$$\text{Effect of treatment} = (O_2 - O_1) - (O_4 - O_3)$$

A regional bookstore chain wants to determine the effect of new display shelves on the sale of children's books. The shelving is temporarily installed in three of their stores (test stores) and sales are compared with those in three comparable stores in which the old shelving is retained. The following sales occurred in the two sets of stores.

$$O_1 = 290 \text{ books} \qquad O_2 = 350 \text{ books}$$

$$O_3 = 285 \text{ books} \qquad O_4 = 320 \text{ books}$$

$$\text{Effect of treatment} = (350 - 290) - (320 - 285)$$

$$= 60 - 35$$

$$= 25 \text{ books}$$

The assumption is that the sales increase in the control stores (35 books) was caused by some extraneous factors. Thus, if this impact is to be subtracted from the change in sales in the test stores (60 books) the resulting value of 25 books can be viewed as the direct impact of the treatment (the new shelving).

After-only with control

This experimental design is the one most commonly used by marketing researchers. It is intended to eliminate the influence of pretesting, so no measurements are taken between either of the groups.

$$\text{EG:} \qquad X \qquad O_1$$

$$O_2$$

A firm wanted to test the success of free gifts as a method of stimulating sales for its detergent product. It posted free sampler packages of its detergent to randomly selected homes in a neighbourhood. A month later it sent coupons offering 25 pence off the purchase of a large package of its detergent to the same group of homes. These coupons were also sent to a control group randomly selected from a comparable neighbourhood but which had not received the free sample. The coupons were coded to enable a count to be made of the number of coupons redeemed by each group. The experimental group redeemed 121 coupons and the control group redeemed 76 coupons. The difference (45 coupons) was felt to be the result of the sampler.

$$\text{Effect of treatment} = O_1 - O_2$$

$$45 = 121 - 76$$

While this design neutralises the impact of pretest, it does not allow any measurement or analysis to be made of the total change that occurred, a situation handled well in the before-after with control design.

Ex-post facto design

This is a variation on the after-only design. The difference between the two is that in ex-post facto design, neither the experimental nor the control groups are chosen until after the treatment is actually applied. This design attempts to create equivalent experimental and control groups but identifies each only after they have been exposed to the experiment.

A group of people who read a certain issue of a particular magazine are contacted. Those who said they read a certain advertisement in the issue are the experimental group; those who did not read the advertisement are the control group. Both are asked about some attribute of different types of the product featured in the advertisement, and the difference in the two groups' ratings of the products determines the advertisement's success. The advantage of this design over the after-only study with control design is that the experimental variable will have exerted its influence in a natural setting, enabling the researcher to study a group which by choice was exposed to the treatment, rather than having been selected to receive the treatment.

Four-group six-study design

This design, also called the Soloman four-group design, is the most sophisticated basic design. It is intended to isolate the effects of various internal validity measures as well as the impact of pretesting. Two experimental and two control groups are randomly selected. The following outline shows how the design operates:

$$EG_1: O_1 \qquad X \qquad O_2$$
$$OG_1: O_3 \qquad\qquad O_4$$
$$EG_2: \qquad X \qquad O_5$$
$$OG_2: \qquad\qquad O_6$$

$$\text{Treatment effect} = [O_5 - 1/2(O_1 - O_3)] - [O_6 - 1/2(O_1 - O_3)]$$

Although it is considered the ideal basic design, it is not very often used by researchers because of its expense and the time it requires.

Time series design

This design uses a series of pre- and post-measurements to determine the impact of the experiment. It attempts to measure the impact over a longer period of time than other basic methods.

The time series design appears as follows:

$$O_1 \ O_2 \ O_3 \ O_4 \ X \ O_5 \ O_6 \ O_7 \ O_8$$

It assumes that the researcher will have continual access to the same test units. Consumer panels are prime examples of the application of this type of experimental design. Figure 9.4 shows some possible outcomes from experiments using a time series design.

Outcome 1: a short-lived positive effect
Outcome 2: a long-term positive effect – market share increased

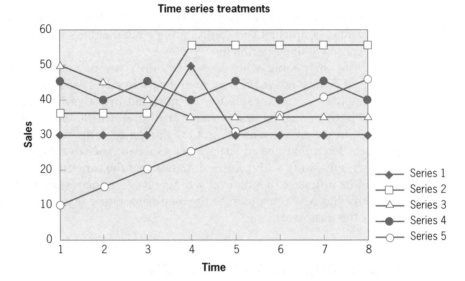

Figure 9.4 Time series analysis

Outcome 3: a positive effect – it halted a decline in sales
Outcome 4: seems to have no effect – fluctuation continues in the same manner
Outcome 5: seems to have no effect – growth continues in the same pattern

Because measurements are made over a longer period of time, such extraneous factors as testing, maturation and regression tend to be neutralised. However, there is always the danger that some other event may have occurred at the same time the experiment took place and this external event could be the real cause of any changes in the observation. The problem of mortality – drop out – also increases as the length of the time series increases.

STATISTICAL DESIGNS

These designs provide a framework for statistically testing the impact not only of the treatment but also of other factors. In the case of statistical designs the researcher randomly assigns treatments to randomly chosen test units and the treatments are then systematically applied. The statistical analysis tool often used with these designs is analysis of variance. This can help to determine whether one factor (the treatment) significantly affects another factor, or whether the observed changes are caused by some other factors or even by chance.

Completely randomised design

In this section we examine statistical designs that are often used with experiments. The design is described, together with the kind of information it can provide.

Table 9.1 Antifreeze sales through motorist DIY outlets

Week	Price £3.89	Price £4.85	Price £5.89
1	19	9	15
2	16	13	20
3	22	20	9
4	24	18	12
Total	81	60	56

Treatments are assigned to test units on a random basis and an analysis is then performed to determine whether the treatments caused a significant difference in the test units. The design can only really measure one type of variance – that occurring between treatments, known as the 'treatment effect'.

Example

A motorist DIY chain is selling antifreeze in all of its outlets, but it does not know the most effective price to charge. It tests three different prices per can – £3.89, £4.85, and £5.89 – and records the sales from each. It randomly assigns these prices to nine experimental stores, three using each price.

The analysis would examine the average amount of the product sold at each price. It could disclose whether the difference in sales at the lower price was a significant one or whether it was caused by chance (Table 9.1).

It fails, however, to take into consideration the influence of such extraneous factors as weather, size of store or competitors' prices. This design assumes that the extraneous variables have had an equal impact on all the test units, which is also a shortcoming of the basic design. Such an assumption might be acceptable in a laboratory experiment where the researcher controls most of the conditions, but it is an unjustified assumption to make for experiments conducted in a real-world environment. This design is not widely used for field experiments.

Randomised block design

This type of design is used when the researcher is interested in isolating a major source of variation in addition to the treatment's influence. In the example above, where three different prices were tested, no allowance was made for the different sizes of the stores, a potentially important influence on the actual sales obtained. The randomised block facilitates the isolation of one extraneous factor from the total experimental error, providing a precise picture of the treatment's actual impact. This additional variable has to be identified and measured at the time of the experiment.

Here we see how the antifreeze example has been expanded to permit the illustration of a randomised block design (Table 9.2). In this case the desire is to control the impact of store size on sales.

Table 9.2 Antifreeze sales in supermarkets at various prices

Store size £'000	Price £3.89	Price £4.85	Price £5.89
1. 100 +	135	100	60
2. 50–100	34	26	15
3. 20–49	17	12	7
4. < 20	5	2	1
Total	191	140	83

Latin square design

This design enables the researcher to isolate the impact of two major extraneous sources as well as measuring the impact of the treatment. It is a complex design and can cost time and money. The additional efficiency it provides must be weighed against the extra costs and the greater expertise needed by the user. It assumes there is no interaction between the factors being measured.

Again expanding on the antifreeze example, this shows how the Latin square design can be used to control for the impact of store size and the type of store selling the antifreeze (Table 9.3).

In using the Latin square design the number of extraneous variables to be controlled must equal the number of treatments. Thus on the example above, three levels of store size are needed and three different types of stores will be involved. The rows and columns of the resulting matrix contain the extraneous variables. The treatment (different prices) is assigned so that each price level occurs only once in each row and column.

Latin square designs are particularly useful in experiments where it is important to establish controls for the effect of store size, the type of store or the time period. The main limitations of the design are:

- It requires equal numbers of rows, columns and treatment levels. This can pose problems when four or five treatments are involved.
- Regardless of the number of treatments, it can still only control two extraneous variables.
- It assumes that the extraneous variables do not interact with each other or even with the treatment – a questionable assumption in many marketing experiments.

Table 9.3 Latin square design

	Size of outlet (weekly sales)		
Type of store	<£5,000	£5,000–£9,999	≥£10,000
Supermarket	Price 2	Price 3	Price 1
Convenience store	Price 1	Price 2	Price 3
Drugstore	Price 3	Price 1	Price 2

Table 9.4 Latin square design in a supermarket grocery

| | Experiment period | | | | | |
| | 20/6–3/7 | | 4/7–17/7 | | 18/7–31/7 | |
	Treatment	Sales	Treatment	Sales	Treatment	Sales
First replication						
Store 1	A	765	B	488	C	410
Store 2	B	330	C	307	A	258
Store 3	C	813	A	579	B	301
Second replication						
Store 1	A	724	C	411	B	308
Store 2	B	366	A	478	C	271
Store 3	C	633	B	366	A	588
Third replication						
Store 1	A	562	B	381	C	322
Store 2	B	308	C	478	A	412
Store 3	C	166	A	233	B	65

Latin square design in a supermarket grocery

The experiment reported below made use of a 3 × 3 design. The rows represented three different stores and the columns represented three time periods. Three replications of the 3 × 3 design were included in the experiment, each comprising a different set of three stores. The treatments consisted of three colour ranges of bananas: treatment A – 'highly coloured green', 75–100 per cent good green colour; B – 'partly green', 50–75 per cent good green colour; and C – 'yellow colour', 50–100 per cent good yellow colour. The performance of treatment A (for example, average sales across the 9 As) can be thought of as a weighted average, where the weights given to each store and day of the week are equal. Treatment B's performance is based on the same set of weights for stores and days of the week that were used to compute the performance of treatment A. This is also true for the weights used to compute the average performance of treatment C.

The results of the experiment indicated that customers most preferred the highly coloured green bananas and least preferred those in the partly green category.

Factorial design

In the previous designs the assumption was that there were one or two major sources of variation and that the researcher wanted to separate them from the total variance. There was no allowance or even assumption that some factors might interact with one another. Indeed, researchers are often interested in the simultaneous effects of two or more independent variables. In the antifreeze example, the researcher might want to see if outlets serving higher-income clientele have greater success with the higher prices than those outlets serving lower-income clientele. A factorial design measures the influence of interacting variables on a dependent variable. In the above, for example, improved sales are associated with both the income of an outlet's clientele and any change in the outlet display used. Factorial designs enable researchers to measure the separate effects of each variable as it works alone. The actual design used can be a randomised block or Latin square, but a more complicated form of variance analysis is applied to the results.

Limitations of experiments

Experiments are often limited to assessing short-term response, whereas long-term response is often more relevant to a problem. Moreover, the long-term response to a particular treatment is often quite different to that of the short-term response. As an example, much advertising is well known to be effective over a period of time which is often difficult, if not impossible, to gauge effectively. Thus to measure its effect over a short period of time may be suspect. Also, the longer an experiment is run, the greater is the opportunity for something to occur that will invalidate it – Murphy's Law of 'if anything can go wrong it will go wrong' is almost certain to apply. Moreover, an experiment often cannot be made sufficiently realistic to be useful.

TEST-MARKETING: AN INTRODUCTION

Test-marketing is about trying something out before making a big commitment to it. It gives the firm producing and marketing the product or service some idea of what is likely to happen should it decide to go ahead with a broader expansion on a regional or national basis. Test-marketing aims to provide estimates of sales volume and market share for a new product, a product extension, or a new marketing device such as a modified advertising campaign, varying media mixes or a change in advertising expenditure.

Conceptually it is very much like holding an experiment. The idea is literally to conduct a test or an experiment to arrive at a sales prediction. This may be done by trying things out in a series of balanced markets under normal conditions and this is the format of the traditional test market. In controlled test-marketing, the research firm forces the distribution of the brand, making sure it is stocked in all selected stores and that stocks are maintained. At another level altogether there is simulated test-marketing – virtually a laboratory situation, in which real stores are seldom used.

The traditional approach to test-marketing

Traditional test-marketing is marketing under 'normal' conditions and the company's own sales force gets retailers to stock the product, give it good shelf position and provide in-store promotion and cooperative advertising. The sales staff also makes sure that the shelves remain stocked.

Homelink

A new process, Homelink, enables accurate and effective targeting to be achieved in a few hours. The process makes use of a database of over 10,000 adults and is one of the most comprehensive, nationally representative research samples available. It makes use of demographic variables and explores the way in which people live, the products they use and the beliefs they hold.

Thousands of new products are launched every year but many of these initiatives fail to come to fruition. Arguably, by fully researching a target audience in the first place, much waste can be avoided. After all, ensuring that products or services match with customer wants, needs and expectations is a critical element in the new product introduction process. Discussions with potential users of a new product, service or sales campaign is an essential part of getting projects of this type off the ground.

Unfortunately, launchers of new ventures often perceive the research process to be over-complex. They often feel that the more targeted the respondents are, the harder they are to locate and the more complex the process of finding meaningful and manageable market data becomes. With Homelink this type of thinking can be shown to be completely out of date.

In order to ensure that the fullest picture can be drawn from their new market research facility, the designers of Homelink have included a wide range of product and service categories. These include such things as baby products, household equipment, pet food, skin-care products, home leisure/entertainment equipment, types of food and much more. This enables people who use specific products and services or who lead particular lifestyles to be identified quickly and cost-effectively. Establishing a baseline from which all aspects of research can be compared is the fundamental question to be answered before the research can begin and Homelink enables this to be done very effectively. Moreover, the framework and database enable information to be gathered from the same respondents over a long period of time which in turn means that sample variability can be reduced. Homelink facilitates the researching of products with both large and small market shares in a cost-effective manner.

Homelink can be used for:

- product or advertisement concept-testing
- evaluating market potential for new or revitalised products or services

- testing new or reformulated products to discover how the current users of those products or users of competing brands rate a new or reformulated product
- discovering how products are used in the home environment
- uncovering customer attitudes towards a particular company and its products

In the case of Homelink no one remains in the database for more than two years, no one tests more than six concepts or products over the course of a year and no one ever tests more than two products from the same product category.

Source: Research Plus.[5]

Traditional test-marketing rests on the premise that if a few reasonably typical communities throughout the country are selected, and the product or marketing method is tried there, results will pretty well predict what will happen when there is a roll-out on a regional or national basis. Moreover, if a simultaneous series of parallel markets is set up, it will be possible to predict which of two or more product variations, copy approaches or the like will work better. One of the greatest problems is the selection of test areas. The idea is to select test markets not too different from the country as a whole.

Matching local markets with national data on sales may not assure comparability. Change may creep in even without the introduction of any known marketing variables. Matching test cities with one another on the basis of causal variables such as regular price, national advertising, couponing, displays and in-store fliers might help matters.

Other important factors include demographics: per capita income, racial composition, etc. The business nature of the community must also be considered. The area should roughly parallel the business composition nationally, by type of business and, usually, medium-sized cities are selected. The advertising media should be representative. The media should be self-contained: they should not have much coverage beyond the test market.

The duration of a traditional market test depends on the nature of the product and the consumers' buying habits. The rule of thumb for packaged goods is an average of three purchases (trial and two repeats). If the product is one with a slow but continuing purchase pattern, the test period has to be long. Competitive pressure also affects the length of the test. A strong competitor means that the marketer must stay in there longer to find out whether it is possible to make inroads into the market.

Competitive action is one of the great risks and uncertainties of the traditional test market. Once a major competitor recognises what is happening, it may decide to make an effort to kill the test by spending heavy marketing funds on advertising and coupons to distort the test results.

Controlled test-marketing

This is a test where sales are measured within a controlled store environment. The length and frequency of the checks are set to parallel the real-life elements of expected product movement, the repurchase cycle of the category and purchase seasonality. The research firm conducting the controlled market test obtains distribution of the product in a representative sample of stores within each market selected for the test. It handles 'sell-in' and guarantees that this will be 100 per cent. It stocks the product in the stores, handling both warehousing and distribution. The research firm maintains retail inventory levels, and handles pricing, shelf conditions and the building and placement of displays.

The approach has several advantages over traditional test-marketing. Costs are far lower and the forced test needs only about six months – the whole process is accelerated. The method also makes it more difficult for competitors to know what is going on, so there is less chance that a competitor can exert a distortion effect.

Simulated test-marketing

Simulated test-marketing is really test-marketing in a laboratory setting. It applies only to a situation where the product and its packaging, pricing and advertising and promotion have been developed in finished form. Although there are variations in practice, consumers are usually invited into a central location facility, such as a research centre in a shopping mall. They are given information – usually in the form of advertising – about the test product, then invited to shop from stocked shelves, which include the test product, with provided funds. Following the first purchase, or lack of it, the consumer is later interviewed to determine repeat buying and frequency of purchase of the test product. Then a computer model of customer behaviour provides an estimate of sales volume for the new product or line extension.

CONSUMER-TRACKING STUDIES

Associated with traditional test-marketing, consumer-tracking studies are diagnostic aids. These studies track what is, or is not, happening as a result of the marketing campaign. They do this by continuing contact with consumers, doing 'waves' of studies, as they are sometimes called, to measure such things as:

- brand awareness
- recall of advertising
- purchase behaviour
- product satisfaction
- intent to repurchase.

Questions about the recall of advertising probe for 'unaided advertising recall'. Typically, the person is first asked about what brands of a product or service they are aware of. The first two brands named are considered by marketers as an indication of probable purchase. Purchase and repurchase behaviour are particularly significant. Overall audit figures report only total sales and market shares. Such reports do not show repurchase behaviour.

Consumer-tracking studies take one of two forms: the one-off study or the panel. Both are carried out in waves, but the one-shot study is conducted with a separate, but comparable, sample of respondents each time. The panel study is conducted with the identical group of people on each wave. Both approaches often make use of the telephone interview method.

Tracking studies must meet rigorous requirements if they are to be useful. Large shifts are rare in tracking studies, so they must be able to measure small differences. Thus the sample design has to include a large and random sample with rigorous controls in execution.

SUMMARY

This chapter has examined a variety of observational methods including those using mechanical means and scanning. It has also looked at experimentation as a research method. Different types of experimental design have been examined, together with a discussion of their limitations, as well as a variety of approaches to test-marketing.

Questions

1   For which weaknesses in the survey method can observation techniques compensate?

2   Enumerate the conditions necessary for effective observation.

3   Indicate the different types of observation procedures that may be used.

4   What is meant by scanning? What use can be made of information gathered in this way?

5   What are the essential features of an experiment?

6   Indicate the kind of evidence needed to demonstrate the existence of a causal relationship.

7   State the three components that should be present in every experiment.

8   Explain internal validity and external validity.

9   State the considerations that affect the internal validity of an experiment.

10   What is the purpose of experimental designs?

11   Distinguish between the different types of experimental design, including statistical designs, indicating the limitations of each one.

12   Indicate the limitations of experiments.

13   What is test-marketing?

14   What factors should be taken into account when setting up a traditional test market?

15   Explain:

   (a) controlled test-marketing

   (b) simulated test-marketing

   How are they different from traditional test-marketing?

16   What are consumer tracking studies? What is their purpose?

Case study 9.1   Soap-sud

Soap-sud is a washing powder brand name for a product marketed throughout the UK. It is produced by one of the two leading multinational soap powder companies. Soap-sud has been around in slightly different forms for many years and has stood the test of time. Periodically, new ingredients have been added to the powder to produce new benefits for the customer, versions have been introduced which have made it more suitable for automatic washing machines and various packaging designs have been used to keep the image of the product in vogue.

The first non-soap detergents were introduced in 1950 with Tide. This was followed by Surf in 1951 and Daz in 1953. They all promised greater cleanliness and whiteness. But at that time Persil had been proclaiming the importance of whiteness for ten years with its famous slogan 'Persil washes whiter'. In 1956 Persil offered perfume for the first time and other changes followed. A scum-disposal agent was added which gave better performance in hard water, a solid suspension agent to prevent dirt being redeposited and more fluorescers to brighten the wash. Persil was the first brand to be advertised on TV in 1956. In the 1960s the growth of washing-machine sales began to accelerate and in 1964 Persil was reformulated to perform even better with machines. At the end of the decade Ariel exploded into the market and captured brand leadership but within a year Persil had regained the position. There have been many changes in the market since 1970 but perhaps none so radical as those of the 1950s and 1960s.

Maintaining market share is an important objective for the brand manager in charge of Soap-sud and in a highly competitive industry this is a difficult thing to do. There is also a problem: the company that owns the brand also has two other soap-powder brands competing alongside Soap-sud in the market place. Bill Carruthers, the brand manager of Soap-sud, is now contemplating a number of changes to the product to give it additional leverage in the market. The changes are as follows:

- The introduction of a special new 'green whitener' ingredient. Tests show that this makes the product even more effective in washing clothes 'whiter than white' and is also environmentally friendly.
- A new television advertising campaign telling users of washing powders of the changes to Soap-sud.

- A brand new package design to promote the idea that the new Soap-sud really is a new product in every way.

Bill is looking for ways of testing out his ideas before making a definite commitment to them.

Question

What advice would you give Bill?

Case study 9.2 | Cheung's chips

Mr Cheung offers a wide range of Chinese food, fried traditional British cuisine, such as fish and chips, and some Italian dishes. Every time he has introduced a new line in the past he has taken a random sample of his customers and asked them whether or not they would be interested in the new line he proposes. If more than 70 per cent of those asked have said they would be interested, he has introduced the new line. He has jotted down the following notes on the last five new products he has introduced.

Line	Percentage saying interested	Weekly average sales turnover (£)
1 Fish and chips	98%	2156
2 Puddings	95%	345
3 Steak pies	94%	213
4 Spaghetti	70%	135
5 Lasagne	71%	123

Mr Cheung wants to set up a method by which he can judge whether it is worthwhile to introduce new lines. He feels that the current method is not very satisfactory and that he may be missing some good opportunities. He also feels that despite the number of people who say they would be interested in buying the new lines, in many instances only a few of them actually do.

Someone has suggested that a good research approach would be to use the response-latency technique. This measures the amount of time a respondent takes to answer a question, with quick answers indicating certainty of preference. The technique is especially useful in telephone interviews since latency can be measured by recording all calls and measuring the time to respond post facto.

Question

What advice would you offer Mr Cheung?

| Case study 9.3 | The Safe 'T' fireproof letterbox |

Barry invented the Safe 'T' out of necessity when an aggrieved tenant poured petrol through his letterbox and set fire to it. Being in the locksmith business, he soon realised there was nothing on the market to protect him against further attacks. He began to sketch out the sort of thing he wanted and the Safe 'T' letterbox began to emerge. The letterbox is able to deal with fireworks, lighted newspaper and almost anything of that nature. If someone pours petrol in, it comes out at the bottom straight on to the culprit's feet. Barry feels that his invention has potential since there are some 80 000 reported arson attacks every year in England and Wales alone.

Source: Business Opportunities World.[6]

Question

Assuming that Barry can find a financial backer to produce and market the invention, how might the idea be tested out among potential customers?

| Case study 9.4 | Thompson Toys |

Thompson Toys manufactures a range of simple toys for pre-school-age children. The toys are robust, colourful and fun to play with, but also take account of sound educational principles – in toy industry parlance, they have high play value. The company has proved successful, exporting toys throughout Europe and Australia, and acquiring in the process a reputation for quality and durability which has stood them in good stead.

Harry Thompson, the founder of the firm, read in the trade press about the Fisher-Price company's crèche in Chicago. At one time, Fisher-Price ran a free crèche at their headquarters where pre-school children were given the company's toys to play with; observers, behind two-way mirrors, observed how the children played with the toys and which toys were most popular. This had proved invaluable for Fisher-Price when developing and marketing new products.

After reading the article, Harry Thompson decided to set up a similar crèche of his own. The crèche would be free for the children of the company's staff, so Harry let his personnel manager work out the details of setting up the project. Initially the crèche had seven children in it, of ages ranging from one year old to four and a half. The crèche was staffed by a fully trained nursery nurse; two observers were hired, and a room fitted out for the purpose. The main difference between Thompson's crèche and the Fisher-Price one was that Thompson used closed-circuit TV to monitor the children rather than two-way mirrors. This not only turned out to be cheaper, but also allowed the observers to record the children's behaviour for later analysis. A further spin-off of CCTV was that it allowed the observers to take breaks or spend time preparing their reports.

The observers either directly observed or recorded all the children's activities throughout the day, in particular observing their approach to playing with the toys.

Although the costs of running the crèche were high, Thompson thought it worthwhile in terms of new product development; several potentially damaging design problems in toys turned up, and some toys which had seemed promising on the drawing-board turn out to be duds with the children. This alone saved the company a fortune in launch costs. The crèche took almost six months to settle down, however, and the researchers detected a number of problems with the set-up.

Firstly, there was a conflict of interest between the nursery nurse's professional training and the needs of the observers. She needed to exercise a degree of control over the children's play, both for educational and nurturing reasons, and also for housekeeping reasons – for example, stopping play when it was time for the children's lunch. The observers, on the other hand, wanted the children to play as freely as possible with the toys. They wanted to observe whether the children spontaneously shared toys with each other, to observe at what point the children became bored with the toys, and to observe what happened if another child tried to take the toy away. Also, the nursery nurse was not comfortable about the children playing with prototypes, because she was concerned about the chances of injury from toys which had not yet undergone full safety testing.

Secondly, the children belonged to the Thompson staff. This meant that most of them were already familiar with the majority of Thompson toys, since staff were allowed to buy toys for their children at very substantial discounts. The observers felt that this might bias the results.

Thirdly, the observers were obtaining so much data from the observations and videotapes that it became impossible to analyse all of it. Choosing which areas should be analysed thoroughly was becoming a nightmare, and the observers were reluctant to perform superficial analysis on such rich data.

Finally, the researchers were not confident that good results could be obtained from such a small sample of children.

Despite these difficulties, Harry Thompson still wanted to proceed with the crèche; already, some very useful feedback had been generated, and he had high hopes for the future running of the crèche once the initial teething troubles had been overcome. The benefits were already outweighing the difficulties – but all concerned with the project knew that even better results could be obtained.

(Case contributed by Jim Blythe.)

Questions

1 How might Thompson Toys resolve the conflicts between the nursery nurse and the researchers?

2 What type of observation would be appropriate in these circumstances?

3 What could be done to overcome the researchers' concerns about sample size?

4 What types of experiment could be substituted for the observation methods used by Thompson?

5 What other factors might affect the validity of the research done at the crèche?

6 How would you design an experiment for Thompson Toys, using the crèche children as experimental subjects?

Further reading

Adler, P and Adler, P (1994) Observational techniques, in Denzin, N K and Lincoln, Y S, *Handbook of Qualitative Research*, Thousand Oaks, CA: Sage.

Cuba, F (1985) Fourteen things that make or break tracking studies, *Journal of Advertising Research*, 25(1), pp 21–3.

Eskin, G (1988) *Setting a Forward Agenda for Test Market Modeling*, New York: Advertising Research Foundation, pp 14–15.

Gibson, R (1992) The fine art of stocking a supermarket's shelves, *Wall Street Journal*, 15 October.

Gibson, R (1993) Broad grocery price cuts may not pay, *Wall Street Journal*, 7 May.

Grove, S J and Fisk, R P (1992) Observational data collection methods for service marketing: an overview, *Journal of the Academy of Marketing Science*, 20(3), pp 217–24.

Kandathil, J (1985) The advantages of electronic test markets: an advertiser view based on experience, *Journal of Advertising Research*, 25(6), pp 11–12.

Langbourne, R (1993) How to reach children in stores: marketing tactics grounded in observational research, *Journal of Advertising Research*, 33, November/December, pp 67–72.

Malhotra, R (1988) *Some Issues and Perspectives on Use of Simulated Test Markets*, New York: Advertising Research Foundation, p 57.

Moult, W M (1988) *The Role of Simulated Test Markets and Test Markets*, New York: Advertising Research Foundation, p 140.

Robson, C (1993) *Real World Research*, Oxford: Blackwell.

Rosenfeld, J (1985) Speeding up test marketing, *Marketing Communications*, June.

Russo, J (1988) Simulated test markets in the real world, *Pre-Test Market Research*, New York: Advertising Research Foundation, pp 118–19.

Rydholm, J (1997) Right on cue: mystery shopping makes sure salespeople sing praises of Yamaha digital pianos, *Quirk's Marketing Review*, Article 234, January.

Seaton, A V (1997) Unobtrusive observational measures as a qualitative extension of visitor surveys at festivals and events: mass observation revisited, *Journal of Travel Research*, 35(4), Spring, pp 25–30.

Test markets: winners and losers, *Advertising Week*, s3, October 1983.

References and notes

[1] Smith, A (1997d) Shoppers under the microscope, *Financial Times*, 5 December.

[2] Hague, P and Jackson, P (1996) *Market Research*, London: Kogan Page.

[3] Collins, L F (1991) Everything is true, but in a different sense: a new perspective on qualitative research, *Journal of the Market Research Society*, 33, pp 31–8.

[4] Cochran, W G and Cox, G M (1957) *Experimental Designs* (2nd edn), New York: Wiley.

[5] Homelink, *Research Plus*, September 1993, pp 8–9.

[6] Safe T letterbox, *Business Opportunities World*, May 1996, pp 64–5.

10 Quantitative data analysis

OBJECTIVE

After reading this chapter you should be able to:

- understand how to identify meaningful patterns in research data;

- understand how to convert into tables data collected with research instruments;

- understand how to code questions;

- understand how to analyse data with statistical methods;

- appreciate how the computer can be used to transform and facilitate the interpretation of research data.

KEY WORDS

interpretation
analysis
tabulation
editing
coding
averages
mean
median
mode
standard deviation
variance
Z test
t test

proportions
non-parametric tests
chi-square
contingency tables
analysis of variance
correlation
regression
multiple regression
hypothesis testing
cluster analysis
factor analysis
conjoint analysis
multidimensional scaling

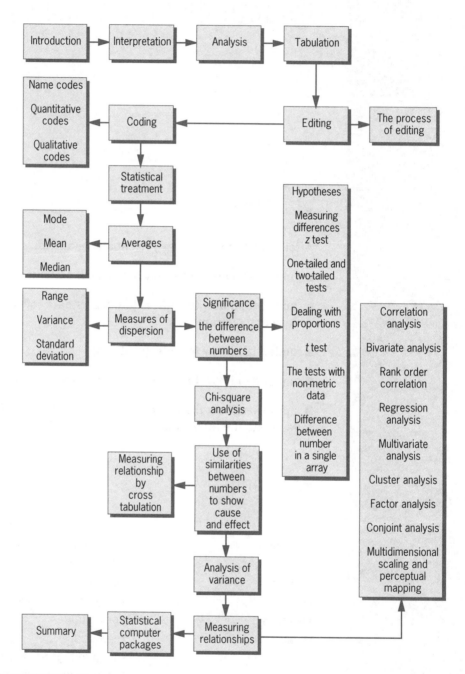

PLAN OF CHAPTER 10

INTRODUCTION

In this chapter we examine how research results are analysed to establish meaningful patterns. The steps involved in converting completed research instruments into tables are examined, together with the coding of answers to questions and the statistical treatment of survey data. Finally, we consider the role of the computer in transforming and facilitating the interpretation of research data.

INTERPRETATION

Interpretation and analysis are closely related. If one or the other is not carried out properly, the success of a study cannot be assured. Consider the cases below. In the first, improper interpretation is the problem and, in the second, improper analysis is the problem.

Improper interpretation

A producer of a branded fast-moving consumer product, which also markets an own-label or private brand version to a large supermarket chain, noted the sales returns shown below from the supermarket.

The figures show that sales of its own brand have been declining steadily for the past two years while those of the private brand have been steadily increasing. The firm concludes that its own brand sales have been dropping because consumers are switching to the private branded label. The company decided to stop supplying its own product to the supermarket.

In fact, what was happening was that another supplier to the supermarket was making huge gains in terms of market share by running very substantial promotions. The decline in sales of the company's brand was due largely to the promotional efforts of the other company. The mistake the company made here was the failure to relate the data it had obtained to other pertinent data – i.e. the activities of its competitor.

		Company brand sales	Private brand sales
1995	1st Quarter	151 234	74 340
	2nd Quarter	146 530	81 188
	3rd Quarter	139 312	83 248
	4th Quarter	131 931	91 430
1996	1st Quarter	125 245	101 121
	2nd Quarter	119 236	110 234
	3rd Quarter	111 125	113 122
	4th Quarter	102 197	122 008

Improper analysis

A firm is trying to determine which of three advertisements is most likely to increase sales of its product. It tests out the three advertisements by running each at different times in newspapers in different areas.

Advertisement	Total sales associated with the advertisement
1	39 005 units
2	31 452 units
3	29 438 units

The sales indicated that advertisement 1 was the most successful. The logical result of the research would be to use the advertisement to promote national sales. However, had an analysis of variance been carried out, it would have indicated that the three advertisements did not in fact differ significantly in terms of their impact on sales. Advertisement 1's apparent success was really due to abnormally high demand in area B. Advertisement 1 was not significantly more successful in the other areas.

Sales impact of the advertisement in four different test areas.

Advertisement	A	B	C	D	Total
1	7072	16 098	8122	7713	39 005
2	7512	7481	7859	8600	31 452
3	7120	7219	9087	6012	29·438

In order to ensure that procedures for analysing the collection of data are given the proper attention, a formal data-analysis plan should be developed in the early stages of the project. Such a plan should identify the following:

1 major variables to be studied
2 methods used to measure the variables
3 analysis procedures that will be used to give meaning to the collected data.

ANALYSIS

The two major approaches employed in summarising the results of marketing research are tabulation and statistical analysis. Tabulation involves laying out data into easy-to-understand summary tables. Tables are the basic way of presenting summary data. Tabulation is the preparation of tables showing the frequency distribution of particular events. Patterns in the data can often be spotted from a cursory examination of data, although when tables themselves are summarised in the form of graphs the patterns are often even more readily discernible. Statistical analysis is undertaken to identify patterns that are not as easy to see in the data. This is often the case when very large amounts of data need analysis.

TABULATION

Three steps are involved in converting completed questionnaires to tables: editing, coding and counting. The procedures involved are called data processing and should be planned at the time of the study design. There are at least three good reasons.

First, the researcher has to think ahead about specific potential results. If this is done, it means that plans for specific tables are made as part of the basic study plan. Second, the data collection method should be designed to provide efficient data processing. This mainly involves the precoding of questionnaires or other research instruments. Precoding is the assignment of codes to various possible responses identified on the research instrument. Whenever possible and reasonable, alternative responses should be identified and listed in advance. Third, if data processing is planned out well, table production is an inexpensive operation.

EDITING

Editing is the inspection of data forms to make a modification or correction of responses. This may seem as if the researcher is making sure that results come out as hoped, but this is not the case. The function of editing is to make the best sense out of what is in hand. One intent is to eliminate or minimise errors in the raw data. There are two basic sources of error: interviewer error and respondent error. Interviewers, for example, may check the wrong response category or not ask the proper flow-through questions. Interviewers can also be poor at recording answers to open-ended questions. Respondents may be inconsistent in their replies: at one point they may indicate they do not drink, yet later talk confidently in the manner of people who drink regularly. Editing gets rid of the inconsistencies and improves the quality of the raw data.

The process of editing

Editing can be done manually or by computer, depending on the method of data collection. In the manual editing, there can be as many as three stages involved: the interviewer, the field editor and the central research office. The computer-editing process starts at the point of data collection. If the respondent or the interviewer enters an inconsistent response, the error must be corrected before the next question appears on the screen. The computer is programmed to recognise the acceptable patterns for sequential questions, what to look for in contingent questions and inconsistent replies and how to handle no-replies. If definitive action for particular corrections can be identified, the computer also issues instructions accordingly.

CODING

Usually in coding a number is assigned to represent each reply to a question on a questionnaire or some other research instrument. Coding translates the answers or responses into a more readily countable form. However, without considerable care about the coding of inputs, the tables that are produced as a result of analysis may be misleading. Three types of coding are required to handle the three basic kinds of data collected in surveys: names, quantitative data and qualitative data.

Name codes

Name codes apply to such things as brands or makes of goods, or even to firms. The names in the list are almost always known in advance. Where a product is being researched, it is simple enough to prelist the brand names that will account for the majority of replies and the same applies to a prelisting of retailers or manufacturers.

Quantitative codes

Quantitative codes are used with questions that request replies in terms of numbers. Categories should be mutually exclusive. For example, too often the question about household income shows categories such as:

£20,000–£25,000

£25,000–£30,000

There is no single place to list a £25,000 income.

Both precoding and postcoding can be applied to quantitative questions. Precoding involves a closed-ended list and postcoding has categories that can be set up only after the answers are in hand. Here are examples of the closed-ended type of quantitative question:

- How many times have you driven your car in the past seven days, not including today?
- What size shirt do you wear?
- Do you own your own house? How long have you owned it?

In each case, answer categories can be set up in advance and the range of answers is known in advance.

In the case of open-ended quantitative questions, even though there may be a rough idea of the range of answers the likely distribution of answers cannot be known in advance. Setting up categories in advance may produce data that destroy the chances to analyse it or, even worse, that actually distort results. Consider the following:

- Where are you intending to go for your holidays?
- Where were you educated?
- What is your favourite TV programme?

Computers take over much of the work in establishing quantitative categories. Each specific response can be entered into the system and totalled for each specific category. These preliminary runs give the researcher or marketer the information needed to set up the quantitative categories that meet all requirements. Appropriate class intervals can be set up and the computer instructed to enter this information for each questionnaire.

Qualitative codes

Qualitative questions usually produce descriptions, explanations and reasons. The question is open-ended and answers can range widely. Setting up codes for qualitative answers calls for much thought in terms of what the particular question is intended to contribute by way of information for the specific study.

STATISTICAL TREATMENT: GIVING MEANING TO SURVEY NUMBERS

Numbers resulting from a piece of research seldom provide much meaning by themselves. Using percentages can facilitate our understanding. A figure of 300 pairs of shoes means little, if anything, completely on its own. However, if we ask 'What is the 300 pairs of shoes a part of?', it begins to assume some meaning, if we are told that out of 1000 sales of shoes over the past month, 30 per cent have been bought within the last three days. It means even more if we know that this 30 per cent is responding to a special promotional offer that was introduced three days ago.

There are pitfalls in the use of percentages, however. Just because they are in an easy-to-understand form of quantifying data does not make them the universal solution to all problems. Percentages from different groups of people should not be averaged unless they are weighted.

Averaging percentages should always involve weighting

The percentage of car owners for three age groups is shown below. We want to determine the percentage of car owners in the first two groups to arrive at a figure showing usage among those aged 18–49. Averaging the two percentages gives a figure of 28.4 per cent.

Percentage of car owners among three age groups

	18–29	30–49	50 and over
Total interviews	100.0%	100.0%	100.0%
Car owners	22.0%	34.8%	65.4%
Average of 18–49	28.4%		

However, if a third column is added to show the total for the combined 18–49 group, as shown below, when the two age groups are combined in terms of their real weights in the study, the resultant correct car-ownership figure for the 18–49 group turns out to be 29.1 per cent. While the difference from the average percentage may not appear all that great, the two figures might be of rather different marketing significance in terms of the particular problem. And the difference between an averaged percentage and a weighted one might be far greater.

Number and percentage of car owners among two age groups

	18–29		30–49		18–49	
	No.	%	No.	%	No.	%
Total interviews	200	100.0	250	100.0	450	100.0
Car owners	44	22.0	87	34.8	131	29.1

AVERAGES

Averages or measures of central tendency come in three forms: the mode, the mean and the median.

The mode

The mode represents the point in an array showing the greatest response level. It is not an average used often in marketing research, but it takes on considerable importance when looking at ordinal data.

The mean

The mean is a commonly used average in marketing research and is readily understood as the sum total of values divided by the number of cases. However, it has one shortcoming: it is affected by a few large or small numbers (skewing), since it is based on all the values in the array. In terms of a product usage-rate study, for instance, the presence of a small number of heavy users in the study could produce mean usage results not truly representative of the typical user in the sample. The mean usage rate is too large to be descriptive of the user.

The median

The median is the value of the middle case in an ordered series. There are as many cases on the higher side as on the lower side. The measure offers the advantage of being unaffected by extreme cases at one end or the other. This again is a useful measure when examining ordinal data.

Using averages – measures of central tendency

The mean, median and mode should first be calculated. If the mean and median are about the same, the mean should be used since the former is the most generally understood. However, if the mean and median are greatly different, the median should probably be used, as it is likely to be a better measure.

Note: it is possible to have more than one modal value in a distribution.

Number of people living in 25 surveyed households

9	7	6	4	3
8	7	6	4	2
8	6	6	3	2

7	6	5	3	1
7	6	5	3	1
Mean 5		Median 6		Mode 6

In marketing research we should use the mean or the median or both. Depending on the nature of the numerical distribution, these may or may not coincide. Taken together they provide a good indication of the average.

MEASURES OF DISPERSION

The most common methods used to describe the dispersion of data are the range, variance and standard deviation. Small values for these measures indicate that the data is compact.

Range

This is the interval from the lowest to the highest value in an array of data. In the number of people living in the sampled households example, the range is $9 - 1 = 8$.

Variance

This is an index that indicates the extent to which the values are dispersed. Were every observation in a data set the same value, the variance would be zero. Variance increases as values differ significantly from the mean. The formula used to calculate variance is:

$$S^2 = \sum_{i=1}^{n}\left(X_i - \overline{X}\right)^2 / (n - 1)$$

where X_i is the individual value in an array, $\overline{X}$ is the mean of the array and n is the number of values in an array.

Standard deviation

This is the square root of the variance and is represented by the symbol S.

THE SIGNIFICANCE OF THE DIFFERENCES BETWEEN NUMBERS

Hypotheses

The first step in tests of significance is to make a claim which one then has to find evidence against. This statement is called the *null hypothesis*. The test is intended to determine the strength of the evidence against the null hypothesis. Customarily, the null hypothesis is a statement of no difference or no effect. The term null hypothesis is abbreviated as H_0 and is usually stated in terms of some population parameter or parameters. For example, suppose that p_1 is the proportion of the whole population of British males who would have been illness free in 2002 if they rode a bicycle to work each day, and let p_2 stand for the illness-free proportion if they went to work in their cars instead. The null hypothesis is:

$$H_0 : p_1 = p_2$$

because this states that riding a bicycle to work has the same effectiveness as travelling by car. The name given to the statement we hope or suspect is true instead of H_0 is the *alternative hypothesis* and it is abbreviated by H_1. The alternative hypothesis in this case is that riding a bicycle to work is more effective than travelling by car. In terms of the population parameters this is:

$$H_1 : p_1 > p_2$$

A test of significance assesses the strength of the evidence against the null hypothesis in terms of probability. If the observed outcome is unlikely under the supposition that the null hypothesis is true, but is more probable if the alternative hypothesis is true, that outcome is evidence against H_0 in favour of H_1 The less probable the outcome is, the stronger is the evidence that H_0 is false.

There are many tests of significance appropriate for different types of hypothesis and for different data collection designs – as well as levels of significance. Some of these are examined later. An outline of what such a test of significance should include is shown in the box.

Steps in a test of significance

1   Select the null hypothesis H_0 and the alternative hypothesis H_1. The test is designed to assess the strength of the evidence against the null hypothesis. H_1 is a statement of the alternative we will accept if the evidence enables us to reject H_0.

2   Select the level of significance. This states how much evidence against H_0 we will accept as sufficient.

3   Select the test statistic on which the test will be based. This is a statistic which assesses how well the data conforms to H_0.

4   Find the probability value that the test statistic would weigh against H_0 at least as strongly as it does for these data, if H_0 were in fact true. If the probability value is less than or equal to the significance level then the test was statistically significant at that level.

Measuring differences

Whenever sample data are being used, we have to compensate for sampling error. Z and t tests are methods used to assess the differences among data while still taking into account the influence that sampling error may have played. The methods are employable when measurement scales are at least interval, observations are independent, two or fewer groups are involved, differences between two means are involved, and, in the case of the t test, where observations are drawn from a normally distributed population.

Provided that these criteria are met, we need to decide which of the two tests is the most appropriate. A Z test is used if the sample size is larger than 30. A t test is appropriate when the sample size is less than 30. If the population variance is not known, then the sample variance is assumed to equate to it and is used instead. The t test is usually employed in marketing research.

One- and two-tailed tests

The tabular value of Z at any level of significance depends on whether a one-tailed or two-tailed test is involved. Where we are looking for equality between two sets of data, $H_0 : \mu_1 = \mu_2$, a two-tailed test is appropriate.

Where we are looking at a situation that involves evaluating whether something is greater than something else, a one-tailed test is appropriate. The same also applies to situations where we are evaluating whether something is less than something else.

Dealing with proportions

If proportions are involved rather than discrete numbers, a different formula is needed – though in other respects the procedure is the same.

The formula used is:

$$Z = (p - P)/\sigma_p$$

where p is the sample proportion, P is the population proportion, $Q = 1 - P$ and $\sigma_p = \sqrt{(P.Q/n)}$ where n is the sample size.

t test

The procedures for using the *t* test are similar to those for using the *Z* test. However, there are different formulae that are applicable in different situations.[1] For example:

$$t = \frac{(\bar{x} - \mu)/s}{\sqrt{(n - 1)}}$$

where *s* is the standard deviation of the sample, $\bar{x}$ is the sample mean, μ is the population mean and *n* is the sample size. When the population data does exist, but the other group is represented by a fairly small sample, this formula should be employed.

The tests with non-metric data

There are several tests depending on the nature of the data and the comparisons made. These include:

- *Mann-Whitney U test*: this is used when comparing two groups, but the basis for comparison is data in ordinal form.

- *Wilcoxon* or *Signed Rank test*: this is appropriate for situations where two matching (non-independent) samples are being compared using ordinal (non-parametric) data.

- *Kruskal-Wallis test*: this is used when more than two independent samples are involved and the data are ordinal.

- *Friedman two-way analysis of data*: this is used when three or more related samples are involved as the data are ordinal.

We have to decide whether the difference between two or more numbers, or sets of numbers, is probably significant, and whether two numbers are causally related.

Difference between numbers in a single array

Suppose that in a survey of 1500, results showed that 64 per cent chose Brand X, 24 per cent chose Brand Y and the remainder made no choice. Are these real differences? Assuming that this was a probability sample, the answer is yes: the sampling error for 64 per cent is some 2.5 per cent, and for 24 per cent it is some 2.2 per cent.

CHI-SQUARE ANALYSIS

Difference between numbers in a series of arrays

In this case a comparison is made between the answers given by people with different sets of characteristics to a particular question. Characteristics of the people include demographics, such as geography, household size, the presence of children, income, sex and age. These are cross-tabulated against such things as awareness or the use of a product category, brand and purchase intent.

Example

Question: Are you aware of brand X washing machines?

Simple inspection of the data would seem to suggest there is a difference between men and women in terms of awareness level. However, we really want to know if the difference observable in cross-tabulating the data is statistically significant: in other words, what the probability is that observed differences could have occurred by chance. In this particular instance we can use the chi-square test to see if this is the case (we should, however, consult standard statistical texts to appreciate the suitability of this test and to understand its theoretical underpinning).

The chi-square statistic is calculated by the formula:

$$X^2 = \sum_{i=1}^{n}(O_i - E_i)^2/E_i$$

where O_i is the observed value and E_i is the Etheoretically expected value, assuming in this case that there is no difference between the occupational backgrounds of respondents.

We hypothesise that there is no relationship. However, X^2 at 2 degrees of freedom at the 5 per cent level = 3.84 and because 13.5 > 3.84 the difference noted in the sample is statistically significant. We must reject the null hypothesis and conclude that the difference in levels of awareness in men and women did not occur by chance.

Table 10.1 Results

	Yes	No	Total
Men	50	200	250
Women	150	300	450
Total	200	500	700

Table 10.2 Aware of the brand

	Yes	No	Total
Men (O = observed)	50	200	250
	$(250 \times 200)/700$	$(250 \times 500)/700$	
(E = expected)	= 71	= 179	
Women (O=observed)	= 150	300	450
	$(450 \times 200)/700$	$(450 \times 500)/700$	
(E = expected)	= 129	= 321	
Total	200	500	700

Note: Expected values are rounded off to the nearest whole number.

$X^2 = (50-71)^2/71 + (200-179)^2/179 + (150-129)^2/129 + (300-321)^2/321$
$= 13.5$ with degrees of freedom $(r-1)(k-1) = 1$

where r = number of rows, k = number of columns.

In the above example, using a 2×2 table it is usually preferable to use *Fisher's exact test* or include *Yates' Correction* where there are a small number of cases. In the latter case the formula is modified to:

$$X^2 = \sum_{i=1}^{n}(|O_i - E_i| - 0.5)^2/E_i$$

Where the sample size is so small that the expected value is less than 5, then chi-square should not be used.

Chi-square is a statistical tool used to evaluate the statistical significance of differences between sets of data. Basically, it compares one or more frequency distributions of data to indicate whether there is a real difference. It compares an actual set of data against a theoretical one to show what would be expected by chance alone.

Chi-square

A market researcher has completed a study of soft drinks. The following table shows the brand purchased most often, broken down by male versus female. The researcher wants to know if there is a relationship between the gender of the purchaser and the brand purchased.

Drink	Male	Female
Coke	66	52
Pepsi	67	48
7 Up	35	38
Dr Pepper	34	21
Sprite	32	41
Lilt	33	31
Blackjack	18	25
Tango	34	24

Chi-square 'Male' 'Female'

Expected counts are printed below observed counts:

	Male	Female	Total
1	66 62.84	52 55.16	118
2	67 61.24	48 53.76	115
3	35 38.88	38 34.12	73
4	34 29.29	21 25.71	55
5	32 38.88	41 29.92	73
6	33 34.08	31 29.92	64
7	18 22.90	25 20.10	43
8	34 30.89	24 27.11	58
Total	319	280	599

$X^2 = -0.159 + 0.181 + 0.541 + 0.616 + 0.387 + 0.440 + 0.757 + 0.863 + 1.216 + 1.386 + 0.034 + 0.039 + 1.048 + 1.194 + 0.314 + 0.357$

$X^2 = 9.533$ df $= 7$

The tabular value of X^2 at 0.05 level of significance and $(8-1)(2-1) = 7$ degrees of freedom is 14.07. The calculated value (9.533) is lower than the tabular value (14.07). There would not seem to be a significant relationship between gender of the purchaser and the brand purchased.

USE OF SIMILARITIES BETWEEN NUMBERS TO SHOW CAUSE AND EFFECT

Another application of numbers in marketing research is in the analysis and understanding of the similarities between variables. Many surveys try to measure the sales impact of advertising or other marketing efforts. One often-used procedure compares the proportion of purchasers among two groups: those who remember seeing or hearing the advertising and those who do not.

The following example represents the data shown in Table 10.1, this time ignoring the gender of the respondents. It also shows brand awareness of the washing machine by those who recall the brand's advertising and those who do not. An obvious but incorrect conclusion from the table is that advertising accounted for the 15 per cent difference in the awareness level. However, the results merely show that there is a correlation between advertising awareness and brand awareness. The correlation may be because people become aware of the brand by other means and then notice its advertising.

Interpreting the meaning of cross-tabulations amounts to more than simply taking the figures at face value. There has to be some underlying logical explanation behind the inferences that are drawn from the numbers alone. In this case, there is some evidence to support the argument presented. In the case of higher-priced items, psychologists have found that people pay attention to advertisements after purchase to help reinforce their purchase choice (allaying post-purchase cognitive dissonance).

Measuring relationships by cross-tabulation

For data provided by marketing research to be useful in making marketing decisions, it is most important that the cross-tabulations that might help to make marketing decisions are identified. For example, differences by age groups, or even concentration on a single age segment, could imply completely different approaches for each target market.

Table 10.3 Brand awareness and advertising recall

	Those remembering advertising (%)	Those not remembering advertising (%)
Total group	100	100
Aware of brand	20	5
Not aware of brand	80	95

ANALYSIS OF VARIANCE

This method is used extensively in evaluating the results of experiments. The general question involves determining the influence of a treatment on a dependent variable. The argument is that the total variance that exists among the data can be apportioned to specific factors by means of formal mathematical techniques. The amount of variance attributable to each factor is indicative of the factor's influence on the dependent variable.

Example

As part of a new advertising campaign, a firm plans a full-page advertisement in one of two media: a news magazine or a sports magazine. The problem is to decide

Table 10.4 Ratio of full-page advertisements to number of pages

Year	News magazine	Sports magazine
1989	0.79	0.60
	0.80	0.46
	0.54	0.38
	0.72	0.42
1991	0.49	0.39
	0.85	0.56
	0.50	0.57
	0.67	0.46
1993	0.36	0.37
	0.65	0.64
	0.47	0.52
	0.68	0.41

Note: the advertisement ratio is calculated by dividing the number of full-page ads by the number of pages in the issue.

Table 10.5 Analysis of variance for advertisement ratio

Source	DF	SS	MS	F	P
Year	2	0.02386	0.01193	0.73	0.494
Magazine	1	0.12615	0.12615	7.76	0.012
Year*Magazine	2	0.03753	0.01876	1.15	0.338
Error	18	0.29265	0.01626		
Total	23	0.48018			

Produced with the student edition of Minitab.
DF = degrees of freedom; SS = sum of squares; MS = mean square; F = statistic; P = probability.

which magazine has the lowest ratio of full-page advertisements to the number of pages in the magazine. It is also important to establish whether there has been a recent change in this ratio.

Three hypotheses are to be tested:

H_0: there is no interaction between year and magazine
H_1: there is an interaction between year and magazine

H_0: there is no difference in the average ad ratios for different years
H_1: there is a difference in the average ad ratios for different years

H_0: there is no difference in the average ad ratio when using different magazines
H_1: there is a difference in the average ad ratio when using different magazines.

We reject the hypothesis when the probability is ≤ 0.05 (decision rule).

Table 10.6 Analysis of variance

Test	Effect	F ratio	P-value	Decision
1	Year*Magazine	1.15	0.338	Do not reject H_0: do not conclude there is significant interaction between year and magazine
2	Year	0.73	0.494	Do not reject H_0: the mean ad ratios are probably the same for the three years
3	Magazine	7.76	0.012	Reject H_0: the mean ad ratios are not the same for the two magazines

For further details of analysis of variance, see McKenzie, et al.[2]

MEASURING RELATIONSHIPS

Regression and correlation both measure the relationship between a dependent variable and one or more independent variables, but each shows this relationship in a different manner. Regression analysis identifies the nature of the relationship using an equation, whereas correlation analysis describes the strength of relationships between variables by means of an index.

Correlation analysis

A coefficient of determination r^2 is computed and indicates the proportion of change in the dependent variable that is associated with changes in the independent variable. For instance, an r^2 of 0.49 means that 49 per cent of the variation in the dependent variable is associated with changes in the independent variable. The square root of the coefficient of determination is the correlation coefficient r and is an index of association between the two variables.

   A strong correlation does not establish causality. There are two major categories of correlation analysis: bivariate and multivariate. Bivariate analysis measures the relationship between two variables whereas multivariate analysis measures the relationship among three or more variables.

Bivariate analysis

Example

The first thing we might do before calculating r or r^2 is to produce a scatterplot of the relationship between the two variables. This is shown in Figure 10.1.

   From the scatterplot we can see that there is some association between the two sets of data, though it may not be very strong. Were there to be a strong degree of association between the two variables, the graph might have appeared as shown in Figure 10.2.

   Notice that where there is a high degree of association, the points lie along a straight line.

   The indices of association r and r^2 are calculated according to the formulae:

$$r = n(\Sigma YX) - (\Sigma Y)^2 / \sqrt{(n\Sigma X - (\Sigma X)^2)(n\Sigma Y^2 - (\Sigma Y)^2)}$$

r^2 is obtained from r.

   In this example correlation of price and alcohol $r = 0.241$.

   The significance of r can be tested using the t test.

Table 10.7 Fourteen brands of cider, their price per glass and alcoholic content per glass

Brand	Price (£)	Alcohol content (%)
1	1.1	4.2
2	1.1	4.2
3	0.9	4.0
4	0.9	3.0
5	1.2	8.5
6	0.9	8.4
7	0.9	4.0
8	0.7	4.0
9	1.1	8.5
10	1.1	8.5
11	0.9	7.5
12	0.9	7.5
13	0.7	7.6
14	1.0	6.0

$$t = r\sqrt{(n-2)/(1-r^2)}$$

$$t = 0.241\sqrt{(14-2)/(1-0.058)} = 0.241 \times \sqrt{(12/0.942)} = 0.86$$

tabular $t = 2.179$ at 0.05 level of significance, 12 degrees of freedom.

Since the computed value is less than the tabular value, the computed value of r indicates no evidence of any association.

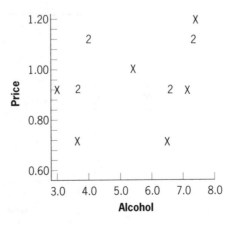

Figure 10.1 Price versus alcoholic content per glass

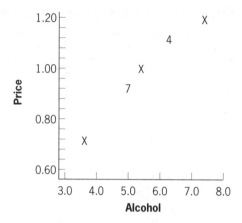

Figure 10.2 Price versus alcoholic content per glass

Rank order correlation

Where we have ordinal data, it is appropriate to use the Spearman Rank correlation method. The formula is:

$$r = 1 = 6\Sigma D^2 / n(n^2 - 1)$$

where D is the absolute difference between rankings and n is the number of observations.

Regression analysis

The first step in regression analysis is to plot the relationships between the dependent and the independent variables on a graph: this is referred to as the scatterplot (as shown in Figures 10.3 to 10.6). This will give some idea of the general kinds of

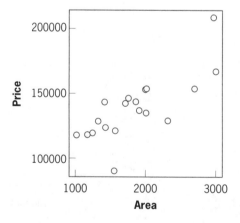

Figure 10.3 Scatterplot – price versus area

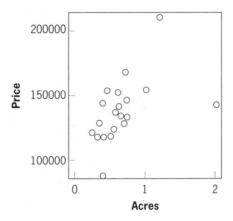

Figure 10.4 Scatterplot – price versus acres

relationship that exist between the data. Once it has been established that a linear relationship exists, it is appropriate to derive values for the equation for fitting a straight line to two variables: $Y = a + b(X)$. Regression analysis fits a line through the data points that minimises the sum of the squared deviations. In order to position the line, two values have to be determined: a, the intercept and b, the regression coefficient.

Suppose we have the following data about houses for sale:

- price
- area in square feet covered by building
- acres of garden
- number of rooms
- number of bathrooms/toilets.

Which of the various factors in Table 10.8 that describe the house are most closely associated with the price?

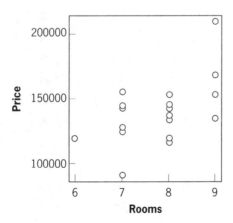

Figure 10.5 Scatterplot – price versus rooms

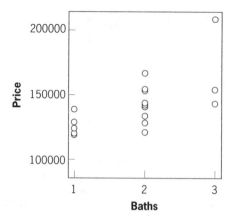

Figure 10.6 Scatterplot – price versus bathrooms

Table 10.8 Houses for sale

Price	Area	Acres	Rooms	Baths
£168,500	2990	0.70	9	2
£122,000	1560	0.24	8	2
£136,000	1990	0.65	9	2
£129,000	1320	0.68	7	1
£136,000	1990	0.70	8	2
£154,000	1980	0.45	8	2
£129,000	2300	0.34	7	2
£118,000	1150	0.32	8	1
£144,000	1400	2.00	7	3
£143,000	1700	0.60	8	2
£120,000	1230	0.50	6	1
£155,000	1990	1.00	7	2
£90,000	1550	0.40	7	1
£154,000	2700	0.60	9	3
£125,000	1400	0.55	7	1
£145,000	1850	0.38	7	2
£146,500	1750	0.72	8	2
£118,000	1000	0.40	8	1
£210,000	2950	1.20	9	3
£138,000	1900	0.57	8	1

Overall we see that there appears to be some degree of positive association between each one of the variables and the price. The clustering of data points along a straight line (indicating the goodness of fit) is perhaps best exhibited between area and price, although acres and price also appear to be well associated. We calculate the regression equation for the relationship between one independent variable and one dependent variable by means of the following equation:

$$Y = a + b(X)$$

where b is the amount of change that takes place in Y for each unit of change in X.

$$b = \frac{\Sigma XY - [(\Sigma X)(\Sigma Y)/n]}{\Sigma X^2 = [(\Sigma X^2)/n]}$$

a is the intercept or the value of Y when X is zero. It is the point where the regression line crosses the Y axis.

Using Minitab 8.0 and SPSSPC, the following bivariate regressions are obtained on the above data (note that figures may show the effects of rounding off), where:

Coef	= regression coefficient
Stdev	= standard deviation
t	= t ratio (statistic)
p	= probability of occurrence
s	= standard error of the estimate
Fit Stdev	= fit standard deviation
Fit	= fit
Residual	= residual
St resid	= standard residual

1. The regression equation is:

Price = 79 312 + 32.6 area

Predictor	Coef	Stdev	t-ratio	p
Constant	79312	12691	6.25	0.000
Area	32.555	6.627	4.91	0.000

s = 16 231 R-sq = 57.3% R-sq(adj) = 54.9%

Analysis of variance

Source	DF	SS	MS	F	p
Regression	1	6356522504	6356522504	24.13	0.000
Error	18	4741927496	263440416		
Total	19	11098450000			

Unusual observations

Obs	Area	Price	Fit Stdev	Fit	Residual	St Resid
13	1550	90000	129772	4091	−39772	−2.53R
19	2950	210000	175349	8233	34651	2.48R

R denotes an observation with a large standard residual.

2. The regression equation is:

Price = 119 815 + 29 593 acres

Predictor	Coef	Stdev	*t*-ratio	*p*
Constant	119815	9623	12.45	0.000
Acres	29593	12767	2.32	0.032

s = 21791 R-sq = 23.0% R-sq(adj) = 18.7%

Analysis of variance

Source	DF	SS	MS	F	*p*
Regression	1	2551202835	2551202835	5.37	0.032
Error	18	8547247165	474847065		
Total	19	11098450000			

Unusual observations

Obs	Acres	Price	Fit Stdev	Fit	Residual	St Resid
9	2.00	144000	179000	17911	−35000	−2.82RX
19	1.20	210000	155326	8547	54674	2.73R

R denotes an observation with a large standard residual.
X denotes an obs whose X value gives it large influence.

3. The regression equation is:

Price = 22 518 + 15 036 rooms

Predictor	Coef	Stdev	*t*-ratio	*p*
Constant	22518	44284	0.51	0.617
Rooms	15036	5682	2.65	0.016

s = 21068 R-sq = 28.0% R-sq(adj) = 24.0%

Analysis of variance

Source	DF	SS	MS	F	*p*
Regression	1	3108768182	3108768182	7.00	0.016
Error	18	7989681818	443871212		
Total	19	11098450000			

Unusual observations

Obs	Rooms	Price	Fit Stdev	Fit	Residual	St Resid
19	9.00	210000	157845	8523	52155	2.71R

R denotes an observation with a large standard residual.

4. The regression equation is:

Price = 94 793 + 24 587 baths

Predictor	Coef	Stdev	*t*-ratio	*p*
Constant	94793	11123	8.52	0.000
Baths	24587	5782	4.25	0.000

s = 17539 R-sq = 50.1% R-sq(adj) = 47.3%

Analysis of variance

Source	DF	SS	MS	F	*p*
Regression	1	5561569565	5561569565	18.08	0.000
Error	18	5536880435	307604469		
Total	19	11098450000			

Unusual observations

Obs	Baths	Price	Fit Stdev	Fit	Residual	St Resid
19	3.00	210000	168554	7970	41446	2.65R

R denotes an observation with a large standard residual.

As predicted by the scattergraph the best relationship is that between area and price.

Knowledge of an independent variable, coupled with the appropriate equation, enables an estimate to be made of the dependent variable. Thus, knowing the area covered by a house can be used to estimate its likely price.

Multivariate analysis

In the preceding sections, simple regression and correlation have been used to determine the association between two variables. However, it is not usual for one independent variable to play such a major part in explaining the dependent variable. Where an r^2 value between two variables is less than 0.8 it is necessary to search for additional independent variables, which can increase the variation explained by the regression or correlation models.

Multiple regression analysis is usually the preferred way of introducing more than one independent variable into the study. The multiple regression model is an expansion of the simple regression model:

$$Y = a + b_1X_1 + b_2X_2 + .. + b_nX_n$$

The number of independent variables used in each model depends on how many are needed to estimate adequately the value of the dependent variable. Most equations usually have fewer than ten independent variables.

Below we show a multiple regression model for the house data above:

Stepwise regression of Price on four predictors (Rooms, Bath, Acre and Area), with $N = 20$

Step	1	2
Constant	79312	69085
Area	32.6	30.1
t-ratio	4.91	5.24
Acres		22800
t-ratio		2.77
S	16231	13859
R-SQ	57.27	70.58

We see that only Areas and Acres are kept in the regression equation. These two independent variables account for more than 70 per cent of the variance in the dependent variable. Since no other independent variables have been included and the total variance accounted for does not come near to 80 per cent, we can only conclude that there must be other factors that are relevant to the house price than those reported here.

For further information on multivariate analysis see McKenzie *et al.*[2] and Hair *et al.*[3]

Cluster analysis

Cluster analysis is the name given to a group of multivariate techniques that identify similar entities from the characteristics possessed by the entities. Objects or variables are identified or classified so that each object is very similar to the others in the cluster with respect to some criteria. The technique examines similarities between observations of entities based on profiles of their scores on a number of measured characteristics. Applications include the following:

- determining the number and composition of market segments;
- facilitating the selection of test markets;
- identifying groups of people with common purchasing interests in segmentation studies. This helps to identify target markets and provides information for establishing product positioning and developing promotional themes.

Example

Various measures of the standard of living in European countries for the end of the 1980s are shown in Table 10.9 and Fig 10.7. On the basis of these measures, countries are clustered according to similarities in the standard of living. The data are

Table 10.9 Measures of standards of living in Europe

	Private per capita	Per '000 population	Per '000 live births	Per '000 ownership		
	Consumption	Doctors	Infant deaths	TV	Cars	Phones
Austria	7434	2.1	8.3	323	370	525
Belgium	8486	3.3	8.6	301	349	478
Denmark	7705	2.7	7.5	386	321	864
France	8733	2.6	7.5	332	394	608
Germany	8120	3.0	7.5	379	457	650
Ireland	5079	1.5	7.5	216	210	265
Italy	8577	1.3	8.9	255	408	488
Netherlands	8133	2.4	6.8	327	348	639
Norway	8224	2.5	8.3	348	388	622
Spain	6443	3.7	7.8	322	263	396
Sweden	8090	3.1	5.8	393	400	890
Switzerland	10181	2.9	7.3	411	419	856
UK	9154	1.4	8.4	534	318	524

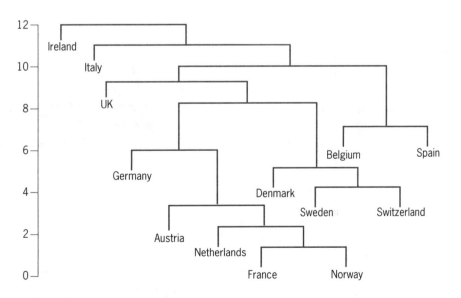

Figure 10.7 Dendrogram showing measures of standard of living in Europe (produced with the aid of S-plus for Windows)[4]

standardised and hierarchical clustering using group average linkage is used to obtain clusters.

From the dendrogram a number of clusters are seen, for example: 'Denmark, Sweden and Switzerland', 'Netherlands, France and Norway', and 'Belgium and Spain'. Subsequent clustering obviously depends on what indicators of the standard of living are taken – a different set of indicators could produce different clustering. Another point is that through standardisation of the data in this example, equal weighting to each of the measures is given. It might be desirable to give more weighting to some measures than to others.

For further information on cluster analysis, *see* Hair *et al.*[3] and Green *et al.*[5]

Factor analysis

This is a generic name given to a class of multivariate statistical methods which undertake data reduction and summarisation. The method analyses the interrelationships among a large number of variables and explains these variables in terms of their common underlying dimensions (factors). For example, a survey questionnaire may consist of 100 questions, but because not all the questions are the same, they do not all measure the basic underlying dimensions to the same extent. Factor analysis enables us to identify the separate dimensions being measured by the survey and obtain a factor loading for each variable on each factor.

Factor analysis may be used to discover a set of dimensions that underlie or underpin a set of variables (Figure 10.8). Applications for factor analysis include:

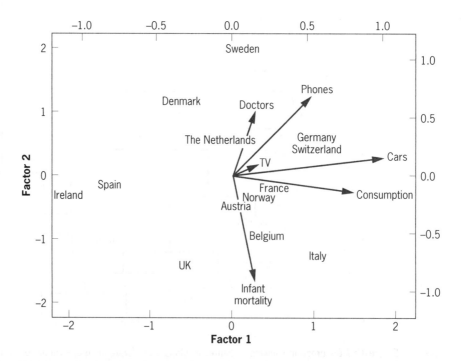

Figure 10.8 Scatterplot of standard of living analysis

- uncovering the factors that influence advertising readership;
- ascertaining which personal characteristics are associated with preferring one brand of product to another;
- uncovering the important dimensions of product/service quality;
- uncovering the factors that need to be taken into account in making decisions about such things as product design and promotion.

The example in Table 10.10 shows a factor analysis of the standard of living data above. Factor 2 represents the health dimension and Factor 1 the spending power dimension.

For further information on factor analysis, *see* Hair *et al.*[3] and Green *et al.*[5]

Conjoint analysis

Conjoint analysis is a method of portraying consumers' decisions realistically as a trade-off among multiattribute products or services. Conjoint analysis helps us to

Table 10.10 Importance of factors in standard of living analysis

	Factor 1	Factor 2	Factor 3
SS loadings	1.644996	1.3791295	1.2124108
Proportion variation	0.274166	0.2298549	0.2020685
Cumulative variation	0.274166	0.5040209	0.7060894

The degrees of freedom for the model is 0

Uniquenesses:

Consump	Doctors	Infant mortality	TV	Cars	Phones
0.08042417	0.7765078	0.3057129	0.3231836	0.1644488	0.1131866

Loadings:

	Factor 1	Factor 2	Factor 3
Consump	0.755		0.588
Doctors	0.108	0.460	
Inf mort		−0.825	
TV	0.176	0.120	0.795
Cars	0.891	0.161	0.126
Phones	0.481	0.665	0.461

Obtained with the aid of S-Plus for Windows using principal axis method.

understand how people develop preferences for products or services. It is based on the simple notion that consumers evaluate the utility or value of something by combining the separate amounts of utility provided by each attribute.

It is closely related to traditional experimentation. In situations where people are involved we often need to conduct experiments with factors we can control. For example, should a chocolate bar be slightly sweet to the taste or very sweet? Should it be promoted as a slimmers' product or not? What price should be asked for the product?

In conjoint analysis the use of experimental design in the analysis of consumer decisions has two objectives. First, the experiments may try to assess how the sweetness of the chocolate bar contributes to the willingness of the consumer to buy it. It may also seek to assess how much change in the willingness to buy can be accounted for by differences between the levels of sweetness. Second, the experiments may seek to establish a valid model of consumer judgements that is useful in predicting the consumer acceptance of any combination of attributes, even those not originally evaluated by the consumer.

Conjoint analysis has been used in the pharmaceutical industry for product positioning close to launch where the product attributes were not changeable. However, it is now used earlier in product development to help define clinical endpoints, and with input into go/no-go decisions.[6]

Conjoint analysis: an illustration

In a furniture polish concept-testing experiment, each respondent has been told about the properties of eight dummy cans of polish to rank choices in order of preference for purchase. The responses for two respondents are shown in Table 10.11.

For simplicity, in applying the technique we will assume an additive model is appropriate and that the overall preference for a combination of attributes is represented as:

$$\text{Preference sib} = \text{PWs} + \text{PWi} + \text{PWb}$$

Table 10.11 Concept-testing experiment: responses

Size	Properties	Brand	Respondent 1	Respondent 2
Small	A	Alpha	1	1
	A	Beta	2	2
	B	Alpha	5	6
	B	Beta	6	5
Large	A	Alpha	3	4
	A	Beta	4	3
	B	Alpha	7	7
	B	Beta	8	8

where the overall preference for a combination of size, properties and brand (Preference sib) is the sum of PWs, PWi, and PWb, the estimated part-worths for the levels of size, properties and brands, respectively.

In order to calculate the coefficients, we have to specify the composition rules and if the additive rule strictly holds, a simple difference from the mean (ANOVA) should apply. The average rank of the eight combinations is 4.5 and we calculate the impact of each factor. For example, the average ranks for the two levels of size are:

$$\text{Small} = (1 + 2 + 5 + 6)/4 = 3.5$$

$$\text{Large} = (3 + 4 + 7 + 8)/4 = 5.5$$

Figures for properties and brand are similarly calculated. Then, for respondent 1 the average ranks and deviations for each factor from the overall average rank (4.5) are shown in Table 10.12.

Higher rank and a more preferred stimulus are usually given a smaller number so the next step is to reverse all the signs so that the positive part-worths now indicate higher preference. Coefficients are then calculated by:

- squaring the deviations and finding their sum (in this case the total is 10.5);
- multiplying each squared deviation by a standardising value calculated as the number of levels divided by the sum of the squared deviations, in this case (6/10.5) or .571;
- taking the square root of the standardised squared deviation to get the actual coefficient.

By way of illustration, for the first level of property (A), the deviation of 2 (reversing the sign!) is squared and then multiplied by .571 to obtain 2.284. To calculate the coefficent for this level, we then take the square root of 2.284 to obtain a coefficient of 1.511. This process yields the coefficients for each level shown in Table 10.13.

The part-worth estimates are in a common scale, so the relative importance of each factor can be computed directly. The importance of a factor is represented by the range of its levels. The ranges are then standardised by dividing each range by the sum of the ranges. For example, for respondent 1, the ranges are 1.512 and .756. The relative importances for size, properties and brand are calculated as 1.512/5.294, 3.022/5.294 and .756/5.294 or 29 per cent, 57 per cent and 14 per cent, respectively.

Table 10.12 Average ranks and deviations for respondent 1

Factor level	Average rank	Deviation
Small	3.5	−1
Large	5.5	+1
A	2.5	−2
B	6.5	+2
Alpha	4.0	−.5
Beta	5.0	+.5

Table 10.13 Coefficients for each level

Size		Property		Brand	
Small	Large	A	B	Alpha	Beta
.756	−.756	1.51	−1.51	.378	−.378

We can follow the same procedures for the second respondent and calculate the average ranks, deviations and coefficients for each level (Table 10.14).

To examine the ability of the model to predict the actual choices of the respondents, we predict performance order by summing the coefficients for the different combinations of factor levels and rank ordering the resulting scores. The calculations for respondent 1 are shown in Table 10.15.

The predicted preference order can be compared to the respondent's actual preference order for a measure of predictive accuracy. The predictive preference orders for both respondents are shown in Table 10.16

In the case of respondent 2, since the weights of zero were calculated for the brand name the compositional rule is unable to predict a difference between brands within the ingredient and can size combinations. Brand name may be a random choice, given size and properties. Moreover, when two or more stimuli have equal total-worth predictions, the rank orders are averaged.

The example illustrated assumes an additive model only as the base for the compositional rule. Original rankings assumed that no interaction effect occurs: for example, the respondent prefers Alpha and normally prefers property A over B. If interaction is thought to have a serious effect, steps have to be taken in the analysis to allow for this.

Multidimensional scaling and perceptual mapping

It is easier to understand the relationships between facts, events or objects if we can visualise these relationships spatially. There are a number of techniques that go under the heading of multidimensional scaling and perceptual mapping techniques which enable us to do exactly that. They allow us to see visually how products and

Table 10.14 Average ranks, deviations and coefficients for respondent 2

Factor level	Average rank	Deviation	Coefficent
Small	3.5	−1	.77
Large	5.5	+1	−.77
A	2.5	−2	1.55
B	6.5	+2	−1.55
Alpha	4.0	−.5	0.0
Beta	5.0	+.5	0.0

Table 10.15 Respondent 1: Calculations

Product description			Predicted value	
Size	Properties	Brand	Part-worth total	Predicted rank
Small	A	Alpha		
.756 +	1.51 +	.378 =	2.644	1
Small	A	Beta		
.756 +	1.51 +	−.378 =	1.888	2
Small	B	Alpha		
.756 +	−1.51 +	.378 =	−.376	5
Small	B	Beta		
.756 +	−1.51 +	−.378 =	−1.132	6
Large	A	Alpha		
−.756 +	1.51 +	.378 =	1.132	3
Large	A	Beta		
−.756 +	1.51 +	−.378 =	.376	4
Large	B	Alpha		
−.756 +	−1.51 +	.378 =	−1.888	7
Large	B	Beta		
−.756 +	−1.51 +	−.378 =	−2.644	8

services are perceived by users in relationship to one another. There are a variety of perceptual-mapping programs and techniques designed to work with the different kinds of data that have been collected.

Below is an example of the use of Multiscale II.[7] In this case the brands of watches were taken in pairs and respondents were asked to judge how dissimilar the brands were *vis-à-vis* each other.

Judgement-similarity measures between products or brands can be used to create geometric representations in multidimensional spaces called perceptual maps. The brands or products are represented by points in the space, while the dimensions represent the attributes used by the customers in making the similarity judgements. Brands located close to each other are judged to be similar on the attributes and thus form a defined market. In Figure 10.9, information about the competitive sets is obtained by the examination of clusters of points. Products A, F and L (Rolex, Jaeger and Ebel) cluster together, but are separate, for example, from M and P (Tag and Breitling), which form another cluster.

Comparing products at the extreme points of both dimensions gives some idea of the name to give to each of the two axes. On the horizontal axis Jaeger at one extreme contrasts with Fossil at the other – perhaps reflecting the status symbol – high-price dimension, while on the vertical axis, Accurist and Roamer contrast with Swatch and Fossil, reflecting the conservatism or lack of it of the brands.

Table 10.16 Predictive preference orders: both respondents

Original rank	Predicted rank order	
	Respondent 1	Respondent 2
1	1	1.5
2	2	1.5
3	3	3.5
4	4	3.5
5	5	5.5
6	6	5.5
7	7	7.5
8	8	7.5

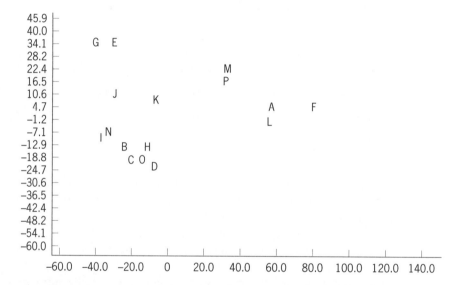

Figure 10.9 Configuration plot for dimension 2 (vertical axis) against dimension 1

SUMMARY

This chapter has examined how research results can be analysed and interpreted to establish meaningful patterns. The steps involved in converting completed research instruments into tables has been examined, together with the coding of answers to questions and the statistical treatment of survey data. Attention has been given to the role of the computer in transforming and facilitating the interpretation of research data. Specific topics covered include the cross-tabulation of data, correlation and regression. Multivariate analysis of variance has also been covered, together with other multivariate techniques such as multiple regression analysis, cluster analysis, factor analysis, conjoint analysis and multidimensional scaling.

Questions

1   What is meant by data interpretation? Discuss the kind of pitfalls that we have to watch for when interpreting data.

2   Explain data tabulation and editing and coding.

3   Calculate the percentage of house owners across all age groups for the whole sample.

Number and percentage of house owners among three age groups.

	Total		
	18–29 No.	30–49 No.	50+ No.
Total interviews	150	230	140
% house owners	36	65	29

4   Calculate the mean, the median and the mode in the following case:

Number of cars per household in 25 surveyed households				
2	2	4	1	1
1	2	0	1	2
0	1	0	1	2
3	3	0	1	1
2	1	2	2	1

Which average best describes the data?

5   What is the range in the data in Question 4?

6   What is the standard deviation and variance of the data in Question 4?

7   In a survey of 281 consumers, the question asked was: Are you aware of brand X? The tally of responses is shown separately below for men and women:

	Yes	No
Men	55	85
Women	65	76

Is there a difference between men and women in terms of their respective levels of awareness of brand X?

8   What are analysis of variance techniques? What do they attempt to measure? In the context of what kinds of problems might they be useful?

9   Fourteen brands of cider and their price per glass and alcoholic content per glass:

Brand	Price (£)	Alcohol content (%)
1	1.71	3.3
2	1.62	3.2
3	1.94	3.1
4	1.81	3.6
5	1.65	4.3
6	1.67	2.2
7	1.56	3.6
8	1.54	1.8
9	1.76	1.7
10	1.88	2.4
11	1.91	2.1
12	1.93	3.2
13	1.72	3.3
14	1.88	3.1

(a)   Produce a scattergraph to show the relationship between the two variables.

(b)   Calculate the Pearson correlation coefficient to measure the relationship between the two variables.

(c)   Calculate the bivariate regression equations (1) using alcoholic content as the independent variable and (2) using the price of cider as the independent variable.

(d)   Interpret and comment on the analysis you have undertaken.

10   The data below is a modified dataset for the one appearing in the text which refers to a different area of the country. Use multiple regression analysis to analyse the data set.

Price	Area	Acres	Rooms	Baths
£128,500	1220	1.50	6	2
£142,000	1670	0.74	7	2
£146,000	1330	0.25	6	2

£159,000	1560	1.38	8	1
£186,000	1430	0.40	7	1
£174,000	1730	1.95	6	2
£119,000	2210	1.34	8	2
£198,000	1780	0.52	9	1
£134,000	1290	2.30	6	2
£153,000	1340	0.70	7	1
£170,000	1810	1.20	8	1
£185,000	1740	1.90	6	2
£91,000	1330	1.76	6	1
£154,000	2700	0.60	9	3
£125,000	1400	0.55	7	1
£145,000	1850	0.38	7	2
£146,500	1750	0.72	8	2
£118,000	1000	0.40	8	1
£210,000	2950	1.20	9	3
£138,000	1900	0.57	8	1

11   Indicate the possible applications, in marketing research, for:

(a) cluster analysis

(b) factor analysis

(c) conjoint analysis

(d) multidimensional scaling.

Case study 10.1   La Gaieté Parisienne

La Gaieté Parisienne owns four boutiques in and around Paris. Recently it undertook a survey of 1000 customers which, among other things, attempted to ascertain whether there was any association between age and the boutique patronised by respondents. A random sample of 250 customers was taken at each boutique between 12 May and 30 May.

If there were any associations between age and boutique patronage, there might be an argument for changing the mix of items offered for sale at each of the boutiques. The following table shows the boutique and the age profile of the respondents interviewed at each boutique.

Boutique	Age				
	Under 18	18–24	25–34	35–44	45 and over
Montparnasse	57	71	61	38	23
St Lazare	48	82	86	20	14
La Fayette	51	66	65	40	28
Madeleine	44	47	54	56	49

Question

What advice would you offer?

Case study 10.2   Summit Motors (B)

Summit Motors' records indicate that less than 40 per cent of its new car buyers remain loyal service customers after the first free service and the dealer is keen to increase the percentage to at least 50 per cent. Some fourteen different attributes have been identified as affecting the patronage of a service facility and a small survey has been conducted among new car purchasers who have bought cars during the past two years. Respondents were asked two questions about each of the identified attributes:

1 How important is the attribute?
2 How well did Summit Motors perform in terms of this attribute?

Mean importance and performance rating from some 311 of 682 contacted previous buyers are shown in the following table.

No.	Attribute	Mean importance rating	Mean performance rating
1	Job done first time	3.79	2.68
2	Complaints dealt with speedily	3.61	2.78
3	Warranty work attended to promptly	3.57	3.11
4	Can do any job required	3.59	2.96
5	Service available when required	3.42	3.02
6	Friendly/courteous service	3.36	3.28
7	Car ready when promised	3.33	3.00
8	Only necessary work performed	3.42	3.06
9	Low service prices	3.26	1.95

10	Clean-up after service done	3.22	2.97
11	Convenient for home	2.46	2.21
12	Convenient for work	2.39	2.47
13	Courtesy cars available	2.32	2.33
14	Maintenance reminders posted	1.99	3.38

A five-point rating scale was used in both cases. In terms of importance, the scale ran from extremely important (5) to not important (0). In the case of performance, the scale ran from excellent (5) to poor (0).

Questions

1 Plot the 28 attribute scores on a two-dimensional graph, the axes being (1) importance of attributes and (2) Summit's performance on the attributes.

2 How might Summit interpret this graphical representation of the data?

Case study 10.3 | **Mr Hungry's Burger Bar**

Mr Hungry's Burger Bar is a national chain of hamburger restaurants with branches in all major cities of the UK and most large towns. The burger bars typically attract three main categories of customer: teenagers looking for a cheap, filling lunch while cruising shopping malls, parents who take young children to the restaurants for a treat or birthday celebration, and office workers and others looking for a quick lunch stop during the day or a pre-cinema snack in the evening.

In an attempt to gauge customer attitudes to the restaurant, each customer is asked to complete a form, which uses a five-point Likert scale to assess responses across a range of issues. The form is as shown below.

At Mr Hungry's we are always looking for ways to improve our service to you, the customer. To help us do this, we would be grateful if you could take a few moments to fill out this form.

	):<	):	I:	(:	(:>
Promptness of service from staff					
Quality of food					
Cleanliness of restaurant					
Value for money					
Facilities for children					

Range of choice on menu

Convenient location

Thank you for your help. We look forward to seeing you again soon at Mr Hungry's!

Returns from the forms tended to be low (less than 10% from most restaurants) but given the very large numbers of customers involved, the firm's customer services department found that they were overwhelmed with forms, with 12 532 usable responses coming in during the first month. A raw tabulation of the forms showed the following pattern.

	):<	):	I:	(:	(:>
Promptness of service from staff	3891	3202	1576	1789	2074
Quality of food	4007	2956	1809	1687	2073
Cleanliness of restaurant	3568	2508	1457	1708	3291
Value for money	4578	3672	1067	1431	1784
Facilities for children	3457	3278	2890	1459	1448
Range of choice on menu	3279	2845	2078	1897	2433
Convenient location	2450	1891	1546	2581	4064

On the face of it, these figures caused some consternation; it seemed that on most measures the restaurants were not doing well. The trend was for customers to be very dissatisfied or dissatisfied with each element of the restaurant, with only the convenience of location coming out well.

Another problem was that the forms could not be segmented; the analysts were unable to tell which sub-category of the firm's target customers had filled in each form. Since the restaurants remained busy, and indeed business seemed to be increasing rather than decreasing, senior management felt that the research must be flawed in some ways. After all, the customers were perfectly capable of voting with their feet by going to any one of half-a-dozen other hamburger outlets; if the restaurants were obviously all right, and the research said the restaurants were all wrong, then the research had to be at fault. The directors of Mr Hungry's told the researchers to look again at the research design and report back.

(Case contributed by Jim Blythe.)

Questions

1 Plot the above figures on a graph, using a separate plot for each attribute. What can you deduce from the shape of the lines?

2 How might the respondents be divided so that the researchers could determine whether responses regarding one attribute of the restaurants relate to responses regarding another attribute?

3 Which of the above attributes show significant correlations with each other? What might be the reasons for these correlations?

4 What are the sources of bias in data of this type?

5 How might the firm improve the form in order to obtain better quality data?

6 How might you check whether the variation shown in the above data is statistically significant?

Further reading

Burdick, R K (1983) Statement of hypotheses in the analysis of variance, *Journal of Marketing Research*, August, pp 320–4.

Cattin, P and Wittink, D (1982) Commercial use of conjoint analysis: a survey, *Journal of Marketing*, 46, pp 44–53.

Curwin, J and Slater, R (1991) *Quantitative Methods for Business Decisions* (3rd edn), London: Chapman & Hall.

Deal, K (1997) Determining success factors for financial products: a comparative analysis of CART, Logit and factor/discriminant analysis, *Service Industries Journal*, 17(3), July, pp 489–506.

Dolan, C V (1994) Factor analysis of variables with 2,3,5 and 7 response categories: a comparison of categorical variable estimators using simulated data, *British Journal of Mathematical and Statistical Psychology*, 47, pp 309–326.

Freeman, P (1991) Using computers to extend analysis and reduce data, *Journal of the Market Research Society*, 33(2), pp 127–36.

Hair, J, Anderson, R, Tatham, R and Black, W (1995) *Multivariate Data Analysis with Readings* (4th edn), New York: Macmillan. Illustrates multivariate techniques using marketing examples.

Huff, D (1991) *How to Lie with Statistics*, Harmondsworth: Penguin Books.

Kaciak, E, and Louviere, J (1990) Multiple correspondence analysis of multiple choice experiment data, *Journal of Marketing Research*, 27, pp 455–65.

Kamakura, W A and Wedel, M (1997) Statistical data fusion for cross-tabulation, *Journal of Marketing Research*, 34(4), November, pp 485–98.

Lenell, W and Bissoneau, R (1996) Using causal comparative and correlational designs in conducting market research, *Journal of Professional Services Marketing*, 13(2), pp 59–69.

Rogers, K (1996) Correspondence analysis: the big picture, *Quirk's Marketing Research Review*, Article 2, April.

Sawyer, A and Peter, J P (1983) The significance of statistical significance tests in marketing research, *Journal of Marketing Research*, 20, May, p 125.

Serious Data Analysis Software, Chicago, IL: SPSS, 1989.

Strutton, D and Pelton, L (1994) A multiple correspondence analysis of telephone contact rates, *The Mid-Atlantic Journal of Business*, 30(1), pp 27–39.

Zeisel, H (1985) *Say It with Figures*, New York: Harper.

References and notes

[1] Kress, G (1988) *Marketing Research* (3rd edn), Upper Saddle River, NJ: Prentice-Hall, pp 260–1.

[2] McKenzie, J, Schaefer, R L and Farber, E (1995) *The Student Edition of Minitab for Windows*, Reading, MA: Addison-Wesley, ch 9.

[3] Hair, J F, Anderson, R E, Tatham, R L and Black, W C (1992) *Multivariate Data Analysis*, New York: Macmillan.

[4] S-Plus for Windows, Statistical Sciences, Inc, 1700 Westlake Av N Suite 500, Seattle, WA 98109, USA.

[5] Green, P E, Tull, D S and Albaum, G (1988) *Research for Marketing Decisions*, Upper Saddle River, NJ: Prentice-Hall.

[6] Winters, P (1996) Of mergers, managers, money, mailsters...and patients too, *Research Plus*, April.

[7] *Multiscale II*, Ramsay, J O, Psychology Department, McGill University.

Qualitative data analysis

OBJECTIVES

After reading this chapter you should be able to:

- understand the general overall approach to qualitative analysis;

- appreciate the types of computer programs that may be used to help in the process of categorisation and other aspects of qualitative research;

- understand how to improve data display;

- convey meaning in the analysis through the use of matrices, networks and diagrams.

KEY WORDS

transcribing data	concordance
indices	matrices
categories	networks
KWIC	causal diagrams
key word in context	cognitive maps
text segments	taxonomy

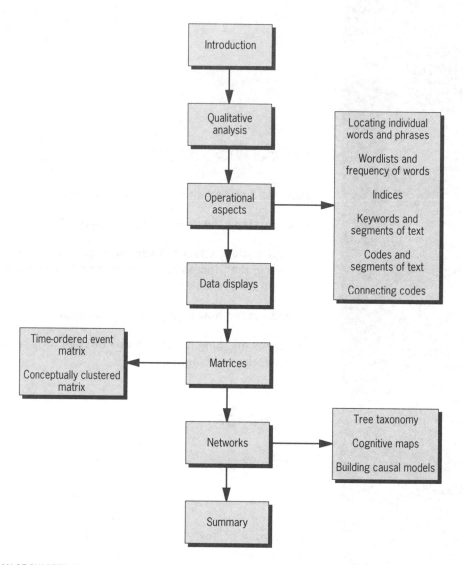

PLAN OF CHAPTER 11

INTRODUCTION

In this chapter we look at how qualitative data might be analysed. Traditionally the approach has been to transcribe notes or recording of meetings and to make an analysis based on visual inspection of the data, quoting what people have said as evidence to support a point of view. The approach has appeared to lack the rigour of quantitative analysis. Recently, however, more analytical methods have been introduced and brought to bear on this form of research and an introduction to these methods is presented here.

The chapter first considers the general overall approach to qualitative analysis, a key aspect of which involves transcribing what has been said or otherwise recorded and then undertaking a detailed analysis of the transcribed written text. This involves searching for keywords and phrases and categorising sections of text. Methods for doing this are reported in the chapter, together with types of computer programs that may be used to help. In quantitative research, tables and graphs are used to display data and convey meaning in the analysis. In qualitative analysis the same effect may be achieved with matrices and networks. The chapter provides some examples of these tools. In the case of networks, attention is also specifically given to the construction of causal diagrams which can do much to help the interpretation of findings.

QUALITATIVE ANALYSIS

Qualitative analysis is a term for the analysis of data that are not numeric. The concept, however, means different things to researchers, depending on the type of approach they take. Not only the nature of the data varies (responses to open-ended questions, narrative fieldnotes, interview transcripts, personal diaries, public documents, etc.) but even if two researchers were to analyse the same text, their strategies and outcomes are likely to be quite different, each justified in the light of their epistemological and research frameworks. It is necessary, therefore, to take into account the variations in the processes that researchers employ when they set about analysing qualitative data. Moreover, qualitative research tends to lay considerable emphasis on situational and often structural contexts, in contrast to quantitative research, which is often multivariate but weak on context. Qualitative research tends to be weak on cross-comparisons.[1]

Despite many practical variations, the stages in qualitative research follow the lines indicated in Figure 11.1. This may include initial background reading of related documents and formal or informal discussions, followed by focus-group or depth interviews, or even open-ended survey questionnaires. Taken together, this constitutes the data-collection stage. The next step involves the subject matter of this chapter: an analysis of transcripts from interviews, discussions and other

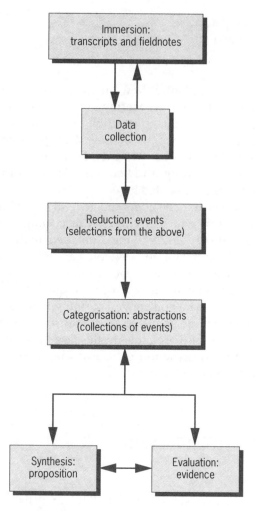

Figure 11.1 Stages of qualitative research

sources. In the analysis the data has first to be reduced into a manageable form and from the more manageable form abstractions from the data, usually referred to as events, are then categorised. This can then lead to the synthesis of ideas and testable propositions.

OPERATIONAL ASPECTS OF QUALITATIVE RESEARCH

First, we consider the major operations required in qualitative research. The following list is not exhaustive and there may be other operations.

Locating individual words and phrases

Suppose we want to locate individual words and phrases for the purpose of cross-tabulation. For example, we might want to establish whether men are more likely to say they use a product for a particular purpose more than women do. In order to establish this, a survey is conducted. If in the first instance we do not have any ideas of the responses people are going to make, the question will have been phrased as an open-ended one. However, after the survey results are made available, it might be quite apparent from cursory inspection that many of the responses do in fact contain a common idea or phrase. It is necessary therefore to code the answers that have been given so that they can be cross-tabulated with other data that have been gathered, such as gender, age, incomes, etc. of respondents.

Where the researcher simply wants to search for words and phrases, word-processing packages or databases may be all that is needed.

Creating alphabetic word lists, counting the frequency of the occurrence of words

This may be used in connection with responses to open-ended questions, to obtain frequency counts. However, it may be much more useful in the context of analysing focus-group interview data or even depth interviews. In order to obtain an initial idea about where the emphasis of discussions has been, it is often useful to compare the frequencies of the occurrence of words and phrases used in discussion and to examine the context in which they have been used.

Several computer programs can help in this particular task, for example, *Longman Concordance*. Such programs produce an alphabetic list with frequency counts.

Creating indices (attaching source information to each occurrence) and key word in context concordance

Where it is important to compare what has been said in one context with what has been said in another context, we could merely compare the frequency of the occurrence of relevant words (content analysis). However, some researchers may prefer to look at a list of locations of each word or phrase. Such a list would be similar to an index in the back of a book, but it would provide information on several levels: document name, chapter number, page and perhaps even paragraph number. In this way, not only can the words be compared across texts, but their locations can be found and the context can be taken into consideration. Techniques that are helpful here involve the researcher creating what is commonly called a KWIC concordance (Key Word in Context). The word is listed and each occurrence is surrounded by a specific range of content.

Constructing key word in context is the sole purpose of the KWIC Text Index. It is a simple, cheap program that makes a list of words in a file or any chunk of it and sorts it alphabetically with reference information. The function is also performed by the *Longman Concordance* program, an illustration of which is given here. The key phrase that was searched in this case was 'Aluminium foil' and a proportion of the 127 abstractions is shown in Figure 11.2.

Attaching key words to segments of texts

In speech or written text, an idea may be verbalised in many ways, without ever using the key word that precisely defines it (such as talking about our various car-servicing experiences without ever using the word 'garage', or 'dealer' or the phrase 'car servicing experience'). If the researcher wants to examine a text for topics it is necessary to break the text down into segments that represent topic units and attach to each the appropriate key word. All the segments that deal with the same topic can then be brought together or assembled by a key word and interpreted. This again is something that can well be applied in analysing the transcriptions of focus-group discussions.

This kind of data manipulation is only possible if the data does not consist of continuous text, but are structured chunks of information that are put into fields: then one or more key words are attached that in some way signify the content of any particular field. A search can then be done using the key word and all fields that have the appropriate content are reproduced. All database systems provide this facility.

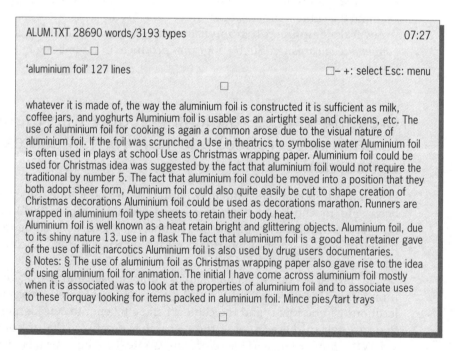

Figure 11.2 Output of *Longman Concordance* program, searching on 'Aluminium foil'

Attaching codes (categorisation symbols) to segments of text

The difference between key words and codes is that key words are one-word summaries of the content of a text segment, while codes are abbreviations of category names. Categories may be thought of as the conceptual equivalent of file folders, each labelled with the name of one aspect of the research project or one topic found in the data. This serves to organise data pieces. These categories may emerge during the analysis, or they may be developed beforehand, or partially both. Key words are complete normal English words, and there can be as many in the study as there are different topics contained in the text. Codes are abbreviations or other made-up fragments.

QUALPRO[2] is the most basic of the qualitative analysis programs. It invites the user to segment and code, then performs searches for the indicated segments and assembles them. An added refinement of the ETHNOGRAPH is that it allows the researcher to search for co-occurring codes and prints out the segments that were coded with both. The ETHNOGRAPH also permits selective searches. In this case the program does not, as usual, search for a particular code or code combination through all data files, but will automatically select only those that satisfy a certain condition.

Connecting codes (categories)

Many researchers want to go beyond mere classification and explore whether or not the subject under analysis possesses a discernible structure, or whether or not linkages exist between or among particular categories. The purpose is to develop propositional statements or to relate concepts in order to discover the underlying principles – often referred to as the generation of hypotheses. Analysing focus-group discussion data in this way can produce questions or hypotheses that might then be answered or tested by large-scale survey work and quantitative analysis.

None of these programs really facilitates 'theory building'. The procedure that theory-building qualitative analysis programs employ is somewhat different to those mentioned previously. Although a code is attached to a particular segment of text, the code 'characterises' the file in which it is present. Codes are therefore thought of as more like 'values' of a variable. For example, if the category or concept is 'relationship with peers' the corresponding codes could be 'competitive', 'cooperative', etc. Any given file will have one of these embedded, perhaps attached to several segments, all of which represent evidence of the 'competitiveness' in the peer relationship, for example. It could also be that among the remaining categories there is one that is concerned with work behaviour. The programs might be used to find that files characterised by competitive relationships with peers are more often than not also characterised by aggressive work behaviour. This might then form the basis of a more formal hypothesis. QSR NUD*IST[3] is a program that facilitates this form of analysis (Figure 11.3). The latest versions of the product are N6 and NVivo.

NUD*IST stands for Non-numerical Unstructured Data Indexing Searching and Theorising. It is a computer package designed to help users handle non-numerical

Figure 11.3 QSR NUD*IST program
Source: QSR NUD*IST[3]

and unstructured data in qualitative analysis. NUD*IST does this by supporting the processes of indexing, searching and theorising.

NUD*IST handles data such as:

- text – for example, reports or minutes, transcripts of unstructured conversational interviews, evidence transcripts, literary documents, personnel records, fieldnotes, newspaper clippings and abstracts
- non-textual records – for example, photographs, tape-recordings, films, maps, plans.

Catterall and Maclaran,[4] in an article examining the use of computers in research, suggest that programs such as NUD*IST take some of the tedium out of exploring qualitative data and therefore help the researcher in this task. However, they also point out that it is important that the program chosen is appropriate to the task in hand and that it remains a tool to assist the researcher and not the driving force of the research. They point out that programs such as NUD*IST are sophisticated tools for the researcher, but the intellectual task of conceptualising data remains the researcher's and will reflect their competence and the quality of the data they have collected.

The same writers point out that such programs encourage the researcher to build detailed and complex coding structures that can be an advantage when exploring complex phenomena. However, they warn that the researcher can get 'bogged down' in its complexities. They warn that such procedure can decontextualise data and make procedure mechanistic. They suggest that there is always an advantage in returning to the original data to gain further insights.

The computer program QSR NUD*IST allows the researcher to build up a complex categorisation system to classify the data under analysis. The document system numbers each line of text for you and brings up the text as a window that allows you to explore it and read each interview thoroughly. Using the indexing system, which allows you to tag and code lines of text with an appropriate term and then store this code in an index tree, you can go through each text indexing lines and assigning line numbers to categories that are created as you go along. These categories are changeable and can be revised over time. As new insights are gained, so you are able to create new codes as the data are explored and a better feel for them is experienced. Another advantage is that it is possible to code one piece of text with several codes. Examples of different categories can often be more than one line long, which means that small sections of text could be assigned a number of different codes if they illustrated several different categories. Thus, NUD*IST allows you to multiple code sections of text and, at the same time, to store each code separately in its own category.

Using computer software in qualitative studies

- Making notes in the field
- Writing up or transcribing fieldnotes or interview proceedings
- Editing: correcting, extending or revising fieldnotes
- Coding: attaching a key word or tags to segments of text to permit later retrieval
- Storage: keeping text in an organised database
- Search and retrieval: locating relevant segments of text and making them available for inspection
- Data 'linking': connecting relevant data segments with each other, forming categories, clusters or networks of information
- Memoing: writing reflective commentaries on some aspect of the data, as a basis for deeper analysis
- Content analysis: counting frequencies, sequences of locations of words and phrases
- Data display: placing selected or reduced data in condensed, organised format, such as a matrix or network for inspection
- Conclusion drawing and verification: helping the analyst to interpret displayed data and to test or confirm findings
- Theory building: developing systematic, conceptually coherent explanations of findings; testing hypotheses
- Graphic mapping: creating diagrams that depict findings or theories
- Preparing interim and final reports

Once the first version of categories is completed, you can go back over all the categories, making reports of them using the indexing system in NUD*IST and revising your initial findings. You can then explore the categories created, to try to gain a better understanding of the phenomena they represented and also to work at better conceptual labels to describe them. This can be accomplished by means of the index system in NUD*IST and a separate report of each category can be produced. The reports can contain all the examples of the categories you have tagged in each transcript and, by exploring these reports, you can refine your thinking about the category and shift, add and delete coding as you feel appropriate. This may be important in places where you have coded things wrongly or where a new category has subsequently been created which better describes an example that had previously been assigned to another category. You can also move the position of the categories within the tree structure to represent what feels more appropriate. As a result, the tree may be simplified as the individual categories became more distinctive.

DATA DISPLAYS

In the context of qualitative analysis a display is a visual format that presents information systematically so that the user can draw valid conclusions and take the required action. In the case of qualitative research the typical mode of display has been extended, unreduced text that the analyst scans through, attaching codes and then extracting code segments and drawing conclusions. The analyst then writes a second form of extended text: a case study report.

Unreduced text by itself is a weak, cumbersome form of display. It makes analysis difficult because data is dispersed over many pages and it is not easy to see as a whole. It is sequential rather than simultaneous, making it difficult to look at two or three variables at once. It is also poorly ordered and can become bulky and monotonously overloading. Making careful comparisons between several extended texts can also be difficult.

Valid analysis requires displays that are focused enough to allow a viewing of a full dataset in the same location and are arranged systematically to answer the research questions at hand. In this sense a full dataset means the condensed, distilled data drawn from a full range of people, events and processes that have been systematically studied. The chances of drawing and verifying valid conclusions are much greater than for extended text: the display is arranged coherently to permit careful comparisons, to detect differences to patterns and themes, and to spot the trends.

Generating formats to display qualitative data is relatively easy. Formats can be as various as the imagination of the analyst permits. They fall into two major types: *matrices,* with defined rows and columns, and *networks,* with a series of nodes with links between them. The data entries can take on different forms: a short block of text, quotes, phrases, ratings, abbreviations, symbolic figures, labelled lines, and so on. The display format and the nature and shape of the entries will depend on what the researcher is trying to understand.

MATRICES

A matrix is effectively the crossing of two lists, set up as rows and columns. A variety of different formats may be of interest to qualitative researchers. The following are illustrative of the kinds of approach that can be taken.

Time-ordered event matrix

Time periods may be defined conceptually and adjusted according to actual happenings. The events may be sorted according to where the event took place, or in some other way (Table 11.1).

The display is helpful for understanding the flow, location and connection of events. It can also be easily compared with similar matrices in other studies. With an analysis and commentary attached, it can also provide a good outline of the process of change that may have taken place.

Conceptually clustered matrix

Many studies are designed to answer a string of research questions – and the string often becomes very lengthy. As a consequence, the performance of a separate analysis and case-report section for each research question is likely to lead to confusion for both the analyst and the reader. The solution is to cluster several research questions so that the meaning can be more easily generated.

A conceptually clustered matrix has its rows and columns arranged so as to bring together items that belong to one another. For example, we may be interested to know whether a relationship exists between people's motives and their attitudes towards purchasing a product. The best way to find out is to cluster the responses to these questions. A format is needed that displays all the relevant responses of all the key informants on one sheet, permits an initial comparison between responses and between informants, lets us see how the data can be analysed further, for

Table 11.1 Time-ordered event matrix

Place	Time period		
	Morning	Afternoon	Evening
Work		Setting up computer program to analyse results	
Home	Analysis of survey results		Checking all final documentation and overheads

Table 11.2 Research questions

Informants	Motives	Attitude to purchasing/stocking brand
Consumers		
C1	Price	Very positive
C2	Price	Fairly positive
C3	Availability	Neutral
Retailers		
R1	Price margin	Neutral
R2	Consumer advertising	Neutral
R3	Price margin	Fairly positive

multicase studies, lends itself readily to cross-case analysis and will not have to be redone and, for multicase studies, provides some preliminary standardisation. Such a display is shown in Table 11.2.

The display matrix possesses on one sheet a format that includes all respondents and all responses to the two research questions. It should be noted that comparisons have been set up between different kinds of informants (customers and retailers). Some preliminary scaling or sorting of responses may be required: types of motive or valence of attitude.

NETWORKS

A network is a collection of nodes or points connected by lines. They can be very useful when it is necessary to focus on more than a few variables at a time. Some examples of the use of networks of different kinds are shown here.

Tree taxonomy

To avoid the implication that concepts are always properly sorted into rows and columns, the tree diagram in Figure 11.4 illustrates how they can also be displayed in a network form. The diagram shows how a respondent might classify motorcars when they are asked the question: 'What kinds of cars are there?' As the respondent continues in the interview, they might next be asked: 'What kinds of cars do you call luxury sport?', or 'What kinds of cars do you call cross-country?', and so on.

Componential analysis may be used as a way to help clarify categories, making it clear why a particular label is assigned to a particular object. We ask for distinctive features of the sort of objects being taxonomised and aim to find the smallest group of features that discriminates them clearly, as shown in Table 11.3.

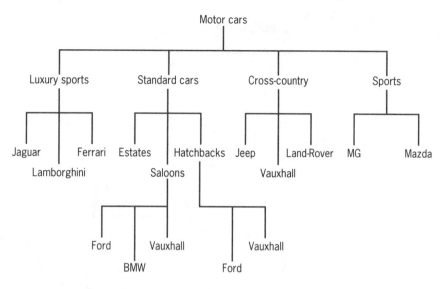

Figure 11.4 Taxonomy of cars

Table 11.3 Smallest group of discriminating features

	Expensive	*Practical*	*High performance*
Lamborghini	+		+
Ferrari	+		+
Jaguar	+		+
Ford		+	
Vauxhall		+	
Land-Rover		+	
MG sports			+
Mazda sports			+

QSR NUD*IST is good at helping to generate taxonomies.

Cognitive maps

It is useful to have displays that show us the complexities of the person. People's minds are not always organised hierarchically, as shown in the taxonomies above. They can be well represented in non-hierarchical network form: a collection of nodes attached by links. A cognitive map displays the person's representations of concepts about a particular domain, showing the relationships among them.

For example, in Figure 11.5's cognitive map we see that the respondent thinks a wrist-watch needs to be fashionable and how this need to be fashionable is reflected in such things as a good quality leather strap, having sports features and having a case made from gold or stainless steel.

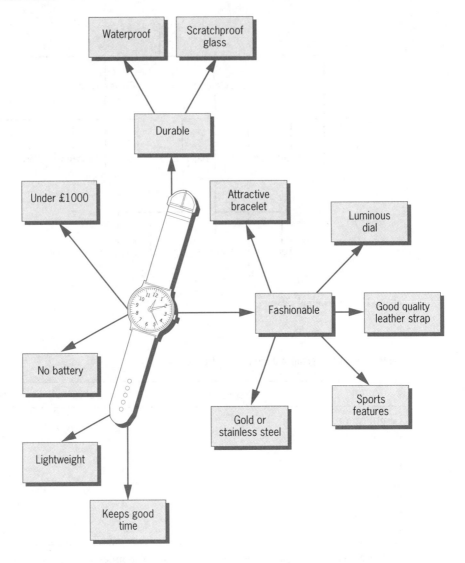

Figure 11.5 Requirements of a wrist-watch

Building causal models

When we are analysing data we might observe that there are associations between elements in the data. The interest is usually to see whether the associations can be integrated into a meaningful explanatory model. To do this it is necessary to apply some heuristics.

The first heuristic involves ordering the model temporally. The questions to be answered then become:

- which variables or events of those found relevant occur first in time?
- which occur along the way during implementation?
- which might be seen as early and late outcomes?

The second heuristic involves considering which variables might reasonably be expected to have a direct impact on other variables, both preceding them in time and having a plausible direct connection. This rule means that we need to think of the mechanisms that could be involved.

The third rule is to check case informants' explanations. What causal linkages do they claim are present? We need to examine our transcripts and fieldnotes very carefully.

The fourth rule is to consider what available research and theories have to say about causal connections.

Using these rules, we have to play with the data for a while. It can help if we put variables or events on cards and move them around into various configurations, looking at the connections that seem sensible. Graphics packages such as Inspiration[5] can also be helpful. Another special program that can help develop causal models is COPE[6] (Cognitive Policy Evaluation). While primarily designed to produce cognitive maps, it enables us to map in two dimensions explanations and consequences of events through a graphic user interface. Since it also has the facility to trace paths throughout the complex network structures that can be constructed, it can also help to establish cause–effect relationships and hence build causal models.

Example

Marketing researchers undertaking focus-group discussions with groups of patients suffering from a specific disease might discover that, in severe cases of loss of appetite, patients are treated in different ways by the GP, depending on whether or not the GP feels they can treat the particular symptom. Where the GP feels confident, a proprietary brand of medicine is prescribed as treatment. Where the GP is unsure, referral is made to the consultant at the hospital who prescribes a non-proprietary brand. The whole process is captured in Figure 11.6.

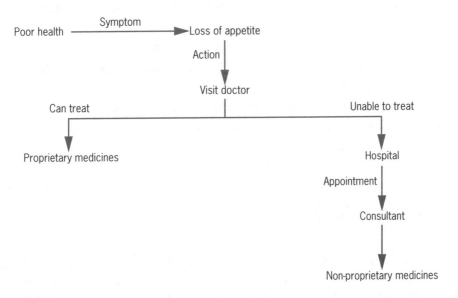

Figure 11.6 Causal diagram

SUMMARY

In this chapter we have examined the general overall approach to qualitative analysis, a key aspect of which involves transcribing what has been said or otherwise recorded and then undertaking a detailed analysis of the transcribed written text. This involves searching for key words and phrases and categorising sections of text. Methods for doing this have been reported in the chapter, together with types of computer programs that may be used to help in this process. In quantitative research, tables and graphs are used to display data and convey meaning in the analysis. In qualitative analysis the same effect may be achieved with the use of matrices and networks. The chapter has given some examples of these tools. In the case of networks, attention has also specifically been given to the construction of causal diagrams that can do much to help in the interpretation of findings.

Questions

1   What do you understand by qualitative analysis? How is it different from quantitative analysis?
2   What are the steps involved in the general process of qualitative research?
3   Indicate some of the operational aspects of qualitative research. What purpose do they serve?
4   Discuss the role that computer programs can play in qualitative research. How can they specifically help with some of the operational aspects?
5   What are data displays?
6   What are the two kinds of data display that can be used in qualitative research? How do they compare with data displays that can be used in quantitative research?
7   To what purposes might cognitive maps be put in qualitative research?
8   What are causal diagrams? What use are they in the context of qualitative research?

Case study 11.1   Cyclist survey

A survey was conducted to ascertain cyclists' views on provisions for them in the town. Cyclists were asked what beneficial improvements were needed. Below are the responses to the survey, together with the sex and age of the respondents.

Sex	Age	Comments
Male	25–34	Improve visibility at A52 road junction with Wellington Road
Female	17–24	More space by the library
Male	17–24	More cycle lanes
Male	25–34	More cycle lanes
Male	17–24	More cycle lanes. No motor vehicles on roads in the city centre at certain times
Male	25–34	Why do cycles have to give way to cars on the A52 roundabout when with no cycle lane they would have priority?!
Female	25–34	More cycle lanes, particularly in the one-way streets
Male	25–34	Enforcement of town/village traffic-speed restrictions
Female	25–34	Very good cycle parking in main streets
Female	17–24	More safe areas for locking bikes – maybe more cycle signs
Male	35–44	More cycle parking racks
Female	25–34	Cycle lanes in and around town and more of them
Male	25–34	Introduce more cycle lanes alongside busy roads and major roundabouts
Male	35–44	More cycle lanes to surrounding towns/villages
Female	35–44	Punishment for those motorists who think the cycle lanes are an extension to the car parks
Female	17–24	Education for drivers. Roads/paths for cycles
Female	25–34	More cycle lanes especially in one-way areas, control parking outside shops
Female	17–24	More cycle paths
Male	17–24	It would help cyclists if the council were to resurface some of the roads
Female	35–44	More cycle lanes
Male	35–44	Road safety by creating cycle route and traffic lights for cyclists
Female	25–34	Cycle paths for as many streets as possible, in as wide an area as possible
Female	25–34	Cycle *priority* lanes in main areas and roundabouts
Male	17–24	Better edges to roads as they are too rough and bumpy
Female	25–34	Resurfacing the whole length of the canal lane
Female	35–44	Increase cycle lanes especially around roundabouts where there are two queues of traffic and little or no room for cyclists. I would like to see improved cycle security facilities at the railway station
Male	25–34	Pay and return lock up facilities
Female	17–24	Against cycle bars (sketch here) or thin street-posts (for parking hours etc.) where I can lock my front wheel and frame to the post, neither of

which are common in town. Maintain the edges of roads better, and avoid putting drains and other obstructions too far out in the road

Male	35–44	More public awareness of the needs of bikers
Male	35–44	More cycle lanes
Female	17–24	In city centre with more facilities to lock a cycle to a fixed object. The speed ramps in Sheldon Road and Park Avenue are extremely uncomfortable for cyclists
Male	25–34	Something more safe round the one-way system
Male	35–44	Try and make car drivers more aware of us cyclists
Female	35–44	Cycle lanes
Male	17–24	More cycle lanes
Male	17–24	The cycle lanes are excellent, could these routes be extended?
Female	17–24	Proper cycle racks outside Army and Navy so that you can lock your bike to something solid. On the A529 we need the cycle path lit because at night the place is a death trap. If you fell off your bike or broke a leg no one would find you till morning
Female	17–24	More cycle lanes at major roundabouts. College Lane desperately needs a cycle lane and road surface improvements
Male	17–24	Perhaps more parking facilities in town centre
Male	35–44	The one-way systems and cycle lanes are unsafe. To cycle in and out of work on the centre of the one-way system is not helped by the cycle lane. The junctions are also dangerous for cyclists
Female	35–44	More cycle pathways
Female	25–34	Add a cycle lane to *all* main roads, and sort out the junction at Southern Road/Westwood Avenue
Female	17–24	Better facilities for leaving bikes
Male	25–34	Pedestrian and cycle crossing or bridge over A52 roundabout
Female	35–44	East Street or North Street cycle rack required
Male	35–44	A52 roundabout: design encourages motorists to not signal on leaving roundabout, into North Street/Dale Road and Lavernum Road
Female	35–44	Worst place to leave cycles in railway station. More cycle lanes
Female	17–24	At the moment it is only a matter of time before there is a fatal accident
Female	35–44	Making sure that vehicles don't keep parking in the cycle lanes
Female	17–24	Cycle parking facilities that are under cover
Male	35–44	Proper cycle lanes. Get rid of the current system at the Fire Brigade roundabout. Cyclists on the roundabout should be given priority over cars leaving the road as any other junction
Female	17–24	More cycle lanes. Promoting more cycle safety
Female	25–34	Somehow improved safety at roundabouts

Male	25–34	I don't think cycling is a problem in the town. London is different
Male	35–44	Cycle lanes on all main roads. Cycle priority on all roads in city especially A52 roundabout
Female	25–34	More bike racks and cycle lanes, and to ease congestion and traffic develop park and ride schemes for motorists
Female	17–24	More cycle lanes, increase other road users' awareness that bikes have a right to be on the road too
Female	17–24	More cycle lanes please
Male	35–44	The new traffic calming humps should have had level gaps in them so that cyclists could ride through them and not up and over them
Male	25–34	More secure facilities at station and other places. Better cycle way, particularly in the dangerous one-way systems. Also traffic lights needed at the junction of Redmayne Drive and Haughton Street
Female	25–34	More cycle lanes
Male	35–44	I think there could be more cycle parks in the four main streets of the town
Female	17–24	Make more cycle paths, as we have in Germany
Female	25–34	Cycle lanes on all major roundabouts and one-way systems
Male	35–44	Cycle lanes beside main roads and greater number of road signs 'Think Bike'
Male	25–34	More cycle racks
Male	35–44	Improve canal towpath cycling. Generally providing better crossing of inner ring road
Male	25–34	More cycle lanes
Female	17–24	In parking facilities, something needed to actually chain bike to
Female	35–44	More cycle lanes and the holes in the roads filled in more often
Male	25–34	Council is lazy and need to sort town before it falls apart
Female	17–24	You need cycling lanes. Cars do not give enough consideration to cyclists
Male	17–24	More cycle paths in town
Female	25–34	More cycle paths through town
Female	35–44	Cycling around roundabouts needs improvement
Female	17–24	Many more cycle lanes needed for safety
Female	35–44	Various parts of the roadside have potholes or cracks which makes cycling both uncomfortable and unsafe
Female	17–24	Supervised parking (preferably sheltered) area near train station
Female	25–34	Make car drivers more aware of cyclists
Female	35–44	Add kerbs to outer cycle lane to prevent drivers encroaching into cycle lanes

Male	17–24	Make car drivers more aware of cyclists on the road
Female	17–24	Everything OK
Female	25–34	*More* cycle parking facilities in town
Male	25–34	Very pleased with cycle route. More of the same would be welcome as although I have never had an accident, the near misses are countless!
Male	35–44	Prohibition of motor vehicles on and within the town centre
Male	35–44	More cycle lanes especially across the by-pass
Male	35–44	More cycle lanes to ring the city and filter lanes for left turns. Additional signs to make motorists aware of cyclists
Female	35–44	A much safer system at A52 roundabout. More cycle lanes on busy roads which don't suddenly peter out
Female	35–44	Lights or bridge over A52 at roundabout. Cycle lanes on all roads
Female	25–34	Additional cycle space throughout town centre. More cycle routes to and from town areas
Male	17–24	Better cycle lanes and more cycle lanes
Male	17–24	More cycle paths, especially by the main roundabouts
Female	25–34	At the roundabout A52 – experience problems with vehicles as fail to indicate when turning off or too close to kerb – roundabout making it very dangerous! Trouble with trucks/lorries and pedestrians in town centre
Female	17–24	Cycle lanes are hopeless on roundabouts as no vehicles indicate where they are going
Female	17–24	A lot more spaces in other parts of town
Male	35–44	Allow cyclists to ride through the pedestrianised parts of town
Male	25–34	Do something about A52 roundabout
Male	35–44	I know it's impossible, but all car drivers should be made to cycle regularly and vice versa
Male	25–34	It would be really useful to be able to cycle though town
Female	25–34	Town centre is particularly poorly served for cycle parking. In other places an increase in spaces would be advantageous to combat overcrowding
Female	25–34	Improvement in road surfaces, especially near the edge of carriageway. Improve vehicle driver awareness to cycles
Male	17–24	More cycle lanes
Male	35–44	I have had four near misses from cars pulling across cycle lane on A52
Male	25–34	Perhaps consider a network of cycle lanes or tracks linking up surrounding villages with town centre
Female	35–44	Improve the edges of the roads
Male	17–24	Provide courses for people to know how to ride safely – as most do not know

Male	35–44	Give cycle priority all the way round the roundabout and do away with the dangerous cycle lane
Male	35–44	Educate car drivers to signal their intentions
Female	35–44	Right of way for cyclists at A52 ring road. Also more cycle lanes in other areas
Male	25–34	Perhaps a cycle lane on the one-way system
Male	25–34	Cycle lanes exclusively for cyclists, especially on busy main roads
Male	35–44	More cycle lanes
Female	25–34	Improve cycle tracks around town
Male	35–44	The two most hazardous spots to cycle in are at the metropolitan roundabout where cyclists give way to motorists and take a chance to cross
Female	35–44	More cycle lanes around fire station
Male	35–44	Maybe there could be a system of padlocking and paying to lock your bike
Male	35–44	Lockable parking outside library
Female	17–24	Raise driver awareness of cyclists and their problems. More and improved cycle ways *away* from traffic
Female	25–34	Extend cycle lanes and improve awareness of motorists – they don't indicate at roundabouts
Male	35–44	More cycle tracks on country roads especially main roads
Male	17–24	Cycle lanes on one-way system roundabouts
Male	35–44	Cycle lane on all roads around town
Male	35–44	City and district generally desperately need more properly designed cycle lanes

Question

Analyse the responses in the best way you can.

Case study 11.2 | Uses of aluminium foil

Respondents were asked to generate as many ideas as they could for uses of aluminium foil. One of the respondents produced the following list of ideas.

1   Covering roast chicken
2   Wrapping potatoes for baking
3   Covering food for storage in a refrigerator
4   Folding it to make a cup to drink out of

5   Using it as a plate
6   Smoothing it out to make a mirror
7   Reflecting sunlight to attract help/send messages
8   Reflecting a heat source for cooking
9   Lining the wall behind a radiator to reflect heat into a room
10   Wrapping up a flower stem for a button hole
11   Making Christmas decorations
12   Making milk bottle tops
13   Stringing small pieces together to make a baby's rattle
14   Making a dish to hold glue
15   Making a dish to hold paint
16   Using under a sleeping bag to stop the cold getting through
17   Wrapping food to cook on a campfire
18   Keeping food fresh without refrigeration
19   Hanging as temporary curtains
20   Sticking on a collage
21   Using to make 'water' for the Brownie Guide pool at Brownie camp
22   Making children's jewellery
23   Wrapping matches to keep them dry
24   Keeping food warm
25   Keeping food cold
26   Screwing it up to make a makeshift ball
27   Making a toy for cats to play with. Foil makes a light but indestructible cat toy
28   Cutting it up into squares to make stepping stones
29   Cutting out fish shapes and having a race to waft them along the hall
30   Cutting a strip to make a bookmark
31   Lining a grill pan to make it easy to clean after use
32   Wrapping up 25th wedding anniversary gifts
33   Wrapping sandwiches for a packed lunch
34   Lining cake-storage tins

Question

Construct a cognitive map showing the respondent's ideas about the possible uses of the aluminium foil.

Further reading

Bryman, A and Burgess, R G (1994) Reflections on qualitative data analysis, in Bryman, A and Burgess, R G (eds), *Analysing Qualitative Data*, London: Routledge, pp 216–26.

Coffey, A, Holbrook, B and Atkinsin, P (1996) Qualitative data analysis: technologies and representations, *Sociological research Online*, 2, http://www.socresonline.org.uk/socresonline/1/1/4.html

Dembhowski, S and Hanmer-Lloyd, S, (1995) Computer applications – a new road to qualitative analysis?, *European Journal of Marketing*, 29(11), pp 50-62.

Denzin, N and Lincoln, Y (1993) *Handbook of Qualitative Research*, Newbury Park, CA: Sage.

Fielding, R and Lee, R (eds) (1991) *Using Computers in Qualitative Analysis*, Berkeley, CA: Sage.

Griggs, S (1987) Analysing qualitative data, *Journal of the Market Research Society*, 32, pp 507–20.

Miles, M B and Huberman, A M (1994) *Qualitative Data Analysis*, London: Sage.

Richards, T and Richards, L (1991) The NUD*IST qualitative data analysis system, *Qualitative Sociology*, 14.

Spiggle, S (1994) Analysis and interpretation of qualitative data in consumer research, *Journal of Consumer Research*, 21(3), pp 491–503.

Strauss, A S (1993) *Qualitative Analysis for Social Scientists*, Cambridge: Cambridge University Press.

Weitzman, E and Miles, M (1995) *Computer Programs for Qualitative Data Analysis*, Thousand Oaks, CA: Sage.

Whipple, T W (1994) Mapping focus group data, *Marketing Research*, 6(1), pp 16–21.

References and notes

[1] Strauss, A S (1993) *Qualitative Analysis for Social Scientists*, Cambridge: Cambridge University Press, p 2.

[2] QUALPRO and ETHNOGRAPH, Qualitative Research Management, 73425 Hilltop Road, Desert Hot Springs, CA, USA.

[3] QSR NUD*IST, Qualitative Solutions & Research Pty Ltd, Box 171, La Trobe University Post Office, Victoria, Australia 3083.

[4] Catterall, M and Maclaran, P (1995) Using a computer to code qualitative data, in *Proceedings of 1995 Annual Conference of the Marketing Education Group 'Making Marketing Work'*, Bradford University, July.

[5] Inspiration, Inspiration Software, Inc., 2920 SW Dolph Court, Suite 3, Portland, Oregon 97219, USA.

[6] COPE, Advertising leaflet/working demo, Department of Management Science, University of Strathclyde.

12 Evaluating, reports and presentation

OBJECTIVES

After reading this chapter you should be able to:

- understand the importance of the presentation to the success of a research study;

- appreciate the preparation of different aspects of the presentation;

- understand how to use some of the visual and electronic aids that are available to the presenter.

KEY WORDS

report   report body
proposal   oral report
executive summary   presentation
outline   visual aids
findings

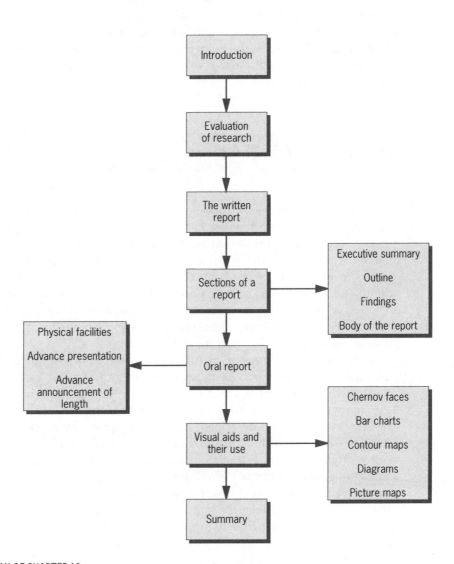

PLAN OF CHAPTER 12

INTRODUCTION

This chapter looks at various ways in which one might evaluate research, and special consideration is given to evaluating research in non-financial terms. The chapter also emphasises how important the presentation is to the success of a research study. It looks at the preparation of the different aspects of the presentation and concludes with a discussion of some of the visual and electronic aids that are available to the presenter.

EVALUATION OF RESEARCH

Marketing research needs to be evaluated *post facto* in order to ascertain its usefulness and cost-effectiveness and to draw lessons from the experience that may prove useful when considering further research. In order to do this the research objectives must be clearly specified in measurable or ascertainable terms so that the degree to which they have been achieved, exceeded or under-achieved can be identified. It may not always be possible to link financial expectations in terms of expected savings or increased profits to the financial cost of carrying out research. In measuring advertising effectiveness, for example, the objective may be to measure increase in product awareness.

There are several ways of evaluating research in non-financial terms. Lincoln and Guba[1] suggest four criteria for evaluating qualitative research – *credibility, transferability, dependability* and *confirmability*. *Credibility* demonstrates that the research was carried out in a manner such that the subject of the research was correctly identified and described. It can be improved by persistent observation to obtain a greater depth of understanding, by triangulation, by using different sources and collection methods of data, and by peer debriefing of colleagues on a continuous basis. This is clearly pertinent to all marketing research studies. *Transferability* is concerned about whether the findings can be applied to another situation that is sufficiently similar to permit generalisation – useful when generating research which may form part of omnibus studies or provide secondary data for other studies. *Dependability* should show that the research processes are systematic, rigorous and well documented. This is an essential foundation upon which all marketing research should be based. It permits subsequent users of the research to ascertain how well the research was conducted. *Confirmability* should be used as a criterion where the study has described the research process fully and it is possible to assess whether the findings flow from the data. Again, this should be a requirement of a marketing research study. Yet another approach to evaluation involves obtaining *respondent validity* for the analysis. This involves discussing findings from the analysis with those who have participated in the study to obtain their reactions and opinions.

THE WRITTEN REPORT

The basic requirement is for a report and presentation that can be believed and trusted by everyone who will be affected by the research (Figure 12.1). The solution to a particular research problem should produce greater efficiency, lower costs and more benefits for the organisation. The presenter of the research results has to convince the audience that the research findings can be acted on for their own benefit. A written report needs to be put together so that interest and belief develop throughout its reading and the recommended action appears as a natural outcome.

It may be beneficial to delete less important questions in order to emphasise the basic problem. Constant attention to the basic problem and its recommendations will make the study and its presentation more usable and interesting in the minds of the listeners and/or the readers of the final presentation. Presenters have the best chance of success if they have planned their research well and meet the expectations of their listeners.

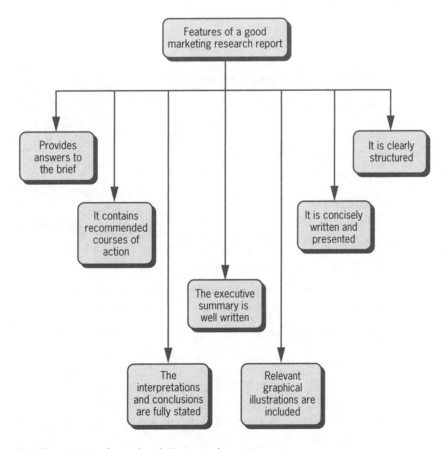

Figure 12.1 Characteristics of a good marketing research report

A good knowledge and understanding of the audience are essential for good reporting. The presenter of a report should know in advance who will receive copies of the written report or who will be at an oral presentation. The report should address itself directly to these people and their needs.

Anticipating objections from people with known mindsets may alter how a report is written – or even how the research is done.

Research studies sometimes tend to deviate from the original problem and proposal. It is often the case that interesting information is uncovered which is peripheral to the study. However, the study should be directed toward the solution of the stated problem and, if research has uncovered another problem that needs looking at, this should be suggested as the basis of another study.

The written or oral presentation must address itself precisely to questions such as:

- Do these recommendations still appear sound?
- Will they affect the needs of the company in the way that was first intended?
- Will the whole study now make sense in the light of conditions when the study was begun?

Contents of a marketing research report

Title page

1   Title
2   Client (optional)
3   Research company (optional)
4   Date

Table of contents

1   Section titles and subheadings with page numbers
2   Table of tables: titles and pages
3   Table of figures: titles and pages
4   Appendices: titles and pages

Management or executive summary

1   Statement of objectives
2   Statement of major findings
3   Statement of conclusions and recommendations
4   Other pertinent information such as limitations of the research or background information.

Introduction

1   Background to the research undertaken
2   People involved in the research, their positions and roles
3   Acknowledgements

Analysis and findings

1   Analytical approach adopted
2   Tables and figures
3   Explanatory text

Conclusions and recommendations

Research methodology

1   Type of study
2   Purpose of study
3   Definition of population of interest
4   Sampling design and method
5   Data collection method adopted and justification for method
6   Questionnaire or other data collection instruments – description and explanation

Limitations

1   Sample size
2   Sample selection
3   Error

Appendices

1   Questionnaire
2   Technical
3   Other

THE SECTIONS OF A REPORT

Executive summary

This is placed at the beginning of the report and allows executives to quickly and easily grasp what has been learned and what is being recommended. Sometimes the digest is bound separately for executives who will not want to read all the details. Experienced presenters often make use of this technique of the separate executive summary.

This executive summary will include the following:

- action implications backed up by key findings;
- discussion of findings for interested middle management;
- a short appendix with a few details of procedures, a sample of appropriate materials, a few detailed tabulations, and statistics.

The outline

The outline should be as complete as possible, since it will greatly facilitate the writing of the final report. All sources of information should be named and details that might seem so obvious that they need not be put on paper should be entered.

The findings

Key findings should stand out, perhaps highlighted by a table, a chart or some other visual aid. The key findings may even form the basis of a separate executive report. Key action recommendations largely stem from the key findings noted.

Details of the procedures followed should be included. These details should include such facts about the study as the research instruments used, sampling methods and the response rate for questionnaires. The procedures should be recorded in enough detail to protect the validity both of the recommendations and of the procedures. This may at some time enable a further study to be made replicating the same procedures so that a comparison can be made with the first study. Once the report has been written up, it can be turned into an oral or a video presentation, or it may even become the basis for a small-group seminar.

The body of the report

The body of the report might include the following:

- a statement of the problem, perhaps slightly modified to allow for changes in instructions and changes caused by early findings in the research;
- a brief account of how the research was conducted;
- a detailed presentation of the findings, but only what is necessary for backing up the recommendations;
- a list of the major recommendations;
- a statement of the implications of the findings and recommendations for specific departments of the sponsoring company.

Objectivity in report writing is of paramount importance. It is a good idea to list the shortcomings of a study since most studies do in fact have them. Style of writing is most important. A research report needs to be sharp, clear and vivid. Simple words are usually best and jargon should be avoided.

THE ORAL RESEARCH REPORT

Only rarely will top executives be interested in the minute details of the recommendations. Later they will want to know almost everything that will affect their firm, if action is to be taken on the recommendations. At this point the recipients of the report will usually want just the highlights of both findings and recommendations.

The physical facilities

The room must be ready with proper lighting, air-conditioning and a sound system that enables everyone to hear. All possibly distracting noises from outside sources must have been eliminated.

Advance preparation of presentation

The presentation must have been well prepared, and all possible interruptions considered. Perhaps several people should participate in the presentation, to relieve the possible boredom of one voice and face.

Advance announcement of length of presentation

Stating how long the presentation will be is a good strategy.

VISUAL AIDS AND THEIR USE

Use of visual aids such as chalkboards, flipcharts and overhead transparencies should be made. Too many visuals, however, can become distracting and often boring. They should be used solely to clarify or reinforce a point. It is a mistake to believe that pictures are always better than words. Visual aids should only be used if they serve a real and necessary purpose.

Figure 12.2 illustrates an overhead transparency that can be prepared with a product such as Microsoft Powerpoint. It shows how a graphic presentation can be combined with key points expressed in words.

There is a wide range of graphical illustrations that can be used. In Figures 12.3–12.5 we show three examples, ranging from the conventional bar chart to the more innovative Chernov face diagram and the contour map.

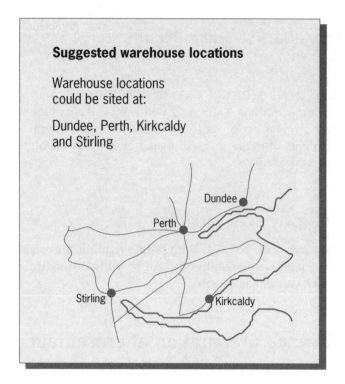

Suggested warehouse locations

Warehouse locations
could be sited at:

Dundee, Perth, Kirkcaldy
and Stirling

Figure 12.2 Text and map in an overhead transparency

Chernov faces

This is a useful way of displaying attitudes to various objects and is more or less self-explanatory. The expressions on the faces reflect the attitudes towards the object (Figure 12.3).

Conventional bar charts

A bar chart is a graph of a frequency distribution (Figure 12.4).

Figure 12.3 Chernov faces of attitude toward various brands of cereal

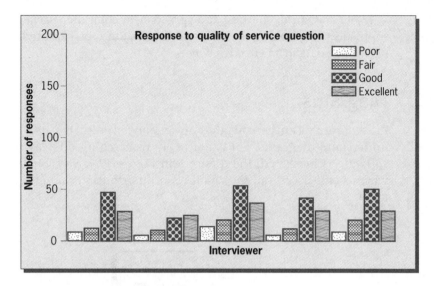

Figure 12.4 Conventional bar chart

Contour maps

Where demographic, attitudinal or other data can be shown to vary geographically by region, area or district, and data points are clustered together into fairly homogeneous groupings, contour maps can be used effectively to illustrate how the data is distributed (Figure 12.5).

Figure 12.5 Contour map

Many statistical, charting and spreadsheet computer packages now have quite sophisticated graphing features and these should be explored to find methods of portraying data in an effective way.

Diagrams

Presentations can be considerably enhanced with the use of simple, easy-to-understand diagrams. For example, in researching the way in which computer software is marketed, the diagram in Figure 12.6 was constructed to show the various end-users and the channels of distribution that could be used to reach them.

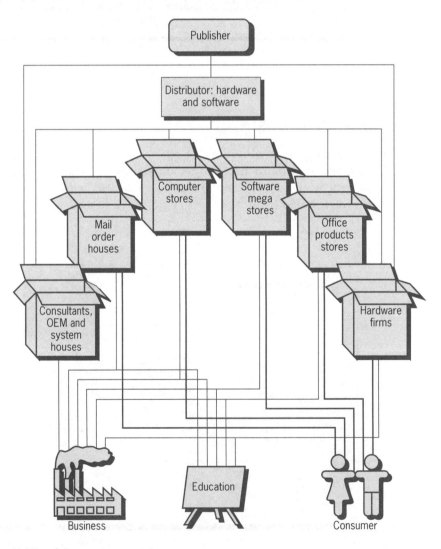

Figure 12.6 Use of diagrams in presentation

In a similar way, diagrams may be used to show how different groups of customers differ in their purchase wants and needs. Figure 12.7 identifies three types of purchasers of bathroom furnishings, together with important, differentiating aspects of their buying behaviour.

Sophisticated computer presentation packages now enable combined displays to be produced. These can be used either as a page for incorporation in a report or as an overhead transparency master. The example in Figure 12.8 captures the original spreadsheet data for expenditure on rent and housing, together with expenditure on food and drink along with the scattergraph showing the relationship between the two. It also shows the distribution of both variables across Europe on a map as well as graphic pictures emphasising the products.

Picture maps

Picture maps are another way of helping to display information in a readily meaningful way (Figure 12.9).

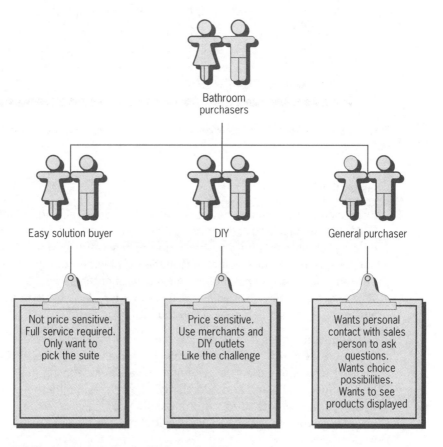

Figure 12.7 Three types of purchasers of bathroom furnishings

	Food, etc	Hsg, etc
AUSTRIA	20	21.1
BELGIUM	23.4	17.1
DENMARK	24	25
FINLAND	18.7	17.1
FRANCE	19.6	19
GERMANY	23.2	25.8
GREECE	36.3	17.3
IRELAND	40.6	10.9
ITALY	23.5	14.8
LUXEMBOURG	22.5	20.1
NETHERLANDS	19.7	27.4
NORWAY	18.6	23.4
PORTUGAL	37	5
SPAIN	29.1	14.9
SWEDEN	22.3	32.3
SWITZERLAND	15.2	17
TURKEY	42.2	25.2
UNITED KINGDOM	14.4	15.7

Figure 12.8 Multiple items on one page or overhead (colour shadings on the map are illustrative only)

Inspiration[2]

Inspiration is a visual idea development tool for developing ideas and plans. It fully integrates an easy-to-use diagram creator and a powerful outliner. We can use the diagram creator to generate ideas, and to plan and produce diagrams and the outline view to organise writing. Inspiration's integration of these facilities through different 'views' gives two different perspectives of the same information: a graphic view and a text view. It provides a single tool for idea development and planning and is useful for developing and communicating ideas.

Inspiration makes it easy and fast to create mind maps, cluster diagrams and idea maps as part of your brainstorming and planning process. These are all visual thinking techniques used for generating ideas and clarifying thinking. Visual maps help stimulate thinking and add clarity. They also simplify the process of moving thoughts into words that communicate your ideas. When writing a report, Inspiration saves time because its powerful outliner helps to revise, edit and format work quickly.

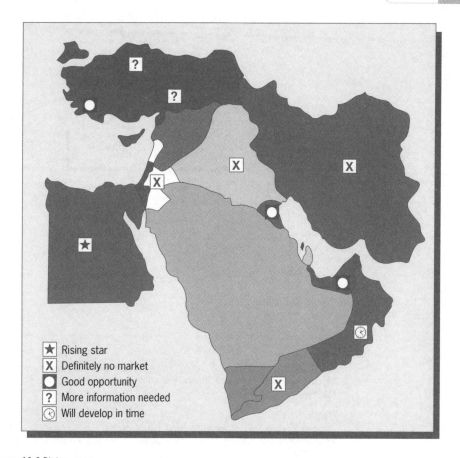

Figure 12.9 Picture map

> Often a picture is the best way to express a concept since it presents its essence instantly. It adds insight by showing the flow of ideas, their relationships and their dependencies. Visual diagrams are a powerful way to communicate an idea or concept, explain a process or procedure, or sell your message.

Figures 12.10 and 12.11 illustrate Inspiration in use. Figure 12.10 shows the various areas that the report is covering. Each of the boxes can be expanded in the outliner view (Figure 12.11).

SUMMARY

This chapter has examined the importance of the presentation to the success of a research study. It looked at the preparation of the different aspects of the presentation and concluded with a discussion of some of the visual and electronic aids that are available to the presenter.

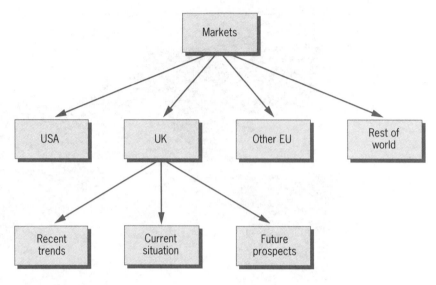

Figure 12.10 Diagram view of Inspiration

I Markets
The report will cover the company's progress and prospects in all the markets in which it operates. More specifically: UK, other EU countries, USA and the rest of the world.

II UK
Recent trends In the last three years the company has made sound progress in all its key product markets. Particularly successful have been sales of compound D to dairy farmers.
Current situation Sales to dairy farmers currently make up some 30% of sales to the UK market.
Future prospects Expansion in sales to dairy farmers in the UK is somewhat limited across the whole product range.

III Other EU

IV USA

V Rest of world

Figure 12.11 Outline view from Inspiration

Questions

1   When preparing a research report, where should you begin? Why?
2   List the various sections that go into making a marketing research report and briefly state what each section includes.
3   How should the oral report differ from the written report?
4   Indicate the types of visual aids that might be used in making an oral presentation.

The St Honoré de Mazarin Restaurant, Paris

A summary of responses to a short questionnaire completed by 24 visitors to the restaurant is shown in the table below. The numbers show the rating given by respondents on a five-point scale (1 is high) on five evaluation criteria.

Table 12.1 Responses to questionnaire

Guest	Country of abode	Age	Varied cuisine	Friendly service	Value for money	Quick service	Pleasant surroundings
1	France	<25	2	4	2	2	2
2	England	65+	3	3	2	3	2
3	Germany	25–34	4	4	2	4	2
4	Italy	45–54	3	3	2	2	2
5	France	25–34	4	4	1	3	1
6	Germany	35–44	2	4	2	3	2
7	Italy	65+	3	4	3	3	2
8	France	35–44	4	4	2	2	1
9	France	45–54	3	2	1	1	2
10	Italy	35–44	3	3	2	2	2
11	England	25–34	4	1	1	3	3
12	Germany	45–54	3	3	2	4	2
13	England	55–64	2	2	1	3	2
14	England	<25	3	2	2	2	2
15	Italy	<25	4	3	3	1	3
16	France	55–64	3	4	2	2	2
17	England	45–54	2	3	2	3	3
18	Italy	25–34	3	2	2	2	3
19	Germany	55–64	4	2	1	1	2
20	England	35–44	2	3	2	3	2
21	France	65+	4	4	3	2	1
22	Germany	65+	3	3	2	3	1
23	Germany	<25	2	2	3	3	2
24	Italy	55–64	1	4	2	3	2

Question

Draw up a report based on the summaries shown above, paying particular attention to the graphical means of summarising the data.

Case study 12.2	Central Training College (C)

Two surveys were conducted to find answers to the research questions indicated in the Central Training College (A) case (see Case Study 5.1). The first survey was among students and the second was among potential business users. The aim of the research was to establish the viability of setting up a recruitment agency under the aegis of the Central Training College which would be of mutual benefit to students and potential employers. In the first of the surveys, students at the Central College were asked for their opinions, while in the second instance potential employees were asked for their reactions.

The student survey sought answers to a comprehensive list of questions. These were incorporated in a well-designed questionnaire that offered possible answers from which the students might select answers or suggest answers of their own. Of students at the 60 colleges contacted, 48.3 per cent returned a completed questionnaire.

The students, 41.4 per cent of them, said that they had used an employment agency before. When asked whether they were satisfied with the service they had been offered, 50 per cent said that they were. Students with experience of using agencies particularly liked a helpful, friendly consultant and career advice. The first factor was mentioned by 50 per cent of students and 16.7 per cent mentioned the second factor. One-third of the students who answered the question complained about agencies' poor communication with students. Consultants would agree to contact a student by a particular time but they would fail to do so and students' costs were therefore increased. Twenty-five per cent of students mentioned the frequency of being sent for an unsuitable position as another source of complaint. Another dislike mentioned by 16.7 per cent of students was being referred to different consultants on each visit. Often, students would have to explain their interests and experience repeatedly to different consultants. Comments written on questionnaires suggested that students felt they were treated very impersonally. Lack of information on pay and holidays supplied by the agencies, the absence of training schemes offered by the agencies to broaden students' skill base and the apparent lack of effort to find the student employment were also cited as shortcomings. However, 37.9 per cent of respondents indicated that they definitely intended using an employment agency in the future and a further 51 per cent said that they would probably do so.

Six people thought that a reputation for being helpful and efficient was the most important consideration when choosing an agency. Five mentioned the need for the chosen agency to have good contacts. Overall reputation, a specialised service for foreign and arts world contacts and a relatively cheap service were each mentioned by four of the respondents. Four thought a personal service, a well-established name and an agency with many branches was important.

Just over half of the students (51.7 per cent) had no idea which agency they intended engaging. Of those who did have some idea, 22.7 per cent stated that they intended to use Kelly, 27.2 per cent said they intended to use Alfred Marks or City Secretaries. Drake and Angela Mortimer each accounted for 9.1 per cent of choices.

Also mentioned were Abacus, Angela Pike, Elizabeth Hunt and Pathfinders. Those who indicated that they were not going to use an agency gave high charges as one of the main reasons.

When asked if they thought it was a good idea for a recruitment agency to be opened in the college, 89.6 per cent said that it was. The most frequent reason given for the idea being perceived as a good one was the belief that the service would be specifically designed for the students of the college. It was thought that an agency in the college might have more flexible consulting times. This flexibility would enable the students to meet consultants on a more frequent and regular basis than would be the case with an agency situated several miles away. Of all the respondents, 37.9 per cent said they would definitely use an agency based in the college and 48.3 per cent said they would probably use it. 10.3 per cent of the respondents usually lived outside the UK and, of the remainder, 80.8 per cent were resident in London. 96.5 per cent of the respondents were female. There were no respondents over 50 years of age and 34.5 per cent were under 20 years of age. 51.7 per cent of the students classed themselves as unemployed, 31 per cent were full-time students and 6.9 per cent were self-employed. 34.5 per cent of the respondents with work experience had obtained it in areas where a college agency might find jobs. One-fifth had book-keeping and accounting experience, two-fifths had experience as secretaries, clerks and receptionists. Just over one-fifth had worked as nannies, waitresses and shop assistants, while 17.2 per cent had teaching experience. A further 17.2 per cent had sales, design or consultant experience. 10.3 per cent of students had no work experience at all. Most respondents were interested in secretarial work: just over 25 per cent were interested in it. Business administration, receptionist and linguistic work were the next popular choices, each accounting for 13.7 per cent of indicated preference. 3.9 per cent were interested in desktop publishing and book-keeping. Accounting and spreadsheet analysis were popular with 1.9 per cent of respondents. 19.6 per cent were not interested in office work at all.

As in the case of the student survey, a well-constructed questionnaire was put together for the survey of firms. This time the survey was by post. Only 30 out of 100 questionnaires were returned. Of those that were returned, 30.3 per cent were not completed but were accompanied by a letter stating that the company did not and would not use employment agencies.

Just over half of the respondents said they had never used a recruitment agency in the past. When used, the most frequently sought employees were secretaries (frequency 15), accounting staff (12), receptionists (4), book-keepers (3) and business administrators (2). 37.5 per cent of jobs offered to the agencies were permanent. The most frequent future need was predicted to be for secretaries – 45.4 per cent of respondents indicated this. However, 45.55 per cent of the respondents said they would be using an agency to hire secretaries and accounting staff in the future. Employers said they would not be using agencies to hire desktop publishers, spreadsheet analysts and linguists. 70 per cent said they would not be using agencies to recruit receptionists.

When asked how many recruits they obtained through an agency, most employers indicated this to be less than one per year. 26.3 per cent hired one person per year through an agency. 60 per cent of respondents who said that they had used a recruitment agency indicated they expected no change in the number of people hired per year in this way in the immediate future. While 6.7 per cent expected an increase, 26.7 per cent expected a decrease.

Most firms did not know how many agencies they employed. There appeared to be no predominantly popular agency. Half of the respondents either did not know or said they used various agencies. 75 per cent said they were satisfied with the service they received.

The feature most liked by the employers was the fact that the ideal person was found. Most employers did not indicate what they disliked about employment agencies. Some, however, mentioned lack of candidate screening and the provision of poor CVs for candidates.

The most common size of firm was 21 to 50 employees –30.3 per cent of the sample fell into this category. 15.1 per cent employed between 51 and 100 employees and 9.1 per cent employed fewer than six people. Some 6.1 per cent of the sample employed more than 100 employees. 27.3 per cent gave no indication of size.

Source: Carol Fry.[3]

Question

Show how you would draw up these findings into a management report and presentation.

| Case study 12.3 | Sunrise Hotels |

Helena Constantine, chief executive of Sunrise Hotels, is keen to ensure that the quality of all hotels in the group is high. As part of a monitoring campaign, 51 completed questionnaires from one of the hotels in the group have recently been returned for her attention. The questionnaire and the summary responses for each item on the questionnaire are shown here.

SUNRISE HOTELS

At Sunrise Hotels, we want to give guests the best service and facilities.

We should like to have your opinions on the service we offer, and would appreciate your thoughts on your stay with us on this visit.

Thank you for choosing Sunrise Hotels and for completing this questionnaire. We look forward to welcoming you back in the near future.

Helena Constantine, Chief Executive

Your name	_____
Your address	_____
	_____
	_____

| From | __ // __ To __ // __ |
| Room number | _____ |

Your age	☐ Under 25 ☐ 25–34 ☐ 35–44 ☐ 45–54
	☐ 55–64 ☐ Over 65
Your sex	☐ Male ☐ Female
What was the primary	☐ Business trip to locality ☐ Overnight stop *en route*
purpose of your visit?	☐ Visiting area, sightseeing
	☐ Weekend break ☐ Other

Our general service and facilities

How well did we match with your expectations?	Excellent	Good	Fair	Poor
On reservation				
Accuracy of information provided	1☐	2☐	3☐	4☐
Your welcome				
On arrival at reception	1☐	2☐	3☐	4☐
In reception				
Speed of check-in	1☐	2☐	3☐	4☐
In the bedroom				
Cleanliness of room	1☐	2☐	3☐	4☐
Overall comfort of room	1☐	2☐	3☐	4☐
General maintenance	1☐	2☐	3☐	4☐
In the telephone service				
Staff telephone manner	1☐	2☐	3☐	4☐
Speed of response	1☐	2☐	3☐	4☐

Have you any specific comments you would like to make? If so, please write them in the box below.

Our staff

How would you rate our staff in terms of the following?	Excellent	Good	Fair	Poor
Courteousness	1☐	2☐	3☐	4☐
Efficiency	1☐	2☐	3☐	4☐

	Excellent	Good	Fair	Poor
Reliability	1☐	2☐	3☐	4☐
Anticipating your requirements	1☐	2☐	3☐	4☐
Attending to your requirements	1☐	2☐	3☐	4☐
Ability to deal with problems	1☐	2☐	3☐	4☐

Please mention any member of staff who made
your stay especially enjoyable

Our dining and bar service

How would you rate our service?

In the restaurant	Excellent	Good	Fair	Poor
Anticipating your requirements	1☐	2☐	3☐	4☐
Range of food and beverages	1☐	2☐	3☐	4☐
Quality of food and beverages	1☐	2☐	3☐	4☐
Quality of service	1☐	2☐	3☐	4☐
Ambience/decor	1☐	2☐	3☐	4☐

Please write any further comments you may have in the box below.

In the lounge or bar	Excellent	Good	Fair	Poor
Anticipating your requirements	1☐	2☐	3☐	4☐
Quality of service	1☐	2☐	3☐	4☐
Quality of food and beverages	1☐	2☐	3☐	4☐
Ambience/decor	1☐	2☐	3☐	4☐

Please write any further comments you may have in the box below.

What do you consider is the hotel's best feature?

What do you think is the hotel's poorest feature?

What is your opinion of the hotel in   ☐ Excellent   ☐ Good   ☐ Fair   ☐ Poor
terms of money?

Thank you for taking the time to complete this questionnaire

Name	From	To	Room	Age	Sex	Purpose	Reservation	Welcome	Check-in	Cleanliness	Comfort	Maintenance	Manner	Response
Sam Jones	08/03/96	12/03/96	69	25–34	Male	Business trip to locality	Good	Fair	Fair	Good	Good	Fair	Fair	Fair
Janet Mills	05/02/96	07/02/96	123	Over 65	Female	Weekend Break	Good	Fair	Fair	Good	Fair	Good	Good	Fair
Ernest Crabbe	04/02/96	07/02/96	109	Over 65	Male	Weekend Break	Good	Good	Fair	Good	Good	Good	Good	Good
John Plant	17/02/96	24/02/96	15	45–54	Male	Overnight stop en route	Good	Good	Fair	Poor	Fair	Good	Good	Poor
William Brown	22/01/96	24/01/96	16	45–54	Male	Overnight stop en route	Good	Good	Fair	Good	Good	Fair	Fair	Fair
Rose Thorne	29/01/96	30/01/96	27	45–54	Female	Weekend Break	Good	Good	Good	Fair	Fair	Fair	Good	Good
Sam Singleton	09/03/96	10/03/96	6	Under 25	Male	Weekend Break	Good	Good	Excellent	Fair	Good	Fair	Fair	Excellent
John Bright	08/04/96	09/04/96	6	55–64	Male	Overnight stop en route	Excellent	Fair	Good	Good	Good	Good	Good	Good
Jim Thickett	24/04/96	27/04/96	11	55–64	Male	Not answered	Excellent	Good	Good	Good	Excellent	Good	Excellent	Good
Jolly Forsyte	07/05/96	09/05/96	2	55–64	Male	Business trip to locality	Excellent	Good	Excellent	Good	Fair	Good	Good	Fair
Juniper Green	10/11/96	15/11/96	1	Over 65	Female	Weekend Break	Excellent	Excellent	Excellent	Good	Fair	Good	Fair	Excellent
Penelope Snow	07/07/96	21/07/96	123	35–44	Female	Visiting area sightseeing	Fair	Good	Poor	Good	Good	Good	Poor	Poor
Wallace Arnold	05/03/96	08/03/96	10	35–44	Male	Weekend Break	Excellent	Good	Fair	Good	Fair	Fair	Good	Fair

Name	From	To	Room	Age	Sex	Purpose	Reservation	Welcome	Check-in	Cleanliness	Comfort	Maintenance	Manner	Response
William Little	09/09/96	24/09/96	29	45–54	Male	Not answered	Fair	Good	Good	Fair	Good	Fair	Fair	Good
Claire Charles	12/07/96	17/07/96	140	Over 65	Female	Visiting area sightseeing	Good	Good	Good	Good	Excellent	Good	Good	Excellent
Cecia Cardwell	05/04/96	07/04/96	17	45–54	Female	Overnight stop en route	Poor	Fair	Good	Fair	Poor	Fair	Fair	Good
Kurt Waldheimer	25/07/96	30/07/96	21	35–44	Male	Visiting area sightseeing	Good	Good	Good	Fair	Good	Excellent	Fair	Fair
Françoise Angouleme	23/08/96	29/08/96	78	25–34	Female	Visiting area sightseeing	Good	Good	Good	Good	Good	Good	Excellent	Good
Peter Pratt	29/04/96	30/04/96	46	45–54	Male	Weekend Break	Good	Good	Good	Good	Good	Excellent	Good	Good
Rene de La Valliere	02/03/96	06/03/96	45	35–44	Male	Overnight stop en route	Excellent	Excellent	Good	Good	Excellent	Excellent	Good	Good
Valerie Carmichael	21/04/96	23/04/96	97	35–44	Female	Weekend Break	Good	Fair	Fair	Good	Good	Excellent	Good	Fair
Thomas Thomas	06/06/96	08/06/96	9	35–44	Male	Weekend Break	Good	Good	Fair	Good	Excellent	Fair	Good	Good
Margaret Lemming	21/08/96	24/08/96	1	25–34	Female	Weekend Break	Good	Excellent	Excellent	Good	Excellent	Good	Good	Fair
Duncan Reddish	05/02/96	07/02/96	199	35–44	Male	Weekend Break	Fair	Good	Good	Fair	Fair	Fair	Good	Fair
Robert Thompson-Smithers	20/02/96	22/02/96	5	Over 65	Male	Other	Fair	Good	Excellent	Good	Good	Fair	Good	Good

Name	From	To	Room	Age	Sex	Purpose	Reservation	Welcome	Check-in	Cleanliness	Comfort	Maintenance	Manner	Response
Arnold Ellis	19/09/96	20/09/96	101	55–64	Male	Not answered	Excellent	Good	Good	Good	Excellent	Good	Excellent	Good
Warwick St. John-Stevenson	03/04/96	06/04/96	200	45–54	Male	Other	Poor	Excellent	Good	Fair	Good	Fair	Fair	Good
Hermione Page	29/01/96	31/01/96	56	25–34	Female	Overnight stop en route	Poor	Poor	Poor	Fair	Poor	Fair	Fair	Poor
Teddie Taylor	21/06/96	28/06/96	17	45–54	Male	Weekend Break	Good	Fair	Fair	Good	Fair	Good	Good	Fair
Ursula Canning	21/12/96	22/12/96	27	Under 25	Female	Overnight stop en route	Fair	Good	Poor	Good	Poor	Good	Poor	Fair
Lionel Clarkson	21/07/96	25/07/96	45	45–54	Male	Business trip to locality	Fair	Good	Poor	Fair	Good	Fair	Fair	Fair
Tania Smith	23/01/96	30/01/96	2	Under 25	Female	Weekend Break	Good	Good	Fair	Fair	Good	Good	Good	Fair
Stella Homer	03/02/96	05/02/96	5	25–34	Female	Weekend Break	Good	Good	Poor	Good	Fair	Good	Good	Good
Ronald Leask	02/09/96	05/09/96	4	55–64	Male	Visiting area sightseeing	Good	Excellent	Fair	Good	Excellent	Fair	Good	Good
François Morrell	02/04/96	05/04/96	2	45–54	Male	Weekend Break	Excellent	Poor	Excellent	Fair	Fair	Poor	Good	Excellent
Audrey Chapman-Harris-Johnson	09/02/96	11/02/96	20	55–64	Female	Weekend Break	Fair	Good	Poor	Poor	Fair	Fair	Good	Good

Name	From	To	Room	Age	Sex	Purpose	Reservation	Welcome	Check-in	Cleanliness	Comfort	Maintenance	Manner	Response
Robin Rutherford	05/03/96	14/03/96	69	25–34	Male	Weekend Break	Good	Excellent	Fair	Excellent	Excellent	Good	Fair	Good
Emily Jackson	23/04/96	26/04/96	180	35–44	Female	Business trip to locality	Excellent	Good	Excellent	Good	Excellent	Good	Fair	Fair
Constance Tucker	05/09/96	10/09/96	13	45–54	Female	Weekend Break	Fair	Good	Poor	Poor	Good	Excellent	Fair	Fair
Sandy Sturgeon	04/01/96	11/01/96	73	25–34	Female	Weekend Break	Good	Good	Excellent	Excellent	Good	Good	Good	Excellent
Morgan Jones	01/04/96	15/04/96	100	55–64	Male	Weekend Break	Poor	Poor	Excellent	Good	Good	Fair	Poor	Fair
David Roberts	24/03/96	26/03/96	1	55–64	Male	Visiting area sightseeing	Good	Good	Good	Excellent	Fair	Fair	Fair	Good
Frederick Cornwallis	24/03/96	26/03/96	4	35–44	Male	Not answered	Good	Good	Fair	Excellent	Good	Fair	Fair	Good
Candice Olsen	24/03/96	26/03/96	16	35–44	Female	Overnight stop en route	Good	Excellent	Good	Excellent	Fair	Good	Fair	Good
Owen Tudor-Williams	24/03/96	26/03/96	34	35–44	Male	Weekend Break	Good	Excellent	Good	Excellent	Excellent	Excellent	Excellent	Good
Janice King	24/03/96	26/03/96	131	35–44	Female	Weekend Break	Good	Excellent	Good	Excellent	Fair	Excellent	Excellent	Good
James Kerr-Jones	24/03/96	26/03/96	77	55–64	Male	Not	Good	Good	Good	Excellent	Excellent	Fair	Excellent	Good

Name	From	To	Room	Age	Sex	Purpose	Reservation	Welcome	Check-in	Cleanliness	Comfort	Maintenance	Manner	Response
Philip Hardborne	24/03/96	26/03/96	79	35–44	Male	Business trip to locality	Good	Fair	Good	Excellent	Good	Fair	Excellent	Good
Rita Davies	22/03/96	23/03/96	79	25–34	Female	Overnight stop en route	Good	Fair	Good	Good	Good	Fair	Excellent	Good
Walter Pidgeon	08/03/96	12/03/96	88	35–44	Male	Visiting area sightseeing	Good	Good	Fair	Good	Fair	Good	Fair	Fair

Name	Prod Comment	Friendliness	Efficiency	Reliability	Anticipate need	Attend need	Resolve problems	Special
Sam Jones	Need better chairs in the bedroom	Good	Good	Good	Fair	Good	Good	Bill the barman
Janet Mills	Chairs in the bedroom uncomfortable; tap drips – needs new washer	Good	Good	Good	Fair	Good	Fair	Bill the barman: brilliantly funny
Ernest Crabbe	Receptionist too slow	Excellent	Good	Good	Good	Fair	Fair	Sue the chambermaid
John Plant	Receptionist needs training	Good	Good	Fair	Poor	Fair	Fair	Bill the barman
William Brown	Telephone service is poor	Excellent	Good	Good	Good	Excellent	Good	
Rose Thorne	Chairs are very uncomfortable	Excellent	Excellent	Excellent	Good	Good	Good	
Sam Singleton	Cobwebs in bedroom; leaking tap in bedroom	Excellent	Good	Excellent	Good	Not answered	Fair	Bill the barman
John Bright		Excellent	Good	Good	Good	Fair	Good	
Jim Thickett	Genial and comfortable	Excellent	Excellent	Good	Excellent	Excellent	Excellent	Bill the barman
Jolly Forsythe	Chairs in bedroom uncomfortable	Fair	Good	Excellent	Good	Excellent	Good	Freda the chambermaid
Juniper Green	Very poor quality chairs – very uncomfortable	Good	Fair	Fair	Good	Fair	Good	
Penelope Snow		Fair	Fair	Poor	Poor	Poor	Fair	
Wallace Arnold	Room rather dark and chairs very uncomfortable	Good	Fair	Good	Fair	Fair	Good	
William Little	Wash basin cracked; cobwebs in room and dust under bed	Good	Fair	Excellent	Good	Fair	Good	
Claire Charles		Excellent	Excellent	Good	Good	Good	Excellent	
Cecila Cardwell	The chairs were less comfortable than church pews and the decor was awful	Poor	Fair	Poor	Fair	Poor	Poor	I wish I could
Kurt Waldheimer	Cleanliness is poor by German standards	Good	Good	Good	Good	Good	Good	
Françoise Angouleme		Excellent	Good	Excellent	Good	Excellent	Excellent	

Name	Prod Comment	Friendliness	Efficiency	Reliability	Anticipate need	Attend need	Resolve problems	Special
Peter Pratt		Good	Excellent	Excellent	Excellent	Good	Good	
Rene de La Valliere		Excellent	Good	Good	Good	Excellent	Excellent	
Valerie Carmichael	More staff needed, I think	Good	Good	Good	Fair	Fair	Good	
Thomas Thomas	Tap dripping all night	Good	Good	Good	Fair	Good	Fair	Bill the barman
Margaret Lemming		Excellent	Good	Good	Excellent	Good	Good	
Duncan Reddish	Lack of insulation – draughts	Fair	Fair	Fair	Fair	Fair	Poor	
Robert Thompson-Smithers	Decor poor	Good	Good	Good	Fair	Fair	Poor	Couldn't get dripping tap in my room fixed
Arnold Ellis		Excellent	Good	Good	Excellent	Good	Good	
Warwick St. John-Stevenson		Poor	Good	Poor	Fair	Fair	Poor	Bill the barman
Hermione Page	Service is very poor and decor is outrageous. The bedroom chairs are hard	Poor	Poor	Poor	Fair	Poor	Poor	
Teddie Taylor		Good	Good	Good	Fair	Good	Good	
Ursula Canning	Very uncomfortable bedroom chairs	Good	Poor	Good	Poor	Good	Not answered	Staff are poor at giving help when needed
Lionel Clarkson		Good	Good	Good	Poor	Good	Not answered	Bill the barman
Tania Smith		Excellent	Good	Good	Excellent	Good	Good	Bill the barman
Stella Homer		Good	Good	Good	Fair	Good	Good	
Ronald Leask		Excellent	Good	Fair	Excellent	Good	Good	Bill the barman
François Morrell	Plumbing very noisy: kept me awake all night	Excellent	Excellent	Good	Good	Good	Excellent	

Name	Prod Comment	Friendliness	Efficiency	Reliability	Anticipate need	Attend need	Resolve problems	Special
Audrey Chapman-Harris-Johnson		Not answered	Good	Good	Fair	Fair	Fair	Bill the barman
Robin Rutherford		Excellent	Good	Fair	Good	Good	Excellent	Bill the barman
Emily Jackson		Excellent	Excellent	Excellent	Good	Good	Excellent	
Constance Tucker	Room was very dusty	Fair	Good	Good	Poor	Poor	Fair	No room service provided
Sandy Sturgeon		Excellent	Excellent	Good	Good	Excellent	Excellent	
Morgan Jones	I couldn't get the blinds in my room to work	Not answered	Good	Fair	Fair	Fair	Poor	No one was able to find the cat in my room
David Roberts		Good	Good	Excellent	Good	Excellent	Good	
Frederick Cornwallis		Not answered	Good	Fair	Good	Excellent	Good	Bill the barman – knew him in the army
Candice Olsen		Excellent	Good	Excellent	Good	Excellent	Good	Bill the barman
Owen Tudor-Williams		Excellent	Good	Excellent	Excellent	Excellent	Good	Bill the barman – knew him in the navy
Janice King		Good	Good	Excellent	Good	Excellent	Good	
James Kerr-Jones		Excellent	Good	Excellent	Excellent	Excellent	Good	
Philip Hardborne		Excellent	Good	Excellent	Good	Excellent	Good	Bill the barman – knew him in the air force
Rita Davies		Excellent	Good	Excellent	Good	Good	Good	
Walter Pidgeon	Need better chairs in the bedroom	Good	Fair	Excellent	Fair	Good	Good	Bill the barman

Name	Anticipate req.	Range food	Quality food	Quality service	Res. decor	Special	Anticipate req. bar	Bar service	Bar food qual.	Bar decor
Sam Jones	Good	Good	Fair	Good	Good		Fair	Good	Excellent	Good
Janet Mills	Good	Good	Fair	Good	Fair		Good	Good	Good	Excellent
Ernest Crabbe	Good	Good	Good	Fair	Fair		Good	Good	Good	Excellent
John Plant	Good	Fair	Poor	Fair	Fair		Fair	Poor	Fair	Fair
William Brown	Good	Good	Good	Excellent	Good		Fair	Good	Good	Fair
Rose Thorne	Excellent	Excellent	Good	Good	Good		Fair	Fair	Fair	Poor
Sam Singleton	Good	Excellent	Good	Not answered	Fair		Good	Fair	Excellent	Excellent
John Bright	Good	Good	Good	Fair	Good		Excellent	Fair	Excellent	Good
Jim Thickett	Excellent	Good	Excellent	Excellent	Excellent		Good	Excellent	Good	Excellent
Jolly Forsyte	Good	Excellent	Good	Excellent	Good		Good	Good	Excellent	Good
Juniper Green	Fair	Fair	Good	Fair	Good		Good	Fair	Good	Excellent
Penelope Snow	Fair	Poor	Poor	Poor	Fair		Fair	Fair	Fair	Poor
Wallace Arnold	Fair	Good	Fair	Fair	Good		Good	Good	Excellent	Good
William Little	Fair	Excellent	Good	Fair	Good		Fair	Excellent	Good	Excellent
Claire Charles	Excellent	Good	Good	Good	Excellent		Good	Good	Excellent	Fair
Ceclia Cardwell	Fair	Poor	Fair	Poor	Poor	I wish I could	Fair	Poor	Poor	Fair
Kurt Waldheimer	Good	Good	Good	Good	Good		Excellent	Good	Good	Good
Françoise Angouleme	Good	Excellent	Good	Excellent	Excellent		Good	Excellent	Excellent	Excellent
Peter Pratt	Excellent	Excellent	Excellent	Good	Good		Good	Excellent	Excellent	Good
Rene de la Valliere	Good	Good	Good	Excellent	Excellent		Good	Excellent	Excellent	Excellent
Valerie Carmichael	Good	Good	Fair	Fair	Good		Good	Fair	Good	Fair

Name	Anticipate req.	Range food	Quality food	Quality service	Res. decor	Special	Anticipate req. bar	Bar service	Bar food qual.	Bar decor
Thomas Thomas	Good	Good	Fair	Good	Fair		Excellent	Good	Good	Fair
Margaret Lemming	Good	Good	Excellent	Good	Good		Good	Fair	Excellent	Good
Duncan Reddish	Fair	Fair	Fair	Fair	Poor		Fair	Good	Fair	Fair
Robert Thompson-Smithers	Good	Good	Fair	Fair	Poor	Couldn't get the dripping tap in my room fixed	Good	Excellent	Excellent	Fair
Arnold Ellis	Good	Good	Excellent	Good	Good		Good	Excellent	Excellent	Fair
Warwick St John-Stevenson	Good	Poor	Fair	Fair	Poor		Good	Fair	Fair	Good
Hermione Page	Poor	Poor	Fair	Poor	Poor		Fair	Poor	Poor	Poor
Teddie Taylor	Good	Good	Fair	Good	Good		Good	Fair	Good	Fair
Ursula Canning	Poor	Good	Poor	Good	Not answered	Staff are poor at rendering help when needed	Fair	Good	Fair	Fair
Lionel Clarkson	Good	Good	Poor	Good	Not answered		Poor	Good	Fair	Good
Tania Smith	Good	Good	Excellent	Good	Good		Good	Good	Excellent	Excellent
Stella Homer	Good	Good	Fair	Good	Good		Fair	Good	Good	Fair
Ronald Leask	Good	Fair	Excellent	Good	Good		Good	Excellent	Excellent	Good

Name	Anticipate req.	Range food	Quality food	Quality service	Res. decor	Special	Anticipate req. bar	Bar service	Bar food qual.	Bar decor
François Morrell	Excellent	Good	Good	Good	Excellent		Good	Good	Fair	Good
Audrey Chapman-Harris-Johnson	Good	Good	Fair	Fair	Fair		Fair	Good	Fair	Fair
Robin Rutherford	Good	Fair	Good	Good	Excellent		Excellent	Good	Good	Good
Emily Jackson	Excellent	Excellent	Good	Good	Excellent		Excellent	Good	Excellent	Good
Constance Tucker	Good	Good	Poor	Poor	Fair	No room service provided	Good	Good	Fair	Fair
Sandy Sturgeon	Excellent	Good	Good	Excellent	Excellent		Good	Excellent	Excellent	Good
Morgan Jones	Good	Fair	Fair	Fair	Poor	No one was able to find the cat in my room	Fair	Good	Good	Fair
David Roberts	Good	Excellent	Good	Excellent	Good		Good	Excellent	Excellent	Good
Frederick Cornwallis	Good	Fair	Good	Excellent	Good		Good	Excellent	Good	Good
Candice Olsen	Good	Excellent	Good	Excellent	Good		Good	Excellent	Excellent	Good
Owen Tudor-Williams	Good	Excellent	Excellent	Excellent	Good		Good	Excellent	Excellent	Excellent
Janice King	Good	Excellent	Good	Excellent	Good		Good	Excellent	Excellent	Excellent
James Kerr-Jones	Good	Excellent	Excellent	Excellent	Good		Good	Excellent	Excellent	Excellent
Philip Hardborne	Good	Excellent	Good	Excellent	Good		Good	Excellent	Good	Fair
Rita Davies	Good	Excellent	Good	Good	Good		Good	Excellent	Good	Good
Walter Pidgeon	Fair	Excellent	Fair	Good	Good		Good	Good	Excellent	Good

Name	Bar Comment	Like most	Like least	Value
Sam Jones				Good
Janet Mills	Bill needs some good assistants to help him with the workload			Good
Ernest Crabbe	Poor Bill is overburdened with work – but he is always cheerful	Cheerful staff	Decor	Fair
John Plant	Food poor			Good
William Brown		Mediocrity		Good
Rose Thorne		Price	Restaurant	Excellent
Sam Singleton	More waiters required in bar	Price	Slightly seedy	Excellent
John Bright	Decoration rather gaudy	Price	Homeliness	Good
Jim Thickett		Price	Drabness	Fair
Jolly Forsyte		Price	Lack of good quality decor	Fair
Juniper Green	More waiters required	Conveniently situated	Rather basic comforts	Fair
Penelope Snow				Fair
Wallace Arnold	Poor range of food			Good
William Little	More staff required	Price	Decor	Good
Claire Charles				Fair
Ceclia Cardwell	I don't drink	None	Everything	Fair
Kurt Waldheimer				Fair
Françoise Angouleme		Price and friendliness	Decor	Good
Peter Pratt				Good
Rene de La Valliere				Good
Valerie Carmichael		Friendliness		Good
Thomas Thomas		Price	Delays in service	Excellent
Margaret Lemming	Decorations need to be improved	Friendliness	Decor	Good
Duncan Reddish	Decor poor	Price	Poor appearance	Poor
Robert Thompson-Smithers		Price	Decor	Good
Arnold Ellis		Friendliness	Decor	Good
Warwick St. John-Stevenson	Poor decor	Price	Decor	Good
Hermione Page	I decided not to eat in the restaurant at all	Has not got one	Everything	Good
Teddie Taylor		Price		Good

Name	Bar Comment	Like most	Like least	Value
Ursula Canning				Good
Lionel Clarkson	Needs a games room	Price	Doesn't cater for vegetarian snooker players	Good
Tania Smith				Good
Stella Homer				Fair
Ronald Leask				Poor
François Morrell	Decor not very tasteful	Price		Good
Audrey Chapman-Harris-Johnson				Fair
Robin Rutherford				Excellent
Emily Jackson				Good
Constance Tucker	Decor awful	Price	No room service	Poor
Sandy Sturgeon		Price		Good
Morgan Jones		It is easy to find in the dark	There was a cat in my room	Fair
David Roberts				Excellent
Frederick Cornwallis		Bill the barman	Price	Excellent
Candice Olsen				Excellent
Owen Tudor-Williams		Easy to find		Good
Janice King		Easy to find	Price	Good
James Kerr-Jones		Price	Hard to find	Good
Philip Hardborne		Bill the barman		Good
Rita Davies	Decor rather gaudy	Price	Gaudy decor	Good
Walter Pidgeon		Easy to find	Decor	Good

Question

Produce a report on the findings of this sample survey.

Case study 12.4 Wallaby Tours

Wallaby Tours operates a tourist bus link between Adelaide and Melbourne. Instead of taking the inland road, which is the most direct route (taking around 24 hours) the company takes three days to travel along the Great Ocean Highway, stopping off at places of interest on the way – although the cost is considerably higher than the commercial bus route, the passengers see a part of Australia which they would miss if the bus followed the 'boring' route. Each bus carries a maximum of eighteen passengers with their luggage; lunch is provided each day, but passengers make their own arrangements for evening meals at the various towns the bus visits. The buses rarely run fully booked, but the service is profitable.

Recently the firm conducted a survey among four groups of passengers – two groups travelling from Adelaide to Melbourne, and two travelling the other way. The directors of the company are hoping to use this information to refine the service offered; one of the directors believes that the company should be offering a different service to people of different age groups, since he believes that older people are less prepared to 'rough it' than are the younger ones. The other director is more concerned about gender issues, believing that women have different needs and expectations than do men.

The passengers were asked to complete a Likert scale, with 1 as the highest rating and 5 as the lowest. The table below shows the responses obtained from the passengers.

Country of origin, age and gender of passenger	Pleasant driver	Route taken	Accommodation	Quality of lunch	Comfort of bus
Bus 1: Ad. to Mel.					
UK: 27: M	2	1	3	2	3
Aus: 42: F	1	2	4	4	4
Italian: 23: M	4	2	4	4	2
Italian: 23: F	3	3	3	4	2
Swiss: 32: F	3	1	1	2	3
UK: 51: F	2	2	4	1	4
Aus: 26: F	2	1	2	4	2
Aus: 28: M	2	1	2	4	2
UK: 24: M	1	1	1	1	1
Singapore: 22: M	4	1	2	3	2
Singapore: 22: M	5	2	1	2	3
Singapore: 21: F	3	1	2	1	4
UK: 48: F	2	2	4	3	4
Bus 2: Ad. to Mel.					
Aus: 31: F	2	2	4	2	1
Aus: 36: M	1	3	2	2	2
Aus: 24: M	1	2	3	2	2
Aus: 24: M	2	3	2	1	3

Aus: 23: M	2	2	1	2	2
Aus: 24: M	3	2	2	3	1
Irish: 28: F	2	1	3	2	2
Irish: 29: F	1	2	3	2	1
UK: 37: M	2	1	3	3	2
UK: 34: F	2	1	4	4	2
Aus: 26: F	1	1	4	3	3
Dutch: 29: F	1	2	5	3	3
Bus 3: Mel. to Ad.					
Singapore: 25: M	3	2	3	4	1
Singapore: 25: F	3	1	3	4	2
UK: 32: M	1	2	3	2	1
UK: 31: F	1	2	3	2	1
Aus: 26: M	3	1	2	3	2
Aus: 24: M	2	2	2	3	2
Irish: 32: M	1	1	2	2	2
Irish: 37: M	2	1	2	1	2
Bus 4: Mel. to Ad.					
Dutch: 43: M	2	1	4	3	3
Dutch: 37: F	1	1	4	3	2
Aus: 47: M	1	1	2	2	2
Aus: 42: F	2	2	4	3	3
UK: 24: M	1	1	3	2	2
UK: 24: M	2	2	2	1	2

Ultimately, the directors will be looking to collect feedback from all the passengers on all the buses; this initial survey is intended to show up major gaps in the services, and also to offer ideas for designing future research studies.

(Case contributed by Jim Blythe.)

Questions

1 Prepare a report based on the above figures.
2 What conclusions can you draw from analysis of the data?
3 What recommendations can you make for Wallaby Tours?
4 How should the report be written in order to meet the needs of the Wallaby Tours directors?
5 What are the key findings of the research?

Further reading

Boland, A (1996) Got report-o-phobia?: Follow these simple steps to get those ideas on to paper, *Chemical Engineering*, 103(3), March, pp 131–2.

Britt, S H (1971) The writing of readable research reports, *Journal of Marketing Research*, May, p 265.

Carnes, W T (1980) *Effective Meetings for Busy People*, New York: McGraw-Hill.

Dwyer, J (1993) *The Business Communication Handbook*, 3rd Edition, Erskineville, NSW: Star Printery.

Eagleson, R D (1990) *Writing in Plain English*, Canberra: AGPS.

Eunson, B (1994) *Writing and Presenting Reports*, Milton, Queensland: John Wiley & Sons.

Fletcher, W (1984) *Meetings, Meetings*, New York: Morrow.

Hague, P and Roberts, C (1994) *Presentation and Report Writing*, London: Kogan Page.

Haynes, M E (1988) *Effective Meeting Skills*, Los Altos, CA: Crisp Publications.

Hibbins, G M (1990) *Stands to Reason*, 4th Edition, South Melbourne, Victoria: The Macmillan Company of Australia Pty Ltd.

Hinkin, S (1995) Charting your course to effective information graphics, *Presentations*, 9(11), November.

Hrisak, D M (1997) Key presentation principles, *Chartered Accountants Journal of New Zealand*, 76(3), April, p 24.

Kauder, N B (1996) Pictures worth a thousand words, *American Demographics* (Tools supplement), November, pp 64–8.

Keys, T (1996) Report writing, *Internal Auditor*, 53(4), August.

Mohn, N C (1989) How to present marketing research results effectively, *Marketing and Research Today*, 17(2), pp 115–18.

Nutting, J and White, G (1992) *The Business of Communication*, 2nd Edition, Roseville, CA McGraw-Hill.

Shait, D I (1994) Report writing, *HR Focus*, 71(2), February, p 20.

Snell, F (1979) *How to Win the Meeting*, New York: Hawthorn Books.

Soroczynski, P (1999) *Technical Communication Handbook*, Darwin: NTU Press.

Sussmans, J (1991) *How to Write Effective Reports*, Hampshire: Gower.

Thomsett, M C (1989) *The Little Black Book of Business Meetings*, New York: American Management Association.

References and notes

[1] Lincoln, Y S and Guba, E C (1985) *Naturalistic Inquiry*, Beverly Hills, CA: Sage.

[2] Inspiration, Inspiration Software Inc., 2920 SW Dolph Court, Suite 3, Portland, Oregon 97219, USA.

[3] Fry, C (1991) Unpublished MBA Dissertation, Department of Management, Keele University, September.

13 Applied marketing research

OBJECTIVES

After reading this chapter you should be able to:

- understand how marketing research may be applied to specific areas of marketing.

KEY WORDS

new products	packaging
ideas for products	market segmentation
evaluation	cartographying
product testing	geographic information system
consumer product testing	motivational research
blind testing	sociological studies
branded testing	anthropological studies
monadic testing	advertising effectiveness
paired comparisons	memory
product delivery	attention
Delphi technique	persuasibility

PLAN OF CHAPTER 13

INTRODUCTION

This chapter looks at some applied areas of marketing research: product research, segmentation research, competition research, promotion research, distribution research and pricing research. These applications of marketing research are substantive enough to warrant specific consideration in their own right. In the case of product research, attention is given to product generation and testing, consumer product testing and packaging research. In the case of segmentation research, attention is given to researching ways of segmenting the market. Attention is given to competition research in which understanding the market strategies of competitors is seen as a focal point. The identification of competitors and sources of information about competitors are also seen as key issues. Next, in promotion research, attention is focused on the ways of assessing its effectiveness. This is followed by a discussion of various approaches to pricing research. Finally, aspects of distribution research are considered.

PRODUCT RESEARCH

Most new products fail, so the use of research in developing and evaluating products is important since it reduces the risk of failure. Product research covers several different kinds of research. The aim of product research is to provide company management with information about the likely acceptance of a new product, a modified product or an existing product. Product research has three roles to play in this aspect of marketing (Figure 13.1):

1 getting ideas for new products;
2 evaluating new product ideas;
3 consumer product testing.

GETTING IDEAS FOR NEW PRODUCTS

Consumers can provide ideas for product improvements and even occasionally identify a new product opportunity in the market place. Focus-group research may be used to generate product ideas, as it reflects the nature of unsatisfied consumer wants. Through focus-group discussion, shortcomings of existing products can be identified as well as desirable new product features (see Chapter 8).

Concept testing means getting reactions to a new product idea or concept and can help eliminate bad ideas. One form of the concept test describes the concept entirely through words. There is a statement about what the product is and does, perhaps listing its major characteristics. Another form is visual, with an illustration (drawing or photograph) presented along with the description. It can even take the form of a draft advertisement, which combines the description and illustration, usually in the form of a print advertisement. A third form of the concept test uses a mock-up of the product. This is something that passes for a prototype, but is really only a dummy product that helps get across the idea of the product.

In the typical concept test, the concept is stated or shown to the consumer and the person is asked about their interest in purchase. It is conducted with a random group of potential consumers and the typical starting sample size is 600. Each respondent is recruited and interviewed at home, then offered the product in a personal call-back interview and for 'real money'. Further sales waves are made by telephone calls and the product is delivered to the homes of purchasers. Sales to the consumer on several occasions over a time period provide an observation of how much the consumer really wants to buy.

Madame Tussaud's

Each additional waxwork figure, or new theme area which is put into the exhibition, is initially a new product – something the public has not seen before. Ideas for new products originate from several sources. The ideas, which will be for a new figure or theme, come principally from a committee consisting of company executives, totalling about eight people, who meet regularly for brainstorming sessions. The committee also canvasses the opinions of other members of staff and takes into account what the marketing department has discovered through its research. The research team conducts a popularity poll, each year, to find out who are the favourite/least favourite figures, and who people would most like to see in the exhibition. These surveys help to overcome the fact that the committee itself is not representative of the people who visit Madame Tussaud's.

The list of possible new figures has to be narrowed down or screened in order to find and drop poor ideas as soon as possible. For Madame Tussaud's it is not so much having to drop poor ideas, as to eliminate the ones that are not practical: for example, the availability of a person, what they look like and what length of life they are likely to have in the exhibition. The question is not so much a monetary one, as one of opportunity cost.

The remaining ideas for figures have to be honed into concepts, because it is these, not the idea, which the consumer will eventually buy. The product concept is what the new product will be and do to satisfy the customers. For Madame Tussaud's concept development consists of deciding where to put the figure, in what pose, in what clothes and whether it will be a 'character' portrayal or not.

Source: Lucy Double.[1]

Hall tests are used mostly in the context of developing new products. They apply to consumer products and involve displaying and testing products on large numbers of possible purchasers. Often the tests take place in or close to shopping centres or precincts and are located in a hall or other suitable area. People are invited to visit the place where the tests are being held and to try the products for themselves and to register their comments and reactions to the products.

Consumer product testing measures what people think of a new or existing product only after the actual trial of the developed product. The testing does not always predict successful products or failures in the market place, for a product may fail because of factors other than the characteristics of the product itself. Even a good product may fail because it lacks the funds to meet the competition, or because a competitor has built up so strong a reputation that no amount of spending on advertising and other forms of promotion can make any impression on it. Indeed, a poor or marginal product, as long as it has even a low level of acceptance, may perform acceptably in the market place as a result of massive spending on promotional efforts.

The nature of the testing varies according to the product. For a food or drink item, the test may be as simple as a one-time taste test, perhaps conducted at a shopping precinct. For a detergent, a longer-term in-home test is required and the brand may be given to people at a shopping centre with a request that they try it at home over an extended time period. In this case, participants in the study are subsequently contacted by telephone to answer questions about the product. You need to decide whether the products in the test are presented on a blind basis (no brand identification) or on a branded basis. Another is whether only a single product is presented to the tester for rating (the monadic test), or whether a pair of products is presented (paired comparison).

Sugar-free Ribena: Smith Kline Beecham

Smith Kline Beecham do a lot of product testing, partly because of the diverse nature of the firm's brands (health, oral care and health drinks) and partly because of the constraints they impose on methods. The way the company tests Lucozade Sports products reflects the fact that they are specially formulated to taste appropriate for sports activities. The firm tries to test the products *in situ*, interviewing sports players in leisure centres directly after taking part in a sport (that is, before they can get to a cafeteria or a bar).

The firm is particularly innovative in brand development and extension and a lot of the product research involves concept product testing. A recent example was a concept product test for the firm's new sugar-free Ribena concentrate before its launch. The main aim of the research was to evaluate two formulation options for the concept and to determine which was the best to develop further or even launch. Because the new product would have to live up to the expectations generated by the Ribena name and the quality of other Ribena products, the firm decided to include standard and light formulations in the test for comparison with the sugar-free products. There was some concern about where the volume of sugar-free was going to come from and whether the other Ribena concentrate products would be cannibalised.

After discussing these issues with the research agency (RSGB), a recommendation was used to include a technique that would give an indication of the possible volume effects of the launch on the firm's other products. RSGB recommended a constant sum-preference exercise, otherwise known as 'The Chip Game'. The Chip Game asks respondents to score different brands and products (and only those within their present or past repertoire) on the basis of which they would prefer. In this case they were asked to allocate marks out of nine between different pairs of products in their repertoire, one pair at a time. The scoring is such that if a respondent prefers brand A to brand B by quite an extent, they might give brand A six and brand B three marks; and if brand A to brand C by a very large extent, brand A might be awarded eight marks and brand C one mark. In this way a total score is built up for each brand within the market, enabling preference shares and therefore volume share estimates to be calculated for each brand, as shown below.

	Brand A	Brand B	Brand C	Total
Brand A	/	6	8	14
Brand B	3	/	5	8
Brand C	1	4	/	5

The exercise can be undertaken twice, once on the current market situation (that is, before the introduction of sugar-free Ribena) and once after the introduction of the new concept, enabling the effects of the launch of sugar-free Ribena on the market and on other brands within the market to be assessed.

The research answered not only the basic objective of product evaluation but also many of the other concerns and issues surrounding the project. The final structure of the test was:

Concept stage

1 Basic background information
2 Chip Game: current situation
3 Evaluation of sugar-free concept
4 Sugar-free Chip Game

Product stage

1 Round Robin product test: four formulations, with each respondent testing two of these
2 Ranking of sugar-free concept against standard and light concepts

The research indicated that the concept of the new sugar-free Ribena would be well received and that one of the formulations would be a slightly better option for the launch. It also gave a clear indication of the likely effects on volume share for the other Ribena concentrates, for the brand as a whole and for other brands within the market.
Source: Sue White.[2]

Blind versus branded testing

There is almost always a need for blind testing, since this really determines how the product, and only the product, is perceived by the tester. It provides basic guidance, when questions about reactions to specific attributes are also asked, as to how the firm can improve its product to make it more acceptable. The branded test also has an important role. The results of such a test provide information about how people react to the product and the brand image. Identified brands typically score higher than blind products, unless the brand is relatively unknown or has a poor image.

Monadic versus paired comparison testing

Monadic testing is the presentation of only one test product at a time, obtaining a rating on that product alone or perhaps against the regular brand used by the consumer. Paired comparison testing means the presentation of two products to be tried, one against the other, and comparative preferences are usually required. In either case, the ratings are not only for overall liking or preference, but usually also cover many attributes or qualities of the product(s).

In conducting the tests, various precautions have to be taken, especially in the case of the paired comparison test. Experience suggests that, all else being equal, the product tried first has a preferred position and may, just because of its sequential position, receive too high a proportion of preferred ratings. The more similar the two products are, the more likely this is to happen. So each product being tested has to be given first position with half of the sample of respondents.

Figure 13.1 Scope of product research

The monadic test reflects the way the real world operates. Consumers rarely make side-by-side choices, although sometimes they do so in a buying situation, particularly with consumer durables. However, experience has shown that the same monadic test may give sharply differing results, probably because those replying have no anchor-point on which to base responses. The paired comparison test provides sharper results, because two definite things are being compared. Under some circumstances, however, these results too are not always consistent. Moreover, paired comparison tests are unsuitable for predicting what will happen in the market place.

Caught in the neighbours' tangled web

Now that everyone in Cyber Street can use a modem and a mouse, it's apparently time to move on to higher things. Microsoft, the software company, has hooked up 30 houses on our north London backwater to the Internet, providing computers, phone lines and plenty of software to let us wander where we will, in an attempt to find out what consumers are going to want from the on-line revolution.

After just four months of being a market research test-bed, everyone is coping with e-mails, bulletin boards and the Internet.

To refresh the process, the street was invited to a convivial evening's networking at an Islington eaterie to meet our 'Microsoft buddies' – the people who keep in touch with individuals and are available for questions – and to be shown what the company was up to in developing its own output. In common with other big companies, Microsoft hopes that in future people will not just sign up for companies that give them an e-mail address and Internet access.

The people passing round the porc au pixil and Chateau Byte were talking animatedly in TV-speak about 'shows' – a word telly people use about everything from News at Ten to Sunday Night at the London Palladium. The 'shows' are the extra product the big computer companies want us to buy: similar to television, it is organised in 'channels' including a news and weather service and magazine programmes on everything from cinema, fashion and health to comics.

Over the tables, the street became introspective and the idea seemed to develop that no self-respecting virtual community was complete without its own web site.

People thought it might be good to be able to call up pictures of their neighbours and even of their neighbours' pets – it's nice to know whose moggie you're chasing from the back garden. We would trade information on the best restaurants, plumbers, interior decorators and chiropractors. To set it all up, the street's very first on-line 'chat' was organised, using the 'chat room' which has lain neglected alongside the street's private bulletin board since the start of the project.

A chat room is a sort of on-line conference call. Instead of speaking and listening, you type in what you want to say in one section of the screen. The names of those taking part are displayed in another panel, and the main bit of the screen shows everyone else's writings as they send them. As a means of communication, it ranks somewhere above hiccuping in Morse code. By the time you type your response to one suggestion, five other remarks have been made, and your offering comes up behind one of those. So your 'I agree' response to some completely sensible proposal appears on everyone's screens just after some misguided soul has tipped Tottenham for the league.

To make matters worse, the cyber-experts have their own language, such as <g>, which is apparently like a slap on the back, but whether this is to approve, say hello, sympathise or dislodge a fishbone from the throat isn't specified. They also like constructing little faces, by typing :-) or :-(to express approval or disapproval respectively. It works really well if you tilt your head through 90 degrees.

The street cantered through its first chat without too much misunderstanding, although this was mainly because there were only seven or eight people on-line at any one time.

The suggested bits of the web site range from the practical – information on shops, restaurants, cinemas and recycling centres – to the avowedly self-indulgent: there was a call for a philosophy column, which isn't a feature of too many other web sites.

Only the residents of Cyber Street would have access to the site, although there is apparently a plan to develop an Islington web site for general use – the council already has a site about its services, but there was a feeling that something a bit racier would be more helpful.

Not that this is a great time to be creating virtual experiences: the street seems to have gone on holiday en masse, possibly to the same part of Tuscany – this is middle-class Islington, after all – and the bulletin board has gone quiet. However, when everyone returns with their cases of duty-free Chianti, there's renewed enthusiasm for organising a street party, one of the first things suggested on the bulletin board way back in April. There has been a marked increase in contact in the street in recent months – it was never noted for neighbourly contact – but the grand street party is taking a bit of building up to. If it does happen, the on-line community will become a lot closer to being a real one.

Source: Tom Lynch.[3]

The one-time sensory test

This form of product test is relatively simple. For example, a flavour test, used to determine which of a product's two flavours is preferred, may require only one central location test, such as in a shopping precinct. In such a high-density traffic location, people can easily be intercepted. Once intercepted interviewers make sure that the respondents are qualified (such as being heavy users of the product category), then they can ask the respondents to sample the product and obtain their reactions to it. Either the monadic or paired comparison presentation of the product(s) can be applied.

PRODUCT DELIVERY

In the discussion that follows, the term 'product' should be construed to mean both product and service. To understand the ways in which marketing research can be helpful in product delivery, it is necessary first to talk about symbolism and imagery, for that is what product delivery is all about: the building of an aura around a particular product.

A symbol is something that stands for or represents something else and it helps create an image. Imagery reflects the way we perceive things, how we screen things to arrive at an interpretation of reality. If a brand is perceived as being poor quality, it is difficult for the supplier of that brand to change people's evaluation. Imagery or perception take on great importance in marketing. The name of the product or service, the package, and the personalising of product delivery all contribute to imagery. It requires considerable understanding and skill about how to use research to develop and measure the impact of these three areas of product delivery. It is unwise to ask people directly how they like a particular logo or brand name: they will probably give an acceptable social reply rather than one they really feel.

The Delphi technique and new product development

When a comparison is made between research projects on new products carried out in 1968 and 1980 (Booz, Allen and Hamilton 1983, ESOMAR seminar) with ones carried out in 1993 (EFO Group, *Marketing News*, 21 June 1993), the percentage of failures still remains extremely high. The Achilles heel in the development process of new products is that consumer needs are measured in a static, not dynamic, way. This means that importance is attached to the analysis of the present without giving adequate consideration to the fact that competitive advantages are achieved by satisfying needs that are still embryonic and whose full benefits have yet to come. Consumers are required to judge new products relative to their current needs, which are usually quite well met by existing products. As a result, new products tend to develop from a priority analysis of the present. Products are derived from the analysis of habits rather than from the study of evolving needs. By changing the perspective and the focus of the analysis from current to future needs, a competitive advantage could be achieved by meeting these emerging needs rather than through a better satisfaction of existing needs. This would gain commitment from trendsetters and arouse the interest of the trend followers.

A method that recognises the so-called market weak signals indicating a current change so that the concept of the new product to be developed can then be based on such signals is the Delphi technique. It was introduced into Italy in the early 1970s and used for a large number of significant research projects carried out for consumer goods and services. One example of its use was to develop a food product with a long shelf-life that did not need cooking or warming up. The research took the following steps:

1 Analysing the Delphi results, mapping out the various evolving consumption opportunities (and their relevant motives) pertaining to the company's business idea. Although food habits are among the slowest to change, the impact caused by the change in working hours and kinds of jobs (less industry and more services), the population's ageing, and a greater attention to health-oriented food are causing changes that will not take many years (five to seven) to occur.

2 Defining the possible alternatives of product concepts, in line with the changes expected in the near future.

3 Identifying the weak signals coming from current behaviours by analysing existing research projects on food habits. Sociodemographic research showed that a few behavioural patterns, for which the Delphi technique expected a wide spread during a span of ten years, were already spreading among population classes with less traditional lifestyles.

4 Confirming weak signals and identification of products. Five product lines were found that shared a few basic elements such as recipes, ingredients, and service level with the new line concept. Sales trends among the five products showed they had small markets, but trends were favourable.

5 Defining the contents of the concept to convert it into a briefing for R&D. Elements were separated into these categories: basic ingredients to use; their qualitative features; importance of organoleptic elements (smell, colour, taste); importance of aesthetic aspects; physical elements of packaging; packaging size; product service level; and emotional elements – naturalness, lightness, taste, health.

   Priorities were assigned to the elements because some of them caused technical or economic problems that were not in line with the product budget.

6 Identifying the positioning, which would influence both the recipe and the advertising. Delphi research provided help in determining which food style would be dominant in the years to come and identifying the value system it was based on so that a particular nutritional area could be chosen.

The next steps were the usual ones: elaboration of the recipes, prototypes at experimental cooking level, and the product-concept test, which showed an extremely high level of consensus on the concept with respect to the results of similar research projects.

Source: Gianni Bolongaro.[4]

NAMING THE PRODUCT

There are three stages in naming the product:

1 defining the need;
2 developing possible names;
3 testing those names.

Definition of the need means that the purpose of the name must be stated in terms of the overall marketing goals, and its expected contribution in such terms as imagery or perception of the firm's own name or that of its product or service.

The basic method of developing possible names is brainstorming. Once potential names have been generated, an image or perception test may be the way to determine the best one.

In developing possible names, the first step is to construct a dictionary of verbal terms and symbol fragments (visible and appropriate elements of existing names in the category). These terms are assembled into a word-making pattern that expresses the product category and messages. These may be natural words (Apricot) or coined words (Natwest). Each promising name is further modified to emphasise impact, aesthetics, memorability, uniqueness, vocabulary fit, internal or external reference and shelf appeal. The final step is a focus-group discussion among the target-market group at which the group is exposed to the names and competitive names. They discuss how well each name describes the product and the kind of images each name puts forward.

The symbol associated with the product is also an important ingredient.

Public puts faith in brand names

Britain has become a nation that puts more trust in brand names than in traditional institutions, according to a report published today by the Henley Centre, the forecasting organisation.

Research carried out for the report, 'Planning for Social Change 1997', found that four in five people would trust food manufacturers such as Heinz and Kelloggs to be honest and fair.

The comparable figures for the police and the judiciary were three in five and two in five. Only a quarter felt they could trust their local council. When people were asked whether they would trust a multinational company to be honest and fair, only 13 per cent gave a positive response.

However, high street retailers also scored highly, with 83 per cent trusting Marks & Spencer, 74 per cent J Sainsbury and 71 per cent Tesco.

Paul Edwards, chairman of the Henley Centre, said the trust in brand names matched other findings in the research. These showed that people felt both 'in and out of control of their lives', he said. While people felt powerful as consumers, they felt they were not in control in their roles as employees or as members of society.

This perception was associated with the transfer of risk from the state and employers to individuals, leaving people to take responsibility for increasingly complex issues such as financial planning.

Mr Edwards said consumers now trusted certain brands so much that they would welcome their extension into new areas in order to help them to cope with increasing demands on their time.

The research suggests that as retailers moved to develop home shopping services, or even to provide services such as household cleaning, they would find a ready market.

The Henley Centre concludes that 'brand management is becoming synonymous with "trust management", demanding strategic attention at the top of the organisation'.

The findings will fuel the debate within the marketing industry about the role of a company's marketing department, and about what type of external adviser – advertising agency or management consultant – should take the lead in giving advice about a company's brand.

Source: Alison Smith.[5] Reprinted with permission.

PACKAGING THE PRODUCT

Packaging, particularly for fast-moving consumer goods, has three functions. First, through visibility and appeal, it helps to focus attention on the shelf. Second, it builds an image for the product. Third, it is for the convenience of storage and use by the consumer.

Good packaging can help the chances of the success of the product in the market place. In the case of fast-moving consumer goods, package design is important and so specialised that most larger companies use a package designer. The designing of the package must start with a good idea of the imagery desired, the importance of shelf visibility and consumer requirements for storage and use. Marketing research should have preceded this design step.

Packaging development

Discussion with consumers through focus groups in the early stages of package development is useful. The process is similar to that adopted in consumer-product research. Drawings or mock-ups of various packages can be shown and discussion in group interviews will produce important points, many of which may not have been previously considered by the firm.

Soft drinks switch to PET leaves industry struggling

Aluminium is under attack in its biggest packaging sector – the drinks industry. Put 50 cents into any of the vending machines at the World of Coca-Cola in Atlanta – housing 'the world's largest collection of Coca-Cola memorabilia' – and the soft drink is delivered in a plastic bottle. A year ago the Coke would have been in an aluminium can. The switch from cans to PET (polyethylene terephthalate) for soft drinks in the US has been so swift and bruising that the aluminium industry is still struggling to come to terms with it.

Aluminium's lightness and flexibility combined with strength, its foldability, good barrier characteristics, non-reactivity in contact with liquids, fats and oils as well as its abundance and recyclability, all make it a formidable packaging material. Innovative design and effective marketing have enabled it to take share in virtually every type of packaging, in spite of its relatively high price, and growth is continuing in many areas.

Cans represent one of aluminium's most important markets, accounting for 20 per cent of global demand. Cans in the US alone account for 10 per cent of worldwide sales of the metal. Now this market is under threat, not only from PET in the soft drinks business, but also because glass bottles are back in favour as beer containers.

In the US the development of micro breweries and the perception that 'premium' beer should be served in glass bottles is having a noticeable impact. Glass's share of the beer package market in the States moved up from 35.8 per cent in 1994 to 38.6 per cent last year while cans slipped from 64.2 to 61.4 per cent.

'Our market research shows that people think glass is classy and that beer tastes better in glass,' says Norman Nieder, group director, packaging technology group at Ansheuser-Busch, the brewing giant. 'A can is a can. It is always the same.'

Robert Budway, president of the US Can Manufacturers' Institute acknowledged the advances glass is making in the beer business but insists that the main threat to the aluminium can is posed by PET bottles in the 'single serve' soft drinks market, primarily in vending. 'In the US this is a market of 15bn to 18bn units and 80 per cent of all new vending business is going to PET,' he warns.

In 1991 aluminium cans accounted for 55 per cent of US soft drinks packages while PET bottles had 34 per cent. Last year the two were neck and neck at 50 and 47 per cent respectively. While the industry had some time to adjust to the PET threat in North America, it has been startled by the way the aluminium can's progress in Europe has suddenly stalled.

Until 1995 demand for aluminium cans in Europe was growing at 9 per cent a year but since then it has levelled off, not only because of the growth in PET bottles but also because the steel industry, not wanting to see the beverage can market go the same way in the US – where aluminium had nearly 100 per cent of the market – had fought back spiritedly. Nick Mason, research manager of the aluminium group at the CRU International consultancy, says: 'Until very recently we thought there was scope for the can to penetrate the European beverage packaging mix a little further, even though we recognise the looming threat of PET. But we estimate that, after three years of steady gains, the share of the packaged beer and soft drinks market taken by cans fell very slightly in 1996 to just more than 15 per cent.'

He points out that it is rare for a product to remain at the top for more than 10 years and that in the US and Europe 'we appear to be at, or close to, the final saturation phase in the life cycle of the can, although I do not believe that precipitate decline is inevitable'.

Another worry for aluminium producers is that the drinks companies, having quickly transferred the PET technology to Europe from the States, might do the same in emerging markets, such as those in Latin America, on which the aluminium industry is heavily relying for future growth in the can business. In soft drinks, for example, two US companies dominate the global business, Coca-Cola, with 47 per cent, and Pepsi with 22.3 per cent. 'One lesson from Europe is that there is a risk, across a whole range of developments in packaging, of a leap to PET,' says Mr Mason. 'Packaging has become a crucial element of brand identity. Over a relatively short period container and material combinations that offer proprietary distinctiveness have acquired tremendous competitive advantages.

'So far the pace has been set by PET bottles.'

Nevertheless, the can remains an excellent container offering, for example, a 30 per cent cost advantage over glass bottles at the filling stage and, at present, competitiveness with PET in the 'single serve' container filled in high volumes.

Mr Mason suggests that a 'two tier market' might emerge, consisting of a high throughput segment in which system economics still dominate – and in which cans retain many advantages – while the other would be the premium part of the market, 'in which the package, as much as the contents, may determine the value of the product to the brand manager'. Ansheuser-Busch's Mr Nieder implies that brewers are still attempting to find a way to win customers by using cans.

'Cans are much more profitable to us than glass bottles,' he points out. His group is experimenting with embossed cans, cans with labels using 10 colours, cans with photographs on them, cans that change colour to show whether they are cold or warm, cans with 'touch-off' tops instead of ring pulls and shaped cans.

However, the plastic producers are now developing bottles made of polyethylene naphthalate (PEN) capable of holding beer, so the plastic threat to the aluminium industry could become even more serious.

Source: Kenneth Gooding.[6] Reprinted with permission.

MARKET SEGMENTATION RESEARCH

A segment is a unique group of customers – or potential customers – who share some common characteristics that make them different from other groups. Different segments may have different needs: they may require different versions of the same product; they may pay different prices; they may buy in different places; they may be reached by different media.

In consumer markets, customers and prospective customers can be grouped together, or 'segmented', by attitude and lifestyle; by age, gender or stage in the family lifecycle; or by job types, level of income and many other relevant variables. In industrial markets, customers and prospective customers are usually grouped together and slotted into a particular segment depending on customer type, customer size, customer culture and customer location. Customers and prospective customers can be further segmented according to whether they are heavy or light users of a particular product or service, and whether they are loyal to a particular competitor.

Segmenting and selecting the optimum market segments is called *target marketing*. This is a vital marketing skill. Target marketing requires an ability to:

- find the key characteristic(s) that break a market into relevant 'actionable' segments;
- identify and quantify which customers fall into which segments;
- target the best segments most likely to give the best results.

Identifying what each segment wants, what it can afford, whether it is loyal to a particular competitor and how it might respond to an offer is vital information. Careful segmentation and accurate targeting keep a firm close to the market. Target marketing reduces waste, finds the best customers and helps to keep them satisfied.

We can segment consumer markets using many different variables which include:

- geographic
- demographic
- geodemographic
- psychographic
- behaviour patterns.

Geographic segments mean location, which can include streets, towns, cities, regions, countries, continents and trading blocks like the European Union and NAFTA.

Demographics, or social statistics, include age, sex, family, lifecycle, job type, socioeconomic and group income level.

Geodemographics mix geographic and demographic data to create categories of house types and locations, for example, people who live in detached houses in exclusive suburbs.

Figure 13.2 Map drawn with the aid of Lotus 1-2-3 showing population figures for 1990

Psychographics attempt to segment according to the psychological profiles of people in terms of their lifestyles, attitudes and personalities, for example, active go-getters.

Behavioural segments address behaviour patterns which include usage (e.g. heavy or light users) and uses: the way a product or service is used – in other words, the benefit enjoyed.

A market can be segmented by the benefits enjoyed: different segments buy the same product for different reasons. Some people use toothpaste for healthy teeth, others to prevent bad breath. Some people buy it for both reasons.

More than one variable can be used when segmenting markets and, indeed, the more variables the better since they help to focus on a tighter target market. Tighter targeting means less waste, more relevant offers to appropriate customers and higher customer satisfaction.

Industrial, organisational or business-to-business markets can also be broken into segments and the most appropriate ones selected as target markets. Different variables are used for these types of markets: customer type, size, location, and how they operate in the corporate culture. Customer type categorises the type of product or service which the customer organisation produces. In the UK, industry type is defined by the Standard Industrial Classification (SIC) code. The size of the customer in terms of sales, number of staff and usage may determine whether or not it is worth targeting. Size of customer is also influenced by whether they are heavy or light users of a particular product or service, and whether they are loyal to a particular competitor.

The basic forms of segmentation

There are three segmentation bases: *consumer*, *business and industrial*, and *geographics*.

Consumer segmentation falls into two groups: syndicated and proprietary. Syndicated services use both primary and secondary sources. The information may be pure demographics, an implied mix of psychographics from demographics, or pure psychographics. Demographics are vital statistics: age, sex, marital status, ethnicity, family size and composition, nature of housing, occupation, education, and other statistical characteristics covered by the census. Psychographics are the psychological attributes that constitute a person's lifestyle and have much to do with the person's self-image and how he or she wants to be perceived. Purely psychographic studies are generally used only in proprietary services, for the sole use of the firm doing the study because any such study has to be tailored for specific needs and uses. The syndicated sources basically use demographic statistics and embellish them in psychographic terms.

Business segmentation is the description of areas or customers in terms of various kinds of statistics, such as nature or size of the business. Business segmentation is not as well developed as consumer segmentation. Firms can readily pinpoint business customers and potential customers and then promote directly to them. Moreover, there are few standard sources for such business and economic segmentation information. Some sources provide data on the general business environment and outlook for a particular community, and others give more detail about specific kinds of business. On a simple basis, business customers may be segmented by SIC code or by classifications within the Yellow Pages.

Geographics. Many people have difficulty arriving at conclusions by inspecting large tables. It is far easier to look at a coded or coloured map to get rapid and lasting impressions. Where tables show data by area one can easily use mapping, and computer technology has facilitated this. Depending on the data source, maps can be displayed in varying colours or shading patterns with almost unlimited possibilities, according to category, such as proportion of potential or actual customers, per capita spending in a particular product or service group, or sales achievement versus potential. Most mapping sources can produce maps on paper, transparency film, slides or colour transparency overlays.

CARTOGRAPHYING GEOGRAPHIC SEGMENTATION

Computer technology has enabled the ready production of maps which display segmentation data effectively. Depending on the data source, the maps can be displayed in varying colours or shading patterns with almost unlimited possibilities, according to category, such as proportion of potential or actual customers, per capita spending in a particular product or service group, or sales achievement versus potential. An illustration of how such maps appear with the aid of a spreadsheet package such as Lotus 1-2-3 release 5 is shown in Figure 13.2. Most mapping sources can produce maps on paper, transparency film or slides, and colour transparency overlays are almost always a possibility.

Geographic information systems

Geographic information systems (GIS) make use of graphical map displays on to which various kinds of data, such as business locations or demographic information, can be superimposed. This enables the user to visualise the spatial relationships between the data. A good GIS can be linked to information databases and can make spatial calculations on the data within the maps. This form of analysis helps users to make business decisions about such matters as where to locate a new outlet, by matching customer profiles and population density to actual geographical physical locations.

MapInfo is a sophisticated GIS which runs on a PC under Windows. It is possible, for example, to select and load multiple files to a map window and we can position several layers of information on to one map. Parts of a map can be clipped for use in presentations and whole maps can be cloned to create different views of our data without changing the original. Labels are stored as attributes of their geographic objects in the map layer, and are saved as such to a workspace where they can be selectively switched to reflect different aspects of data.

MapInfo has worked hand-in-hand with Microsoft to achieve full compatibility with MS Office. Excel now includes MapInfo's Data Map: a subset of MapInfo which enables the user to map Excel data. MapInfo fully supports ODBC and OLE which enables us to connect directly and simultaneously to remote database servers, and to paste a map into a report, word-processor file or presentation and edit the map *in situ*. The product treats all data, including maps, as tables, and it is possible to view data as tables, maps or graphs. We can also open more than one view of our data simultaneously. These views may be synchronised and all views are automatically updated when any change is made.

The program has extensive statistical and analytic tools and MapBasic (a separate software package) provides programming functions should these be required. MapInfo also includes *The Geographic Tracker*, a MapBasic application from Blue Marble Geographics which allows us to link and track Global Positioning System (GPS) data in real time and place it on top of a background map within MapInfo. The system does need a GPS receiver.

MapInfo can visualise and segment data, but acquiring useful data is time-consuming, time-critical and expensive. MapInfo provides a CD-ROM Data Product Viewer containing a valuable set of maps and sample data. MapInfo can also supply a huge range of more detailed datasets.

Source: MapInfo.[7]

COMPETITION RESEARCH

Understanding the marketing strategies of competitors

Understanding competition is central to making marketing plans and strategy. A firm has to be regularly comparing its products, prices, channels of distribution and promotional methods with those of its competitors in order to ensure that it is not at a disadvantage. In so doing it can also identify areas where it can gain a competitive advantage.

In order to establish a sustainable competitive advantage in the market place it is necessary to know and understand the strategies adopted by competitors. This is more than noting in which markets/segments the competition is operating and their respective market shares and financial performance. In addition it is important to consider how competition will develop in the future and thus to ascertain the focus of the strategies that competitors are pursuing.

Firms need to monitor competition continually. The main need is for information regarding:

- sales
- market share
- profit margin
- return on investment
- cash flow
- new investment.

In addition, knowledge of competitors' financial performances is useful.

Such information enables firms to gain comprehensive impressions of their rivals that may be useful in predicting short-term strategies to be adopted by competitors. A knowledge of competitors' specific objectives would be very welcome since these would give clues as to future strategies that competitors are likely to pursue. This kind of information may be difficult to obtain but may be inferred from present or past activities.

Identifying competitors

The first step, however, is to identify the competition. This may seem a simple question for most firms to answer. For example, at first sight a book publisher's main competitors might appear to be other book publishers. This is, of course correct. However, product substitution has also to be considered. This involves looking more broadly at the types of business in which the firm operates. If this is done one can identify many producers of goods and services that people use for leisure, education and other informational needs. Many of these products could be potential competition for the publisher. Many of these products could be used instead of the publishers' books – i.e. they can be substituted.

Sources of information about competitors

Decision-making can be improved by an adequate supply of relevant information, and a knowledge of good sources of information is an important first step. A suitable starting point is to examine what competitors say about themselves and what others say about them. Sources of information fall into four categories:

- public
- trade
- government
- investors.

Public sources

Advertising, promotional materials and press releases are prime sources of information on what competitors have to say about themselves. Articles and newspaper reports provide a good source of information on what others have to say about them. None the less, one does have to be wary of the information gleaned since it may be biased or even distorted.

Trade and professional sources

Courses, seminars, technical papers and manuals prepared by competitors can give detailed insights into competitors' activities. However, it can take a considerable amount of time to distil and analyse this information. Distributors, the trade press and even customers can be good sources of information about what others have to say about competitors.

Government

In the UK companies have to lodge their annual reports at Companies House in London and the contents of these reports provide insights into the operations of competitors. In addition, lawsuits, government ministries and national plans are useful sources of information.

Investors

Annual meetings, annual reports and prospectuses are primary sources of what competitors have to say about themselves. Credit reports and industry studies provide an outsider's viewpoint.

Newspapers are a source of information about competitors

Nike

Is Nike no longer cool? Its shares certainly are not. The sportswear group, a stockmarket star for much of the 1990s, has underperformed the S&P 500 by over 70 per cent this year. Even Reebok, its smaller and more fragile rival, has not done quite as badly. The two companies have blamed their recent profit warnings on Asia, and with some justification since the Far East has been an important source of growth in recent years.

More significant, however, are the sudden problems in the US, which still accounts for over half of sales at both. Some slowing was inevitable. Nike's torrid growth, based on winning market share and ramping up prices in a fundamentally static athletic footwear market, was always going to plateau. But few investors expected footwear sales and orders to start declining, as they did last quarter. That probably reflects resistance to this spring's sharp price increases. Many of Nike's shoes sell for well over $100 a pair, while competitors such as Converse and Adidas have launched ranges at $80 to $100. But the real worry would be if Nike was ever to lose its touch with the notoriously fickle teenagers who set the trends in the sportswear market.

Nike will bounce back. It has a strong balance sheet, a great brand and is branching out into new market segments like golf and soccer. But with no big new product launches until early 1999, and plenty of unwanted stock to unload until then, its comeback will take time.

Source: Financial Times.[8] Reprinted with permission.

PROMOTION RESEARCH

Much of promotional research is aimed at the development of advertising appeals. The type of research this requires may be classified as psychological (or motivational), sociological (focus groups) and anthropological (observation).

Psychological (motivational) studies

Motivational researchers usually employ psychological approaches within the framework of individual interviews. This involves talking with people in depth about what a product may mean to them: products may often evoke strong emotional feelings. It is often possible to discover what a product symbolises in this way.

Sociological (focus-group) studies

In Chapter 8 we have examined the use of focus-group technique. Group interaction may lead to ideas that a single person would be unlikely to generate.

Anthropological studies

The anthropological research approach may be applied to observe a small number of people in order to understand how a product fits into their life and what retains their interest in a particular brand. The method has also been used as an in-depth tool to obtain better understanding of consumers. It can provide a way of getting past the level of responses to questions by observing what people actually do, instead of merely listening to what they say.

The effectiveness of poster advertising

Some 300 people aged between 18 and 55 were shown ten current posters and asked whether they remembered seeing them before. They were also asked to indicate how much they liked each poster by giving a mark out of ten. More than 80 per cent recognised at least one poster, ranging from 61 per cent for Esso Price-watch to 9 per cent for the National Lottery 'National Heritage' advertisement. Four posters – Esso, Peugeot 406, Silk Cut 'German' and Foster's Lager 'Ambre Solaire' – were recognised by one-third of respondents.

Men were twice as likely as women to have noticed one poster before – but this may have been caused by the rather masculine nature of the products. Male recall was particularly high for the Royal's 'Batman' advertisement and for the Littlewoods FA Cup advertisement for which men make up 70 per cent of the recognisers. Of Channel 4's NBA poster, and the Silk Cut and Orange campaigns, the under 25s are similarly important.

The Esso and Royal Insurance poster advertisements tied for top position in the survey, with Esso taking first place among the females and over 35s.

Poster	Liking marks out of 10	Ranking	Recognition % saying	Rank
Royal Insurance	5.4	1	20	8
Esso	5.3	2	61	1
Peugeot	4.9	3	47	2
Silk Cut	4.9	3	47	2
Toyota	4.7	5	22	7

Foster's	4.7	5	35	4
Littlewoods	4.5	7	27	5
Channel 4 NBA	4.5	7	25	6
National Lottery	3.8	9	9	10
Orange	2.8	10	19	9

Source: Poster watch.[9]

MEASURING ADVERTISING EFFECTIVENESS

The measurement of the effectiveness of advertising and promotion is one of the most difficult aspects of marketing research. Many factors influence sales besides advertising. The other factors include all the elements of the marketing-mix, together with the availability of the product and the effect of competition. It is perhaps only when people place orders in response to advertisements, however, that we can be reasonably sure about its effectiveness in terms of producing sales.

Advertising must, however, provide information and it must persuade. Various available copy-testing research services are essentially built around these two premises. Most leading agencies provide services to measure awareness-creation ability, information retention and persuasability of advertisements. Another service provides guidance on how the particular advertisement might be modified to be more effective.

Advertising content research tests an advertisement's ability to project the desired message to the target audience. The design and layout of an advertisement is tested together with the basic theme: the copy platform. Different kinds of communication appeal are tested out in this kind of research. Measurements can be taken at two stages: pre-publication and post-publication. At the pretesting phase, emphasis is placed on ideas and methods of publication; at post-testing, the emphasis is on measuring how effectively communication concepts were received by the intended audience.

The pretesting of advertisements can involve:

- direct rating where a consumer panel is shown different advertisements and asked to rate them on their attention-getting power, whether it encourages the recipient of the message to listen, watch or read further, the clarity of the message, the effectiveness of the appeal and whether it suggests follow-through action.
- portfolio tests where the participant is presented with a collection of advertisements and asked to recall their content. Recalling an advertisement reflects its ability to be understood and remembered.
- laboratory tests which are used to measure the consumers' physical reaction to advertisements. Pupil-dilation tests, changes in heartbeat, etc., reflect an advertisement's ability to attract attention.

Post-testing emphasises the recall and recognition of advertisements. It may be either aided or unaided recall. In the case of unaided recall, people are shown a series of advertisements and then asked to recall the messages. In the case of unaided recall, people are questioned about whether they have seen a particular advertisement and, if this is the case, they are asked to state what impact it has had on them.

Advertising campaigns have a number of objectives and advertisers want to know how effective they have been in reaching these objectives. Changing awareness, knowledge and preference about a brand may be the objectives for a campaign. The use of models such as the Lavidge and Steiner[10] hierarchy of effects model may enable researchers to specify the kind of advertising research that is appropriate. Researchers may try to assess how successful an advertising campaign has been in terms of, say, creating an awareness of a product or giving people information about a product or service that will move them further along the ladder of purchase intent. Similar measures may be taken for creating a liking, developing a preference, bringing about conviction and, where relevant, actual purchase.

Current thinking about advertising effectiveness suggests that four elements are generally regarded as extremely important:

1 *Awareness.* A variety of studies of assessing awareness point to its importance. Studies by the Dutch organisation NIPO[11] through its brand-monitor system demonstrate a high correlation between brand-loyal buying behaviour scores and aggregate brand awareness. They also found a high correlation with brand awareness and the numbers of people who claim that their next purchase of a durable will be a given brand.

2 *The customer liking or finding an advertisement appealing.* The Advertising Research Foundation's *Copy Research Validation Study* suggested that the 'likeability of a commercial was the single best predictor of sales effectiveness'. The use of a likeability scale claims to predict sales winners 97 per cent of the time.[12] Factors such as ingenuity, meaningfulness, energy and warmth were found to underpin likeability. The relative importance of each one of these factors appears to vary across products.

3 *Interest.* Finding an advertisement really interesting is suggested as being even more important than liking the advertisement.[13]

4 *Enjoyment.* The extent to which an advertisement is enjoyed has been found to be a better pretest measure than short-term recall.[14]

These advertising-effectiveness predictors are often used today by market research companies, usually under the direction of the advertising agency. The predictors are linked to the customer's emotional thoughts.

Advertising media research

Research here tries to eliminate waste in advertising by systematically examining the media available for promoting products and services.

Press research

This mainly takes the form of readership surveys, for example, the National Readership Survey, which is based on a stratified random sample of 28 500 adult interviews over a continuous period of twelve months. Businesses making use of this survey obtain breakdowns by demographic characteristics, regional distribution, television viewing, cinema attendance, commercial radio listening and special interests. Average issue readership is provided for each publication, together with a regional analysis. The National Readership Survey is administered by the Joint Industry Committee for National Readership Surveys (JICNARS).

Television advertising research

The Joint Industry Committee for Television Advertising Research (JICTAR) appoints a research organisation to provide a research service based on a television panel of UK households. The service releases information on the size of audiences at different times of the day and week by projecting the viewing patterns of the sample panel. A measure is also taken of the audience appreciation of TV programmes.

Radio research

A Joint Industry Committee for Radio Audience Research (JICRAR) follows the pattern set by JICNAR and JICTAR. The JICRAR survey is based on seven-day diaries distributed among random samples of persons aged 15 or more living in private households within a radio station's designated area. The diaries are placed and collected by the interviewers.

Cinema audience research

This is covered mainly by the National Readership Survey administered by JICNARS.

Poster research

The Joint Industry Committee for Poster Advertising Research (JICPAR) commissions a research organisation to estimate both pedestrian and vehicular audiences for all posters. Information is also provided on types of area, shops and commercial characteristics so that posters can be strategically sited.

Television audience measurement

Measuring methods used are diaries, set meters and people meters. A media research diary involves participants keeping records of their television viewing in a structured form. It usually is kept for a week and covers, by day of the week and time of day, station and programme identification. Diaries are on a household basis, with a diary for each household set. Every person 12 years of age or over, or an adult surrogate, is asked to fill in the diary. Viewing of younger children is also recorded.

The set meter is an electronic device attached to the individual television set in the home. It automatically records the time, whether the set is on or off, and the channel to which it is tuned – all reported on a minute-by-minute basis. The data are recorded in a home storage unit and are transferred to the research firm's central computer the next day, through telephone lines. Since the participating home needs an expensive installation, this is operated with a relatively small panel of houses.

The people meter is a special form of the set meter. In this case, each family member pushes buttons on a keypad to indicate viewing, and these data are automatically recorded simultaneously with set usage.

Each of the three methods presumes to measure total audience size. The straight set meter measures only whether the set is on or off. Figures showing total audience size and size by nature of household demographics are produced but specific viewers and their demographics cannot be identified. Such measurements are not specific enough to permit an advertiser to pinpoint its desired individual market. Diaries and people meters provide demographic definitions for individual audiences. People meters have added a method of measuring the demographics of the audience to a particular show.

Magazine audience measurement

The method usually used to measure the audience involves taking the person through the magazine, and asking aided recognition questions. The researcher has a deck of cards, each containing the logo of one of the magazines being covered. The deck is handed to the respondent, who is asked to sort the cards into two piles, placing in one pile those he or she might have read or looked into in the past six months, and in the other pile those the person is sure that he or she has not read or looked into. For each magazine that the respondent 'might have read or looked into', a stripped issue (containing up to nine articles) is shown. The issue is sufficiently dated to permit time for the magazine to accumulate its total audience. The person is shown each of the articles and then asked whether the particular issue was seen. Then follow other queries such as where the publication was seen and the overall rating the respondent would give. Reports generated show, for each magazine, summaries of audience accumulation and reach, net unduplicated audiences for combinations of magazines, total and in-home audiences by demographics and psychographics, and qualitative measures of readership.

Newspaper audience measurements

Newspaper measurements usually call for two interviews with each respondent, separated by a short time interval, and employs the 'yesterday reading' method. For daily newspapers, respondents are first asked what newspapers they have read or looked into during the past six months. Then, excluding the day of the interview, they are asked when they last looked into an issue of the particular paper, and the amount read (but only the replies of those reading yesterday are counted). The same general procedure is followed for Sunday newspapers, with necessary changes. Qualitative questions about place of reading and how the paper was obtained may also be asked.

SELLING RESEARCH

Research into selling is examined by Moutinho and Evans[15] and there are various models reported in the literature which discuss, among other things, how to allocate territories to representatives (see, for example, Lilien et al.[16]). The illustration in the box, however, shows research in action in terms of the more qualitative dimensions of selling.

Getting feedback on selling

Pharmaceutical firms depend primarily on the sales force as the means of communication with both existing and potential customers. In order to provide information of the effectiveness of representative detailing, 'follow-up research' has developed. The research aims to contact those healthcare professionals who have been visited by the representatives and to question them about their recall of the interview. Research interviews with professionals are usually conducted over the telephone and last 10 to 20 minutes each.

The analysis of the results is usually presented in a series of quantitative measures of various parameters used to assess the effectiveness of the detail. The parameters might include:

■ recall of the detail taking place
■ recall of the key communication objectives
■ reaction to the information provided
■ impact on usage.

A wide spread of interviews is obtained by limiting the number of interviews conducted for each representative in the fieldforce. For an average fieldforce of 50 to 60 representatives, a sample of two interviews per representative is a reasonable target. This works well for larger samples and where most of the questions can be precoded. Much more, however, can be learned from a detailed follow-up survey, particularly when interviews are tape-recorded. Verbatim transcripts of interviews show the depth and richness of the answers.

Although the results of a detailed follow-up survey are useful in their own right, they are made much more useful when comparisons are made with other detailed follow-up surveys conducted for the same company and with surveys conducted by competitors. Standard norms of performance may be developed for both levels of recall of a product, the number of key communication points that are recalled and the impact on usage. Through the use of these comparisons, an effective measure of the success of the detail can be obtained.

Source: Andrew Scott.[17]

PRICING RESEARCH

Research into pricing explores pricing approaches both for new products before they are launched and for any proposed changes once they have been launched. There are two general approaches to pricing research. The first (Gabor and Grainger[18]) involves presenting different prices for a product to respondents who are then questioned about whether or not they would buy. A 'buy-response' curve of different prices associated with positive purchase intentions is then constructed. Another approach involves people being shown different sets of brands in the same product category, at different prices. They, too, are then asked which ones they would buy. This latter approach enables competitors' brands to be taken into account by respondents.

Statistical analysis of data is useful for helping to sort out the effect of price versus that of other variables on quantities sold. The main technique used is regression analysis. Data obtained from consumer panels can be analysed with regression analysis to assess the impact of price changes.

Another commonly applied approach is to make use of survey data. A question might be included in a survey such as 'By how much would your sales increase (or decrease) if prices were increased (decreased) to ...?' Such a question would be aimed at distributors but similar questions can be put to consumers. But obtaining response curves in this way can be subject to error. Distributors may readily exhibit bias and consumers are usually unable to give reliable answers to questions about how price affects their brand purchase and preferences.

Yet another approach is to make use of laboratory experiments and simulated test markets. This usually involves having a simulated store where prices are altered experimentally and their effects on purchase levels assessed. This is a relatively inexpensive way of estimating the demand for a product at different prices, but getting a sense of reality into the simulation can be difficult and the simulation may not represent the real world at all well.

The standard test market also offers an approach to pricing research.

Pricing pharmaceuticals in Europe

Despite the fact that controllers of drug budgets can exert an influence over what physicians prescribe, the latter have to believe that a product has a 'perceived value' that is commensurate with its price if they are to prescribe it. Some countries are now following the example set by France in requiring firms to examine the volume projections for a new product and using it as a basis for price-setting. The danger in this is underlined by the sales history of the anti-depressant Prozac. As sales in France exceeded forecast, Lilly was forced into reducing its price. Eventually the price in France was cheaper than that in the UK and other countries and led to parallel importation despite an initial pan-European approach to pricing.

Marketing research is needed to determine the price/volume ratio required to focus as much if not more on the patient's willingness to pay as the physician's willingness to prescribe. In the future investigations using consumer pricing research techniques, such as the Gabor and Grainger method,[18] will probably become more and more popular. Such studies will also benefit from the 'perceived value pricing' approach developed since 1989 at Martin Hamblin Research. In this latter connection the adoption in the last two years of choice-based conjoint techniques enables the researcher to examine a variety of scenarios that might affect the market in the future: for example, what happens if important competitors reduce their prices. Choice-based conjoint is a valuable procedure for exploring the potential action that prescribers and buyers would take, given a change in market circumstances. Bowditch and Fitall (1995)[19] describe how Janssen used the method when examining a number of alternative line extensions for one of its leading products, enabling the firm to develop a forecasting model. The model not only established the impact on the product and the competitors from the alternatives tested, but also helped to establish the projected profit and loss for each one.
Source: A J Bowditch.[20]

DISTRIBUTION RESEARCH

A variety of research can be conducted to cover distribution. The relevance of such research often reflects whether the sponsors are engaged in business-to-business or consumer marketing. There are many commonalities in terms of requirements. Possibly the main difference reflects to the fact that research is required at the retail level – the consumer interface – in the case of consumer-goods marketing.

Research can also be divided or categorised according to whether it is in connection with physical distribution decisions or with channel selection and management. In the case of physical distribution there are obvious overlaps with the broader subject area of operations management and operations research techniques, which help to optimise the management process. For example, inventory management may be regarded as part of the distribution system (or part of the production system) depending on whether it is at the factory or at a distribution warehousing facility. The topic of inventory optimisation is well covered in the operational research management literature. Warehouse location and layout for optimal efficiency are also discussed extensively in the operational research literature, as are models to facilitate the optimal transportation of goods policies (see, for example, Taha[21]) although Moutinho and Evans[15] do discuss warehouse-location research and retail-outlet location research. Lilien *et al.*[16] provide a good overview of the kinds of models and information requirements useful in both physical-distribution and channel-strategy decisions.

In consumer marketing Crimp[22] discusses retail audits in general and the use of syndicated trade research in the assessment of performance compared with that of

competitors through the retail audit. Retail marketing perhaps offers more opportunities for the traditional market researcher through the medium of shopping
surveys. These tend to be restricted to retailing generally and to service marketing
where there is a mixing of customers – hotels, restaurants and the like. In these
studies, a fieldworker poses as a customer and makes mental notes on aspects of
customer service. The shopper may note which aspects of service were or were not
present, or they may note the quality or rating of service. Some of the aspects
typically covered are:

- product or service quality
- facility quality
- personnel courtesy
- personnel efficiency
- personnel service
- personnel promotion of selected brands, items, features, benefits
- items stocked, offered, on display
- prices.

Such studies are usually handled by an outside specialist firm.

Electronic revolution in the retailing world

More sophisticated sales strategies and strong interest in electronic commerce are
fueling a boom in IT use among retailers.

The retail sector is a battleground where the effective deployment of information
technology can make the difference between victory and defeat, and where recent
advances in information systems and the prospects for electronic commerce are
bringing about the most rapid changes in retailing for decades.

Meanwhile, in an attempt to differentiate their services and retain customer
loyalty, retailers are using IT systems to personalise their offerings and switch from
demand-led to customer focused strategies.

'Consumers have become incredibly demanding,' says Deloitte & Touche
Consulting. 'They have high expectations for ever-improving quality, better
information, better service at lower real prices – and they are getting it. They are
able to enforce these demands because of the information explosion and the
increasing competitive alternatives available to them today.' Retailers, already under
tremendous pressure on margins, are trying to reduce labour costs, improve
customer retention and fine-tune pricing and inventory. To achieve this, they are
deploying a wide range of IT systems ranging from demand forecasting and
logistics software, to self-scanners, electronic labelling systems and huge data
warehouses.

'There is already a sustained pressure in the retail supply chain to reduce cost
and this trend is set to continue,' says IBM, one of the leading suppliers to the retail

sector. 'Overall, the strategic trend by the retailer is to move from "product-led" to "market-led" by improving knowledge of the consumer and consequently increasing margins by more effectively positioning products.'

Demand-chain management software, such as Industri-Matematik's System ESS, is based on the principle that customer 'pull' through the demand chain has primacy over the desire of manufacturers to 'push' products through the supply chain. It is increasingly seen as a key to delivering business benefits such as improved customer service, better financial performance and differentiated products.

According to a recent *Harvard Business Review* study, most retailers estimate the cost of carrying inventory for a year is equivalent to at least a quarter of what they paid for the product. Therefore a two-week inventory reduction represents a cost saving of nearly 1 per cent of sales and a significant boost to profits.

IT systems also help retailers monitor 'customer traffic' using infra-red or video-tracking systems to follow shoppers' movements, identify 'cold spots' in the store and help to ensure adequate staffing levels in service-critical areas.

Meanwhile, loyalty cards – increasingly likely to be smartcards – are being used to boost what analysts call 'frequency of shop', especially in the food retailing sector.

Other back-office systems sort out 'customer activity' by hoping to classify shoppers by 'type of purchase' and promoting goods that will appeal to them while in that frame of mind by product positioning or related discount offers.

'Overall, there are two big vectors in retailing,' says Julian David, marketing director for IBM Europe's distribution industry business unit. 'Digitisation, in all its forms, and personalisation.' In spite of reduced market growth expectations, companies in Europe's retail and distribution industries plan to increase their IT investments by up to 10 per cent this year, according to a survey sponsored by IBM. In large companies, IT spending is being driven by the challenges of improving overall infrastructure, cost competitiveness and customer service, with investments focused mainly on supply chain management, targeted marketing and globalisation.

For example, Benetton, the fashion retailer, signed a worldwide agreement with IBM in July, which will eventually link point-of-sale terminals in 7,000 shops and five continents. 'Operational management of the business will be simplified and it will be possible to distribute IT services from our central data processing system to the point-of-sale,' says Bruno Zuccaro, Benetton's computer systems director.

Existing IT investments are also being used differently. When electronic point-of-sale (Epos) systems were introduced over a decade ago, they were mostly used for stock control and inventory management. Now, however, retailers are using the data they collect in different ways – to identify trends and target individual consumers.

'IT in retailing is moving from being an operational tool, primarily aimed at improving inventory control and front-end technologies, to become an enterprise-wide mechanism for increasing efficiency throughout the supply chain,' says Andy Cummins, retail marketing manager for Siemens Nixdorf in the UK.

'With the merchandise pipeline geared for rapid response, the priority of many retailers is to identify customer requirements and shopping habits using the most recent relational database systems and data mining techniques,' he says.

Retail-based data warehouses manage the records of individual transactions from a variety of processing systems and information sources such as electronic cash registers, inventory systems, weather records and customer demographics. They then enable users such as store managers to query the database. 'Retail is detail,' says Tony Fano, senior vice-president of NCR's Atlanta-based retail group.

NCR, a leading data warehouse provider, says retailers typically begin asking the data warehouse about the company, then about individual stores, followed by inquiries about individual items and prices. They then demand historic data so they can examine trends by season or region. Such information allows retailers to do market-basket analysis, looking at each customer's entire transaction history to design loyalty programmes, determine display space, and judge the effectiveness of promotions. Wal-Mart, which claims to operate the world's largest commercial data warehouse, uses the vast amounts of information stored there to guide its business. It is expanding the warehouse, based on the NCR Teradata system, from 7.5 terabytes to more than 24 terabytes – the equivalent of 6bn pages of text.

'Our business strategy depends on detailed data at every level,' says Randy Mott, senior vice-president in charge of information systems at Wal-Mart. 'Every cost, every item is carefully analysed, enabling better merchandising decisions to be made on a daily basis.'

Among the UK-based stores, Safeway has already deployed its 'Shop and Go' self-scanning service in more than 130 stores and plans to roll it out in another 35 stores by the end of 1997.

Self-scanning systems have been on trial for more than 10 years but with mixed results. Analysts believe it is only now as customers become familiar with high-tech systems that the concept seems to have taken off. It has been much the same with multimedia kiosk systems which first appeared in the early 1980s using cumbersome 12-inch video disks.

Numerous schemes have been tested since then and most have failed, but interactive media now seems to be gaining more popular acceptance. Kiosks are seen by many analysts as simply one of a range of channels to market which retailers will deploy in the future. Clearly, the Internet, and the World Wide Web in particular, represents another important and rapidly emerging channel.

Although many early entrants in the home shopping arena, such as Time Warner's Dream Shop, IBM's World Avenue, comprising 20 retail 'shops', and e-Shop Plaza have been slow to take off or have failed, many specialist Internet-based stores are flourishing and most market research firms predict a bright future for electronic commerce. Nevertheless, forecasts for business-to-consumer electronic commerce vary wildly from a conservative $6.6bn in 2000 from Forrester Research to around $200bn from IDC and Input. Despite this, a Cap Gemini sponsored survey of

European retailers published in March suggested the greatest uptake of electronic shopping by retailers will come not in the longer term, but over the next two years.

According to the Cap Gemini survey, most retailers outside traditional mail order expect 13 per cent of their sales to be via home shopping within two years rising to 26 per cent in 10 years, yet despite these bullish forecasts, almost 60 per cent said this would not affect their existing store operations. In other words, most retailers hope to run their physical outlets and electronic channels profitably side by side.

Internet shopping in particular is forecast to increase its share of total sales dramatically with 70 per cent of retailers expecting to be receiving customer orders via the Web within two years.

'Over the next decade, Internet shopping will steadily build for traditional store-based retailers to 14 per cent of total sales, and just over half of home shopping sales,' says the Cap Gemini report. 'Television shopping – via both dedicated and interactive channels – is also expected to enjoy major growth after the next two years.'

Source: Paul Taylor.[23] Reprinted with permission.

SUMMARY

This chapter has examined several applied areas of marketing research: product research, segmentation research, competition research, promotion research, pricing research and distribution research. In the case of product research, attention has been paid to product generation and testing, consumer product testing and packaging research. In the case of segmentation research, attention has been given to researching ways of segmenting the market. In promotion research, attention has been focused on the ways of assessing its suitability and effectiveness, and various approaches to pricing research were examined. Finally, attention was paid to some aspects of distribution research.

Questions

1   Explain how marketing research can be used in product generating and testing.
2   What is product delivery? What is the relevance of marketing research to this topic?
3   Discuss the role of the Delphi technique in product research.
4   How might marketing research help in naming a product?
5   Indicate what is covered by packaging research.
6   What is market segmentation research? What actually takes place?

7   Describe the role played by cartographying in geographic segmentation.

8   What is a geographic information system?

9   Discuss the problems involved in identifying competitors and indicate how firms might obtain information about competitors' strategies and intended strategies.

10   Indicate the different marketing research methods that have been successfully applied in promotion and advertising research.

11   What is meant by measuring advertising effectiveness?

12   What is involved in media research?

13   Discuss the various approaches to pricing research.

14   Indicate how marketing research can help with distribution decisions.

15   Describe the types of information gathered by retail audits.

16   Explain the type of research that can be conducted into selling.

Case study 13.1   The Ford Probe

The design of the Capri was not entirely new: it was inspired by the Mustang which had been launched in the USA some five years earlier. 'The car you always promised yourself' was the slogan Ford used in 1969 to launch the Capri in Europe. Ford had previously introduced a car with the same name earlier in the 1960s but it was a complete flop. Launching a new model under the 'Capri' label might have been considered by some people to have been an unnecessary gamble.

The Capri was effectively an adaptation of the Cortina chassis, fitted with a sleek, eye-catching coupé body. It had the appearance of a sports car but had full four-seat accommodation. The car was built until 1987, achieving nearly two million sales in total. In 1987, however, the only sizeable remaining market for the car was in the UK and sales volumes did not justify developing a model based on the Cortina's replacement, the Sierra.

Enthusiasts mourned the passing of the Capri and, while fast hatchbacks like the Escort XR3i were bought by those who wanted something fast and distinctive, an unfulfilled desire in the market place remained. The hot hatchbacks were seen as too expensive to insure, too attractive to young criminals, and too flash for comfort in the politically correct 1990s: they could not fill the gap left by the Capri.

The Ford Probe is a sports coupé now making an entrance to the market. The idea for the model again comes from the USA. The Probe is made by Auto Alliance International, a joint venture between Ford and Mazda in Flat Rock, Michigan. The body is styled by Ford of America, although it is in effect a Japanese design. On the mechanical side the engines, transmissions and major mechanical components originated at Mazda. Technically the Probe is very similar to the Mazda MX6 coupé.

Unique among Ford's offerings to the European market and quite different to the old Capri, the Probe's chief rival is perhaps the Vauxhall Calibra. However, having been purpose-built as a sports coupé, the Probe is very different to the Calibra. With the Probe, Ford hopes to regain the Capri's old position as Britain's bestseller in this class. However, in contrast to the Calibra, a restyled Cavalier with full four-seat accommodation, the Probe is a 2 + 2. In designing the Probe, all the emphasis has been placed on the driver and frontseat passenger: there is very little room in the back.

The Probe is possibly more like cars such as the Volkswagen Corrado, Honda Prelude, Toyota Celica, the forthcoming Coupé Fiat and the Mazda MX6. It will probably appeal to many people since it feels more special than the Calibra and has more aggressive looks and better responses than the Mazda MX6. Although its ride at low speed is harsh enough to be uncomfortable on some bumpy roads, the Probe is fitted with wide, low-profile tyres that provide plenty of grip and its cornering on smooth roads is a confidence-building experience.

Under the bonnet the powerful V6 engine is impressive. It comes in two sizes:

- The 165 bhp 24V engine produces a top speed of 136 mph and a 0–60 mph acceleration time of eight seconds.
- The 115 bhp 16V engine produces a top speed of 127 mph and a 0–60 mph time of ten seconds.

Whichever version of the Probe is chosen it will be an enjoyable tourer for two or even a family with small children. The Probe is priced directly against the Calibra with a tag of around £16,500 for the 2-litre engine and around £19,500 for the larger engine.
Source: R Hutton.[24]

Question

Describe the kind of research that would have taken place in finding out how to position the Ford Probe.

Case study 13.2 | **South Africa**

The Sotho word, *Gauteng*, translates into English as 'place of gold'. It is the new name given to the Pretoria–Witwatersrand–Vaal Triangle, one of the largest industrial regions in the southern hemisphere. In 1886, on a patch of windswept veld, an unemployed miner came across a stone containing traces of gold. From this event came the discovery of the world's richest natural treasure house. Speculators, prospectors, fortune-seekers and adventurers arrived in the area from all over the world and, in a comparatively short space of time, the pastoral landscape was completely transformed. First, shanty towns sprang up as goldrush fever gripped the area. Then these shanty towns rapidly changed into modern concrete cities. Johannesburg became known as the 'Gold capital of the world' and the entire country became the centre of an economic boom. The revenues generated by gold in the world's export markets enabled the country to develop its impressive industrial, commercial and financial strength.

South Africa is home to an extraordinary variety of ethnic groups, cultures, creeds and languages. The background to this human diversity extends over thousands of years to the original inhabitants – the Stone Age hunter–gatherers known as the Bushmen. Black migrants arrived from the north to take their place and they, in turn, were followed by European and Indian immigrants. Gauteng is a dynamic, cosmopolitan kaleidoscope representing most of these different cultural components.

Johannesburg is *nouveau riche* territory: a modern, cosmopolitan metropolis packed with vitality and verve. In quiet, leafy suburbs, baronial mansions in manicured gardens lined with limousines testify to the fact that the city, at the top of the supertax bracket, is a very affluent society. In the central business district, the astute make daily fortunes on the Stock Exchange. Skyscrapers tower over chic boutiques, aromatic Indian bazaars and African *muti* (medicine) shops where traditional healers dispense advice and herbal remedies.

Some 50 km north of Johannesburg, Pretoria is well known for its colourful gardens, shrubs and trees. The city developed more slowly than Johannesburg but now boasts high-tech shopping centres, museums, art galleries and multiculinary restaurants. The city has four universities and several scientific institutes, including the Council for Scientific and Industrial Research and the Onderstepoort Veterinary Research Institute, both of which are famous worldwide.

Soweto (South Western Township) is a huge sprawling township, estimated to be inhabited by more than two million people. Homes range from affluent mansions to makeshift shacks. Soweto residents belong to nine ethnic groups, among whom Zulus and Xhosas predominate. The township has the Baragwanath hospital which is reputed to be the largest hospital in the southern hemisphere. Here high-quality training and medical standards are provided. The hospital attracts patients not only from the rest of South Africa but also from countries as far north as Nigeria. Despite this, it is estimated that between 80 per cent and 85 per cent of Soweto residents consult traditional healers. Commercial activities in Soweto are expanding rapidly. New supermarkets, retail chains, banks and shopping complexes are constantly being developed.

In the north of the country lies the Northern Province. The Venda, who inhabit the eastern part of the Soutpansberg, are thought to be descended from chiefs who travelled south from Central Africa towards the end of the seventeenth century. They are an intensely superstitious people who place great store on rites and rituals. For example, in the python dance, barebreasted teenage girls perform a slow, rhythmic dance to the throb of tribal drums. The drum is central to traditional Venda religious belief.

Scattered throughout the Northern Province are to be found the North Sotho people who live in small settlements with family homesteads clustered around their cattle kraals. The most famous member of this tribe was the legendary Rain Queen, Modjadji, who was believed by many to be immortal. Small numbers of the Tsonga people also inhabit the Northern Province. In rural areas they pursue a leisurely pace, spending time on arts and crafts. Unlike other tribal people, the Tsonga are also keen fishermen. Pietersburg is the commercial and cultural hub of the region, featuring impressive art exhibitions and elegant historical buildings. It also possesses wide streets, jacaranda and coral trees, colourful parks and sparkling fountains. In the vicinity, the countryside is the setting for some of the most prosperous cattle ranches in South Africa.

Mpumalanga (the former Eastern Transvaal) is steeped in the history of pioneers, hunters and fortune-seekers and gold-rush towns abound. Barberton and Pilgrim's Rest are among the most famous. The Middleveld region is inhabited by the Ndebele people who are renowned for their strikingly attractive dress, characterised by vivid colours, metal rings and beaded hoops. They are also notable for the exceptional quality of their beadwork and the strong geometric designs on the walls of their homes. The capital of the region is Nelspruit and revenues from the extensive fruit-growing which has taken place in the region have played a vital role in its development. The town shows the signs of the opulence generated by the natural wealth of the region produced by the fruit growers.

KwaZulu-Natal is the main home of South Africa's Indian population. Languages, especially among the older generation, include Tamil, Telegu, Hindustani, Gujarati and Urdu. The strictly regulated patriarchal, extended family is not as evident today as at one time and Indian languages tend to be heard less often. Younger people tend to speak English as a first language and lead an increasingly Westernised life. Members of the Indian community are found throughout the upper echelons of commerce, industry and the professions. Durban has good shopping centres where you can buy anything from photographic equipment to couturier clothes and rare antiques. Fleamarkets and craft trails attract leisurely browsers, while discount stores offer quality merchandise at bargain-basement prices. Within a stone's throw of the city centre, oriental bazaars, fragrant with spice and incense, offer silks, saris, unusual jewellery and ornaments. Theatres and concert-halls present avant-garde and ethnic programmes.

Although most of the South Sotho (Basotho) people live in the Kingdom of Lesotho, a self-contained mountain kingdom in the middle of South Africa, many of them live in Qwaqwa and in other parts of the Free State. Marriage customs among traditional South Sotho people involve the exchange of *lobola*, whereby the bridegroom gives a specified number of cattle to the bride's parents. Marriage between relatives is allowed for the simple reason that this keeps wealth within the family. Old tribal traditions still continue in the mountains where the people are fairly isolated. Farmers till the fields with hand-held ox-drawn ploughs. Bloemfontein originated at a spring which at various times was a source of water for Bushman hunters, Sotho farmers, Voortrekkers and enormous herds of game. For many years it remained a tranquil agricultural settlement, but it has recently developed into a prosperous commercial and industrial city – the capital of the Free State and the judicial capital of South Africa. With its stately old buildings dominated by skyscrapers, the city has many facets, ranging from sophisticated up-market shopping centres, restaurants and theatres to vestiges of the gracious Victorian ambience that once prevailed. Surprisingly, for a city that was formerly the capital of a Boer republic, Bloemfontein has many British features – legacies of the Anglo-Boer War when the town was occupied by British forces. In the north of the Free State is the attractive garden-city of Welkom, which lies at the centre of the Freestate goldfields. It has good shopping malls and restaurants, an airport and a thriving theatre. Winburg, steeped in Voortrekker history, is the oldest town and first capital of the former Republic of the Orange Free State. The Voortrekker Monument symbolises five major trekker groups.

In the early days of European settlement in South Africa, groups of Malays were brought to the Cape by the Dutch East India Company. Among the many talents the Malays brought with them were exceptional cooking skills and this has exerted considerable influence over the cuisine of the Western Cape. Over the past 340 years, their lifestyle has become a unique blend of East and West – but much of the mystique remains, as Malay culture is firmly rooted in the Muslim religion. Although Malays are found throughout the Western Cape, the area on the lower slopes of Signal Hill, known as the Bo-Kaap, is the place most closely identified with Malay culture. With its majestic Table-Mountain backdrop, Cape Town is one of the most magnificent cities in the world. Between high-rise office blocks, Edwardian and Victorian buildings have been meticulously preserved and many outstanding examples of Cape Dutch architecture are to be found. Narrow cobblestone streets and the strongly Islamic ambience of the Bo-Kaap enhance the cosmopolitan sense of the city. Cape Town's shopping provision includes elegant malls, antique shops, craft markets and fleamarkets. Specialist boutiques offer an enticing array of unusual items that are not readily obtainable elsewhere. Gourmets and lovers of fine wines have a treat in store.

The Xhosa are a diversity of Eastern Cape tribes of Nguni origin who moved south across the Kei river from KwaZulu-Natal before the seventeenth century. While the Xhosa are increasingly moving into towns and adopting the white man's lifestyle, those who remain on the land cling to their old tribal systems and timeless traditions. Each rural family lives in a group of huts known as a kraal with a cattle byre and a small garden. In every kraal a man lives with his wife and children, together with his married sons and their wives and children. Cattle, sheep and goats play an important role in their social life and its rituals. A man counts his wealth in cattle: his daughters are valuable assets, for their bride price is paid in cattle.

Kimberley is in the Northern Cape and its diamond mines were largely responsible for financing the Witwatersrand goldfields. Today, Kimberley is a modern city with broad, treelined streets, attractive parks and gardens, comfortable hotels and busy shopping centres.

Source: South Africa Tourism Board.[25]

Question

Discuss the kinds of problems that would be encountered in segmentation research in South African markets.

Case study 13.3 | Lengthy effect of advertising

There are good reasons why current advertising research practice is not resulting in better advertising. It really is a case of asking whether research can really objectively assess whether an individual advertisement will be effective. It is quite common to see immediate benefits in sales just after an advertisement has been run, but the extra sales revenue – or, more to the point, the extra profit – does not usually pay back the cost of the extra time, particularly when the brand has been around for a long time in a mature market. Individual advertisements do not change perceptions about brands. All the tracking study companies agree that shifting perceptions requires continued activity and time. It is clear that the real value of advertising lies in long-term campaigns.

Source: Simon Sylvester.[26]

Question

Do you agree with the point of view expressed in this case? Explain your reasons.

Case study 13.4   Bronco Jeans

Bronco Jeans distribute their denims direct to retailers. The firm produces and markets a single line of jeans under the brand name Bronco and sells them to retailers at a list price of £8 per pair. Total fixed costs amount to £1,000 per week and variable unit costs are £2.00. Various discounts are given to retailers for bulk purchases and the early settlement of debts. Retailers put a 100 per cent mark-up on the list price + VAT. Demand has been quite strong at the retail level and Bronco has been able to sell 1,000 pairs of jeans per week. It wants to expand production and at the same time it feels that because it can sell all it produces, it may be pricing itself too low. Most of its competitors' jeans are retailing for around £20 a pair, including VAT at 17.5 per cent.

In an effort to get some hard data to help it reach a decision, the firm has asked the 250 retail outlets it supplies to estimate the impact on demand that various changes in the list price might have. The answers are summarised below.

Question

On looking at the results of the survey, the firm feels that it should increase its prices by 20 per cent. Do you think this would be a good idea? Explain your reasons.

Price change (%)	Change in demand mean (%)	Standard deviation (%)
−10	+5	2.1
−5	+2	1.0
+5	0	0.0
+10	−5	1.1
+15	−10	1.5
+20	−25	2.5

Case study 13.5 | British divided into four types

A third of Britons are unhappy with their lot, struggling with life in the modern age, according to market research released yesterday. The group – dubbed resistors – make up 36 per cent of the population. They are offset by embracers, the 1990s' successors to the 1980s' yuppies who see new technology as a style statement. Embracers are physically and socially active but decidedly selfish. Only a third of this group, who make up 27 per cent of the population, believe it is their responsibility to help people worse off than themselves. In the middle are the pragmatists – the 'ordinary' men and women who adopt new technology when they believe it offers them proven benefits and are more concerned with the community than a computer – and the traditionalists, the smallest group, at 15 per cent. Generally the oldest, generally well off, they are 'a happy self-confident bunch', according to Michael Svennevig, the project's research director.

The classifications come from futura.com, a research project run by Leeds University in partnership with the Independent Television Commission and Ogilvy & Mather and sponsored by a string of big companies including Unilever, IBM, Guinness and Ford as well as the Department of Trade and the Central Office of Information.

Source: Nicholas Timmins.[27] Reprinted with permission.

Question

Discuss how the above classifications might be used in segmentation research studies.

Case study 13.6 | Skoda cars

Skoda is, by one measure, the third oldest car manufacturer in the world. It is the biggest Czech industrial company, and is far and away the biggest employer in the country – some 30 per cent of the Czech workforce are either employed directly by Skoda, or owe their jobs to the firm, working for suppliers or firms servicing the company. During the 1930s the company's cars were regarded as prestige automobiles; they were the BMWs of their day, and the Skoda company was the flagship of the then-buoyant Czech economy. Czechoslovakia was then the fifth richest country in the world in terms of per-capita wealth, and thus had a strong domestic market; unfortunately, the Second World War and the advent of communism changed all that.

During the ensuing forty years of communist rule in Czechoslovakia the company suffered badly from a lack of innovation, from a lowering of quality standards, and a poor image elsewhere in the world. The cars acquired a reputation for being unreliable, uncomfortable, and hard to resell – in the UK, 'Skoda jokes' became fashionable, with the car as the butt of the humour. The cars could only be sold by being the cheapest available, and even then sales were somewhat disappointing.

In 1989, communism collapsed in eastern Europe, and in 1991 Volkswagen acquired Skoda and set about changing the firm's products and image. Research showed that the Skoda image was one of unreliability and poor quality; since this was the opposite of VW's image (which is very much one of quality and reliability) the company began by stressing the link with VW at every opportunity. Skoda's advertising campaign used the slogan, 'We've changed our cars – can you change your mind?' The target audiences for this campaign were not only the potential buyers for the cars, but also the public at large; the company hoped to stem the flood of Skoda jokes and make Skoda purchase a matter for congratulation rather than ridicule. The next move in the campaign to re-invent Skoda was to invest heavily in the factory, introducing better quality control and modern manufacturing equipment. Skoda's design team were moved from the dingy corner of the factory they had occupied in communist days, into new offices where they were given the facilities to redesign the cars.

Skoda's UK managing director, Dermot Kelly, said, 'We did image analysis before and after the marketing campaign to assess our progress. While VW is a strong trigger, it doesn't create a strong brand image but it takes away a negative one.'

Currently, the brand is multi-faced across Europe; Alfred Rieck, the Dutchman who was appointed as marketing manager of Skoda, aims to create a single brand image across the continent. This will be achieved on the back of the Skoda Octavia, the company's flagship vehicle, which has been well received by motoring writers and the general public alike.

The company's greatest accolade might be the influential JD Power Survey, an American research programme which surveys customer satisfaction. The survey canvasses customers' opinions of their cars and the dealerships two years after purchase, and is regarded as highly influential on consumers' decision-making. In 1994 Skoda was rated 21st in the survey; in 1995 in came 13th, in 1996 7th, in 1997 it came 6th, and finally in 1998 Skoda was rated first in total overall satisfaction.

So far, Skoda's policies appear to be paying off; in 1994, 170,000 cars were built. This had risen to 357,000 by 1997, and 422,000 by 1999. European demand has been so high the company has been forced to cut deliveries to Asia, and the Skoda factory at Mlada Boleslav in Bohemia works 24 hours a day, six days a week to satisfy demand. Having moved from their 1991 position of having to pay potential customers £10 to induce them to take a test-drive, Skoda is now in a position of being unable to meet world demand for the cars. From being the butt of everyone's humour in the 1970s and 1980s, Skoda has again become a force to be reckoned with in the world's automobile markets.

(Case contributed by Jim Blythe.)

Questions

1 What role has market research played in the success of Skoda?

2 How might Skoda research a new market, such as China?

3 What techniques might be used to monitor the image of the cars?

4 Although the JD Power Survey has been very positive about Skoda, what are the potential problems with relying on a survey of this kind?

5 What are the market research implications of trying to develop a pan-European image for the cars?

Further reading

Brown, G, Copeland, T and Millward, M (1973) Monadic testing of new products – an old problem and some partial solutions, *Journal of the Market Research Society* (15)2, April, pp 112–31.

Cooper, L and Nakanishi, M (1988) *Market Share Analysis: Evaluating competitive marketing effectiveness*, Boston: Kluwer Academic Press.

Cox, W E (1979) *Industrial Marketing Research*, New York: John Wiley.

Day, E and Stafford, M R (1997) Age-related cues in retail services advertising: their effects on younger consumers, *Journal of Retailing*, 73(2), pp 211–33.

Douglas, S P and Craig, C S (1983) *International Marketing Research*, Upper Saddle River, NJ: Prentice-Hall.

Geo-Visual Solutions for Today's Business (1990) Mt Olive, NJ: Intelligent Charting.

Gordon, W and Corr, D (1990) The space between words: the application of a new model of communication to quantitative brand image measurement, *Journal of the Market Research Society*, 32(3), pp 409–35.

Green, P E and Krieger, A M (1989), Recent contributions to optimal product positioning and buyer segmentation, *European Journal of Operational Research*, 41, pp 127–41.

Green, P E and Krieger, A M (1992), An application of a product positioning model to pharmaceutical products, *Marketing Science*, 11(2), Spring, pp 117–32.

Grover, R and Srinivasan, V (1987), A simultaneous approach to market segmentation and market structuring, *Journal of Marketing Research*, 24(May), pp 139–53.

Hammond, K, Ehrenberg, A S C and Goodhart, G J (1996) Market segmentation for competitive brands, *European Journal of Marketing*, 30, pp 39–49.

Kamakura, W and Russell, G J (1989) A probabilistic choice model for market segmentation, *Journal of Marketing Research*, 26(Nov), pp 379–90.

Lewis, D B (1983) Advertising research and measurement, Chapter 6 in *Marketing Manager's Handbook*, Chicago, IL: Dartnell, pp 6–7.

Lewis, P H (1989) When maps are tied to data bases, *New York Times*, 28 May, p 10.

Malhotra, N K (1995) *Marketing Research: An application orientation*, Upper Saddle River, NJ: Prentice-Hall.

Marks, A P (1990) The Sinclair C5 – why did it fail?, *Management Decision*, 28(4), pp 9–14.

Mitchell, V (1995) Using astrology in market segmentation, *Management Decision*, 33(1), pp 48–57.

Moskowitz, H R (1985) *New Directions for Product Testing and Sensory Analysis of Foods*, Westport, CT: Food & Nutrition Press, p 171ff.

New products, *The Number News*, June 1990, p 8.

Newton, S (1993) From hearses to horses: launching the Volvo 850, *Journal of the Market Research Society*, 33, pp 153–62.

Proctor, S, Papasolomou-Doukakis, I and Proctor, T (2001) What are TV advertisements really trying to tell us? A postmodern perspective. *Journal of Consumer Behaviour*, 1(3), pp 246–55.

Studies of Media and Markets (1989), New York: Simmons Market Research Bureau.

Uncles, M D, Hammond, K A, Ehrenberg, A S C and Davies, R E (1994) A replication study of two brand-loyalty measures, *European Journal of Operational Research*, 76, pp 375–84.

Workman, J P (1993), Marketing's limited role in new product development in one computer system firm, *Journal of Marketing Research*, XXX (November), pp 405–21.

References and notes

[1] Double, L (1991) Unpublished MBA dissertation, Department of Management, Keele University, September.

[2] White, S (1993) Get a helping of the sugar-free chip game, *Research Plus*, September, p 3.

[3] Lynch, T (1997) Caught in the neighbours' tangled web, *Financial Times*, 15 August.

[4] Bolongaro, G (1994) Delphi technique can work for new product development, *Marketing News*, 3 January, p 11.

[5] Smith, A (1997c) Public puts faith in brand names, *Financial Times*, 13 October.

[6] Gooding, K (1997) Soft drinks switch to PET leaves industry struggling, *Financial Times*, 22 October.

[7] MapInfo, Centennial Court, Easthampstead Road, Bracknell, Berks, RG12 1YQ. Tel: 01344 482888.

[8] *Financial Times*, 20 December 1997.

[9] Poster watch, *Marketing Week*, 26 April 1996, p 58.

[10] Lavidge, R J and Steiner, G A (1961) A model for predictive measurements of advertising effectiveness, *Journal of Marketing*, 25, October, pp 59–62.

[11] Stapel, J (1990) Monitoring advertising performance, *ADMAP*, July/August.

[12] Biel, A (1989) Love the advertisement, buy the product?, *ADMAP*, October.

[13] Stapel, H (1991) Like the advertisement but does it interest me?, *ADMAP*, April.

[14] Brown, G (1991a) Modelling advertising awareness, *ADMAP*, April.

[15] Moutinko, L and Evans, M (1992) *Applied Marketing Research*, Harlow: Addison-Wesley.

[16] Lilien, G L, Kotler, P and Moorthy, K S (1992) *Marketing Models*, Upper Saddle River, NJ: Prentice-Hall, ch 9.

[17] Scott, A (1996) The launch went fine – then the devil's in the detailing, *Research Plus*, April, p 14.

[18] Gabor, A and Grainger, C (1966) Price as an indicator of quality, *Economics*, 33, pp 43–70.

[19] Bowditch, A J and Fitall, S (1995) Through the looking glass: primary research in multicountry forecasting, *Proceedings of the EphMRA/ESOMAR Pharmaceutical Marketing Research Conference, Geneva*, Amsterdam: ESOMAR, pp 141–63.

[20] Bowditch, A J (1996) In Europe's complex market, check the price is right, *Research Plus*, April, pp 12–13.

[21] Taha, H A (1992) *Operations Research: An introduction* (5th edn), New York: Macmillan.

[22] Crimp, M (1990) *The Marketing Research Process* (3rd edn), Hemel Hempstead: Prentice Hall.

[23] Taylor, P (1997b) Electronic revolution in the retailing world, *Financial Times*, 3 September.

[24] Hutton, R (1994) Best of the bunch, *Scottish Business Insider*, March, pp 662–3.

[25] *South Africa: A world in one country*, South Africa Tourism Board, 1996.

[26] Sylvester, S (1993) Don't ask consumers to supply your answers, *Research Plus*, November, p 8.

[27] Timmins, N (1997) British divided into four types, *Financial Times*, 5 September.

14 Marketing research settings: business-to-business, services and internal marketing

OBJECTIVES

After reading this chapter you should be able to:

■ understand the differences and similarities between consumer marketing research and business-to-business marketing research;

■ appreciate how marketing research can be applied to the marketing of services;

■ have an understanding of the concept of internal marketing and the role that can be played by marketing research within such a context.

KEY WORDS

business-to-business markets
SIC
shopping surveys
service quality

service satisfaction
service delivery
SERVQUAL
internal marketing

PLAN OF CHAPTER 14

INTRODUCTION

This chapter looks at business-to-business marketing research, services research and internal marketing research.

In the case of business-to-business marketing research, the differences and the similarities with consumer marketing research are explored. Business-to-business marketing research has changed considerably in recent years and employs many of the approaches that were at one time the domain of consumer research. The changing nature of business-to-business marketing research is explored further.

The chapter explores the role of marketing research in service marketing, looking specifically at shopping surveys, customised, full-scale studies of service satisfaction to provide measurement of customer reactions to the delivery of service, and SERVQUAL, designed to assess service quality.

The last section looks at the role of marketing research in internal marketing. Market research can be adopted for use to gain feedback to management about working conditions, company policy in general and workers' own understanding about what comprises quality for the customer. The relationship between organisational sub-units and also their relationship to top management is also important. This can be assessed by a variation of the SERVQUAL instrument mentioned above.

BUSINESS-TO-BUSINESS MARKETING RESEARCH

Business-to-business marketing research is very similar in many ways to consumer marketing research. Both forms of marketing research use primary and secondary sources, qualitative and quantitative techniques, and internal and external sources of data. Both forms of research use telephone interviews and face-to-face interviews but organisational marketing research does not use street surveys, door-to-door interviews or hall tests. However, there are some major differences between consumer and business-to-business markets. For example, when developing the marketing mix, different strategies are needed for business-to-business customers than for final customers – a difference that significantly affects their research activities.

The business-to-business market

Business-to-business markets are composed of those organisations and agencies that purchase goods and services either to aid in the production of other goods and services or for resale purposes. This includes manufacturing firms, government agencies, public utilities, and educational institutions as well as intermediaries such as retailers and wholesalers. Consumer markets, by contrast, comprise individuals, families or households who purchase goods and services for their own final consumption.

The demand for business goods is derived from the demand for final consumer goods. If the domestic car market has a bad year the car components industry will also suffer because its sales are closely tied to the demand for cars. Because of this relationship, the demand for business-to-business goods can be very volatile and business-to-business marketing research has therefore to be concerned with general business and economic conditions, levels of inventory and the prices of raw materials.

It is quite common in business-to-business markets to have a small number of customers account for the vast majority of a firm's sales. Often 80 per cent of the business comes from 20 per cent of the customers. Such a relationship influences the type of sampling procedures used in business-to-business markets since a great deal can be learned from surveying only a few large customers.

When trying to determine which factors influence purchase decisions, the business-to-business researcher's task is made more difficult by the fact that more than one person is often involved in making such decisions. It is not possible from one interview in a company to ascertain key buying influences.

Quality of service, availability of supplies, and consistent quality of materials are critical factors in the purchase decisions made in the business-to-business market. Businesses-to-business buyers are usually more knowledgeable about their own needs and are swayed less by promotional appeals than are consumers.

Many business-to-business products are engineered or designed specifically for a customer. In these situations the supplier must identify the specific needs of the customer but it also means that there is less need for research of mass markets.

When conducting consumer research, the persons to be surveyed or observed can usually be identified and contacted fairly easily. In business-to-business markets not only are the appropriate respondents hard to identify because of multiple buyers but once identified these people may be difficult to reach directly: many are senior managers and are shielded from would-be interviewers by assistants and secretaries. Senior managers also tend to be less accessible since they travel frequently and possess little uncommitted time. The fact that they are being contacted for their business knowledge usually prevents making such contacts in the evening hours or during weekends.

Most manufacturers of consumer products, especially those in high-tech products, adopt the marketing concept: that is, they attempt to build their product marketing offerings around identified customer needs. The concept, however, is not as prevalent among business-to-business firms primarily because their research activities are strongly influenced by technically oriented people who appear to place more emphasis on distinctive features and technological breakthroughs.

Consumer product firms can purchase information from Nielsen that will afford them a monthly review of how their products, as well as their competitors' products, are doing in terms of unit sales and market share. No similar type of information exists for business-to-business products from either syndicated firms or the firm's own research staff. There appears to be less interest in continuous monitoring of the sales of business-to-business products. This may be due to characteristic sales patterns – infrequent sales – but it could also be due to a difference in outlook of the executives of business-to-business organisations.

Because the costs of developing and producing prototypes of some business-to-business products are quite high, test marketing is not usually an important research tool within business-to-business markets. Some firms also do not like to have proposed products on display in test situations where competitors can observe their operation and usage.

Overview of research

Business-to-business marketing research tends to emphasise the use of internal staff and internal records as a major source of research information. Market intelligence is also a more significant aspect of the marketing information system than in consumer goods marketing. The explanation for this perhaps lies in the fact that business-to-business activity involves being more directly in touch with the market than is usual in the case of consumer goods marketing, where the nature of the distribution system creates a physical separation between the manufacturer and consumers. Close contact with the market makes it advantageous for a business-to-business marketing organisation to maintain a marketing intelligence system that makes use of feedback from the sales force as a mechanism for reporting customer views.

Desk research has more significance in business-to-business marketing than in consumer marketing. Government publications, trade information, published sources and so on, contribute an important part of the data input for marketing planning and decisions. Where the consumer researcher is interested in the census of population, for example, the business-to-business researcher is more likely to be interested in the census of production. As far as syndicated and omnibus research services are concerned these are unlikely to be available in any but the largest and most sophisticated markets.

Business-to-business marketing researchers are more likely to make use of postal research and telephone research in conducting quantitative surveys. Telephone research has traditionally been an important technique for business-to-business marketing researchers and its major advantage over personal interviewing in this case is that a geographically dispersed sample can be more economically contacted and produce better response rates than postal research.

Depth interviews figure predominantly in qualitative research in business-to-business marketing research. It is difficult to get a small group of business executives in the same room at the same time for the purpose of a research group discussion. Nevertheless, group discussions are used and can be useful, but they are the exception rather than the rule. Expert informants in particular fields are valuable for their information, and their participation in depth interviews at the exploratory stage of research study is of particular significance in business-to-business marketing research.

In business-to-business marketing, business directories or even internal customer lists or business mailing lists are often used as sampling frames. Stratification as a sophistication of random sampling and to some extent quota sampling methods are used. In this case the allocation of sample segments might be based on appropriate criteria such as the Standard Industrial Classification (SIC) or size of organisation in terms of sales turnover.

One sampling problem, however, concerns who is actually to be asked the questions. The business-to-business marketing researcher has to know which individual in the firm should be asked the questions or to whom a postal or telephone enquiry should be addressed in order to ensure the best chance of getting valid and reliable information.

Types of research undertaken

There is in fact a great deal of similarity between the types of research undertaken by consumer product firms and business-to-business product firms. The following similarities and differences should be noted:

1 Consumer product firms are much more involved with all types of research related to advertising.
2 Both groups are heavily involved with economic and sales forecasting.
3 Both groups are heavily involved with most aspects of product research – but business-to-business product firms are less concerned with packaging.
4 Both groups are heavily involved with sales and market analysis.

Ball-Bearings

A well known ball-bearing firm established its early reputation on an innovative self-aligning ball-bearing. The tolerance provided by the bearing permitted rolling bearings to be employed where inaccuracies in the manufacture and assembly methods then used were too destructive for conventional deep-groove bearings.

By the 1980s it was thought that the product might be approaching the end of its lifecycle. The market was researched at some length across a wide range of applications using two levels of research team members chosen for their specific knowledge of the specific target sectors. Results indicated that while few firms would admit that their own manufacturing processes were inaccurate or that their assembly was hit and miss, many still were glad of the flexibility which the bearings design permitted. Indeed the concept had proved so valuable that a whole new generation of compact aligning bearings has been developed.

Source: Peter Gorle.[1]

Differences in research applications

The market for most business-to-business products is composed largely of other manufacturers or intermediaries. Information on these firms is usually contained under SIC headings and includes such information as total shipments, number of employees, and size of payroll. In order to put SIC data to good use, the researcher needs to understand the numbering process of the system.

In this classification system all places of business are classified into one of ten divisions covering the entire range of economic activity. These are:

1   agriculture, forestry and fisheries
2   mining
3   construction
4   manufacturing
5   transportation, communication, electric, gas and sanitary services
6   wholesale and retail trade
7   finance, insurance and real estate
8   services
9   government
10   all others.

The principal divisions are divided into several major groups such as printing and publishing, chemicals and allied products, with each major group having assigned to it a two-digit SIC number. Further classification is achieved by means of three-and four-digit numbers (see Figure 14.1). By using the SIC system business-to-business markets can be divided into relatively small, medium or large market segments.

Some example SIC classifications

SIC code	Description
25	Furniture and fixtures
251	Manufacturers of household furniture
2514	Manufacturers of metal household furniture

Figure 14.1 Standard Industrial Classification

Most firms belong to one or more trade associations and the publications of these associations are a major source of statistics about a particular industry. The publications also cover a variety of topics relevant to their member firms.

Many business-to-business firms serve unique markets and for this reason appropriate secondary data may be difficult to obtain. The firms often make use of the services of indexing services, such as *Chemical Abstracts* or *Engineering Index*, to obtain information on unique topics or groups of customers. These agencies search many data sources, such as journals and association publications, to locate articles of possible value to their clients.

Of the methods that may be used to obtain primary data, the survey method is most important for business-to-business researchers. The complexity of the buying process in most business-to-business markets usually precludes the use of either observations or experiments. Personal interviews are favoured on account of the small size and geographical compactness of respondents, the uniqueness of information sought, the

Table 14.1 Differences between business-to-business and consumer marketing research

	Consumer	*Business-to-business*
Population	Large – usually unlimited	Small
Respondent accessibility	Fairly easy. Can interview at home, in the street, on the telephone or using mail technique	Difficult. Available usually only during working hours at place of work. Usually has other priorities
Respondent cooperation	Has become more and more difficult. Millions still never interviewed	A major concern. Danger of being over-researched
Sample size	Can usually be drawn as large as deemed necessary since the population is so large	Usually much smaller than consumer sample but the statistical confidence is equal due to the relationship of the sample to the total population
Respondent definitions	Usually fairly simple. Users of a brand, demographic characteristics, etc. The ultimate purchaser is also a user for most consumer products and services	Can be difficult. The user and the purchasing decision maker in most cases are not the same
Interviewers	Easily trained. They are familiar with the area under investigation for most categories	Difficult to find good executive interviewers. A working knowledge of the subject being researched is absolutely essential
Research costs	Key factors are sample size and incidence of usage categories (low incidence categories)	Lower incidence levels and difficulties in locating the right respondent are key factors

frequent need for demonstrations in interviews, and the greater amounts of information that can usually be obtained within the time constraints.

Extensive use of probability sampling is not made among business-to-business marketing researchers because most markets are fairly small and can be completely surveyed, or the surveys concentrate on the bigger customers in the market. Many business-to-business researchers ignore sampling altogether: they prefer to obtain information through a series of interviews until satisfied that they have obtained an accurate picture of the market. When sampling is used it tends to be judgement sampling.

Since less emphasis is placed on sampling there is less use of sophisticated methods when analysing data. Attitudes merely reflect such conditions as fewer firms in the market, less emphasis on probability sampling, and an emphasis on qualitative data.

Changes in business research

Business-to-business market research emerged from the protective cloak of consumer market research in the 1960s as being a more appropriate approach to the research needs primarily of business-to-business goods manufacturers. The techniques required for business-to-business markets were very different from those required to measure the brand share of fast moving consumer goods.

The rigid separation between business-to-business and consumer research – further enhanced by the Business-to-Business Market Research Association remaining a separate entity from the Market Research Society – continued through the 1970s and early 1980s, when the emergence of the business services sector prompted a fundamental re-examination of which approaches were most relevant to this dynamic sector. By the 1990s the needs of the business-to-business and business services community had moved substantially away from a need to quantify market size and structure to a pre-occupation with retaining and satisfying customers. This environment has encouraged a return to a more consumer research oriented approach. IMRA is no more and the interests of business-to-business market research are now handled by the Business-to-Business Group, a special interest group within the Market Research Society.

Many attempts have been made to quantify the market for business and business-to-business market research. Few are made with much conviction, given the breaking down of boundaries between business and consumer research from an agency perspective and the grey areas of what actually constitutes consumer as opposed to business-to-business research. Some of the most exciting data-capture developments emanate from the business-to-business sector. This is well demonstrated by the development of audiotext as a data capture tool, the use of predictive diallers in customer satisfaction surveys and cheque book size computers as self-completion tools – all developed and pioneered by leading UK business-to-business agencies. In the field of sampling, data capture and processing – and especially in the larger surveys – consumer research approaches are being used increasingly and are improving efficiency and accuracy for the research customers.
Source: D Jamieson.[2]

RESEARCH INTO SERVICES

There are many different kinds of services and they demand the full spectrum of research activities. In this section we will consider some of the rather specific kinds of research which are only applicable to services.

Shopping surveys

Shopping surveys are related to retailing and to service marketing where there is a mingling of customers (hotels, motels, restaurants, and the like). In a shopping survey, a field worker poses as a customer and, following a list of predefined steps, makes mental notes. The shopper may simply note what aspects of delivery were or were not delivered. In addition, he or she may note the quality or rating of delivery. Major users of such surveys may be retailers such as fast food outlets and hotels. Here are some of the aspects typically covered (both for the organisation and its major competitors):

- Product or service quality
- Facility quality in various aspects
- Personnel courtesy
- Personnel efficiency
- Personnel service
- Personnel promotion of selected brands, items, features, benefits
- Items stocked, offered, on display
- Prices.

Such studies are generally handled by an outside specialist firm. There are three reasons. First is impartiality: the outside firm has no pre-formed dispositions. Second is skill. It can assist in determining what has to be checked and how to check it. Third, there is much less chance of the shopper's being detected by the employees, since it is most unlikely that any employee might know the individual.

Customised, full-scale studies of service satisfaction

Some marketing research firms are offering customised, full-scale studies to provide measurement of customer reactions to the delivery of service. This is a continuing service aimed at firms that have continuing and 'formal' service satisfaction systems (i.e. where consumer reactions funnel in to a single central location. It is used to conduct a day-after telephone interview with the customer to measure reaction while the experience is still fresh in the customer's mind. Because of the day-after telephone feature, the service has particular value to utility, financial and health care organisations.

Other customer/client reaction research studies

Studies of customer/client reaction are often used by small-scale retailers or service firms as well as by the larger firms. They are typically do-it-yourself research projects.

Deceptive appearance

There always seems to be at least one moving walkway out of order at London's Heathrow airport. When I asked Sir John Egan, chief executive of BAA, the owner of Heathrow, why this should be, he said it was because so many people used them. But help was at hand, he said. BAA was empowering its engineers to fix the walkways as they broke down. The night I arrived to catch a flight, the engineers had apparently used their new empowerment to go to the pub. Not only was there a dysfunctional walkway, there was also something unpleasant smeared on the ground outside the airport's third terminal. The check-in area was strewn with litter, while the gents' toilets were flooded and the hand towels needed replacing. The lines of passengers waiting to have their hand luggage X-rayed were long because only a few security machines were in use. The carpet in the security area was dirty.

A short distance away, however, on the other side of the machines, we could see a glittering world of plenty. Swatch and Burberry signs twinkled at us from Heathrow's shops, like a glimpse of cold war West Berlin from the wrong side of the Wall. I am not the only one to have noticed the contrast between the public areas and the shops at the world's busiest international airport. Sir Terence Conran, the retailer and restaurateur, wrote in *The Independent* newspaper last year of a visit to Heathrow's Terminal One: 'All is glossy and new, clean and tidy in the shopping areas; in the walkways and the departure lounge, however, it's an altogether different story. They are fitted with stained, worn-out carpet held together with odd lengths of black tape, patched plastic tiles, odd wires hanging all over the place, broken chairs with their stuffing hanging out, cigarette burns on table tops, rubbish on the floors. The check-in desks are falling to pieces. Even a third world country would feel disgraced by the squalor and shabbiness.' Before boarding my flight from Terminal Three, I filled in a complaints card and posted it in one of the boxes BAA has put up around the airport. That was over two months ago. I have heard nothing.

Des Wilson, the veteran radical activist who now heads BAA's public relations effort, agreed it was unacceptable that I had had no response. But he strongly contested my view that Heathrow was in danger of becoming a slum. Heathrow's 56m passengers did not feel that way, he said. He sent me to see Stan Maiden, BAA's research director. Before meeting Maiden at Heathrow, I wandered around the terminals. Two moving walkways were out of order, although the empowered engineers were hacking away at one of them. Terminal One's public areas were bright and clean; Terminal Two, largely because it is the oldest, was dark and gloomy; and Terminal Three still looked shabby. Did my complaints, I asked Maiden, really make me one in 56m – or two in 56m, counting Sir Terence? Not quite, he said. Heathrow attracts its share of complaints and tries to act on them. BAA is investing £1m ($1.6m) a day at Heathrow, and its managers' pay is partly tied to what passengers say about the airport. To find out what they think, BAA did a lot of market research, Maiden said. If its activities in this area were a stand-alone operation, BAA would be one of the top 20 market research companies in the UK.

BAA's most basic customer feedback comes from the complaint and comment cards at the airport. Heathrow receives about 7,000 complaints a year. The airport's policy, which broke down in my case, is to reply to all of them. Heathrow also receives compliments on the cards, but people were more likely to complain, said

Maiden, 'as in any other field'. He uses the cards to identify clusters of complaints, such as a shortage of luggage trolleys or long lines in the security area. The cards are an unsatisfactory form of feedback, however, because they rely on passengers taking the trouble to fill them in. In addition to reading the cards, BAA interviews 26,000 Heathrow customers a year in a range of languages. They are asked to rate everything from flight announcements to public telephones on a scale of one to five, where five is excellent and one is very poor.

He showed me some recent results, which had the airport receiving a score of four in many areas and over 3.5 in almost all. One of the few areas scoring below 3.5 was passengers' perception of the distances they had to walk in the airport. Smokers gave smoking facilities in one part of the airport a mark of only 3.4, but non-smokers judged the same arrangement a 3.7. And Heathrow would rather satisfy the non-smokers? 'Well, there are more of them,' Maiden said. A fairly creditable performance, if BAA's methodology is sound. Maiden insisted it was. Brussels and Vienna airports have asked BAA to implement its survey methods there. The group also carries out market research on specific areas, such as whether customers prefer lifts or escalators. Which do they prefer? 'It rather depends on their age,' Maiden said. BAA also asks passengers to compare Heathrow with other airports. This gives Heathrow an opportunity to compare itself with competitors such as Amsterdam's Schiphol and Singapore's Changi.

On issues such as availability of trolleys and flight information, Heathrow is somewhere in the middle, below Schiphol and Changi, but above both Paris airports and New York's JFK. Heathrow's cleanliness is rated average, as is seat availability in departure lounges. Heathrow's catering, shops and the attitude of security staff all receive high international ratings. The least critical Heathrow customers are elderly American and British passengers who travel infrequently. And the most critical? 'Regular British business travellers,' Maiden said through clenched teeth. 'People like you.'

Source: Michael Skapinker.[3] Reprinted with permission.

SERVQUAL

In 1985 Parasuraman *et al.*[4] published their now classic article which led to a revolution in the way that service quality is monitored. The results of their exploratory research included a statement of ten service quality determinants. These represent the basic dimensions that a consumer uses to evaluate a service. In order to improve 'true quality' in a service organisation the first step is to identify the quality determinants that are most important or relevant to the company's target market[5] and then assess their own and their competitors' performance. This early work formed the basis for the development of SERVQUAL[6] with the ten determinants mapped onto five underlying factors, which are: tangibles, empathy, responsiveness, reliability and assurance.

There are claims that SERVQUAL can be used or adapted to measure service quality in a variety of service settings. However, one should note that there are some who hold reservations about this.[7]

Service positioning

A service organisation is interested in how its image is positioned in the minds of customers and the trade *vis-à-vis* competition. It wants to know what kinds of people prefer to be its customers and how they compare with non-customers in terms of service perceptions and preferences, benefits sought, lifestyle and demographics. It also wants to know what is happening to its positioning from a more or less dynamic stand-point. For instance, it wants to know from which competitors it is gaining customers and to which competitors it is losing them. Service positioning is of major interest to management and it is here that perceptual maps of how customers see various providers as being similar or different are useful. The maps can help to show what combination of attributes customers prefer in their choice of service.

In-house marketing research in firms' district banks

Consumer behaviour research in banks and the financial sector is becoming a focus of interest. Here we will look at some of the more informal and day-to-day marketing research that can be done in-house in banks and other similar types of service organisation which serve a local community.

The most common decisions that bank executives have to make related to customers are simple but at the same time may become complex due to the lack of information to enable the decisions to be made with real confidence. For example decisions such as:

- Will this advertising convey the information the bank wants the potential customers to have?
- Will the advertising be credible to the potential customers?
- Will an advertising message motivate customers of other banks to visit it?
- How will customers react to a new product?
- Will the interest rates promoted in a particular promotion motivate customers to increase their deposits?
- Why is a branch not attracting enough customers?
- Where are the bank's customers?
- How can the bank best give customers access to services?
- What image should be projected into the customer's mind when positioning the bank as a lender?

The answers to such questions may be obtained through in-house marketing research and information gathered every time it thinks it has doubts about its customers. There are several ways to do this.

The customer's map

It is useful to know where customers live and work. A road map of the area served should be covered in transparent foil and mounted on card. The foil is attached to the top of the map with office adhesive tape. Up to four overlay foils can be used on the same map to view four kinds of information simultaneously. For example: customers, competitors, transportation and housing.

On the first overlay of the map you mark with an ink marker, lets say red in colour, a point at the addresses of a sample of customers. The best way to do this sampling is to mark the opening account card in any place in the file and from there on count a set of cards and extract the next. The count quota is established by dividing the total number of customers by the size of the sample. For example, if a branch has 1500 customer cards and you want to make a map with 100 customers, then you will have to extract the residential address of every 15th customer. This produces clusters of points where customers live. This can be repeated with working address. You take the next foil and start the same process with a blue marker. Then you might use another overlay to mark the competitor's and your branches, let's say with a green marker. Finally, you may want to know where are the bus stops. We take the last foil and mark them in black.

Now, if you place the branch and transportation overlays together on the map, you can find opportunities to open branches and place automated teller machines (ATMs) near bus stops. Now if you place the branch foil with the working address one can see how vulnerable your customers can be if they are far from you and near to the competitor's branches.

If one places the residential and working address overlays on the map, then one can see areas where customers are not being served, blockades of natural and man-made obstacles (bridges, rivers, highways, etc.) that make the customers' journey a round-about way in order to reach the branch. If you have also the approximate population of districts, an overlay with this information on top of the overlay foils will indicate the areas where the bank is not present and a high population density exists. This system works very well for malls, commercial centres, for department stores and for shops in general.

RESEARCH FOR INTERNAL MARKETING

Internal marketing is based upon the idea that every individual in an organisation, particularly a service organisation, should recognise that they have customers to serve. In addition it implements the philosophy that all internal customers must be convinced about the quality of the service being provided and be content in their work.

The relationship between internal and external service quality

The link between internal service quality and external service quality and hence customer satisfaction, customer loyalty and the profitability of the organisation has been proposed by Heskett et al.[8] They propose that high quality internal services lead to increased employee satisfaction which in turn leads to increased service value, leading to increased external customer satisfaction. This is supported by Brooks and Smith,[9] Brooks[10, 11] and Davis.[12] Magidson and Polcha[13] also discuss the problem of the inferior quality of many internally produced products and services having a direct relationship with the ability of companies to adjust to changing customer needs and meet competitive challenges. Equally, Azzolini and Shillaber[14] propose that quality service to internal customers converts to quality service to external customers. Furthermore, Hart[15] discusses how internal service is related to external service. In his paper he proposes that internal service guarantees ultimately benefit the (external) customer and the bottom line.

Internal marketing will allow the company to improve the quality of the services and products produced internally and so improve both internal and external customer satisfaction. This assumes that the quality of the internal exchange can be measured.

Role of marketing research

Market research traditionally involves identifying the needs and wants of customers in a systematic manner and monitors the impact of marketing activities upon them. The same process can be adopted with employees. Personnel can be given the opportunity to give feedback to management about working conditions, company policy in general and workers' own understanding about what comprises quality for the customer. The information might be obtained by using questionnaires or focus groups or in-depth interviews with employees. Although surveys of employees need careful handling, they not only provide employees with a measure of satisfaction but can identify early breakdowns in communication.

The relationships between organisational sub-units and their relationship to top management are also important since the quality of support they receive from each other impinges on the overall quality of service that is eventually given to the customer. This can be assessed by a variation of the SERVQUAL instrument mentioned above which is constructed to measure the quality of support organisational sub-units provide to each other (see Figure 14.2).

In service organisations those involved in dealing with customers are in a unique position to identify trends and business opportunities. Marketing research or an 'internal marketing' information system can be used to good effect in helping to collect such information and provide it to senior/top management for action.

SUMMARY

The chapter has examined business-to-business marketing research and internal marketing research. In the case of business-to-business marketing research the differences and the similarities with consumer marketing research have been explored. Business-to-business marketing research has changed considerably in

---

INTERNAL CUSTOMER QUESTIONNAIRE

Instructions

With regard to the following statements there is a six-point answer scale with a brief indication of what the numbers on the scale represent. For each of the statements you are asked to provide an answer for each of the organisational departments or sections with which you come into contact. Fill in as many questionnaires as there are departments or sections.

Name of your department or section

....

Name of the section/department with which you come into contact

....

Scale:

Fails altogether to meet our expectations	1
Fails to meet our expectations in many ways	2
Fails to meet our expectations in one way or another	3
Nearly always meets our expectations	4
Meets our expectations in full	5
Surpasses our expectations	6

The way this section/department keeps us informed about progress, problems or changes which affect us. ☐

The ability of this section/department to perform first time and correctly the service we require. ☐

The comprehension this section/department has of our needs and problems along with the constraints we have. ☐

The courtesy shown by members of this section/department towards us. ☐

The speed of this section/department in responding to our requests. ☐

How this section/department is organised so as to be able to meet our requirements. ☐

The condition of work, documents and material which it passes to us for further progressing. ☐

The extent to which it keeps us informed about matters which are of mutual interest. ☐

Figure 14.2 Internal customers' questionnaire

recent years and employs many of the approaches that were at one time the domain of consumer research.

Service marketing research includes shopping surveys. In a shopping survey, a field worker poses as a customer and, following a list of predefined steps, makes mental notes. Major users of such surveys are retailers and hotels. Such studies are generally handled by an outside specialist firm. It also makes use of customised, full-scale studies of service satisfaction to provide measurement of customer reactions to the delivery of service. Other customer/client reaction studies are often used by small-scale retailers or service firms as well as by the larger firms.

Parasuraman *et al.* published their now classic article which led to a revolution in the way that service quality is dealt with. In that paper the results of their exploratory research were presented, including a statement of ten service quality determinants that appeared to be relevant. In order to improve 'true quality' in a service organisation the first step is to identify the quality determinants most important or relevant to the company's target market and then assess their own and their competitors' performance. This early work formed the basis for the development of SERVQUAL.

Internal marketing is based upon the idea that every individual in an organisation, particularly a service organisation, should recognise that they have customers to serve. There is a positive link between internal service quality and external service quality and hence customer satisfaction, customer loyalty and the profitability of the organisation. Market research can be adopted for use with employees. Personnel can be given the opportunity to give feedback to management about working conditions, company policy in general and workers' own understanding about what comprises quality for the customer. The relationships between organisational sub-units and their relationship to top management are also important. This can be assessed by a variation of the SERVQUAL instrument mention above.

Questions

1   What is business-to-business marketing research?
2   How does it differ from consumer marketing research?
3   What types of research are undertaken in business marketing research?
4   How might marketing research vary with the nature of a service which is being studied?
5   Discuss how shopping studies can help decision-making in a large retailing organisation.
6   Consider how SERVQUAL might be used in an organisation of your own choice.
7   Discuss the role of marketing research within the context of internal marketing.
8   Examine how marketing research which looks at internal marketing might interface with that which looks at external customers.

Case study 14.1   Obtaining expertise

Companies often insist that the researcher needs to have worked in the specific industry sector for the last ten years. Researchers often maintain that it is the method that matters and not the knowledge of the sector or process that matters.

Both views have their merits in the right circumstances and perhaps lead to the argument that when you really know what you want to know, get someone less expensive to ask the questions. This leads to the *cascade approach.*

In the cascade approach the defining questions are asked by experts with the cascade being applied through several layers. At the final level the questions may be put to the majority of the sample in fully structured pre-coded form by well-briefed interviewers. Some business-to-business research addresses so many different concepts at a time that this final structured level is not a practical proposition, but it should be a target for researchers since it can save money.

Large business-to-business companies with specialist market research departments often provide the technical and strategic levels of the cascade from their internal resources and only use interviewing once the questionnaire has been defined so that it can be handled easily. The need for technical or business specialists at the research company level arises when the in-house team does not have the time or experience to cascade the work down to this level.

Source: Peter Gorle.[16]

Question

How widely do you think this approach can be applied throughout the business sector?

Case study 14.2 | Orchestras aim to pass the baton

The lights dim in the concert hall of the Colorado Symphony Orchestra, and the audience falls silent. Conductor Martin Alsop raises his baton to direct a piece by composer Scott Bradley, and over the performance stage a camera image is projected. Tom and Jerry, the famous duo, scamper across the screen.

What are Tom and Jerry doing at a classical music performance? The symphony orchestra hopes they – and other marketing innovations – will bring in larger and younger audiences.

Symphony orchestras are not the only US entertainment form facing an increasingly grey-haired clientèle.

But the demographics of symphonic attendance are striking. A study of concertgoers released last year by the National Endowment for the Arts found audiences declining for every age group under 50. According to the St Paul Chamber Orchestra, only 6 per cent of its audience is under 35.

An ageing audience eventually means more empty seats. Eight symphony orchestras have closed in the US in the last ten years. Last year alone, the orchestras of San Diego and Sacramento shut down.

What's needed, say observers, is a complete overhaul of marketing strategy. Eugene Carr, president of Culture Finder, a Net information service about the arts, says he realised just how little symphony orchestras have changed when the New York Philharmonic recently presented a concert nearly identical to a performance a century ago.

Previously foreign concepts like 'building a brand image', 'measuring customer satisfaction' and 'creating name recognition' are finding their way into classical music parlance.

The Oregon Symphony, for instance, has conducted market research to find out what appeals to its viewers. 'Our theory is, the music's not the problem, it's how it's presented,' says Don Roth, director of the orchestra. To attract a younger clientèle, the Oregon Symphony has introduced concerts under a new 'brand' name, *Nerve Endings*. 'We did it this way because it lets people know that these concerts will be different from your standard fare,' says Maureen O'Connor, in charge of marketing for the orchestra. Under the auspices of the new brand, the Oregon Symphony is venturing on to new ground. A February concert featured a corpse in the lobby, cordoned off with police tape. The corpse was a dummy of Mozart, a display designed to create a mood for that night's Mozart programme.

Another *Nerve Endings* performance featured a Flamenco-inspired classical music programme, complete with dancers, videos of Flamenco singers, and discounts to Flamenco parties at local night clubs.

Source: Victoria Griffiths.[17] Reprinted with permission.

Question

Suggest a programme of marketing research that could be useful in helping an orchestra develop a good marketing strategy.

Case study 14.3 | # The decline and fall of frills

Companies are spending more money on business travel but their employees are gaining little of the benefit as they continue to cut the costs of each trip, Scheherazade Daneshkhu writes.

Euromonitor, the London-based market research group, says that costs are being reduced through shorter trips. Business travellers are also holding back from spending a night in their destination to save on hotel bills. The main reason for the increase in corporate business travel spending is because of the rise in flight costs, according to Euromonitor.

Some companies are continuing to cut the number of trips their employees take as well as trading down the class of air travel. Carlson Wagonlit, the business travel agent, says that 35 per cent of UK companies questioned for its survey in January said that they had changed their policy to allow for a lower class of travel.

The number of companies willing to pay for long-haul business-class travel has been in general decline over the past three years, according to Carlson Wagonlit. There has been a corresponding rise in economy fares. Most of those it questioned said they were prepared to travel on less expensive no-frills flights on short-haul routes, but wanted greater comfort on longer flights.

The latter wish appears not to be granted. The number of those flying in business or first class on long-haul flights dropped compared to last year, while economy class travel has increased.

But there is some room for optimism. More than two-thirds of the travellers questioned said they expected to make more business trips over the next 12 months – a 36 per cent increase from last year.

Source: Scheherazade Daneshkhu.[18] Reprinted with permission.

Question

How might marketing research help the travel business to unravel some of its problems which are as yet unresolved?

Case study 14.4 | The Jasmine Hotel, Dubai

The Jasmine Hotel is located in the Deira district of Dubai in the United Arab Emirates. It is about ten minutes' drive from the airport and within a short walk of the shops. The Gold Souk is a short taxi drive away and the hotel is within walking distance of most of the city on the Deira side of the creek. A complimentary shuttle service operates between the hotel and the public Al Mamzar Beach Park where full beach club and water sports are available for a small fee.

Within the hotel itself there is a good choice of bars and restaurants and there is also a coffee shop. Leisure facilities include a small roof-top swimming pool, a fitness room, sauna and spa. The central atrium is light and spacious and is the focal point of this very recently built hotel.

Dubai enjoys a very hot and dry climate, being sub-tropical and close to the desert. Temperatures for most of the year exceed 100 degrees Fahrenheit during the daytime and are more than 80 degrees Fahrenheit after sunset. It is not unknown for daytime temperatures to soar to 120 degrees Fahrenheit in July and August. Acclimatisation can take visitors to Dubai a little while to achieve. While locals brave the daytime sun, all the year round visitors from more temperate climates can find the climate unbearable during the day during July and August.

The accommodation comprises some 250 rooms which are spacious and well furnished with bath and shower, air-conditioning, telephone and television and mini-bar. The hotel has three restaurants: Indian, Thai and Chinese. All are well appointed in traditional style. Guests pay separately for all meals and use of the mini-bar. A typical room costs between 30 and 50 pounds sterling per night, depending on the time of year. The breakfast buffet costs around 12 pounds sterling. Canned soft drinks from the mini-bar cost around 3 pounds sterling a can while beer is around 4 pounds sterling a can. In the neighbourhood there are many good quality restaurants offering meals at low prices and soft drinks can be bought locally from stores for as little as 10 pence per can.

The hotel employs a large number of staff. These range from several receptionists and door-men to house boys, chamber maids, waiters and cooks. The hotel is keen to improve the level of service it offers to customers and at the same time is also anxious to ensure that it has a fully motivated staff to meet the needs and wants of the wide variety of guests that it entertains. Guests come from all over the world and the hotel also hires out its conference suite on the top floor to both local and foreign clients.

Question

Design a marketing research system that will help the hotel maintain the level of service quality that it is hoping to achieve. Account should be taken of both the hotel's internal and external customers in designing the system.

Case study 14.5 | ## Banking in Portugal

Northern Portugal is the cradle of the nation's entrepreneurial spirit. Business people in the region consider themselves to be the real wheeler-dealers of the Portuguese economy, running mainly small to medium-sized businesses, and having a certain air of contempt for their counterparts in Lisbon and further south. According to the northern Portuguese, Lisbonites are mere employees of multinationals who spend their time on politics and parties while the real deals are done in the North.

Of course, in common with most other capital cities Lisbon is where the power and money gravitates; like the multinationals, banks have a strong presence there. However, the Portuguese have a saying that banks are born in Oporto and die in Lisbon, where deal-making skills become blunted and attention to detail becomes lax. For this reason, Banco Portugues de Investimento keeps its headquarters in Oporto.

BPI is an exclusive merchant bank set up in 1981 by Artur Santos Silva; Senhor Silva has, in the meantime, set up or acquired a string of subsidiary banks between Oporto and Lisbon. Two of these, Banco de Fomento e Exterior and Banco Fonsecas & Burnay, have head offices in Lisbon, while a third, Banco Borges & Irmao, remains in Oporto. Borges & Irmao is focused towards Northern Portugal, which is where the bulk of its branches are, and Fonsecas & Burnay focuses in the South.

Both subsidiary networks have been briefed to develop consumer lending niches such as credit cards and car purchase loans, segments where BPI claims it has developed key products. The business in the North has the added bonus of using its retail activities to scout for corporate finance – so many of its retail customers are business people running small and medium enterprises. Typically, the banking groups in Portugal divide their markets into three main segments: small and medium enterprises, universal banking, and large corporations. BPI believes that the delivery of tailor-made services to specific segments is the key to success in domestic banking.

Banking executives are painfully aware that there is a lot of work to be done in restructuring the industries of Northern Portugal – they talk in terms of identifying products and standardising them, of joint marketing projects, and of pooling companies together for research and testing of projects. Aiding management buy-outs and merger and acquisition deals are seen as ways of ensuring continuity in businesses, and they are looking towards cross-border transactions with companies in Northern Spain as a way of consolidating businesses.

So far, progress has been slow; the Northern business culture is not receptive to involving banks in their activities. The family businesses in the North tend to be mistrustful of banks, are suspicious of marketing ideas, and usually employ one graduate to look after the banks – there is a widespread belief that the less the company has to do with the bank, the stronger is the business. Successful firms are perceived as those that neither give nor receive credit, deal in cash only, and which keep their business dealings close to their chests. There is, fortunately, a growing realisation that these practices might work well for small firms, but will not be effective if the firm is to grow beyond a small family concern. 'Small family companies tend to have opaque accounts which makes risk evaluation very complex; they are also, by definition, very individualistic', is how one Oporto banking analyst expressed it.

In the near future, the banks are expecting some medium to large firms to emerge in Northern Portugal as the merger process accelerates. Better able to compete on a world stage, these firms will probably be engaged in the traditional industries of textiles and leather, but will be better managed and better financed than the present companies. If this is the case, the banks expect to be sharing in their success, and in the growth of Northern Portugal as a player on the world business stage.

(Case contributed by Jim Blythe.)

Questions

1   What kind of secondary sources might be useful to the banks in identifying business customers?
2   How might banks decide which retail customers are also potential corporate clients?
3   What would be the main difficulties in researching the corporate market in Northern Portugal?
4   How might the banks research the market for retail customers?
5   What secondary sources might be useful for the banks in identifying customers within their chosen niche markets of credit cards and car loans?

Further reading

Anderson, E W (1993) Firm, industry and national indices of customer satisfaction: implications for services, in Swartz, T and Brown, S W (eds), *Advances in Services Marketing Management: Research and practice*, Vol. 2, Greenwich, CT JAI Press, pp 87–108.

Anderson, E W, Fornell, C and Rust, R T (1997) Customer satisfaction, productivity, and profitability: differences between goods and services, *Marketing Science*, 16(2), pp 129–45.

Andreasson, T W (1994) Satisfaction, loyalty and reputation as indicators of customer orientation in the public sector, *International Journal of Public Sector Management*, 7(2), pp 16–34.

Donnelly, M, Wisniewski, M, Dalrymple, J F and Curry, A (1995) Measuring service quality in local government: The SERVQUAL approach, *International Journal of Public Sector Management*, 8(7), pp 15–20.

Eklof, J A, Hackl, P, and Westlund, A (1999) On measuring interactions between customer satisfaction and financial results, *Total Quality Management*, 10(4–5), pp 514–22.

Flanagan, T A, and Fredericks, J O (1993) Improving company performance through customer satisfaction measurement and management, *National Productivity Review*, Spring, pp 239–58.

Gronroos, C (1990) *Service Management and Marketing: Managing the moments of truth in service competition*, Lexington, MA: Lexington Books.

Gulledge, L G (1991) Satisfying the internal customer, *Bank Marketing*, 23, pp 46–8.

Gummesson, E (1993) Quality management in service organizations: an interpretation of the service quality phenomenon and a synthesis of international research, *International Service Quality Association*, Karlstad, Sweden.

Hague, P (1985) *The Industrial Market Research Handbook* (2nd edn), London: Kogan Page.

Hallowell, R (1996) The relationship of customer satisfaction, customer loyalty and profitability: an empirical study, *International Journal of Service Industry Management*, 7(4), pp 27–42.

Piercy, N (1996) The effects of customer satisfaction measurement: the internal market versus the external market, *Marketing Intelligence and Planning*, 14(4), April, p 9.

Piercy, N and Morgan, N (1995) Customer satisfaction measurement and management: a processual analysis, *Journal of Marketing Management*, 11, pp 817–34.

Schneider, K C and Johnson, J C (1995) Stimulating response to market surveys of business professionals, *Industrial Marketing Management*, 24, pp 265–76.

Sirkin, A F (1995) Maximizing customer satisfaction, *MLS: Marketing Library Services*, 9(4), June, pp 3–4.

Smith, A M (1995) Quality aspects of service marketing, *Marketing Intelligence and Planning*, pp 25–32.

Sutherland, K (ed.) (1994) *Researching Business Markets*, London: Kogan Page.

Swindley, D (1992) Retail buying in the United Kingdom, *The Service Industries Journal*, 12, pp 533–44.

White, D M and Abels, E G (1995) Measuring service quality in special libraries: lessons from service marketing, *Special Libraries*, 86 (Winter), pp 36–45.

Zeithaml, V A, Berry, L L and Parasuraman, A, (1996) The behavioral consequences of service quality, *Journal of Marketing*, 60, April, pp 31–46.

References and notes

[1] Gorle, P (1995) The cascade theory that shows practical gains, *Research Plus*, October, p 11.

[2] Jamieson, D (1995) Now business research is every agency's research, *Research Plus*, October, pp 4–5.

[3] Skapinker, M (1997) Deceptive appearance, *Financial Times*, 3 February.

4 Parasuraman, A, Berry, L L and Zeithaml, V (1985) A conceptual model of service quality and the implications for future research, *Journal of Marketing*, 49, pp 41–51.

5 Berry, L L, Zeithaml, V A and Parasuraman, A (1985) Quality counts in services, too, *Business Horizons*, May–June, pp 44–52.

6 Zeithaml, V, Parasuraman, A and Berry, L (1990) *Delivering Quality Service*, New York: Free Press.

7 Buttle, F (1996) *Relationship Marketing*, London: Paul Chapman, pp 59–60.

8 Heskett, J L, Jones, T O, Loveman, G W, Sasser, W E and Schlesinger, L A (1994) Putting the service profit chain to work, *Harvard Business Review*, March–April, pp 164–74.

9 Brooks, R F and Smith J V (1993) Service from within, *TQM Journal*, October, pp 41–5.

10 Brooks, R F (1993) Internal service quality – a manufacturing perspective, *Proceedings of the Marketing Education Group*, Loughborough, pp 93–4.

11 Brooks, R F (1995) Internal service quality – a theoretical development, *Proceedings of the Marketing Education Group*, Bradford, pp 80–90.

12 Davis, T R V (1992) Satisfying internal customers: the link to external customer satisfaction, *Planning Review*, 20(1), pp 34–7.

13 Magidson, D and Polcha, A E (1992) Creating market economies within organisations, a conference on internal markets, *Planning Review*, January–February, pp 37–40.

14 Azzolini, M and Shillaber, J (1993) Internal service quality: winning from the inside out, *Quality Progress*, November, pp 75–8.

15 Hart, C W L (1995) The power of internal guarantees, *Harvard Business Review*, January–February, pp 64–73.

16 Gorle, P (1995) The cascade theory that shows practical gains, *Research Plus*, October, p 10.

17 Griffiths, V (1997) Orchestras aim to pass the baton, *Financial Times*, 20 May.

18 Daneshkhu, S (1997) The decline and fall of frills, *Financial Times*, 28 April.

15 Global marketing research

OBJECTIVES

After reading this chapter you should be able to:

■ appreciate how marketing research is organised and conducted in global markets;

■ understand how global marketing research may differ from research in the home market.

KEY WORDS

international segmentation   functional equivalence
target market   conceptual equivalence
market selection   ethnic influences
concentration   instrument equivalence
diversification   instrument translation
culture   desk research
developing markets

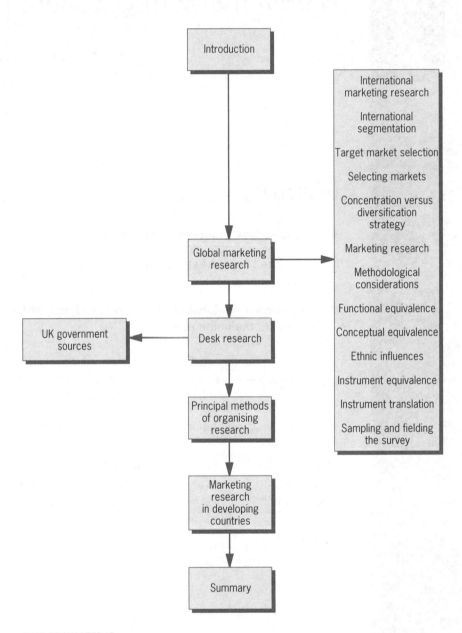

PLAN OF CHAPTER 15

INTRODUCTION

This chapter looks at how marketing research is organised and conducted in global markets. Segmentation and targeting are considered along with the selection of markets. Attention is given to methodological considerations when operating in an international context. Desk research is an important source of information and attention is given in the chapter to identifying fruitful sources of information. How marketing research is organised is also covered in the chapter. We then go on to look at the additional difficulties involved in undertaking marketing research in developing countries where the situation is also worsened by a lack of requisite research skills and a poor appreciation of the value of marketing research. Often, few indigenous organisations possess marketing research departments and comparatively few commercial marketing research services exist.

GLOBAL MARKETING RESEARCH

Most firms involved in international marketing activities at least know the destination of their goods. Clearly, this means that such firms really need to understand the foreign market place in the same way as they understand the domestic market place. It would seem sensible that before undertaking international marketing firms should undertake analysis of what marketing opportunities exist. A variety of factors should then be taken into account when screening potential international marketing opportunities to enable a sensible decision to be taken about which, if any, of the opportunities should be pursued.

A company engaged in international marketing needs to know foreign government policies about importing the range and type of products it produces together with information on tariffs and quotas. Because of the complexity of international marketing, knowledge of legal and financial regulations is essential. The marketing and commercial infrastructures of countries differ considerably and it is imperative to understand how these vary from country to country.

As far as consumer behaviour is concerned we can not assume that what applies in the home market will also be applicable in different foreign markets. Lifecycle patterns, bases of motivation, cultural values and lifestyles may be very different from what we are used to and require an entirely different marketing approach. Many blunders have been made by firms that have failed to study local customs carefully. In some countries it is considered unacceptable and even offensive to portray physical contact between the sexes in promotional material. In Thailand, for example, a firm was trying to introduce a mouthwash but was unaware that the foregoing comments were applicable in that country and showed, in its advertisements, a young couple holding hands. This caused offence but by changing the advertisement so that two women were portrayed holding hands the commercials were then considered to be acceptable.[1]

Marketing communication channels must be studied in order to identify how information relating to products and services can be brought effectively to the consumer's attention. Common barriers include those posed by literacy and language and have to be overcome.

A key factor, however, is the capacity of the market to pay for the goods and services supplied. This is influenced by such things as personal disposable income and government restrictions on the expenditure of foreign currency reserves. In the case of larger items and business-to-business projects, loan terms, interest and capital requirements are also important factors.

International marketing research

Most marketing research work is usually carried out by local researchers but the entire process is directed and coordinated by headquarters staff. Headquarters staff also have to put considerable effort into 'country market screening' – looking at the relative size of each potential market, the size of its purchasing power and its concentration, and the likely rate of future growth. In addition an assessment of the competitive forces at work in each potential market has to be made.

Rise of international research

Consumer marketing has penetrated to most cities in most countries in the world, and, along with marketing and advertising, market research is commonplace. Recently, Mary Goodyear sat in a small house in a black township in Capetown with a group of young men whose prospects seemed limited to casual labour and, possibly, crime. One of the young men chided Mary for showing the group a dull advertisement. 'Surely you must remember AIDA,' he said, 'Attention Interest Desire Action – well I don't see much of Interest and Desire in that advert.'
Source: M Goodyear.[2]

Transitionary markets

Millionaires on the French Riviera are to be expected but it may be surprising to know that there are over 500,000 dollar millionaires in the People's Republic of China and that there is also an emerging middle class in China (those with annual incomes in excess of $15,000 equivalent) which numbers more than 35 million people.

The common view is that China's growing consumer market is tied to its urban population, which represents about 20% to 25% of the nation's 1.2 billion people. With annual disposable income of about US$465 a head (and much more in purchasing power), urban dwellers reportedly earn about 2.5 times as much as their rural cousins. However, this picture not only undercounts city dwellers but also misses a huge adjunct to the main consumer market: an increasingly affluent suburban economy that has sprouted on the fringes of the cities but is often classified as part of the rural economy. Suburbanites and better off peasants make up some 384 million people and they enjoy average per capita incomes of US$450, almost as much as urbanites. Urban and suburban groups taken together make up some two thirds of China's population and account for 80% of its gross domestic product. Their purchasing power helps to explain why real retail sales on the mainland continue to grow at 10% per annum despite the nation's recent austerity measures.

Indeed, while European retail sales languish in the doldrums many Asian retail markets are experiencing annual sales growths of more than 10%. Of course the stage in development of the market may vary considerably from country to country, even within a particular region of the world. Malaysia in 1994 was a buoyant retail economy, but some of its neighbours such as Thailand, Cambodia, Vietnam and Laos did not share the same fortune.

It is possible to characterise the stage of economic development in a country and relate it to levels and types of marketing activity. The following typology is suggested by the Henley Centre:

■ The first stage is where the formal cash economy is hardly developed and most consumption is of unbranded commodities.

■ At the second stage incomes are in the range $2,000 to $3,000 per annum; brands consciousness develops and consumption patterns are influenced by a desire to emulate.

■ At the third stage consumption is characterised by the demands of an individualistic middle-class and people seek to express their individuality. The mass markets that are typical of the second stage are supplemented and even replaced by market niches.

■ Stage four sees gender, class, family or caste-based stereotypes disintegrate as individuals act and buy in a way which is alien to the norms of the group to whom they have been traditionally affiliated.

■ Stage five sees individuals buying brands for occasions. Often more differences exist between the same individual on two different occasions than between two different individuals on the same occasion.

Many of the developing markets of Asia appear to be somewhere between stages one and two. However, notable exceptions are Hong Kong and Singapore, where living standards are above those of Ireland and Portugal. Malaysia and Indonesia are developing rapidly and other Pacific Rim countries are likely to develop swiftly as political stability takes root.

Sources: B Tyrrell,[3] G Korents.[4]

International segmentation

Market segmentation amounts to dividing markets into groups of consumers with similar buying needs and who are likely to respond, as a group, to specific marketing mixes.

Segmentation helps firms to market their products in the most effective ways. It is important to note that all segments should be measurable, accessible and of reasonable size. The international marketing strategist seeks to consolidate numerous small segments across a number of countries into a slice of the global market that is worth serving.

Target market selection

The process involves narrowing down potential country markets to a feasible number of countries and market segments within them. It is argued that instead of trying to appeal to everyone, firms best make use of their resources by identifying potential markets for entry and expanding selectivity over time to those that are considered attractive. The four stages of screening are:

- preliminary screening
- estimation of market potential
- estimation of sales potential and
- identification of segments.

Preliminary screening relies on secondary data and in particular indicators of overall buying power in country markets are useful. Estimation of market potential is often undertaken with the aid of secondary-data-based analytical techniques that focus on or utilise demand patterns, income elasticity measures, etc.

Estimating sales potential involves assessing the market share likely to be achieved. Information on competition, degree of relative product advantage and access to retail outlets must figure predominantly in these assessments.

Selecting markets

It is often the case that opportunities in foreign markets present themselves to would-be exporters/international marketing firms from time to time. In such a case, one has to evaluate each case on its merits. It may also be, however, that a firm is actively searching for such opportunities and in either case it should bear in mind the points outlined below.

The kind of information that needs to be obtained should answer questions about the following points:

- the approximate size of the market production/imports/exports/consumption;
- the products which are currently available (how well they satisfy tastes, habits, etc.);

- the leading competitors, their market shares, promotion methods, services and facilities offered;
- the channels and costs of distribution;
- the legal requirements, standards, etc.;
- tariffs, quotas, import licences (contact the British Overseas Trade Board (BOTB) for details);
- ease of transportation (speed/frequency/costs);
- the political/economic stability of the market (BOTB *Hints to Exporters* booklets are a good source);
- the growth trends in the market.

Concentration versus diversification as a strategy

A firm's major alternatives are to concentrate on a small number of markets or to achieve growth by diversification in a large number of markets in the early stages of international market expansion. The choice of expansion strategy is influenced by market-related, mix-related factors.

National attitudes to antibiotics

People were consulted about their beliefs about infections and their problems in taking antibiotics in a large survey of attitudes. The study, conducted in France, Belgium, Italy, Spain, Turkey and the UK involved some 3,610 people. Respondents had taken an antibiotic, or given one to their child, for a respiratory tract infection (RTI), such as colds, sore-throats, catarrh, 'flu and earaches in the previous 12 months. 200 respondents were drawn from each country in each of three groups: working adults, elderly adults over 55 years and mothers of children under 12 years.

More than 50% of those interviewed thought that antibiotics should be prescribed for any respiratory tract infection with the exception of a simple cold. The percentage in Turkey, France and Spain was higher than that in the UK, Belgium and Italy. These differences in expectations were related to patients' perceptions of antibiotics (in particular their fears about their effects), and the extent of their knowledge about antibiotics.

Cultural attitudes underlie individual behaviour and practices in taking courses of antibiotics. Medical opinion strongly advises that a whole course should be used to prevent the development of resistant bacteria and recurrent infection. However, in Spain there was a widespread belief that part of a course could be saved and used for a subsequent illness. Indeed, the proportion of patients who claimed not to have taken the whole of the antibiotic course showed distinct variations across countries. Compliance was high in the UK, France and Belgium, but was lower in Italy and Spain. The main reason for stopping taking the antibiotic before the end of the course was completed was 'feeling better'. In Italy and Spain it had become the norm to stop taking the medicine once you felt better. Differences in the rates of compliance across countries reflect social norms and attitudes, and this has profound implications for community health. The research uncovered a natural rhythm in antibiotic taking related to the patient's intrinsic timetable for visiting the doctor, getting antibiotics, then feeling well and consequently stopping the medication.

Ideas about improving antibiotics reflected concern firstly about fewer side-effects (52%) and then improved efficacy (35%) and speed of action (34%). Interest in shorter courses (32%) and fewer daily doses (28%) was also expressed. Interest in reducing the duration of treatment and number of doses was greatest in the UK and Spain but in Italy most were concerned with side-effects.

Nowadays people expect effectiveness and quick results from modern technology. Producers of consumer products, by corresponding closer to patients' lifestyles and the expressed desire for shorter courses of treatment, would not only meet patients' wishes but would also achieve significant medical benefits through improved compliance.

Source: A Branthwaite and J Bruggemann.[5]

Marketing research

Many factors add to the complexity and diversity of conducting marketing research in international markets. They are outlined in the following subsections.

Understanding the culture

A thorough understanding of the culture is necessary if the researcher is to obtain satisfactory response rates. Quite apart from the problems associated with high rates of illiteracy, in some cultures a woman will not consent to an interview by a stranger, let alone a man. In other cultures men will be reluctant to discuss topics such as personal hygiene or preferences in clothing because they feel that this would be beneath their dignity – and they will definitely not address these issues in the presence of a female interviewer. In addition it is difficult for respondents to answer questions concerning goods and services that have never been available or are not commonly used in the community, or whose use is not well understood.

Lack of secondary data

The usually large amounts of secondary data that characterise countries such as the USA are in most cases not available in every other country. This is particularly the case in developing or transitional countries. Even if data is available it will be of variable quality. For instance, population censuses in some countries are frequently made by people who are not professionals and data on income and sales from tax returns can be totally inaccurate in countries where such information is often undeclared or under-reported.

Cost of collecting primary data

One soon discovers, when trying to collect data in international markets, that the cost of collecting it can be considerably higher without a network of established marketing firms. Many countries lack companies that are experienced in collecting information, which means that a sponsoring firm will have to invest in the development of sampling frames and other materials and in the training of interviewers and other necessary personnel.

Research can be rained off for the day in India

One of the first things that strikes one about a country such as India is its diversity. It has a population of 900 million people across 26 states, with 16 official languages and over 1,600 minor languages and dialects and numerous different religions.

At a general methodological level, there are a number of considerations when conducting marketing research in India. Clearly with such a population and massive regional differences, selecting an appropriate sample of the population in terms of both size and survey centres is a considerable feat to achieve. In addition with the large number of different languages there is considerable opportunity for misunderstandings or misinterpretations to arise and qualitative research requires executive teams who can speak all of the local languages that may be required.

With respect to data collection methods, postal research in India is a non-starter until the postal system within the country is improved significantly. In addition because of cultural traditions the telephone is rarely used for lengthy discussions. This being the case a relatively cheap labour force usually makes face-to-face interviewing the most appropriate method to employ.

There are also other logistical factors to be taken into account. For example, when it rains in India it pours and because research is conducted through personal interviews it makes it impossible to carry on working. Religious festivals also present obstacles that one would not encounter in the West. There are so many of them and the level of devotion practised is so high that scheduling fieldwork requires significant juggling skills.

Source: Sue Bunn.[6]

Marketing research in Central and Eastern Europe

Within only five years the countries in Central and Eastern Europe have moved from state-led command economies to consumer-led demand economies. During this time Western products and services have been actively marketed to the local population. Consumers have had to get used to the new economic situation and its marketing tools: advertising, promotions and branding. The majority have learned to differentiate not only between local and Western brands but also among Western brands. Value for money, an almost unknown concept in 1992, is now part of the everyday vocabulary. Moreover, local brands are increasing in popularity and increasing in quality.

Research existed in the region before the collapse of Communism and most countries have a tradition of government sponsored research. At the end of the 1980s the value of commercial survey research commissioned by Western companies in the region was probably less than US$100,000 but by 1995 it had risen to more than US$30 million. In the more developed countries some 65% of the commissions are from locally based companies, primarily multinationals. In the less developed areas about 60% of the commissioning companies are based outside the country in which research is undertaken. In the Czech Republic, Hungary, Poland and Russia there are some 10 to 20 companies offering full service qualitative and quantitative research. In addition there are many others that claim to provide some elements of the marketing research service. There are at least three to five full service marketing research agencies in each country in the region. In the Czech Republic, Hungary, Poland and Russia major marketing research suppliers are forming associations and considering quality standard systems for field work. Most major companies are investing in their future by training staff in Western Europe and America. In most countries there is at least one viewing facility for qualitative research, one monthly omnibus service, one consumer or specialist panel and one CATI facility. Moreover, several companies in the region are testing or piloting CAPI methods of data collection.

Source: Mia Bartonova.[7]

Methodological considerations

A number of methodological considerations affect the construction of question-naires and other research instruments to be used in international research studies. The problems arise from two sources:

1 The complex cultural differences in the meaning of products and activities
2 The lack of standardised data collection instruments to measure marketing-related variables.

Functional equivalence

The extent to which the same product is used for the same or a similar function in two or more countries is called functional equivalence. However, possessions tend to be used for different functions in different societies. In India, for example, the accumulation of jewellery represents less an interest in the display of social status than in security and accumulation of wealth. Refrigerators, used to store food in some countries, are used primarily for chilling water and soft drinks in some other countries.[8] When General Mills entered the UK breakfast cereal market, a box featured a freckled, red-haired, crew-cut kid saying 'Gee kids, it's great'. What General Mills failed to recognise was that the British family is not as child-oriented and permissive as the American family to which it was accustomed, and that British parent–child relationships tend to be more authoritarian; consequently, the package had no appeal to the British housewife.[9]

A similar blunder was made by Binoca when it launched a talcum powder advertisement in India. The advertisement showed an attractive, seemingly naked, woman dousing herself with talcum powder. The caption, covering strategic portions of her body, read: 'Don't go wild – just enough is all you need of Binoca talc'. The highly conservative Indian public found the advertisement distasteful and developed strong negative associations with the brand name.[9] To ask proper questions requires that the researchers understand the functional equivalence, or lack of it, of the activities being investigated.

Conceptual equivalence

The extent to which the same concept (e.g. family) has the same meaning in two or more countries is known as conceptual equivalence. However, concepts can have totally different meanings in different cultural environments. This requires the careful choice of words used to convey the meaning of what the researcher is attempting to explore. The word 'family', for example, means something different in the US, where it typically refers to only parents and children, than it does in many other cultures, where it can extend to grandparents, aunts, uncles and other relatives.

Ethnic influences

Researchers need to understand how the cultural values of a society will affect the approach to the research issue of interest. It may be possible to research problems in one culture but not in another because of cultural taboos and different levels of abstraction. For example, researching attitudes and behaviour concerning personal hygiene products may simply not be possible in some cultures where the norm clearly proscribes public discussion of such issues.

Instrument equivalence

It may not be possible to use the same measuring instrument in every culture. For this reason the researcher may choose to use what are called 'emic' instruments. An emic instrument is one that is constructed specifically for investigating an attitude in a specific culture. Closed-ended questions, for example, may not work well in one culture, but because of cultural differences may work well in another. Certain categories may have to be omitted while others may have to be added. Open-ended questions may also pose some problems, especially in countries where the level of literacy is low and where interviewer bias is significant. Other methods of interviewing, such as focus groups and consumer panels, may face problems because of strong social acquiescence tendencies that are the cultural norm in some countries.

In some instances the researcher may construct 'etic' instruments, ones that are transcultural in application, relating to the behavioural analysis of attitudes considered in isolation. This would permit direct comparison of the same variable across cultures. Attempts at developing etic instruments have employed non-verbal instruments such as picture completion, TAT instruments, and semantic differentials.[8]

Instrument translation

It may seem obvious to suggest that a survey developed in one country be carefully translated into the language of the country where it is going to be administered and assessed: however, mistakes can happen even in the case of literal equivalence. One classic example is a US airline's advertisement of its Boeing 747 'rendezvous lounge' that translated into Portuguese as the 'prostitution chamber'.[9]

Special translation methods have been applied in international research projects:

- *Direct translation*. The survey undergoes a single translation from one language into another by a bilingual translator. This method, however, exposes the instrument to all the problems mentioned above.

- *Back translation*. This is a variation of direct translation that requires the translated survey to be translated back into the original language by another bilingual translator. This lets the translator correct any meaning problems between the original and retranslated instruments. Note that back translation requires that equivalent terms for words or phrases exist in the other language, which may not always be the case.

- *Decentring*. A hybrid of back translation, this method involves a successive iteration process: translation and retranslation of an instrument, each time by a different translator. The back-translated versions in the original language are compared sequentially. If discrepancies occur, the original is modified, and the process is repeated until both show the same or similar wordings. Generally each iteration should show more convergence.

Sampling and fielding the survey

In many countries telephone directories, census tract and block data, and detailed socioeconomic characteristics of the target population will not be available or will be outdated. This adversely affects the ability to draw non-probability as well as probability samples and to conduct personal interviews of any variety. For example, lacking age distributions for the target population, it is difficult for a marketing researcher to set representative age quotas. Moreover, in certain cultures, convenience samples are doomed to failure. In Saudi Arabia, for example, because of the seclusion of women, shopping mall interviews produce all-male samples.

Inadequate mailing lists and rudimentary postal and telephone services can make marketing research in some countries extremely difficult. In many countries only a small percentage of the population possesses telephones, and an alarmingly large percentage of telephone lines may be out of service at any one time. Mail surveys suffer from similar problems. Delivery delays of weeks are common, and in certain countries, expected response rates are lowered considerably because the questionnaire can be mailed back only at the post office.

The obstacles in conducting international marketing research studies can be formidable. Understanding the cultural environment in which the research is taking place is a necessary condition for success. The researcher must also avoid the tendency to blindly apply conventional research techniques and practices. Designing and implementing international research projects can be done effectively. It just takes effort and sensitivity to ask questions in a manner that increases the likelihood that respondents will provide the desired information.

DESK RESEARCH

Desk research is particularly important in export research. This type of research should be fully explored before considering field research. A great deal of desk research can be conducted in the UK where extremely valuable information is freely available from government and other sources. The British Overseas Trade Board is concerned with giving directions for the development of British export activities and establishing priorities in these areas. Some of its main ways of helping British exporters are shown below.

The export marketing information service of the Department of Trade and Industry (1–19 Victoria Street, London, SW1H 0ET) has available the following resources:

- *Foreign statistical publications.* These are produced by both national statistical offices and international organisations, covering a range of topics including trade, production, prices, employment, population and other economic data. The centre can also undertake some searching of selected trade statistics on-line.

- *Foreign trade directories.* Included among these are telephone directories for most countries and specialised directories covering particular sectors of industry.

- *National development plans.* These are issued by many countries and most are available for loan to exporters.

- *British overseas trade information system.* This is a database for exporters of information on products and markets, overseas contacts, export opportunities and promotional events. This includes:

1 The product data store – a computerised microfilm database of product and industry information on overseas markets. Sources include unique market reports researched by British Embassy staff. Coverage varies from country to country but falls within three broad areas of interest: market size, structure and share.
2 The Overseas Contacts Service, which provides details of potential agents, distributors, importers, retailers and others supplied by British embassies.

The export intelligence service

This service sends export-related information to interested subscribing companies, trade associations, and other similar organisations. Its main objective is to secure export orders for British companies by bringing individual export opportunities to their attention. It also supplies market information such as changes in tariff rates and import regulations. Each subscriber is profiled to receive only those notices that are personally relevant – by commodity, overseas market and type of notice.

Other UK government services

There are a number of journals and booklets that provide a wealth of information useful to exporters. These are summarised in Table 15.1.

There are many other sources of data, including:

- National Economic Development Office
- Central Office of Information
- Foreign embassies
- British Export Houses Association
- British Standards Institution
- Institute of Export
- London World Trade Centre
- The Market Research Society.

Professional advice on export marketing research is obtainable from organisations such as:

Table 15.1 UK government services

Source	Content
British Business	Markets, tariff changes, import regulations, overseas trade missions. Special market surveys, details of trade fairs and exhibitions. Covers world markets.
Hints to Exporters (Department of Trade and Industry)	Booklets that cover all export markets, giving a rapid overview of trading customs, travel facilities, etc.
Economic Surveys (The Stationery Office)	Detailed appraisals of local economic conditions.
Overseas Trade Bulletin (CBI)	
European Union Information Office (8 Storey's Gate, London, SW1P 3AT)	
Export and Import Statistics (Statistical Office)	
OECD: Foreign Trade Statistics Bulletin	
Euromonitor	
CBI Overseas reports	

- The European Association for Business to Business Marketing Research
- The Market Research Society
- The Business to Business Marketing Research Association
- The British Overseas Trade Board.

PRINCIPAL METHODS OF ORGANISING RESEARCH

Research for export marketing can be undertaken in a variety of ways, and a brief outline of the principal methods is given below.

1 Use of own staff or importing agents.
   (a) The first objection to this methodology is lack of objectivity; sales staff are usually incapable of giving an unbiased opinion about the likely success of their product.
   (b) The second objection is that agents may have other interests which prevent them from giving an objective assessment of the market.
   (c) Research is a specialist's job which requires particular training and expertise.
   (d) This method may, perhaps, be the only feasible way of researching in some markets.

2 Using research agencies in overseas markets.
   (a) Selection of these may be difficult and risky.
   (b) Where several markets are involved, multiple agencies may have to be used to cover the whole export programme.
   (c) A big advantage is that national research organisations should possess intimate knowledge of their own home market.

3 Using a marketing research organisation based in the UK plus the services of a locally based research firm
   (a) This method is rather cumbersome and offers few advantages over method 2.
   (b) It could be useful where manufacturers have no trained research staff (as is often the case in smaller companies).

4 Using the services of a consortium of research agencies.
   (a) Superficially attractive, but member firms can vary considerably in the quality of those services.
   (b) Closely related to this method is that of an international research organisation linked with advertising agencies over principal markets. This is generally effective.

Several of the larger marketing research companies – i.e. Gallup, BMRB via its associated company MRBI, IFT, and Research Services Ltd – are active in multi-country research.

MARKETING RESEARCH IN DEVELOPING COUNTRIES

There are additional difficulties involved in undertaking marketing research in developing countries. The rapid rate of change occurring in such countries creates problems in maintaining adequate data bases. Moreover, as countries develop, there is an increased requirement for both secondary sources of data and primary data collection research skills. The situation is also worsened by a lack of requisite research skills and a poor appreciation of the value of marketing research.

Often, few indigenous organisations possess marketing research departments and comparatively few commercial marketing research services exist. Government departments make inadequate use of marketing research and are unlikely to be really useful sources of information in this respect. Until adequate documentary detail and data agglomeration infrastructures are set up in such countries the situation cannot improve.

The overall process of marketing research still applies and with modification to take account of cultural, economic and other environmental considerations, research can produce useful results. Secondary sources are a prime source of data and are used extensively despite their limitations. Field research can be hazardous and there is a propensity to rely upon certain methods and techniques in order to obviate sampling and non-sampling errors.

SUMMARY

Emphasis has been placed on how marketing research is organised and conducted in global markets. Desk research is an important source of information and attention has been given in the chapter to identifying fruitful sources of information. There are additional difficulties involved in undertaking marketing research in developing countries and the situation is also worsened by a lack of requisite research skills and a poor appreciation of the value of marketing research. Often, few indigenous organisations possess marketing research departments and comparatively few commercial marketing research services exist.

Questions

1   How is the majority of international marketing research conducted?
2   Explain international segmentation research.
3   What is involved in selecting target markets in international markets?
4   Compare and contrast concentration and diversification as strategies.

5   What are the main factors to take into account when undertaking international marketing research?

6   Indicate the main sources of desk research material made available by the UK government and the use to which it may be put.

7   What are the principal methods of organising international marketing research?

8   Examine the problems of undertaking marketing research in developing countries.

Case study 15.1	Michel Herbelin

At the end of the Second World War, a young self-taught watchmaker named Michel Herbelin opened a workshop in Charquemont in the Jura Mountains just across the border from Switzerland. He chose Charquemont principally because his main suppliers were close at hand. Only 15 km away as the crow flies was La Chaux-de-Fonds, centre of Swiss watchmaking for a couple of hundred years and home to some of its most prestigious brands.

To start with he assembled 'private label' watches for other companies, concentrating particularly on the precision of his manufacture. Very soon, Michel Herbelin gained a reputation for not only the reliability and quality of his products but also for their aesthetic appeal. He longed to have his own brand, however, and in 1968 he launched his first collection under the name Michel Herbelin. These watches were extremely well received and during the course of the 1970s under the direction of his elder son Jean-Claude the brand began to acquire an international reputation. Today it has a presence in 80 countries throughout the five continents and more than 60 per cent of the factory output goes abroad. The majority of sales are to the Middle East and Far East although the brand is well known in Europe. But it is in France that its main success lies. In France it is the leading independent watchmaker and has a 12 per cent share of the under £1,000 retail price bracket. Moreover, in each of the past two years it has achieved a 25 per cent increase in sales turnover.

Michel Herbelin retired from active participation in the business in 1993 and the firm is now in the hands of his two sons, Jean-Claude and Pierre-Michel. It employs 80 workers who produce around 120,000 pieces annually of which 90 per cent use quartz movements. The accent has always been on reliability and to this end the firm utilises ETA movements for 80 per cent of its production. The majority are the popular Flatline movements with the Valjoux 7750 automatic chronograph movements in the more complicated models. Quartz movements from France Ebauches, France's largest supplier, are used in certain ladies' models such as the fashionable Chic collection.

The aesthetic appeal of the whole range is the responsibility of a design team under the personal direction of the Managing Director, Jean-Claude. With a careful eye on fashion trends the team creates two collections a year – rather like their couturier contemporaries in Paris – and work to a distinctive house style notable for its emphasis on softness of line and harmony of dimension enhanced by subtle refinement of detail. The 350 exclusive models of the collection fall into three main ranges. The classic range features traditional styles with simple uncluttered lines. The jewellery range consists of original and elegant designs. The sports range has a strong nautical flavour of ships' wheels and ropes and sea-blue dials and straps.

Jean-Claude's concern for quality ensures that every watch is individually finished by craftsmen and has to undertake 50 quality control procedures during its journey through the factory. Considerable attention is given to protection against moisture penetration, seals being fitted to the crystal, case back and even bezel. Water resistance to 30 metres is standard and verified individually by the routine compression tank immersion and droplet test. Gold plating is another operation where the accent on quality is paramount. 19 microns of anti-corrosion alloy are laid over the base metal, followed by 5 microns of 18ct gold plating which in turn is covered by a 1 micron layer of 23.7 gold for finish and resistance. The rhodium plating process is equally meticulous.

Michel Herbelin originally entered the UK market in the 1970s but failure to meet the targeted growth led the parent company to withdraw around 1990. It was re-launched under its present Sales Director, Peter Gauntlett, in 1993, since when it has achieved considerable acceptance by the trade, with some 80 stockists covering the country. Peter Gauntlett indicated that the company had found that a number of go-ahead independent jewellers look on Michel Herbelin as a splendid platform to help them launch their business onwards and upwards. The brand received an encouraging reception at a recent International Jewellery Fair at Earl's Court. Quite a few new accounts were opened and a number of repeat orders were taken.

Source: Frank Edwards.[10]

Question

What kind of marketing research do you think would be beneficial to a company such as Michel Herbelin in its attempt to get a strong foothold in the UK market?

Case study 15.2 | China

Before the outbreak of the Second World War Shanghai was referred to as the 'Paris of the Orient' but after the communist revolution of 1949 its significance diminished. Today, however, there is talk of it surpassing even Hong Kong in the not too distant future as a capital of enterprise. In the first four months of 1993 business-to-business output surged by more than 20 per cent. American firms such as AT & T, Dupont, Merrill Lynch, Hilton, and Sheraton have made their way to Shanghai, joining Volkswagen, Hitachi, Pilkington and many others.

It is on the east side of the city in the Pudong New Area that the business-to-business activity is most in evidence. During the past three years more than a thousand foreign firms have located there and investments have approached nearly five billion dollars. The Chinese government has chosen Shanghai to become the trade and banking centre not only of Asia but of the whole world by 2010, or at least to surpass Hong Kong as a financial giant. Commercial advertising in Shanghai is gaining in importance. In 1992 advertising appearing on city buses alone sold for more than 10 million yuan. There are some 16 million hoardings on Shanghai's public transport buses every workday.

In Shanghai today, chic, young Chinese promenade on the Bund, the waterfront where European, US and Japanese colonial powers built one of the first commercial enclaves in China. Along Nanjing Road a million people pass every day. There the shops are full of foreign luxury items. New businesses in Shanghai are being established at the rate of five an hour. But this growth in the business-to-business and commercial sector has created cost of living rises of around 20 per cent a year. Moreover, the bill for a couple of drinks in a luxury hotel can amount to more than half a month's income for a Chinese peasant.

Chinese women, like their Western counterparts, take a great deal of interest in their appearance and cosmetics are much valued. However, cultural factors have a very strong impact on their tastes, beliefs and attitudes. For example, in 1988 an exhibition in a northern city produced information which revealed that a cosmetic was required that would both moisturise the face and whiten it. To meet this requirement, a new product 'Xiafei Gold Brand Special Whitening Honey' was developed and introduced to the market, breaking the sales record with 20 million items sold in four years.

'Xiafei' and 'Olice' feature among the most well-known brands of cosmetics in China. Both products were introduced to the market by Cao Jianhua, who has just introduced yet another new product, 'Chaotian'. 'Xiafei''s success is attributable to its middle price position and suitability for a wide range of people. 'Olice' was formulated by adapting a product and adding a biological ingredient known as SOD, which was supposed to protect middle aged women from signs of age. With the name 'Blue Noble', the packaging was given the image of elegance in order to satisfy the customers' desire for fashion and modernity and the product was an immediate success. 'Chaotian Beauty Treasure' was introduced in 1993 into the top ten department stores in Shanghai and this too has been an immediate success.

The brand names, supportive of the positioning strategy adopted, were considered very important to their success. The names sound bright and modern in Chinese – 'Xiafei' means 'the brightening of a colourful morning glow' and names such as 'Whitening Honey', 'Blue Noble' and 'Beauty Treasure' give the impression of safety, nutrition and grace associated with expected levels of product quality.

Source: Rushuang Xiong.[11]

Question

Discuss the kind of marketing research that might well be undertaken with regard to fast-moving consumer and fashion goods in China.

Over the past year, WPP has started up market research businesses in China, Indonesia and South Korea. We have set up a joint venture in healthcare marketing services in Japan. Earlier this month we bought the largest sales promotion and direct marketing agency in Taiwan.

These initiatives are a sign of our commitment to the so-called 'emerging markets', more aptly named 'fast-growing markets'.

Asia Pacific, Latin America, central and eastern Europe, Africa and the Middle East accounted for about one-fifth of WPP's business last year. This year they will account for almost a quarter, and in five years' time, I would be disappointed if the proportion were not at least one-third.

It seems to me that consumer-driven businesses in the West are preoccupied with the development, or lack of it, of our own markets and so miss out on opportunities elsewhere.

Unilever is a rare exception among multinationals in setting the objective that half of its business comes from Asia Pacific, Latin America, Africa and the Middle East within five years, instead of the one-third currently generated.

It also seems to me that most major multinational businesses are not pursuing global strategies in the way they would have us believe. The average US-based multinational still derives only 20 per cent of its sales from outside the US. Coca-Cola is the exception not the rule, with 80 per cent of its business outside the US.

Yet over the next ten years world-wide geographical expansion must be a strategic priority. Many consumer goods and services companies promise growth of 5, 10 or 15 per cent in earnings per share or a similar measure. When the world's population is growing at less than two per cent a year on average, this means finding new international opportunities.

As we have seen in the case of Vietnam, with a market of around 75m people, and with South Africa and its market of around 40m people, unprecedented foreign investment flows in as soon as political conditions allow. The same will be true for Burma's 45m people market and Cuba's 11m people. As a result of greater economic stability, more welcoming governments, and harder working people, Asia Pacific still retains the lead in terms of interest among multinationals. Latin America is a close second. Within Asia Pacific, only China remains an enigma, with significant revenue growth but limited profitability.

Western businesses should not assume that these markets are simply awaiting their arrival.

Besides the dominant Japanese financial institutions, some of the leading Korean chaebols – conglomerates such as Samsung, Hyundai, LG and Daewoo – have grown as big as or bigger than IBM in a shorter time.

President Foods, one of the world's biggest food companies, based in Taiwan, and San Miguel, the Philippines-based brewing company, are both capable of developing global brands.

Latin America is also witnessing the development of significant global forces. In the media and communications sector, for example, the Azcarraga family, the

Marinho family and John Malone of TCI have all collaborated with Rupert Murdoch on pan-regional projects or companies.

Against this background, if we in Western companies don't develop our businesses, products and services in the new, faster-growing markets, we will ultimately suffer competitively as the growing forces invade our own backyards.

The author is chief executive of WPP Group.

Source: Martin Sorrell.[12] Reprinted with permission.

Question

Discuss the kind of marketing research that might be undertaken in the various markets mentioned above. What kinds of problems do you think researchers will encounter in each case?

Case study 15.4	European laundry statistics

Detergents are big business, and the world market is dominated by a few very large companies. America's Procter & Gamble, and Britain's Unilever, are among the biggest. Economies of scale (notably in the construction costs of the huge drying towers used to convert liquid detergents into powders) mean that it is difficult for small firms to enter the powdered detergent market.

It may be a commonly held view that detergents differ very little from one to another, but in the fact the differences in washday habits between countries are often very marked, and detergent manufacturers need to take account of these differences if they are to be successful in capturing their share of the global market.

Research conducted on behalf of American detergent manufacturers showed that European clothes-washing practices not only differ from American practices, but also differ between European countries. Procter & Gamble's Walter Lingle had said as early as 1955, 'Washing habits vary widely from country to country. We must tailor products to meet consumer demands in each nation. We cannot simply sell products with US formulas. They won't work – they won't be accepted.'

The main differences revealed by the research were as follows:

1 European washing machines are normally front-loading, with a horizontally rotating drum. The typical US washing machine is top-loading, with a central agitator.
2 European machines have a smaller water capacity, usually around 3–5 gallons rather than the 12–14 gallons used by American machines.
3 European machines have a 90–120 minute wash cycle, whereas US machines cycle in about 20–30 minutes.
4 Water temperatures are much higher in Europe, with 'boil washes' using water hotter than 60 degrees centigrade being commonplace. In some countries, the washing machines do not heat the water, so the powders need to work at lower temperatures, and in still other countries hand-washing is common.

5 Americans use more synthetic fabrics than Europeans do, and also tend to wash their clothes more often.
6 Although many Europeans do not own a washing machine, those that do tend to use more detergent than Americans use, so that the total detergent consumption in Europe is some 30 per cent above US levels.

The problem for the detergent companies has several aspects. Firstly, the front-loading machines made liquid detergents harder to use. Secondly, the much slower washing cycle of European machines meant that the washing powders or liquids needed to remain stable in the water for longer. Thirdly, the higher washing temperature meant a different formulation for the product – or a programme of re-educating the consumers to wash at lower temperatures. Fourthly, European clothing purchase trends would need to be monitored carefully to see whether there would be an increase in the wearing of synthetics.

Fifthly, and more positively, the European market is clearly an attractive one for US detergent manufacturers since consumption levels are high. The manufacturers were interested in the possibilities of opening up a market for liquid detergents; the reason for this is that liquids are much easier to manufacture, and the companies were afraid that if they did not establish strong brands in the market fairly quickly, small manufacturers would be able to enter the market and establish a presence. This would create competition in an industry which had previously had very little competitive pressure, due to the high capital costs of establishing plants to manufacture powder detergents. In the meantime, the difficulty of using liquids in European machines was working to the advantage of the major manufacturers.

Although many Americans tend to regard Europe as being one place (in the same way as many Europeans ignore cultural differences between American states), the more sophisticated marketers within the detergent companies realised quickly that separate strategies would need to be worked out for each country, and even for regions within each country. This meant that several separate research programmes would need to be carried out, both nationally and regionally. In some cases cultural similarities cross borders; for example, Bavarians often have more in common with Austrians than they do with their fellow-countrymen in northern Germany.

Striking a balance between finding economies of scale in manufacture and the need to differentiate the product would prove difficult, but the detergent manufacturers did not see these difficulties as being insuperable. What they needed to do was to identify segments within the European market as a whole, ignoring borders, and develop products which would meet the needs of consumers within those segments.

(Case contributed by Jim Blythe.)

Questions

1 What are the main difficulties in designing a research programme for the European detergent market?
2 How would you research the acceptability of low-temperature detergents?

3 What problems might arise when collecting secondary data within Europe?

4 The European market can be segmented by methods other than nationality; in other words, segments exist which cut across national borders. How might you go about identifying these segments?

5 What methods might be available for monitoring pan-European fashion-buying trends?

Further reading

Brock, S E (1989) Marketing research in Asia: problems, opportunities and lessons, *Marketing Research*, September, p 47.

Cateora, P R (1993) *International Marketing* (8th edn), Homewood, IL: Irwin, ch 11 'Researching global markets'.

Douglas, S P and Craig, C S (1983) *International Marketing Research*, Upper Saddle River, NJ: Prentice-Hall.

Greenbaum, T L (1996) Understanding focus group research abroad, *Marketing News* 30(12), June, p 3.

Hart, S J, Webb, J R and Jones, M V (1996) Export marketing research and the effect of export experience in industrial series, *International Marketing Review*, 11(6), pp 4–23.

Johansson, J K and Nonaka, J (1987) Market research the Japanese way, *Harvard Business Review*, May–June, pp 16–22.

Keillor, B, Owens, D and Pettijohn, C (2001) A cross-cultural/cross-national study of influencing factors and socially desirable response bias, *International Journal of Market Research*, 43(1), pp 63–84.

Kinsey, J (1988) *Marketing in Developing Countries*, London: Macmillan, ch 4 'Marketing research in developing countries'.

Malhotra, N K, Agarwal, J and Peterson, M (1996) Cross-cultural marketing research: methodological issues and guidelines, *International Marketing Review*, 3(5), pp 7–43.

Mattson, J (1990) Measuring inherent product values, *European Journal of Marketing*, 24(9), pp 25–39.

Munson, J and McIntery, S (1979) Developing practical procedures for measurement of personal values in cross cultural marketing, *Journal of Marketing Research*, 16.

References and notes

[1] Ricks, D A, Fu, Y C and Arpan, S (1974) *International Business Blunders*, Columbus, OH: Grid.

[2] Goodyear, M (1996) The world shrinks, maybe, but there's still the need to travel, *Research Plus*, May, p 12.

[3] Tyrrell, B (1994) Eastern promise is worth all the pain of red tape, *Marketing*, 3 February, p 5.

[4] Korents, G (1996) China's other consumers, *Business Week*, 13 May, p 11.

5 Branthwaite, A and Bruggemann, J (1996) Why we won't keep taking pills, *Research Plus*, April, pp 8–9.

6 Bunn, S (1996) Now that India's got GATT, a massive market beckons, *Research Plus*, April, pp 10–11.

7 Bartonova, M (1996) The markets are emerging – and research is hard on their heels, *Research Plus*, January, pp 4–5.

8 Choudry, Y A (1986) Pitfalls of international marketing research: are you speaking French like a Spanish cow?, *ABER*, 17(4), Winter, pp 18–28.

9 Ricks, D A, Fu, Y C and Arpan, S (1974) *International Business Blunders*, Columbus, OH: Grid.

10 Edwards, F (1995) The French connection, *International Wrist Watch*, 31, pp 46–8.

11 Xiong, R (1994) Moving towards market economy and marketing application in China, Unpublished MBA dissertation, Department of Management, Keele University.

12 Sorrell, M (1997) The future lies abroad, *Financial Times*, 30 June.

16 Marketing decision-support systems

OBJECTIVES

After reading this chapter you should be able to:

- appreciate the nature of marketing decision-support mechanisms;

- appreciate, in particular, the use of traditional management science/operational research tools in marketing.

KEY WORDS

marketing intelligence	new product
decision-support mechanisms	linear programming
electronic data interchange (EDI)	transportation models
forecasting	assignment models
mathematical models	network models
expert systems	decision trees
market demand	inventory models
time-series analysis	queuing theory models
exponential smoothing	Markov analysis
moving average	simulation
statistical demand analysis	game theory

PLAN OF CHAPTER 16

INTRODUCTION

This chapter presents the main components of a marketing information system. It covers both objective and subjective approaches to market measurement and forecasting and the use of traditional management science/operational research tools in marketing decisions.

First we take a systematic look at the overall concept of a marketing information system and then explore its various components in more detail. Attention is directed to methods of market measurement and forecasting and then to examining the range of management science and operational research techniques that can be used to help improve our marketing decisions. Finally, we look at the possible uses for expert systems as part of the decision-support mechanism.

MARKETING INFORMATION SYSTEMS

Marketing information systems exist to help marketing management make good decisions. When the marketing environment is undergoing rapid change, initiative in decision-making is necessary. An efficient marketing information system records the relevant changes taking place in the market place and prevents management suffering from an overload of redundant information.

A marketing information system supports marketing decisions by facilitating interlinkage and integration between functional departments of the business. Customer perceptions of new products, for example, may be collected by the sales force and disseminated to product-development groups by way of the system. The marketing information system enhances the organisation's ability to respond to a dynamic business environment. For example, as a result of information provided through a link with retail scanners, price changes can be immediately initiated in response to the actions of competitors. A well-designed information system enables the efficient handling, organisation and storage of data and leads to improvements in customer service through increased responsiveness to customer needs.

A marketing information system might comprise the following subsystems[1] (Figure 16.1):

- An internal reporting system containing data on such things as sales, inventories, cash flows and accounts receivable, all of which can be used to measure current activity and performance.
- A marketing intelligence system that collects everyday information about developments in the external environment and, in particular, problems and opportunities.

Figure 16.1 The marketing information system

- A marketing-research system which gathers, evaluates and reports information on a specific environmental situation facing a company and provides sufficient information to minimise guesswork.
- An analytical marketing system which is able to undertake the complex analysis of business problems.

The *analytical marketing system* consists of a set of statistical tools and mathematical models. We have already looked at the statistical tools in earlier chapters. The mathematical models help executives to generate better marketing decisions. These tools and models comprise the *decision support* mechanisms.

Information on competitors' activities and on customers' wants and needs can be obtained from sales persons' reports. These can be entered into the information system in electronic form and this calls for the design of electronic forms which can easily be completed by sales staff. Sales reports tend to be filled in at home at weekends or in hotel bedrooms during the working week. A portable laptop computer directly connected by a modem to the firm's mainframe computer provides an attractive solution to the problem. The communication link is also two-way. Information that the company has on the information system can be fed to sales staff in the field. This includes information that is either internal or external to the firm. While internal data is collected as a matter of course as business proceeds, data on the environment and competitive activity can often be bought from consultants and marketing-research agencies, which is often already in an electronic form (see Chapter 3 on secondary data).

It is better to store data in a disaggregated form in the database. This allows anyone to manipulate and analyse the data to suit their own particular purposes. Any summary statistical analyses can be kept in a separate file within the database. Having a computer-based information system means that information in the form of reports can quickly be made available to management.

SNAP is a useful computer program which incorporates questionnaire design, storage of data based on surveys using the questionnaire and data analysis (Figure 16.2). The features of the program are shown in the box.

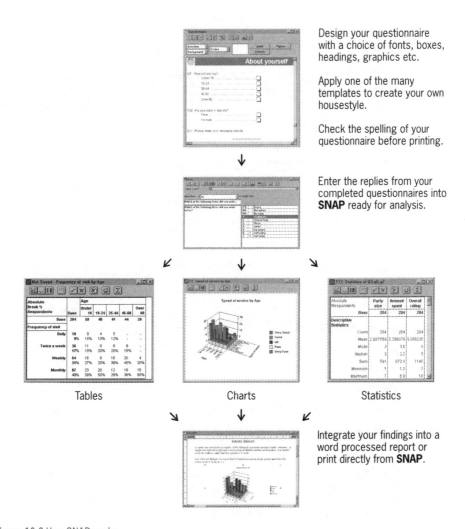

Design your questionnaire with a choice of fonts, boxes, headings, graphics etc.

Apply one of the many templates to create your own housestyle.

Check the spelling of your questionnaire before printing.

Enter the replies from your completed questionnaires into **SNAP** ready for analysis.

Tables   Charts   Statistics

Integrate your findings into a word processed report or print directly from **SNAP**.

Figure 16.2 How SNAP works
Source: Mercator Systems.[2]

Users and uses of a marketing information system

Sales management is one of the prime users of the marketing information system. The information system can help with the effective allocation of tasks to the sales force. It also facilitates the assessment of the performance of sales. Sales staff, too, benefit from being able to access the system easily and to get support and information about such things as:

- the quantity of the product on hand
- prices and price discounts
- status information on invoices, time of delivery and back orders
- delivery dates
- complete product specifications.

SNAP

SNAP Professional is an integrated survey design and analysis software program providing on-screen questionnaire design, data entry, analysis and presentation of results in the form of tables and charts. It operates in Windows 95, NT, 2000, ME and XP environments.

Questionnaire Design Choice of WYSIWYG on-screen questionnaire design or alternative survey variable definition.

Single or multiple column page layout.

Predefined question styles which are customisable and re-usable.

Choice of Single, Multiple, Date, Literal and Quantity responses.

Up to 250 answer choices per question.

No limit to the number of questions per survey.

Variety of question numbering schemes.

Question renumbering feature.

Changes may be made to questions even after data entry has begun.

Questionnaire data view shows completed respondent questionnaires.

Questionnaire analysis view shows counts or percentage survey results.

Bitmap backgrounds can be shown behind questions and notes.

Each code of a question has an optional 'GoTo Q...' routing tag.

Questionnaire editing includes a spell-checker.

Style Templates that enable a complete questionnaire style to be saved or loaded.

Links seamlessly with optional Internet and Scanning modules.

Use predefined questions from SNAP surveyPaks.

Use other questions from your own surveys.

Data Entry Up to 100,000 respondents per survey.

Four modes of data entry – Questionnaire, Interview, Prompted and Fast.

Customisable data verification in all three modes.

Automatic routing following logic set up through questions.

Configuration of non-response strategy.

Changes may be made to questions even after data entry has begun.

Filtering to select cases for browsing and/or printing reports.

Search and replace feature for data cleaning. Import and export data to/from other SNAP surveys, spreadsheets, databases and other survey software.

Data entry spell-checker.

Links seamlessly with optional Internet and Scanning modules.

General Analysis features (applies to both Tabular and Graphical Analysis).

Analyses based on respondents or responses, with or without missing and 'not asked' results.

Unlimited level of filters to tabulate subsets of data.

Weighting capabilities enable weighting by other questions, factors or to targets.

Question responses may be dynamically split, combined and regrouped to construct multi-way analyses. Specification of derived variables to group quantity, date and literal response variables or to combine categories from any number of other single and multiple response variables.

Batch operation to generate large volume reporting in a 'macro' style.

Tables and charts can be saved for future quick reference.

Optional Internet module generates tables for publication on the WWW.

Tabular Analysis Choice of cross-tabulations, frequency tables, grid tables and holecounts.

Predefined table presentation styles which are customisable and re-usable.

Selection of row, column, total per cents, index and expected values, suppress zeros and order rows.

Calculation of score statistics (mean, standard error and confidence) on cross-tabulations and grid tables.

Descriptive statistics: count, sum, mean, mode, median, minimum, maximum, range, standard deviation, variance, standard error, skewness and kurtosis.

Additional statistics on cross-tabulations: Chi square, Cramers V, Phi coefficient, Contingency coefficient. Tables of means, with optional T-test significance results.

Graphical Analysis Choice of 2D and 3D bar, pie, line, area, step, scatter, radar, hi-lo and donut charts. Predefined chart presentation styles which are customisable and re-usable.

Optional inclusion of titles, footnotes, bar and sector labels, values and percentages, coloured backgrounds. Creation of pictograph bar charts using BMP and WMF image files.

Perspective rotation and modification of light source location and intensity on 3D charts.

Source: Mercator Systems.[2]

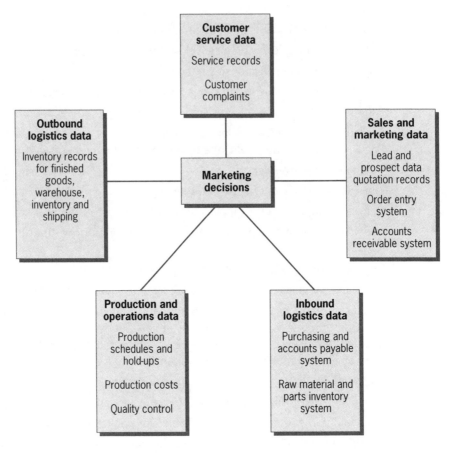

Figure 16.3 Sources of internal data

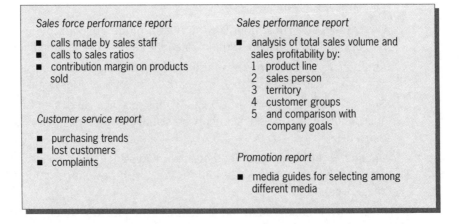

Figure 16.4 Marketing information system reports

Useful sources of internal data

The information system can help to produce sales forecasts and marketing budgets which form the basis of sales strategies and quotas. The sales forecasts facilitate the planning and control of manufacturing, distribution, advertising and promotion activities.

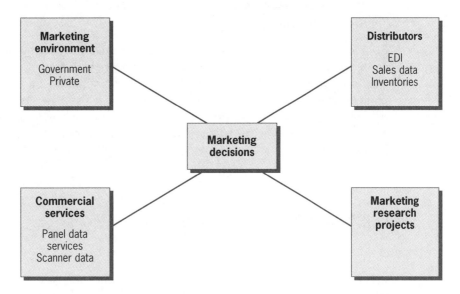

Figure 16.5 Sources of external data

Electronic data interchange

Electronic Data Interchange (EDI) improves the process of distribution for both producers and retailers. With the aid of technology a constant communication link is forged between manufacturers and retailers, making the process of supply much more efficient and cost-effective. It means that instead of going through the tiresome and time-consuming process of assessing demand, making an order and waiting for it to be processed, retailers can allow sales information provided by EPOS to be instantly transmitted to suppliers through EDI. This gives the supplier the opportunity to respond immediately to demand, despatching stock as and when required by the retailer.

EDI confers several potential improvements on the process of distribution:

■ EDI enables a supplier to use 'real-time' processing as opposed to batch processing. As a result, an order can be despatched when the need is identified, rather than at a regular processing point (usually, the end of the day)

■ The system can improve customer service, since goods will be in stock when customers require them

■ EDI reduces operating expenses, since orders are handled more efficiently and more rapidly as there are fewer repetitions involved. Once data is input at the point of sale (via EPOS), there is no need for a re-entry at the supplier end and this reduces costs

■ Where a process is a long one, there is more chance of error. In the case of EDI, there is the need for only one point of data entry and the risk of error is substantially reduced

EDI can help manufacturers gain a competitive advantage in the market. First, it enables them to gain access to valuable information held by retailers about consumer tastes and behaviour. This in turn helps manufacturers regain some contact with the ultimate consumer – contact that has been lost as a result of growing retailer power. Second, manufacturers are able to use their technical resources as an incentive to attract retailers to stock their brand.

Source: A Samways and K Whittcome.[3]

DECISION-SUPPORT MECHANISMS

Marketing decision-support mechanisms are a collection of tools and techniques, with supporting software and hardware. With it, an organisation gathers and interprets relevant information from business and the environment and turns it into a basis for marketing action. The remainder of this chapter examines the various decision-support mechanisms that can be used. The main areas covered are:

1 forecasting tools
2 mathematical models
3 expert systems.

FORECASTING DEMAND

Forecasting amounts to estimating some future event that is outside the control of the organisation and that provides a basis for managerial planning. The estimates produced often form the basis of production planning, sales force planning, setting advertising appropriations, estimating cashflow and assessing the need for innovation. Marketing plans are only useful if the size of current and future markets is carefully measured and estimated. Such information is a useful starting point from which to determine how resources should be allocated among markets and products or services.

Defining market demand

Demand can be measured at several different levels:

- product levels: product-item sales, product-form sales, product-line sales, company sales, industry sales, national sales;
- space levels: sales to individual customers, sales by territory, area, country, or world sales;
- time levels: short-range, medium-range, long-range sales.

There are many different ways of describing a market. The current number of users of a product or service and the sales volume they generate constitutes the 'penetrated market'. Secondary data sources may provide information on this or it may be necessary to establish this figure by sample survey. This measure does not take account of those people who have an interest in buying the product or service, but who currently do not buy the product. The latter are important, since in looking at future demand they provide a measure of the 'potential market'. A further stipulation is that customers must be able to afford the product or service. In assessing the 'potential market' this too must be established and will lead to a redefinition of the market size. The ability to use a product or service affects the size of the market. If it is not possible to use a product, this will obviously restrict the market size and taking this into account will define the 'available market'. Finally, a firm has only a limited amount of resources at its disposal, so it chooses only certain market segments where it feels it has the capacity to compete effectively and where the market size is sufficiently attractive. This becomes the 'served' or the 'target market'.

Predicting future demand

The following considerations should be borne in mind when choosing the most appropriate forecasting technique:

- Time horizon. The technique must be suitable for use over the period of time required.
- Technical sophistication. The people doing the forecasting must be comfortable with the technique used. They must have the knowledge to understand its use and limitations.
- Cost. Greater accuracy in forecasting may only be possible at extra cost. We have to assess whether the extra cost of accuracy is worthwhile.
- The data that can be used. The extensiveness, currency, accuracy and representativeness of the availability must be assessed before choosing a technique.

Firms can adopt a variety of approaches to sales forecasting but the basic approach is to:

1 Make an environmental forecast about inflation, employment, interest rates, consumer spending and saving, business investment.

2 Make a forecast of sales and profits to be earned by the industry, using the data in 1 together with other information that links industry figures to environmental trends.
3 Make a company sales forecast, using the data in 2 and assuming a given market share.

Often, however, firms may not know the industry sales level. In such cases sales forecasts are made at the company level at stage 2 and stage 3 is not used.

When forecasting the sales for established products two approaches are possible, both of which have a number of variants. First, there are methods that rely on asking people questions and, second, there are methods that involve the statistical or mathematical analysis of historical data.

Asking people questions

Surveys of buyers' intentions

Some market-research organisations, and even businesses themselves, conduct periodic surveys of buying intentions. Using the results produced by regular sample surveys, predictions of the likely demand for various items or activities can then be made. This method can be applied effectively by producers of many business products and services, particularly industrial plant, machinery and supplies.

Composite of sales force opinion

The sales team makes contact with the distributors and/or customers in the market place and is well positioned to provide estimates on potential sales demand. When making use of estimates produced by the sales force, account needs to be taken of any bias that may exist. The sales force may be biased either in the direction of pessimism or of optimism. We also have to remember that the sales force may not really appreciate the larger economic factors that may influence sales. However, providing we can identify the sources of bias and compensate for them in interpreting predictions, it is possible to make use of these estimates.

Expert opinion

Expert opinion is another method of forecasting. Experts may include dealers, distributors, suppliers, marketing consultants and even trade associations. A key factor that influences patterns of sales in a country is the state of an economy. Various economic experts can provide their opinions and a government produces its own economic forecast.

Analysing past data

Firms tend to base their forecasts on what they have achieved in the past. This approach to forecasting offers few opportunities for mistakes except where there are large variations in sales from one year to the next. There are two basic methods of forecasting, each of which has a number of versions.

Methods that adopt a solely time-dependent approach

Classical time-series analysis

The first sets of methods are those based on time-series analysis, which assumes that sales simply vary as a function of time. The time effects are divided into:

- cycle – fluctuations every few years, for example, the effect of trade cycles as various major economies in the world are hit by booms and slumps.
- trend – a general upward, downward or static (no trend) pattern, for example, the upward trend of sales of video-recorders during the growth phase of the lifecycle.
- seasonal – systematic variations at certain times of the year, for example, additional sales of swimsuits in the summer months.
- erratic – unpredictable or random variations, for example, demand interrupted by an industry-wide strike.

Erratic variation is taken into account when making forecasts, but we do not attempt to predict it exactly. We merely express it as the error we attach to the sales forecast. This method is most suitable for forecasting the sales of products where the unexplained variation is small.

The trend component results from developments in a population, the formation of capital and developments in technology. It is evidenced by a general upward or downward shift in the pattern of sales. If there is no such pattern, there is assumed to be no trend.

The cycle depicts the wavelike flow of sales over a number of years and is most useful when examining data for use in intermediate range forecasts (3–7 years). Traditionally, the cycle represents swings in economic activity.

The seasonal component refers to recurrent sales patterns that may exist within the period of a single year. This will reflect things such as weather factors, holidays and seasonal buying habits.

Erratic variation comprises such things as strikes, fashions and other unforeseen circumstances. These factors are unpredictable and need to be removed from past data in order to inspect the other three elements. Time-series analysis consists of decomposing the original sales data into its trend, cyclical, seasonal and erratic components. The series is then recombined to produce a sales forecast.

Example

Imagine that Table 16.1 represents quarterly data on shipments of a particular commodity.

Table 16.1 Quarterly data

Period	Year	Sales (tonnes)
1	1993	436
2		291
3		357
4		529
5	1994	386
6		304
7		333
8		471
9	1995	383
10		336
11		365
12		539

More than one way to forecast time-series data such as these exists. One method is to use dummy variables and multiple regression analysis. Multiple regression is a statistical tool that can be applied to past data to discover the most important factors influencing sales and their relative influence. The dummy variables in this particular case represent the factors influencing sales. The approach consists of creating a variable for each of the four quarters and the following equation is then estimated by multiple linear regression analysis:

$$\text{Sales} = B_0 + B_1 \text{ Time} + B_2 \text{ Winter} + B_3 \text{ Spring} + B_4 \text{ Summer}$$

One of the dummy variables has to be left out so that the regression can be solved by computer: in this case 'Autumn' is omitted.

The values obtained are:

$$B_0 = 510.5 \; B_1 = 0.3125 \; B_2 = -110.396 \; B_3 = -202.042 \; B_4 = -161.021$$

Substituting values into the equation for subsequent periods enables a forecast of sales to be made. For example:

$$\text{Period 13 forecast sales} = 510.5 + 0.3125 \times 13 - 110.396 \times 1 = 404$$

Moving average

This is one of the simplest methods. Trend, seasonal or cyclical patterns are not usually included in it, although in the more advanced methods it is possible to do so.

Table 16.2 Multiple linear regression analysis

Time	Sales	Winter	Spring	Summer	Autumn
1	436	1	0	0	0
2	291	0	1	0	0
3	357	0	0	1	0
4	529	0	0	0	1
5	386	1	0	0	0
6	304	0	1	0	0
7	333	0	0	1	0
8	471	0	0	0	1
9	383	1	0	0	0
10	336	0	1	0	0
11	365	0	0	1	0
12	539	0	0	0	1

The average demand is the arithmetic mean of demand from a number (N) of past periods.

$$A_t = [D_1 + D_2 + \ldots + D_{t-(N+1)}]/N$$

The forecast demand for period $t + 1$ is a projection of the past average demand. The number of periods included in the average can be increased to give more importance to past demand (referred to as damping). In order to fine-tune the sensitivity of the moving average to certain periods, a weighting factor W_t can be applied to those periods:

$$F_{t+1} = A_t = W_1 D_1 + W_2 D_2 + \ldots + W_N D_{t-(N+1)}$$

where $W_1 + W_2 + \ldots + W_N = 1$

Exponential smoothing

Many businesses produce many hundreds or thousands of products. Notable examples are the firms operating in the pharmaceutical industry. For such firms, a simple forecasting technique is required which requires the minimum of data. In its simplest form exponential smoothing requires only three pieces of information:

1 the period's actual sales Q_t
2 the current period's smoothed sales q_t
3 a smoothing parameter a, a value between 0 and 1.

The sales forecast for the next period is given by the formula:

$$q_{t+1} + 1 = aQ_t + (1 - a)q_t$$

Forecasts of this kind are handled by computer. Using an iterative procedure (trial and error), the computer program can regularly determine that value of a which gives the most satisfactory results in making forecasts. The value is the one that gives the best fit to past sales. Once the system has been set up, all we have to do is to add new sales figures to the database as and when they occur. There are a number of more sophisticated variants on this approach, such as double exponential smoothing and exponential smoothing incorporating seasonal and trend components.

Statistical demand analysis

So far, the statistical or mathematical approaches we have considered treat the factors that seem to influence sales as regularly recurring phenomena. The difficulty with this approach is that some patterns do not reappear at regular intervals. For example, while there are economic booms and slumps from time to time, their patterns are not so precise as to enable accurate forecasts to be made.

Statistical demand analysis attempts to identify the source of all influences on demand so that more accurate forecasts can be made. The basic statistical method to take account of such factors is multiple regression analysis. Experience indicates that the factors most commonly considered are price, income, population and marketing promotion.

The first stage in a regression analysis is to build a causal model in which we try to explain sales in terms of a number of independent variables. For example, we might conjecture that industry sales of umbrellas are related to their relative price (P), personal disposable income (I), relative advertising expenditure and the absolute level of rainfall (R). We would express this relationship in the form of an equation:

$$S = a_0 + b_0P + b_1I + b_2A + b_3R$$

We need to estimate the parameters for a_0 and for b_1 to b_3 and apply them to quantifications of P, I, A and R for the period of the forecast.

In principle, demand equations of this variety are acquired by fitting the best equations to historical or cross-sectional data. The coefficients of the equation are estimated according to what is called the 'least squares criterion', according to which the best equation is the one that minimises a measure of the error between the actual and the predicted observations. The better the fit, the more useful will be the equation for forecasting purposes.

Although this is a popular technique, it needs to be used with care. There must always be an adequate number of observations: in making annual forecasts, 10–15 years data is not unreasonable, where there are four independent variables. Independent variables can sometimes turn out to influence each other and are not independent at all. For example, relative price and relative advertising expenditure may well influence each other, since advertising costs can be reflected in the selling price. There are also other pitfalls to be watched for.

Forecasting sales of new products

To forecast sales of new products we need some initial sales figures with which to work. Given that early sales data is available, it is usually possible, by using one or other of a variety of mathematical models or 'curve-fitting routines' to make some prediction for sales over a specified time period. Alternatively, it may be possible to look at sales histories of similar new products and make predictions by analogy. There are many examples of these models (see, for instance, Kotler and Lilien[4]).

Example

The epidemic model of initial sales is a useful tool to have to hand when trying to make a sales prediction for certain kinds of new products. The model developed by Bass,[5] which he specifically tested out on a range of consumer-durable goods, is illustrative:

$$p_t = p + q/M(Y_t)$$

where p_t is the probability of purchase given that no previous purchase was made, Y_t is the total number who have tried the product, M is the total number of potential buyers (saturation level), q is a parameter reflecting the rate of diffusion of the model and p is the initial probability of first-time purchase.

The model can be estimated by running a regression of current versus past sales (Table 16.3):

$$Sales_t = c_0 + c_1 Y_t + c_2 Y_t^2$$

Analysis of the sales in Table 16.3 gives the forecasting model:

$$Sales_t = 2.06 + 1.016 Y_t - 0.00464 Y_t^2$$

Table 16.3 Current versus past sales

Year	$Sales_t$ '000	Y_t '000	Y_t^2 '000
1	1	0	0
2	2	1	1
3	4	3	9
4	10	7	49
5	20	17	289
6	36	37	1,369
7	48	73	5,329
8	58	121	14,641

Forecasting sales of new products in retail outlets

Large retail chains often add new lines to their stock. Most of these retailers have benchmarks against which to judge whether a product is likely to be successful or not. A common practice is to offer the product for sale for a limited period in one of its shops. If the product fails to achieve level of sales within the specified period, it is withdrawn and is not put on sale in other outlets.

APPLICATIONS FOR MATHEMATICAL MODELS IN THE MARKETING DECISION-SUPPORT SYSTEM

Mathematical models are those referred to in the operations research literature. The main models are:

1 Linear programming
2 Transportation model
3 Assignment model
4 Network model
5 Decision tree
6 Inventory model
7 Queuing theory model
8 Markov analysis
9 Simulation
10 Game theory.

The various models or techniques have been applied in a wide variety of settings and can help to find solutions to problems in many different areas of marketing. Below, examples are shown (usually omitting calculations) of how these techniques may be applied to marketing problems.

Linear programming

Linear programming helps to determine how to minimise costs or maximise profits (or minimise/maximise some other factors) subject to a set of constraints.

Example

A marketing executive has a budget of £5000 and wants to maximise the 'reach' of magazine advertisements. The reach of magazine 1 is 8000 potential customers and that of magazine 2 is 5000 potential customers. The number of potential customers with incomes of less than £10000 per annum is 1000 and 400, respectively, per column inch advertising seen in each magazine. The cost of an advertisement in magazine 1 is £600 per column inch and £1000 per column inch in the case of 2. The manager would like to reach at most 4500 potential customers whose incomes are less than £10 000 per annum. How many column inches should be bought in each of the magazines in order to maximise profits?

This problem is expressed as follows:

Objective: maximise $Z = 8000 X1 + 5000 X2$

subject to $X1,X2 \geq 0$ (negative amounts not allowed)

and $£600 X1 + £1000 X2 \leq £5000$ (budget constraint)

and $1000 X1 + 400 X2 \leq 4500$ (reach constraint).

Applying linear programming gives the answer:

3.29 column inches in magazine 1

3.03 column inches in magazine 2

and the number of readers reached is 41 470.

Transportation model

The transportation model may be considered a special case of the linear programming model. A special algorithm is developed to solve such problems. Essentially, the idea is to allocate the flow of objects to sources and destinations in such a way as to minimise costs or maximise profits (or some other measure relating to minimisation/maximisation).

Example

A company ships goods from three factories to three distribution outlets. The supply capacities of the factories, the demand requirements of the three outlets and the shipping costs (£/tonne) are shown in Table 16.4.

How should supply be equated with demand in order to minimise costs? The solution suggested is shown in Table 16.5.

The solution value = £2,260 (cost minimised).

Table 16.4 Transportation model

	To distribution outlet			
From factory	1	2	3	Supply (tonnes)
1	12	14	7	160
2	13	6	18	40
3	7	4	5	90
Demand (tonnes)	140	50	100	290

Table 16.5 Transportation model: Solution

		1	2	3	Total
Supply plant	1	60.00	0.00	100.00	160.00
	2	0.00	40.00	0.00	40.00
	3	80.00	10.00	0.00	90.00
Demand		140.00	50.00	100.00	290.00

Assignment model

The assignment model helps to find the minimum or maximum pay-off associated with matching one set of items to a second set. The items may be people, projects, jobs, contracts or territories. For example, we might be concerned with assigning people to jobs, assigning various contracts to people making bids or assigning sales people to territories. An assignment problem is one where only one from a set of items is assigned to only one from a set of other items.

Example

This problem involves getting a marketing-research project completed in the shortest possible time. A marketing-research department has received a request to carry out a study of the market for eight different products. The department manager asks individual members of the department to estimate how long (in days) it would take each of them to complete each of the projects (one for each product). The estimates shown in Table 16.6 were provided.

Table 16.6 Assignment model

	Product							
	1	2	3	4	5	6	7	8
John	4	3	4	3	6	3	M	7
Paul	5	4	3	2	5	4	6	7
Bill	3	M	5	4	4	5	7	6
Sam	4	6	6	3	3	2	8	6
Helen	2	7	7	M	5	3	5	7
Mary	4	4	3	6	4	6	6	8
Winifred	5	5	4	5	M	5	5	8
Alice	4	5	5	4	4	M	3	7
Arthur	3	4	M	3	5	3	7	6
Mark	6	3	4	4	6	2	7	4

Entries marked 'M' signify that the person would not have the skills or experience to carry out that particular study.

The objective is to accomplish the task in the shortest possible time. In this case, the firm wants to have only one individual per project since experience indicates that this is usually the quickest way to get things done. In the past the firm has conducted this exercise by assigning tasks according to the shortest available time indicated in each person's product-study column, provided they have not already been previously allocated to one of the other tasks. Thus the assignment made, based on such an heuristic, might be as shown in Table 16.7.

This would give a completion time of 24 days. Using the assignment model and minimising the amount of time, the solution indicates that the tasks *can in fact be completed in 23 days* with a different assignment of personnel (Table 16.8).

Table 16.7 Assignment: solution 1

Product study	Name	Time
1	Helen	2
2	John	3
3	Mary	3
4	Paul	2
5	Sam	3
6	Mark	2
7	Alice	3
8	Bill	6

Table 16.8 Assignment: solution 2

Product study	Name	Time
1	Helen	2
2	John	3
3	Mary	3
4	Paul	2
5	Sam	3
6	Arthur	3
7	Alice	3
8	Mark	4
		= 23 days

Network model

There are a variety of different network models including Critical Path and PERT models. Here we consider a simple type of network.

Example

A particular market research study includes ten activities, which have the durations and precedences shown in Table 16.9.

The objective is to determine the minimum time that the project would take to complete. This is calculated to be:

$$A B E G I L 1 + 4 + 2 + 7 + 3 + 2 = 19 \text{ days}$$

The minimum time of 19 is on the *critical* path. In order to shorten the time to complete the entire project, an element on this route or *path* has to be shortened. It would be no use shortening C, D or K, for instance (Figure 16.6).

Decision tree

Decision trees evaluate the expected pay-off of different alternatives. The example shown below is a simple one, and much more complex ones can be built. The expected pay-off of the various alternatives are calculated and evaluated.

Table 16.9 Network model

Activity	Duration (days)	Immediately preceding activities
A		1
B	4	A
C	5	A
D	6	A
E	2	B
F	1	B
G	7	E
H	4	F
I	3	G, H
J	5	G, H, C and D
K	6	D
L	2	I, J and K

Note: Activities D, G and H must be completed before the commencement of J.

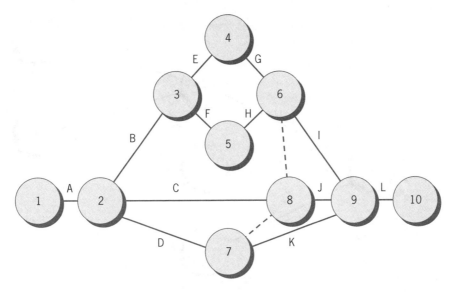

Figure 16.6 Network model

Example

A marketing manager is deciding among a number of alternatives:

1 Launch a new product that has a 0.3 probability of a £5 m profit if it is successful and a 0.7 probability of losing £1 m if it is unsuccessful.
2 Cut prices temporarily and stimulate market share. This would generate an additional £0.7 m.
3 Do nothing for the present, so that there would be neither a gain nor a loss.

Which of these alternatives should be chosen?
    The expected values of the three alternatives are:

1 $(0.7 \times -1.0) + (0.3 \times 5.0) = £0.8$ m
2 £0.7 m
3 £0

Alternative 1 is the best (see Figure 16.7).

Inventory model

Inventory models are employed to assess the best level of stocks to maintain, the frequency with which to place orders and the quantities to buy. These models provide information on how to minimise the total cost of the inventory system. The total inventory cost is the sum of total ordering costs and shortage costs. Ordering costs refer to the costs connected with placing orders and receiving inventory – salaries in

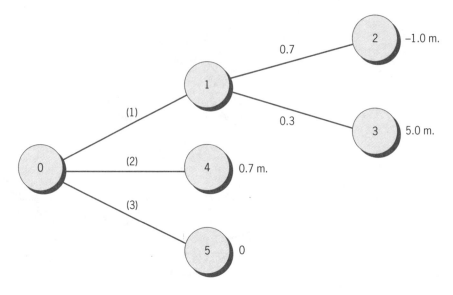

Figure 16.7 Alternative 1

purchasing and accounting departments, wages in the receiving area. Carrying costs are those associated with storage, such as warehouse rent and fuel costs. Shortages are the costs associated with a lost sale and loss of customer goodwill.

Inventory models can be quite complex and take into account a variety of different factors such as quantity discounts, backorders and economic lot sizes. The best-known and the simplest model is the Economic Order Quantity (EOQ) model, the purpose of which is to determine the optimum order quantity. The model assumes a demand pattern that is deterministic and at a constant rate, the instantaneous replenishment of inventory, constant inventory costs and no shortages. The algorithm used is:

$$Q^* = \sqrt{2DC_0/C_h}$$

where Q^* is the optimum order quantity, D is the annual demand in units, C_h is the holding cost per unit per year and C_0 is the ordering cost per order.

Unfortunately, the basic EOQ model may be unsuitable for many real-world situations where the basic assumptions of the model do not apply. Further refinements to the model can enable these difficulties to be overcome.

Queuing theory model

Queues arise because facilities cannot meet the demand for the service the facilities have been set up to provide. The purpose of applying queuing theory models or techniques is usually to facilitate the identification of an adequate but not-too-liberal service facility. If the service provision is too generous, the service facility will often be idle and incur unnecessary costs, such as idle employees. On the other hand, where excessive waiting time exists because the facility is inadequate, customer dissatisfaction can occur and a loss of important goodwill ensues. The aim of these techniques is to establish the economic equilibrium between the cost of the service and the cost associated with the possible loss of goodwill.

Solutions to queuing problems may be determined by common formulae. However, the situations in which they occur are complex and it is often preferable to use simulation methods (see below) to obtain a solution.

Markov analysis

Markov analysis has mainly been restricted to brand-switching behaviour and the impact it has had on market share.

Example

Research data shows the probabilities that a person will buy a particular brand of soap, given that they purchased a specific brand on the previous occasion (Table 16.10).

The current market shares of the brands are as follows:

Amy's	20%
Bebe's	30%
Celia's	50%

The task is to estimate the long-run market-share positions, given that the brand-switching probabilities remain constant. This can be done in several ways. One way is to multiply out the matrices thus:

$$1\begin{pmatrix} .5 & .5 & .4 \\ .2 & .4 & .3 \\ .3 & .1 & .3 \end{pmatrix}.\begin{pmatrix} .2 \\ .3 \\ .5 \end{pmatrix} = \begin{pmatrix} 0.45 \\ 0.31 \\ 0.24 \end{pmatrix}$$

$$2\begin{pmatrix} .5 & .5 & .4 \\ .2 & .4 & .3 \\ .3 & .1 & .3 \end{pmatrix}.\begin{pmatrix} 0.45 \\ 0.31 \\ 0.24 \end{pmatrix} = \begin{pmatrix} 0.476 \\ 0.286 \\ 0.238 \end{pmatrix}$$

Table 16.10 Markov analysis

Transition matrix	Next purchase		
Last purchase	Amy's brand	Bebe's brand	Celia's brand
Amy's brand	0.5	0.2	0.3
Bebe's brand	0.5	0.4	0.1
Celia's brand	0.4	0.3	0.3

$$3 \begin{pmatrix} .5 & .5 & .4 \\ .2 & .4 & .3 \\ .3 & .1 & .3 \end{pmatrix} . \begin{pmatrix} 0.476 \\ 0.286 \\ 0.238 \end{pmatrix} = \begin{pmatrix} 0.476 \\ 0.281 \\ 0.243 \end{pmatrix}$$

$$4 \begin{pmatrix} .5 & .5 & .4 \\ .2 & .4 & .3 \\ .3 & .1 & .3 \end{pmatrix} . \begin{pmatrix} 0.476 \\ 0.281 \\ 0.243 \end{pmatrix} = \begin{pmatrix} 0.476 \\ 0.28 \\ 0.244 \end{pmatrix}$$

$$5 \begin{pmatrix} .5 & .5 & .4 \\ .2 & .4 & .3 \\ .3 & .1 & .3 \end{pmatrix} . \begin{pmatrix} 0.476 \\ 0.28 \\ 0.244 \end{pmatrix} = \begin{pmatrix} 0.476 \\ 0.28 \\ 0.244 \end{pmatrix}$$

The solution is:

Amy's = 0.476
Bebe's = 0.28
Celia's = 0.244

The main limitation of the model is the assumption of a stationery transition matrix.

Simulation

The idea behind simulation is to find a satisfactory or close-to-best solution to a problem by using a mathematical model of the problem situation and testing it out by varying the various parameters to the model. Simulation does not employ an optimisation algorithm but simply portrays the performance of a particular system, given a set of input parameters. Simulation is usually employed when the problem under study is too complex to be treated by optimisation techniques. A problem may be judged to be too complex when it either cannot be expressed mathematically or the formulation is too involved for economic or practical purposes.

Simulation has been widely used by practitioners because of the degree of realism that can be included in simulation models and the ease with which such models can be explained to non-technical decision-makers.[6] In comparison with analytic techniques, such as queuing theory, simulation models do not require the stringent assumptions necessary for tractable solutions. The logic and mathematical relationships are usually more easily understood.

Since simulation models the expected behaviour of a system, the model has to be built from the perspective of the executive who is studying the system. The executive can then experiment with different factors and different scenarios to decide which gives the most satisfactory results. The executive can then experiment with a model rather than interfere with a system in order to understand its behaviour.

The technique of simulation consists of taking random samples from the probability distribution that represents the real-world system under study. Many real-world phenomena are 'normally' distributed and so in many cases probability estimates using the normal curve can often be employed. In the case of queues, however, other kinds of distributions may be more appropriate – such as a uniform or a random distribution – and we first need to establish how the events are distributed in reality. The inputs to the model consist of the observed values and the probabilities associated with each event.

Recent software developments for desktop and laptop computers have made it possible for simulations to be developed with comparative ease. An excellent software package is MicroSaint.[7] Illustrations of its use can be found in Proctor.[8, 9]

An excellent simulation package is available from Decision Support Laboratory[10] and an illustration of its use is given in Figure 16.8. Here, sales demand for a product is being simulated over a period of time. Decision Support Laboratory is a visual spreadsheet. It provides an easier and faster way to build, edit and explain a spreadsheet model. The basic building block of traditional spreadsheets is a cell. The basic building block of DS Lab is an element. With DS Lab, you define your model in the same way you would think through a problem, using symbols for elements such as inputs, variables, constants, series and tables to define the data with which you work.

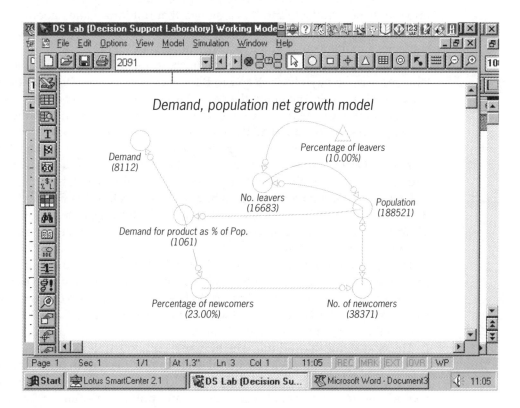

Figure 16.8 Simulation model

DS Lab shows graphically the logic of the model by letting the user represent and manipulate the data with symbols connected by arrows. The symbols (elements) display the data one step at a time, while leaving all the data accessible in an instant with the click of a mouse. The arrows display the relationship between the elements. DS Lab easily manages hundreds of elements over thousands of steps. Time is the parameter most commonly defined for these steps, so DS Lab provides a built-in calendar to define days, weeks, months or years. Steps may be defined as something other than time, such as geography or product type, by simply creating a list of items. The software will then automatically generate the values for each step of the user-defined parameters.

Game theory

Game theory has been found to be useful when considering marketing strategy problems. It helps to determine the best strategy that competing firms can adopt. Games can be constructed for any number of 'players' and the simplest of these to understand is the two-person game.

Example

In the model presented here (Table 16.11) there are two players, A and B. Each has three strategies available and it is assumed that full information about the outcome of each possible pair of strategies is available. The two players decide their strategies simultaneously and it is a one-shot game.

The usual way of showing this form of the game is indicated in Table 16.12. The table records the pay-offs to A and to B for each possible combination of strategies. For example the cell containing the pay-off 6,4 denotes a pay-off of 6 to A and 4 to B.

Examination of the pay-off table shows, by trial and error, that there are two strategy pairs (A1,B2) and (A2,B3) that satisfy the Nash equilibrium condition that each player's strategy is a best response to the other's. In order to model this game on a spreadsheet, it is necessary to use the data from the pay-off matrix to construct two separate pay-off tables for A and B, as shown in the main table.

First, the pay-off data for A has to be entered into cells C6 to E8. Next, the pay-off data for B has to be inserted into cells I6 to K8. To find A's best response to each of B's strategies, the column maximums for A's pay-off table have to be found. Enter @MAX(C6..C8) in cell C10.

This formula should then be copied from C10 to cells D10 and E10. The column maximum signifies the pay-off to A when it chooses its best response to B's strategy corresponding to that column. To find B's best response to each of A's strategies, the row maximums for B's pay-off table have to be found. Enter @MAX(I6..K6) in cell M6 and then copy the formula to M7 and M8.

The next step is to find out which, if any, pairs of strategies correspond to both a column maximum for A's pay-off table and a row maximum for B's pay-off table. This is accomplished by first identifying which cells in the pay-off tables contain the column and row maximums, respectively, and putting the number 1 in these cells. This identifying code (1) is put in cell G11.

Table 16.11 Game theory

	A	B	C	D	E	F	G	H	I	J	K
1											
2											
3		Payoff				Tables					
4	To A						To B			Row	
5		B1	B2	B3			B1	B2	B3	Max.	
6	A1	6	7	2			4	5	3		5
7	A2	4	2	6			5	4	7		7
8	A3	6	4	2			4	9	3		9
9 Col.											
10 Max.		6	7	6							
11						1 = code number					
12											
13		B1	B2	B3			B1	B2	B3		
14	A1	1	1	0		A1	0	1	0		
15	A2	0	0	1		A2	0	0	1		
16	A3	1	0	0		A3	0	1	0		
17											
18		B1 B2	B3								
19	A1	– NE	–			NE	–	Nash			
20	A2	– –	NE					Equilibrium			
21	A3	– –	–					Strategies			

Table 16.12 Pay-off matrix A,B

Strategies	B1	B2	B3
A1	6,4	7,5	2,3
A2	4,5	2,5	6,7
A3	6,4	4,4	2,3

We next create a new set of pay-off matrices in rows 14 to 16. In cell C14, enter @IF(C6=C$10,$G11,A11).

This will cause the number 1 (from cell G11) to appear in C14 if C6 equals the column maximum in C10 and 0, from cell A11, if it is not. This formula can now be copied from C14 to C15 and C16 as the row 10 is anchored with the $. In this example the code 1 appears in C16 as strategy A3 is A's best response if B plays B1.

To code A's best response to B2 and B3 copy from the three cells C14..C16 to the column sections commencing D14 and E14. To code B's best response to each of A's strategies it is necessary to indicate which cells in B's pay-off matrix correspond to the row maximums in cells M6 to M8. In cell I14: Enter @IF(I6=$M6,$G$11,$A$11).

Copy the formula from I14 to J14 and K14, then copy the three cells I14..K14 to the row sections commencing I15 and I16.

Nash equilibrium conditions are satisfied when each player receives the maximum pay-off possible, taking into account the other player's strategy. This means that there will be a 1 in both the coded pay-off matrices for this strategy combination. Nash equilibrium pairs in the final matrix can be coded NE in a single matrix of strategy combinations by adding the two matrices already coded and finding cells whose value is 2, i.e. where the strategy combination is both a column maximum for A and a row maximum for B. In cell C1: Enter @IF(+C14+I14>G11,H19,I19).

This last entry displays the code NE from cell H19 when the value in C19 is greater than the value 1 in cell G11, i.e. when it equals 2. The dash in I19 is displayed when C19 has the value less than 2. Copy this formula from C19 to the rest of the cells in the matrix C19..C21.

Using the basic principles developed, more complex games can be constructed. Such games might contain pay-off tables with larger numbers of rows and columns (see, for example, Rosser[11]). It would also be possible to consider other forms of pay-off. For example, the objective may be to minimise the maximum gain of the other player. In such a case a 3,4 strategy would be preferable from A's viewpoint to a 7,8 strategy. Alternatively, minimising the relative gain might be the object, in which case a 7,8 strategy would be preferred to a 2,4 strategy. While the construction of the pay-off tables and principles of calculation would be similar in all these cases, the rules to be applied would be different.

EXPERT SYSTEMS AND DECISION SUPPORT

An expert system provides expertise to help problem-solving. It can represent the best thinking of the top experts in the field that can lead to solutions to problems that are imaginative, accurate and efficient. An expert system has predictive modelling power and can act as an information-processing model of problem-solving in marketing, providing the desired answers for a given problem-solving situation and demonstrating how they would change for new situations.

Expert systems are most appropriately used in the following circumstances:

1 Where the key relationships are logical rather than arithmetical. Generating new ideas is more appropriate for an expert system. Advising on action to be taken in specific situations is another example.

2 Where the problem is semi-structured rather than structured. For structured problems, a traditional algorithm approach will do; for unstructured problems there may not be sufficient knowledge in the knowledge base to provide satisfactory results.

3 Where the knowledge in the domain is incomplete. Expert systems are most applicable in the domains of incomplete knowledge.

4 Where problem-solving in the domain requires a direct interface between the manager and the computer system. Situations of decision urgency and on-line decision support are most appropriate for expert system use.

The three major components of an expert system are:

- a user interface
- a knowledge base
- an inference engine.

The knowledge base includes the definitions of the objects and variables in the system, including data, assumptions, production rules (if–then statements), heuristics and models. The inference engine manipulates the elements in the knowledge base and combines it with information from the user to solve a particular problem.

Expert systems can be used for a variety of purposes. These include:

- *Interpretation*: inferring situation descriptions from sensor data. This is useful in observational market-research studies.

- *Prediction*: inferring the likely consequences of given situations. This is useful in forecasting.

- *Planning – designing actions*: campaign planning or even marketing planning is an area of application.

- *Diagnosis and monitoring*: inferring system malfunctions from observables. This is useful in the context of marketing control, monitoring performance against targets or budgets set.

- *Debugging*: prescribing remedies for malfunctions. Recommending contingency action when plans are not achieved.

- *Design*: configuring objects under constraints. Product design is an area where expert systems can be applied.

- *Repair*: putting contingency plans into action.

Given the wide array of applications for expert systems in marketing, it is not appropriate to discuss or illustrate expert systems in the generic sense. However, there are different commercial packages available that suit specific purposes. A good example is that provided by project-management systems software that incorporates an applications generator capable of facilitating the production of a marketing plan.

In marketing, expert systems have been used to examine single source data for trends, to filter marketing data for quality problems, to develop forecasting models, to set sales quotas, to qualify sales prospects and to train sales personnel.[12, 13]

McCann[14] has described several expert systems that have been useful to consumer packaged goods brand managers.

Neural networks

Whereas expert systems parody experts' thinking processes, neural networks are computer applications that mimic the human brain. One important aspect of neural networks is their ability to learn from their past activities in the sense that records of the system's past performance can influence processing in order to improve future performance. Theoretically, such systems could be self-improving.

The growth of interest in neural networks comes about as a result of the fact that they emulate not only the brain's reasoning but also its learning capabilities. Although neural network applications in marketing are sparse just now, researchers have documented several interesting applications. Kestylyn[15] has studied how neural networks can be used to identify the best sales prospects for a telemarketing operation to call from a list of customers who have not been active recently. Westland[16] has presented systems that save busy executives time by identifying and organising environmental and internal information for them. Proctor[17] has also suggested a potential application of neural networks in evaluating new product opportunities.

Breakthroughs in business intelligence

Neural networks and data mining software can now mimic human thought when processing vast amounts of sales data, thus allowing large companies to save millions of dollars, enter new markets, retain customers, track fraud and generally become more competitive.

Neural networks and artificial intelligence were among the hot issues in the fast-moving information technology industry in the early 1980s. But when they failed to deliver the instant wins that venture capitalists and others were seeking, neural computing and AI fell out of fashion and out of the high-tech spotlight.

Even Japan's much vaunted Fifth Generation computer project, which was begun in 1982 and was to use parallel processing and AI techniques to develop next-generation 'intelligent' machines, faded from sight.

But in spite of these early setbacks, neural computing, parallel processing and AI techniques have all made substantial advances in recent years aided, in part, by the dramatic advances in microprocessor power.

Although many researchers and high-tech start-ups now shun the AI tag, these advances coupled with more realistic expectations, have ensured that neural computing and AI have not been forgotten. Indeed, many of the technologies pioneered by AI researchers at the Massachusetts Institute of Technology and other laboratories on both sides of the Atlantic have begun to be incorporated into mainstream business applications.

Unlike conventional computing techniques, neural computing is modelled on the biological processes of the human brain and has many human-like qualities. For example, neural computers can learn from experience and do not need to be programmed with fixed rules or equations. They can analyse vast quantities of complex data and identify patterns from which predictions can be made.

They also tend to be more robust than their conventional counterparts. They have the ability to cope well with incomplete or 'fuzzy' data, and can deal with previously unspecified or new situations. As such, they are ideally suited to real world applications and can provide the solution to a host of currently impossible or commercially impractical problems.

In addition, the time needed to develop a neural application is often less than with a conventional programme because there are no algorithms or rules to define. The scope and accuracy of the finished application are also often improved since the neural computer can be exposed to many more examples than can be assimilated by a single human 'expert'. International Business Machines has, for example, integrated neural network and artificial intelligence technology into software applications, such as data mining packages.

Mr Evangelous Simoudis, a scientist at IBM's Almanden Research Center, says such techniques enable business users to sift through vast quantities of raw data in order to spot hidden trends or anomalies which might otherwise be missed. IBM's business intelligence and data mining software can mimic human thought when processing information called the 'verification model' or go beyond human logic to discover correlations between seemingly disparate data called the 'discovery model'.

The verification model confirms or refutes the hypothesis of a savvy business person while the discovery model reveals patterns that human logic might not see. The classic example was the unexpected connection between beer and nappies discovered during a data mining experiment on a US supermarket database. The study revealed that the people purchasing nappies on a Friday also tended to buy beer.

Before neural networks and artificial intelligence were used in business intelligence applications, companies lacked the ability to leverage the information they were collecting in data warehouses. They were unable to connect consumer-buying patterns, customise promotions to target a range of customers with different needs or identify potentially fraudulent insurance claims based on past behaviour.

At best, information analysis was done manually, perhaps as much as 90 per cent of analysts' time was spent gathering information, leaving only 10 per cent of the time to digest and analyse the data. With IBM's business intelligence technology, however, customers are now able to save millions of dollars, enter new markets, retain customers, track fraud and generally be more competitive.

Among IBM's customers: Merrill Lynch developed a Trusted Global Advisor (TGA) network that gives up-to-the-minute information on customer portfolios and investments. With access to information in real-time, brokers can help customers make better decisions about their financial futures.

Cadbury's saw its market share of the chocolate market slip from 33 per cent to 28 per cent, but an IBM business intelligence solution helped the company focus attention on those product lines that appealed to customers and Cadbury's market share is now back up to 30 per cent.

The Safeway supermarket chain in the UK is improving customer service by tracking product purchases – a system created by IBM in only a few weeks. Preferred customers receive marketing information that appeals directly to their individual needs and tastes.

Southern California Edison uses IBM database technology to identify unanticipated opportunities that saved millions of dollars for the United States' second largest utility. One application that looked at credit collection and overdue accounts helped recover more than $8m. The company says its overall return on investment for its databases is 600 per cent.

Neural computing and AI techniques also lie behind many of the sophisticated search engines and intelligent agents found on the Internet and corporate intranets. As Mr Mike Lynch, founder and managing director of Autonomy, the Cambridge-based intelligent agent pioneer, notes: 'In business today, the ability to access the right information at the right time is absolutely critical. The problem is that technologies which promise this ability, namely the Internet and corporate intranets, are flawed in their delivery. Rather than giving users the tools to assimilate the right information into useful knowledge, they are overloading them with too much irrelevant dross.' Autonomy's latest products include server products designed to deliver personalised information to Internet and intranet users in a dynamic fashion. They use the dynamic reasoning engine technology developed by Cambridge Neurodynamics, a recognised world leader in the application of neural network and pattern recognition technologies.

AI and neural computing techniques are used in 'case-based reasoning' tools such as those developed by California-based Inference for intelligent problem solving in help desk, customer support and other computer-telephony integration packages.

Other AI and neural computing-based systems are used for credit scoring and to help pinpoint and prevent fraud in areas as diverse as equity trading and cellular telephone networks.

Meanwhile, Neural Technologies, a Hampshire based start-up has launched a software package called Prospect Explorer. The product, developed in conjunction with Australia's Straits Resources group, is a geological exploration tool with the capacity to analyse a range of different types of raw exploration data and automatically detect and prioritise anomalies. 'Neural computing and other forms of intelligent technology are providing leading edge solutions to complex business problems,' says Mr Nick Ryman-Tubb, chief executive of the Neural Technologies. 'From manufacturing, banking and finance, defence, telecommunications, pharmaceuticals to the holiday industry, we have already applied neural computing to a wide variety of commercial and industrial applications – particularly those which have, until now, been either impossible or commercially impractical for conventional computing to address,' says Mr Ryman-Tubb.

Nevertheless, even neural computing enthusiasts concede that neural networks will not replace conventional computers. 'Neural computing should not be viewed as a competitor to conventional computing, but rather as a complementary technique,' notes Neural Technologies.

The most successful neural computing applications to date have been those which operate in conjunction with other computing techniques. For example, using a neural network to perform a first pass over a set of incoming data, then passing the results over to a conventional system for subsequent processing.

However, with the growing emphasis on autonomy, intelligence and an increased amount of information required by businesses, traditional computer processing technology can only cope through faster hardware with more complex, bespoke software. With this approach, the question is: how long is it going to take to write this software, how many different versions for each variation and once written, how safe is it from bugs? As Neural Technologies notes in its white paper: 'The problem, growing towards the millennium, is that engineers no longer have the luxury in development to calculate all the algorithms or identify all the rules in these complex systems. In fact, most of these systems are so chaotic that doing so would be futile and prone to failure.'

'Neural computers, with their ability to learn from examples, rather than needing to be explicitly programmed, offer a means of making such tasks tractable to a machine.'

Source: Paul Taylor.[18] Reprinted with permission.

Other applications in marketing

Neuroshell is an expert system shell that can operate in binary or analogue mode. Thus far we have examined its use only in the analogue mode. The binary mode enables us to set up an expert system that uses essentially categorical data. Kotler[1] provides an illustration of how a firm might respond to a competitor cutting its price. The conditions and corresponding actions can be set into a decision table (Table 16.13).

The top half of the table shows the various conditions that can occur – the actions that can be undertaken by competitors (inputs). A 'Y' indicates the presence of the condition, whereas an 'N' or a blank space indicates the condition's absence. In the bottom half of the table the reactions (outputs) to the conditions are shown as a 1 in the appropriate column.

The seven cases can then be entered into Neuroshell in its binary mode of operation and the pattern of inputs and outputs learned. After learning has taken place, if we then enter into the programme the nature of the competitor's action, the programme will respond with the appropriate output – what action should be taken (the lower half of the table).

Table 16.13 Decision table showing reaction to a competitor's price cut

Reaction to competitor cutting price	1	2	3	4	5	6	7
Competitor cuts price	N	Y	Y	Y	Y	Y	Y
Competitor's price stable		Y					
Price cut likely to have a significant effect on sales		N	N	Y	Y	Y	Y
Cut is likely to be a permanent cut		N	Y	N	Y	Y	Y
Price has been cut by more than 4%					Y	N	N
Price cut between 2.1 and 4.0%					N	Y	N
Price cut less than 2%					N	N	Y
Drop the price to competitor's price					1		
Offer self-liquidating premium to steal limelight from competitor						1	
Run temporary cents off to dilute the effect of the price cut							1
Hold our prices at present level: continue to watch competitor's price	1	1	1	1			

Source: Kotler.[1]

The ability of neural network shells to work with binary data opens up all kinds of applications for routine strategic decision-making.

Further information on neural nets

Eberhart and Dobbins[19] present a comprehensive text on neural network developments and include C source code for several types of neural networking models. This includes the feed-forward backward propagation model discussed in this article. More material is available from Roy Dobbins on request. McClelland and Rumelhart[20] have also produced a useful handbook that includes source code and diskettes. The work includes material on the backward propagation model and provides tutorial assistance. The major limitation on applications using PC-based neural networking software just now is that imposed by the hardware. The complexities of some types of pattern make it difficult for software to learn the pattern within a reasonable timespan. Ward Systems[21] has tried to overcome this problem with respect to Neuroshell by offering a piece of hardware that accelerates the process. However, it may only be that when parallel programming becomes available on the PC, a step will have been taken in the direction of solving this particular limitation.

Statistical tools and decision support

See Chapter 10.

SUMMARY

Marketing information systems exist to help marketing managers get to grips with the volumes of data with which they are constantly bombarded. The marketing information system provides management with a variety of reports to help its decision-making.

Marketing planning requires the size of current and potential markets to be carefully measured and estimated. There are several approaches to forecasting. Some methods rely on asking questions of people, while others involve the statistical analysis of historical data.

An indication and examples of how management science/operational research techniques and tools can be applied to marketing problems is given. Methods considered included linear programming, transportation models, assignment models, network models, decision trees, inventory models, queuing theory models, Markov analysis, simulation and game theory.

A growing area of interest and importance in the area of decision-support systems are expert systems. There are many opportunities for the implementation of expert systems in marketing.

Questions

1   How would you define a marketing information system?

2   How does a marketing information system differ from marketing research?

3   What are marketing decision-support mechanisms? How do they relate to the marketing information system?

4   Indicate the various ways in which sales management can make use of a marketing information system.

5   Why is it important to be able to measure the size of current and future markets?

6   What are the various levels at which market demand may be measured?

7   When forecasting future demand for products or services, what should be the nature of the basic approach?

8   Under what circumstances might it be appropriate to undertake a survey of buyers' intentions in order to establish the nature of demand for a product?

9   When might expert opinion be an appropriate forecasting method?

10   Time-series analysis is a method of statistical forecasting. What are the four components of a time series?

11   Multiple regression analysis is one of several ways of forecasting with the aid of time-series analysis. Explain the principles involved in applying multiple regression analysis to time-series forecasting.

12   Under what circumstances might exponential smoothing be a useful way of forecasting demand?

13   Statistical demand analysis employs multiple regression analysis to explain variations in demand for a product or service. How might it be used to forecast future demand?

14   Explain the principles involved in using epidemic models to forecast the demand for new products.

15   How might we forecast the sales of a new product through multiple retail outlets?

16   Indicate the kinds of marketing problems to which the following might be usefully applied:

   (a)   Linear programming
   (b)   Transportation models
   (c)   Assignment models
   (d)   Network models
   (e)   Decision trees
   (f)   Inventory models
   (g)   Queuing theory
   (h)   Markov analysis
   (i)   Simulation
   (j)   Game theory

17   Suggest potential applications for expert systems in marketing management.

Case study 16.1 Demand for agricultural tractors

Average farm size (acres)	Number of farms	AV hp tractors sold	Farms income index	Tractor population	AV price of tractors (units)	Sales of tractors (units)	Average tractor horse power (all producers)	Average big tractor horse power (all producers)	A&B share small tractor sales	A&B share big tractor sales	Year
232	7256	51.2	100	10425	100	1114	48.0	58.3	12.3	11.5	77
233	7103	51.4	101.5	10200	100	1108	48.2	59.1	12.5	11.6	78
235	7002	51.7	101.6	10000	101.5	1196	48.5	60.2	12.8	11.7	79
238	6874	52.4	98.3	9987	101.6	1024	48.8	61.2	13.2	11.8	80
240	6687	52.8	96.2	9915	101.8	1056	49.2	62.3	13.4	11.3	81
246	6502	53.1	95.3	9824	102.1	995	49.4	62.7	13.5	11.8	82
253	6411	54.8	97.2	9810	102.7	1087	49.3	62.8	12.9	12.0	83
258	6301	56.7	96.3	9786	103.5	1056	49.6	63.4	13.2	12.5	84

260	6218	57.5	95.1	9752	104.5	1034	50.1	64.2	13.4	12.8	85
263	6154	58.3	96.5	9664	106.8	1025	50.7	65.3	13.4	12.0	86
268	6058	59.5	97.2	9615	105.6	1048	51.6	66.8	13.6	12.4	87
270	5947	60.5	100.5	9611	105.7	1189	52.3	68.1	13.8	11.8	88
272	5821	61.2	101.2	9588	105.7	1205	54.6	69.0	13.8	12.1	89
275	5714	61.8	102.4	9615	106.4	1314	55.0	69.5	13.9	12.4	90
278	5621	62.4	103.5	9623	108.6	1412	55.1	70.0	13.7	12.5	91
281	5545	62.7	102.0	9625	110.5	1248	55.3	71.2	14.1	12.4	92
284	5432	63.1	100.5	9634	111.5	1232	55.6	72.1	14.0	12.4	93
287	5308	63.8	96.2	9651	112.4	1145	56.1	72.5	13.8	11.8	94
290	5126	64.5	98.5	9667	112.4	1045	56.8	72.8	14.0	12.1	95

Question

Prepare forecasts of sales of all tractor sizes for the next five years.
Hint: Use the regression feature in Lotus 1–2–3, Aseasyas or some other spreadsheet to help with your calculations.

Case study 16.2   Kenbrock

Kenbrock Timber Finishes Pty Ltd manufactures a range of Cabot's timber treatments. The firm thinks of itself as being one of the smaller national Australian brands, and claims 25 per cent of the total national paint market in Australia. Being in the wood-finishing business, the company reckons its main rivals market paint, wallpaper and other decorative material. It counts on four major competitors, among whom are Dulux and Bristol, both of whom sell Kenbrock's products in their own stores and are important Kenbrock customers. Besides distributing nationally throughout all the States, Kenbrock obtains export orders, mainly from Thailand, which account for roughly 3 to 4 per cent of its total sales volume. In pursuance of its strategy of full market penetration, the company manufactures more than 250 individual products with different features, colours and sizes.

In the past, the company experienced difficulties with its approach to forecasting. Even though the company possessed such a large product range that was distributed nationally, it continued to use a simple naïve twelve-month moving average on each product to forecast and schedule production requirements. However, from the analysis of past sales data, a seasonal pattern corresponded closely to the weather conditions observed in each State.

As a result of using a simple moving average method, the company's forecasting system failed to incorporate the seasonal pattern into its forecasting process which produced misleading forecast results. It was taken for granted that the rolling average was valid, but in the real world some product ranges varied between 25 and 30 per cent either side of the average with the seasonal variations. As the problem existed it led to a combination of increased inventory cost (caused by a build-up of stock) and failure to meet customer demand at peak times. Such a situation impeded the company's market competitiveness.

Source: D Waddell and A S Sohal.[22]

Question

Suggest how the firm might have resolved its forecasting difficulties.

Case study 16.3   Restaurant strategies

Two restaurants, A and B, are positioned at either end of a village and compete with one another for business. Each can adopt one of three strategies with respect to the evening menu and each restaurant has full information about the outcome of each possible pair of strategies available. Both restaurants decide their strategy for the evening meal simultaneously and can only change the strategy for the next evening meal – it is a one-shot game. The table below records the pay-offs to restaurant A and restaurant B for each possible combination of strategies.

Pay-off matrix A,B (evening meal sales turnover '£00)

	b1	b2	b3
a1	2,1	3,2	6,1
a2	4,2	4,2	5,3
a3	4F,4	3,4	1,3

Question

Which strategy leads to each restaurant receiving the maximum possible pay-off, taking into account the other restaurant's strategy?

Case study 16.4   Brand switching

Studies indicate the following probabilities that a person will buy a particular brand of jam, given that they purchased a specific brand on the previous occasion, as follows:

| | *Next purchase* | | |
Last purchase	A	B	C
A	.6	.1	.3
B	6	.2	.2
C	4	.3	.3

Question

Given that the current market shares of the brands are:
A 40%
B 30%
C 30%
estimate the long-run market share position.

Case study 16.5 | # Simon Theodolou, hairstylists

Simon Theodolou runs two large hairdressing salons in the Midlands. Each salon operates as a separate limited company, with Simon owning half the shares in each one and the salon manager owning the other half. Services such as materials purchase and laundry are provided centrally, and economies of scale help ensure that the salons remain highly profitable. The salons' reputation in terms of the quality of the hairdressing is one of the best in Britain, with stylists being regularly entered in competitions, and Simon also operates a training school for his own staff and for hairdressers from other salons.

As a regular routine, each salon collects daily data on the number of clients seen (including a breakdown of the services bought), the daily takings, and the takings for each stylist. These figures are aggregated weekly and monthly, and comparisons are made with previous months and years. Comparisons are also made between the salons, so Simon and his co-directors can assess whether the individual salons are improving or worsening, and whether they are doing better or worse in comparison with each other.

In the short term, the directors are planning to open a third salon in Wolverhampton; in the longer term, the intention is to expand through the Midlands, or even nationally. Each director is well aware that expansion of the group will strengthen the individual salons, not only because of the economies of scale in central services, but also because of the greater impact on public perceptions that membership of a large chain would imply. The problem for Simon is that he finds it hard to predict whether a new salon will be a success or not; experience has shown that it takes about a year for business to build up to its permanent level.

Simon also finds it hard to benchmark performances; in other words, he doesn't know whether his salons could be doing even better overall than they are, because he only makes comparisons one with another. Aware that his present systems, though better than most hairdressing salons', are still somewhat naive, he decided to call in a firm of consultants, Midlands Marketing, to re-analyse his figures and come up with some new recommendations. The aggregated figures for the previous twelve months for each salon are as laid out below.

Birmingham (12 stylists)

Month	Perms	Cut & B/dry	Highlights	Tinting	No. of clients	Av. clients per stylist	Takings (£)	Takings per stylist (£)
Oct	75	1002	98	384	1559	130	42,393	3,533
Nov	110	1235	97	342	1784	146	49,552	4,129
Dec	125	1104	98	374	1701	142	51,730	4,311
Jan	62	804	73	205	1144	143	32,432	4,054
Feb	77	843	76	227	1223	153	34,966	4,371
Mar	84	837	74	229	1224	153	37,430	4,679
Apr	79	997	87	260	1423	142.3	40,555	4,055
May	93	1055	78	273	1499	149.9	44,970	4,497
Jun	104	973	84	285	1446	144.6	46,272	4,627
July	73	904	78	240	1295	144	34,317	3,813
Aug	83	944	72	248	1347	150	36,908	4,100
Sept	97	904	70	243	1314	146	39,157	4,351

Coventry (8 stylists)

Month	Perms	Cut & B/dry	Highlights	Tinting	No. of clients	Av. clients per stylist	Takings (£)	Takings per stylist (£)
Oct	60	798	75	210	1143	143	32,678	4,085
Nov	79	837	78	210	1204	151	34,820	4,353
Dec	114	970	92	246	1422	178	45,504	5,688
Jan	42	605	54	207	908	114	22,700	2,838
Feb	62	698	54	193	1007	126	27,586	3,448
Mar	73	620	56	208	957	119	28,953	3,619
Apr	82	980	75	241	1378	172	37,895	4,737
May	93	995	72	235	1395	174	37,386	4,673
Jun	82	825	71	198	1176	147	31,125	3,891
Jul	75	807	64	208	1154	144	33,408	4,176
Aug	73	798	61	183	1115	139	29,938	3,742
Sept	48	809	67	210	1134	142	30,448	3,806

Simon asked Midlands Marketing to come up with ideas for improving his systems, and also to forecast what his businesses will be doing over the next year. He also wants to know how he can predict the performance of the proposed new salon in Wolverhampton, and other salons in the future.

(Case contributed by Jim Blythe.)

Questions

1 Using the above figures, predict the takings for the next twelve months for each salon.

2 What seasonal trends can be discovered within the above data?

3 If Simon were to open his new salon next March, and employ six stylists to begin with, what would be a reasonable expectation for the salon's turnover in the second year?

4 What other information could Simon collect in order to make the predictions more accurate?

5 What differences are apparent between the two salons in terms of the business done?

Further reading

Ashill, N and Jobber, D (1999) The impact of environmental uncertainty perceptions, decision-maker characteristics and work environment characteristics on the perceived usefulness of marketing information systems (MkIS): a conceptual framework, *Journal of Marketing Management*, 15(6), pp 519–40.

Attaran, M (1992) *Management Science Information Systems*, New York: Wiley (includes a disk on which there are various management science tools, including a simulation program).

Cohen, M A, Jehoshua, E, Teck, H H (1997) An anatomy of a decision support system for developing and launching line extensions, *Journal of Marketing Research* 34, February, pp 117–29.

Goff, M (1997) Mapping out markets, *Provider*, 23(10), October, pp 79+ (2 pp).

Hoover, S V and Perry, R F (1989) *Simulation: A problem-solving approach*, New York: Addison-Wesley.

Jones, J W and McLeod, R (1986) The structure of executive information systems: an exploratory analysis, *Decision Science*, 17, pp 220–49.

Kotler, P A (1966) A design for the firm's marketing nerve centre, *Business Horizons*, Fall, pp 63–74.

Li, E (1997) Perceived importance of information system success factors: a meta analysis of group differences, *Information and Management*, 32, pp 15–28.

McConagle, J J and Vella, C M (1990) *Outsmarting the Competition*, Naperville, IL: Sourcebooks.

Marshall, K P (1996) *Marketing Information Systems*, Danvers, MA: Boyd & Fraser.

Mohanty, R P and Deshmukh, S G (1997) Evolution of a decision support system for human resource planning in a petroleum company, *International Journal of Production Economics*, 51(3), September, pp 251–61.

Morris, S (1990) *Using Personal Computers in Marketing*, Oxford: NCC Blackwell.

Pereira, R (1999) Factors influencing consumer perceptions of web-based decision support systems, *Logistics Information Management*, 12(1/2), pp 157–81.

Watson, H J and Blackstone, J H (1989) *Computer Simulation*, New York: Wiley.

Yava, U (1996) Demand forecasting in a service setting, *Journal of International Marketing and Marketing Research*, 21(1), February, pp 3–11.

References and notes

[1] Kotler, P (1988) *Marketing Management: Planning, analysis and control* (6th edn), Upper Saddle River, NJ: Prentice-Hall, p 525.

[2] SNAP software, Mercator Systems, 5 Mead Court, Bristol, B35 3UW. Tel + 44(0) 1454 280800; Fax + 44(0) 1454 281216; http://www.mercator.co.uk.

[3] Samways, A and Whittcome, K (1994) UK brand strategies, *A Financial Times Management Report*, p 108.

[4] Kotler, P and Lilien, G (1983) *Marketing Decision-Making: A model-building approach*, New York: Harper & Row.

[5] Bass, F (1969) A new product growth model for consumer durables, *Management Science*, 15 January, pp 215–27.

[6] Hoover, S V and Perry, R F (1989) *Simulation: A problem-solving approach*, New York: Addison-Wesley.

[7] MicroSaint: Rapid Data Ltd, Crescent House, Crescent Road, Worthing, West Sussex, BN11 5RW (computer software).

[8] Proctor, R A (1994a) Queues and the power of simulation in helping with business decisions and problems, *Management Decision*, 32(1), pp 50–5.

[9] Proctor, R A (1994b) Simulation in management services, *Management Services*, 38(1), January, pp 18–23.

[10] Decision Support Laboratory, *The Visual Spreadsheet*, DS Group, Inc, 474 North Street, Greenwich, CT 06830–3449, USA, Version 2.0.

[11] Rosser, M (1995) Modelling game theory with spreadsheets, *Cheer*, 9(2), pp 15–18.

[12] Schmitz, J D, Armstrong, G D and Little, J D C (1990) Cover story: automated news findings in marketing, *Interfaces*, 20(6), Nov/Dec, pp 29–38.

[13] Steinberg, M and Planck, R E (1990) Implementing expert systems into business-to-business marketing practice, *Journal of Business and Industrial Marketing*, 5(2), pp 15–26.

[14] McCann, J M (1986) *The Marketing Workbench*, Homewood, IL: Dow-Jones Irwin.

[15] Kestylyn, J (1992) Application watch, *AI Expert*, January, pp 63–4.

[16] Westland, J C (1992) Self-organising executive information networks, *Decision Support Systems*, 8, pp 41–53.

[17] Proctor, R A (1992) Marketing decision support systems: a role for neural networking, *Marketing Intelligence and Planning*, 10(1), pp 21–6.

[18] Taylor, P (1997a) Breakthroughs in business intelligence, *Financial Times*, 7 May.

[19] Eberhart, R C and Dobbins, R W (1990) *Neural Network PC Tools*, London: Academic Press.

[20] McClelland, J L and Rumelhart, D E (1988) *Explorations in Parallel Distributed Processing: A handbook of models, programs and exercises*, Cambridge, MA: MIT Press.

[21] Ward Systems (1989) *Neuroshell: Neural Network Shell Program*, Ward Systems Inc., 228 W Patrick Street, Frederick, MD 21701, USA.

[22] Waddell, D and Sohal, A S (1994) Forecasting: the key to managerial decision-making, *Management Decision*, 32(1), p 46.

Further case studies

Watching paint fly

ICI Paints aims for global coverage and 30 per cent returns by the millennium. Paint has become more critical to Imperial Chemical Industries than ever in the company's history. Before the demerger of Zeneca, paint accounted for seven per cent of the old ICI group profit. It is 23 per cent now and has become crucial to improving financial performance. Moreover, ICI Paints has been ordered to climb a mountain by Mr Charles Miller Smith, who was appointed ICI's chief executive two years ago with a brief to shake up the group. The paint business's annual average return on net assets for the past decade has been 18 per cent. Many in the industry regard this as, at least, reasonable – and some wish they could do as well. Mr Miller Smith wants the returns at a regular 30 per cent before the millennium. The man charged with this task is Mr Peter Kirby, who succeeded Mr Herman Scopes as chief executive of ICI Paints in 1995. Mr Scopes had presided over ICI's emergence as the world's biggest paintmaker during the previous 10 years, but had not been rewarded with a seat on the ICI main board and decided to retire.

The change at Slough, where ICI Paints is headquartered, is palpable. This was a business that mirrored the 'imperial' part of ICI's name. Slough was the centre of a world painted increasingly dark blue – the corporate colour – as ICI expanded by acquisition. There was a strong element of expatriate control, with visiting potentates fanning out to far parts of the empire. Mr Kirby has rapidly changed things.

ICI Paints is now run by a widely scattered team consisting of a Brazilian, who looks after the Mercosur region, a Malaysian Chinese woman, who looks after Asia, an American, a British planner and a Scots-Canadian, all captained by Mr Kirby, a Johannesburg-born Australian who moved from his home in Melbourne to take the job, unencumbered by years of British-based corporate conditioning. Only Mr Kirby and Mr John Thompson, the business's chief planner, are based in Slough.

The team meets en masse, in person, once a quarter but holds frequent videoconferences. ICI Paints is now run globally. Mr Kirby questioned whether Slough should remain the world HQ but, since it is 20 minutes from London's Heathrow Airport, Slough is as good as anywhere else. None of this detracts from Mr Scopes's achievements. He led the pioneering stage of development; a new approach is needed now.

ICI made its most significant leap forward in paint in 1986 when it spent $550m acquiring Glidden of the US. Both were in the world's top 10 league as paintmakers, but ICI had a big geographical hole in its markets by not being in the US. Glidden brought ICI US market share, thereby making it a genuine world player.

Other chemicals giants were in the same race: for example, BASF of Germany was similarly acquisitive in the Americas, while PPG of the US was breaking out of its domestic market in the opposite direction. Courtaulds has used its great technical strength in marine paints to dominate the niche worldwide.

Driving this rush for empire was the process of globalisation, particularly in automotive markets. Global manufacturers wanted global suppliers. Moreover, entry costs were rising. 'It cost $300m to set up a new laboratory to service the automotive industry. It is no wonder there are no new entrants into the sector,' observes Mr Neville Petersen, chief executive of Courtaulds Coatings.

It was not just about getting bigger, however. The paint business is highly segmented. Half is concerned with decorative or architectural paints, but the rest of the market is made up of high technology industrial coatings for niche users.

ICI Paints was spread too thin. It dropped out the paints used for agricultural, construction and earthmoving equipment, for instance, as well as aerospace coatings. For five years it persevered with a joint venture with DuPont to try and break the grip of BASF, PPG and Herberts – a subsidiary of Germany's Hoechst, Europe's largest chemicals group – on car factory paint shops but, in 1994, left DuPont to carry on alone. Now ICI is in only three paint sectors – decorative, vehicle refinish (or VR, products used for car paintwork repair) and packaging, which is mainly concerned with cans, which not only have to be decorated on the outside, but coated internally with a thin layer of inert lacquer to stop the metal of the can contaminating the contents.

In general, high technology, specialised niches provide good margins, while decorative coatings are high-volume products and are much nearer the commodities end of the paint business. Many paint giants – notably PPG, Courtaulds and Herberts – have exited decorative markets altogether. The question is whether ICI now has enough muscle to achieve 30 per cent on net assets given its products and market mixes. Geographical spread – but in depth and in emerging as well as mature markets – will be essential, enabling ICI to sell its superior decorative products to more people. Mr Kirby says that, in mature economies, the paint industry grows at three-quarters of the rate of growth of gross domestic product. In developing countries, growth is between one-and-a-half and twice the rate of GDP. South American and Asian markets are therefore the key to high and higher returns, although it is equally necessary to strengthen share in mature economies, if only to try and keep prices stable. With this in mind, Mr Scopes initiated the purchase of Grow, another large US paintmaker, just before he retired, plus a smaller one, to improve ICI's share of US decorative markets to 15 per cent. Since then, Bunge has been acquired to provide a way into South America and more recent purchases have been made in Puerto Rico and Vietnam. An attempt to buy into India's Asian Paints last month has so far been repulsed.

ICI's strengths in paint are both technical and managerial. The company is widely respected in the industry for its consumer marketing skills and distributive know-how. Mr Kirby's team runs VR and packaging – the two industrial niches – as self-contained businesses in their own right. Decorative markets are organised geographically and run by local nationals, attuned to local culture but versed in ICI marketing skills.

Car repairers are being trained at ICI centres in more than 30 countries, new factories have been opened in China and Thailand, to complement others in Pakistan, India, Malaysia, Singapore, Indonesia, Taiwan, the Philippines and Vietnam. There are research and development laboratories in Malaysia, Slough and Strongsville, Ohio.

With the global framework in place all now depends on the people running the businesses. Mr Kirby thinks they will succeed, not least because of the way ICI Paints has changed the way it runs itself. 'Brits have very creditable flexibility but sometimes lack of determination,' he says. He believes that the multinational structure has plugged any weaknesses.

Source: Ian Hamilton Fazey (1997) *Financial Times*, 25 September. Reprinted with permission.

Question

Outline a role for marketing research within ICI Paints. What specific tasks for marketing research would you consider imperative?

Case study 2 | ## China's future dragons

Guests for dinner at the headquarters of Sichuan Changhong, China's largest television producer, are offered a rare treat – pan-fried leopard followed by braised bear in soy sauce.

But then Changhong itself is an unusual creature: a profitable, state-owned business which, unlike most of China's loss-making state enterprises, has beaten back foreign competitors in its domestic market. Now it wants to follow in the footsteps of Japan's exporters and South Korea's conglomerates, and become another of Asia's world-beating companies. Between mouthfuls, Mr Li Tibin, Changhong's chief financial officer, outlines the company's plans. 'By 2005,' he says, 'Changhong aims to be one of the top 500 companies in the world.' The group expects to take a third of the Chinese colour TV market this year and has announced plans to start selling Changhong TV sets in the US from 1999. The company is just one of a band of Chinese state enterprises hoping to establish themselves as international competitors, with their own brand names. Take Qingdao Haier or Guangdon Kelon, the two largest makers of refrigerators in China. Both have increased their share of the home market (to a combined 45 per cent) in spite of the numbers of international white-goods makers pouring into China.

Now Qingdao Haier, having established its first overseas facility in Indonesia, is involved in talks to set up factories in South Africa and Mexico. The company said it sold 200,000 refrigerators outside China last year, and claims to be Asia's largest refrigerator exporter to Europe. Or take Legend, China's best-selling personal-computer maker. In the first six months of this year, it sold 133,360 PCs, increasing its market share from 8 per cent in the first half of 1996 to 10.4 per cent. In the same period, IBM's share fell from 7.9 to 6.7 per cent and Compaq's fell from 8.2 to 6.2 per cent.

Or consider Wuxi Little Swan, which sells 40 per cent of all automatic washing machines in China. It has operations in South-East Asia and is investigating opportunities in Europe.

The mystery is how a clutch of thriving firms has emerged from the debris of China's failing state sector. The challenge for the companies is how to handle the next transition, from national champions to global competitors. Their ability to meet this challenge will matter not only to world trade and to the companies they want to compete with. It will also make a difference to China's government, as it struggles to cope with the problems of the state sector as a whole.

Half of China's state-owned industrial companies incurred net losses last year, up from one-third two years ago. Profits of state-sector companies have fallen from 6 per cent of gross domestic product in the early 1980s to less than 1 per cent in 1996. State companies account for one-third of industrial production, but employ roughly two-thirds of the urban workforce. The management of thousands of failed state enterprises – and the potential for social unrest in the face of looming mass redundancies – is therefore one of the thorniest problems facing China. The country's Communist leadership is now gearing up for next month's Party Congress – which is held every five years and is the most important event of the Chinese political calendar. Reform of the state sector is top of the Congress's concerns. China's leadership appears to be edging towards agreement that some state companies must be privatised to give them greater scope. But since the government is fearful of being criticised for selling off the family silver, the process is likely to be slow.

The question is, though, why has a handful of state-owned, or predominantly state-owned, companies broken the mould? There are three explanations.

First, commercial independence. The few profitable Chinese state businesses have all, for different reasons, been spared the worst of state interference.

Guangdong Kelon, the white-goods maker, is the most successful township and village enterprise in China. (TVEs are loosely controlled by local authorities rather than the central government.) A company official says it has been left largely to its own devices: 'As a TVE we don't get much favourable treatment, but then we don't get burdened with the social and commercial responsibilities which many state-owned enterprises suffer.' Other companies have been left alone even though they have ties with national or provincial bodies. Changhong has close links with the military (it used to be a big equipment supplier to the People's Liberation Army). Wuxi Little Swan is connected to the government of Jiangsu province. But both were left alone at first – and their success has won them greater freedom.

Changhong, for example, holds great sway over the municipal government in Mianyang, western China, which has experienced the worst reported case of labour unrest this year following the failure of state businesses. Bureaucrats have little incentive to interfere with the winning formula of the one local company that generates sizeable revenues and employment.

Second, managerial flair. Mr Brewer Stone, the chief representative in Shanghai of Prudential Securities, a US brokerage, says: 'There seems to be a myth that there are no great managers in China. But there is a small pool of people with real drive, who have vision, who are micro-managers, who eat, live and breathe their work.'

Given a little room to manoeuvre, they have succeeded in introducing fundamental, but previously foreign, business principles to long-cossetted Chinese companies.

Mr Zhang Ruimin, Haier's president, has been a stickler for quality control. In the 1980s he instilled in the workers the importance of reliability by forcing them to destroy faulty refrigerators by hand. The emergence of Hongta Tobacco from the ranks of China's many provincial cigarette makers is credited to the leadership of the former president Mr Chu Shijian and his insistence on buying state-of-the-art tobacco-rolling machinery, rather than cheap, second-hand goods. Hongta is now the largest cigarette producer in Asia (though, since tobacco is a heavily protected market, it is hard to tell how competitive it really is).

Third, the challenge of foreign competition. The domestic-appliances sector is full of competitive state-owned enterprises. That is no accident. It is one of the few markets that has been almost fully opened to foreign companies, forcing domestic companies to hone their production and marketing skills.

'The government does not protect our industry,' says a representative of Little Swan. 'As long as wolves are coming into the sheep pen, the sheep have to stand up and fight back.' Similarly with colour TVs. Mr Stephen Young, general manager of Sound and Vision for Philips in China, says:

'Standards are improving in China every day and as far as consumer electronics are concerned there are some very competitive, very progressive Chinese companies.'

In rare cases, Chinese companies owe their success to a competitive advantage that foreign companies find hard to duplicate. Erdos Group, for example, produces nearly a third of the world's cashmere and looks set to increase its dominance thanks to its location in Inner Mongolia – home of half the world's cashmere-producing goats. Founder Group, a software company established by people from Beijing University, leads the world market in electronic publishing and software in Mandarin Chinese. It has opened subsidiaries in Singapore, Malaysia, Japan, Canada and the US. To compete internationally, China's would-be world-beaters know they have a number of problems to overcome.

'Chinese management can have an exaggerated sense of its own abilities,' says Mr Stone at Prudential. 'They can get complacent, a kind of managerial hubris.' He is worried by the tendency of good companies to diversify from their core businesses into the current commercial fad. Haier, for example, is understood to be developing a pharmaceutical subsidiary to add to its white-goods businesses.

Chinese companies are also weak in product innovation (like other Asian exporters before them). According to Mr Hoong Lik Yuen, head of ING Barings in Shanghai, even China's successful consumer-appliance manufacturers will have to start investing more heavily in research and development and bring quality products to market 'otherwise, they will find the competitive advantage they enjoy, which is basically price, is temporary'.

But the biggest problem the Chinese will have to overcome lies back home: their relationship with the government. This year, even companies that have enjoyed the most autonomy have been faced with the government's enthusiasm for building conglomerates through mergers. Some people think this is a strategy for creating national champions. Others fear it is simply a ruse to foist the welfare responsibilities of failed state-owned enterprises on to the most successful ones.

Baosteel, for example, is one of Asia's largest steel companies. It has been encouraged by the Shanghai municipal authorities to merge with the failed Shanghai Steel, taking on the welfare responsibilities for thousands of redundant workers. HG Asia's Mr Richardson says that until now the authorities 'have been careful not to kill the goose that lays the eggs'. But it is not clear if their self-restraint will continue. Back in Changhong's dining room, when conversation turns to the issue of government-directed mergers, Mr Li stops eating. Changhong has just absorbed the local Mianyang Battery factory, taking on double the workers it needs to run a factory in a sector where it has no previous experience. But Mr Li insists the expansion, although ordained by the government, has sound business logic, arguing that the factory has potential. 'As far as restructuring is concerned, big fish can eat small fish, quick fish will eat slow fish, but we do not want to eat dead fish.'

Changhong, Mr Li promises, will remain state-controlled and commercially successful.

Source: James Harding (1997) *Financial Times*, 14 August. Reprinted with permission.

Question

If Chinese companies are weak in innovation, what kind of role can marketing research play to help compensate for at least some of these weaknesses?

Case study 3 **When time means money**

Gisele Rufer is stuck. She has a concept, a good one, one that many former colleagues in the sophisticated Swiss watchmaking industry have admitted was long overdue. She also has a market which has said it will absorb whatever she can give it.

The problem: her first production has sold out, and it did not produce the capital or the cash flow with which to get a second, larger going. The eldest daughter of a watchmaker, Rufer left school early to help in her mother's shop, only returning to her studies after her marriage. 'I made the children and the Baccalaureate together,' she says. She became an artist. Art, however, produced little income and Rufer decided to return to school to qualify as an engineer, aged 39. Her first work experience was not encouraging, however. 'I was a woman. They asked me to make the coffee,' she says.

So she returned to her roots in the watchmaking industry and, while working for Omega, was given the task of promoting a new concept in children's watches. After three years her results were so good that she was given carte blanche to create new watches for women.

Only the carte didn't prove to be quite so blanche after all. 'In this business men make women's watches,' she says. They make them along the same lines as men's ranges, except with more delicacy and colour. After extensive research she had settled on two original designs particularly liked by women, but the men in the business thought otherwise. 'They said is was not the image of Omega.'

Deeply frustrated by the lack of enthusiasm for her women's watch designs, Rufer and freelance designer Carol Gygax decided to push ahead with the concept on their own – at this stage, just for the fun of it. 'We did it like two little girls in kindergarten. We both like everything to be beautiful, and suddenly we didn't have men telling us what we couldn't do.' The watch, she says, took on a symbolic meaning. 'Perhaps you can say it is post-feminist,' Rufer says. 'What it symbolises is that women can struggle through.'

But her own struggle was destined to continue. By December 1994 the design was complete, and Rufer went back to university yet again, this time to do a five-month entrepreneurship course at Neufchatel. She still hadn't decided to set up business on her own. Instead, she created a 'very good business plan' and hawked it around all the big watchmaking brands. Their response was scathing. 'Do you think we need you to make watches for women? We've been doing it for hundreds of years,' was a typical reply. After three months of this she had had enough. Angry, and increasingly determined, she decided to make the watches herself and market them under her father's name, Delance, establishing the company in April 1996. With her husband's support, Rufer collected 'all the money we had and some we didn't have', totalling SFr100,000 (£42,000). Carol Gygax is a 50 per cent owner of the designs and will receive royalties, but is not involved in running the company.

The money raised was not nearly enough to launch the Delance design and Rufer knew it. But she had another idea. 'By chance, I read how women in Africa help each other by pooling their expertise, so I asked all my friends in the industry if they would help me.' All of the women she approached said they would help. Some have given very long credit, some have been promised a share of any eventual profits, some have been paid in watches, while others have worked for free. Rufer estimates the services-in-kind amount to £300,000 in labour costs.

Meanwhile, Rufer went in search of the people needed to make her design a reality. One was the case-maker. The design of the Delance watch with its curved, almost sculpted, lozenge shape is technically very challenging. 'Impossible' was the grunted verdict of most executives in the industry. Rufer approached Pretat, the best steel case-maker in the country. But she wanted gold. It so happened that demand for steel designs has been in decline while gold is on the increase, and this case-maker needed to diversify to compete. The Delance watch was the perfect opportunity. After much hard work Rufer had 250 watches completed by the beginning of 1996, 50 in gold and 200 in steel. She had only paid for the moulds and the materials, while Pretat, keen to promote its ability for working with gold, worked for free.

A year on, that first output has all been sold, despite prices that range from SFr1,250 for the basic steel model right up to SFr22,000 for a gold Delance covered in jewels. Several watches had to be given away for marketing purposes, others were given as repayment for original investment in the first production run, and 80 per cent of sales have been made by Rufer. Delance has not yet made any profit.

In the past year Rufer has taken the product to the trade. In Switzerland, a large distributor has agreed that there is a niche in the market, and would at some point take Delance watches; and in the US, J.J. Hubacher, a distributor, has said it is happy with person, product and price. But in both markets Rufer says she faces a problem that is typical for any business start-up: the product needs to show it will sell before the big distributors will take orders from her.

Distributors also expect her to have at least 1,000 watches complete for a decent launch. But to make 1,000 pieces Rufer needs to raise SFr1m. So far Rufer's main fund-raising brainwave has been to launch a Participation Certificate scheme. Investors do not become company shareholders but instead are able to buy watches at a substantial discount, and receive a twice-yearly Delance newsletter.

Participation also means they have indirectly helped the Women's World Summit Foundation, a Swiss-based charity helping women entrepreneurs in developing countries, which receives any dividends on the certificates. Certificates sell at SFr100 each.

So far Rufer has sold 200 certificates and raised SFr20,000. She, her husband and children own 75 per cent of the company, the remainder is owned by a scattering of shareholders.

Rufer recently has also received some free and expert advice. At a conference on financing start-ups at the Ecole Politechnique in Lausanne, she met Anne Southam-Lingjaerde, a founder-partner of Genilem, a small business promoter established 18 months ago on a non-profit basis by a group of Swiss companies. Genilem's aim is to increase new enterprise in the Geneva region, nursing newcomers through their first three years, free of charge.

With Genilem's expertise in marketing and drawing up business plans, Rufer has been targeting potential business angels, investors or partnerships in Switzerland and France, in search of that much-needed cash injection. But time is of the essence. Supporters of the project who gave Rufer generous loan terms are starting to ask for their money. She knows, and Genilem knows, that in the end it is largely a question of surviving for long enough to convince an ultra-conservative business environment that the product is a sound prospect.

Delance Ltd, 201 Route Principale, Ch-2532 Macolin, Switzerland. Tel: 0041 32 3236401, fax: 0041 32 3236827.

Source: Andrew Eames (1997) *Financial Times*, 24 May. Reprinted with permission.

Question

Delance is struggling towards profitability. Could systematic marketing research have helped at all? Why or why not?

Case study 4 | # The growing business: same aims, different strategies

Innovation is a challenge in any company, and all the more so in a business controlled by the same family for decades. It helps, though, when the boss is a former management consultant in his thirties eager to test out his theories.

Colt of the UK and Seidenader in Germany are both run by former Bain consultants. Paul O'Hea is the grandson of Colt's founder, Nik Seidenader the great grandson in the family dynasty. Mr O'Hea was seconded to Bain for a spell in the 1980s, while Mr Seidenader spent three years at the consultancy working in industries such as automotive and glassmaking. Each company is a technology leader and operates globally. But in seeking fresh impetus outside their companies' core areas, Mr O'Hea and Mr Seidenader are following two quite contrasting routes.

A specialist in ventilation and related equipment used in construction, Colt's most visible product is probably the 40m tall pyramid-shaped ventilation unit on top of Canary Wharf, the UK's tallest building. The company has annual sales of around £110m, and Mr O'Hea's approach is to graft on new thinking from the outside. Through five joint ventures or acquisition, the UK company has added new ideas in areas as unrelated as noise control and solar energy.

At Seidenader, a company about a tenth of the size which makes image analysis systems used for checking quality in the pharmaceuticals industry, innovation is being sought inside the company. In a more measured, though no less risky, process, it is splitting itself in two to re-direct some of its energies into new business sectors including confectionery and orthopaedics. For Mr O'Hea, the impetus for change was the realisation that 'organic growth was not going to be sufficient to keep us moving'. Hence its initial joint venture in 1990 with Holland Heating, a Dutch leader in large 'air handling' systems that fan fresh air through buildings such as department stores.

Next came a link with a Swiss company called Fabrisolar, which provided expertise on how to add solar cells to the shading systems it already manufactured, providing a source of electrical energy. Two other projects are still at an early stage. They include joint ventures with Albers and Digisonix, two small US companies which have respectively developed new low-energy air-conditioning systems and electronic 'anti-sound' equipment for cutting noise in buildings such as paper mills. In the past few weeks Colt has also acquired Braat, a Dutch company that makes specialised glazing systems that can be used in conjunction with the shading and solar equipment.

With this rush of new ideas, a big job for Mr O'Hea will be to integrate the thinking from the outside with existing products and management structures. He says a quarter of Colt's 1,000 staff will have to involve themselves in some way with the new 'technology packages' brought in by the outsiders. At Munich-based Seidenader, the challenge is in some ways the other way around. It wants to forge divisions rather than bridge them. Virtually all its DM20m (£6.8m) annual sales come from the pharmaceutical industry, with just 15 per cent of its revenues from Germany, and 30 per cent from the US. Customers include Hoechst, Glaxo Wellcome, Schering Plough and Merck. Roughly half the sales are in the form of image analysis equipment (checking, for instance, pills at the end of the production line) and the rest from cleaning and sorting machinery.

Of these areas, by far the fastest growing is image analysis, which depends heavily on software research and linkages with highly accurate camera systems.

Under its new structure, the 102-year-old company will have one division concentrating on pharmaceuticals and a second (with joint headquarters in Munich and Pennsylvania) trying to 'spin out' some of its image analysis ideas for use in other sectors.

Although technology links will be close, the new unit will have a distinct management identity. 'To be free to act (in the new division) we have to get away from our pharmaceutical bias,' says Mr Seidenader. One of his goals is to develop systems that can check during the factory production process the quality of items. Another is to use image analysis software to 'look' for patterns in the sprays of paint and other materials used in coating systems in industry.

The software could form part of the control equipment in these businesses, while another development at the pilot stage is to use Seidenader's software techniques to capture images of feet, to be used in surgical applications and methods to cure walking disorders.

How this will work out is still unclear. But Mr Seidenader has high hopes; he thinks he could grow the new division's annual sales of more than DM5m over the next few years.

Source: Peter Marsh (1997) *Financial Times*, 23 December. Reprinted with permission.

Question

Discuss how marketing research may be organised and undertaken in such a company. What do you see as the major difficulties that market researchers are likely to encounter?

Case study 5   Canal Satellite disappoints

Canal Satellite, one of France's two leading satellite services, made losses above expectations during the first half of 1997, paving the way for a recapitalisation with help from Time Warner of the US, writes Andrew Jack. Results at Pathe revealed that Canal Satellite, in which it has a 20 per cent stake, had losses ahead of interest, tax and depreciation of FFr186m for the six months to June 30, compared with FFr37m in the same period of the previous year.

The service was launched in April 1996.

Jerome Seydoux, Pathe chairman, said yesterday that a recapitalisation of the company with Time Warner – which some analysts expect to be for about 10 per cent of the total equity – was 'in the pipeline'. He also confirmed that Générale des Eaux, which owns 10 per cent, would sell its stake to the existing investors – Canal Plus, with 70 per cent, and Pathe – to ensure they could maintain their existing holdings. Mr Seydoux said losses at Canal Satellite were the result of higher marketing and promotion costs for the service, which had been forced to compete aggressively by the launch of the rival TPS service at the end of last year.

Source: Andrew Jack (1997) *Financial Times*, 12 September. Reprinted with permission.

Question

What kind of post facto marketing research do you think might be beneficial in this case? What do you consider to be the key issues and how might they be explored?

Case study 6   Saffron revivalists turn to genetic engineering

Saffron is as quintessentially Spanish as paella – the spice's ochre-tinted filaments provide colour and flavour to the country's emblematic rice dish. But uncontrolled foreign imports and poor domestic yields have sharply reduced its cultivation.

Land devoted to saffron – the world's most expensive condiment – has shrunk from more than 4,000 hectares in 1989 to less than 2,000 hectares. A combination of climate, applied agronomy and marketing could, however, revive domestic farmers' interest.

Heavy rains last autumn ended a prolonged drought on Spain's central plateau and with the new year a blanket of snow has covered the plains of La Mancha around Albacete where saffron is painstakingly produced. Irrigation, which can double the crop yield, will now be possible next October when harvesting starts.

As the climate swings in favour of saffron, efforts by people such as Ms Ramona Maria Munoz, a young agronomist, and Mr Tomas Gomez, a dealer in agricultural products, to promote its cultivation look increasingly relevant.

Ms Munoz, who is attached to Albacete's Agronomy Institute, has started clonal breeding of the purple-coloured crocus, the *Crocus oficinalis*, whose dark orange stigmas, just three on each flower, produce saffron. The genetic research conducted by Ms Munoz seeks to increase the yield of the crocus and offset the cost of its highly labour-intensive harvesting and production.

'We know practically nothing about this plant,' she says, 'and the first objective is to create a more uniform crocus.'

Mr Gomez, a veteran Albacete wholesaler who specialises in saffron, is calling on the Spanish government to award a *Denominacion de Origen* guarantee, a seal of authenticity equivalent to the *Appellation Contrôlée* of French wine, to the locally produced spice.

His campaign aims to end an escalating adulteration business – based on blending the local produce with cheaper, but inferior quality, saffron imported mainly from Greece and Iran – that has depressed the price paid to local producers.

In 1989, when just 25,000 kg of saffron were produced in Spain, 70,000 kg of 'Spanish' saffron were exported, mostly to the Middle East. Since then, in spite of lowered crops, exports have risen steadily. There are compelling reasons to justify a revival of domestic cultivation.

Top quality La Mancha saffron commands astronomical prices. Farmers can earn up to Pta130,000/kg ($1,000/kg) and wholesalers, who pack the filaments in one gramme sachets, can sell it for three times that.

Spanish wholesalers currently obtain saffron from Greece for around Pta100,000/kg and for as little as Pta60,000/kg from Iran, but Mr Gomez believes that strict quality controls could restore a saffron economy based on the more intense colouring and greater fragrancy of the local product. The prices reflect the high processing cost of producing saffron. The crocuses are harvested early in the morning when their petals bloom and it takes two experienced pickers – bent double to grasp the flowers – 15 days to pick the 150,000 or so crocuses from 0.8 hectares which in turn produce one kilogramme of fresh stigmas.

Plucking the stigmas from the flowers is an even more wearisome process. It takes seven hours to separate these filaments from the 500 crocuses picked over a two-hour period.

In the final stage of the process the end product all but disappears. The stigmas are lightly toasted to extract their moisture (once toasted the saffron will retain its qualities in an airtight jar for years) and one kilogramme of the extracted filaments is reduced to just two grammes. Given such labours, it is small wonder that, at a time of lower prices, caused by cheaper imported saffron, and of poor yields, caused by the years of drought, local farmers have been put off cultivating crocuses.

'Everyone in my village used to have some land set aside for saffron but virtually everybody has now switched to vines,' says Ms Munoz, who was born in Caca-Ibanez, 50km north of Albacete. 'Until my clones increase the yield, saffron won't be worth the trouble.'

Mr Gomez says the Agronomy Institute is doing good work. 'But what we can do straight away is equip ourselves with proper labelling and decent marketing so that consumers know they are the genuine article,' he adds.

Source: Tom Burns (1997) *Financial Times*, 15 January. Reprinted with permission.

Question

Can marketing research help the saffron growers of Spain? If so, how can it help?

Case study 7 | World tyre industry may face shake-out

After five years of consolidation, the world's tyre industry is likely to face another round of restructuring over the next decade, according to new research by the Economist Intelligence Unit.

Analysing the performance of the 12 largest tyre companies, accounting for more than 80 per cent of world sales, the EIU concludes that it is the companies ranking immediately below the 'Big Three' – Bridgestone, Michelin and Goodyear – which face the fiercest competition. They lack the economies of scale of the biggest companies and are most at risk from aggressive emerging country producers, the EIU says, although its analysis is unlikely to go uncontested by the industry itself. Continental of Germany, Sumitomo of Japan and Pirelli of Italy – ranked fourth, fifth and sixth – are all substantial businesses and themselves account for nearly a fifth of the industry's $70bn turnover. However, they have many of the disadvantages of size without the compensating advantages, the researchers say. Because each has tyre sales of much less than half of that of each of the 'Big Three', marketing and research and development costs have to be spread over much smaller production volumes.

'They have a world presence but typically they are significant players in only two or three regions and they do not dominate or lead in any region. In this situation it is difficult to earn the profit margins enjoyed by the industry leaders. And these companies show signs of being squeezed between the really large companies, which enjoy economies of scale, and the smaller, more focused companies which are growing through concentration on niche products or specific geographic areas.'

The point is made by reference to operating profit margins. The research shows that those of the 'Big Three' averaged 7.8 per cent last year, compared with 4.7 per cent for Continental, Sumitomo and Pirelli. Nevertheless, it also shows that the three smaller companies have fared better than the top three in improving their margins over the past three years. The top three's 7.8 per cent is only marginally better than the 7.6 per cent achieved in 1994, whereas the three smaller companies have improved from just 3.7 per cent.

Pirelli, for one, says its improving margins show that its strategy of increasingly targeting high value-added, niche performance tyre business – while retaining a state in more mainstream business – is paying off. And new flexible manufacturing technology, allowing commercially viable production of tyres in batches of as low as 150–200 units, means that 'Pirelli no longer feels particularly disadvantaged at the lack of scale economies enjoyed by the Big Three,' according to Mr Giuseppi Bencini, managing director of Pirelli Tyres.

Mr Bencini points to the company's exclusive supply contract, for Jaguar Cars' new XK8 sports car, of a tyre developed with Jaguar engineers from scratch specifically for the XK8, as further evidence of the strategy working.

Like Germany's Continental, Mr Bencini maintains that collaboration between companies on specific projects is as likely a route to viability as further big takeovers.

One example is provided by Continental itself, which is collaborating with Michelin. Continental is providing Michelin with budget tyres from its low-cost plants in eastern Europe, while Continental has secured the right to use the Michelin-owned Uniroyal brand name for Continental-produced premium tyres throughout Europe.

However, the EIU says the big second-tier companies also face a potential squeeze from below, in the form of aggressively expanding concerns from the Asia-Pacific region, notably Kumho and Hankook of South Korea. Kumho is already ranked tenth in the world with sales of $1.1bn. Hankook is only marginally behind in 11th place but has boasted of its intention to rank fifth within a few years.

The EIU warns that, just like South Korea's car industry, both are in danger of expanding too fast for their own resources. 'But providing they continue to survive they pose a real threat to the medium-sized players, particularly Sumitomo and to the other Japanese tyre makes such as Toyo and Yokohama.' The industry and EIU research find common ground, however, in predicting that some competitive pressures should be offset by steady growth in demand for tyres as vehicle use increases in the emerging world.

Total demand, covering both original and replacement tyres is projected to rise by about 19 per cent between last year and 2005. However, only 8 per cent growth is forecast for the developed markets of Western Europe and North America, compared with a rise of 36 per cent for developing world markets. (The World Tyre Industry: A New Perspective to 2005. The Economist Intelligence Unit, 15 Regent Street, London, SW1Y 4LR. £595/$945.)

Source: John Griffiths (1997) *Financial Times*, 14 March. Reprinted with permission.

Question

What use might Kumho and Hankook make of marketing research in their quest to improve their competitive position?

Case study 8 | Lake Lucerne Navigation Company (SGV)

The Lake Lucerne Navigation Company (SGV) is Switzerland's largest steamship and motor ship operator. Its fleet of five nostalgic paddle steamers and fifteen elegant salon cruisers can accommodate 13 000 passengers and seat 3200 on-board restaurant guests. The ships connect Lucerne with the lake's popular holiday resorts year-round. Scheduled links also provide excellent service to all the mountain rail and cable systems with lakeside terminals. More than two million passengers a year make the SGV Central Switzerland's key transit authority, second in volume only to the Swiss Federal Railways.

Lake Lucerne offers a varied landscape ranging from the fertile shores of the lowlands and the steep slopes of the Alpine foothills to the vertical rock faces of the towering Alps surrounding Lake Uri. In the same area visitors can also find the Swiss Path, a walking trail created in 1991 on the occasion of Switzerland's 700-year anniversary.

Main routes and operating times of the Paddle Steamers

In Lucerne, Brunnen, Flüelen and Alpnachstad, the lake is connected to the Swiss and European railways and fully integrated in their system of schedules and fares. Around the lake you will find parking for cars and coaches. On the main routes:

- Lucerne – Weggis – Vitznau – Beckenried – Gersau – Brunnen – Rütli – Flüelen
- Lucerne – Kehrsiten (– Bürgenstock) – Stansstad – Alpnachstad

departures are scheduled approximately every hour. Visitors have a very attractive choice of cruises lasting between one and six hours.

In summer, the following main routes are operated with Paddle Steamers:

09.15	to Flüelen	Daily
10.15	to Alpnachstad	On Sundays as well as daily in July and August
11.15	to Flüelen	On Sundays
11.20	to Flüelen	Daily from 1st May to 28th October
13.15	to Flüelen	Daily
14.00	to Alpnachstad	On Sundays as well as daily in July and August
15.20	to Vitznau	Daily

(Schedules are subject to change)

Winter-Steamer-Cruises 2000/2001

Like in the millenniums-winter Paddle Steamer 'Uri' will be in scheduled service again this winter. This is the timetable: 24th December 2000 departure from Lucerne to Rütli at 10.32. 25th and 26th December 2000 as well as 1st and 2nd January 2001 departure from Lucerne at 13.15 to Flüelen. From 27th until 30th December 2000 departure from Lucerne at 10.32 to Rütli and at 16.25 to Beckenried. Festive menus as well as warm and cold specialities are available on board. Fondue Cruise on Friday, 29th December 2000. Daily Steam & Cream from 27th to 30th December 2000.

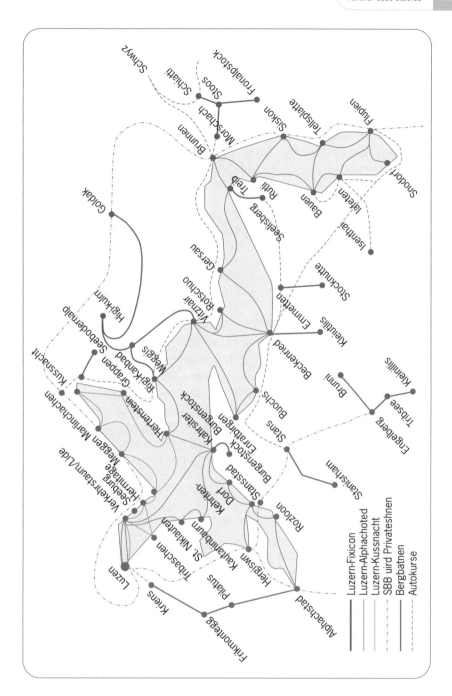

Paddle Steamer 'Uri' Celebrations

Switzerland's oldest Paddle Steamer is celebrating its 100th birthday in the year 2001. The 'Uri' was built by Sulzer Bros., Winterthur, in 1901. The 'Uri' is still in regular scheduled service on Lake Lucerne. The first cruise of PS 'Uri' will take place on 1st January in the course of the Winter-Steamer-Cruises. 93 years after the first maiden voyage on 4th May 1901 under the command of Captain Anton Koller, on 30th April 1994 the second maiden voyage took place under Captain Beat Kallenbach. This voyage was preceded by a total revision lasting $2^1/_2$ years in the Navigation Company's own shipyard. The navigation cabin and chimney were restored in their original form, so that since then the 'Uri' has been unable to sail under the Acheregg Bridge in Stansstad. The 1st class saloon is built in the new-baroque style, and its interior with floral decorations is reminiscent of a garden hall from the turn of the last century. The etched glass inserts on the saloon doors are particularly valuable. A detailed guide to the regular and special anniversary sailings will be issued during the course of winter.

10 years Swiss Path

10 years ago, the scenic Swiss Path walking trail was opened. The Swiss Path is a joint cantonal effort in commemoration of Switzerland's 700th anniversary (1291 to 1991). It starts at Rütli Meadow, birthplace of the Confederation, and ends at Brunnen. Each canton has designed one segment of the trail (there are 5mm of trail for each inhabitant). The trail is accessible via 8 boat landings, 3 railway stations, a funicular railway and 4 bus lines.

From 8th April to 28th October 2001, SGV considerably increases the number of its Lucerne – Lake Uri trips. The Hike-Express 'Swiss Path' leaves Lucerne at 8.32 in the morning in order to bring the hikers to the trail in good time. But also on Sundays and holidays during winter, the stop-overs Rütli, Bauen, Isleten-Isenthal and Flüelen are served twice daily in both directions. A special brochure featuring all details about the trail and its sights is offered by SGV at the price of SFr. 1.—.

The Swiss Path was ceremonially inaugurated on 4th May 1991. On 5th May 2001, special anniversary events will be held all around Lake Uri.

The *new* 'Titlis'

In 1951 the motorship 'Titlis' was built in the Navigation Company's own shipyard, with a capacity of 400 passengers. Since the launching of MS 'Waldstätter' in 1998, the 'Titlis' has been used pimarly for special occasions. The last day of service was 29th April 2000, before the start of the reconstruction in the Navigation Company's own shipyard in Lucerne. The passenger capacity was reduced from 400 to 250 passengers. On the main deck the 2nd class saloon contains 62 restaurant seats and 70 outdoor seats. The saloon 1st class holds 28 restaurant seats. On the upper deck are 60 outdoor seats available, reached through the elegant staircase made of glass. From August 2001 on, MS 'Titlis' is ready for scheduled and charted cruises departing from Brunnen. Photos of the reconstruction can be seen in the Internet (www.lakelucerne.ch, photo gallery).

On board gastronomy

On all main routes, we offer refined service for breakfast, lunch, coffee/cakes, and dinner.

Breakfast cruise: Every Sunday morning, as well as on official holidays, passengers can enjoy a breakfast buffet. Spring, summer and autumn: Departures in

Lucerne to charming Lake Küssnacht at 10.20, Winter: Departures at 9.15 (see section 12 for details). Breakfast is also available daily on all other ships leaving Lucerne or Flüelen before 10.20.

The year-round **lunch cruise** is very popular. It departs from Lucerne daily at 12.03 and returns at 13.44. The trip goes to Weggis and Vitznau along the Rigi. Daily on board: large, varied salad buffet à discrétion with twelve crisp salads, various sauces, garnishing and bread (SFr. 15.50), as well as three different lunches (meat, fish or vegetarian). Prices with salad buffet SFr. 22.— to SFr. 30.—, without salad buffet SFr. 17.— to SFr. 25.—.The round trip costs SFr. 21.50 with the Half-Fare Travel Card (SFr. 28.— without Half-Fare Travel Card). In 2nd class only SFr. 14.50 (SFr. 24.—).

SUSHIP – the Sushi-Ship: Evening cruise departing from Lucerne with large fish and vegetarian buffet as much as you can eat. The dates for 2001 are being planned.

Cruise with fondue chinoise: Every Friday evening from 13th April until 18th May 2001 and from 27th September until 26th October 2001. Evening cruise with salad buffet, fondue chinoise à discrétion and other fine dishes. Lucerne departure 19.15, cruise on a panoramic motorship, arrival 21.44.

The **daily sunset dinner cruise** is already a successful tradition: 19th May to 23th September 2001. An elegant salon motorship departs from Lucerne at 19.15 and returns at 21.44. The culinary offer lends to this round-trip a touch of ocean cruise luxury. Every Tuesday (in July and August also every Wednesday) operated by Paddle Steamer.

The Family-friendly Lake Lucerne Cruises

The Junior Card issued by the public transport authorities (SFr. 20.—) under the motto 'Accompanied children up to 16 years old travel free' is, of course, also valid on Lake Lucerne. In addition, SGV has no steamer surcharge, which can be expensive for families. With the travel guide 'Walking trails for Baby Carriages' the SGV demonstrates its friendliness towards families.

Evening-Cruises

- **Night Boat** offering music, dancing, Swiss folklore and special Swiss menus.
  Daily from May to September, Departure at 20.45, arrival at 22.15.
  Happy hour Cruise: 17.30 – 18.30
  All cruises on request. For further information and reservations, please call 041 / 319 49 78.

- **Evening cruises with music and gastronomy**.
  Special tickets between SFr. 24.— and SFr. 30.—. People celebrating their birthday travel for free! **Every Friday in July and August** with Paddle Steamer. Departures from **Lucerne** (19.20), **Kastanienbaum, Hergiswil and Stansstad**. Dixieland, evergreens or folklore, according to the special programme. **Further cruises** from **Buochs, Beckenried, Vitznau, Weggis, Brunnen, Seelisberg, Gersau** and **Flüelen.** Music according to special programme.

Lucerne Concert Hall is accessible by boat

The inauguration of the new Lucerne Concert Hall was held on 18th August 1998. Some of the SGV landing stages by the main railway station are located directly under architect Jean Nouvel's spectacular projecting roof. The proximity of the landing stage to the KKL offers a range of attractive combinations (side programmes, exhibitions, various events, transfers etc.).

Combination lake/lift trips

All mountain cable and rail systems can be reached quickly and conveniently by our boats:

- **Rigi cogwheel railway**: Lucerne – Vitznau, approx. 60 minutes
- **Pilatus cogwheel railway**: Lucerne – Alpnachstad, approx. 80 minutes
- **Klewenalp aerial cablecar**: Lucerne – Beckenried, approx. 90 minutes
- **Seelisberg funicular**: Lucerne – Treib, approx. 110 minutes
- **Bürgenstock funicular**: Lucerne – Kehrsiten, approx. 40 minutes
- **Stanserhorn and Titlis lifts**: Lucerne – Stansstad, approx. 60 minutes
- **Seebodenalp aerial cablecar**: Lucerne – Küssnacht am Rigi, approx. 60 minutes

Ideal combination options for round trips and walks. Bargain package rates including ship fare, lift fare and snack are available for trips to Bürgenstock/Felsenweg, Seebodenalp, Rigi and Klewenalp.

William Tell Express: the only alpine express by boat and train

The William Tell Express is a top tourist attraction connecting two of the most fascinating Swiss regions – Central Switzerland and Ticino. The trip starts in Lucerne as you board a magnificently restored, nostalgic Paddle Steamer and cruise to Flüelen on Lake Lucerne in about $3^1/_2$ hours. As you enjoy a gourmet meal in the first class restaurant, you can watch secluded bays, picturesque villages and historic landmarks such as the Rütli and the Tellsplatte silently glide by on the starboard and port sides. In Flüelen, only a few steps away from the pier, our guests board air-conditioned, first class panorama compartments or travel as economy passengers in modern, air-conditioned second-class compartments of the Swiss Federal Railways. The trip continues through deep ravines and precipitous cliffs on the world famous Gotthard line to Lugano or Locarno.

In 2001, the William Tell Express will operate daily from 1st May to 28th October and in 2002 from 1st May to 27th October. Departure from Lucerne at 11.20, arrival in Lugano at 17.23 (in Locarno at 17.30, change in Bellinzona). With this timetable the William Tell Express can be included in many package tours, as an appealing link between Switzerland and Italy for example in conjunction with Bernina and Glacier Express.

The William Tell Express surcharge of Sfr. 45.— includes a three-course meal, a travel guide, reserved seating and an attractive souvenir. All tickets boat 1st class, train 1st or 2nd class are valid. Reservations can be made at all Swiss rail stations or through SGV. Tour and bus operators worldwide offer special round trips with the William Tell Express.

Lake Lucerne is in season all year round!

During the winter months, SGV offers daily 7 lake cruises leaving Lucerne for Hertenstein, Weggis, Vitznau (Rigi), Beckenried (Klewenalp), Gersau, Treib (Seelisberg) or Brunnen. Besides that the piers at Rütli, Bauen, Isleten-Isenthal and Flüelen along Lake Uri are served twice a day in both directions on Sundays and holidays. Winter-Steamer-Cruises see section 2. The following offers are especially attractive:

- **Lunch cruise**: Departs from Lucerne daily at 12.03 and returns at 13.44. Enjoy a relaxing break on this midday cruise with business lunch and salad bar (see section 6).
- **Sunday breakfast cruise**: Departs from Lucerne every Sunday morning, as well as on official holidays, at 9.15 featuring a generous breakfast buffet. Ideal as a feeder to the Rigi and Klewenalp ski areas or as a round trip (arrival in Lucerne 11.44).
- **Fondue cruise**: Every Friday evening from 3rd November 2000 until 6th April 2001 and 2nd November 2001 until 22nd March 2002. Departure from Lucerne at 19.15. The after-dark cruise with candlelight, accordion music and fondue à discrétion has become a popular classic (arrival in Lucerne 21.15).
- **Rigi and Klewenalp snow specials**: Hit the slopes by ship! The budget prices include transportation plus a full-day lift pass for skiers. The packages will also appeal to sledding and hiking fans (extra services provided).
- **Have some cake on the lake**: The floating temptation. Lake excursions from Lucerne at 14.25 to 16.44. Daily 30th October 2000 until 7th April 2001 as well as from 29th October 2001 until 28th March 2002 with delicious cake varieties – Sweet greetings from Lake Lucerne!

Source: The Lake Lucerne Navigation Company

Question

The Marketing Manager is keen to find out visitor attitudes and opinions about what the company presently provides. Outline a number of research studies that might provide the company with useful information in this respect.

Case study 9	Gondolas for Liverpool

Liverpool is a big city but like most cities its centre is relatively small. The only problem with Liverpool is that the centre is on two sites. The old centre around Lime Street, the James Centre and the City (as far as the Town Hall) and the new centre on the waterfront around the Pier Head and the Albert Dock. For the new centre there have been several recent proposals for expansion including a vast shopping complex and a new site for Everton football stadium. In addition the new centre has an industrial complex and residential up-beat apartments built in what were once the old dockland buildings.

Liverpool has an underground railway system which traverses the river Mersey but there are only four underground stations on the Liverpool side of the Mersey – James Street (city), Moorfields, Lime Street and Central. The latter two are in the heart of the old shopping area. During the 19th century Liverpool was among the foremost cities in Britain in terms of innovation of travel around the city. The city's network of tramcars rivalled that of modern day San Francisco while its overhead railway which ran the length of the docklands rivalled that of modern day New York. Sadly both of these latter two systems of transportation are no more. Buses and taxis ply their trade where once these transport systems ruled supreme.

Recently, on a visit to Switzerland, Liverpool City Councillor Dan Smith encountered the gondola transportation system in operation at the foot of Mount Pilatus near Krienz next to Lucerne. The red gondolas are an impressive site as they continually ply their way from the terminus station at Krienz, through an intermediate dropping off point, to the higher station some 4500 feet above sea level (an ascent of some 3500 feet) two thirds of the way up Mount Milatus. The journey covers several miles and takes around half an hour to complete. Dan was not able to count the number of the gondolas on the continuous belt system system but he reckoned it to be several hundred. Each gondola could carry four persons so that the whole system must have been able to carry at least 1000 people at any one time. A gondola is a bit like a four seater bubble car which is suspended from a cable which runs in a continuous loop-over circuit and is supported by pylons. The gondolas at Krienz can be up to 100 feet above the ground though more often the distance is 20 to 30 feet.

Dan felt that perhaps a gondola transportation system might be the answer to what Liverpool really needed. Such a system would be highly innovative in the UK and be an attraction which would outperform the new tram systems in Sheffield and Manchester. He felt an obvious first route would be from Lime Street to the Pier Head with maybe an intermediate station in the city close to the Town Hall. The system might also be extended to other parts of the city in due course. e.g. Anfield and the Liverpool football ground, the Liverpool University and John Moores University campuses.

Dan mulled these ideas over in his mind and decided that perhaps some sort of feasability study would be required. At the next meeting of the City Council he put forward his ideas and suggested that perhaps a feasibility study would be worthwhile. His colleagues were quite interested in the idea but pointed out that they could not really waste ratepayers' money on a 'pie in the sky' scheme. Dan said he thought it might be worthwhile to find out ratepayers' attitudes to such a scheme in the first place. If these were positive, he argued, then his idea would have some support and it would be worthwhile taking the scheme on to the next stage where one might assess its costs and benefits.

Questions

1 Is Dan right in suggesting one should assess customer attitudes to such a scheme prior to undertaking a cost–benefit analysis? Explain.

2 Draw up a research proposal indicating how you would set about measuring ratepayers' attitudes as Dan suggests.

3 In making a decision about this project what information is required? What role would marketing research play in providing the relevant information – i.e. What further information is required?

Glossary

aided questions Questions that provide clues to help respondents recall more accurately.

aided recall Respondents are asked if they remember an advertisement for a particular brand.

alternative hypothesis A competing hypothesis to the null.

analysis of variance A method of testing hypotheses of no differences among means for more than two independent samples.

attitude A learned predisposition to act in a consistent manner with respect to a given object.

audit A formal examination of the movement of goods at the retail level or in and out of stock in warehouses.

balanced scale Scale employing an equal number of favourable and unfavourable categories.

blind testing Tests where the brand name of the product under test is not disclosed.

branded testing Test where the name of a product is made known.

causality The effect of one variable creating change in another.

census A complete enumeration of the pre-specified group.

chi-square test statistic Measures the goodness of fit between the numbers observed in the sample and the numbers which should have been evident in a sample were the null hypothesis true.

cluster sampling Design where one first selects a sample of clusters and next decides on which sampling unit to include.

coding Involves the assignment of an alphanumeric symbol or a numerical value to represent a specific response to a question. It also includes the column position that the designated code occupies on a data record.

comparative scaling Sometimes called non-metric scaling, it requires the respondent to compare a set of stimulus objects directly against one another.

concept Something intended to satisfy customers' wants and needs.

concept evaluation test A test for screening new product ideas or alternative end benefits for products.

concept tests Data on purchase intentions, attribute ratings and likes/dislikes with respect to ideas for new products or repositioning of existing ones.

construct validity Assessment of whether the variables measured in a study adequately represent the intended theoretical constructs.

content validity Assessment of whether scale items adequately reflect the entire spectrum of the construct under examination.

continuous rating scale Involves the respondent indicating a rating by placing a mark at an appropriate position on a line.

continuous tracking A study whereby the measurements are taken during the entire length of the campaign.

copy recall The number (percentage) of respondents who can recall the copy in an advertisement being tested.

copy testing Advertising effectiveness research.

cross-sectional surveys Data obtained by survey from a number of different respondents at a single point in time.

debriefing Respondents' explanation of answers to questions, interpretation of meanings and nature of problems encountered during the conduct of a study.

dependent variable The response measure which is being studied in a research exercise.

depth interview A one-to-one interview in which feelings and opinions are discussed. Usually intended to uncover motivations, prejudices and attitudes.

diary panels Households that agree to give information regularly for an extended period of time. Respondents record events as they occur, e.g. purchases.

double-barrelled questions Requests for information which simultaneously try to elicit answers to two questions.

electronic scanner services Services that record information on purchases made with the aid of electronic optical checkout devices.

emic instrument An instrument that investigates a cultural construct.

ethnography Systematic recording of human cultures.

etic instrument An instrument to make comparisons of the same variable across different cultures.

experimental design The particular approach adopted in an experiment to minimise the effect of different sources of error.

exploratory analysis No prior assumptions are made and the data itself allows for the findings that are obtained.

extended-use product test In-home tests where a product is tried out for an extended period of time.

external validity The extent to which research findings can be generalised to and across populations of interest in different situations and at different times.

filter questions Questions posed to determine the route to be followed through a questionnaire.

follow-ups Means of contacting respondents from time to time after an initial contact.

funnel sequence In an interview or questionnaire, the process of asking questions of a general nature followed by questions of a more precise and pointed nature which refer to the topic being explored.

hypothesis An assumption a researcher is making about a characteristic of or a relationship in a population of interest.

independent variable A factor which has influence on the values adopted by the dependent variable in a phenomenon being explored.

inverted funnel sequence Moving from the specific to the general when exploring a topic in a questionnaire or interview.

itemised questions (closed ended) Questionnaire format in which the respondent is allowed a number of predetermined descriptions and requested to select the one which he or she prefers.

judgemental data Data reflecting perceptions or preferences.

judgemental sampling A sample selected for study because it is considered to be representative of the population of interest or because they fit with the requirements of the research study.

laboratory experiment Experimentation under artificially created conditions in which the experimenter has direct control over most of the factors that influence the outcome of the experiments.

latent theoretical construct A construct which is not directly observable.

loaded questions Questions which suggest what the answer might be or express the researcher's own position on the matter.

longitudinal design A research design in which time is an important variable.

longitudinal surveys A survey in which respondents are questioned at different points in time.

market testing Test designed to assess the impact of a change in a marketing mix element.

market tracking studies Provide performance benchmarks by examining performance of competitors.

maturation The changes that take place in the dependent variable under study in research with the passage of time and that are unrelated to the influence of the independent variable.

monadic product tests Product tests undertaken without comparison to other products as benchmarks.

mortality Drop out or loss of respondents in the course of a longitudinal research project.

multicollinearity The correlations which exist among independent variables and which makes it difficult to assess the true impact of individual independent variables on the dependent variable.

multiple item formats Attitude scaling measures requiring the subject to respond to several items (usually statements) of belief, feeling and intention.

non-comparative scaling (monadic scaling) A scaling method in which the respondent is asked to evaluate each object on a scale independently of the other objects being evaluated.

non-probability samples A sample where there is no way of assessing what the probability is of selecting any particular element or unit into the sample.

non-response error Error which is introduced because not all the respondents included in a sample do in fact respond. It reflects the possibility that the responses of non-respondents may well be different to those of people who actually respond and hence the results produced are not representative of the whole population of interest.

null hypothesis The hypothesis that is tested.

open-ended questions Questions which allow respondents freedom to express their answers in whatever format they choose.

optical scanning Direct machine reading of numerical values or alphanumeric codes and transcription into electronic storage devices.

order bias A condition whereby responses to stimuli (questions, pictures, objects, etc.) is influenced by the order in which they are shown.

paired comparison scale A scale which presents the respondents with objects two at a time requesting the respondent to select one or other of them according to some criterion.

positioning A means of determining how to set the marketing mix elements so as to maximise the appeal of a particular product in the minds of a specific target population.

protocol analysis A procedure in which the subject in the research verbalises his or her thoughts while answering questions.

qualitative research Methods of research, usually involving small samples, which attempt to elicit descriptive information about the thoughts and feeling of respondents on a topic of interest to the research.

quantitative research methods An approach usually involving large samples which are designed to generate data that can be projected to the whole population.

random sampling error Error produced because the selected sample is not a perfect representation of the overall population.

recall A measure of the number of people who can remember having seen an advertisement.

recognition A measure of whether respondents can recognise the name of a particular brand.

reliability The extent to which measures are free from random error and give consistent results.

response error Error occurring as a result of inaccurate or wrongly re-coded answers.

response rates The percentage of people who respond positively to requests to participate in the research.

sampling frame List of members of the population of interest that is eligible for inclusion in a sample.

sampling unit Elements that make up a population.

spurious association Inappropriate assumption that a causal relationship exists between observed events.

structured interview Method of interviewing where the questions are entirely predetermined.

syndicated research services Suppliers of market research data which is collected on a regular basis through standardised procedures. The data is sold to individual clients.

target population The set of people, products or objects that possesses the information of interest to the researcher.

tracking System which permits the assessment of key sales components of customer awareness and trial and repeat purchases.

treatment Refers to manipulation of the independent variable – especially in experiments.

Type I error A situation where the null hypothesis is true but it is rejected on the basis of the sample data.

Type II error A situation where the null hypothesis is not rejected when in fact the alternative hypothesis is true.

unaided questions Questions that do not provide any clues as to the answer.

unbalanced scale A scale which uses an unequal number of unfavourable or favourable scale categories.

unstructured interview An interview wherein questions are not entirely predetermined and the interviewer can probe for details and underlying thoughts.

validity The extent to which instruments measure that which they are intended to measure or research findings reflect reality as we might know it.

verification Procedures aimed at ensuring the accurate transcription of research data.

Bibliography

Abdel-Ghany, M and Sharpe, D L (1997) Consumption patterns among the young–old and old–old, *Journal of Consumer Affairs*, **31**(1), Summer, pp 90–112.

Abraham, M and Lodish, L (1990) Getting the most out of advertising and promotion, *Harvard Business Review*, **68**, p 3.

Achrol, R S and Stern, L W (1988) Environmental determinants of decision making uncertainty in marketing channels, *Journal of Marketing Research*, **25**, pp 36–50.

Adcock, C J (1997) Sample size determination – a review, *Statistician*, **46**(2), pp 261–83.

Adler, P and Adler, P (1994) Observational techniques, in Denzin, N K and Lincoln, Y S (eds), *Handbook of Qualitative Research*, Thousand Oaks, CA: Sage.

Advertising Association (published annually) *The Marketing Pocket Book*. The Advertising Association in conjunction with NTC Publications, Farm Road, Henley-on-Thames, Oxfordshire, RG9 1EJ. Also *The Lifestyle Pocket Book*, *The Media Pocket Book* and *The Regional Marketing Pocket Book*.

Albaum, G (1987) Do source and anonymity affect mail survey results?, *Journal of the Academy of Marketing Science*, **15**, pp 74–81.

Albaum, G and Strandskow, J (1989) Participation in a mail survey of international marketers: effects of pre-contact and detailed project explanation, *Journal of Global Marketing*, **2**(4), pp 7–23.

Albrecht, T L, Johnson, G M and Walther, J B (1993) Understanding communication processes in focus groups, in Morgan, D L (ed.), *Successful Focus Groups: Advancing the state of the art*, Newbury Park, CA: Sage pp 51–63.

Allison, B, O'Sullivan, T, Owen, A, Rice, J, Rothwell, A and Saunders, C (1996) *Research Skills for Students: Transferable and learning skills*. London: Kogan Page.

AMA (1987) New marketing research definition approved, *Marketing News*, **21**, pp 6–8.

Anderson, E W (1993) Firm, industry and national indices of customer satisfaction: implications for services, in Swartz, T and Brown, S W (eds), *Advances in Services Marketing Management: Research and practice*, **2** Vol 2, Greenwich, CT: JAI Press, pp 87–108.

Anderson, E W, Fornell, C and Rust, R T (1997) Customer satisfaction, productivity, and profitability: differences between goods and services, *Marketing Science*, **16**(2), pp 129–45.

Anderson, P F (1983) Marketing, scientific progress, and scientific method, *Journal of Marketing*, **47**(4), pp 18–31.

Andreasen, A. (1983) Cost-conscious marketing research, *Harvard Business Review*, **61**, p 4.

Andreasson, T W (1994) Satisfaction, loyalty and reputation as indicators of customer orientation in the public sector, *International Journal of Public Sector Management*, **7**(2), pp 16–34.

Arnett, R (1990) Mail panel research in the 1990s, *Applied Marketing Research*, **30**(2), pp 8–10.

Aschenbaum, A A (1993) The future challenge to market research, *Marketing Research: A Magazine of Management and Applications*, **5**(2), pp 12–18.

Ashill, N and Jobber, D (1999) The impact of environmental uncertainty perceptions, decision-maker characteristics and work environment characteristics on the perceived usefulness of marketing information systems (MkIS): a conceptual framework, *Journal of Marketing Management*, **15**(6), pp 519–40.

Attaran, M (1992) *Management Science Information System*. New York: Wiley.

Azzolini, M and Shillaber, J (1993) Internal service quality: winning from the inside out, *Quality Progress*, November, pp 75–8.

Bachmann, D P (1987) Cover letter appeals and sponsorship effects on mail survey response rates, *Journal of Marketing Education*, **9**, pp 45–51.

Bailar, B A (1997) Does sampling work?, *Business Economics*, **32**(1), January, pp 47–53.

Baker, K (1989) Using geodemographics in market research, *Journal of the Market Research Society*, **31**, pp 37–44.

Barrie, C (1996) Second rescue for spluttering Reliant, *The Guardian*, 6 April, p 2.

Bartonova, M (1996) The markets are emerging – and research is hard on their heels, *Research Plus*, January, pp 4–5.

Bass, F (1969) A new product growth model for consumer durables, *Management Science*, **15** (January), pp 215–27.

Bates, B (1996) Quality will mark the route to deeper client relationships, *Research Plus*, March, pp 9 and 14.

Bekesi, J. (1997). Gruppe Phänomenologie. Society for the Advancement of the Critical Development of Phenomenology and its Impulses. http://gph.freezope.org.

Berry, L L, Zeithaml, V A and Parasuraman, A (1985) Quality counts in services, too, *Business Horizons*, May–June, pp 44–52.

Berry, L L, Zeithaml, A and Parasuraman, A (1989) Five imperatives for improving service quality, *Sloan Management Review*, **31–32**, pp 89–91.

Bhaduri, M, de Souza, M and Sweeney, T (1993) International qualitative research: a critical review of different approaches, *Marketing and Research Today*, **21**(3), pp 171–8.

Biel, A (1989) Love the advertisement. Buy the product?, *ADMAP*, October.

Blattberg, R and Deighton, J (1991) Interactive marketing: exploiting the age of addressability, *Sloan Management Review*, **33**, p 1.

Blattberg, R and Hoch, S (1990) Database models and managerial intuition: 50% model + 50% manager, *Management Science*, **36**(8), pp 887–99.

Blum, A G and Law, K (1984) Making focus groups even more effective, *Agri Marketing*, March, p 24 ff.

Bogda, P and Meyers, G C (1991) Grab a partner for more effective research, *Marketing News*, 7 January, p 2 ff.

Boland A (1996) Got report-o-phobia?: Follow these simple steps to get those ideas on to paper, *Chemical Engineering*, **103**(3), March, pp 131–2.

Bolongaro, G (1994) Delphi technique can work for new product development, *Marketing News*, 3 January, p 11.

Bolton R (1991) An exploratory investigation of questionnaire pretesting with verbal protocol analysis, *Advances in Consumer Research*, **18**, pp 558–65.

Bolton, R N (1994) Covering the market, *Marketing Research: A Magazine of Management and Applications*, **6**(3), pp 30–5.

Booth-Kewley, S, Edwards, J E and Rosenfeld, P (1992) Impression management, social desirability and computer administration of attitude questionnaires: does the computer make a difference?, *Journal of Applied Psychology*, **77**(4), pp 562–6.

Bowditch, A and Fitall, S (1995) Through the looking glass: primary research in multi-country forecasting, *Proceedings of the EphMRA/ESOMAR Pharmaceutical Marketing Research Conference*, Geneva, Amsterdam: ESOMAR, pp 141–63.

Bowditch, A J (1996) In Europe's complex market, check the price is right, *Research Plus*, April, pp 12–13.

Branthwaite, A and Bruggemann, J (1996) Why we won't keep taking pills, *Research Plus*, April, pp 8–9.

Britt S H (1971) The writing of readable research reports, *Journal of Marketing Research*, May, p 265.

Brock, S E (1989) Marketing research in Asia: problems, opportunities and lessons, *Marketing Research*, September, p 47.

Brooks, R F (1993) Internal service quality – a manufacturing perspective, *Proceedings of the Marketing Education Group*, Loughborough, pp 93–4.

Brooks, R F (1995) Internal service quality – a theoretical development, *Proceedings of the Marketing Education Group*, Bradford, pp 80–90.

Brooks, R F and Smith, J V (1993) Service from within, *TQM Journal*, October, pp 41–5.

Brown, G (1991a) Modelling advertising awareness, *ADMAP*, April.

Brown, G (1991b) Big stable brands and advertisements effects, *ADMAP*, May.

Brown, G, Copeland, T and Millward, M (1973) Monadic testing of new products – an old problem and some partial solutions, *Journal of the Market Research Society*, **15**(2), pp 112–31.

Brown, S (1996) Art or science? Fifty years of marketing debate, *Journal of Marketing Management*, **12**(4), pp 243–67.

Bryman, A and Burgess, R G (1994) Reflections on qualitative data analysis, in Bryman, A and Burgess, R G (eds), *Analysing Qualitative Data*, Routledge, London, pp 216–26.

Bunn, S (1996) Now that India's got GATT, a massive market beckons, *Research Plus*, April, pp 10–11.

Burdick R K (1983) Statement of hypotheses in the analysis of variance, *Journal of Marketing Research*, August, pp 320–4.

Burns, T (1997) Saffron revivalists turn to genetic engineering, *Financial Times*, 15 January.

Butcher B (1994), Sampling methods – an overview and review, *Survey Methods Centre Newsletter*, **15**, pp 4–8.

Butler, P (1994) Marketing problems: from analysis to decision, *Marketing Intelligence and Planning*, **2**(2), pp 4–13.

Buttle, F (1996) *Relationship Marketing*, London: Paul Chapman, pp 59–60.

Byers, P Y and Wilcox, J R (1991) Focus groups: a qualitative opportunity for researchers, *Journal of Business Communication*, **28**(1), pp 63–78.

CACI (1989) *Market Analysis,* London: CACI.

Cahill, D (1998) When to use qualitative marketing research: how about at the midpoint?, *Marketing News,* **32**(1), 5 January, pp 15, 17.

Campbell, S (1997) Management: marketing wake-up, *Financial Times,* 3 June.

Carnes, W T (1980) *Effective Meetings for Busy People,* New York: McGraw-Hill.

Cateora, P R (1993) *International Marketing* (8th edn), Homewood, IL: Irwin, ch 11 'Researching global markets'.

Catterall, M and Maclaran, P (1995) Using a computer to code qualitative data, in *Proceedings of 1995 Annual Conference of the Marketing Education Group* 'Making Marketing Work', Bradford University, July.

Cattin, P and Wittink, D (1982) Commercial use of conjoint analysis: a survey, *Journal of Marketing,* **46**, pp 44–53.

Chapman, R G (1989) Problem definition in marketing research studies, *Journal of Services Marketing,* **3**(3), pp 51–9.

Chisnall, P M (1992) *Marketing Research* (4th edn), Maidenhead: McGraw-Hill.

Choudry, Y A (1986) Pitfalls of international marketing research: are you speaking French like a Spanish cow?, *ABER* **17**(4), Winter, pp 18–28.

Churchill, G A (1979) A paradigm for developing better measures of marketing constructs, *Journal of Marketing Research,* **16** (February), pp 64–73.

Churchill, G (1995) *Marketing Research: Methodological foundations* (6th edn), Fort Worth, TX: Dryden.

Churchill, V B (1988a) How good is mail panel research?, *Address before Advertising Research Foundation Conference.*

Churchill, V B (1988b) Learning to live with continuing household panels, *Telenation Reports,* Summer, pp 1–2.

Clark, L G (1986) Focus groups are a phone call away, *Marketing News,* 3 January.

Cochran, W G and Cox, G M (1957) *Experimental Designs* (2nd edn), New York: Wiley.

Coffey A, Holbrook, B and Atkinsin, P (1996) Qualitative data analysis: technologies and representations, *Sociological Research Online,* 2, http://www.socresonline.org.uk / socresonline/1/1/4.html.

Cohen M A, Jehoshua E and Teck, H H (1997) An anatomy of a decision support system for developing and launching line extensions, *Journal of Marketing Research,* **34**, February, pp 117–29.

Collins, L F (1991) Everything is true, but in a different sense: a new perspective on qualitative research, *Journal of the Market Research Society,* **33**, pp 31–8.

Collins, M (1997) Interviewer variability: a review of the problem, *Journal of the Market Research Society,* **39**, pp 67–84.

Colwell, J (1990) Qualitative market research: a conceptual analysis and review of practitioner criteria, *Journal of the Market Research Society,* **32**.

Cooper, L and Nakanishi, M (1988) *Market Share Analysis: Evaluating competitive marketing effectiveness,* Boston, MA: Kluwer Academic Press.

Cooper, Z (1991) Unpublished MBA dissertation, Department of Management, Keele University, September.

COPE, Advertising leaflet/working demo, Department of Management Science, University of Strathclyde.

Cowan, C D (1991) Using multiple sample frames to improve survey coverage, quality and costs, *Marketing Research: A Magazine of Management and applications*, **3**(4), pp 66–9.

Cowan, D (1994) Good information, *Journal of the Market Research Society*, **36**(2), pp 105–14.

Cox, W E (1979) *Industrial Marketing Research*, New York: Wiley.

Creswell, J W (1994) *Research design: qualitative and quantitative approaches*, London: Sage.

Crimp, M (1990) *The Marketing Research Process* (3rd edn), Hemel Hempstead: Prentice Hall.

Crouch, S (1985) *Marketing Research for Managers*, London: Pan Books.

Cuba, F (1985) Fourteen things that make or break tracking studies, *Journal of Advertising Research*, **25**(1), pp 21–3.

Curwin, J and Slater, R (1991) *Quantitative Methods for Business Decisions* (3rd edn), London: Chapman & Hall.

Daneshkhu, S (1997) The decline and fall of frills, *Financial Times*, 28 April.

Davis, G (1997) Are Internet surveys ready for prime time?, *Marketing News*, 7 April, p 5.

Davis, T R V (1992) Satisfying internal customers: the link to external customer satisfaction, *Planning Review*, **20**(1), pp 34–7.

Day E (1998) Know consumers through qualitative research, *Marketing News*, **32**(1), 5 January, p 14.

Day, E and Stafford, M R (1997) Age-related cues in retail services advertising: their effects on younger consumers, *Journal of Retailing*, **73**(2), pp 211–33.

De Bono, E (1992), in Peter, T, *Liberation Management*, New York: Macmillan, p 635.

Deal K (1997) Determining success factors for financial products: a comparative analysis of CART, Logit and factor/discriminant analysis, *Service Industries Journal*, **17**(3), July, pp 489–506.

Dembhowski, S and Hanmer-Lloyd, S (1995) Computer applications – a new road to qualitative analysis?, *European Journal of Marketing*, **29**(11), pp 50–62.

Deming, W E (1950) On errors in surveys, *American Sociological Review*, **9**(4).

Dent, T (1992) How to design for a more reliable customer sample, *Business Marketing*, **17**(2), pp 73–6.

Denzin, N and Lincoln, Y (1993) *Handbook of Qualitative Research*, Newbury Park, CA: Sage.

Dillman, D A, Singer, E, Clark, J R and Treat, J B (1996) Effects of benefits appeals and variations in statements of confidentiality on completion rates for census questionnaires, *Public Opinion Quarterly*, **60**(3).

Directory of On-Line Databases, Gale Research International, PO Box 699, North Way, Andover, Hampshire, SP10 5YE.

Dolan, C V (1994) Factor analysis of variables with 2,3,5 and 7 response categories: a comparison of categorical variable estimators using simulated data, *British Journal of Mathematical and Statistical Psychology*, **47**, pp 309–26.

Donnelly, M, Wisniewski, M, Dalrymple, J F and Curry, A (1995) Measuring service quality in local government: the SERVQUAL approach, *International Journal of Public Sector Management*, **8**(7), pp 15–20.

Double, L (1991) Unpublished MBA dissertation, Department of Management, Keele University, September.

Douglas, S P and Craig, C S (1983) *International Marketing Research,* Upper Saddle River, NJ: Prentice-Hall.

Dutka, S and Frankel, L R (1988) *Techniques for the Cost Efficient Sampling of Small or Rare Populations,* New York: Audits and Surveys.

Dwyer, J (1993) *The Business Communication Handbook* (3rd edn), Erskineville, NSW: Star Printery.

Eagleson, R D (1990) *Writing in Plain English,* Canberra: AGPS.

Eames, A (1997) When time means money, *Financial Times,* 24 May.

Easterby-Smith, M, Thorpe, R and Lowe, A (1991) *Management Research: An introduction,* London: Sage.

Eberhart, R C and Dobbins, R W (1990) *Neural Network PC Tools,* London: Academic Press.

Edwards, F (1995) The French connection, *International Wrist Watch,* **31**, pp 46–8.

EFO Group (1993) *Marketing News,* 21 June.

Eklof, J A, Hackl, P and Westlund, A (1999) On measuring interactions between customer satisfaction and financial results, *Total Quality Management,* **10**(4–5), pp 514–22.

Embree, L (1997) What is phenomenology? Center for Advanced Research in Phenomenology, http://www.phenomenologycenter.org/phenom.htm.

Eskin, G (1988) *Setting a Forward Agenda for Test Market Modeling,* New York: Advertising Research Foundation, pp 14–15.

Eunson, B (1994) *Writing and Presenting Reports,* Milton, Queensland: Wiley.

Eurostat Catalogue: Publications and Electronic Services, Office for the Official Publications of the European Communities, L-2985 Luxembourg.

Fazey, I H (1997) Watching paint fly, *Financial Times,* 25 September.

Fielding, R and Lee, R (eds) (1991) *Using Computers in Qualitative Analysis.* Berkeley, CA: Sage.

Findex, available through Euromonitor, 87 Turnmill Street, London EC1 5QU.

Fishbein, M and Azjen, I (1975) *Belief, Attitude, Intention and Behavior,* Reading, MA: Addison-Wesley, p 6.

Flaherty, J (1990) Computer administration of questions: more desirable or more socially desirable, *Journal of Applied Psychology,* **75**, pp 310–14.

Flanagan, T A and Fredericks, J O (1993) Improving company performance through customer satisfaction measurement and management, *National Productivity Review,* Spring, pp 239–58.

Fletcher, K (1995) Jump on the omnibus, *Marketing,* 15 June, pp 25–8.

Fletcher, W (1984) *Meetings, Meetings.* New York: Morrow.

Fletcher, W (1997) Why researchers are so jittery, *Financial Times,* 3 March.

Freeling, A (1994) Marketing is in a crisis – can marketing research help?, *Journal of the Market Research Society,* **36**, pp 97–104.

Freeman, P (1991) Using computers to extend analysis and reduce data, *Journal of the Market Research Society,* **33**(2), pp 127–36.

Fry, C (1991) Unpublished MBA dissertation, Department of Management, Keele University, September.

Gabor, A and Grainger, C (1966) Price as an indicator of quality, *Economics*, **33**, pp 43–70.

Gabriel, C (1990) The validity of qualitative marketing research, *Journal of the Market Research Society*, **32**, October, pp 507–19.

Geo-Visual Solutions for Today's Business (1990) Mt Olive, NJ: Intelligent Charting.

Gibson, R (1992) The fine art of stocking a supermarket's shelves, *Wall Street Journal*, 15 October.

Gibson, R (1993) Broad grocery price cuts may not pay, *Wall Street Journal*, 7 May.

Goff, M (1997) Mapping out markets, *Provider*, **23**(10), October, pp 79–80.

Gofton, K (1997) If it moves measure it, *Marketing*, 4 September, p 17.

Gold L N (1996) Do it yourself interviewing, *Marketing Research: A Magazine of Management and Applications*, **8**(2), Summer, pp 40–1.

Gooding, K (1997) Soft drinks switch to PET leaves industry struggling, *Financial Times*, 22 October.

Goodyear, M (1996) The world shrinks, maybe, but there's still the need to travel, *Research Plus*, May, p 12.

Gordon, W and Corr, D (1990) The space between words: the application of a new model of communication to quantitative brand image measurement, *Journal of the Market Research Society*, **32**(3), pp 409–35.

Gorle, P (1995) The cascade theory that shows practical gains, *Research Plus*, October, p 11.

Government Statistics: A brief guide to sources, Norwich: Office for National Statistics.

Green, P A, Tull, D S and Albaum, G (1988) *Research for Marketing Decisions*, Upper Saddle River, NJ: Prentice-Hall.

Green, P E and Krieger, A M (1989) Recent contributions to optimal product positioning and buyer segmentation, *European Journal of Operational Research*, **41**, pp 127–41.

Green, P E and Krieger, A M (1992) An application of a product positioning model to pharmaceutical products, *Marketing Science*, **11**(2), pp 117–32.

Greenbaum, T L (1984) Keys to improving the effectiveness of focus group research, *Marketing Review*, June–July, p 23.

Greenbaum, T L (1988) *The Practical Handbook and Guide to Focus Group Research*, Lexington, MA: Heath.

Greenbaum T L (1996) Understanding focus group research abroad, *Marketing News*, **30**(12), 3 June, p 3.

Griffiths, J (1997) World tyre industry may face shake-out, *Financial Times*, 14 May.

Griffiths, V (1997) Orchestras aim to pass the baton, *Financial Times*, 20 May.

Griggs, S (1987) Analysing qualitative data, *Journal of the Market Research Society*, **32**, pp 507–20.

Gronroos, C (1990) *Service Management and Marketing: Managing the moments of truth in service competition*. Lexington, MA: Lexington Books.

Grove, S J and Fisk, R P (1992) Observational data collection methods for service marketing: an overview, *Journal of the Academy of Marketing Science*, **20**(3), pp 217–24.

Grover, R and Srinivasan, V (1987) A simultaneous approach to market segmentation and market structuring, *Journal of Marketing Research*, **24**, pp 139–53.

Gulledge, L G (1991) Satisfying the internal customer, *Bank Marketing*, **23**, pp 46–8.

Gummesson, E (1990) *Qualitative Methods in Management Research*, London: Sage.

Gummesson, E (1993) *Quality Management in Service Organizations: An interpretation of the service quality phenomenon and a synthesis of international research*, Karlstad, Sweden: International Service Quality Association.

Hague, P (1987) Good and bad in questionnaire design, *Industrial Marketing Digest*, **12**(3), pp 161–70.

Hague, P (1993) *Questionnaire Design*, London: Kogan Page.

Hague, P and Jackson, P (1996) *Market Research*, London: Kogan Page.

Hague, P and Roberts, C (1994) *Presentation and Report Writing*, London: Kogan Page.

Hague, P N (1985) *The Industrial Market Research Handbook* (2nd edn), London: Kogan Page.

Hahlo, G (1992) Examining the validity of re-interviewing respondents for quantitative surveys, *Journal of the Market Research Society*, **34**, pp 99–118.

Hair, J F, Anderson, R E, Tatham, R L and Black, W C (1992) *Multivariate Data Analysis*, New York: Macmillan.

Hair, J F, Anderson, R E, Tatham, R L and Black, W C (1995) *Multivariate Data Analysis with Readings* (4th edn), New York: Macmillan (illustrates multivariate techniques using marketing examples).

Hallowell, R (1996) The relationship of customer satisfaction, customer loyalty and profitability: an empirical study, *International Journal of Service Industry Management*, **7**(4), pp 27–42.

Hammond, K, Ehrenberg, A S C and Goodhart, G J (1996) Market segmentation for competitive brands, *European Journal of Marketing*, **30**, pp 39–49.

Hammond, M (1986) Creative focus groups: uses and misuses, *Marketing and Media Decisions*, July, pp 154–5.

Hannabuss, S (1995) Approaches to research, *Aslib Proceedings*, **47**, January, pp 3–11.

Harding, J (1997) China's future dragons, *Financial Times*, 14 August.

Hart, C W L (1995) The power of internal guarantee, *Harvard Business Review*, Jan–Feb, pp 64–73.

Hart, S J, Webb, J R and Jones, M V (1994) Export marketing research and the effect of export experience in industrial SMEs, *International Marketing Review*, **11**(6), pp 4–23.

Haynes, M E (1988) *Effective Meeting Skills*, Los Altos, CA: Crisp Publications.

Heskett, J L, Jones, T O, Loveman, G W, Sasser, W E and Schlesinger, L A (1994) Putting the service profit chain to work, *Harvard Business Review*, Mar–Apr, pp 164–74.

Hibbins, G M (1990) *Stands to Reason* (4th edn), South Melbourne, Victoria: Macmillan.

Hill, A, Roberts, H, Ewings, P and Gunnell, D (1997) Nonresponse bias in a lifestyle survey, *Journal of Public Health Medicine*, **19**(2), June, pp 203–7.

Hinkin, S (1995) Charting your course to effective information graphics, *Presentations*, 9(11).

Hirschman, E C (1986) Humanistic inquiry in marketing research: philosophy, method and criteria, *Journal of Marketing Research*, **23**, pp 237–49.

Hoinville, G, Jowell, R and Associates. (eds) (1978) *Survey Research Practice*, London: Heinemann, ch 4.

Holtgraves, T, Eck, J and Lasky, B (1997), Face management, question wording and social desirability, *Journal of Applied Social Psychology*, **27**(18), pp 1650–71.

Homelink (1993) *Research Plus*, September, pp 8–9.

Hoover, S V and Perry, R F (1989) *Simulation: A problem-solving approach*, New York: Addison-Wesley.

Hrisak, D M (1997) Key presentation principles, *Chartered Accountants Journal of New Zealand*, **76**(3), April, p 24.

Huff, D (1991) *How to Lie with Statistics*, Harmondsworth: Penguin.

Hutton, R (1994) Best of the bunch, *Scottish Business Insider*, March, pp 662–3.

IBM's Butterfly gets crushed on the wheel (1996) *PC Direct*, May, p 57.

Infoplus, PO Box 12, Sunbury on Thames, Middlesex TW16 7UD.

Inspiration, Inspiration Software, Inc., 2920 SW Dolph Court, Suite 3, Portland, Oregon 97219, USA.

Jack, A (1997) Canal Satellite disappoints, *Financial Times*, 12 September.

Jackson, P (1994a) *Buying Market Research*, London: Kogan Page.

Jackson, P (1994b) *Desk Research*, London: Kogan Page.

Jamieson, D (1995) Now business research is every agency's research, *Research Plus*, October, pp 4–5.

Jick, T D (1979) Mixing qualitative and quantitative methods: triangulation in action, *Administrative Science Quarterly*, **24**, pp 602–11.

JICNARS *National Readership Survey* (1981) London: JICNARS.

Johansson, J K and Nonaka, J (1987) Market research the Japanese way, *Harvard Business Review*, May–June, pp 16–22.

Jones, J W and McLeod, R (1986) The structure of executive information systems: an exploratory analysis, *Decision Science*, **17**, pp 220–49.

Kaciak, E and Louviere, J (1990) Multiple correspondence analysis of multiple choice experiment data, *Journal of Marketing Research*, **27**, pp 455–65.

Kalton, G and Schuman, H (1982) The effect of the question on survey responses: a review, *Journal of the Royal Statistical Society*, **145**, Part 1, pp 42–73.

Kamakura, W A and Wedel, M (1997) Statistical data fusion for cross-tabulation, *Journal of Marketing Research*, **34**(4), November, pp 485–98.

Kamakura, W and Russell, G J (1989) A probabilistic choice model for market segmentation, *Journal of Marketing Research*, **26**, pp 379–90.

Kandathil, J (1985) The advantages of electronic test markets: an advertiser view based on experience, *Journal of Advertising Research*, **25**(6), pp RC 11–12.

Kauder, N B (1996) Pictures worth a thousand words, *American Demographics* (Tools supplement), November, pp 64–8.

Kaushik, M and Sen, A (1990) Semiotics and qualitative research, *Journal of the Market Research Society*, **32**, pp 227–43.

Keillor, B, Owens, D and Pettijohn, C (2001) A cross-cultural/cross-national study of influencing factors and socially desirable response bias, *International Journal of Market Research*, **43**(1), pp 63–84.

Kerlinger, F (1973) *Foundations of Behavioral Research*, New York: Holt, Rinehart & Winston, ch 2.

Kestylyn, J (1992) Application watch, *AI Expert* (January), pp 63–4.

Keys, T (1996) Report writing, *Internal Auditor*, **53**(4), August.

Kinsey, J (1988) *Marketing in Developing Countries*, London: Macmillan, ch 4.

Korents, G (1996) China's other consumers, *Business Week*, 13 May, p 11.

Kotler, P (1966) A design for the firm's marketing nerve centre, *Business Horizons*, Fall, pp 63–74.

Kotler, P (1988) *Marketing Management: Planning, analysis and control* (6th edn), Upper Saddle River, NJ: Prentice-Hall, p 525.

Kotler, P and Lilien, G (1983) *Marketing Decision Making: A model building approach*, New York: Harper & Row.

Kress, G (1988) *Marketing Research* (3rd edn), Upper Saddle River, NJ: Prentice-Hall, chs 8 and 9.

Lafferty, F (1997) Management: The English Bear Company – partners, *Financial Times*, 28 April.

Langbourne, R (1993) How to reach children in stores: marketing tactics grounded in observational research, *Journal of Advertising Research*, **33**, November/December, pp 67–72.

Larson, E (1992) Watching Americans watch TV, *The Atlantic Monthly*, March.

Lautenschlager, G and Flaherty, V L (1990) Computer administration of questions: more desirable or more social desirability?, *Journal of Applied Psychology*, **75**, pp 310–14.

Lavidge, R J and Steiner, G A (1961) A model for predictive measurements of advertising effectiveness, *Journal of Marketing*, **25**, October, pp 59–62.

Lenell, W and Bissoneau, R (1996) Using causal comparative and correlational designs in conducting market research, *Journal of Professional Services Marketing*, **13**(2), pp 59–69.

Lewis, D B (1983) Advertising research and measurement, in *Marketing Managers Handbook*, Chicago, IL: Dartnell, pp 6–7.

Lewis, P H (1989) When maps are tied to data bases, *New York Times*, **28** May, p F10.

Li, E. (1997) Perceived importance of information system success factors: a meta analysis of group differences, *Information and Management*, **32**, pp 15–28.

Likert, R (1932) A technique for the measurements of attitudes, *Archives of Psychology*, 140.

Lilien, G L, Kotler, P and Moorthy, K S (1992) *Marketing Models*, Upper Saddle River, NJ: Prentice-Hall, ch 9.

Lincoln, Y S and Guba, E G (1985) *Naturalistic Inquiry*, Beverly Hills, CA: Sage.

Locander, W, Sudman, S and Bradburn, N M (1976) An investigation of interview method, threat and response distortion, *Journal of the American Statistical Association*, **71**, pp 269–75.

Lynch, T (1997) Caught in the neighbours' tangled web, *Financial Times*, 15 August.

Macht, J (1999) The new market research, *Inc*, **20**(10), pp 86–94.

Magidson, D and Polcha, A E (1992) Creating market economies within organisations, a conference on internal markets, *Planning Review*, Jan–Feb, pp 37–40.

Malhotra, N K (1995) *Marketing Research: An application orientation*, Upper Saddle River, NJ: Prentice-Hall.

Malhotra, N K, Agarwal, J and Peterson, M (1996) Cross-cultural marketing research: methodological issues and guidelines, *International Marketing Review*, **13**(5), pp 7–43.

Malhotra, R (1988) *Some Issues and Perspectives on Use of Simulated Test Markets*, New York: Advertising Research Foundation, p 57.

MapInfo, Centennial Court, Easthampstead Road, Bracknell, Berks, RG12 1YQ. Tel: 01344 482888.

Marek, D (1998) We all need to address declining respondent co-operation, http://www.mra-net.org.

Market Search, Arlington Publications, 25 New Bond Street, London W1Y 9HD.

Markland, R E (1983) *Topics in Management Science,* New York: Wiley.

Marks, A P (1990) The Sinclair 5 – why did it fail? *Management Decision*, **28**(4), pp 9–14.

Marsh, C and Scarborough, C (1990) Testing nine hypotheses about quota sampling, *Journal of the Market Research Society*, **32**, October, pp 485–506.

Marsh, P (1997) The growing business: same aims, different strategies, *Financial Times*, 23 December.

Marshall, K P (1996) *Marketing Information Systems,* Danvers, MA: Boyd & Fraser.

Mathews, A (1997) Academic xenophobia and the analysis of focus group data, *Journal of Targeting, Measurement and Analysis for Marketing*, **6**(2), pp 160–71.

Mattson, J (1990) Measuring inherent product values, *European Journal of Marketing*, **24**(9), pp 25–39.

Mayer, M (1990) Scanning the future, *Forbes*, 15 October.

Mazzella, G F (1997) Show and tell focus groups reveal core boomer values, *Marketing News*, **3**(12), p H8.

McCann, J M (1986) *The Marketing Workbench*, Homewood, IL: Dow-Jones Irwin.

McCann, P (1996) Commercial TV audiences rise…, *Marketing Week*, 26 April, p 15.

McClelland, J L and Rumelhart, D E (1988) *Explorations in Parallel Distributed Processing: A handbook of models, programs and exercises.* Cambridge, MA: MIT Press.

McConagle, J J and Vella, C M (1990) *Outsmarting the Competition,* Naperville, IL: Sourcebooks.

McCulough, D (1999) Why marketing research is a waste of money (and what you can do about it), *Marcom Today*, November.

McDaniel, C and Gates, R (2002) *Marketing Research: The impact of the Internet* (5th edn), Cincinatti, OH: South-Western.

McDonald, W (1993) Focus groups research dynamics, *Journal of the Academy of Marketing Science*, **21**(2), pp 161–8.

McKenzie, J (1988) Study of characteristics of ex-directory telephone owners, *Market Research Newsletter*, December.

McKenzie, J, Schaefer, R L and Farber, E (1995) *The Student Edition of Minitab for Windows*, Reading, MA: Addison-Wesley.

Mehta, R and Sivadas, E, (1995) Comparing response rates and response context in mail vs electronic mail surveys, *Journal of the Marketing Research Society*, **37**(4), pp 429–39.

Miles, M B and Huberman, A M (1994) *Qualitative Data Analysis,* London: Sage.

Mitchell, V (1995) Using astrology in market segmentation, *Management Decision*, **33**(1), pp 48–57.

Mohanty, R P and Deshmukh, S G (1997) Evolution of a decision support system for human resource planning in a petroleum company, *International Journal of Production Economics*, **51**(3), September, pp 251–61.

Mohn, N C (1989) How to present marketing research results effectively, *Marketing and Research Today*, **17**(2), pp 115–18.

Morris, S (1990) *Using Personal Computers in Marketing*, Oxford: NCC Blackwell.

Morton-Williams, J (1978) Questionnaire design, in Worcester, R and Downham, J (eds), *Consumer Market Research Handbook*. Wokingham: Van Nostrand Reinhold.

Morton-Williams, J and Sykes, W (1984) The use of interaction coding, *Journal of the Market Research Society*, 26(2), April.

Moskowitz, H R (1985) *New Directions for Product Testing and Sensory Analysis of Foods*, Westport, CT: Food and Nutrition Press, p 171 ff.

Moult, W M (1988) *The Role of Simulated Test Markets and Test Markets*, New York: Advertising Research Foundation, p 140.

Mouncey, P (1996) With growing demands for data, will purity prove only theoretical? *Research Plus*, May, p 9.

Moutinho, L and Evans, M (1992) *Applied Marketing Research*, Wokingham: Addison-Wesley.

Munson, J and McIntery, S (1979) Developing practical procedures for measurement of personal values in cross cultural marketing, *Journal of Marketing Research*, 16.

Murray, P J (1997) Using virtual focus groups in qualitative research, *Qualitative Health Research*, 7(4), pp 542–9.

Nairn, G (1997) Golden nuggets on a long and winding road, *Financial Times*, 3 December.

Newton, S (1993) From hearses to horses: launching the Volvo 850, *Journal of the Market Research Society*, 33, pp 153–62.

Nicholas, R (1994) Avon ads praise the real woman, *Marketing*, 27 January, p 6.

Number News, The (1990) New products, June, p 8.

Nuttall, C (1996) Research needs more creativity, *Marketing Week*, 29 April, p 32.

Nutting, J and White, G (1992) *The Business of Communication* (2nd edn) Roseville, CA: McGraw Hill.

Ohanian, R (1990) Construction and validation of a scale to measure celebrity endorsers' perceived expertise, trustworthiness and attractiveness, *Journal of Advertising*, 19(3), pp 39–52.

On-Line Business and Company Databases, ASLIB, 20 Old Street, London EC1V 9AP.

On-Line Business Source Book, Headland Press, 1 Henry Smith's Terrace, Headland, Cleveland, TS24 0PD.

Oppenheim, A N (1984) *Questionnaire Design and Attitude Measurement*, London: Heinemann.

Oppermann, M (1995) E-mail survey – potentials and pitfalls, *Market Research*, 7(3), pp 29–33.

Osgood, C, Suci, G and Tannenbaum, P (1987) *The Measurement of Meaning*, Urbana, IL: University of Illinois Press.

Parasuraman, A, Berry, L L and Zeithaml, V (1985) A conceptual model of service quality and the implications for future research, *Journal of Marketing*, 49, pp 41–51.

Parker, L (1992) Collecting data the e-mail way, *Training and Development*, pp 52–4.

Payne, S L (1951) *The Art of Asking Questions*, Princeton, NJ: Princeton University Press.

Pereira, R E (1999) Factors influencing consumer perceptions of web-based decision support systems, *Logistics Information Management*, 12(1/2), pp 157–81.

Perrott, N (1995) Research that becomes part of a company's strategy, *Research Plus*, October, p 6ff.

Perry, C, Reige, A and Brown, L (1999) Realism's role among scientific paradigms in marketing research, *Irish Marketing* Review, 12(2), pp 16–23.

Peter, P J and Olson, C (1989) The relativist/constructionist perspective on scientific knowledge and consumer research, in Hirschman, E (ed.), *Interpretive Consumer Research*, Provo, UT: ACR, pp 24–8.

Piercy, N (1996) The effects of customer satisfaction measurement: the internal market versus the external market, *Marketing Intelligence and Planning*, **14**(4), p 9.

Piercy, N and Evans, M (1993) *Managing Marketing Information*, London: Croom Helm.

Piercy, N and Morgan, N (1995) Customer satisfaction measurement and management: a processual analysis, *Journal of Marketing Management*, **11**, pp 817–34.

Poster watch (1996) *Marketing Week*, 26 April, p 58.

Proctor, R A (1992) Marketing decision support systems: a role for neural networking, *Marketing Intelligence and Planning*, **10**(1), pp 21–6.

Proctor, R A (1994a) Queues and the power of simulation in helping with business decisions and problems, *Management Decision*, **32**(1), pp 50–5.

Proctor, R A (1994b) Simulation in management services, *Management Services*, 38(1), January, pp 18–23.

Proctor, S, Papasolomou-Doukakis, I and Proctor, T (2001) What are TV advertisements really trying to tell us? A postmodern perspective, *Journal of Consumer Behaviour*, **1**, p 3.

Proctor, T (1992) *Essential Marketing*, London: Collins Educational.

Proctor, T (1999) *Creative Problem Solving for Managers*, London: Routledge.

QUALPRO and ETHNOGRAPH, Qualitative Research Management, 73425 Hilltop Road, Desert Hot Springs, CA, USA.

QSR NUD*IST, Qualitative Solutions & Research Pty Ltd, Box 171, La Trobe University Post Office, Victoria, Australia 3083.

Raudsepp, T (1987) Establishing a creative climate, *Training and Development Journal*, April, pp 50–3.

Rebondir (1996) Un restaurant de gambas ouvrir un commerce, no. 12.

Reed, D (1996) The data game, *Marketing Week*, 3 May, pp 47–51.

Rees, J (1996) PepsiCo needs new strategy for iced tea, *Marketing Week*, 16 April, p 23.

Reports Index, Business Surveys Ltd, Osmington Drive, Broadmayne, Dorset, DT2 8ED.

Research propels innovation (1994) *Marketing*, 27 January, pp 33–5.

Richards, T and Richards, L (1991) The NUD*IST qualitative data analysis system, *Qualitative Sociology*, 14.

Riche, M F (1990) A bigger role for telephone interviews, *American Demographics*, September, p 17.

Rickards, T (1974) *Problem Solving through Creative Analysis*, Aldershot: Gower.

Rickards, T (1988) Creativity and innovation: a transatlantic perspective, *Creativity and Innovation Yearbook*, Manchester Business School.

Ricks, D A, Fu, Y C and Arpan, S (1974) *International Business Blunders*, Columbus, OH: Grid.

Robson, C (1993) *Real World Research*, Oxford: Blackwell.

Robson, S (1991) Ethics: informed consent or misinformed compliance?, *Journal of the Market Research Society*, **33**, pp 19–28.

Rogers, K (1996) Correspondence analysis: the big picture, *Quirk's Marketing Research Review*, Article 2, April.

Rosenfeld, J (1985) Speeding up test marketing, *Marketing Communications*, June.

Rosser, M (1995) Modelling game theory with spreadsheets, *Cheer*, **9**(2), pp 15–18.

Rothenberg, R (1989) The trouble with mail interviewing, *New York Times*, 16 August.

Rowland, M L and Forthofer, R N (1993) Adjusting for non-response bias in a health examination survey, *Public Health Reports*, **108**(3), May–June, pp 380–6.

Russo, J (1988) Simulated test markets in the real world, *Pre-Test Market Research*, New York: Advertising Research Foundation, pp 118–19.

Rydholm, J (1997) Right on cue: mystery shopping makes sure salespeople sing praises of Yamaha digital pianos, *Quirk's Marketing Review*, Article 234, January.

Safe T letterbox (1996) *Business Opportunities World*, May, pp 64–5.

Samways, A and Whittcome, K (1994) UK brand strategies, Financial Times Management Report, p 108.

Sanderson, T (1996) How a spoonful of research helps the medicine go down, *Research Plus*, April, pp 6–8.

Sawyer, A and Peter, J P (1983) The significance of statistical significance tests in marketing research, *Journal of Marketing Research*, **20**, May, p 125.

Schindler, R M (1992) The real lesson of new Coke: the value of focus groups for predicting the effects of social influence, *Marketing Research: A Magazine of Management and Applications*, December, pp 22–7.

Schmitz, J D, Armstrong, G D and Little, J D C (1990) Cover story: automated news findings, *Marketing Interfaces*, **20**(6), pp 29–38.

Schneider, K C and Johnson, J C (1995) Stimulating response to market surveys of business professionals, *Industrial Marketing Management*, **24**, pp 265–76.

Scott, A (1996) The launch went fine – then the devil's in the detailing, *Research Plus*, April, p 14.

Seaton, A V (1997) Unobtrusive observational measures as a qualitative extension of visitor surveys at festivals and events: mass observation revisited, *Journal of Travel Research*, **35**(4), Spring, pp 25–30.

Semon, T T (1994a) Save a few bucks on sample size, risk millions in opportunity loss, *Marketing News*, **28**(1), p 19.

Semon, T T (1994b) A good sample of accounts may not always be a good sample of your customers, *Marketing News*, **28**(9), pp 8–11.

Shait, D I (1994) Report writing, *HR Focus*, **71**(2), p 20.

Shea, C Z and LeBourveau, C (2000) Jumping the hurdles of marketing research, *Marketing Research*, **12**(3), pp 22–30.

Sheehan, K B and McMillan, S J (1999) Response variation in e-mail surveys: an exploration, *Journal of Advertising Research*, **39**(4), pp 45–54.

Singer, E, Von Thurn, D R and Miller, E R (1995) Confidentiality assurances and response. A quantitative review of the experimental literature, *Public Opinion Quarterly*, **59**(1), pp 67–77.

Sirkin, A F (1995) Maximizing customer satisfaction, *MLS: Marketing Library Services*, **9**(4), pp 3–4.

Skapinker, M (1997) Deceptive appearance, *Financial Times*, 3 February.

Smith, A M (1995) Quality aspects of service marketing, *Marketing Intelligence and Planning*, **8**(6), pp 25–32.

Smith, A (1997a) Baby boomers get the message, *Financial Times*, 26 May.

Smith, A (1997b) Opinion polling faces new scrutiny, *Financial Times*, 21 March.

Smith, A (1997c) Public puts faith in brand names, *Financial Times*, 13 October.

Smith, A (1997d) Shoppers under the microscope, *Financial Times*, 5 December.

Smith, L A and Gupta, S (1985) Project management software in P & IM, *P & IM Review and APICS News*, June, pp 66–8.

Snell, F (1979) *How to Win the Meeting*, New York: Hawthorn Books.

Soroczynski, P (1999) *Technical Communication Handbook*, Darwin: NTU Press.

Sorrell, M (1997) The future lies abroad, *Financial Times*, 30 June.

The Source Book, Keynote Publications, 72 Oldfield Road, Hampton, Middlesex TW12 2HQ.

South Africa: A world in one country (1996) South Africa Tourism Board.

Spiggle, S (1994) Analysis and interpretation of qualitative data in consumer research, *Journal of Consumer Research*, **21**, December, pp 491–503.

Spindler, R (1991) Unpublished MSc dissertation, Odense University.

Stapel, H (1991) Like the advertisement but does it interest me?, *ADMAP*, April.

Stapel, J (1990) Monitoring advertising performance, *ADMAP*, July/August.

Steinberg, M and Planck, R E (1990) Implementing expert systems into business to business marketing practice, *Journal of Business and Industrial Marketing*, **5**(2), pp 15–26.

Strauss, A and Corbin, J (1990) *Basics of Qualitative Research*, London: Sage.

Strauss, A S (1993) *Qualitative Analysis for Social Scientists*, Cambridge: Cambridge University Press, p 2.

Strutton, D and Pelton, L (1994) A multiple correspondence analysis of telephone contact rates, *The Mid-Atlantic Journal of Business*, **30**(1), pp 27–39.

Studies of Media and Markets (1989) New York: Simmons Market Research Bureau.

Sussmans, J (1991) *How to Write Effective Reports*, Aldershot: Gower.

Sutherland, K (ed.) (1994) *Researching Business Markets*, London: Kogan Page.

Swindley, D (1992) Retail buying in the United Kingdom, *The Service Industries Journal*, **12**, pp 533–44.

Sykes, W (1990) Validity and reliability in qualitative marketing research: a review of the literature, *Journal of the Market Research Society*, **33**, pp 3–12.

Sylvester, S (1993) Don't ask consumers to supply your answers, *Research Plus*, November, p 8.

Synodinos, N E and Brennan, J E (1988) Computer interactive interviewing in survey research, *Psychology and Marketing*, **5**, Summer, pp 115–38.

Taha, H A (1992) *Operations Research: An introduction* (5th edn), New York: Macmillan.

Taylor, H (2000) Does Internet research work? Comparing online survey results with telephone survey, *International Journal of Market Research*, **42**(1), pp 51–63.

Taylor, P (1997a) Breakthroughs in business intelligence, *Financial Times*, 7 May.

Taylor, P (1997b) Electronic revolution in the retailing world, *Financial Times*, 3 September.

The Teleconference Network (1990) Orangeburg, NY: The Market Navigator.

Test markets: winners and losers (1983) *Advertising Week*, 3 October.

Thomsett, C (1989) *The Little Black Book of Business Meetings*, New York: American Management Association.

Tillet, L S (2000) A 24-hour focus group – sites dig into search queries to learn consumer preferences, *Internet Week*, no. **808**, 10 April, p 170.

Timmins, N (1997) British divided into four types, *Financial Times*, 5 September.

Tse, C B, Tse, K C, Yin, C H, Ting, C B, Yi, K W, Yee, K P and Hong, W C (1995) Comparing two methods of sending out questionnaires: e-mail vs mail, *Journal of the Market Research Society*, **37**(4).

Tull, D S and Hawkins, D I (1990) *Marketing Research: measurement and method*, New York: Macmillan.

Tyrrell, B (1994) Eastern promise is worth all the pain of red tape, *Marketing*, 3 February, p 5.

UK Marketing Source Book, NTC Publications, Farm Road, Henley on Thames, Oxon, RG9 1EJ.

Uncles, M D, Hammond, K A, Ehrenberg, A S C and Davies, R E (1994) A replication study of two brand-loyalty measures, *European Journal of Operational Research*, **76**, pp 375–84.

Vinten, G (1997) The threat in the question, *Credit Control*, **18**(1), pp 25–31.

Waddell, D and Sohal, A S (1994) Forecasting: the key to managerial decision making, *Management Decision*, **32**(1), p 46.

Warner, S L (1965) Randomised response: a survey technique for eliminating evasive answer bias, *Journal of the American Statistical Association*, **60**, pp 63–9.

Watson, H J and Blackstone, J H (1989) *Computer Simulation*, New York: Wiley.

Watson, M A (1992) Researching minorities, *Journal of the Market Research Society*, **34**(4), pp 337–44.

Weible, R and Wallace, J (1998) Cyber research: the impact of the Internet on data collection, *Market Research*, **10**(3), pp 19–27.

Weinman, C (1991) It's not an 'art', but marketing research can be creative, *Marketing News*, **25**(8), pp 9–24.

Weitzman, E and Miles, M (1995) *Computer Programs for Qualitative Data Analysis*, Thousand Oaks, CA: Sage.

West, C (1995) Marketing research, in Baker, M J (ed.), *Companion Encyclopaedia of Marketing*, London: Routledge.

Westland, J C (1992) Self-organising executive information networks, *Decision Support Systems*, **8**, pp 41–53.

Wheatley, K and Flexmer, W A (1987) Option Technologies, Inc., *Marketing News*, 27 February, p 23.

Whipple, T W (1994) Mapping focus group data, *Marketing Research*, **6**(1), pp 16–21.

White, D M and Abels, E G (1995) Measuring service quality in special libraries: lessons from service marketing, *Special Libraries*, **86** (Winter), pp 36–45.

White, S (1993) Get a helping of the sugar-free chips game, *Research Plus*, September, p 3.

Wilkinson, S (1998) Focus group methodology: a review, *International Journal of Social Research Methodology*, **1**(3), pp 181–203.

Winters, P (1996) Of mergers, managers, money, mailsters... and patients too, *Research Plus*, April.

Workman, J P (1993) Marketing's limited role in new product development in one computer system firm, *Journal of Marketing Research*, XXX (November), pp 405–21.

Xiong, R (1994) Moving towards market economy and marketing application in China, Unpublished MBA dissertation, Department of Management, Keele University.

Yava, U (1996) Demand forecasting in a service setting, *Journal of International Marketing and Marketing Research*, **21**(1), February, pp 3–11.

Zeisel, H (1985) *Say It with Figures*, New York: Harper & Row.

Zeithaml, V, Berry, L and Parasuraman, A (1993) The nature and determinants of customer expectations of a service, *Journal of the Academy of Marketing Science*, **21**(1), pp 1–12.

Zeithaml, V A, Berry, L L and Parasuraman, A (1996) The behavioral consequences of service quality, *Journal of Marketing*, **60**, April, pp 31–46.

Zeithaml, V, Parasuraman, A and Berry, L (1990) *Delivering Quality Service*, New York: Free Press.

Zemke, R (1978) How market research techniques can pay off for trainers, *Training*, **15**(12).

Index

Numbers in **bold** indicate glossary entries.